# Voltaire and the Cowboy

*The Letters of Thurman Arnold*

# Voltaire and the Cowboy

## *The Letters of Thurman Arnold*

*Edited by* Gene M. Gressley

COLORADO ASSOCIATED UNIVERSITY PRESS

BOULDER

Library of Congress Card Catalog Number 76-15772
ISBN 0-87081-073-1
Printed in United States of America
Designed by Bruce Campbell

For the University of Wyoming—
students, faculty, staff, administration,
trustees and alumni—
who have made their University into the educational
institution that Thurman Arnold dreamed about—

# Illustrations



*Courtesy Western History Research Center,*
*Laramie, Wyoming, unless otherwise credited.*

# *Contents*

# *Preface*

My first contact with Thurman Arnold came in 1958. I wrote him what was at once both a diffident and presumptuous letter, gently inviting him to consider the Archives of the University of Wyoming as a possible repository for his papers. Three days after my letter had been postmarked (September 8th), he replied. "I have your request for my papers," he wrote. "Of course you may have them if you want. As soon as I have a chance to go over them and take out the more recent material, which I may need."

A month after this exchange, I visited Thurman Arnold in the Arnold, Fortas and Porter offices at 1229 19th N.W., Washington, D.C., the first of several visits over the next decade. This was not to lay claim to a long, intimate friendship, for I never presumed that I ever really knew Thurman Arnold. I respected him. In common with hosts of his friends, I delighted in his wondrous, torrential conversation. Arnold always had time for a visitor from the West, especially if that visitor came out of Wyoming! For Thurman Arnold possessed a nostalgic, almost to the point of naivete, reverence for his memories of life in the West. A minor though vivid illustration of Arnold's sentiment came at a luncheon at the International Club in Washington (then next door to 1229 19th N.W.), when Arnold introduced his friend to Henry Munroe. "You know he is from Wyoming," and before Thurman could finish, Munroe interjected, "and *you* know for Thurman that's enough!" And it was.

Over the next ten years, I mentioned the opportunity of editing the Arnold correspondence to a couple of scholars who I thought might be persuaded to undertake the task. They were intrigued, and both pondered the idea at length before saying "maybe"—someday. In 1970, I decided that if the Arnold family would give its consent I would do the editing. A letter to the executrixes of the Arnold estate, Mrs. Thurman Arnold and Mrs. Carolyn Agger Fortas, brought back the warm response, please proceed.

It has proven a challenging assignment, although I was from the first aware of the difficulty of impressing the image of Thurman Arnold's personality on paper. The introduction aspires to catch the complex, elusive, brilliant, blustering individual who was Thurman Arnold, but it is in his letters that the real Thurman Arnold comes closest to being revealed. The insecure college student out of the West, the young, practicing, bored attorney, the miserable doughboy, the western "probate and real estate" lawyer and aspiring politician, the zestful academician and political theorist, the successful administrative innovator, the restless judge, and finally, the corporate lawyer—all kinescopes of a life come into view with the turn of each page. For an intellect whom others found obtuse and fuzzy, his letters are remarkably straightforward, uninhibited prose. In his correspondence, his moods switched from the solicitous friend to the devil's advocate to the prankster to the dutiful son to the persuasive counselor and to the irritated administrator. In these pages, Thurman Arnold is endowed with a naturalism that would elude the most perceptive portraitist.

Thurman Arnold wrote then, as we have come to realize through the years of immersion in his literary legacy, a much more felicitous autobiography in his correspondence than he did in his half-hearted try at autobiography, *Fair Fights and Foul.* This roaring, dynamic, courtroom performer turned into a blushing self-conscious author when he attempted to write about himself. Indeed, in *Fair Fights and Foul,* his "squirming" can be deciphered in sentence after sentence. He simply detested autobiographical writing; his readers knew it, and his reviewers knew it.

The editor's challenge came in selecting the precise number of letters from the mass of over 17,000 communications which would most accurately portray Thurman Arnold and at the same time spotlight his era. A different editor obviously would have made different selections. In many instances the choice was apparent; numerous Arnold letters would attract attention at a glance. Fortunately Thurman wrote few superfluous communications. Bread-and-butter letters appear with amazing infrequency; acknowledgments of a stream of unsolicited literature were, for the most part, perfunctory. Thurman Arnold was simply not given to writing discursive letters for letter writing's sake. Nor did he write with posterity in mind, as did his friend Harold Ickes. It will be left to the readers (and even more to those who may eventually scan the unpublished Arnold correspondence) to judge how successful the editor has been.

The usual canons of editorial scholarship have been adhered to. Each document appears exactly as Arnold wrote it, with a few minor exceptions which have been noted. For the sake of clarity, the punctuation, in a limited number of instances, has been altered. Each letter has been annotated when it was deemed essential to identify correspondents, personalities, places, and/or events. An effort was made to restrict the footnoting by incorporating extensive biographical and historical background into the introduction. Finally, some may wonder at the dearth of representation from the 1920-1927 period. Unfortunately, the Arnold correspondence from this era as a practicing attorney in Laramie is nonexistent. Arnold thought that his good friend from his Harvard Law School days, Philo Calhoun, had retained the letters which he sent to Calhoun during the twenties. The estate of Philo Calhoun, after an exhaustive search, has failed to locate this Arnold correspondence.

Anyone undertaking a project of this scope inevitably accumulates to his friends and colleagues debts which can never be repaid; this editor is no exception. Earl Pomeroy, who has all too often been assaulted with the writer's prose, read the entire introduction. I have profited, as I have frequently in the past, from his wise and perceptive comments. Another friend, Robert O'Neil, of Indiana University, gave the introduction a critical reading, with the benefit of his legal expertise. Bob O'Neill, whose interest in Arnold extends back to his graduate school days, has an unrivalled understanding of Arnold's legal theory and procedures. Several fellow historians graciously consented to review portions of the introduction. Unanimously they offered helpful and constructive comments. My deep appreciation to Robert Burke, Leonard Bates, Ellis Hawley, Thomas Krueger, Donald McCoy, and Paul L. Murphy.

Without the benediction of the Arnold family, this project would have remained a figment of the editor's imagination, although in no sense should the product be interpreted as having their endorsement. They have not suggested one change in the introduction or text, but they have been ever willing to respond to the editor's garrulous and unceasing questions. My sincerest thanks to Mrs. Thurman Arnold and her sons, George and Thurman Jr.; and to her sister-in-law, Mrs. Olga Moore Arnold.

The partners of Thurman Arnold's firm, Arnold and Porter, could not have been more supportive. They gave their enthusiasm, insight and hours to what from the beginning was obviously another pro bono imposition. In all their interviews, they were consistently candid and reflective in their responses to what, on occasion, could only be described as delicate questions. If they could not answer (and I recall only three refusals) they said so forthrightly. I am especially indebted to William McGovern, who not only made room on his calendar for two time-consuming interviews and read the introduction, but also made arrangements for the editor to use the attractive garden room, the site of so many delightful soirees of the Arnold and Porter firm. Carolyn Agger Fortas, Milton Freeman, one-time partner Victor Kramer, Abe Krash and Paul Porter spent hours with the editor, patiently explaining "the" Thurman Arnold whom they individually knew. Marguerite O'Brien, the loyal, devoted and diplomatic secretary, was of immense help in describing Thurman Arnold's work habits and administrative talents.

Arnold friends and former associates all appeared eager to share their memories of Thurman. The late Hugh Cox, one of the ablest members of the American Bar, unraveled the complexities of the antitrust period and Arnold's legal philosophy on two long, hot summer afternoons. In addition, he responded several times with a lengthy analysis of some of the more enigmatic phases of Arnold's thought. Another intimate friend and colleague, Abe Fortas, made the remarkable offer to the writer to provide "as much time as you want." Then he courteously consented to read the manuscript, providing clarifications, particularly in regard to Arnold's Vietnam position. Judge Gerhard Gesell shared his reminiscences of Arnold's career at Yale. Benjamin V. Cohen, one of the most influential of President Roosevelt's advisors, gave his appreciation of that "remarkable character," Arnold. Cohen, who has suffered through a parade of historians crossing his threshold at 1727 Massachusetts Avenue, never once (audibly) complained about yet one more historical pest.

To Mrs. Esther Kelley, who keeps the office running in spite of her associate, and to Mrs. Norma Mai, who typed the manuscript far too many times, my sincerest thanks.

Finally my gratitude to Joyce and our two descendants, David Randolph and Deborah Ellyn, who put up with my vacant stares at the dinner table—fixed gazes, which they interpreted as, "Father's at the library talking to Thurman again!"

Years ago, Joseph Alsop and Robert Kinter wrote what remains one of the ablest assessments of Arnold, in an article in the *Saturday Evening Post.* In their essay they quoted the then attorney general, Robert Jackson's, description of Arnold, as "a cross between Voltaire and the cowboy, with the cowboy predominating." It still is the most graphic, and perhaps accurate, one-phrase representation of that man from Laramie.

Gene M. Gressley

January 31, 1977
Laramie, Wyoming
Windy, clear, 34°

# Introduction

# Introduction

The place—the United States District Court House, Philadelphia, a typical gray "courthouse Gothic" structure, with hallways built for the passage of regiments, and ceilings of a height that cavalierly disregarded cost and acoustics. The date—the winter of 1942–43. The scene—a courtroom where a legal contest had been under way for the better part of two years. The case—*U.S.* v. *The Pullman Company.* The Pullman Company had displayed at its table a battery of legal talent headed by Ralph Shaw of Winston, Strawn, & Shaw of Chicago, and Seth Richardson of Davies, Richberg, Beebe, Busick, & Richardson of Washington, D.C. Hovering in the back of the courtroom was the star performer for the defense, George Wharton Pepper. Pepper remained mute during the trial until the stage of summation. An ex–United States senator, Pepper's silent presence permeated the atmosphere of the entire courtroom; few trial lawyers in the country exceeded Pepper in his forensic powers. The advocates for the government were represented by Fowler Hamilton, William McGovern and Paul Fitting. The two sets of opposing legal gladiators had been circling and thrusting at each other through the past winter of discontent.

William McGovern found himself in that Philadelphia court of justice as the result of answering a summons from his former professor-mentor, Thurman Arnold, then currently assistant attorney general in charge of the Antitrust Division of the Department of Justice. When McGovern received his invitation from Arnold, he did not debate the merits of the offer but quickly packed his bags and headed for Washington.[1] The morning after his summons, McGovern arrived at the Antitrust Division with eager expectancy and even a tinge of euphoria. Arnold barked at him, "McGovern, ever hear of the Pullman case?" McGovern admitted that he might have vaguely heard of such a case. Arnold shot back, "Get on the train immediately, go up to Philadelphia. Fowler Hamilton called for assistance."

McGovern, with suitcases still packed, headed for Philadelphia. He recalled in later years that he arrived at the old Pennsylvania station with "a heart full of hope and a mind full of emptiness." Fowler Hamilton filled in his new recruit on some of the intricacies of the case in their dilapidated rooms at the Ben Franklin. In many ways the Pullman case was a classic antitrust suit. The Pullman Company, a holding company, comprised two basic operating companies: one, the Pullman Car Manufacturing Company, which constructed passenger and sleeping cars, and two, the Pullman Company, which operated the cars on the railroads. If a railroad wanted Pullman service, and obviously every railroad with passengers did, the railroads had to sign an exclusive contract with the Pullman Company. Part of the fine print in their contracts read that the Pullman Company reserved the right to supply service on cars of their own selection—cars, quite naturally, that their "sister" company manufactured.

For years the coffers of the Pullman Company had been full to overflowing with the royalties paid in by American railroads. Indeed, the Pullman Company had one of the most profitable monopolies ever conceived in the fertile imagination of an entrepreneur. Then a David appeared on the scene, Edward G. Budd by name, who threatened to liquidate completely the treasury of the Pullman firm. Budd, whose company had a wonderful reputation for its technical achievements in the automotive world, had gone on holiday to Europe in the early nineteen thirties. There he rode on clean, streamlined aluminum railroad cars that were vastly superior to any equipment on American railroads. He returned to Pennsylvania determined to build a lightweight, beautifully articulated aluminum train. Enroute to Chicago, Budd attracted the interest of one of the most progressive railroad leaders of the twentieth century, Ralph Budd [no relation], president of the Chicago, Burlington and Quincy Railroad. Together these two innovative industrial leaders set out to implement Edward Budd's European vision.

Ralph Budd approached the Pullman Company, asking them to operate his new cars. The Pullman Company politely refused, pointing out that their contracts specified that they provide both the cars and the service. Utilizing his close connections with the Franklin Roosevelt administration, Ralph Budd vigorously protested the Pullman Company's action in the halls and offices of the Interstate Commerce Commission in Washington. As a result of the pressure applied by Ralph Budd, the Pullman Company agreed to draft a separate contract for ten aluminum cars. The contract was so crammed with onerous provisions that it made it absolutely uneconomical for any other railroad to buy Edward Budd—manufactured cars. With no market, Edward Budd stopped producing railroad cars.

Edward Budd went to Washington for a redress of his grievances. First he went to the Federal Trade Commission, which offered him great empathy but little action. Then Budd decided to see Thurman Arnold in the Antitrust Division. Arnold detected a tailor-made antitrust violation, and immediately filed in Philadelphia an indictment against the Pullman Company.[2] Over the next several months, the courtroom of the U.S. District Court House in Philadelphia rang with the bullhorn voice of Seth

Richardson. A "tall, cadaverous looking guy," McGovern remembered Richardson, with "a fantastic voice that could have been heard in Washington." When Richardson tired, the stage was taken by Ralph Shaw, who loved to sprinkle his speech with a lexicon straight out of the robber-baron era of Chicago, and who tenaciously, sometimes viciously, cross-examined the government witnesses.

A quarter of a century later, McGovern still was convulsed with laughter at the remembrance of Shaw's courtroom pyrotechnics. One morning about halfway through the case, Shaw had been snapping at a witness for about a half hour, insisting that the witness recall in detail conversations some four years in the past. Finally, the witness said, "Well, really, Mr. Shaw, I cannot recall whether that particular point came up or not." Shaw retorted, "You cannot recall whether it happened?" "No, sir," the witness replied, "I can not." Then Shaw yelled at the witness, "Well, sir, you wouldn't say it wasn't so, would you!" McGovern, muttering an oath and thinking, "Thurman never taught me this," violently objected.[3] The judge laughed and said, sustained.

As the case wound down into the late winter of 1942–43, McGovern became increasingly confident that the government had the case won. Then one morning in the coffee shop of the Ben Franklin Hotel, McGovern picked up a copy of the Philadelphia *Bulletin*. He turned to one of the inside pages and read the shocking news that Thurman Arnold had resigned from the Antitrust Division to take an appointment as judge on the United States Circuit Court of Appeals for the District of Columbia. Still in a state of shock, McGovern placed a call to Arnold. After an exchange of bantering, McGovern said, "Thurman, I've got this case won, I could be wrong, you frequently say don't count your chickens before they come home to roost [Arnold delighted in mixing homespun moral fables]. The final argument is next week, why don't you come up here and make the summation, telling us why the Pullman Company is an evil influence on the American scene, etc. You could make this your grand finale!" Arnold, sensing an opportunity to give free rein to his histrionic and combative instincts, quickly consented. "All right, all right, McGovern, I will be up there on Monday; I will take my train, you know my train."[4] For some reason, unfathomable to his wife, friends and associates, Arnold loved to take the midnight Pennsylvania sleeper from Washington to New York, a train which dumped him off at the Pennsylvania station at about five-thirty in the morning.

Monday morning arrived with the final summation on behalf of the defendant to be delivered by George Wharton Pepper, and the reply for the plaintiff by Thurman Arnold. To William McGovern on that crucial Monday, George Wharton Pepper's physical stature seemed twice as impressive as his awesome legal reputation. Over six feet tall, with silver streaked through his hair, lean, with a handsome chiseled countenance, George Wharton Pepper's mere presence dominated any group that he joined. As Pepper rose to address the court, the hum in the courtroom subsided; the spectators leaned forward to listen to one of the brilliant orators of the American bar. They were not disappointed: after a half hour of Pepper's presentation, McGovern recalled, "I want to tell you, that as much as I was persuaded that we had the case won in the terms of antitrust principles. . . that son-of-a-gun, after about thirty minutes shook me, and shook me badly."[5]

Pepper began his discourse by pointing out that this was the first occasion in over a year and a half of sitting in the courtroom that he had taken the liberty of addressing the court. He first called the attention of the court to the fact that he had participated in many antitrust cases, and "with all modesty I can say in some major antitrust cases." In line of this experience he wanted to compliment his young friends from the Department of Justice. "They have presented this case with great elan, perhaps a little overzealous, but this is the overzealousness of youth." Pepper came to Edward G. Budd, pointing out that he had known Budd all his life. "I would go to the grave an unhappy man," Pepper assured the court, "if it occurred to me that in any time in the course of my career as professional lawyer, I had ever taken a position or said a thing that was designed to injure in any way Edward G. Budd. He is a great man. He is everything the government said he was."[6] But the question was, Pepper reminded the court, neither the honor nor the good character of Edward G. Budd, but whether Budd had the right to force his railroad cars on a company with which he was not at all associated. Pepper's booming voice sounded throughout the courtroom for more than three hours while he presented "just a few insights" into the Pullman Company case.

As McGovern sat there listening to Pepper's masterful performance, he believed that for the first time he had some appreciation for what Ulysses had endured listening to the Sirens. In concluding his oration, Pepper again reminded the court that he had stayed above the "storm and stress of the trial," but he "simply hoped that perhaps I have been able to bring to your honors some perspective on this case that your honors might find helpful in deciding it."

As Pepper sat down a hush fell over the courtroom. Suddenly, the still silence erupted with a harsh , nasal twang, perhaps a roar, from the government table. "Your honors." The judges, lulled by Pepper's soliloquy, jerked like Jack-in-the-boxes, to the right and to the left. "Your honors, my good friend Senator Pepper states that by sitting in the back of the courtroom, he has remained above the storm and stress of this trial, and that somehow this has made him objective and given him perspective. As your honors know I have been one-hundred-fifty miles away from this case, and if sitting in the back of the courtroom makes you objective, your honors, I can claim that I have more objectivity than Senator Pepper on this case. Furthermore, I just happen to have in my pocket here, my appointment by the president of the United States to the Circuit Court of Appeals; so if your honors will move over, I will get up there and help you decide this case."[7] The judges laughed; the courtroom audience roared.

The mellifluous spell of George Wharton Pepper had been smashed by a Western-born lawyer who knew intuitively how to slice through banalities. McGovern considered Arnold's performance not only a perfect antidote to Pepper but one of the most masterful tours de force that he had ever encountered in a courtroom. After his opening comments, Arnold proceeded to assure the judges that this case was just like the Alcoa case, the Coca-Cola case, and a long row of other precedents. As a matter of fact, there were very few similarities with the Alcoa case, or the Coca-Cola case; McGovern and Fitting had spent several hours trying to disabuse Arnold of these analogies. But Arnold, once he had a mental set, refused to be switched.

Arnold's summation in the Pullman case illustrates two distinctive traits of his mental patterns. First, he had an unerring sense of the essential, the heart of the matter. He demolished Pepper, and won the judges over to his side, with one of his most potent and frequently employed weapons—satire. Second, Arnold's courtroom arguments could be completely disorganized. Forgetful of names, whether of clients or cases, he reduced more than one court to chaos by his habit of handing one set of documents to a judge, a different set to a jury, and sometimes yet another to a witness. The point to be remembered is that somehow all this turbulence did not seem to make any difference. For Arnold could, as he did so beautifully that Monday morning in Philadelphia with one or two brilliant ripostes, completely demolish a well-phrased argument and annihilate the opposing counsel's composure.

The slayer of George Wharton Pepper's argument began life in the style of most beginners—inauspiciously, in Laramie, Wyoming on June 2, 1891. Even the local press, the Laramie *Boomerang* (named after onetime editor Bill Nye's errant mule), failed to note the momentous arrival of Thurman Wesley Arnold at the Constantine Peter Arnold home, 812 Grand Avenue. However, not everyone ignored the birth on Laramie's main street. The first University of Wyoming commencement, lasting three to four days, was held that June. According to one eyewitness, the stage contained so many flowers that they all but hid the orators. At the conclusion of the festivities, one of the two graduating seniors, William Bramel, took flowers to Mrs. C.P. Arnold in "honor of the newly-arrived son."[8]

Thurman Arnold as a young boy.

Thurman's father, C.P. Arnold, renowned for his command of the law and of poetry.

Long after Thurman left Laramie, he looked back on his life there with tremendous nostalgia and emotion. He wrote in the first sentences of his autobiography, "I will never get over my love for that wild semiarid country. . . ."[9] In fact, the opening chapter of his memoir is one of the best descriptions to be found of a Western town at the turn of the century. Laramie in the 1890s had a population of some 6,338 souls.[10] The economic base mixed a merchant-ranch economy with a sprinkling of industry—the Union Pacific, the tie plant, the rolling mill. The geographic setting is magnificent with the Snowy Range of the Rockies thirty miles to the west, incredibly stark in their whiteness, and to the east, lower and greener, the Laramie range, which during the nineteenth century was often referred to as the Black Hills.

As Thurman so vividly described in his autobiography,[11] the Laramie of his youth was populated by numerous town "characters," people of the ilk of the infamous Colonel E.J. Bell, whose Millbrook Ranch his father, C.P. Arnold, later acquired. Rotund, short, and profane, Colonel Bell had the disconcerting habit of aiming heavenward any firearm that might be handy, and firing off a shot at the Almighty. What infuriated the good Colonel most was having the heavy rains come down on his newly-mown hay, or not having the rains come at all, leaving his crops to wither away. To a society that stood in mortal fear of eternal damnation from an immensely personal God, such actions, as Thurman observed, "chilled us to the bone." In a lightning storm one stayed clear of trees and Colonel Bell!

Another of the town's "select" individuals was Elmer Lovejoy; Elmer was Laramie's Thomas Edison and Henry Ford rolled into one unforgettable character. In 1895, twenty-three-year-old Elmer constructed Laramie's first gasoline "horseless" carriage. Elmer sped around Laramie's byways at the incredible velocity of eight miles an hour in this carriage resembling a beer wagon and powered by a one-cylinder, two-cycle marine engine. Deciding that the ride was far too rough, Elmer placed balloon tires on his vehicle twenty-five years before they became commonplace on American autos. Lovejoy also invented the steering gear knuckle, which was in use in cars for the next five decades. Unable to obtain financing for a patent, he sold it to the Locomobile Company for $800 and one Locomobile steamer. Having established a garage in Laramie, Elmer maintained the Franklin agency for years. Then in 1917, he patented the first electric automatic garage door opener, manufactured the doors for a few years, but lost interest and went back to being a garageman. Elmer died in 1960, one of those mechanical geniuses, a square peg in a round hole, who never really discovered his "take-off" stage.[12]

Contemporary with Elmer Lovejoy and E.J. Bell, and on anyone's list of Laramie's incredible characters, is the name of Grace Raymond

Hebard.[13] Civil engineer, suffragist, historian, librarian, golf champion, secretary of the University board of trustees, she led a fantastic career. Grace R. Hebard migrated from Iowa to Wyoming in 1882, first to Cheyenne, where she found employment in the state engineer's office for nine years. During her life in Cheyenne, she lobbied, according to her account, for women's suffrage, this activity resulting in the passage of the first state women's voting legislation. In 1891 she joined the faculty of the University of Wyoming as a member of the political economy department, plus accepting an appointment as secretary of the board of trustees. Miss Hebard, in effect, was her own employer. This astounding situation continued for the next eighteen years! Few individuals in the history of the University of Wyoming have had more political power than this lady historian. Rumors persist to the present that the "scalps" of at least two University presidents could be laid at Dr. Hebard's door. An author of some seven volumes on the history of Wyoming and the West, her research habits were unorthodox to say the least. Fascinated by the history of Shoshone Indians, she saw nothing incongruous about "tipping" a member of the tribe to tell her tales of old. When the stories ran down, another gratuity produced more imagination. This formidable lady made her greatest contribution to the University in bequeathing her collection of Western books and manuscripts to the University of Wyoming Library. Today the Hebard Collection forms the nucleus of an outstanding Western history collection.

One could enumerate the names of other "individualists" of Laramie in the early twentieth century. A frequent cliché which permeates many histories of the West is that the West fostered the eccentric individualist, the loner. Admittedly the bonds of social conformity were looser than in Eastern drawing rooms, yet such analysis misses the main point; the prime reason for the benevolent toleration of the Lovejoys, the Hebards and the Bells centered on the elemental fact of a sparse population. Wisdom and common sense dictated that one cherish his neighbors; in a limited society one did not cultivate enemies. Survival required interdependence. Viewed from this reserve position, the social controls and covenants of Western social conformity may have been even tighter than their Eastern counterparts.

Regardless of the social stratification, Laramie of the 1890s was a wonderful place for a boy to grow up. As a youth and as an adult, Thurman was entranced with the adventures of Tom Sawyer and Huckleberry Finn. The Laramie plains bore little resemblance to the banks of the Mississippi, but for a boy with the imagination of Thurman, the rolling land could be turned into the land of Alnaschar. There were few rafts or canoes, and no steamboats, but there were mountains to hike in, grasslands to explore, and Indian artifacts to pick up. On a summer

Saturday afternoon, just by squinting at the horizon one could see Chiefs Washakie of the Shoshone and Red Cloud of the Sioux come sweeping across the plains. True, there came an age when one no longer related these visions at the supper table, but by that time life had lost a lot of dreams.

After what Thurman always remembered as an idyllic boyhood, he left Laramie to enroll in Wabash College, Crawfordsville, Indiana, in the autumn of 1907, a couple of months short of his sixteenth birthday. Wabash accepted 51 quarter hours of transfer credit from the University of Wyoming that Thurman had accumulated while a student at the preparatory school of the University.[14] Academically Thurman excelled at Wabash, taking courses in Greek drama, elementary German, rhetoric and inorganic chemistry. By the end of his first year, he had accumulated 99 quarter credits of 188 for graduation. However, by the spring of 1908 nothing could have persuaded Thurman to stay another year in Indiana. Socially the experience had been so miserable that afterwards he seldom referred to Wabash and omitted reference to that year in his various autobiographical sketches.[15]

Thurman returned to college in the fall of 1908; this time he selected Princeton. He could never recall why he chose Princeton, except for some vague ideas about its "Presbyterian leanings" and its quality reputation. Again he excelled academically. By the time he graduated with the class of 1911, he had absorbed heavy doses of Italian, German, history, economics, and political science, plus a smattering of mathematics, Latin, philosophy, logic, physics, psychology and French.[16] At commencement he received the kudo of being elected to Phi Beta Kappa with "High Honors in Politics." Socially, Princeton represented only a slight improvement over Wabash. Fifty years later he recalled the uncomfortable situation of being a young Western "cowboy" in an Ivy League atmosphere. "My Western clothes, mannerisms, and speech did not fit. I was immediately classed as a queer character. I was not admitted to any club; indeed I was never admitted to anything at Princeton. . . . My years at Princeton were chiefly remarkable for their loneliness."[17]

After a summer in Laramie, Thurman returned to academic life, this time enrolling in the Harvard Law School. For the first time Thurman found his pursuit of higher education rewarding and challenging. His teachers transcended the narrow confines of a classical curriculum, "eternal verities and absolute certainties" fell by the wayside. Thurman reveled in the hard work, "something no one ever did at Princeton."[18] Again he did well academically, immersing himself in civil procedure, contracts, criminal law, property and torts the first year. The second year he crammed with classes in bankruptcy, bills and notes, damages, equity evidence, property, public service and sales. The third year rounded out his curriculum with conference of law, constitutional law, corporations, equity, suretyship and mortgage and trusts.[19]

Thurman having lost "enough of my Western manners," Harvard became his first pleasant social experience in the East. He went so far as to purchase a tuxedo so that he would be properly attired for symphonic concerts. He even encountered Eastern crime; at an outing on Revere Beach a pickpocket managed to relieve him of his monetary possessions.[20] Typically resourceful, Thurman pawned his Phi Beta Kappa key for carfare to go to Cambridge and for the first and last time was properly impressed with the high academic honor: after all, if a Phi Beta Kappa key was negotiable, one could not regard the organization as completely useless. At Harvard he acquired numerous friends, among them Philo Calhoun, who became a lifelong friend.

When we read Thurman's remarkable letter home describing the Christmas of 1912 in the Calhoun home,[21] we can recapture the warmth radiated, the feeling of peace and well-being which enveloped Thurman. All of the nostalgia and the romanticism of a holiday season in a seemingly uncomplicated era is in every line of Thurman's portraiture—long walks and animated conversations with Philo, reading contemporary novels, movies, feasting and more reading. Particularly engraved in Thurman's memory was a night ride back from Stamford: "It was one of those sharp winter evenings, when every star seems etched in diamond point in the frosty sky, and the bare arms of the trees seemed like frozen moonlight, as we whizzed past them on the beautiful roads at 50 miles an hour."[22] For the first time he had been made to feel as much at home in the East as he would have been in Laramie.

During Thurman's last year at Harvard, he expended considerable time with the Harvard Legal Aid Society, where he received a glimpse into the problems of a metropolitan practice among the indigent. Divorce cases were "a nuisance, as I have to trot around to strange places to get affidavits, and it takes a lot of time." More often than not his efforts came to naught "because my clients have not as yet succeeded in raising enough money to pay the initial costs, which I have heartily refused to put up for them."[23]

In the winter of 1914 Thurman engaged in a game of mental gymnastics about his future. The West had a strong emotional pull, yet if he returned to Laramie he knew that his practice, while more remunerative than that of the clients furnished by the Harvard Legal Aid Society, would be of the same genre—collections, divorces, probate. The deciding factor came through in a carefully composed letter to his father: ". . . to go home seems like drifting with the current and taking the easiest course out."[24]

After consulting with several friends about the best of all possible urban worlds, Thurman selected Chicago in which to settle. Then, even as now, the Windy City seemed to many to be the Chicago of Carl

Sandburg—hustling, raw, violent, dynamic. For Thurman it had an added appeal: it was farther West. Arriving in Chicago in August of 1914, he temporarily "took quarters" at the Wilson Avenue YMCA. Twenty minutes from the Loop, a swimming pool and a good gym, all for the price of thirteen dollars per month, made the "Y" a good home for a "broke" young aspiring lawyer, in spite of the "exceeding diminutive character of the rooms."[25]

The struggling young lawyer image was not an aphorism as far as Thurman was concerned. The years in Chicago consisted largely of wearisome routine practice, with the accompanying challenge of making ends meet. Even though Thurman was often exhausted by the work load, it was more from boredom and loneliness than from accomplishment. His legal tasks accumulated into one long treadmill of divorce, collection and criminal cases. One exciting episode came early in 1915, when a large Wisconsin lumber company teetered and then collapsed into bankruptcy.[26] The legal complexities, compounded by fraud, stimulated Thurman's imagination.

On the assumption that the rewards, both economic and professional, might be greater if they were on their own, Thurman and two friends created the firm of O'Bryan, Waite and Arnold in January of 1916. They rented office space in the New York Life building, more sumptuous quarters than they could afford. For the first few months, O'Bryan, Waite and Arnold were kept afloat by Arnold's former firm of Adams, Follansbee, Hawley and Shorey, which, out of a mixture of kindness and pity, "subcontracted" its routine legal research.[27] After six months, Thurman assured his parents that they were encouraged by the progress of their new firm, for their finances showed a steady progression upward. The first month they collected $293.00 in cash; the second month, $197.00; and in May they reached the munificent amount of $301.85. They had managed to acquire other assets, including $275.00 in uncollected fees, plus $200.00 worth of stock in a motor lock company, "which looks to me to be a very fair proposition."[28]

Twelve days after Thurman had written home so optimistically, he wrote again to say that his artillery battery of the Illinois National Guard had been called up. Thurman was decidedly dejected about joining Battery C, First Field Artillery, for Pershing's punitive expedition against Villa. He noted to his father, "It seems rather a wasteful method of patrolling the border with men who have an earning capacity of over $5,000 a year when it could be done as well by a standing army getting $2.00 a day. But that is the way they do things in this country."[29]

If Thurman had doubts about the wisdom of his residence at Fort Sheridan, just north of Chicago, he had even more misgivings when he finally arrived on the Mexican border. Although he gave the impression that he thrived on the heat, soon the inaction, the unpalatable food and the misery of his follow soldiers all combined to make him thoroughly disgusted with President Wilson's Mexican adventure. Fortunately, the emergency did not last long; by late September, he had exchanged the burning sun of Texas for the cool wind of Wyoming. On the assumption that the populace of Laramie would enjoy hearing tales of Villa and the Mexican fracas, Thurman's father scheduled a public lecture for Thurman. On the broadside printed up for the occasion, C.P. Arnold billed his son as "The Man from Mexico."

After the welcome Wyoming respite, Thurman returned to his Chicago practice. By December his future in Chicago appeared bleaker than ever. The cash flow for O'Bryan, Waite and Arnold came to $51 in November, "skyrocketing" in December to $110.[30] The day before Christmas of 1916, Thurman wrote his father, "No very rosy sunset closes the year with O'Bryan, Waite and Arnold. Poverty still lurks in every corner."[31] In spite of the evil threat of penury, Thurman expropriated ten dollars of the Christmas check from his parents for dancing lessons. While he scorned the ballroom, ". . . still one cannot afford to be too different from one's fellow creatures."[32] Tortuously, Thurman was making some accomodation to the social mores of a sophisticated society.

By March of 1917 Thurman's spirits, along with the firm's financial situation, improved, although the uncertainty surrounding America's involvement in the First World War threw a pall over their plans for the future. The indecisive moment did not last long; on May 13, 1917, Thurman reported to Fort Sheridan. After spending most of the summer in training, he left for New York with orders to sail for France on September 8th. While he waited in New York to leave for Europe, Thurman's emotions were in more of a turmoil than he would admit to his family or friends. In fact, the only hint of his mental state was contained in the last sentence of a letter home on August 24: "I've been in a state of indecision as to whether to wire Frances to come and stay with the Calhouns for a few days. Maybe I will."[33]

Evidently Thurman's debate with himself was quickly resolved. In Chicago, Frances Longan was dining with her sister at the Blackstone Hotel when she received a wire from New York requesting that she come immediately to Gotham to become Mrs. Thurman Arnold. Frances hesitated just long enough to horrify her sister, cash a draft at Marshall Field's and board a train for New York.[34] After a series of misadventures that included Thurman's unexplained absence from New York and his leaving his billfold on a train, Thurman and Frances were married on September 4, 1917. Six days later Thurman sailed for France.

Frances Longan Arnold had grown up in Sedalia, Missouri, where her father was a prominent and affluent attorney and judge. Mrs. Longan, a very proper lady, possessed a well-honed code of social conduct. One of the strongest commandments in that code stated that young Southern ladies, regardless of the attractiveness of their swain, did not run off and get married. Over the years, no matter how often they retold the story, Frances and Thurman always found high humor in relating Mrs. Longan's reaction on that fateful morning. As Frances Arnold recently told the anecdote, the telegraph operator in Sedalia, renowned for his officiousness, called the Longan home and in a solicitous tone asked, "Mrs. Longan, is the Judge there?" She replied, "No, Mr. McGreney." "Well," said the telegraph operator, "That's too bad; I am sorry he's not with you." Now very worried, Mrs. Longan said, "Well, what's the matter, is there bad news?" The operator replied, "I don't know how the news will affect you, but . . ." Mrs. Longan, becoming highly exasperated, said, "Well, go ahead and tell me about it, because the Judge has gone to the office, and I have to know sooner or later." The operator then blurted out, "Well, it seems Frances has gotten married." At this point Thurman usually interrupted, "Mother then took to her bed and didn't get up for three weeks!" And she truly did, Frances added![35]

While Mrs. Longan was doing her best to adjust to her daughter's new state, Thurman was discovering life as a doughboy in France. He always recalled the war as one of the worst periods of his life. In *Fair Fights and Foul* he comments, "The chief discomforts were the cold and the wet, which I shall never forget."[36] Sentence after sentence, in his letters home, revealed his disgust with the inanity of war. On March 4, 1918, he wrote to the Arnolds in Laramie, "This war seems such an endless business. Both sides lodged in almost impregnable positions, shooting millions of dollars worth of ammunition, consuming incredible quantities of supplies, and accomplishing nothing—not even in a military way. Everyone seems so settled in the war. Seems a normal method of existence almost. Except one gets so weary of the cold, the lack of civilized comforts, and the endless ruin everywhere."[37] Interlaced with his commentary on the war, in common with thousands of other soldiers, would be requests for cigars ("can't get good ones here"), heavy pajamas and woolen socks ("lost all I had"), milk chocolate ("can't get it here"), and smoking tobacco ("terrible").[38]

By August of 1918 Thurman had been ordered back to the United States to serve as an instructor for new units. However, to no one's surprise, a change of orders occurred, and Thurman's 35th Field Artillery was ordered to the front. Before they could get there, the Armistice was signed.

With the conclusion of the First World War, Thurman again confronted the question that had plagued him when he left Harvard: Where should he practice? This time he did little agonizing over the alternatives but returned immediately to Laramie to enter his father's law office. There are several reasons for his decision. First, his father, who owned the Millbrook Ranch, had cast a covetous eye on three sections of land adjoining it. If Thurman, his brother Carl and another friend would just homestead these lands for a year, Father Arnold promised to reward them amply. Of course, as Thurman never ceased to point out to his father, this was patently illegal. Nevertheless they all agreed to participate in Father Arnold's "fraud." Second, Thurman had tried big city practice and found it wanting both financially and professionally. With a bride to consider, he felt he could no longer afford the luxury of experimenting with his future. So while the return to Laramie may have been made with some apprehension, actually there were few other possibilities.

As Thurman later remembered, the Laramie of the 1920s seemed much like the Laramie of his youth, "a wild and woolly place." According to the 1920 census, the Gem City of the Plains had some 6,300 inhabitants.[39] What the census did not disclose was the strong personal life-style among the residents. Not only did everyone know his neighbor but was frequently related to him; he usually knew what "Laramieites" had done yesterday, what they were engaged in today, and what they planned for tomorrow. In essence, Laramie society resembled any small Western or Midwestern town. Sherwood Anderson could have found Winesburg in Laramie as easily as in Clyde, Ohio. What is less realized is that the Laramie of the seventies still retains much of the social flavor of the twenties. True, as Thurman pointed out, the Laramie of the forties and fifties contained far fewer "individualists" than thirty years earlier; yet personal relationships still count heavily in a state with a population of 340,000. This one-to-one relationship has made life in Wyoming rewarding for some and for others frustrating.

If one were to take the society columns of the two Laramie newspapers, the *Boomerang* and the *Republican*, literally and seriously, the impression would be that Laramie had an extremely active, as well as stratified, social life in the 1920s. Seemingly there was an unending round of social club affairs, especially those centering on the performing arts. The musicales of the Tuesday Music Club were a favorite, although the plays of the drama club were well attended.[40] For one of these Jester Club performances, C.P. Arnold wrote a play on the theme of world peace, entitled "Merrie Christmas," which, according to the *Boomerang*, brought a "beautiful, and at the same time an original message."[41]

If Laramie socialites became bored with their own imaginations, there were always church functions and bridge clubs to attend. The names of the Arnold families, both the father's and the son's, surface continuously in the newspaper columns. Frances Arnold was an enthusiastic member of the Friday afternoon bridge club, and occasionally Thurman joined

Panoramic view of Laramie's city center (Second Street and Garfield) in Thurman Arnold's youth, early 1900s. Courtesy of Mrs. Frances Arnold.

The Arnold horse and buggy in front of the C.P. Arnold home, 812 Grand, Laramie. Courtesy of Mrs. Frances Arnold.

in the supper-bridge festivities. At these gatherings, gossip about the local moonshine raids provided additional entertainment. One particularly memorable event, whispered about for months, came in the wake of a "cruel fire" in the Binford Forest, northeast of Laramie. When the fire had run its course, there in stark nakedness for all to view was "a big moonshine still," replete with the accoutrements of "two large copper kettles, four barrels of mash, a gasoline stove, yeast, coloring dyes," and other paraphernalia.[42]

As a family, the Arnolds found themselves participating in an active, if slightly disorganized, social calendar. One of the favorite yearly gatherings of the Arnold clan and friends was C.P. Arnold's winter picnic. Oldtimers in Laramie still recall these frigid but convivial outings. C.P. Arnold usually held the picnic in February at the Millbrook Ranch. He would frequently write a long poem commemorating the event. After reciting his verse, "C.P." would then lapse into an extensive monologue on the wonders of the West, the beauty of Wyoming and how fortunate they were to be living amidst these gorgeous natural surroundings.[43]

As delightful as the horseplay at the Elks Club, winter picnics and bridge parties may have been, for Thurman life in Laramie did not pivot on these social affairs but on the intellectual stimulation he received and exchanged with numerous friends on the University of Wyoming faculty. These friends included Fred Nussbaum, an internationally known historian with an engaging, barbed wit; Wilson Clough, a pioneer in the American Studies movement in the United States who had a stringent, satirical view of life; and Samuel "Doc" Knight, who created a geology department that ranked among the finest in the world. Knight, Clough and Nussbaum remained lifelong friends. Thurman cherished these relationships. They are why he always remembered Laramie of the 1920s as intellectually stimulating.

These friendships also reveal another one of Thurman's strong traits of personality. He made friends easily, and he retained them, for he was always extremely loyal to his friends and associates, displaying a loyalty that was inevitably reciprocated. An engrossing aspect of Thurman's comrades derives from their extreme catholicity.[44] In the political spectrum, they ranged from Alfred Landon and Robert Taft to Max Lerner and Harold Laski.[45] Among the legal profession his friendships ran from the most conservative, stolid members of the bar to the most brilliant and stimulating. There was a simplistic philosophy underlying Arnold's fraternity of friends; to use a crippled aphorism—he liked people and they responded in kind.[46] Many of his associates instantly trusted him. This quality was vividly exposed during the New Deal days, when his relations with the fourth estate were solidly grounded on mutual confidence.

Revelers at one of the famous Constantine Peter Arnold Winter Picnics.

Laramie natives who found their recreation on picnics, at University cultural affairs, and in civic clubs sought their employment in a variety of small industries, specifically: the Midwest Refinery, the Monolith plant, the forest treating company, the Union Pacific Railroad and the University. Laramie has always maintained an economy which has fostered slow but steady growth. Laramie in 1972, with a population of 23,000, ranks third in size among the urban communities of Wyoming. Thurman Arnold, in his autobiography as elsewhere, emphasized the lack of economic opportunity in Wyoming, and the Eastern colonialism in the West as a number of the local businesses were absorbed into national corporations.[47] Arnold further ascribes this lack of economic future as one of the motivating forces behind his leaving the West. His friends of that era, however, do not recall that he had a preoccupation with Eastern exploitation. Nevertheless, Arnold was correct; Laramie's economy historically has been dominated by outside capital—a feature that Laramie has in common with hundreds of other communities.

While Thurman may have been concerned with the stagnant economy of Laramie, the only overt way he participated in Laramie's progress was in the political arena. Local politics for Thurman were far more than a diversion; he pursued elective office purposely and intensely. First, Thurman knew instinctively that if he wished to increase his practice, politics presented a broad billboard. Further, although his political career could never be described as a roaring success, it is obvious that he enjoyed campaigning. Finally, while we may debate the degree of his commitment to the princples of progressivism, there is little doubt that Thurman wanted to practice what he preached to his friends on Saturday night at the Elks Club.

Within less than two years after his return from the First World War, Thurman launched his first political campaign for a seat in the Wyoming House of Representatives. He came in third among a field of six candidates, and thereby won one of the four seats of Albany County.[48] The immediate reward was a trip to Cheyenne on a bitterly cold January morn over the long, steep, icy Sherman hill. Thurman Arnold's performance at the opening session of the sixteenth legislature on January 11, 1921 has become engrained in the political folklore of Wyoming. As Thurman recalled the scene fifty years later, he sat in the House chamber enduring a number of flowery and long-winded speeches extolling the virtues of first one and then another candidate for the speakership. As the lone Democrat in the entire House, Thurman decided that it was his moral obligation to redress matters. So he rose just as the final vote was about to be taken and said, "Mr. Speaker, the Democratic party caucused last night, and when the name of Thurman Arnold was mentioned, it threw its hat up in the air and cheered for fifteen minutes. I, therefore, wish to put his name in nomination for speaker of the House." Thurman sat down, quickly rising again to second the nomination, with the sterling, emotion-packed words, "I have known Thurman Arnold for most of my life, and would trust him as far as I would myself." Then with the House in a hilarious uproar, and the speaker pro tem in a state of befuddlement, Thurman rose a third time and, with a magnanimous flourish, said, "Mr. Speaker, some irresponsible Democrat has put my name in nomination and I wish to withdraw it."[49]

After that unforgettable introduction to the Wyoming legislature, Thurman settled down to more mundane legislative matters. The Wyoming electorate, along with the rest of the nation, was in a mood for economy. Joining a number of Republicans, Thurman proposed a raise for all state officials. A majority of Republicans opposed the raise "as playing politics." Representative Mercer from Big Horn County pointed his finger at Arnold and roared, "Representative Arnold would like to see us raise salaries, for it would be a black eye to the Republican party. But we must not do it."[50] After a substantial oratorical display, the Republican party decided a caucus was required. Again Arnold, sensitive to an opportunity, rose and called for a Democratic caucus, "The Democratic caucus will be held in the hall just outside, and all disgruntled Republicans are invited to join in the deliberations of the Democratic caucus. We will treat them well."[51]

The other fiscal fight centered on the overall reduction of the state budget, with the University of Wyoming budget being slashed by twenty-five percent across the board. Arnold, reflecting his constituency along with his own personal convictions, vigorously protested the University's reduction—all to no avail.[52]

In view of Arnold's later career, the most intriguing bill that he sponsored and that the legislature passed provided stiff penalties for conviction of individuals whose property was used for prostitution, gambling and the dispensing of liquor. Arnold obviously wanted his constituents to know that he was on the side of morality, especially since his candidacy had been endorsed by the prohibition elements in Laramie.[53] In addition, what many commentators had overlooked about Arnold is that he personally endorsed the same standards of morality as his neighbors on Fifteenth Street. As one of his close friends and partners in Arnold and Porter later emphasized, "Never forget, Thurman was always for God, country and mother's apple pie."[54]

Unequivocally committed to Edgar Guest's ideals, Arnold was never so simplistic as to assume that one could outlaw sin by legislative fiat. However, one of Thurman's favorite maxims—which he never tired of telling students—was that all that was necessary to transform the world into a moral heaven was one law prohibiting all sin. If this law could be passed and enforced, all the rest of the statutes in the cosmos would be superfluous.

Thurman's personal endorsement of public virtue aside, the abatement act, as this legislation became known, was aimed at Laramie's populace.[55] Further, how much the act enhanced Arnold's political fortunes is highly debatable. We have been able to uncover only one public comment about Arnold's arrow aimed at sin, and that a brief editorial by his longtime friend (later a foremost leader of Wyoming Democracy), Tracy McCracken.[56]

Perhaps the best indication of the populace's approval came in November 1922, when Thurman won the mayoralty election by forty-four votes.[57] The campaign had been a hotly contested one with the primary issue focusing on the employment of the Republican candidate, Frank Blair, by the local Standard Oil (Indiana) refinery. The Democrats, in a "whisper" campaign (so screamed the Republicans), were insidiously suggesting that a vote for Blair was a vote for Eastern exploitation and bossism.[58] Blair, in a paid political advertisement in the *Boomerang,* argued that on the contrary, "a connection with such a corporation is indeed a great influence on one's ideas of how a municipal corporation can be better managed."[59]

Thurman ran a very issue-oriented campaign spelling out in newspaper columns and speeches a specific platform directed to answering Laramie's municipal problems. Slyly noting that "unlike most candidates . . . I can not claim that I was forced into the race by admiring friends,"[60] he announced his program: the removal of the fish hatchery to stop a source of local pollution; the erection of a viaduct over the extensive Union Pacific yards; the continuation of a sewer construction program; the compelling of the Intermountain Railway Light and Power Company to give up its street railway franchise on expansion of "feeder" lines; the continuation of improvement of city streets; the enlargement of the Union Pacific depot; and the practice of economy. Arnold concluded by reminding the citizenry, "I represent no corporation whose interest by way of taxation or otherwise conflicts with the interest of this city."[61]

Three days before Christmas of 1922 Thurman outlined to his neighbors the philosophical structure for accomplishing his ambitious program. First, he observed that city government was "usually good or bad in proportion to the amount of interest taken in it by the citizens." Therefore, he hoped to form a city planning club, whereby all citizens would gather together to discuss civic welfare. From time to time, he anticipated publishing articles in the newspapers giving "State of Laramie" messages.[62]

Two weeks later at his first city council meeting Thurman amplified his municipal ideology. Good municipal government, he claimed, rested on three supports: "leadership; intelligent interest and co-operation of the citizens and taxpayers; and expert technical advice on numerous technical problems which arise.'"[63] Thurman described the implementation: the first goal of leadership he hoped to provide; the second goal of citizen involvement would come through publicity and education; and the third aim would be accomplished through hiring outside consultants.

Then Arnold tackled the moral climate of Laramie. "There are two problems of equal importance in the enforcement of the prohibition law. The first is the problem of the bootlegger, which is a police problem. The second, and equally important one, is the problem of the purchaser, which must be dealt with by an educated and organized public opinion. Moral conditions in Laramie are not bad but there is room for improvement."[64] For Laramie's elite this represented a unique and uncomfortable twist to their consciences. Arnold not only damned the bootlegger, who was fair game for all, but he had the audacity to suggest that Laramie society should be equated with the supplier of moonshine!

Arnold's program was a translation of progressivism in its purest state. Indeed, one of the few clear ideological strains in Arnold's thought which he carried throughout his life focused on the progressive creed. To a Westerner, acutely aware of the impact of colonialism on his region, Brandeisian economic doctrine made sense. Time and again, in speech after speech, and essay after essay, the shibboleths of progressivism emanated from Arnold's voice and pen. Nor should it be surprising that Arnold chose the mayoralty period as the first testing of his personal progressivism. The twenties saw the emergence of municipal reform on a broad front. A dozen or more articles on the subject of municipal regeneration appeared in national periodicals in 1921 alone. Two of these authors espoused programs very similar to the one Arnold announced to his fellow citizens.[65] Whether Thurman read these specific essays or not is unimportant; what is obvious and well known is that progressivism was part and parcel of urban theory during the twenties. He could not have ignored Brandeis, the *New Republic,* and the other bastions of progressivism, had he wanted. Furthermore, for Arnold the ideas endorsed by Walter Lippmann and cohorts held a strong appeal.

Now that Arnold had prescribed progressivism as the cure for Laramie ills, what happened? The answer is simply nothing. Discussion of civic participation through city planning clubs stopped. No outside consultants were employed to offer their brand of efficiency. In fact, if one peruses the *Boomerang* and the *Republican,* what is striking is the somnolent atmosphere that enshrouded city affairs. Little opinion, pro or con, appears in daily and weekly columns.

This is not to say that all civic progress ceased. The paving of Grand Avenue proceeded, the fish hatchery and the water supply were separated, and a proclamation was issued concerning resident water use.[66] A blow for righteousness was struck by Arnold when proceedings were instituted (under the abatement act) against a couple of members of the local radical "Wobblies." One of the "Wobblies" was taken into custody on the charge of "using profane and abusive language."[67] Yet most of Arnold's program, let alone his progressive philosophy, did not surface during his tenure as mayor. To the obvious question of why, there is no obvious answer.

The entrenched financial and political leadership of Laramie may have blocked Arnold's path to reform. If so, the opposition was more covert than overt. Another plausible but not too convincing answer is that Arnold may have himself become bored with the implementation of progressivism. Perhaps the tenable explanation for the abortion of Arnold's civic program is a combination of both factors, plus the political apathy of Laramie's citizens.

The first opportunity for the voters of Laramie to express their opinion of Arnold's mayoralty came in the summer of 1924, when Thurman announced his candidacy for county prosecuting attorney in the Democratic primary.[68] For some months the town gossips had spread the rumor that Arnold had his eyes on a seat in Congress. When the primary ballot was tallied in August, Arnold came in fourth among a field of four, two Republicans and two Democrats.[69] Thurman's ego suffered from his first political defeat. He was so disappointed that his wife,[70] in retrospect, believes that this premature consignment to political oblivion may have been a major factor behind his eventual interest in leaving Laramie.

Upon handing the reins of Laramie's government over to the new mayor, C.E. Blair, on January 3, 1925,[71] Thurman devoted his entire energy to building up the practice of Arnold and Arnold. In some ways, the task more than matched the challenge of establishing a political career. Thurman's father had the disconcerting habit of throwing clients with whom he disagreed out of his office![72] While such behavior may have relieved C.P. Arnold's frustrations, the attendant publicity did little in the way of attracting new business. Frances Arnold, who remembers her father-in-law with affection, nevertheless refers to him as being extremely authoritarian with his family—a benevolent tyrant.[73] Even today among Laramie's senior citizens there are almost as many stories about Father Arnold as there are about his sons.

Over the years "C.P." amassed a battery of imaginative courtroom acrobatics. A favorite device, which he employed shamelessly when he sensed that he was losing an argument, was to recite poetry for the edification of the entire courtroom. Usually he began with a monologue, emphasizing to judge, jury and witness that twentieth-century America should honor poets and poetry. Then he followed up by reciting as many verses of his favorite poems as the benevolence of the judge and the opposing counsel would allow.

So when Thurman returned from the First World War he faced the Herculean task of overcoming the antipathy generated by his father. One of the legends that persists most about Thurman was that he really knew little about the mechanics of law and could not care less. One of Thurman's closest and most perceptive friends dissents from this view: "He had a knowledge of details, of the technical branch of the law, which he never made any point of, and nobody knew anything about, but you would discover it if you started talking to him about technicalities; I attribute that to his experience in Laramie."[74] Thurman's success in his Laramie practice buttresses Hugh Cox's assessment. In *Fair Fights and Foul*, Arnold painted a bleak picture of the economic privations and lack of opportunities for a small-town barrister. According to Arnold, an attorney on America's Main Street confronted a dull and unrewarding life of collections and divorce cases with an occasional injury suit.[75] Of course he was right, but what Thurman failed to record was that many small-town lawyers became prosperous in this fashion. Frances Arnold believes that the Arnolds did not exceed the income they had received in Laramie for almost a decade after they left there.[76]

In the late summer of 1926, Thurman received a telephone call from Charleston, West Virginia, altering the direction of his life. A Harvard classmate, David Howard, had an investment group of West Virginia businessmen as clients. This investment company held a few scattered oil leases in the Big Horn Basin of Wyoming and required the services of some local attorney for consultation on land titles in Wyoming. Remembering his classmate from the Wild West, Howard phoned Arnold to ask if he would accept a retainer. Thurman's initial reaction was far from enthusiastic. First of all, he did not have the vaguest memory of one David Howard. Secondly, Thurman definitely lacked interest in travelling three hundred miles in order to investigate a legal matter for clients fifteen hundred miles away. Typically, Thurman decided that he would have fun. When Howard finished his description of the legal complexities of the assignment, Thurman replied, "Well, we are living in this little house in a sod yard [then, as now, the Arnold home, which he and Frances built at 318 South Fifteenth, was one of Laramie's more attractive residences]. I just haven't the resources to go off on a jump like that, so I would have to have my expenses paid in advance."[77] Howard, undoubtedly a bit nonplused over the mannerisms of a Western attorney, quickly agreed to send a check, also guaranteeing a flattering fee. Subsequently, Arnold made two trips in the autumn of 1926 and the spring of 1927 to the Big Horn Basin and one to Charleston.

Thurman not only satisfied Howard's clients but he made a lasting impression on Howard. Indeed, when Dave Howard received an appointment to a committee to select the new dean for the University of West

Thurman and Frances Arnold with their sons Thurman, Jr. (on his mother's lap) and George, in their home at 318 S. Fifteenth Street, Laramie, in the 1920s. Courtesy of Mrs. Frances Arnold.

Virginia Law School, he called Arnold inviting him to Morgantown for an interview. Thurman met with the president and the board of governors the last week of June 1927. Within twenty-four hours he was offered the position. After placing a call to Frances he accepted the offer. Over forty years later, Frances Arnold still remembered her immense surprise at Thurman's decision. "He telephoned me and said, 'You know I really like this place, I think maybe I would like to come in from Wyoming and take on the deanship of the Law School.' I was really astonished. I hadn't thought he would ever leave Wyoming. Most people thought he would never leave. . . that he would become U.S. senator after Kendrick."[78]

Frances could not have been more amazed than the townspeople of Laramie. After breaking the news in his column, the editor of the local paper commented, "This announcement will come as a great surprise to most of Mr. Arnold's follow citizens. . . . The willingness to help in every worthwhile civic or community enterprise which Thurman, as he is always known to his friends, has always manifested and above all his good comradeship, will make his intimates especially lament his subtraction from the life of the town."[79]

After a series of seemingly unending farewell picnics, bar association dinners and private parties, the Arnold family tumbled into their Dodge and headed east over Sherman Hill.[80] Thurman later described the scene, "I packed my family in our car and drove away, never to return except for casual visits. How we hated to leave that wonderful combination of rolling plains and blue, snow-capped mountains that we knew as Wyoming. My wife wept continuously for the first thirty miles, and the children looked as if they thought I was selling them down the river into slavery."[81]

With these accumulated memories, the Arnold family's arrival in Morgantown, a much more staid community than Laramie, must have been a rude shock. On one of Thurman's first days in the law school, the janitor stopped him in the hall, and in no uncertain terms informed him that "cigar smoking was not allowed on the premises."[82] Regardless of the impression Thurman made on the custodial staff, he immediately settled down to make an impact on the legal profession in West Virginia. His interest, as Douglas Ayer has shown,[83] converged on two areas: one, the procedural reform of the West Virginia courts, and two, the upgrading of the University of West Virginia Law School. Thurman once described procedure as the "art of speeding law up or slowing it down".[84] Arnold was totally convinced that the administration of justice in West Virginia, as in most states, was not only cluttered but antiquated. In effect, this inefficiency offended Arnold's progressive ethic.

To reform the judiciary and put it on a more businesslike basis, Arnold proposed the formation of a judicial council. The main obligation of this assortment of experts—composed of representatives of the bench, bar and

The College of Law, University of West Virginia, where Thurman Arnold made a notable impact as dean. Courtesy of College of Law, University of West Virginia.

the University Law faculty—would be to review the procedural rule and administration of the courts, then submit suggestions for improvement.[85] Arnold further expanded the scope of the judicial council to the promulgation of rules pertaining to pleading and practice in West Virginia courts. While Arnold conceded that rule-making properly came under legislative jurisdiction, he found legislatures deficient instruments for judicial reform. Why? Arnold quickly enumerated the reasons: one, only a body of experts independent of political pressures could arrive at intelligent decisions; two, legislatures, even if qualified to enter the maze of judicial procedure, did not have the time to expend on such precise matters; and finally, judicial statistics were the foundation for any revision of procedural rules. Arnold categorically stated that legislatures could not gather or interpret such statistics.

Arnold's fascination with the quantitative approach to law derived from his association with Charles E. Clark of Yale University. Clark, enamored with the revision of procedural rules, had been diligently gathering statistics in Connecticut prior to Arnold's arrival in West Virginia. Quite logically, when Arnold began to consider paths to reform in West Virginia, he turned to Clark's work in Connecticut. Similarly, Clark became intrigued with Arnold's enterprise in West Virginia. Soon Clark began financing summer legal research institutes at Morgantown. Clark did more than send Yale dollars to West Virginia; he visited Arnold, spoke to the local bar association, and brought Arnold's work to the attention of his (Clark's) friends in New England.

Nor did Arnold limit his activities to collecting row upon row of digits. He presented his ideas so forcefully and lobbied them through with such adroitness that soon arrangements were made between the bar association and the law school faculty whereby the latter was "acting as a research bureau, investigating problems of state-wide interest."[86] Going further, Arnold argued to Clark that since the cooperation between Yale and West Virginia had been so beneficial, the program should be broadened to include other law schools.

Therefore, in the fall of 1929 Arnold wrote Clark at length, suggesting that Yale establish a permanent summer institute along the lines of the Yale–West Virginia format. Arnold proposed that Yale invite as many faculty as feasible from law schools over the country, expose them to Clark's quantitative techniques, and thus spread procedural reform nationwide. Arnold concluded, "I believe the future of law reform in this country is going to be greatly influenced by investigative work done by state and national law schools."[87]

Along with his preoccupation with reforming the West Virginia judicial system, Arnold set out to revise radically the law school curriculum and admission requirements, with the obvious objective of raising its standards.

First, he proposed the requirement of three years of collegiate preparation as a prerequisite for law school admission.[88] Arnold appointed a committee composed of both faculty and representatives from the bar to review the curriculum. He told Dave Howard, "as you and I know there is far too much nonsense in law school courses. So do not hesitate to slice away, wherever you see stupidity."[89]

From the standpoint of intellectual development and professional recognition, the West Virginia years were profitable for Thurman. Within an amazingly brief time after leaving Laramie, Arnold had made a lasting impression on law in West Virginia and had attracted the attention of the legal profession nationwide. Personally, Thurman was restless and unhappy in West Virginia. Two years after arriving in Morgantown, he wrote his Laramie friends the Nussbaums, "Loneliness often develops more affection than constant association—and I have been lonely here the past year. Out of the entire community I have not made one intimate friend."[90]

Frances Arnold retained a vivid memory of social life in West Virginia as being very formal and puritanical in atmosphere. "Thurman and I, and the dean of agriculture, who had just come in from Virginia Polytechnic Institute, were the only people on the faculty [it seemed] under seventy-five. They were all old, doddering and very conservative."[91] After the freewheeling, casual life in Wyoming, Thurman found living in Morgantown as confining as his grandfather's high, starched clerical collar.

Yet all was not boredom in West Virginia. Thurman and Frances did form a lasting friendship with the rector of the local Episcopal church and his wife, Rev. and Mrs. W.J. Gehri.[92] The Arnolds had a very comfortable home on a beautiful site—a bluff overlooking the Monongahela River. Morgantown was also where Thurman, perhaps out of desperation, began his lifelong absorption with the cinema. "Talkies" had just arrived. Thurman and Frances spent many an evening at one of the local movie "palaces." Here again the Tom Sawyer in Thurman refused suppression. Upon entering the local palladium, Thurman would march down the aisle to the front, select a seat as near the middle as possible, then crane his neck upward at the screen.[93] Years later, when he attended the New York theatre, he invariably purchased tickets in the orchestra section as close to the stage as possible.[94] Thurman had a strong enchantment for the dramatic arts in any form, although his emotional and intellectual involvement was far from uncritical. After viewing a motion picture or a stage play, he would inevitably spend hours pouring out a torrent of conversation which dissected the plot, acting, scenery and so on.

Thurman's captivation with the stage may have derived from his telescopic view of life as a theatre, with the curtain always up on a dozen simultaneous performances. In the theatre with his imagination unharnassed Thurman could give free range to his plastic perception of life. He always possessed the wonderful gift of looking at the world upside down and inside out. For any play, he could and did devise a half dozen endings along with basic alterations in the scenarios. For Thurman the theatre was far more than an evening's entertainment; what he saw across the footlights held the reality of life itself.

When Charles Clark invited Thurman to come to Yale as a visiting professor in the fall of 1930, Thurman accepted with alacrity. By November Clark, who had recently become dean of the law school, asked Thurman to accept a permanent appointment. The decision was an easy one for the Arnolds. Thurman found the Yale Law School in the thirties, as did many young lawyers, the most exciting law school in the nation. The brilliant faculty was studded with such nonsectarian and free-thinking minds as Willian O. Douglas, Wesley Sturges, Walton Hamilton, Arthur Corbin and Underhill Moore. Across the Yale commons walked the most stimulating and exciting legal talent in the nation—at least so it seemed to Thurman.

If the pull from Yale had been minimal, the push from West Virginia would have been enough to move Arnold from Morgantown to New Haven. First, he sincerely believed that he had accomplished about all he could hope for in West Virginia. After all, he possessed only so many lances to break against the bastion of an entrenched legal establishment. Further, he had long since lost his fascination with statistics and procedural reform. Considering Thurman's circus-like mind, it is difficult to believe that he had ever been entranced with quantification. In fact, in later life he seldom missed a chance to poke fun at "those piles of statistics" that he had so assiduously amassed at both Yale and West Virginia. In his autobiography he noted, "We then proceeded to count everything that happened in the courts in Connecticut. . . . They had only one flaw. Nobody then and nobody yet has ever been able to think of what to do with them. They are presently enshrined in a government archives awaiting the coming of the Prince who will awaken their true beauty."[95]

On December 23, 1930 Arnold wrote President John R. Turner of the University of West Virginia that he had decided to stay at Yale. Thurman's most revealing evaluation of his tenure at West Virginia came in *Fair Fights and Foul,* describing his entire era there in one sentence: "In 1930, after two years as dean of the West Virginia University College of Law, an excellent school, I accepted an appointment to the law faculty of Yale."[96]

In the compass of three months, after Arnold resigned from West Virginia and accepted the post at Yale, he had attractive offers from Wisconsin and Harvard. After a sumptuous dinner at the Century Club in New York, Roscoe Pound invited Thurman to join the Harvard law faculty to head a study of the trial courts of the country. Arnold asked Pound

The Yale Law School as it looked during Thurman Arnold's tenure. Courtesy of Yale Law School.

what precisely he had in mind. "This led to the astonishing discovery that Pound didn't have the faintest idea as to what it was all about, but was quite sure that I knew just what should be done. I let it go at that. I could think of nothing more apt than Manuel in the *Figures of the Earth,* with his white feather. Someone had presented me with a white feather, and I just couldn't convince them it was just an ordinary feather, no matter how much I talked (I'll admit that I didn't try very hard to convince them)."[97] On April 18 Arnold wrote to Glenn Frank, the spats-wearing president of the University of Wisconsin, declining the deanship of the University of Wisconsin School of Law.[98]

In retrospect, Arnold's decision to accept the Yale offer was a fateful one for him. However, as Arnold recalled long after he was ensconced in the firm of Arnold, Fortas and Porter, the decision was inevitable.[99] Yale was just too exciting a place for Arnold to think of leaving after six months. To legal theorists and the avant garde of legal philosophy in the 1930s, Yale was the amen of legal realism. When Arnold's very close friend and brilliant associate Abe Fortas was asked recently about Arnold's place in the legal realist system, he replied, ". . . that term [legal realism] really has no meaning."[100] Fortas, with his usual uncommon perception, had diagnosed the dominant feature of the legal realist school—namely its diversity. As Karl Lewellyn observed, the distinguishing trait of legal realism was its heterodoxy.[101]

Yet admitting their intellectual disorder, the legal realists as a group did hold in common certain theses, if not canon.[102] Foremost, the legal realists emphasized their preoccupation with discovering the "nature of the decision-making process in law." In divining the mysteries of law they became devotees of the social sciences. Anthropologists, sociologists and political scientists united with their friends in the legal world to undertake the search for reality. The legal realists possessed a thorough-going skepticism towards rules, facts and precedents. Realists were skeptical of rules on two premises: a) in any litigation legal authority can be uncovered for opposing decisions; as a result many judicial opinions are based on hidden views of social policy; b) the choice between two conflicting opinions can often be made only after considering the magnitude of the social outcome.

Coupled with rule skepticism in the minds of some realists was fact skepticism, which was the specific contribution of Jerome Frank. Fact skepticism, as intricately conceived by Frank, fundamentally meant that the "facts" as perceived by a court, whether judge or jury, had little or no relation to actual facts. Furthermore, the specific reaction of a judge or jury was inherently unpredictable. Most legal theorists, including many realists, found Frank's extreme relativism totally capricious and self-defeating.

Nevertheless, in assailing the subjectivity of the court, particularly the judge, Frank had accurately underlined the maximal tenet of legal realism. Underhill Moore, William O. Douglas, Karl Lewellyn, and Thurman Arnold all emphasized the non-objective factors innate in judicial teleology.

Legal realism at Yale meant incorporating not only philosophical realism as evolved elsewhere but also a heavy coloration of pragmatism. The obvious example on the Yale faculty was Charles Clark. Clark became totally enamored with statistics, primarily because he fervently held that procedural reformers were blinded by the opium of conjecture. Underhill Moore, Wesley Sturges, and William O. Douglas saw little point in pursuing the traditional legal curriculum of corporations, mortgages and property, but decided that the "truths" of those subjects should be revealed through the analysis of profit and economic distribution. Accordingly, Douglas, in conjunction with George Bates of the Harvard Business School, developed a four-year course on the interaction of law and business economics. Underhill Moore became so frustrated with the symbolic overtones of the banking and financial vocabulary that he for a time tried out an experimental lexicon. Case books—which many realists at Yale and elsewhere regarded as the main villians in legal education—were tossed aside in favor of moot courts and the cheaply reproduced syllabi of the individual faculty members.[103]

How did Arnold fit into realism in general and the Yale brand of realism specifically? In some respects, the most doctrinaire of realists would have endorsed Arnold's realism. Intrigued with the interplay between law and social sciences, Arnold originated a course with Edward S. Robinson, a psychologist at Yale, entitled "The Judicial Process from the Point of View of Social Psychology." Arnold soon attracted a galaxy of social scientists and legal theorists with an interdisciplinary bent. At one time or another, those who appeared in front of Arnold's classroom blackboard included: George Soule, H.L. Mencken, Myres McDougall, Fred Rodell, Max Lerner and Jerome Frank.

After Robinson's tragic and untimely death in 1935, Arnold joined with Henry Stack Sullivan, the renowned psychiatrist, in holding a seminar that examined maturity and the loss of infantilism.[104] Arnold never tired of quoting from Sullivan's last lecture to the class, "And now, young gentlemen, when you have lost your taste for adventure, when you have forgotten romance, when the only things worthwhile to you are prestige and income, then you have grown up, then you have become an adult."[105] Later Arnold and Eugene Kahn, a psychiatrist from the University of Vienna, attempted to delve into the criminal mind to divine whether criminals should be held responsible for their acts. Arnold quickly decided that his experimental seminar resulted in only cross-sterilization rather than the anticipated cross-fertilization.[106]

Arnold has been referred to as the most popular teacher on the Yale law faculty in the 1930s; undoubtedly he was the most unorthodox. Arnold's mastery of the Yale classroom was not always evident. One of his former students (a later colleague) recalls that Arnold spent his first year on the Yale campus wandering about in an apparent daze, insecure, associating with graduate students more than faculty.[107] The student left for three years, and when he returned he was astounded at the transformation in his former teacher. Students were not only flocking to his classroom, but Arnold was the acknowledged intellectual leader of the Yale law faculty.

Today his students vividly remember Arnold's classes with a strange mixture of reverence, embarrassment, fear and affection. One of Arnold's favorite teaching techniques was to take a simple and seemingly obvious legal procedure and force the students to examine it from an entirely new, previously inconceivable, perspective. He might walk into a class, five minutes or more late, throw his handkerchief on the floor, and bellow at the bewildered assemblage, "Get that handkerchief into evidence!" Some befuddled student might timidly inquire, "Well, sir, what is it?" Arnold would quickly and loudly retort, "What the hell difference does it make what it is, get it into evidence, I am the judge now."[108] Then Thurman would explode with that marvelous torrent of words and ideas all scrambled up, skipping whole phrases, for his mind always raced ahead of his vocal cords. Arnold had the further disconcerting habit of mentally jumping into an argument in the middle only to move in both directions at once. This could be effective in the classroom for the student who had the curiosity and several hours to decipher the Arnold intellectual scrabble.

This is not to say that every student left Arnold's classes enthralled by the preceding hour. Far from it; Arnold simply did not appeal to the conventional mind. His greatness as a teacher came from conquering the greatest challenge a teacher ever confronts—he forced his students to think! He excited them. By asking his classes to follow his mental gymnastics, he led them to intellectual maturity and sophistication, a result to which many teachers aspire but few achieve.

One of Arnold's singular contributions to the Yale Law School was his development of the moot court. In common with other realists, Arnold had a scorn for case-book instruction. Arnold steadfastly believed that case books induced a mental rigidity, cementing the mind in "unholy" orthodoxy. If one expected to train young lawyers in courtroom theory and practice, why not at least try to simulate reality?

When Arnold contemplated establishing a moot court, he wrote to the circuit courts of appeal requesting the excess copies of records they had from recent cases.[109] Arnold was not interested in the opinions or briefs but the actual court transcripts. Then he moved a step further to courtroom fidelity: why not have actual judges try these cases? Soon students were presenting factual cases before judges who sometimes had decided the original cases. In the moot court concept, we again have clear evidence of the engrained pragmatism that ran so deeply in Arnold's thought. Indeed, what could be more classically pragmatic than the "learning by doing" philosophy of the Yale moot court?

While Arnold's legal theory followed the line of the realists at Yale and elsewhere, in several ways he detoured significantly from the realist formulations. First, Arnold scorned the realist contention that a specific knowledge of the "facts" was either wise or even necessary. In fact, just to the contrary, the myths and symbols of law serve an enormous function as preservers of the potency and prestige of the judiciary. Thus Arnold would argue in his *Symbols of Government,* "Law is primarily a great reservoir of emotionally important social symbols."[110] Ironically, Arnold continued, the realists had adopted what they most denounced. "Realists prove incontrovertibly that there can be no objective reality behind the law as a brooding omnipresence in the skies—only to find their own writings swallowed up and becoming a part of that brooding omnipresence which they are insistently denying."[111]

Against this backdrop of Arnold's speculation on realism, it is more than a little surprising that thirty-two years later his sparkling memorial essay on Jerome Frank should have created such a furor.

Arnold had no hesitation in praising Frank as a warm, highly intelligent, delightful human being. As a judge, Arnold frankly admitted that Frank's espousal of relativism bothered him. "Certainly it is true that the idea of federal judges roaming the stormy fields of economics, sociology, psychiatry and anthropology, their black robes flapping in the winds of controversy, is a disquieting one, even to the writer."[112] Harking back to that "brooding onmipresence in the skies" Arnold found Frank's emphasis on the shedding of irrational mysticism as materialistic and inane. For after men cast off the beliefs that frustrate them, they must find "a new faith that inspires them." Arnold conceded that realism had its usefulness in the sick society of the nineteen thirties "But realism, despite its liberating virtues, is not sustaining food for a stable civilization."[113]

Those who expressed shock at Arnold's seeming divorce from realism in the 1950s might have suffered less had they realized that the marriage between Arnold and realism had never occurred in the first place. Arnold could be far more undeviating than his friends or detractors realized, just as he could be consistently inconsistent. Arnold's mental patterns are analogous to the Pyramid of Khufu; the structure is there for all to see, but the mechanics of construction are hidden.

Arnold's relation to realism aside, it was during the Yale years that he first moved on to the national scene via the publication of two volumes,

*The Symbols of Government* and *The Folklore of Capitalism.* Arnold clearly stated the purpose and the quest of *Symbols* in the preface when he wrote, "In this book, we propose to examine law and economics, not as a collection of truths, but as symbolic thinking and conduct which condition the behavior of men in groups."[114] Arnold, by stepping into the role of a Don Quixote, intended to strip away the symbols in law and economics with one swipe, and at the same time dramatize the essentiality of these symbols for American institutions.

Arnold decided to commit to paper the outgrowth of this thinking on legal and economic institutions. Thoughts had been maturing in his mind since his days on Fifteenth Street in Laramie, a fermentation that had reached its greatest effervescence in the seminars that he carried on in tandem with Edward S. Robinson and Henry Stack Sullivan. The message of *Symbols* was unusually lucid. Economics becomes the guardian of society's vested interests, and law lends a permanence to them and to society. In a striking sentence, the essence of which he repeated in his essay on Jerome Frank, Arnold depicted the rule of law as "the belief that there must be something behind and above government without which it cannot have permanence or respect. Even a dictator cannot escape the psychology of his time. He does not quite believe in his own government unless he is able to make gestures toward this prevailing ideal."[115]

Law then provided the mortar, the theology, for the body politic. All his life Arnold delighted in describing the secular world in ecclessiastical metaphors. Jurisprudence is law's Holy Ghost; the liturgy in the cathedral corresponds to the ritual of the courts, the creed to the legal codes, and so on. One wonders whether this fascination with the mysticism of theology derived from his Calvinist grandfather, that worthy divine whose great spiritual crisis came when he had to wrestle with the Lord over whether to switch his faith from the Congregational to the Presbyterian church. Whether he or the Lord won out will never be known, but at least Peter Franklin Arnold served as pastor of Laramie Presbyterians for several years.

In the final chapter of *Symbols,* entitled "A Philosophy for Politicians," Arnold leaves his readers with what he hopes will be the operative message for his time. Arnold proposed that what is desperately needed in these dispiriting years is a new set of symbols to inspire Americans to dedicate themselves to a practical, efficient course in their search for some solution of their economic ills.

*Symbols of Government* received a polite, if reserved, approval from reviewers and the general public. Its immediate impact, like its sales, was modest. Two years after the appearance of *Symbols,* Arnold published *The Folklore of Capitalism.* In contrast with *Symbols, Folklore* became an immediate hit, a topic of conversation at cocktail parties whether in New

Haven or Washington.[116] No one has quite understood why *Folklore* struck the chord that it did in popular response. Basically, in *Folklore* Arnold restated, rephrased and expanded the same themes that he had expounded in *Symbols.* While Arnold always skirted a mechanistic philosophy, in *Folklore,* as in *Symbols,* he insisted that social progress must come through a pragmatic approach to government.

Never one to scorn philosopher-kings in government, for all his playful musing and ideological juxtapositions Arnold always avoided taking his own Socratic analogies as solemnly as did many of his readers. This one fact explains, more than anything else, why Fred Rodell,[117] William E. Borah and others were dumbfounded with Arnold's nomination as assistant attorney general. How could a man who had ridiculed the Sherman Act and antitrust efforts of the past be placed in charge of enforcing this same antitrust legislation? Thurman Arnold, with his inside-out, upside-down, satirical way of examining institutions, completely confounded more than one would-be interpreter. Politicians, academicians, friends and foes all thought they knew what Arnold was saying. However, if they, sans two martinis, were closely questioned, most of these would-be seers admitted to lack of comprehension and sometimes to complete bafflement. Even today many of Arnold's associates and friends will begin their reminiscences of him with the phrase, "Thurman was an authentic genius—I think!"

One of the perpetual traps for those who pondered Arnold's words, printed or oral, was that they simply took him far too seriously. They assumed that he meant literally what he said—that those marvelous posturings, ridiculous metaphors, and that deluge of fanciful illustrations were parts of a sophisticated, rational system. The element of the unexpected, always a threat in Arnold's thought, ensnared more than one unwary listener. His audiences commonly found themselves trying to understand one idea, two or three paragraphs back, while Arnold's mind raced ahead pouring out, in confused snytax, one exuberant image after another.

As his former student and intimate friend, Edward Levi, wrote, Thurman Arnold was far too complex a man to yield to easy capsulization.[118] One of Arnold's most frequently remembered and commented upon characteristics was his distinctive manner of examining life, ideas, and the milieu around him. One of his closest friends, Hugh Cox, recalls the time that he and Thurman, after finishing their business, had one of those leftover Saturday afternoons in New York City. Cox suggested that they visit one of the museums which had a showing of Leonardo da Vinci drawings. After a few minutes there, Thurman burst out to his friend, "You know they say that this man is the first modern; that is a mistake. He was not the first modern at all; he was the last of the medievalists.

Look at these devices of his. He tried to design a flying machine, but he designed something like a bird; that is not the way the Wright brothers went about it."[119]

Stories illustrative of the remarkable functioning of Thurman's mind tumble out of the reminiscences of his friends. Abe Fortas emphasized the originality of Arnold's intellectuality, equating it with the freshness of a child's outlook on life. Like many children, Thurman did not see life through the impediments of encrusted preconceptions.

If one were attempting to define the originality of Arnold's mind, encompassed in that definition would be that he simply saw problems, situations and human events in a way that differed from the conventional. These discernments could be extremely provocative, stimulating and significant. They could also enmesh and stupefy those individuals who had the audacity to try to systematize Arnold's thought. His world was not neat, orderly or systematic; it was rather a brilliantly lighted stage, crammed with characters, jumbled scenery, flashing lightning, and an unending play—a drama that, viewed from the front row seat, held all the excitement, satire, humor, optimism, dreams and hope that incredible mind could imagine. Little wonder that those devoid of his gift discovered only the blurred script and none of the nuances that provided the revelation of understanding.

His wife, Frances, and his sister-in-law, Mrs. Carl Arnold, both emphasized Thurman's tremendous breadth of intellectual involvement.[120] He had a proclivity for transferring superficial interests into hobbies, as in his absorption with the cinema and the theatre; later he developed a passion for photography. He always derived pleasure from music, playing competently the piano by ear; his favorite opera, "Der Rosenkavalier" by Richard Strauss, was frequently on the phonograph when friends visited. Perhaps his greatest and abiding obsession was conversation. The Arnold family home at 812 Grand, Laramie, is remembered by friends as a scene of constant vocal uproar. There were long-winded, dogmatic discourses on topics varying from the value of money, politics, the bicycle versus the horse, one-way streets, cattle breeding, astronomy, plus a myriad of other subjects.[121] The family domicile offered an excellent setting for mental calisthenics that Thurman's students, readers and clients later watched with a mixture of bemusement, horror, fascination and sometimes understanding.

Today it is the search for comprehending Arnold that makes reading the reviews of *Folklore of Capitalism* such an intriguing digression. Not a single reviewer would admit that he had difficulty deciphering Arnold's sermon, although the depth of their statements often betrayed their lack of discernment. Most reviewers, politicians and assorted political pundits hailed the author of *Folklore* as a new Jeremiah. In an age full of prophets,

Arnold's diagnosis of society's ills had the obvious touch of originality, even if the reader remained more than slightly confused about the scripture.

What appealed to many readers of *Folklore*, whether they realized it or not, was Arnold's conservative prescription for society. Arnold saw no reason to throw out capitalism, not even in exchange for a mild version of Norman Thomas's tomorrow. Arnold believed capitalism to be as valid as any economic system; the problem was to make it work. For those readers who had absorbed the moral fable in *Symbols*, Arnold's answer to society's maladies was self-evident. Our civilization must exchange old symbols, old folklore for new myths and more original folklore. Such an analysis seemed eminently sane, sensible and safe. All Arnold advocated was finding a practical way of altering society without upsetting our traditions. No wonder that Robert Taft, many years after *Folklore's* publication, told Arnold that he had recently read *Folklore* with profit, and expressed amazement at how valid Arnold's inquiry was for the 1950s.[122]

*Folklore* and *Symbols* not only brought Arnold a national audience, but they helped pave his way to a place in the Washington bureaucracy. In the priesthood of professors swarming around the capitol during the New Deal, a man with stimulating, safe ideas automatically attracted attention. Furthermore, by the time Arnold's books appeared, he had been shuttling back and forth from New Haven to Washington for a number of years; his broken gait was a familiar sight in the offices and halls. In the federal court in San Francisco in 1933, Arnold tried the first case on behalf of the Agricultural Adjustment Administration, involving the constitutionality of the Agricultural Adjustment Act. Arnold, Abe Fortas and James T. Fly all served at the defendant's table for the Department of Agriculture.[123] They won the case.

Arnold spent the summer of 1934 in the Philippines advising Governor General Frank Murphy in the administration of the Jones-Costigan Sugar Act, which imposed a quota limitation system on the production of sugar. Arnold found the Philippine sugar refiners affable and enlightened men who argued over nothing that Arnold proposed, signed all the documents in front of them and then lavishly entertained their guest. After Arnold departed for the states, the refiners blithely ignored all their signed agreements![124] In succeeding summers, 1935 and 1936, Arnold served in Washington as a trial examiner for the Securities and Exchange Commission, headed by his intimate friend and former Yale colleague, William O. Douglas. Taking a sabbatical from Yale in 1937, Arnold again trekked to the capitol, this time to try six cases before the Supreme Court for the Tax Division of the Department of Justice, then directed by Robert Jackson. Through these sequential stints in Washington, Arnold collected an assortment of friends and acquaintances, including Benjamin

Cohen, Thomas Corcoran, Rexford Tugwell, Jerome Frank, Harold Ickes and Homer Cummings. Neither friends nor Washington gossip columnists were surprised to hear repeated rumors through the spring of 1938 that Arnold was about to receive a major appointment. As the celebrated author of *Folklore,* and as one eminently acquainted with the capitol power structure, it seemed intimately reasonable, if not foreordained, that Arnold would soon receive the official baptism from the White House.

The shock came over the specific nomination. When President Roosevelt announced Arnold's nomination as assistant attorney general in charge of the Antitrust Division of the Department of Justice, no one was more upset than the old progressive senator from Arnold's neighboring state of Idaho, William E. Borah. Borah made little effort to disguise the fact that he seriously questioned the wisdom of putting a man who had so recently belittled the antitrust laws in charge of enforcing them. As a potent member of the Judiciary Committee, Borah held a strategic position from which to review Arnold's past, present and future. At 10:30 A.M. on March 11, 1938, in Room 324 of the old Senate Office Building, the hearings on Arnold's appointment began.[125] Borah did not wait long before he waded into Arnold, reading passages from *Folklore* which dramatized Arnold's disenchantment with antitrust legislation.

Aware of Borah's irritation, Arnold prepared a clever, if obvious, defense. In answer to Borah's persistent needling, Arnold adopted the position that all he was doing in *Folklore* was merely describing the effect of the antitrust laws on the nation's economy. All would be different, of course, "once I was in office."[126] The senator from Idaho and Arnold exchanged one spirited sally after another. At one point, Borah asked incredulously, "The book [*Folklore of Capitalism*] in its philosophy is no indication of what your views will be or what your action will be in the Department of Justice?" Mr. Arnold: "The philosophy of the book and the point of view of the book has a limited utility. It has only utility for diagnosis. That is, I am describing what has happened. I think that it is helpful in order to determine what will happen in the future: but describing what has happened is just the first step."[127]

Adding to Arnold's discomfort in the hearing was his acute recollection of what he now could only consider a decidedly unfortunate reference to the good senator from Idaho in *Folklore of Capitalism.* As Arnold sat in the witness chair that March morning he could not help but wonder how much of Borah's prickliness derived from this passage: "The antitrust laws remain as an important symbol. Wherever anyone demanded a practical regulation, they formed an effective moral obstacle, since all the liberals would answer with a demand that the antitrust laws be enforced. Men like Senator Borah founded political careers on the continuation of such crusades, which were entirely futile but enormously picturesque, and which paid big dividends in personal prestige."[128] Arnold mentally replayed that sentence time and again as he faced Borah's steady gaze.

Whatever Borah's personal estimation of the author of *Folklore* may have been, the subcommittee quickly confirmed Arnold's appointment. Both Borah and Arnold had a good friend in Senator Joseph C. O'Mahoney of Wyoming. As chairman of the subcommittee, O'Mahoney may have poured oil on troubled waters when the subcommittee went into executive session. Arnold always attributed the ease of his confirmation to O'Mahoney, but the senator from Cheyenne kept his own counsel.

When Thurman Arnold took the oath of office on the morning of March 21, 1938, he inherited an antitrust policy that could only be described as ambiguous.[129] The enforcement of antitrust legislation since the Sherman Act of 1890 had been vacillating and sporadic in approach—confused in policy.[130] This was especially true during the thirty years after 1900. From the well-publicized trust busting of the insurgency period, through the anti-monopolistic views propounded by Wilson, to the business-oriented trade-association movement of the 1920s there was little to suggest that a uniform philosophy of antitrust enforcement had been developed in the United States.

Franklin D. Roosevelt's "New Deal," arriving on the political wave that followed the traumatic shock of the crash of the stock market, did little initially to alleviate the confusion surrounding antitrust enforcement. The first comprehensive legislation to remedy industrial dislocation was the National Industrial Recovery Act (NIRA), which negated the antitrust laws in some areas of industry.

So widespread was the belief that antitrust prosecution would be suspended entirely that Attorney General Homer Cummings issued a statement on July 6, 1933 to counteract the multitude of rumors. Cummings emphatically asserted:[131]

> There seems to be an impression in some quarters that the antitrust laws have been repealed or suspended in whole or in part. This is an entirely erroneous impression. Industrial and other groups must abide by the terms and conditions of the antitrust laws unless and until they obtain actual exemption from certain of the requirements thereof by formulating a code under the National Recovery Act, and obtaining its approval by the President.
>
> A large number of industrial activities and arrangements which are prohibited by the antitrust laws, do not come in any sense whatever within the purview of the exemptions contemplated by the National Recovery Act.

Cummings, as shown later in the revelations of the Temporary National Economic Committee, was whispering in a cave-of-the-winds.[132] A

Attorney General Homer Cummings, right, administers oath of office as assistant attorney general, Antitrust Division, to Thurman Arnold, March 22, 1938. Newly appointed Solicitor General Robert Jackson looks on. Copyright by Harris & Ewing.

significant element of the business community during the short and unhappy life of the NIRA regarded antitrust legislation as nonenforceable. Some large industrial firms exploited the relaxation of the antitrust laws to increase their share of the market at the expense of smaller concerns.[133]

After the Schechter case nullifying the NIRA in 1935, antitrust enforcement reflected the ambivalence of the Roosevelt administration. The president wavered between the trade association–NRA arguments[134] of Henry Wallace, Adolph Berle, Jerome Frank, and Donald Richberg and the increasingly vocal antimonopolistic position voiced by Felix Frankfurter, Robert Jackson, and Homer Cummings. The Justice Department kept up an unceasing barrage of memoranda that decried the market power of large corporations in the American economy—a situation equated in the public mind with "monopoly."

Slowly the antimonopoly partisans succeeded in gaining the president's favor. The recession of 1937 greatly assisted their case. Roosevelt's political antennae sensed the general discontent in the country. Why not spotlight the monopoly issue? Public uneasiness at economic conditions in the country had been increased by intellectuals who were producing a spate of tomes on economic concentration in the United States.[135] Politically, it appeared to be an opportune time to launch an investigation.[136]

A most effective pressure on the president for renewed emphasis on antitrust policy came from Congress, where the progressive bloc, albeit disorganized, was in open revolt. Senators O'Mahoney, Nye, Borah, and La Follette had all contested presidential leadership on a variety of issues. Borah and O'Mahoney especially were attempting to gain political advantage over the chief executive on the monopoly issue by again proposing the old idea of federal licensing for all interstate corporations.

Roosevelt, with his usual political adeptness, had no desire to surrender the initiative on the monopoly issue to Congress; just the opposite, he determined to steal the thunder of the progressive bloc.[137]

It was against this background of dissent that two events occurred that signaled a radical departure from the NRA philosophy. On October 22, 1937 Roosevelt wrote Assistant Attorney General Robert Jackson.[138]

> One of the problems that continues to require attention is the inadequacies and defects in our anti-monopoly laws, which I have often reviewed informally with you and others. I want to ask you to undertake, with the help of such others in government service as you wish from time to time to enlist, to assemble for me the following:
>
> 1. The important facts bearing upon the success or failure of our present anti-monopoly laws, their economic and social results, and the necessity for revision or amendment.
>
> 2. The different proposals or alternatives worthy of practical consideration, with the advantages and disadvantages of each.

This letter marked a significant step which finally resulted in Roosevelt's famous anti-monopoly speech of April 29, 1938[139] and the subsequent Temporary National Economic Committee (TNEC) investigation.

Six months after his famous letter to Jackson, Roosevelt named Arnold to the Department of Justice. From the minute Arnold stepped behind his desk at the Antitrust Division, he insistently told the press that the administration was unified in its antitrust approach. Nevertheless, seeds of dissent sown by a few remnants of the old believers in NRA still played upon Roosevelt's latent faith in the trade-association philosophy. In April 1938 Donald Richberg, during one of the moments he was in temporary favor, wrote to Roosevelt:[140]

> The philosophy of the NRA was wholly consistent with the New Deal. The philosophy of the fanatic trust busters, their hostility to all large enterprise, their assumption that co-operation is always a cloak for monopolistic conspiracy, this philosophy is wholly inconsistent with the New Deal.

Three months after Richberg wrote Roosevelt that the antitrust program was the antithesis of the NRA, the *United States News* carried a column refining the position outlined by Richberg. The antitrust philosophy was not diametrically opposed to the NRA, according to the *News*:[141]

> President Roosevelt, reversing the tactics of earlier years, now is turning loose the Department of Justice in a quest for industrial recovery.
>
> The Department's quest consists of searching for what it determines to be criminal practices on the part of business men. The attack on these practices—the White House is convinced—will improve the chance for achieving prosperity through the program of spending that is about to be started.
>
> All of this is in sharp contrast to the procedure followed in 1933. At that time business men were encouraged to forget the nation's 45-year-old antitrust laws and to get together to plan their operations through consultation.

Besides the opposition Arnold inevitably met within the governmental bureaucracy,[142] his definition of the role he should play as an enforcer of antitrust laws confused even some of his close associates. They were apparently imbued with the belief that he proposed to remake the structure of American industry in conformity with some economist's competitive model.[143] Arnold, however, insisted both in *The Folklore of Capitalism* and in public utterances that he was a diagnostician of institutional decay and not an economic practitioner. Arnold had an innate skepticism of "preachers"[144] with manufactured economic panaceas.

While Arnold was more than a legal and economic technician he emphatically did not want to promote legislation. His function, as he saw it, was to enforce and suggest corrective measures. Whether his immediate success in antitrust suits would have been greater had he followed more of a policy-making role is a moot question; that his influence on New Deal economic policy might have been greater is another matter.

While associates, fellow bureaucrats, and the general public may have been hazy on the specific outlines of Arnold's antitrust policy, the assistant attorney general had a well-defined conceptual framework for what he desired to accomplish. Writing to Charles Seymour, president of Yale, on July 4, 1939 Arnold stated that he was not interested in "trust busting for the sake of trust busting"; quite the contrary, he intended to give the Antitrust Division a constructive purpose. The creation of a positive antitrust program had three facets, according to Arnold: (1) a statement of a uniform well-publicized policy was essential; (2) the building up of an effective antitrust organization; and (3) "the elimination of partisan politics from the Division was desired." "I have refused to make a single political speech during my term of office, or to become identified with any exclusively New Deal group."[145]

During his first year in office Arnold made amazing progress in maneuvering to accomplish these goals. He quickly admitted to one and all that the Sherman Act[146] was an imperfect tool at best, but that he was convinced that the "sole weakness of the enforcement of the Sherman Act in the past has been the lack of an enforcement organization."[147] Revision of the law was not the answer, Arnold maintained, but more funds for personnel in the Antitrust Division were essential.[148] In the first two years, his sizable budget requests received generous congressional support.

In effect, admitting the inadequacy of his organizational analysis of the enforcement problem, Arnold also blamed the general climate of opinion which historically had regarded the antitrust laws as a moral and emotional rather than an economic problem.[149] It was this ignorance of the economic ramifications of the antitrust laws that particularly piqued the head of the Antitrust Division.[150]

The social aspects of the antitrust policy, the remnants of progressive attitudes toward trusts incorporating moralistic and ethical considerations, annoyed the Arnold of 1937. He believed that these were attitudes outmoded by the complex industrial system of the twentieth century; the United States could no longer afford to be a nation of economic illiterates. Arnold's good friend, H.L. Mencken, perhaps in silent sympathy with Arnold's reasoning, thought this analysis far too sophisticated. For Mencken the solution to the antitrust problem was characteristically simple and clear: the men who wrote the Sherman Act made just one mistake—they forgot to provide for capital punishment.[151]

Recently described in a memorial tribute as the "Perfect Advocate," Hugh Cox was special assistant to the assistant attorney general, Antitrust Division, from 1935 to 1943. Courtesy of Mrs. Hugh Cox.

Accepting the Sherman Act as a workable one, Arnold formulated a procedure for handling antitrust cases. Utilizing the machinery which had long been available for enforcement, he undertook two courses. First, he revived use of the consent decree, which involved dropping indictments in return for the adoption of basic remedial practices by the industry in question, and, second, he stepped up criminal prosecution. Arnold contended that the consent decree, as employed in previous years, was nothing more than a subterfuge.[152] Historically, the government had used the consent decree to accomplish the objective of litigation without going through a lengthy court proceeding. Having secured evidence of an antitrust violation, the government would give the potential defendant an opportunity to make a private compact whereby, in return for the government's dropping a criminal indictment, the subject of the action would promise not to commit specific violations in the future. Arnold deemed this use of the consent decree "absurd."[153] Instead, Arnold developed a new approach to the consent decree. In the future no prosecution would be dismissed categorically on the basis of announced good intentions. Instead, Arnold advanced a plan whereby the defendant would present, as formerly, a plan to the court, but this scheme must now not only incorporate sufficient redress of the indictment but, more importantly, offer genuine reorganization on a company or industry-wide basis that would be more beneficial to the general public than would the results of a criminal prosecution.[154]

The consent decree represented one of Arnold's most striking contributions to antitrust philosophy. He brilliantly refashioned an age-old concept by adding a dimension of flexibility that enabled him to widen his enforcement program. Numerous contemporary observers and historians later have frequently commented on the daring "operative planning" nature of Arnold's enforcement tactics. Actually, much of the originality ascribed to his enforcement methods issued from his imaginative utilization of the consent decree.

This is not to denigrate Arnold's concrete and permanent contribution to antitrust policy. In the preceding forty years, the Justice Department had launched mercurial attacks on industrial giants, with some degree of success but without stopping violations in our entire industry.[155] Arnold saw the crux of the monopolizing power in the system of distribution. Speaking to the Advertising Federation of America in Detroit, Arnold noted the adverse effects of the power of producers over distribution. "Incredible as it may seem, in order to keep prices up, industry is choking off its own avenues of distribution, decreasing employment and widening the disparity of prices."[156] The solution prescribed was a comprehensive prosecution at the distribution level in an attempt to remove the artificial "roadblocks." Joseph Alsop and Robert Kinter described Arnold's attack on distribution as one of "hit hard, hit everyone and hit them all at once." [157]

There just was no over-all magic potion that could be administered in one massive dose by the Justice Department to the industrial economy. The most rewarding prosecution formula promised to be the case-by-case indictment.[158] Arnold logically contended that restraints of trade in the movie industry would have little relevance to restraints in the steel industry, while artificial "tolls" in the milk industry in Detroit would differ often from the abuses in the same industry in Chicago. The basic requirement was a pliable policy molded to the necessities of the individual prosecutions. Arnold's imaginative ability at selecting prototype cases and administering the antitrust laws in a kaleidoscopic fashion, instead of being bound by inflexible precedents, was one of his most brilliant achievements.

A practical consequence of undertaking a case-by-case approach was the necessity for a huge legal staff. Arnold was able during the first two years to obtain sufficient appropriations to increase the number of lawyers in the Antitrust Division from 48 to over 300. Congressional approval of the antitrust program was in large measure due to the tremendous publicity resulting from the indictments—plus Arnold's unabashed demonstration that for every dollar appropriated to his Division, two or three dollars flowed into the Treasury in fines received from indicted defendants.

The widespread publicity buttressed Arnold's program in a variety of ways, not only by stimulating consumer pressure on congressional delegations for increased appropriations, but as a powerful catharsis on industry in general. Arnold saw nothing surprising about the fact that often a successful suit in one sector of business resulted in lower prices in other sectors. In an article in the *New Republic* he wrote:[159]

> We do not think there is anything mysterious about our results. An antitrust proceeding suddenly confronts the members of an industry with an appraisal of the industry's performance from the point of view of the public interest. It is sharp enough to shock, to induce self-questioning; and there is no reason for surprise that business men with public spirit and imagination sometimes alter their pricing policies as a result of such examination.

The very scope of the Justice Department's suits was justification enough for such business reactions.

Within three years the Antitrust Division had sought indictments in the movie, construction, tire, fertilizer, newspaper, tobacco, shoe, and petroleum industries, not to mention suits against trade unions, the American Medical Association, and various agricultural marketing agencies.[160] In all, Arnold and his colleagues instigated 215 investigations and brought 93 suits. No wonder he trumpeted in 1940 that in "the entire history of the Sherman Act there has never been such support for its enforcement."[161]

Concurrently with the antitrust campaign, a broad congressional inquiry had been launched concerning the character and extent of economic concentration in America. The idea for the Temporary National Economic Committee germinated in the recession of 1937[162] but originated directly from President Roosevelt's famous message of April 29, 1938 to Congress on monopoly. The president's message ended with the frequently quoted phrase, "Idle factories and idle workers profit no man." This expression set the tone of the TNEC probe; the committee was assigned the implied task of uncovering the causes of the depression. Leon Henderson, on the staff of the TNEC, offered a more precise definition of the committee's goals in a memorandum to Roosevelt on September 3, 1939. "The committee plans to outline, in detail, the facts about control in finance, insurance, industry, natural resources—the methods and devices of control—instances of abuses, and to recommend proper legislation."[163]

The TNEC hearings began on December 1, 1938 and lasted until March 11, 1941.[164] The testimony of 552 witnesses filled 37 impressive volumes; the various economic studies by the TNEC staff were collected in another 43 volumes. As in other investigations of this type, the recommendations were feeble indeed in relation to the comprehensiveness of the inquiry. The main prescription, which had been pointed to from the beginning of the hearings, was the necessity of a vigorous and militant enforcement of the antitrust laws. This was an anti-climatic conclusion after more than two years of questioning and cross-examination. Yet there was a significant by-product of the hearings in that American economic strengths and weaknesses were widely publicized. As David Lynch has pointed out, at least the committee brought up-to-date our knowledge of competitive practices.

While Arnold sympathized with the TNEC's objectives, a division developed between his personal relationship to the committee and the Antitrust Division. The more Arnold came to regard the TNEC investigation as a "study group" grinding out academic monographs, the less he became interested in expending his time with the committee. Arnold's posture toward the TNEC hearings was probably inevitable. He was just too much of an activist to be interested in following the contorted involutions of 17,000 pages of testimony. In addition, the mounting pressures of the rapid expansion of the Antitrust Division and numerous speechmaking forays left Arnold few hours for any other diversion, including the TNEC.

Just as Arnold's program was producing dramatic results, he was effectively undermined. The administration withdrew support for his requests of 1941 and 1942 for increased budgets. In three short years the Antitrust Division had been remarkably successful, in fact too successful perhaps for its own perpetuation. One does not have to ferret out the subsurface motives for the administration's severely diminished enthusiasm for the antitrust program. The most crucial and obvious explanation was the war in Europe. As early as July 6, 1940 Arnold was cognizant of the political and economic pressures that would utilize the war as a lever to impede antitrusts suits. In a letter to a Scripps-Howard columnist, Arnold succinctly stated his position:[165]

> If some combination is imperative to the interest of national defense, if it is a reasonable combination which requires no waiver of the law to get this result, fine. However, I fail to see any possibility of the things we are now prosecuting standing the test.

Arnold concluded his letter by noting that the president was in agreement with this statement.

By the fall of 1940 Arnold was not as sanguine regarding the administration's attitude. It became increasingly clear that attack on monopoly was being given a holiday. Attorney General Francis Biddle made a mild protest over the suspension of the antitrust program in the spring of 1942, which was promptly lost in the noise of creating an arsenal of democracy.[166] Arnold for his part became quite vocal on the relaxation of antitrust enforcement. In the Baxter Memorial Lectures delivered at the University of Omaha in 1942, he presented the case for wartime surveillance of monopoly.[167] Because of cartel tendencies inherent in any national emergency, Arnold argued that antitrust prosecution should be increased, not abated.

Three years after the war terminated, Arnold was still bitter about being forsaken by the president. Writing on the subject, "Must 1929 Repeat Itself?" Arnold commented:[168]

> F.D.R. recognizing that he could have only one war at a time, was content to declare a truce in the fight against monopoly. He was to have his foreign war; monopoly was to give him patriotic support—on its own terms.
>
> And so more than 90 percent of all war contracts went to a handfull of giant empires, many of them formerly linked by strong ties with the corporations of the Reich. The big fellows got the contracts, the little fellows were dependent upon subcontracts with the big boys.

As potent as the war in shooting down Arnold's antitrust program was the fanatic opposition of the labor unions.[169] From the moment he took the oath of office as assistant attorney general, Arnold had repeated ad infinitum, in press conference after press conference, in speech after speech, that he would attack the economic concentration of power, whenever and wherever he located it.[170] Publicly, President Roosevelt never once dissented from Arnold's barrage against big business; indeed, he may have privately applauded Arnold's activity. While the president was highly amused at Arnold's indictment of the American Medical Association, he found little humor in Arnold's slashing fusillades against labor. After all, the labor movement comprised a major component of the "Grand Alliance" of the New Deal's political house. Without a great deal of daydreaming, the president could envision the disintegration of his carefully constructed Democratic party coalition.

The major blow to Arnold's labor prosecution fell in the winter of 1941. In the preceding year a jurisdictional dispute had taken place in St. Louis between the machinists' and the carpenters' unions. The disagreement centered on whose right it was to dismantle specific pieces of machinery in the Anheuser-Busch plant. The machinists' union received the contract, whereupon W.H. "Big Bill" Hutcheson, president of the carpenters' union, invoked a secondary boycott on Anheuser-Busch. After placing a picket line around the brewery, Hutcheson inaugurated a campaign to urge the American people to stop purchasing Anheuser-Busch beer. Arnold saw this secondary boycott as a classic example of restraint-of-trade, plus injury to the general welfare. Arnold asked the Court to declare the secondary boycott a violation of the Sherman Act.

On February 4, 1941 the Supreme Court announced their decision in the *U.S.* v. *Hutcheson* ruling in a six-to-two majority against the government. Ironically, Justice Frankfurter wrote the majority opinion, while the two conservatives on the Supreme Court bench, Chief Justice Hughes and Mr. Justice Roberts, dissented. The majority of the Court found it difficult to escape the argument propounded by the counsel for the carpenters' union, that if competition between business firms is meritorious, rivalry between unions cannot be a crime. The crux of the issue, so the Supreme Court majority announced, was whether under the Sherman Act and the Norris–La Guardia Act a jurisdictional strike was illegal. The Court admitted that most of the precedents were with the assistant attorney general, but they concluded that so long as a union acted in its own self-interest and did not ally with a non-labor organization, it was exempt from prosecution.

When Arnold received the Supreme Court decision, he was astounded, annoyed and discouraged. Arnold perceived the ruling as simply legally condoning a wide spectrum of labor abuses in the future. Seven days after the Hutcheson decision, he summarized for Attorney General Robert Jackson the immediate problems: "One, the protection of the employer from retaliatory action when he deals with a legitimate union. Two, the protection of the right of collective bargaining of the workman himself from exploitation by labor dictators, who charge him for his right to work. Three, the effect of such activities on national defense."[171]

On the same day he wrote the attorney general, Arnold sent off an impassioned letter to his longtime friend, Professor T. Reed Powell of the Harvard Law School. In the Powell epistle, Arnold dropped all pretense of a measured and judicious argument. "I never dreamed that the Norris–La Guardia Act would be interpreted to take away the criminal remedy. . . . Public indignation is rising in all parts of the country. However, I am getting the support of everybody except a few so-called liberal papers. The trouble with liberals today is that they are unable to see any individuals. They see unions and they see labor movements. When individuals are crushed they think no more of it than Mr. Hitler does who is also working for an ideal system in which there is a place for everyone, and everyone has his place."[172]

When Arnold desired to dramatize his definition of liberalism, he returned again and again to the inherent rights of the individual. During the McCarthy malaise, he constantly stressed to his friends and partners his horror at the destruction of the individual under the sledgehammer tactics issuing from this national paranoia. To this Westerner, reared at the base of the Rockies and bathed in progressivism, the protection of individual prerogatives held a special meaning. Seventeen years after the Hutcheson decision Arnold remained firmly convinced that the exclusion of unions from antitrust prosecution had hindered the growth of unionism and weakened the economy. To political pundit Arthur Krock, Arnold commented, "The exemption of labor has actually worked to the detriment of unions like Walter Reuther's and to the enchancement of the power of unions like the teamsters'."[173]

The opposition of labor and Hitler was too great for Arnold to overcome. Roosevelt silently, but not so slowly, began withdrawing his tacit support of the antitrust program. Besides labor and war, there were other cumulative influences that abetted attacks on the Antitrust Division. In trying to apply the antitrust laws Arnold had made numerous enemies.

Disillusioned, Arnold resigned and accepted Roosevelt's appointment as judge of the United States Circuit Court of Appeals. *Business Week*, interviewing Arnold in 1949, asked,[174]

> "Judge Arnold, although you are in private law practice now, your ideas haven't changed a great deal since you were in the Department of Justice?" Arnold retorted, "Well, I don't know why they should."

Although Arnold's ideas on antitrust policy may have remained stable, certainly his political beliefs during the 1940s underwent a metamorphosis. In the early 1930s he bridged the philosophies of Justices Holmes and Brandeis. Arnold agreed with Holmes that economic concentration was not intrinsically a curse; however, he deviated from Holmes's doctrine of the totality of countervailing power. Arnold was not convinced that the public interest was adequately safeguarded by competition of industrial giants. On the other hand, he sympathized with Brandeis as to the desirability of humanizing competition with modifications. He wrote to the editor of the *Saturday Evening Post* in 1942:[175]

> When our whole thinking is dominated by a search for security, I believe that we have lost the greatest stimulus to industrial activity that exists, and that is the belief. . . the driving force of a society must be based on the preservation of opportunities to succeed or to fail. I am committed to a politics of opportunity versus a politics of security.

Arnold dissented from Brandeis's opinion that big business was an evil to be destroyed and small business a positive good to be preserved.

By the early 1940s Arnold was beginning to sound like a resurrected Western progressive;[176] the tinge of Wilsonianism was there, but fading. In an amazing letter to William Allen White, he summed up his philosophy:[177]

> I expect you have little realization of how you have caught the imagination of that peculiar brand of liberal who comes from the Middle West and who believes in the simple philosophy that our institutions are fundamentally sound and, therefore, all we need to do is to attack entrenched special privileges. The economic planners are always too complicated for me. They were bound to get in power during a period of frustration when people were afraid to face a world in which they had to take a chance of failure on their own efforts. But now, in spite of all the reactionary influences, I begin to feel a new spirit rising in this country. I believe that men like Henry Kaiser, who I got to know very well in my efforts to prosecute the steel companies for preventing him from getting into production on the Pacific Coast, are going to get strong enough through this war that they cannot be stopped. If they do, liberalism in this country is going to change from faith in Government bureaucracy to the sort of thing that you have represented for so many years.

Whether the shift in Arnold's political philosophy was the result of five years of give-and-take in Washington politics, the result of estrangement from the administration regarding antitrust programs, or sprang from the fact that he was forced to assume an increasingly defensive position that terminated in an inflexible stand, it is obvious that the Arnold of 1937 was not the Arnold of 1943. By the time he donned judicial robes, Arnold was for sustaining twentieth-century industrialism, at the same time protesting strongly the loss of economic individualism—a stand that a young Hiram Johnson, of three decades past, would have applauded.

Guests at testimonial dinner honoring Thurman Arnold as departing head of the Antitrust Division, held in the Presidential Room of the Statler Hotel, March 9, 1943. Arnold is on the left. Copyright by Harris & Ewing.

In retrospect, it appears that a folklore around Arnold often obscured his antitrust objectives. What then was Arnold's antitrust ideal? The answer is surprisingly simple: his entire antitrust program was oriented toward the benefit of the consumer. In one sentence he summed up his aim: "The idea of antitrust laws is to create a situation in which competition compels the passing on to the consumers the savings of mass distribution and production."[178] It is mystifying that Arnold's goal should have been so largely ignored by so many commentators.[179] Perhaps its very simplicity confused those who were in search of a more sophisticated or complex motivation. On the first page of *The Bottlenecks of Business* the purpose of the book was outlined as an exploration of how the consumer could benefit from an equitable distribution of goods. In fact, the whole book was an economic and political platform for the consumer.

The question remains: what was Arnold's motivation in raising the consumer placard? Undoubtedly he was aware of the political advantage of casting the consumer in the role of the forgotten man. Roosevelt most certainly was conscious of the political promise of an antitrust crusade. Yet Arnold was enough of a political pragmatist to know as did the president that the amorphous body of consumers was a capricious political force at best, its whims frequently shaped by special interest lobbies. Furthermore, it is difficult to accuse Arnold of courting popularity; the wide-ranging indictments against industry and labor alike belie any attempt to be among the political elect. The only clear rationale is that Arnold was sincerely convinced that proper enforcement of the antitrust laws provided the means for economic and social justice.

When Arnold donned the robes of an associate justice of the United States Court of Appeals, he did so with mixed emotions. In later years, he would refer to his period on the bench as one of the more frustrating times of his life. Abe Fortas, in a felicitous metaphor, put Arnold's reaction most eloquently, "For him, the appellate robes were like a halter on an eagle."[180] In *Fair Fights and Foul,* Arnold quoted a story of George Wharton Pepper's which precisely summed up his own sentiments on a judicial career. After leaving the circuit court, Arnold encountered Pepper one day, and the latter probed as to why he had left the sanctuary of the court. For once Arnold did not have an appropriate response so he began fumbling for the right remarks. Pepper interjected, "Let me help out—I think I know. Some years ago I was offered an appointment to the bench—it wobbled me. I was almost ready to accept. But I finally decided that I would rather make my living talking to a bunch of damn fools than listening to a bunch of damn fools."[181]

Arnold allotted only three pages of his autobiography to his court service, but in concluding that brief account, he offered his own explanation for leaving the circuit court of appeals. "I think it was my preference for partisan argument, rather than for impartial decision, that made me dissatisfied with a career on the appellate court. Furthermore, I was beginning to doubt whether a person of my temperament could ever be an ornament to the bench. I was impatient with legal precedents that seemed to me to reach an unjust result."[182]

As restless as Arnold may have been on the bench he had, as his article on Jerome Frank spotlighted, a deep reverence for the majesty of the law. He could scorn precedents, he could revolt at inane arguments, he could be impatient with obtuseness in his colleagues, but Arnold maintained an abiding respect for the court system and the role of the judge as an instrumentality of that legal organism.

In the little more than the two years Arnold sat on the circuit court he wrote sixty-seven opinions: four were dissents, one a concurrence, and the rest were for the majority of the court. Most of the opinions were brief: thirty-four of them ran three columns or less.[183] In two areas, obscenity and insanity, Arnold wrote three notable and quotable opinions which influenced legal precedents. The two significant opinions that revealed Judge Arnold's perception on insanity and the law were *Holloway* v. *U.S.* and *Fisher* v. *U.S.* In *Holloway* v. *U.S.*, the appellant was convicted of rape. In his opinion Arnold noted that the appellant appealed on the sole ground that his medical history indicated that he had been mentally ill for a substantial period. The psychiatric evidence left little room for doubt that the accused suffered from mental illness. In spite of this overwhelming evidence, Arnold affirmed the conviction. In doing so he offered an apologia for a judicial system that threw its cloak of approbation over this injustice. Arnold argued, "The issue of criminal responsibility of a defendant suffering from mental disease is not an issue of fact in the same sense as the commission of the offense. The ordinary test of criminal responsibility is whether the defendant could tell right from wrong." Then Arnold captured the dilemma with a simile so striking that one finds it appearing forever after in footnotes and texts of law journals on this subject. Arnold wrote that the ordinary man, when he probes into human behavior, discerns ". . . a separate little man in the top of one's head called reason whose function it is to guide another little unruly man called instinct, emotion or impulse in the way that he should go." Arnold emphasized that modern psychiatry had destroyed these common assumptions about human behavior. "For the purposes of conviction," wrote Arnold, "there is no twilight zone between abnormality and insanity. An offender is wholly sane or wholly insane." In essence, the function of a jury is a moral one, not therapeutic or diagnostic. Arnold finished his opinion by stating that if legal theory embraced the finding of psychiatrists, it would violate and corrupt society's respect for criminal law.[184]

In *Fisher* v. *U.S.* Arnold followed the carefully balanced opinion that he had worked out in *Holloway.* Fisher, annoyed by his employer because she had reprimanded him, proceeded to murder her with all the thoroughness of the murders of Rasputin. First he bludgeoned the lady with a piece of firewood and then he stabbed her with a knife. Pyschiatric examination proved beyond a reasonable doubt that Fisher was an impulsive, aggressive psychopath of low mental competence. The appeal rested on the sole ground that the evidence was not sufficient for the jury to have found the defendant guilty of premeditated murder. Reverting to *Holloway,* Arnold gave weight to the fact that no testimony was given that indicated the defendant did not know the difference between right and wrong. Arnold distilled the essence of the issue in one sentence, "In the determination of guilt age-old conceptions of individual moral responsibility cannot be abandoned without creating a laxity of enforcement that undermines the whole administration of criminal law."[185] In sum, the necessity to protect the whole of society from criminal acts is greater than the obligation to the individual offender. These were hardly the words of a legal revolutionist.[186]

Judge Arnold held little brief for his opinion in either *Holloway* or *Fisher.* Arnold abhorred the legal necessity of rejecting the findings of modern psychiatry. Those two little men labeled impulse and reason, the Gog and Magog of his allegory, jabbed at his consciousness for years.

Six years after the Fisher case, the decision in *Monte W. Durham* v. *U.S.* resolved Arnold's disquietude.[187] Durham was convicted of housebreaking and grand larceny. A psychiatrist testified that at the time of his trial Durham was of unsound mind. However, when the psychiatrist was asked the age-old legal test for insanity—did the defendant know the difference between right and wrong?—he replied as had his colleagues for years: he simply was unable to tell whether Durham knew right from wrong. A decision was made to appeal the case to the United States Circuit Court of Appeals for the District of Columbia. Since Durham was indigent, Arnold's partner, Abe Fortas, was appointed by the court to take the appeal. Fortas argued the inevitable: specifically, that the right-and-wrong test for insanity was clearly archaic in the face of modern depth psychology.[188]

The court then faced the self-imposed quandray that the judges knew would arise from Fortas's appeal. Should the court persist in holding to the right-and-wrong test for insanity, they would be excluding all psychologists from the courtroom. No reputable psychologist would testify on whether an insane criminal knew the moral difference between right and wrong. Chief Judge David Bazelon wrote the opinion, which ruled that the hoary M'Naghten precedent was obsolete. The courts, henceforth, must mesh their decisions with the scientific findings of psychologists. From that moment on, juries would be instructed that if the criminal act resulted from mental illness, the jury must acquit the defendant via the reason of insanity. Immediately, some attorneys and politicians warned that the Durham decision would forever paralyze criminal law. For criminals of this mentality, the syllogism went, since law should be based on moral principles and since there were no moral credos in the Durham decision, the case had obviously pulled the entire underpinning out from under criminal litigation. The Durham rule stood. Arnold succinctly summarized its importance as giving "a trial on the issue of insanity the appearance of justice achieved by scientific methods."[189]

The other major social area where Judge Arnold's reasoning had a profound impact came over the issue of obscenity and the law. Today if one mentions Arnold and the *Esquire* or *Playboy* cases in the offices of Arnold and Porter, one of the first expressions from any partner will be how titillated, delighted and intrigued Arnold was by the entire question of obscenity. All of his former colleagues, Hugh Cox, Milton Freeman, Abe Fortas, Abe Krash, Carol Agger Fortas, and William McGovern refer to Arnold's penchant for scoffing at the role of sex in American society.[190] The entire question of sex and the law appealed to Arnold's sense of the ridiculous. The obscenity issue provided a wonderful vehicle with which to expose pretentiousness and hypocrisy in society. Thurman reveled in quoting a judge who came up with what must be conceded as a highly original definition of obscenity. This judge, after presumably long and prayerful meditation, decreed that a naked lady was not necessarily obscene per se; however, if she were fat and ugly, that sight was obscenity![191]

Thurman had little patience with the extreme position taken by people on the obscenity question. The blatant, vulgar and crude public expressions of sex bored and annoyed him, every bit as much as the mores depicted by a Grant Wood's "American Gothic." Arnold's views on obscenity unmask another captivating side of his personality: his charm. He detested what he most commonly called cant or pretense, whether in institutions, society or individuals. He delighted in exposing the phoniness in men.

While Thurman could brutally expose fraud in individuals, he could also be kind with bumbling, inept, insecure people. Milton Freeman remembers one episode when Arnold, Fortas and Porter received a visit from a lawyer residing in a Midwestern city. The visitor spent an unholy amount of time ballyhooing his legal conquests, his brilliant courtroom performances, ad nauseam. When their guest departed, Freeman commented to Arnold, "You know he really annoyed me the way he went on like that." Arnold quickly replied, "Well, you shouldn't be upset about that; this fellow just wanted us to know that he was somebody too."[192]

No one, regardless of his eminence, was safe from an Arnold riposte. Arnold became convinced during one of his exchanges with a distinguished Supreme Court justice that the justice possessed serious inhibitions about the subject of sex. Arnold, in fact, thought the justice's discussion of obscenity plainly ridiculous. In reliving the conversation with this justice, he would tell his friends that the only trouble with Mr. Justice "Smith" was that his beard was on the inside of his head.

The obscenity cases, for Arnold, presented a rostrum from which to expose one of society's foibles. In two cases, *Esquire, Inc.* v. *Walker,*[193] and the *Playboy* case, *State of Vermont* v. *Verham News Corporation,*[194] Arnold unveiled his personal viewpoint on obscenity. The most systematic clarification of his opinions on obscenity came in the *Esquire* case during his tenure on the bench. In a brilliant tightly reasoned decision, Judge Arnold first defined the question. The postmaster general had revoked the second-class mailing privileges of *Esquire,* not for reasons of obscenity but because he was righteously convinced that the magazine's editorial policy was to publish literature and illustrative material that the postmaster general identified "in that obscure and treacherous borderland zone where the average person hesitates to find them technically obscene, but still may see ample proof that they are morally improper and not for the public welfare and the public good."[195] As the result of this dictum from the postmaster general, *Esquire* would be charged with an additional postage totaling some half a million annually. Pro forma, *Esquire* would cease publication entirely.

Arnold proceeded to riddle the postmaster general's logic. He dismembered the government's case on the power to invoke what amounted to censorship not on moral but economic grounds. The government, wrote Arnold, in making "this extraordinary contention" insists that it has the power to charge *Esquire* another half a million a year unless the periodical conforms to the postmaster general's notion of the public good."[196] In opening up a window into the postmaster general's mind, Arnold stated that the only rationale he could conceive for Walker's position was that the postmaster general regarded second-class mailing rights as "unique privileges." Devastatingly, Arnold commented that the postmaster general's action could be compared to that of those who awarded the Navy "E" for special merit. The postmaster general appeared to be bent on bestowing a croix de guerre on those editors who resisted "the temptation to publish material which offends persons of refinement."[197]

Arnold continued his lecture, "But mail is not a special privilege. It is a highway over which all business must travel."[198] Then Arnold gave full rein to lampooning the absurd. The real origin of the difficulty, the Judge continued, was embedded in the hidden recesses of persecuted mentalities. "The first source of confusion is, of course, the age-old question when a scantily clad lady is art, and when she is highly improper. Some refined persons are hopeful that an answer to this vexing riddle may some day be found. Others are pessimistic."[199]

Thurman Arnold at Florida State Bar Association meeting, Miami Beach, May 1944.

Moreover, Arnold observed, "A second course of confusion in determining what kind of literature furthers public welfare is the dividing line between refined humor and low comedy." To illustrate the deep seriousness of this very perplexing challenge, Arnold quoted a colloquy between the counsel for the postmaster general and the counsel for the beleaguered *Esquire:*

> Mr. Bromley: I would like to know, Mr. Hassell, if you don't mind telling me now, just what it is in that article you don't like. I can't find it.
> Mr. Hassell: I would be glad to read to the counsel.
> Mr. Bromley: Thank you.
> Mr. Hassell: Third column at the bottom of page 144. "He noticed how large the uniform made her behind look."

The third abuse in this no man's land centered on the question, where did censorship cease? One could reverse Arnold's dialectic and ask, where should censorship begin? Arnold quickly admitted that the postmaster general, after obvious long and prayerful reflection, had considered this very dilemma and had deduced a startling conclusion. Arnold rephrased Walker's verdict to read, "An occasional indifference to the public welfare may be indulged by an editor provided that it is not so frequent as to be classed a habit." At this juncture, Arnold's sketch of the absurd fairly leaped off the page. Now imagine, Arnold said, if a court, by some intuitive means, acquiesced in attempting to pass sentence on the artistic and literary merit of a controversial literary piece. There remained a definite practical matter to consider: "Opinion on such matters differs so widely that if the evidence in the record before the Post Office were to be weighed each side would have to continue calling witnesses indefinitely in order not to be outweighed by each other."[200]

Judge Arnold ended his opinion by emphasizing that he intended no criticism of the counsel for the Post Office. After all, they were faced with an impossible task! However, if the Post Office sought a balm for its wounds, it was there. "We believe that the Post Office officials should experience a feeling of relief if they are limited to the more prosaic function of seeing to it that 'neither snow, nor rain, nor heat, nor gloom of night stays these couriers from the swift completion of their appointed rounds.' "[201]

Blithely ignoring centuries of testimony to the inherent difficulty of defining obscenity, legally or otherwise, let alone the recent history of Judge Arnold's *Esquire* opinion, the postmaster general again tried to confer martyrdom on a publisher. This time the postmaster general's righteous wrath fell on an enterprising entrepreneur of male fantasies in the country of Theodore Dreiser. The accused—Hugh Hefner and his golden publication, *Playboy,* a magazine Arnold wittily described as dedicated to proving that most women were mammals. This time the postmaster general decided to classify *Playboy* as outright obscenity, banning it entirely from the mails. The case came to William McGovern at Arnold, Fortas and Porter, by referral from a Chicago attorney.[202] When McGovern walked into Arnold's office and outlined the *Playboy* complaint, he recalls, Arnold's face "lit up all over" at the opportunity of again jousting with the Post Office on the obscenity issue.

Arnold learned one morning at two A.M. that the Post Office was stopping the mailing of the current *Playboy.* With a million or more copies in warehouses, Hefner faced bankruptcy. Arnold obtained a temporary restraining order requesting an administrative hearing. At that juncture, the postmaster general, either wary or bored, dropped the issue. The magazine reached its million-or-so pop-eyed readers. Soon thereafter Arnold received another frantic call from Chicago. The Post Office had again barred *Playboy* from the mails and had set an administrative hearing for the following morning at ten A.M. Wearily, Arnold once more obtained a restraining order, on the premise that a hearing on this short a notice amounted to a legal farce. When finally the date came for the hearing, the postmaster general appeared and requested that the case be dismissed. Paul Porter protested the dismissal, insisting that after two retraining orders, the postmaster general's tactics were capricious and that therefore the case should be heard. The Judge disagreed; the case was summarily dismissed.

The final drama of Hefner and his unclad ladies was acted out in Vermont. The attorney general of Vermont indicted the Verham News Corporation for selling *Playboy* and other allegedly "salacious" periodicals. In contrast to his eight-page *Esquire* brief, this time Arnold and his staff prepared an elaborate presentation, tracing the history of obscenity. Arnold discussed at length the historical, philosophical and legal evolution of our moral heritage. Arnold emphasized, as he did time and again throughout his life, the anthropological subterfuges that man erected to protect his cultural taboos. "Such laws [against obscenity] are passed because men are stimulated by erotica and at the same time they are ashamed of it. Society requires a public denunciation of this almost universal sin whether or not it leads to positive harmful conduct."[203] These sentences reverberated back to his earliest days at Yale, when his students recall Arnold noting that in reality all society needed was one law to outlaw all sin. If humanity would obey that law, self-evidently no other statutes would be needed.

Arnold continued his lecture by indicating a few of the numerous contradictions in legislation passed on obscenity. One way that politicians had tried to varnish over these legislative burlesques was to plead the commonplace theory that erotic literature insidiously weakened the moral fiber of the young. Arnold argued this was simply attempting to prove the unprovable. "The moral censor who tries to make all literature decent is like a man who wants everything up and nothing down."[204] After reviewing the major obscenity cases, Arnold fairly burst with delight over the "spectacle of a judge pouring over the picture of some nude, trying to ascertain the extent to which she arouses purient interests, then attempting to write an opinion which explains the difference between that nude and some other nude, has elements of low comedy."[205] After solicitously assuring the justices of the Supreme Court of Vermont that they would be exposing themselves to ribald jesting if they so much as even tried to decide this case, Arnold added his final bon mot, "Besides, 'Justice' is supposed to be a blind Goddess."[206] He followed that by stuffing in a footnote one of Paul Porter's great puns, "No nudes is good nudes."

The case attracted national attention and comment. While the maelstrom swirled about them, the Vermont justices, as if following Arnold's prepared text, refused to ask one question or offer one comment. They listened to the arguments in stony silence. When the Supreme Court of Vermont handed down its decision, the case was remanded to a lower Vermont court on the premise of a legal technicality. The attorney general of Vermont, undoubtedly perceiving the wisdom of Arnold's warning, dropped the case.

As Judge Arnold sat listening to the opposing counsel in the *Esquire* case he pondered his future, which seemed far removed from the erotic effrontery to society that so worried the postmaster general. Twenty-six days after the *Esquire* decision, Thurman Arnold resigned from the bench of the United States Circuit Court of Appeals. For months preceding his departure he had been debating his future. Some of his friends in the New York City bar urged him to join them in practice. Arnold concluded that if he went into private practice, he would stay in Washington. His contacts were there; besides he and Frances had deep roots in the capital city. Thurman commented in a letter to his father in November of 1938, "Frances blossoms like a flower under her social activities. The small, intimate dinner with the president was very pleasant. There were only eight at the table. She sat on his right and got very chummy indeed, reaching over several times to pat his arm. He seemed to like it and they got along like a pair of old schoolmates. Nothing could be more delightful than the informality of the president's small dinners."[207]

Frances Arnold was celebrated on the Washington social scene for her novel parties, her witty, sometimes outrageous remarks. One of the Arnolds' festive soirees featured liquor bottles tied on ropes at the end of a windlass in their garden well. The head knocking that occurred among the guests as they peered into the murky depths of the well echoes three decades later through the conversations of those invited.

Frances Arnold during her husband's years as assistant attorney general. Courtesy of Mrs. Frances Arnold.

For a short time in the spring of 1945 Thurman thought that after he had established a thriving law practice he might return to Wyoming and run for the Senate. After all, Laramieites in 1925 had assumed that he was heir apparent to Senator Kendrick. In June of 1945, Thurman wrote his close friend and Laramie attorney, Joseph R. Sullivan:

> I spoke to you briefly about forming a firm in Wyoming. I would expect no share in your business but the connection would be valuable to me. I have in mind—and this is very confidential indeed—the possibility that I might get a chance to run for the Senate. Whether this would work out or not is hard to tell, but I want to have an anchor out that way. My theory is that if I can get a firm started, with a substantial business, and some men to carry on, I will be in a financial position so that I can make a race, if things worked out in a couple of years. . . . Don't breathe a word of this to anybody, even my Mother, because if it didn't work out I would look foolish."[208]

Along with exploring the option of a Senate seat, for several months before he left the court Thurman sounded out his acquaintances in the business community on the feasibility of obtaining retainers. By the summer of 1945 he was assured of a $25,000 retainer from the Coca Cola Company, arranged by his friend Robert Woodruff. Then out of the "clear sky" came a $12,500 retainer from the Chesapeake and Ohio Railway Company, "the hub" of the Robert Young railroad empire, and $12,500 from the Otis Banking Company of Cleveland, Ohio. Thurman gossiped to Joe Sullivan in Laramie that the last two retainers came via individuals in both companies having read a new book, *Justice in Transportation* by Arne Wiprud.[209] At the request of Wiprud, Arnold had written an introduction to the volume. Wiprud had been head of the Transportation Section of the Antitrust Division during Arnold's tenure. Understandably, Arnold took Wiprud into partnership, as "he knows more about the railroad problem than anybody else in America and he will be very necessary."[210] Arnold had received further assurances from Otis and the Chesapeake that over the years their firm would receive in "the neighborhood of about $100,000 from these two concerns.

With high hopes and the comforting thought of a $50,000 cushion, Arnold and Wiprud moved into the former office of General "Wild Bill" Donovan at 821 Fifteenth Street. Arnold was delighted with his new quarters: "We are buying the furniture lock, stock and barrel, at an evaluation which will be put on it by appraisers. The building is air cooled and is the best law building in Washington."[211]

It did not take long for the new firm to begin to earn its retainer from Young, for the Pullman Company again entered Arnold's world. After the

Present-day office of Arnold and Porter, 1229 19th Street NW, Washington, D.C. Thurman Arnold's office was the enclosed porch barely visible on the second floor, extreme right of photograph.

government had won its suit in Philadelphia, the Pullman Company had been ordered to divest itself of either the manufacturing or operating of Pullman cars. The Pullman Company, after long deliberation, decided to sell the operating side of the business. Robert Young, the free-wheeling impresario of a railroad kingdom, entered a bid for the Pullman equipment and service. The American Association of Railroads, having a decidedly jaundiced view of any project conceived by the febrile mind of Robert Young, vehemently opposed his offer. Most railroad executives felt that it was bad enough having Young as a competitor, let alone as a partner in their business.[212] Young's rivals quickly formed a pool and placed a competing bid for the Pullman Company assets. Arnold and Wiprud contended that the very existence of such a combination by the railroads was a violation of the Sherman Act. Young lost his case; the railroads' bid was accepted.[213] Arnold appealed to the Supreme Court; the justices split equally, thereby affirming the lower court's decision.

In his autobiography, Arnold remarked that at this juncture, with no other transportation business in sight, "Arne Wiprud, whose sole interest was in transportation law, dissolved our partnership to pursue his own speciality."[214] Most of Arnold's friends today regard the divorce of Arnold and Wiprud as destined. The firm represented a merger of dissimilar talents and temperaments. Had there been no preoccupation with a legal specialization, the two partners probably would have eventually gone their separate ways.[215]

Casting about for a new associate, Arnold discovered that Abe Fortas was planning on leaving his post as undersecretary of the interior. Arnold invited Fortas to form a new firm. Fortas consented, Arnold and Fortas officially came into being on April 18, 1946. Arnold always maintained that his proposal to Fortas was "the smartest decision I ever made. . . . His decision [Fortas' acceptance] was by all odds the luckiest thing that ever happened to me."[216] At Thurman's memorial service, Abe Fortas recalled, "For twenty years we were law partners. We began with nothing but ourselves. Able and devoted young lawyers joined us."[217] In a few months, Paul A. Porter, lately ambassador to Greece, joined their firm.[218] By the end of the first year, Walton H. Hamilton, Reed Miller, Milton Freeman and Norman Diamond had all cast their futures with Arnold, Fortas and Porter.

Arnold's role in his own firm has been the subject of considerable speculation by watchers of Arnold, Fortas and Porter. Actually, a few minutes of conversation with any of his partners, past or present, will quickly dispense any mystery surrounding Arnold's place in the firm.[219] First and foremost, Arnold was not, nor did he ever claim to be, an orthodox corporate attorney. As Fortas observed, "Thurman was not a corporate lawyer, and he did not have the perverted taste that I have

Mr. Justice Abe Fortas, co-founder of the firm Arnold and Fortas. A Chase Ltd. photograph, Washington, D.C.

for working out intricate problems, just because they were intricate. He was not a craftsman in that sense. . . . Thurman's interest was much more in the broader and more passionate aspects of the law, which more directly reflect the characteristics of human behavior."[220] Another partner in Arnold and Porter agreed: "You ask whether he [Arnold] was a business getter and the answer is no, primarily for the reason I have suggested he was really very naive about how to deal with businessmen."[221] Furthermore, McGovern pointed out, Arnold had a reputation as a great trust buster, a reputation that was not apt to endear him to corporate clients. Thurman also had a proclivity for going about the country, much as he did before entering private practice, making speeches and writing articles, many of which annoyed vast segments of the corporate community. Another Arnold partner and associate during the antitrust days, Victor Kramer, seconded Abe Fortas's comments: "Thurman just did not have the patience or interest in the usual aspects of corporate law."[222]

It would have been paradoxical if Arnold had been preoccupied with the complexities of corporate law. Arnold did not have a systematic philosophy, nor was he an organic scholar in the conventional sense. While his partners readily recognized Arnold's limitations as a corporate attorney in the classical connotation, they were just as quick to divulge his unique endowment to the firm. Abe Fortas recalled that he found Arnold extremely useful in two ways: First, Fortas would go to Arnold with a seemingly impossible legal puzzle. After a few minutes of highly stimulating conversation, Arnold was likely to produce several ideas that at first blush appeared absolutely inane. However, after being exposed to one of Arnold's intellectual gypsy sessions, Fortas found himself several days later discovering that Arnold's deductions made sense. Arnold simply possessed an unfathomable depth of resourcefulness and imagination. Secondly, Fortas, particularly in the McCarthy years, found Arnold's courage a tremendous bulwark. A certain comfort and reassurance came from having ten feet down the hall an individual who plainly refused to be intimidated by the hysteria of the age.[223]

Besides his sagaciousness and fearlessness, Arnold's contribution to Arnold, Fortas and Porter can be measured in other ways. Victor Kramer and Abe Krash emphasized Arnold's ability to judge and attract able, young, dedicated lawyers to the firm.[224] In his antitrust days, Arnold was widely recognized in Washington, as one of the au fait administrators of the New Deal, for his ability to recognize talent, hire and retain bright young attorneys. Hugh Cox and Victor Kramer both recall the tremendous sense of freedom in the Antitrust Division, the absence of the burdensome weight of excessive bureaucracy.[225] Each member of the Division was encouraged, indeed strongly urged, to give full rein to his own creativity. Arnold's attorneys in the field knew that he would be behind them, supportive even in their faux pas.

A typically smiling Paul Porter. His joining the firm of Arnold and Fortas created Arnold, Fortas and Porter.

Arnold lacked the passion or the precision for unraveling the ambiguities of corporate statutes, but as an advocate he had an uncanny ability. His annihilation of George Wharton Pepper in the Pullman case was but one example. He might and frequently did mix up the names of his clients, jumble the exhibits, and back into his arguments with excessive glee; but when the case was finished he would have managed by some mysterious means to have convinced both judge and jury of the justice of his position. In the courtroom, he had an unerring instinct for human psychology: the right argument, the most convincing sentence would come tumbling from his lips.[226] He had little hesitation in quite emphatically instructing a judge on the alternatives available on which to decide a case. He did just that in the *Playboy* and Fort Monmouth cases. Few lawyers would have had the temerity to try, let alone have gotten away with, such courtroom antics. Thurman Arnold managed to retain his credibility for two basic reasons. First, as an ex-judge he understood the workings of the judiciary, a past he made evident to the judge before whom he was presenting a case. Secondly, and perhaps more significantly, Thurman Arnold was not another lawyer pleading his client's cause, he was Thurman Arnold—genius. Admittedly, no judge, any more than Arnold's friends, could have told how they knew that paunchy individual with a rumpled suit and cigar ashes strewn about was a mental giant. They just knew or thought they knew. Some clients were repelled by this mystique. Arnold did not attract business to the firm as did Paul Porter with his unlimited reservoir of charm. Nor did he devote himself to building up the firm's business in the orderly manner of Abe Fortas. Most of the present-day members of the firm quickly admit that it was Fortas whose frenetic energy, zealous application and brilliance created the business foundation of Arnold, Fortas and Porter. The firm's clients appreciated Fortas's genius for comprehending the supposedly incomprehensible legal tangles. Victor Kramer illustrated Arnold's lack of business sense when he said, "For one thing Thurman never knew what to charge a client; it was as basic as that."[227] Fortunately for Arnold, Fortas and Porter, others in the firm never found themselves unable to imagine what a bill should be.

In reviewing the past for the readers of the *Yale Law Journal,* Fortas wrote, "The purpose of the firm was to provide a means for its two partners to make a living. Neither partner quite knew how this was to be done. At the outset, neither had a single client or any prospects; but both were dedicated to the great cause of economic survival which they had undertaken." The time, the economy, as Fortas observed was propitious. The mass of regulatory law and agencies, spawned by the Second World War, sent many a businessman scurrying into a lawyer's portal. A guardian to light the way through the complexity of regulatory policy was not a luxury—it was essential for survival. Thurman Arnold and Abe Fortas, with their immense number of friends sprinkled about the bureaucracy, were in a strategic situation to be of benefit to their prospective clients. Arnold's pragmatism never led him to scorn the firm's regulatory business but he never adjusted philosophically to his role in the interplay between businesses and regulatory agencies in the mid-twentieth century. Cynicism may be too potent a term to define Arnold's reaction, but he did become increasingly sardonic about the "regulating" powers of regulatory agencies.

Of course, Arnold's conceptual framework regarding regulatory bodies derived from the New Deal. When he first came to Washington, Arnold foresaw, as did many, that regulatory agencies, under the blanket of antitrust enforcement, would maintain a continuing surveillance over business practices. At the beginning era of his Washington service, Arnold was especially optimistic about the power of regulatory instrumentalities. He could look toward the Securities and Exchange Commission and William O. Douglas, or to the Agricultural Adjustment Administration and Jerome Frank, or to Henry Friendly and the Civil Aeronautics Board, and so on. These men were able dedicated public servants, not easily intimidated by their fellow man. Arnold fervently believed that these regulatory agencies, guided by men of vision, would be great solvents for the malaise of the business sector. What Arnold and others came to realize was that the regulatory agencies gradually began to be molded by their clientele. Slowly the consequences of the marriage of the regulatory agencies and their publics came through with brilliant clarity. The regulatory agencies, instead of supervising business in the public interest, actually reversed their covenant and began governing public interest on behalf of business. Arnold's disenchantment with regulatory commissions increased over the years as these bodies were given the authority to immunize areas of the economy over which theoretically they had been given jurisdiction. The enforcement of antitrust laws became continuously frustrated and this situation particularly annoyed Arnold.

Arnold did not allow his skepticism over government-business relationships to degenerate into despondency. Part of Arnold's attractiveness was that he never lost his optimism, his great anticipation for the future.[228] Whether he was discussing business, American institutions, youth or international relations, tomorrow was not only a new day, it was a better day. Gloom never enshrouded Arnold—at least for long. One should not interpret his opinions on regulatory commissions as being anti-business. What most businessmen would never believe, and what many of his friends misinterpreted, was that Arnold was not being facetious when he entitled one of his articles, "I Like Big Business."[229] Arnold held the deep conviction that his antitrust action was abetting, not hindering, the free enterprise system.

Arnold never subscribed to an anti-business mentality. For instance, he argued that the affluent entrepreneur had as much right to counsel as a pauper and the pro bono client. Some of Arnold's populistic admirers across the country automatically associated wealth with evil: individuals should be graded morally on the basis of their wealth, especially concerning the source of their riches. Arnold never embraced that amazingly simplistic and ignorant fable. In 1969, with stinging scorn, Arnold roasted the Yale professor who wrote him that because Arnold and Porter represented a tobacco company, he had been deprived of "hope for achieving a decent society in this country." Arnold reminded the Yale chemistry professor that his firm had represented Owen Lattimore, Dr. John P. Peters, and established the Durham and Gideon precedents. Arnold then underscored his main case: "During the course of these cases we have been subjected to hundreds of comments like yours. How can a reputable firm justify representing such despicable people?" The analogy was transparent even for the Yale professor as Arnold concluded, "Whatever may be the ultimate solution of the cigarette problem it will not be furthered by establishing the principle that in any sort of legal controversy either side should be deprived of the services of the best counsel he can obtain. Your idea is a dangerous doctrine; once established, it will sap the very foundations of the American ideal of a fair trial."[230]

For Arnold those were not stagnant platitudes to be chiseled on a public building. They had possessed a vital meaning and a deep emotion since his youth on the Laramie plains: canons that held a glaze fired by the hysteria of the McCarthy period.

It is difficult, if not impossible, to recreate for those who did not live through it the violence of emotions, the national paranoia, the morbid excitement of the McCarthy era. Even for those who experienced this time of madness, the feverish convulsion of those years is blotted out. The horror and insanity has been cauterized, but scars on the body politic remain. Perhaps three vignettes from that time can transmit in some minor degree the schizophrenia that afflicted America. A young mother in Boulder, Colorado, one Saturday evening decided to visit a neighborhood grocery store to purchase a few items for the evening meal. She placed a red "farmer's" handkerchief on her nine-month-old daughter, picked her up in her arms, and dashed to the store. As the young wife was checking out, an elderly woman walked up to her, took one glance at her daughter, and burst out, "Any mother who puts a red kerchief on her daughter must be a Communist!" The mother, too stunned and horrified to reply, quickly paid her bill and dashed to her apartment. She did not have the presence of mind to reply with the perfect squelch: her daughter was dressed in blue jeans, a white T shirt and a red bandana—red, white and blue! One can suggest that her accuser was self-evidently a senile and/or demented person. Yet there were millions who suffered from this conspiratorial fear that permeated society.

Twelve hundred miles east of Boulder, in Chicago, another incident revealed the temper of the times. A young wife who edited her sorority magazine at home had the habit of posting her manuscripts at the neighborhood post office after dinner. Her small son had received a toy gun as a recent Christmas gift. One evening when she was about to leave for the post office her little boy said, "Mommy, take my gun." The mother, pleased by this expression of thoughtfulness in her usually selfish child, thanked him profusely and carried the toy weapon to please him. A few days later an FBI agent called on her—a very nice man in IBM attire. They chatted about her husband's work, her editorial employment, how she enjoyed living in Chicago, plus several other innocuous subjects. Finally the agent blurted out, "You seem to be a very nice person, but there's something that I have to ask you: what work do you do that is so secret that you go armed at night?" The young mother quickly explained the story of the toy gun, the agent departed, apparently satisfied that nothing sinister was afoot.[231]

The theatre now shifts sixty miles west of Chicago to the stable farming community of Sycamore, Illinois. A young social studies teacher heard that a boyhood acquaintance and next-door neighbor had returned to Sycamore for a visit. The instructor, knowing his former neighbor is now an organizer for the National Maritime Union, assumes that Harry Bridges' follower will have something of value to relate to his students on twentieth-century labor policy. He does, and the message is leftist; by the last class of the day, the labor organizer's talk is replete with actual or allegorical references to class revolution. By nightfall, the telephone wires in Sycamore are humming—a scene reminiscent of the famous Norman Rockwell painting of the town gossips! A real live Communist in Sycamore!

The teacher, bewildered, alarmed and yet horrified that this 1984 ideology had been enacted in his home town, tenaciously fought back. School board meetings were convened. The teacher was fired. However, after a new school board election, with new faces, the board decided the previous board's action was premature and unwise (perhaps even silly?). After all, many residents of Sycamore had known the teacher since the first grade and they had never noticed any subversive activity before; within three months the teacher was rehired. All was not forgotten, but at least a personal tragedy had been avoided.

These three episodes, variations on a common theme, were acted out hundreds of times in the McCarthy era. Commonly, the individual paid the bounty; in terms of financial, physical and emotional cost the price was incalculable. Reputations were destroyed with a whisper, longtime friendships sabotaged. One's neighbor, one's co-worker were not only potential enemies but informers. America had turned into a massive psychological snake pit.

Congress, the Executive and, to an extent, the Supreme Court legitimatized this reign of terror by a series of repressive measures designed to implant suspicion into American institutions. In November of 1946

President Truman gave the first official blessing of the federal machinery by setting up the Temporary Commission on Employee Loyalty.[232] Conservatives and liberals both damned Truman's orders. The conservatives pointed out that by his action the president had confessed to a serious loyalty problem in government. The liberals, with the righteousness of Tom Paine, saw sinister control over private lives.

A year later, Truman again yielded to the pressures created by the FBI and other political forces and promulgated Executive Order 9835. By administrative fiat he established a comprehensive federal security and loyalty program. Technically, all federal employees could be under surveillance for their loyalty beliefs, with secret information, regardless of the sources, as the basis for dismissal from government service.

Still, this was not enough for those who saw strangers in the night; in 1950, Congress passed the Internal Security Act, with its hapless, hopeless, muddled provisions. Truman vetoed the bill. Congress passed it over his veto. Three years elapsed; a new president, Dwight Eisenhower, sought to pre-empt the security issue. On April 27, 1953 the president by executive order created a new loyalty program. Now an employee could be fired from government service if the individual's actions, speech, or, presumably, thoughts were not "clearly consistent with the interests of national security." A year went by; under the leadership of civil libertarian Hubert Humphrey, and with the vigorous support of later liberals John F. Kennedy and Eugene McCarthy, Congress passed the Communist Control Act. The ostensible aim of the legislation was to outlaw the Communist Party; membership in the party would now be a crime against the state.

It was the depths of this Robespierrean terror, ratified by Congress and the Executive, that Abe Fortas referred to in his eloquent eulogy at the Arnold memorial service. "Joe McCarthy gave us what turned out to be our opportunity—the opportunity to be men as well as lawyers. It *was* an opportunity, although, as we saw it then, it was a dangerous and fearful summons—a call to duty which we could not ignore."[233]

Arnold, Fortas and Porter became entangled in the loyalty program in much the same way that many firms are caught up in causes: a client walked across their threshold. Not long after the black lettering had dried on the office doors of suite 928 in the Bowen Building, Morton Friedman appealed to the firm for advice. On September 12, 1944 Friedman had been dismissed from his position as chief of the Classification Division of the War Manpower Commission. The basis for Friedman's dismissal came from the United States Civil Service Commission, which "had determined that there was a reasonable doubt as to his loyalty." Friedman then sued in the United States District Court of the District of Columbia for reinstatement. The district court dismissed the suit and the circuit court, in refusing to review the Civil Service Commission ruling, offered the opinion, "We are not concerned here with the question as to whether Friedman was in fact disloyal under the regulation; he could be removed from service if the commission had reasonable doubt as to his loyalty."[234]

What then was the rationale of the circuit court for end-running the Friedman case? Toward the conclusion of the majority opinion the raison d'etre of the circuit court judges surfaced: "It is beyond our province, and it was beyond the province of the district court, to review the finding of the Civil Service Commission that it had reasonable doubt as to whether Friedman was loyal to the government, because it has long been held that the Courts will not review managerial acts, not clearly arbitrary, of executive officials performed within the scope of their authority."[235] So, by hiding behind a hundred-and-six-year-old precedent, the circuit court had skirted the loyalty problem.

Arnold, Fortas and Porter then petitioned the Supreme Court for a writ of certiorari. In making their petition Arnold contended that the government had every right to discharge Friedman, after notifying him of the charges, for non-performance or unsuitability for his position. But Arnold argued, "The government. . . could not fire an employee and then put upon his record a charge akin to treason, and thus not only get rid of him, but also ruin his career in other fields."[236] The Supreme Court refused to grant a writ of certiorari; so automatically the lower court's decision was affirmed.[237]

Arnold suspected that the reluctance of the court to hear the *Friedman* v. *Schwellenbach* case derived from the principle "that one of the main functions of the court is to keep out of trouble." Arnold's observation was a none too subtle swipe at Mr. Justice Frankfurter and those justices who endorsed Frankfurter's philosophy of judicial restraint.[238] Frankfurter, who could never forget that the heavy hand of history rested on his shoulder, as the occupant of the seat of the magisterial Holmes and Cardozo, constantly lectured his brethren on the bench on the academic value of legal self-restraint. As Mr. Justice Holmes had championed legal restraint in the economic area, so Frankfurter advocated the same Holmesian position be extended to civil liberties cases. For his admirers who recalled Frankfurter's courageous stand in the Sacco-Vanzetti case, Frankfurter's civil libertarian view of the fifties not only did not make sense, it plainly mystified them.

As Congress and the Executive raced to see who could make the most political capital out of the loyalty issue, Arnold, Fortas and Porter found themselves in the unenviable spot of seeing in their anteroom more and more individuals with loyalty difficulties. Paul Porter, whose facility as a raconteur is unrivalled, remembers that one morning he arrived at his office to find a postal employee waiting for him. The postal worker immediately accosted Porter with the query, "Suh, I understand this is where one comes to get his loyalty fixed." Highly amused and yet taken back by the ingenuousness of the remark, Porter replied, "Yes sir, you have come to the right place; please come in."[239] Fortunately for the employee his case was a minor one; a letter was sent and the problem solved.

When asked whether Arnold, Fortas, and Porter ever consciously decided to take civil liberties cases, the partners from this era were unanimous in their opinion that no specific decision was ever executed. On the contrary, Milton Freeman recalls that at one of the office gatherings one of the partners almost plaintively asked why Arnold, Fortas and Porter had to become involved in the loyalty mess. Abe Fortas quickly replied, "Because if we do not no one else will."[240] When asked about Arnold's legal activism in relation to the loyalty cause, Abe Fortas responded, "I do not think that Thurman would have gone out of his way to get involved in an activist role in the McCarthy fight. Profoundly as he disliked and profoundly as he was opposed to it. . . it came and so we did it. . . . We were scared, but on the other hand it was there to be done, and you could not call yourself a man and not do it. It was as unromantic as that, really."[241]

Actually, Arnold, Fortas and Porter cast their die, consciously or unconsciously, when they accepted the first loyalty case. Once the firm acquired the reputation of taking loyalty clients, they were flooded with supplicants. One of the earliest as well as most publicized cases concerned one Dorothy Bailey. An old friend of Milton Freeman, Dorothy Bailey naturally thought of Arnold, Fortas and Porter when she encountered the loyalty problem. Miss Bailey, thirty-eight years of age, received on February 11, 1949 a letter removing her from her position as a training officer in the United States Employment Service of the Federal Security Agency. At the time of her dismissal, Miss Bailey received an annual salary of $7,911. Dorothy Bailey was not surprised at this action, as she had been warned six months previously that her security was in jeopardy. Between February 11 and July 28, 1949 she was accorded two oral hearings, the first before a panel, the Fourth Regional Loyalty Review Board of the U.S. Civil Service Commission, and the second before the U.S. Civil Service Commission Loyalty Review Board.[242]

At neither of these hearings, nor subsequently, was Dorothy Bailey ever informed of the exact nature of the accusations against her. No prosecutor appeared at these hearings, nor did anyone testify against Miss Bailey in regard to her performance, character or conduct.[243] All the intelligence she gleaned from these two boards was that five or six reports came from informants, certified by the FBI, that she had been a member of the Communist Party from 1935 to about 1943. Before both review boards, Miss Bailey was represented by counsel. Her minister and numerous witnesses testified to her impeccable character. She further stated orally and under oath that she was not then or ever had been a member of the Communist Party.

A month and a half after her firing, Miss Bailey filed complaint for injunction and declaratory judgment in the district court. The district court sustained the government. Then Miss Bailey appealed to the United States Circuit Court of Appeals for the District of Columbia. Judge Prettyman upheld the lower court but ordered a decree entered, "holding invalid those sections of the orders of the Loyalty Boards and the Federal Security Agency, which would ban Miss Bailey from employment for three years, and holding valid those sections which accomplished her removal from the rolls and from the office in classified civil service."[244] In an extremely strong dissent, Judge Edgerton brought into sharp relief the basic constitutional issues intertwined in the Bailey case. "Without trial by jury, without evidence, and without even being allowed to confront her accusers or to know their identity, a citizen of the United States has been found disloyal to the government of the United States." Edgerton continued, "No witness offered evidence, even hearsay evidence, against the appellant. No affidavit against her. The record consists entirely of evidence in her favor."[245] Then Edgerton summarized the constitutional issues in the case, enumerating the identical points that Thurman Arnold had forcefully hammered upon in his appeal to the circuit court. Specifically, Executive Order 9835 required the introduction of substantial evidence and an opportunity for cross-examination. Second, any dismissal for disloyalty is extra punishment, and necessitates all the safeguards inherent in any judicial trial. Third, Miss Bailey's freedom of speech and assembly was abridged by her ouster.

As an example of disregard for the First Amendment, Judge Edgerton quoted an incredible exchange in the transcript of the Regional Loyalty Board examination: "Mr. Blair: Did you ever write a letter to the Red Cross about the segregation of blood? Miss Bailey: I do not recall. Mr. Blair: What was your personal position about that? Miss Bailey: Well, the medical—Mr. Blair: I am asking yours."[246] Judge Edgerton concluded his eloquent dissent with the sentence, "We cannot preserve our liberties by sacrificing them."[247]

When they read the decision of the court of appeals, Arnold, Fortas and Porter asked for and received from the Supreme Court a writ of certiorari. The case was argued before the full court. Again, Thurman Arnold pleaded impassionately that no one in the entire judicial proceedings had so much as hinted that Dorothy Bailey had a fair trial.[248] Therefore, Arnold, under the due process clause of the Fifth Amendment, requested that the entire action of the Loyalty Board be nullified. The government contended that, since Judge Prettyman had stricken the Loyalty Board's ruling that Miss Bailey was ineligible to take competitive examinations, Miss Bailey had every opportunity to secure federal employment. Arnold responded that the right to take competitive examination in no way removed the stigma of disloyalty.

When the government attorney insisted that Dorothy Bailey had every chance for a position in government, Justice Jackson sharply questioned him. "I do not mind being amused, but I don't want to be made a laughing stock of. Do you mean," Jackson asked, "that Dorothy Bailey can get a job?" Solicitor General Perlman conceded that pragmatically Miss Bailey would not be considered for employment, but theoretically she was eligible. Mr. Justice Jackson then said, "Does the government actually wish to win the case on that point?" Perlman replied, "No sir, we have other points."[249] The court wrestled with the Bailey case for several months; finally a decision came down on April 30, 1951. One judge had disqualified himself, and the court split four to four; hence, the court of appeals was sustained.[250]

Thurman Arnold was disheartened and frustrated by the Supreme Court ruling. Hugh Cox, Abe Krash and other friends of Arnold during the early fifties remember the intense indignation and unmitigated disgust that Arnold had for the procedures of the entire loyalty program. What riled Arnold most was the effect on the individual caught up in the brawling upheaval of the security crisis.[251] Arnold never perceived the McCarthy inquisition from a class action basis. Of course he, like many others, commented on the destruction of freedom, the undermining of the Republic and the vital threat of totalitarianism. What incensed Arnold most was the senseless destruction of careers and lives, the ignominious and baseless character assassination of Owen Lattimore, John P. Peters and Dorothy Bailey on sleazy, inaccurate and frequently fraudulent evidence. No one in Laramie, Wyoming, would have termed this anything but high injustice, and as far as Arnold was concerned the progressive creed of Laramie in 1910 retained its validity in the 1950s.

The next loyalty case, in which the constitutional principles presented a striking similarity to those in the Bailey case, focused on Dr. John P. Peters of Yale University Medical School.[252] A specialist in metabolism, for a number of years in the late 1940s and into the 1950s Dr. Peters served as a special consultant to the United States Public Health Service of the Federal Security Agency. In April of 1953 the activities of the Federal Security Agency were absorbed by the Department of Health, Education and Welfare. Approximately four to ten days a year Peters journeyed to Washington to advise the surgeon general on research proposals and grants to medical schools and organizations. By no stretch of the imagination could Dr. Peters's interest in metabolic consumption or his consultation with the surgeon general be classified as sensitive to the security of the United States, unless one assumed that a Communist conspiracy existed to destroy America by producing corpulent citizens.

In January of 1949 Joseph E. McElvain, chairman of the Board of Inquiry on Employee Loyalty of the Federal Security Agency, wrote to Peters that they had received derogatory data concerning Peters's loyalty. An investigation ensued, with Dr. Peters being completely cleared of disloyalty. Two years later, in May of 1951, the case was reopened under the procedure outlined by Executive Order 9835. This time Dr. Peters received a letter describing sixteen charges, including membership in the Communist Party. A hearing at New Haven by the Loyalty Board of the Federal Security Agency followed on the first and second of April, 1952. As if the power structure were replaying the Dorothy Bailey case, the only evidence offered was presented on behalf of Dr. Peters. Under oath, Peters testified he had never been a member of the Communist Party. On May 23, 1952 the board, for the second time in three years, informed Dr. Peters that "there was no reasonable doubt" of his loyalty.

Then the unbelievable happened, explicable only in terms of the hysteria fogging the Capitol in these years. The Federal Loyalty Review Board decided to initiate a "post-audit" of the Agency's board's findings. After a hearing, at which the identical evidence of the two previous hearings was introduced, the Federal Loyalty Board reached the astounding conclusion that there existed a reasonable doubt of Dr. Peter's loyalty. Further, he was "barred from the Federal Service" for three years dating from May 18, 1953. At this point, the bedeviled Dr. Peters sued.

Arnold, Fortas and Porter decided to assail directly the denial of civil liberties by the secret witness pattern of the Truman Loyalty Boards. Dr. Peters's case followed the same legal route, exhibiting many of the identical arguments that had resounded on the ears of the judges in the Bailey case. The district court and the court of appeals both affirmed the Loyalty Review Board's action. So for the second time in three years, Arnold, Fortas and Porter requested a writ of certiorari before the United States Supreme Court. Chief Justice Warren stated that certiorari was granted "because the case appeared to present the same constitutional questions left unresolved by this court's action in *Bailey* v. *Richardson*."[253]

Against the backdrop of that statement, the Court's majority opinion is all the more astounding as the Court decided the Peters case, not on the grounds of constitutionality, but on a legal technicality. Reliving the Peters case, Thurman Arnold recalled his immense surprise when Mr. Justice Felix Frankfurter questioned him whether he thought the Federal Loyalty Review Board was properly constituted. Arnold and Assistant Attorney General (now Chief Justice) Warren Burger both responded that they did not wish to win the case on this point. Mr. Justice Frankfurter assured Arnold that "it made no difference on what grounds I wanted the case decided on."[254]

Forewarned, Arnold and Burger should have been forearmed; nevertheless, they were both astonished when the Supreme Court decided in favor of Dr. Peters, on the mechanistic detail that the Federal Loyalty Board did not have jurisdiction in the case. Mr. Justice Douglas reluctantly concurred with the majority, opening his remarks with the comment, "With all deference, I do not think we can avoid the constitutional issue in this case." Then Douglas' famed indignation flared:

> Dr. Peters was condemned by faceless informers, some of whom were not known even to the board that condemned him. Some of these informers were not even under oath. None of them had to face Dr. Peters. So far as we or the Board knew, they may be psychopaths or venal people like Titus Oates, who revel in being informers.
>
> They may bear old grudges. Under cross-examination their stories might disappear like bubbles. Their whispered confidences might turn out to be yarns conceived by twisted minds or by people who, though sincere, have poor faculties for observation and memory. . . . Confrontation and cross-examination under oath are essential, if the American ideal of due process is to remain a vital force in our public life.[255]

The third major case in which Arnold, Fortas and Porter had the challenge of arguing the question of secret witnesses and the Bill of Rights brought Arnold into direct confrontation with the army. Thirty-one scientists at Fort Monmouth, New Jersey engaged in military research were accused of subversive activity and fired. The charges against these scientists ranged from membership in the American Veterans Committee (a purple guilt they shared with fellow member Dwight D. Eisenhower) to the mind-boggling accusation of failure "to take an active stand against Communist sympathizers." Ten of the scientists who received a hearing before a loyalty review board heard evidence introduced from a growing legion of faceless informers. Now the inconceivable transpired—the army adamantly refused to reveal to the scientists or to their counsel the names of the reviewing tribunal. Such tactics brought back vivid memories of the 1930s, for this was a ploy worthy of a Goebbels in Germany or a Beria in the U.S.S.R. Scenes like this appear one after another on the pages of Zola, Kafka and Herling. Still incredulous a decade later, Arnold wrote,

> The proceeding thus outdid the Dreyfus case. Not only was the evidence against the accused kept secret, but also it was reviewed

> and weighed by a secret tribunal. If there are any other spectacles like this in the history of American or English jurisprudence, I have been unable to find them.[256]

Arnold, Fortas and Porter, following the slash marks through the legal bramblebush of previous trials, brought the case before the U.S. District Court of the District of Columbia. The district court sustained the Loyalty Review Board. Arnold then appealed to the circuit court of appeals. This time he made a plea that only an ex-judge could have made, indeed, only an ex-judge by the name of Thurman Arnold. Milton Freeman, who was with Arnold that day in the circuit court, remembers the tableau vividly.[257] For a minute Freeman had difficulty believing his ears when Arnold concluded his summation by telling the judges, "Now, gentlemen, you have to decide this case in our favor." Why? "Because," Arnold stated, "the issue is the same as in the Bailey and Peters cases: secret witnesses." Arnold then told them what they already knew, that Arnold, Fortas and Porter had been to the Supreme Court twice on this subject, and twice the Supreme Court had refused to decide it. However, Arnold boomed at his attentive listeners, "they will decide this case as they did the Peters case. In favor of our clients." So Arnold reasoned, why should the Supreme Court be bothered? "Let me give you three or four grounds on which you can render a decision in our favor."[258]

Freeman, closely watching the reaction of the circuit court judges, believed that Arnold's argument appeared to move them. Whatever impact Arnold's courtroom virtuosity may have had was soon dispelled by a startling development. The government counsels, afraid that a ruling would force them to reveal the names of secret witnesses, suddenly moved to drop the case, consenting to a judgment in favor of the plantiffs. The scientists were paid $80,000 in back wages, with the stipulation that they resign from government service. So ended another unreal case in an age of hallucinations.

The most histrionic and publicized loyalty case that Arnold, Fortas and Porter consented to handle during the McCarthy reign of terror was that of Owen Lattimore. In 1950 Lattimore was director of the Walter Hines Page School of International Relations at The Johns Hopkins University. In foreign policy centers and in the academic world, Lattimore had the reputation of being one of the nation's ablest experts on the Orient. Lattimore had held a number of governmental or quasi-governmental positions during the forties. President Roosevelt had selected him to serve as his personal political adviser to Chiang Kai-shek in 1941. From 1942 to 1944 Lattimore had charge of Pacific operations for the Office of War Information.

Against this long background of service to his country, one can imagine the stupefaction of Lattimore's family, friends and associates when Senator

Joseph McCarthy on the morning of March 21, 1950 disclosed to the Tydings Committee that Owen Lattimore,[259] on the basis of a reputed FBI file, was "definitely an espionage agent." Carried away by his own imagination, McCarthy further asserted that Lattimore was ". . . the top of the whole spy ring of which Hiss was a part. . . . I think he is the top Russian spy."[260]

Receiving the news of McCarthy's defamation in a primitive hut in Afghanistan, Lattimore immediately flew back to defend himself before the Tydings Committee. At Mrs. Lattimore's request, Abe Fortas had consented to act as Lattimore's counsel. The Tydings Committee, a subcommittee of the Senate Committee on Foreign Relations, was formed to investigate "persons who are disloyal to the United States and are or have been employed by the State Department." The public and executive hearings extended from March 8 to July 7, 1950. The committee reached the conclusion at the end of four months "on the evidence before us that Mr. Lattimore is not an employee of our State Department, that he is not the architect of our Far Eastern policy, and that he is not a spy."[261] The Tydings Committee had completely exonerated Owen Lattimore of all the charges brought against him by Senator McCarthy.

Senator McCarthy had trumpeted at the opening of the Lattimore inquiry that he "would stand or fall" on the Lattimore case; unfortunately and typically he did not bother to honor his own pledge. In this and in numerous other ways McCarthy differed from the collegiate football coaches, who have a penchant for resigning after a poor season or that "crucial game."

Unhappily, there was little resemblance between the emotional frenzy of a winning or losing football season and the paranoia of the early fifties. Arnold wrote to his friend on the Harvard law faculty, George K. Gardner, at the height of the McCarthy fever, "Washington today is in a state of hysteria, which you wouldn't believe unless you were here. The fantastic cloak and dagger intrigue, the bribery which we suspect surrounds the Lattimore case, is unthinkable. It is getting so attorneys are afraid to handle these cases for fear of losing respectable clients and the tragedy of it all is that I have very good grounds to believe that it is the Communists themselves who are turning into the FBI and Congressional Committees accusations against persons who are in their way."[262]

After the Tydings Committee hearings, Owen Lattimore basked in the euphoria of having survived the onslaught of one of America's most effective demagogues. Lattimore's relaxed mood was rudely jolted when he learned of the appointment of the Internal Security Subcommittee of the Senate Judiciary Committee, the so-called McCarran Committee.[263] The first target of McCarran was the Institute of Pacific Relations. As the

McCarran Committee formulated its own mandate, it had two obligations: one, the discernment of whether the Institute of Pacific Relations was influenced or controlled by Communist agents; two, whether in turn these agents had infiltrated United States Far Eastern diplomatic policy. The Institute had been the recipient of sizable public and private philanthropy. But what appealed to the McCarran committee as most insidious of all was that Owen Lattimore had served as editor of the Institute's quarterly, *Pacific Affairs*, 1934-41.

The McCarran Committee conducted hearings and held sessions for almost one full year, from July 25, 1951 to June 20, 1952. The first five months of the McCarran Committee's activity was consumed by examining the massive records of the Institute, which had been dramatically seized in a raid on a barn in Lee, Massachusetts.[264] Then the McCarran Committee turned to its prize, Owen Lattimore. Finally, after the committee had sat for over six months, it allowed Lattimore to defend himself on the witness stand. For thirteen days, the members grilled Lattimore, setting a record for the longest interrogation of any one person in all congressional history. The committee badgered, harassed and accused Lattimore of distortion. In addition, they demanded that he recall minute details of events in his life fifteen years ago. The committee hearings bore a startling resemblance to the Spanish Inquisition.

The exchanges between Lattimore and the committee, sometimes vitriolic, were always hostile. The committee gave Lattimore a list of individual names and requested that he pin a label on each name, Communist, non-Communist or in the happy hunting ground between. When Lattimore challenged the committee's definition of "Communist," the committee counsel rephrased the question in so many ways that the hearing almost collapsed under the weight of semantic doubletalk.[265] Abe Fortas, frustrated and annoyed by the committee's discourtesy and harassment, interrupted Lattimore during his attempt to read a fifty-page prepared statement, with the plea, "But gentlemen, these proceedings are a tremendous strain. I have seen that with people that I have handled, and I beg you to keep that in mind and let this man lay out these reasons which will retraverse many of the things which have been already asked."[266]

The committee continually goaded Lattimore, time and again warning him to offer no opinions, only "tested" facts. A furious exchange took place between Senator Willis Smith of North Carolina and Lattimore on this very point.[267]

> Mr. Lattimore: Senator, a great many statements of opinion against me have been freely entered into the records. Am I not allowed to state my opinions?

> Senator Smith: No, you state facts. That is what we want. If you do not have a foundation of fact, then do not state it."

To those who peruse the nine hundred sixteen pages of Lattimore's testimony, twenty-two years removed from the event, the impact remains one of depression mixed with horror. Of the millions of pages of congressional transcripts, it is doubtful that there are another thousand pages that offer a better glimpse of an Orwellian future. Time after time the interrogator and interrogee exploded with exasperation. Toward the end of the second day of hearings, Owen Lattimore summed up his regard of the McCarran investigation by reading from his prepared transcript. "The personal damage that has been done to me by the way in which this subcommittee has allowed malicious testimony to be stacked against me is probably beyond repair. But much more important is the damage that has been done to my country."[268]

Senator McCarran returned the compliment at the end of Lattimore's hearings:[269]

> Chairman: Then the hearings of the witness, Owen Lattimore, are now closed. But the Committee has something to say. What I am going to say now comes from the unanimous Committee that has heard this hearing. . . . The Committee has been confronted here with an individual so flagrantly defiant of the United States Senate, so outspoken in his discourtesy, and so persistent in his efforts to confuse and obscure the facts, that the Committee feels constrained to take due notice of his conduct.

When silence fell on the McCarran Committee room on that evening of June 20, 1952 had the McCarran Committee said categorically that Owen Lattimore was a Communist? Incredibly, they never did accuse Lattimore of being an outright Communist. The closest they came to such an accusation was when among the "listed conclusions" of their report the McCarran Committee stated, "Owen Lattimore was from some time beginning in the 1930s a conscious articulate instrument of the Soviet conspiracy."[270] Far more injurious to Lattimore personally than this unsubstantiated accusation was the recommendation to the Department of Justice that a grand jury investigate whether he had committed perjury.

The Lattimore case now moved into its third phase, with the grand jury indicting Lattimore on seven counts of perjury in his testimony before the McCarran Committee. With the exception of three days, Abe Fortas had borne the burden of representing Lattimore before the committee. With the shift from committee room to courtroom, Fortas took a less public role in the case; Thurman Arnold and Joseph C. O'Mahoney, Arnold's friend and recently defeated senator from Wyoming, became the advocates in the district and circuit courts.

With two decades of hindsight, anyone today reading the seven counts of perjury in the Lattimore indictment must be struck by the flimsiness of the charges and wonder if Lattimore's prosecutors could really have been serious, as indeed they were. On December 19, 1952 Owen Lattimore pleaded not guilty, denying emphatically that he had committed perjury before the McCarran Committee on the following items: one, that he had knowingly promoted Communism; two and three, that he was unaware that certain obscure persons were Communists; four, that he had published numerous articles by bona fide Communists when he edited the *Pacific Affairs;* five, that he had gained access to China in 1927 through the influence of the Communist Party; six, that he had had a luncheon engagement with Soviet Ambassador Oumansky in July of 1941; seven, that he had, at the request of Lauchlin Currie, undertaken to answer Currie's correspondence while Currie was absent from the White House.[271] This was the indictment of a man who held a dagger poised at America's security in the 1950s. The first judicial move in the Lattimore case came in the United States District Court for the District of Columbia on May 11, 1953. Arnold moved to dismiss the entire indictment. Judge Luther Youngdahl, former governor of Minnesota, overruled the motion. However, Judge Youngdahl held that the first, third, fourth and seventh counts of the indictment were invalid; and that the second, fifth and sixth counts were so ambiguous that the defendant should receive a bill of particulars on which he could defend himself.[272]

The government counsel appealed Judge Youngdahl's ruling. Judge Prettyman of the United States Circuit Court of Appeals sustained Judge Youngdahl on the first and seventh counts, but reversed him on the third and fourth counts, holding that these were valid.[273]

Then the Department of Justice heightened the drama of the case and at the same time made a monumental misjudgment. Operating under the theory that any judge who did not rule for them was obviously unfit to rule at all, the attorney general filed an affidavit of prejudice against Youngdahl. The Department of Justice, with transparent calculation, relied on the adverse publicity to force Judge Youngdahl to disqualify himself. Incensed at the government's political ploy, Youngdahl issued a stinging rebuke to the Department of Justice and struck the affidavit from the record.[274] In reprimanding the counsel for the Justice Department, Judge Youngdahl was quick to press home that four of the nine appellate judges had endorsed his position in toto. Eight of the nine had sustained his action on the vital first count. Finally, the government did not request the Supreme Court to review the Court of Appeals decision; hence, the government must have thought no valid challenge to his ruling existed. Then Judge Youngdahl, full of indignation, came to the heart of the matter, "At the bottom, the affidavit is based upon the virulent notion that a United States judge who honors and adheres to the sacred constitutional presumption that a man is innocent until his guilt is established by due process of law has 'a bent mind' that disables him from conducting the fair and impartial trial to which both the accused and the government are entitled."[275]

Shunning the personal attack, Judge Youngdahl turned to hearing the Lattimore case on the two counts of perjury that the circuit court had returned. Again, Judge Youngdahl found it difficult to take the indictment at face value. In closing his decision, Youngdahl wrote,

> The Government seeks to establish that at some time, in some day, in some places, in all his vast writing over a fifteen-year period, Lattimore agreed with something it calls and personally defines as following the Communist line and promoting Communist interests.
>
> With so sweeping an indictment, with its many vague charges, and with the existing atmosphere of assumed and expected loathing for Communism, it would be neither surprising nor unreasonable were the jury subconsciously impelled to substitute its own understanding for that of the defendant.
>
> To require the defendant to go to trial for perjury under charges so formless and obscure as those before the Court would be unprecedented and would make sham of the Sixth Amendment and the Federal Rule requiring specification of charges."[276]

Among the impassioned pleas of Lattimore's counsel and Youngdahl's wrath there had been moments of comic relief. In one of Thurman Arnold's more animated flashes, when he was enthusiastically propounding the glory of the First and Sixth Amendments, U.S. Attorney Leo Rover interrupted him. Rover had lost track, several tributaries back, of Arnold's stream of consciousness, so with more than a small degree of frustration Rover addressed the court, "Well, all I can say around here is, I don't understand the arguments of Mr. Arnold. Of course, I did not have the advantages of having a Harvard Law School education; perhaps that accounts for it." Arnold, seizing the moment to jump into this wide-open opportunity, replied, "Your honor, I am not going to spend any time on the U.S. Attorney's education, or lack of it."[277]

The amount of unfavorable publicity that Arnold, Fortas and Porter received in the loyalty era was unbelievable. Paul Porter recently recalled another anecdote from those days. An acquaintance, at a country club in suburban Washington, accosted Porter with the yell, "Paul are you still representing Communists and homosexuals?" Porter fired back, "What's the matter, John, are you in trouble?"

Seven months before the U.S. Circuit Court's last ruling on the Lattimore case, Senator Joseph C. McCarthy was censured by his Senate colleagues. McCarthy's downfall had been brought about by two New

Englanders, a witty dour, righteous Boston lawyer, Joseph Welch, and a flinty, independent senator from Vermont, Ralph Flanders. The nation awoke from its nightmare almost as rapidly as it had gone to sleep.

As friends returned to smiling at friends, as luncheon partners ceased viewing their neighbors as potential informers, as politicians quit cowering before the image of a Wisconsin senator; indeed as the country escaped from the terrifying hand of Kafkaesque oppression, Thurman Arnold returned to the daily pursuit of corporate law. Although Arnold, Fortas and Porter seldom mentioned it, they felt much satisfaction in having protected freedom of speech and expression in one of the most threatening totalitarian periods of our history.

They had not sought martyrdom, for they had as much to lose (if not more) that the average citizen or attorney. They had not petitioned for the role of guardian of the First and Sixth Amendments. All the present members of the firms who endured those dark days of the fifties agree that no one in the firm eagerly coveted the chance to assail the establishment. Why would they? They committed themselves because they could not be men if they shirked their responsibility. True, they were frightened men; they were human.

Whether Thurman Arnold expressed it vocally or not, he could with pride view this period as his finest hour. Arnold, Fortas and Porter may have had a country-club-golf-course reputation for serving society's misbegotten, yet surprisingly enough they lost few corporate clients. Perhaps the corporate world admired their courage, even if they disagreed with their cause—although many executives undoubtedly, if dimly, realized that their freedom was being threatened as much as that of Peters and Lattimore.

As Arnold's life came to a close, he would increasingly voice cynicism, though not of the conservatives, for these he could understand. What disturbed him far more than the people who looked under their beds every night for agile Communists were the "pseudo-liberals" who hid under their beds. With clarity and a touch of "bitters," Arnold expressed his thoughts to Ernest Angell in 1968.

> I recall the Dorothy Bailey case, which this firm defended and lost, where a career was ruined on evidence which was not disclosed to the accused; the Fort Monmouth spy case, where scientists were discharged on secret evidence, which this firm defended and finally won, but not until the careers of twenty-six scientists had been irretrievably damaged. In those days noisy people like Dr. Spock and Chaplain Coffin were entirely silent. It was impossible to raise among college professors a fund to defend Lattimore. Arthur Schlesinger [Jr.] , who was accused of being soft

on Communism on the floor of Congress, was sufficiently frightened to prove his virtue by writing a column attacking Lattimore."[278]

With the nation's return to sanity, Thurman Arnold returned to dividing his time between corporate law, speeches, and a flow of articles on subjects sweeping from legal realism through antitrust to international law. A major preoccupation of his time after 1960 was the writing of his autobiography, *Fair Fights and Foul.* One of his more spirited intellectual encounters happened when Arnold picked up his copy of the *Harvard Law Review* for November 1959.[279] This issue contained an article by Henry M. Hart, Jr., a member of the Harvard law faculty. Professor Hart was disturbed. After reviewing the Supreme Court docket for the 1958 season, he came to the conclusion that the justices were heavily overworked—worse, the justices lacked good judgment, for they were expending their time on the wrong judicial subjects. By some inspired calculation, Hart determined that a justice in a typical thirty-six-week Court session allotted 1,728 hours to his job; this led Hart to ask the rhetorical question: should men in their fifties, sixties and seventies be expected to work in excess of an eight-hour day, six days a week?

Having established to his satisfaction that Supreme Court justices suffered from extreme mental and physical exertion, Hart deduced the serious implications of this situation. The oral arguments before the Court represented half the time the justices assigned to a case. What "intellectual respect," Hart wondered, can one have for precedents, when decisions are reached this rapidly? Historically, professors with prolific publishing records have been denounced for exploiting their graduate students. Similarly, Hart suggested that law clerks played a major role in the framing of questions for decision. Finally, the Supreme Court unwisely and to the detriment of the judicial system persisted in hearing cases involving the Federal Employer's Liability Act, "involving nothing of importance except an appraisal of the evidence in the particular litigation." Was there any wonder that the decisions of the Supreme Court were inferior in quality and sparse in quantity? In one paragraph Hart provided his coup de grace. "The opinions of the Justices, if one turns to them, confirm the conclusion that the Court is trying to decide more cases than it can decide well. Regretfully and with deference, it has to be said that too many of the Court's opinions are about what one would expect could be written in twenty-four hours."[280]

Arnold considered Hart's article fallacious and pompous—a titillating target. Arnold proceeded to demolish Hart's thesis with a mixture of surgical skill and sledgehammer blows.[281] Some of Arnold's partners conjectured that a couple of Arnold's friends on the Supreme Court prompted the reply. Motivation aside, Arnold relished the chance to take Hart to task. First, Arnold ridiculed as simply nonsense Hart's proposal

Thurman Arnold strikes a Napoleonic pose, late 1950s. Courtesy of Mrs. Frances Arnold.

that the Court should refuse certiorari in FELA cases. How could the Court abdicate its appellate jurisdiction when Congress had conferred on the Court that specific obligation and power? Even should one concede Hart's point, Arnold pounded, no area of law affected more people than the law of negligence. Then Arnold came, with the inexorableness of Graham Greene, to the centrifuge: "The plain and simple fact is that they [the Supreme Court justices] are not overworked and that, in my judgment, their opinions nevertheless rank higher than the articles which appear in the *Harvard Law Review,* whose authors have limitless time available."[282]

Further, Arnold proposed that via the same methodology that Professor Hart employed in his article, Arnold could positively prove that Hart had not expended the necessary time in collective thought and deliberation to frame his attack on the Court. Arnold admitted that he could demonstrate the point to his satisfaction, but never to Professor Hart or those who endorsed Hart's views. What irked Arnold most was not Hart's strictures against the Court on the utilization of their days, but the broad generalizations that "discredited other opinions, never mentioned, of the members of the Court who have shown the most courage in defending civil liberties in a time of national hysteria."[283] Arnold believed that the courts, especially at the upper levels of the judiciary, had saved the Republic; how could one censure a judiciary to which one owed so much so recently? Arnold found the very thought repugnant and myopic.

Arnold's reverence for the judicial system, plus his basic conservative patriotism, forced him into a position where he lost ground with the younger generation. The Vietnam war, like the prohibition movement of a younger America, became the watershed issue. Among many of the young idealists, if one were against the Vietnam war that was all that counted; everything else that one might be for or against was thrown aside. From the beginning Arnold took a hawkish stand on Vietnam. Murkiness drowns the motivation behind Arnold's assessment of the Vietnam conflict. A close friend, to whom Arnold would confide from time to time, thought Thurman's mood on Vietnam came from a fundamental distrust of those who clothed their position in high moral and abstract principles. Arnold became very impatient with the religiosity surrounding the Vietnam war.

Arnold was not as doctrinaire as many of his fellow hawks. When a friend suggested that, on political grounds alone, we should admit we made a mistake in Vietnam and get out, Arnold quickly replied that such a statement was perfectly reasonable and rational. He respected it, and even admitted that there was a great deal to be said for it. What Arnold had no patience with was what he termed the halfway measures: that if you stop the bombing you will be able to negotiate, etc. Arnold's opinion on the war could be capsulated in one phrase, "If you are going to fight, you fight, if you are going to get out, you get out."[284]

Another colleague submitted that one had to look no further than Abe Fortas and Lyndon Johnson to understand why Arnold espoused the Vietnam quagmire. The equation goes this way: Fortas and Johnson were confidants; Arnold and Fortas were intimate; Arnold always believed in closing ranks behind one's friends; sine qua non, Arnold supported Johnson. If this actually charted Arnold's thought it would explain in part why Arnold was a dove on the Korean war and a hawk on Vietnam war.[285] Yet other friends of Arnold insist that Arnold never allowed friendship to sway his opinion on such a basic issue.

The young attorneys who joined Arnold, Fortas and Porter in the early 1960s did not pause to cogitate on the intricacies of Arnold's thought. The crisis on Vietnam in Arnold's firm came when one of the young attorneys was asked to defend a man in the cadre surrounding Dr. Spock. Arnold, quite distraught that the firm should defend such a person, vacillated for a long time. Finally, he gave his consent, providing the firm had total control over the defense. By that time, the prospective client had gone elsewhere, and had been acquitted at the district court level.[286]

How could a man who had so fearlessly fought McCarthyism surrender on Vietnam was the question that most distressed the young in Arnold's firm. What these associates missed was that for Arnold the two periods in our history could not be equated. He drew a sharp line between the eras, clearly and unequivocally. In a famous letter to Ernest Angell of the American Civil Liberties Union, Arnold spoke of his disenchantment with the ACLU in its defense of the dissenters on Vietnam. Reviewing the ACLU during the McCarthy era, Arnold had high praise for its actions. "In those days," wrote Arnold, "the ACLU although constantly being charged with subversion stood up to its guns—and I was proud of it. Today we do have freedom of speech in the sense that anyone can hire a hall or teach a course in a university or express views in Government without danger to his career; in other words, the battle for civil liberties in the sense of free expression of opinion has been won." Now Arnold moved to the vital center of his personal protest. "It is regrettable that the ACLU should now be pushing the cause of civil liberties into what, in my view, amounts to a defense of civil disobedience."[287] That was the hard rock issue. In no way could Arnold see the riots of university students, interference with the war effort, and disruption of the draft as adding up to anything but anarchy and bordering on treason. Civil liberty did not translate into the right to destroy the laws of the land.

Undoubtedly a great deal of Arnold' skepticism about the Vietnam dissenters emanated from his almost contemptuous view of campus disorder. He never forgot or some say forgave, the American intellectual community for what he considered its deadly hush in the early fifties. Now that the battle had been won, those very intellectuals were exploiting the victory by jeopardizing the specific rights Arnold had fought to preserve.

Arnold formally delineated his position in a speech delivered at Valparaiso University on Law Day, April 28, 1967.[288] Arnold described America's Vietnam stake in the moralistic terms of the appeasement debate of the 1930s. The main principle was the violation of international law. Our world constitution had been trampled on by an aggressor nation; we had no alternative but to defend international order by repelling this attacker. With that foundation, Arnold fleshed out his argument. Who were the appeasers of the 1960s? Arnold, borrowing a term from Walter Lippmann that had recently been popularized by Professor Lewis C. Feur,[289] characterized them as "alienated intellectuals." Who were these misguided persons? With little hesitation Arnold ticked them off—Walter Lippmann, John Kenneth Galbraith, Henry Steele Commager, Senator William Fulbright. What did this intellectual elite advocate? They had codified "dissent" as an inherent good in itself, Arnold shouted to his audience. "They have advanced a new doctrine of dissent based on the premise that dissent deserves special consideration, immunity from criticism, and the right to shout down persons who disagree with them."[290] There is little use arguing with such people, Arnold told his listeners. He would dismiss them with a line of poetry, appropriately enough from Rudyard Kipling, "The poor little street bred people who vapor and fume and brag, They are lifting their heads in the stillness to yelp at the English flag."[291] Arnold finished his speech that spring day in northern Indiana by stating that whether he was right or wrong, there was no place to hide. Safety and isolation were separate, not integrated, postulates, and Americans must be one of the protectors of international law and peace.

The Valparaiso address brought an instantaneous, stormy reaction. The conservative press embraced Arnold. The Chicago *Tribune* applauded Arnold, not once, but twice, in editorials. The liberals expressed horror and indignation; what had happened to the Arnold of yore, they wondered; had senility set in? His old friend Rexford Tugwell politely, almost plaintively, wrote to him inquiring if he had actually said what the press reported.[292] Tugwell was not the only one to say sadly in effect, "Tell us, Thurman, it isn't so."

Arnold's reply to Tugwell may have been some comfort to the former member of Roosevelt's brain trust, but it was more than a little disingenuous. "Although my speech has been so interpreted, I never intended to attack intellectuals as such, or to claim that they were always wrong or always alienated." Then Arnold defended his moralistic philosophy. "I do not think that the terms 'right' or 'wrong' should apply to the expressions of social ideals as an advocate. As an advocate, I am in favor of attacking all pacifists. As a philosopher, I would feel the world would be greatly disadvantaged if it were not for the continual expression of pacifist ideals."[293] Arnold conceded that part of the confusion came from his role as an advocate, as his entire life in law had been devoted to oversimplification of the issues so that he might convince judge and jury. Undoubtedly he had overstated his case at Valparaiso; but if he were to present it persuasively, that result was inevitable.

Three months later, after a couple of other exchanges with Tugwell, Arnold wrote that he was not downhearted about America's future, far from it:

> I am tremendously optimistic about the present process of change in our society. Spurred on by the Negro problem, architects are planning cities. Housing is being studied. Sociologists for the first time in history are making meaningful studies. The necessity of international leadership by the United States was tacitly admitted when Fulbright and his crew notified Vietnam we are *not* going to get out of the war. The population explosion is being seriously studied. And, best of all, the vital ideal that there must be a war on poverty is being accepted by Republican conservatives. . . . Real work is being done on every pressing American problem."[294]

This did not sound like a bitter, tired, disillusioned retreaded liberal!

So we return, as we began, to the man Thurman Arnold, who cast his spell on all who knew him. He is remembered, as he lived—a personality of marvelous incongruities. As an intellectual, he could penetrate obtuseness with a dazzling swiftness that astounded. An unerring sense of the essential was his. He had little sympathy for "chasing rabbits," as he put it, for those minds that bogged down in details, trapping with high glee the insignificant. Horribly impatient with abstract moral arguments, his major weakness as an attorney was his inability to master detail and parade it in an organized, formal presentation. His mind could not stop racing long enough to show others what he had long since mastered, extracted and thrown aside. Yet his brilliance as an advocate came from his ability to convince judge and jury that his arguments were the correct ones. Having long since convinced himself of the merit of his position, he found it an easier challenge, than do many, to convince others.

He remained, in the memories of his students, one of the legendary teachers of the Yale Law School, not for driving home rows of facts, but for teaching his students how to speak, how to handle themselves, how to discover truths. One of his favorite phrases, in and out of the classroom, was "the emperor has no clothes." Woe be it to the student in the moot court who forgot that aphorism. Finally, as a teacher Arnold had that trait that is common to all great teachers—he could be counted on for the unexpected. He was, simply, dynamic and interesting.

Once he expressed loyalty to a friend or an idea, he was totally, enthusiastically committed. He abhorred pomposity or, to use his favorite term, "cant." To Arnold, Fortas and Porter he brought a boldness, a bigness, humor and decency—a grandeur of spirit and purpose—that is now missed by his older friends and partners. Above all at 1229 19th Street he is remembered for the courage which sustained his colleagues during the delirium of the early fifties.

He was a Western progressive all his life, but far more politically conservative than most of his friends or detractors ever realized. No "sockless" Jerry Simpson or Joe Hill, Thurman never thought in terms of a political revolutionist. One of his great contributions to the New Deal was that he made the ideal of competition acceptable to the liberal community.

He was a deeply patriotic man, a man who revered the law as one of civilization's noblest institutions. He was a man who lampooned man's devotion to rituals and theological assumptions and an iconoclast who believed deeply in the usefulness of the social cements of society's ceremonies and liturgies. He had no hesitation in challenging, as he did in the McCarthy period, the all-powerful druids who espoused a ritual that he considered inimical and fallacious.

The passions of his person won him an enormous following of friends and not always a select number of enemies. He was a romantic, whose favorite poems were Matthew Arnold's pessimistic "Dover Beach" and Alfred Lord Tennyson's optimistic "Ulysses," both of which he could and would recite on almost any occasion. That his favorite opera was *Der Rosenkavalier* was not accidental. Richard Strauss's lace and frills ended the age of romantic opera, vanquished by the slaughterhouse of the First World War. For all of Thurman's jesting about the good old days that never were, he had a nostalgic feeling for the past. He knew and loved the seemingly uncomplicated pre-World War era.

They brought Thurman Arnold back to Laramie on a frosty, clear, windy November day, three days after he had died peaceably in the early morning hours of November 7, 1969. He had spent a lifetime returning home.

# The Letters

# I

## COLLEGE & CAREER

## 1910 – 1918

---

*To Mrs. C.P. Arnold*

Hamburg, Germany, Sept. 3, 1910

Dear Mama:

I arrived in Hamburg all right last night and am now safe in the arms of various relatives too numerous to mention.[1] They are all glad to see me and try to do everything in their power to amuse me. Uncle Carl was here and left this morning for Breslau, where I will go tomorrow. I do not think I will have to use the draft that you sent Uncle Godfried for I borrowed enough from him to tide me over emergencies not knowing whether there would be any money here or not.

This morning I went down to perform the last sad rites over my steamer ticket. I do not think that the relatives here are overwhelmed by my business acumen. They do not seem to realize the amount of sagacity involved in a transaction by which one pays $55 for a piece of paper and then holds it for an indefinite time to receive $27.50 back, but never mind. When I am making $10,000 a year I can point with pride to these humble beginnings.

Uncle Godfried took me this morning to a botanical garden of which he is very fond. We stood in the pouring rain and examined the spots where certain signs with Latin names, indicate that plants will be put there in the near future. The signs we examined were on places engaged by plants which are due to arrive next spring. However, Uncle Godfried told me that they are very beautiful when visible. He asked me if I could tell the plants by their Latin names and I told him I could. This was not strictly true, but I had to do it. After my venture in the field of ticket speculation, something has to be done to uphold the family reputation, which looks pretty feeble.

This afternoon it was still raining, but these Hamburgers are just like ducks, and the plan was for Hannah, and another relative, whom I have not spotted as yet, to take me to the Zoo. Now I have a bad cold, I was tired, and I don't care a whoop for the Zoo, even though I realized that there was a band of real Sioux Indians camped there. But fate had me in her iron paw. I am here in Hamburg to be amused, and they are going to amuse me if it kills me. They could not understand my protestations, so off we started in the pouring rain for the animals and the Sioux Indians. Hannah asked me what animals I liked best, and we would remark those with particular care. She had been there many times and did not care over which ones we lingered. I intimated that I was a regular reformed Ancient Mariner in my love for all things great and small, and could not bear to show particularity. This was poor judgment. I should have picked out a few animals who were caged inside, and made a particular study of them. My two guides immediately jumped at the conclusion that my one desire was to gaze at the buffalo who were anchored outside, and at the fake Indians who were camped in the rain. So we stood there and remarked these wonders of nature while the heavens wept. At last I got away from the Zoo and am back at the house drying out and writing this letter. I enjoy Hamburg and the fine collection of relatives very much, however, Carlyle was right when he said that life would be bearable if it were not for its amusements.

I am a little discouraged about the German language. The longer I stay in Germany, the less German I seem to know. I had better hurry up and get out of here or it will be all gone.

My finances are on the blink as usual. I have my passage back, and ticket to Rotterdam from which port I sail for Liverpool. I have spent the $350 dollars with which I started, and also the $25 sent me to cover the trip to Hamburg. Now, if I could get along without spending another cent the dream of my life would be realized. For once in my brief career I would have kept within my allowance. But, not so. I must go to Breslau, there is no way back to Liverpool, though my fare is all paid. If only the ticket accident had not occurred I would have sailed direct from Hamburg. My allowance would not have been exceeded, and I would have had about $20 left when I got to Princeton. But my ticket mix up has cost all the money I thought I had saved, and my trip to Breslau will carry my expense over my allowance. I am awfully sorry; something always seems to happen which makes pie out of my good intentions. I either forget I have my bills to pay, or invest in obsolete steamer tickets, or do something else. I don't wonder you get discouraged. True, I learn a little more each time. I will not run any more bills, or buy any more premature steamer passages, but fate will get me in some unknown way, and Carl will see his gloomy forebodings realized one by one. I think that the only solution is that I should have a nurse. I have an account kept every day but if you wish to know in a general way how the money has gone I send the following figures:

| | | |
|---|---|---|
| Passage | 109 | 375 |
| Extra money spent in | | 215 |
| fixing up passage | 20 | 160 |
| R.R. Fare in England | 12 | This 160 dollars has |
| R.R. Fare in France to Geneva | 15 | been scattered over 70 |
| R.R. Ticket thru Italy | 30 | days at the rate of |
| Down the Rhine | 8 | $2.40 per day |
| R. trip to Hamburg | 10 | |
| Total | 193 | |
| Pictures bought | 15 | |
| Shoes, socks, Hdkfs. | 7 | |
| Total | 215 | |

*With love*

P.S. If you don't know I repeat that I sail 3rd class on the Mauretania on the 10th (the best I could get) and leave for Liverpool from Rotterdam on the 8th of Sept.

---

## *To Mrs. C.P. Arnold*

Cambridge, Mass., March 10, 1912

Dear Mama:

I have just come out of the infirmary where I have been confined for the past three days with a sore throat and headache.[2] There was nothing in particular the matter with me except General Debility was in command, having received his appointment through a protracted cold. He is not a great general in any respect, even tho he does wear gold epaulets. However I am out now and feeling all right. I have four days work to do, and will be kept pretty busy for the next week.

The infirmary is a nice place, and you can lounge around in your bath robe and converse with the other invalids, being interrupted every little while by a nurse who will give you something to gargle. It appears that gargling is the one great standby and cureall. Every one is compelled to gargle at least six times a day no matter what he has been stricken with. All the eight inmates of my ward spent most of their time gargling. The food that they give you there is fine and they serve it on trays in bed. It is quite a luxury to have your breakfast in bed. Then you can sit around and read all day, or play simple games with the other poor weak mental and physical wrecks, cast derelict on the shore by the busy and strenous whirl of college life. Most of the invalids seemed to have nothing at all the matter with them. It is quite the popular method of taking a vacation. The only trouble with going there is that they will never let you out of the place when you are well. I had to argue with the doctor about fifteen minutes before he would give me my clothes.

I have tried many typewriters in my time but this one is altogether the poorest that I have ever seen. The touch is so heavy that I am unable to hit the keys heavy enough. My own typewriter is sadly on the blink, and I am looking for a heavy bill when it comes back from the repair shop.

I must get to work now to make up the four days I lost in the infirmary.

*With lots of love*

P.S. Tell papa that I got his letter in the infirmary and got Norry to tend to it. The Dean said that he would see [Roscoe] Pound and get him to send the examination questions.

---

## *To C.P. Arnold*

Cambridge, Mass., May 19, 1912

Dear Papa:

I have attained the proud record of eleven hours a day for the last week, but I am getting stale, and can't work any more. My efforts to work today have been a futile failure. I got the hundred dollar check and the letter about your trip to Denver yesterday.

The examinations here close on the 15th, at which date I have my last exam. Dick Valentine[3] wants me to come down to his home about fifty miles from here for a few days after examinations, and I would like to do it, for it may be a long time before I will get another chance of seeing him. You will probably remember him as the wild C.E. who went to dinner with us at the Princeton Inn when you were in Princeton last. He has been working down in New Jersey somewhere this winter trying to get enough money to get married on, which he expects to do sometime this year. If you are not in too much of a hurry to see me I would like to stop a couple of days there, and start for home on the 19th. Write me if you have any objections.

I am too dopey and tired to write a good letter, and there is absolutely no news to tell, so I will close,

*With much love*

---

*To Mrs. C.P. Arnold*

Cambridge, Mass., June 8, 1912

Dear Mama:

One week more and the nervous strain of the examinations will be over. I still have criminal law and pleading left. Pleading promises to be the hardest of the lot. The trouble with the exams is that they give you such a hopelessly inadequate time to answer them. I think that I know the law all right, but my mind refuses to work fast enough and I make boneheads which I could easily see and correct if only I had more time. I will be so glad however to get them over with that I have ceased to care about the marks. Another week of them would reduce me to a wreck.

Saturday I had torts, and went out to Revere Beach[4] to recuperate. I had a good swim in the ocean, though the water was rather cold, and after having supper in one of the little places on the beach, we started to ride on the roller coasters. We were having a great time, and had spent all our change and at about half past nine we decided to go home, and I went up to buy the tickets with a five dollar bill which I had stowed away in my wallet. They handed out the tickets, but on investigation I found both the wallet and the five dollar bill absent. Someone had picked my pocket in the crowd, and the three of us were absolutely without funds, unless six cents which we managed to scrape up could be dignified by that term. The problem of getting home immediately assumed serious proportions, and after much consultation I came to the front and hocked my Phi Beta Kappa key, and thus saved the day. Fortunately that and my watch had been overlooked by the acquisitive individual who had taken my wallet. Thus we see that the industrious youth who studies in college need never suffer for want of cash. I will have to find some one who is going out there this week to redeem the key from the low browed uncultured pawnbroker person who has it at present, as I will not find time myself.

The examinations close on Saturday the 15th, and I will go to Stafford Springs[5] on the 16th. I will only stay there two days and will leave for home on the 19th at the latest. This ought to bring me home on the 22nd or 23rd, or at the latest the 24th. I suppose that if I take the round trip by way of Montreal it will take a day more to get there. I wrote you about the $66.50 rate, round trip to Laramie by way of Montreal, and am expecting to hear from you any day as to whether you think I had better take it. It is good till the 3rd of October, and I save about ten dollars on it. I can hardly wait till I get home, and I think that it will look pretty good to me when I get there.

I received quite a shock this evening. I went around to see Borden, the fellow who traveled through Europe with us. I had not seen him for about a week, and the last time he complained about feeling unwell. He looked so healthy however that I thought nothing about it, but this evening I found that he had died last Thursday. It appeared that he was only sick two days. I don't know what was the trouble, and the fellows who roomed in the dormitory knew nothing of it save that he was dead. Due to their confounded Harvard indifference a man can room across the hall from another all year here, and know nothing about him. It is as bad as a New York City flat. Borden was a fine fellow, with a rare artistic appreciation. He was writing a book on something or other, and had only got it half finished. He was to receive his Ph.D. degree this next week.

It is getting late now so I must close,

*With love*

---

*To C.P. Arnold*

Cambridge, Mass., June 15, 1912

Dear Papa:

I have just finished my last examination. It was very hard. I answered all the points that I saw, but the questions were so complicated that I suppose there were a good many that I did not see at all. I got your check this last mail. I really needed a hundred, but it is my own fault for not letting you know. I have been so worried during the last few weeks that I have not done the things I meant to. I intended to write you and thought that I had done so, but I guess that I must have left it out of my last letter. I can easily borrow twenty dollars from Pierson.

I intend to leave for Stafford Springs tomorrow, and will come back to Boston on Wednesday and leave directly for home. I think that I will take the round trip through Montreal. The reason that I asked you about it was that there was some doubt when I left whether I would come back here another year. If I do there is no doubt that I had better take the round trip because otherwise it will cost me about fifteen dollars more in railway fare. I therefore will take a chance and buy the round trip for $66.50. This will make my trip home, including meals and berth come to about $90.00. It will cost me about six dollars to go to Stafford Springs.

I will write you from Stafford Springs. I only intend to stay there for two days. I leave here tomorrow morning, so I am very busy packing up this afternoon.

*With lots of love*

---

## *To C.P. Arnold*

Cambridge, Mass., Oct. 16, 1912

Dear Papa:

I received your letter from Rawlins this morning. The young lady you speak of is unknown to me, but if it will aid the cause I will inform her by immediate mail on which side to enlist. I wish that I were on the campaign with you.[6] From the letters which mama has sent me it must be great sport. I read your letter about the snow storm to some of my friends to give them an idea of campaigning in the wild and woolen west.

But little is happening in Boston except the world's series in baseball, which has just been won by Boston.[7] It is absolutely wonderful how these fool people go crazy over the antics of the hired thugs on the baseball field. Then none of them come from Boston, nor do I see just what credit their winning reflects on Boston, but an average of 40,000 people pay exorbitant prices to see them play, and go absolutely crazy when they win. They have just got thru giving them triumphal processions, led by the mayor, and the prominent citizens, and have taken them to Fanueil Hall to worship them. Politics, death, and salvation take a second place to them. Boston is the champion of the world. They have won the world's series, socalled I suppose because of the interest that it excites in Afghanistan and points east. A strange person is the baseball fan.[8]

Politics are much discussed here, and election bets registered with great frequency, in spite of the fact that law students well know that gambling contracts are void. The odds are about four to one on Wilson, which is supposed to be a fair indication of his chances.

A writ of mandamus is now before the Massachusetts Supreme Court to compell the city of Cambridge to allow the hitherto disenfranchised Harvard student to vote. It appears that the Harvard student has hitherto not been allowed to vote, not because he lacked intelligence, but because he lacked domicile. The petitioner however claims that he has both of these elements, and should vote. It appears that the English view of domicile, holds that a man is domiciled in a place, only when he has an intention of staying there permanently, and some even go so far as to hold that he has to have an intention of dying in the place before he can acquire a domicile. This according to Beale is absurd, and the prevailing American view is that a man may have a domicile in a place if he intends to remain there a certain length of time. He is domiciled in that place for that time. However there are dicta in the Mass. cases which seem to hold that they prefer the English view. Besides these dicta, there is a hoary old decision, handed down in 1813 in which it is held that a man is domiciled with his parent so long as he receives his support from that parent. This is manifestly absurd on principle. On that theory a woman who lived in New York and was married, would still be domiciled in San Francisco if her father sent her money from there. This case, and the dicta above referred are all that keep me from voting next election, and it looks as if there was a good chance that the writ of mandamus would issue and I would get a chance to vote for Wilson.

It is getting late now, and I will close in order to go to bed.

*With much love*

---

## *To C.P. Arnold*

Cambridge, Mass., Dec. 23, 1912

Dear Papa:

I find that I left out of my last letter the bill which I said that I had enclosed. It is rather late now, so I enclose it with only a short note. You can give it to mama, and she can send the amount on to the college office, or send it to me and I will take it around, just as she sees fit. Since the money has to be sent however, she might just as well send it to the office direct. I am in no need of money for myself.

I am sorry to say that mama is one hundred dollars off in her accounts. I received one hundred dollars between October 5th, and Nov. 11, which she did not put down apparently. This makes $575 which I have received, and after $50 is deducted for traveling expenses, it makes $525 applied on the allowance for the year. I do not just see how I got the amount as $535. I think that it is a mistake, but I have not time to hunt it down now. I think that I counted $10 of my own. I cannot give the exact date that I deposited this $100 which I refer to, because I lost my bank book on my Christmas vacation with the rest of my accounts.

I got the coyote skin, and Norry was much pleased. We were also much amused by the typewritten sketch of Bill Nye. I am rather busy this week as I have to argue a case next Friday. When I get through then I will have to start in reviewing for the midyears.

It is after twelve, and time that I got in bed, so I will make this letter very short.

*With lots of love*

---

*To Mr. and Mrs. C.P. Arnold*

Cambridge, Mass., Jan. 7, 1913

Dear Mother and Father:

I sit down to write a more or less belated account of my journeyings about the East during the Christmas holidays, which on no account are you to publish in the *Boomerang*, or *Republican,* or in another paper, either of greater or less merit.

I started with my suit case laden with dress suit, tuxedo, and various books, which I brought along ostensibly to study, but which were destined to see little hard usage on the vacation. Saturday night before Christmas, I sent off the few remaining Christmas presents, and went to the symphony concert, hearing a most splendid concert, of Mozart and Mendelssohn. I then visited around till about three in the morning with Cy Wilson, talking over the possibility of starting in Boston, and the advisability of same. He tells me that he will be able to get me a job in his firm, paying at the start $50 per month. He has been with them three years, and is now getting $2,000. It is one of the best firms in Boston. But enough of this. Late or early, as you choose to call it, I went to bed, and arose in feverish haste to catch the 8 o'clock train for Bridgeport, which Norry had recommended to me, looking it up carefully with his great brown eyes in the time table. I sweated, and ran, with my ponderous luggage, but got down fives minutes too late for the train. My feelings when I learned that the train did not run on Sunday are difficult to describe. Is it better to miss a train which does exist, or run for a train which does not exist? I leave this to deeper philosophers than myself. The general sense of irritation accompanying either is difficult of analysis.

Suffice it to say that I got in Bridgeport that evening, and spent it around the fire with the family, discussing various subjects in a more or less frivolous way, and went to bed. The time before Christmas I spent variously; playing golf out at the country club, which I do worse the more I try, and go wild with envy at Katherine's efficiency; taking walks and talking with Philo:[9] smoking pipes of indescribable filthiness in the immaculate bedroom of Mrs. Calhoun, while she wrote letters and mended stockings; reading that most delightful of modern novels "Joseph Vance" by de Morgan;[10] and running errands; going to picture shows, eating, reading, and smoking some more, and generally loafing around the premises, to the great pleasure of myself and the family, who like to have me around. Christmas day passed with its usual chorus of exclamations over the perfectly useless presents that people will send, including books with thick pages and limp leather bindings which flop over the edges, to publish which ought to be a crime punishable by some slow and painful method of incineration of both the book and the publisher, and various lacy filmy feminine things whose use no one knows, nor dares ask. The evening was less pleasant, consisting of a dinner of the Calhoun relatives, lasting from 5 till 7:30, during which so much food is consumed that the participants can scarcely rise from the table. Why should people take the occasion of Christmas to make such gourmands of themselves, and curses upon the blackened soul of the infernal misanthrope who ever invented family dinners. Relatives invariably bore each other, and the presence of many in conjunction is nothing more than torture to the simple outsider. There are in addition invariably present, various infants, of the most muling variety, who monopolize the attention of the feminine contingent, whose horrid little persons one is asked to hold, whose disgusting pink toes are exhibited without regard to decency or propriety, and who invariably bawl lustily when one playfully pokes an embarrassed finger at their idiotic little countenances, just in order to seem interested. They seem to sense some inner and hidden streak of depravity in me, which causes them to bawl when I try to make up to them. The little dears,—they know,—you can't fool them by a polished and smiling exterior. They realize the accumulated hate and bitterness that is masked behind my immobile countenance. Ergo they bawl. Their mothers don't realize this, and sit them next to me, seated on accumulated dictionaries, from which they continually topple off, and have to be reinstated, which operation causes them to bawl again. Just as reason is about to totter on its throne, and digestion is about to go on a perpetual strike, relief comes, and everyone rises from the table, and waddles into the next room, too full to do anything but grunt.

The Saturday after Christmas, I disappeared in the direction of New York, to meet Red O'Gorman, one of the very best fellows in all the world, whom I had not seen since the first year in law school, when I got acquainted with him. He is waiting for me in a Packard limousine, and informs me that he desires my opinion on the girl with whom he is in love. (He is always desparately in love with someone and so I was not surprised.) We collect her in the limousine, and go to the Plaza for lunch. She seems a plausible enough girl, rather pretty, expensively dressed, and shooting the same general line of conversation that is customary at lunches at the Plaza. But to Red she is a fiery constellation of stars, and far be it from me to undeceive him. We then rode over to his home in Jersey City, and met his family who are most charming people. His father is president of the Carpentier Steel Corporation, and is a delightful rock ribbed old reactionary, firmly convinced that the country is going to the dogs under Woodrow, and that solid and substantial men of business will be utterly ruined by the combined suicidal folly of the tariff and the currency bill. His mother is a very beautiful southern woman, and is much more reasonable, due chiefly to a delightful sense of humor. Philo and Norry wandered into New York at 6 P.M. from Hartford where they had been taking bar exams, and we had a regular old reunion with Red, among the glittering lights of Broadway, and then were motored swiftly back to Jersey City where the four of us spent the night. Sunday morning we had the most magnificent breakfast imaginable, consisting of many courses, the chief and most substantial one being magnificent fried chicken, for which their chef is particularly noted. We then left for Stamford, where we were all due for Sunday dinner. That afternoon we all motored up to Bridgeport in the Pierson's car, and had supper there, and motored back to Stamford in the evening. It was one of those sharp winter evenings, when every star seems etched with a diamond point in the frosty sky, and the bare arms of the trees seemed like frozen moonlight, as we whizzed past them on the beautiful roads at 50 miles per hour. Everything shot past, like a shrill wind, except the sky, and that remained silent and immovable, and very still.

I went back to Bridgeport the next day, and did various things till New Year's, among them attending a dance, at which I had the poorest imaginable time. The modern dance is not a program affair, but is one continuous dance, and you cut in to get your partner, and dance with her till some one takes her away from you, or some great force of nature separates you. Nothing is danced but the tango, and various allied steps, and so, of course I did not attempt it. But I was compelled to talk hours with various girls, whom no one else dared speak to lest they be burdened with them all evening. At the modern dance, if you get an unpopular girl on your hands you might just as well marry her and be done with it. Nothing can ever separate you. You are doomed to live and die in each other's company. No scheme can be devised for getting rid of her. And so for one hour and a quarter I was compelled to struggle with a certain Miss Warner, whose dress was shockingly low, and whose general average was the same. I prayed for relief, but none came till supper. She is, incidentally the daughter of the man who makes all the corsets in the world, and is worth untold millions in her own right, but they add but little to her charm unless one is thinking of marrying her. And even then I doubt if it is worth it. Making corsets is such an indelicate business anyway.

On New Year's day Philo and I entrained for Montclair, New Jersey, at which home of the wealthy and predacious, various big doings were scheduled to be pulled off. I confess that I went with many misgivings, for a dance was among them, but I was finally pulled toward the train, after Katherine had packed my suit case for me and Philo had dragged me out of the house. Katherine went down with us. She was scheduled to go to some big New Year's dance and dinner in New York. Such is the modern family. They never go to the same places, or even travel in the same set. Each lives his or her independent existence and they see each other at meals.

We arrived in Montclair anon, and proceeded to the home of Mrs. Platt. Imagine a comparatively small entrance hall, dimly lighted with a beautiful old Florentine lamp, dating from the 16th Century, whose murky gleams shine through old wrought iron work with a mellow luster. An attentive butler takes your coats and hats, and you step down the hall, through heavy old velvet curtains, into the main living room, and pause on the threshold. The room is about 40 feet long, and along the sides, in pairs, in true Florentine style, are heavy Corinthian columns, hung with brackets covered with roses which make the walls seem to blossom cut flowers. In the center, surrounded by beautiful Persian rugs, is a huge carved table, dark with the luster of centuries. It was taken directly out of a Florentine Palace, and who knows what dark plots were hatched over its dull and richly wrought surface. Further down the room a delicately wrought iron balcony adds just a touch of lightness to the room, giving a vista of a dining room. It was taken out of a palace in Verona, and I do not think that there it had a more splendid setting. On the one side, between the columns, great curtained glass doors show glimpses of formal gardens, skeleton-like on the wintry night, with a fountain playing in the center. And down at the end of the room a huge old marble fireplace, big enough to hold great logs, blazes cheerful warmth into the dusk and rose perfume of the room. The room is entirely lit by candles, set in strangely wrought old candlesticks, and as you walk down the room toward the great mantel with its beautiful glowing log, you are taken back over the centuries, and think that you are some crude Goth, from the wilds of Germany, come to hold audience with a renaissance prince. And then a door at the end of the room opens, and out of it steps the Duchess (for what else can you call her) gowned exquisitely, in old rose, with dull gold ornaments, and strange gems. She is in perfect keeping with the illusion created by her beautiful palace. And then you step forward to greet her, and sit down by the fire.

She is a very charming and cultured lady, as the decoration of the house would indicate. Mere wealth can never produce such beautiful effects as she has achieved in their room. Mr. Platt, the owner of the estate, was in Wyoming in the early seventies, and became very reminiscent when I informed him that it was my domicile of origin.

We had supper there, and then were reluctantly dragged to a dance at some other huge place in Montclair. This place was nothing other than a very large and expensively fitted out mansion. It lacked the exquisite and distinguished taste of the Platt's house. I did not have as poor a time at the dance as I expected. I discovered a very charming Southern girl who had water on her knee and was therefore temporarily laid out of the dancing game. We sat around a fire for most of the evening, and she told me all about their old southern cotton plantation, life on which appears to be one continual glad round of song, and carping care appears but little. I shot the various lines that I have for such occasions: (a) humorous, (b) general culture, (c) music, (of which I know absolutely nothing), (d) art, (on which my ignorance is completely absymal). She ran the same general kind of a bluff. Each of us knew that the other was a complete and unholy fraud, but we were kind enough not to mention it to the other. So the evening passed. At twelve o'clock, by dint of the most diplomatic and polished tactics, Philo and I managed to break away from the affair which was due to last until three, and were carted back to the Platt's, where a big fire was waiting in the room, lit by candles, and covered with roses, and the host's splendid, 50 cent cigars, lay in profusion on the sideboard. With one of these superior articles in my mouth, I listened to Philo play sentimental melodies on the piano, and Harry, the attentive butler, brought us food, and splendid old wine. I know that papa will tear his hair at the mention of this, his preference being for bad whiskey taken in bar rooms, but the truth must be told. At an unconscionably late hour we retired.

Philo had to leave the next morning, and I went with him, tho they were kind enough to urge me to stay. Nice people they are, and very attentive. For example, both of the family cars being busy, our host thoughtfully orders a taxicab, for us to take to the station. Money of course, to us, just as to him, is absolutely immaterial, a mere boring detail. So we bribe the servants heavily, and enter the cab, and are whizzed off, and waiting till we get down the street about a mile, and around a couple of corners, we stop the taxi, alight, and empty the contents of our purses in the hands of the chauffeur. We then soberly walk the rest of the way to where a plebian train takes us out of the land of luxury and expense.

In New York, I proceed up to see the Slossons,[11] stopping on the way to purchase roses for Mrs. Slosson, who I think deserves them if anyone does. At that humble flat, great excitement prevailed. Both of the Laramie ladies, Helen and Gladys, were due on the scene in the afternoon. Neither of the Slossons know them, their recollection of them being merely as muling infants. I am immediately drafted into service, and appear promptly on deck at the station, but no girls. With the train they did not come, and at the hour they were not there, as the poet hath it. I therefore was compelled to meet all the trains which thundered into the station from Washington all the afternoon. They finally arrived, and I took them up to the Slossons where we had supper.

After supper at the Slossons, a strange and pitiful scene occurred, in which your son bore himself manfully and refused to be roped in tho the odds became very heavy against him and he was sore pressed. It was the manifest desire and intention of the two young ladies to see the sights of New York that evening, they being simple young ladies, and unused to the sights of the great metropolis. Cabaret shows appealed to their fancy, as I inferred from various broad and jesting talk. Glitter of all kinds appealed to them, and the idea of a gay time titillated their very souls. I stolidly agreed with them, assuming the air of a hardened cynic, to whom the pleasures of a quiet evening by the fireside outweighed the flesh pots of Egypt, and the decadent gaiety of Babylon. Nor did suggestion of invitation, nor hint of escort, escape my guarded lips. For with my lightning-like mind I figured that two young ladies on Broadway in the evening, meant a deficit in the treasury of at least $5.00 and probably more, in fact almost certainly more, and if you infer from the account of my previous adventures that they were not expensive, and that money did not fly in all directions, in hundreds of ways, you err, sadly do you err. I therefore felt that caution was the best policy, and became as the silent and uncommunicative clam, clammy, and evinced a total lack of interest in the conversation. I was doing pretty well, when attack came from a new quarter. Mrs. Slosson, who shows a surprising lack of tact on some occasions, said that it would be lovely if we could all go down town that evening, referring, not to herself and Dr. Slosson, but to me and the girls. I looked vacantly at the ceiling and said "Oh I don't know," in a vague sort of way, neither agreeing or disagreeing, and walked in the other room and engaged in an earnest discussion with Dr. Slosson, while the girls figited. It did not take a mind reader to see that I was getting in wrong and how long I could have held out is uncertain, had not help arrived. Two young men from Laramie blew in, who had heard that the girls were to be in town, and I drew a great breath of relief. For lo it was their intent that all were to go down town. Whereas I gracefully stepped down and out, on a plea of great and overwhelming fatigue, and bid them god speed, maliciously suggesting Shanley's as the best place to go, because the cabaret show there was unequaled—as I look back that was a mean thing to do, because a sandwich at Shanley's costs 60¢ with other things in proportion. I then spent the evening playing chess with Preston.[12]

The next morning I went around with the girls to see Mrs. Daley, and then departed, with much regret because I could not go to the Laramie dinner at the Waldorf that evening. For lo, I had an engagement to meet Katherine, and take her to dinner and the opera, and also to lunch and to hear Kreisler play in the afternoon. I suppose that this party would be considered foolish—in fact it was by Mrs. Calhoun, Philo, and also

Katherine, and was pulled off only after overcoming the most emphatic and pronounced opposition on the part of all concerned. But apparently nothing could stop this fatuous youth, and pulled off it was, and in style. Find what mercy you can in your heart for your erring and expensive son.

That night I arrived in Bridgeport at 2:00 A.M. with Katherine, and the next day left for Cambridge, where I still am, extremely busy, for I have two examinations, coming in only two weeks, in as many half year courses. Please do not look for a letter from me until these are over because I have a tremendous lot of work to do.

I have also started two divorce suits, which will be tried some time in March. They are great nuisances when you are busy.

*With much love*

---

## *To Mrs. C.P. Arnold*

Cambridge, Mass., Oct. 5, 1913

Dearest Mother:

It is now Sunday of the second week here. It is astonishing how quickly the time passes when you have routine work to do. I attend classes four hours in the morning, work three hours in the afternoon, take an hour's exercise, eat supper, and work an hour in the evening, making an eight hour day, which is strenuous enough for concentrated work. That is my schedule, and I have kept to it fairly well, but you know how I am at keeping to a schedule. I got a cheerful letter from Carl,[13] howling for the cat skin, which I had forgotten about completely. I will send it to him at once. He seems very cheerful from the tone of his letter and has apparently plunged heavily in a canoe. He ought to have a great time with it. I am seriously debating whether I ought to take some of the money I earned this summer and go down to cheer him up, and see if there was anything that I could do. This would be a great personal sacrifice, but one should not consider himself in these matters. By a singularly unfortunate coincidence, which I am unable to explain, the Harvard-Princeton football game occurs in Princeton on the very Saturday on which I had planned to go down. However I shall not let this interfere with my plans if I decide to go. I have a sneaking premonition however that I will stay here and stick to the study of the law.

I went down town last night and had a Welsh rarebit with Sidal and Norry. It was raining, and the night was just falling over the city streets. Hence I composed the enclosed poem while I was sitting on a bench in the Boston Common, waiting for the other two to show up.

The Twilight and the Rain.

Up the gleaming pavements wet, quiver shafts of light,
Growing bright and brighter yet, with the touch of night.
With a quiet gladness, twinkling through the mist,
Glean the happy street lamps that the rain has kissed;
While the Ugly City, rushing through the day,
Like a great unwieldy Caliban at play,
Seems to grow more gentle, suddenly made sane,
By the soothing magic of the twilight and the rain.

Like a low born woman, in a costly dress,
Which gives to haggard features the touch of comliness,
And the lovely garment, for a little while,
Changes smirks and laughter to a quiet smile,
Guilty thoughts and pleasures, even want forgot,
In a wistful yearning for a beauty she has not,
With a wistful comfort that her yearning's not in vain,
When clad in jeweled splendor of the twilight and the rain.

*With much love*

---

*To Mr. and Mrs. C.P. Arnold*

Cambridge, Mass., Nov. 16, 1913

Dearest Mother and Father:

I suppose that you all are anxiously awaiting a word from me about the trip I took down to Princeton, et al. After going down there with at least the fictitious purpose of having an unselfish end in view, i.e. that of giving a report on the condition and welfare of the youngest scion of our line, I suppose that I have been guilty of laches in not getting in a report earlier. But I returned from the trip only to find that I had a rather severe attack of tonsilitus (spelling does not look right, but never mind—I had what the above sounds like.) The novelty of this new ailment riveted my attention to the exclusion of all else for a couple of days, and resulted in my getting behind in my work. The combination resulted in my getting very much behind in the filial duty that I owe to the folks at home. I therefore crave the pardon and indulgence of said folks, and hope that they are not as much wrought up about it as they were about my not sending the coyote skin promptly. (How upset you all were about that anyway.)

To begin with I left Cambridge on Thursday afternoon, because I could not resist the temptation of stopping off at Bridgeport for just one evening. I found the family away except the younger generation, but managed to have quite a delightful time in smoking huge quantities of Mr. Calhoun's expensive cigars before a log fire with Philo and his exceedingly lovely sister. (I am ashamed to figure up how many I smoked. They were very small and very expensive, but Katherine has the fixed idea that no man is normal, unless he is puffing huge clouds of smoke out of his disgusting and tobacco pickled mouth.) I tore myself away with some difficulty the next morning and left for Princeton.

Arriving in Princeton I found the Kid bro and Bickford awaiting me at the station, and we went to the graduate school for dinner. The Graduate College is one of the most beautiful things in America in the way of architecture. Built in the form of a great quadrangle, with cloistered sides running around on the court in the interior, it embodies every idea of the perpendicular Gothic. The great tower shoots up at one corner, with four graceful pinnacles, and beautiful gothic tracery, and the fretted roofs of the cloisters help along the idea of monastic seclusion, and lead the mind irresistibly to thoughts of a semi-poetic and philosophical nature. The architecture represents the ideals of scholarly seclusion worked out by scholars of a bygone era. There is only this difference. In those days the simple and heavy oaken beams and furnishings represented plain living and high thinking. Today they represent high living and plain thinking.

Dinner was served in the beautiful dining hall. It has a wonderful window at one end, an elaborately carved oaken screen at the other, and huge carved oak beams vaulted above, grotesquely wrought into grinning gargoyles which smile down with gentle irony at the gothic provender which is served by gothic waiters. The food is unquestionably gothic. I would prefer just a touch of renaissance in the menu, just a hint of that liberal spirit of Epictetus, just a flavor of the spirit of the well fed Horace on his sabine farm. But no. A rigid spirit of conformity with the monastic architecture seems to inform the cook. A delightful carefree disdain of the wants of the body has made the mashed potatoes lack most of the elements that grosser spirits deem essential to mashed potatoes, and the cook has undoubtedly been pondering on synthesis of Hegel when he cooked roast beef. However, these are but the maudlin remarks of one accustomed to board at $8.50 a week.

To abandon description and resume narration, we smuggled the Kid into an academic gown, which are required at the dinners, listened to a Latin benediction, consumed the food described supra, and retired to the room of said Kid bro. I immediately called a gathering of the clan, and assembled them in one of the rooms with the professed purpose of looking them over. They responded cheerfully, and I talked to them in the patronizing way which should be assumed by grads when dealing with nothing but Freshmen. They are a plausible bunch of youths into which our young hero has been injected. Good natured, carefree and their smooth brows unwrinkled by a single thought. Nourse who rooms at the house has more maturity than the rest, but for that very reason does not associate with them so much. The Jackman boys are not too impressive to the casual observer. Garvey who seems to be the most intimate with Carl is the one that I thought as much of as any of them. I am glad that Carl has taken up with him. He seems an intelligent and likable fellow. I only fear that he has lots of money, which is unfortunate for Carl, unless Carl has a corresponding amount of judgment. On the whole they are a good average bunch of fellows, and Carl seems to be having a good time with them. The ideals of scholarship do not seem to weigh down their youthful spirits to any extent, but what can you expect of Freshmen. Carl is happy, and college only comes but once in a life time anyway.

At ten o'clock I left Carl to partake of a feed which someone was giving in the house, and retired to the graduate schools, where some of the old-time spirits of my class had gathered. We sat around a fire until three in the morning, going over the time when we used to make life worth while in the South entry of West College Dorm, recounted with sorrow the fact that Mallet, Old Tweedle–Dick's dog which chewed up 15 dollars worth of engineering books–had joined the ranks of the departed, dwelt exhaustively and with great joy on the time that the great Al Urban had attempted to break into the room of the studious M. P. Miller, and to do so had placed both feet on the door, at about the height of the knob, bracing his back on the opposite wall of the entry and had gone sailing into the room lighting on the small of his back in the middle of the floor, to the great discomfiture of the said Al Urban, but the lifelong joy and amusement of his compatriots; commiserated at great length with Jim Collard and Bill Eves and Bill Abbotts, who were all there and coyly announcing their engagements–(Bickford and I immediately named them The Storm Birds of Passion, after the well known passage from Swinburne)–and thus we talked and smoked till the grey light began to etch the faint outline of the beautiful tower against the sky. Such evenings are worth travelling far for, and treasuring long after you have had them. It isn't so much the follows, for I have far better friends than they are here in Cambridge, but it's the spirit of the old times, mellowed and tinted by memory, with all the little unpleasant features blotted out. It's like being a simple undergraduate once more, out of touch with everything real, forming expensive habits, going to lectures, reading poetry and trying to write it, and wasting time generally.

It is a sad commentary on a calloused conscience how little I regret the time I wasted in College.

The next day I went to the game. Princeton lost, but I did not care so much as I used to. This shows that I am learning to face the hard knocks and the sudden and sickening calamities of real life with philosophical equanimity. I ate with Carl at the Commons, and quite agree with Carl that the food deserves no enthusiastic eulogies. However, the other Freshmen stand it, and think of the poor Russians. I spent the evening with Carl, and told him that the main object of going to College was to acquire confidence in himself and not to allow himself to be bluffed by anything. He was a little timid about going out for debating, but I told him to get busy and go at it, and he said he would. I tried to stimulate him to try something hard and win at it, a thing which his poor brother never did. His poor brother had just enough facility at the things he did in College, so that he did not work hard for anything, and succeeded only in a mediocre fashion at the things that were easy for him. There was too much inertia and dolce far niente in his make up. Carl has the same temperament, and College is a poor place to overcome it. However, let us hope for the best.

Sunday I left, and could not resist the temptation to stop over in Bridgeport for the evening. I got up here Monday morning, and immediately acquired the tonsilitis which is just taking its leave of the lower regions of my throat. Verily, those learned sages who have opined this is but a vale of tears have come nearer the truth than they wotted of.

This evening I have done a little work for tomorrow, and written this letter. The wind has been howling around the corner in a rather chill and biting way. Curiously enough it is the South wind. The following has just occurred to me.

Oh South Wind that's winging from over the sea,
Strange songs for a South Wind you're singing to me.

Sped from the tropical Isles are your wings,
Where you sang the strange loves of the Cannibal Kings;

Bourne on your breath have been petals of flowers,
Languidly bathered thru langorous hours;

Wistfully toying with fragments of tunes,
Lazily lisped to the low lying dunes.

Ah where have the smiles and the rose leaves been lost,
Since you joined the grim ranks of the King of the Forest,

Traitor to all the fair regions of Gold,
Adding your might to the legions of Cold,

You have wrecked the tall ships that have crossed in your path
and you wail but the dirge of the deeds of your wrath;

Singing only the song of the roll of the tide,
Chanting only the chant of the waste places wide.

Traitorous South Wind, from over the sea,
Little of South Land you're bringing to me.

*Love*

---

## *To Mrs. C.P. Arnold*

Cambridge, Mass., Nov. 24, 1913

Dearest Mother:

The preceeding Saturday has been one of great excitement in Cambridge, due to the Yale-Harvard game. The town was full of people, and Boston was full of people last night. Philo [Calhoun] was up in Boston to see the game, and the four of us had a very pleasant dinner in town Saturday night. I expect that the Laramie girls would have given their souls to have seen the game, but I feel that I have done my duty like a little man already.

I got an invitation from Mrs. Slosson to Thanksgiving dinner in New York. Carl and the Laramie girls, and Howell are going to be there. I was very sorry to decline, but I had already promised to come down to Bridgeport. I will write Carl to come to Bridgeport the day after Thanksgiving, if he cares to come. I got a letter from Carl saying that he had been up to the Yale-Princeton game in New Haven. Leslie Jacobs came in the other night and I learned that he had been down to the Princeton-Harvard game in Princeton, and had taken a girl to the same. Verily there is some speed to our young Laramie freshmen, and little that they miss.

I have voted myself a vacation for the weekend of Thanksgiving, since the faculty here refused to give me but one day, and I am going, as alleged in paragraph one of this instrument, down to Bridgeport. I have my work fairly well up, and feel that I need the change that I would get by going away more than the change that I would save by staying here. (Rotten pun but I could not help it.)

My two divorce cases are rather of a nuisance, as I have to trot around to strange places to get affidavits, and it takes a lot of time. I have not filed either of them yet, because my clients have not as yet succeeded in raising enough money to pay the initial costs, which I have heartedly refused to put up for them.

I had a rather amusing case the other day. A ladies' maid came in to the office, and put up a tale of woe about how her mistress was trying to do her out of $12.50 wages, including her fare from New Brunswick where said hard hearted mistress had left her to find her own way home. I listened with sympathy and dispatched the usual note to the lady, saying that doubtless she had overlooked the little matter, and if she wanted to avoid the unpleasantness of a suit, etc. The next day I received a special messenger, asking me to come down to the office of the Legal aid at 5 o'clock. I appeared as per contract, but my client refused to come, saying that she would rather have me settle it. I had a faint glimmering of why my client preferred the solitude of her own society to coming with me, when a large limousine purred up to the door, and a huge lady of the Dreadnought type, incased in a fur coat emerged with a meak looking husband following at her heals. In she sailed under a full head of steam, and sinking in a chair began to blow off surplus pressure. She was loaded to the gunwalls with wrath of the most virulent type, and she had been taking on more every minute since she had received my curt note. Never it appeared, had she had been so outrageously treated. Few people on this green footstool had received the motherly affection, and tender solicitude given to this girl. Said maid had been loaded with gratuities, and had been kept on at great expense during the summer, when it was her custom to cut down her retinue to three servants. I saw that it was no use even trying to get a word in edgewise, and so I adopted a sympathetic tone, alleging that in the heart of every maid, black ingratitude lay coiled like a snake ready to strike. It was the nature of the race to be unappreciative of kindness and to ferociously chaw at the delicate and loving hand that nourished them. Gradually she calmed, and began to show me documentary evidence. It appeared that the girl had first sent in a bill of $4 which had not been answered because mistress was away. She then raised it to $6 and then to $12.50, without having any other grounds, than her natural perversity. I finally settled for $6, which is more than the girl deserved, and the couple sailed off, beaming at me. The lady was so taken by my sympathy with her troubles that she turned and said with great emotion in her voice. "You are a fine young man." I was reluctantly and much against my will compelled to admit the truth of her statement. Just about at the end of the interview her husband turned to me and asked "Do you know where I courted this woman?" I replied with a statement of utter ignorance as to the place where, etc. "On 5th Ave. New York, next to John D. Rockefeller's house," he replied beaming at his wife, who beamed at him in return.

With that extraordinary information they arose and departed, and I watched the chauffeur start the huge car and purr away. Some class to the clientele that I am getting.

*With much love*

---

## *To C.P. Arnold*

Cambridge, Mass., Feb. 15, 1914

Dear Papa:

I have been over hearing Sherman Whipple,[14] who is one of the leaders of the Boston bar, talking on legal procedure. He has shocked the conservative William Taft, by his proposal to abolish privilege between attorney and client, and to abolish the hearsay rule, leaving only a rule of probative value, which should be governed by the discretion of the judge. What he said seemed to me sound, though a trifle radical.

The offer in the firm of Hurlburt, Cabot, and Jones, is still open, and I have not completely decided what to do about it. I have however decided not to come home to practice law. The reasons governing me in this are not entirely the fact that Laramie is a place of rather limited opportunity so far as the law is concerned, but to go home seems like drifting with the current and taking the easiest course out. I will simply go into a place made for me, and there will be little incentive to get down and do any real hard work. There will be no push of necessity, and I feel that I had better get out and see what I can do. Of course there is always home as a sort of sheet anchor, if things get too hard elsewhere.

The reason I am tempted by the Boston offer, is that life would be so much more pleasant in Boston among friends, living with a man that I like very much, than in going to Chicago, and this makes the choice harder.

I'm afraid that my advice on whether to hang on to the Scoville ranch would not be much good.[15] My instincts are like mama's, to hang on to land. There is something about being a landed proprietor that appeals to our imaginations. Mamie sent me a box of candy, which was thoughtful and nice in her and all that, but I wish she wouldn't, as I would rather buy my own candy, and not have to write complicated letters of thanks. However we must take people as we find them, and I suppose that the letter must be written some time.

*With love*

---

La Salle at Madison St.

# Hotel La Salle

Chicago June 19 1914

Dearest Mother:

Thank you for your telegram. I have been to about 25 big offices in the last two days. ~~The tentative~~ Two tentative offers have appeared, and one definite offer carrying with it the staggering salary of $5 per week. Also heaps of advice. Most of them tell me to go back home. Some say to stay. The outlook on the whole is not encouraging. It is a long hard unremunerative uphill pull to get anywhere here. And a lawyer making $10,000 a year is nowhere. to is expenses eat up his income, and he had better be making $5000 in a small town. Two lawyers who said they were making that told me so. They handed out a blue line of talk and told me to go home.

## *To Mrs. C.P. Arnold*

Chicago, Ill., June 19, 1914

Dearest Mother:

Thank you for your telegram. I have been to about 25 big offices in the last two days. Two tentative offers have appeared, and one definite offer carrying with it the staggering salary of $5 per week. Also heaps of advice. Most of them tell me to go back home. Some say to stay. The outlook on the whole is not encouraging. It is a long hard unremunerative uphill pull to get anywhere here. And a lawyer making $10,000 a year is nowhere. His expenses eat up his income, and he had better be making $5,000 in a small town. Two lawyers who said they were making that told me so. They handed out a blue line of talk and told me to go home. On the other hand a lawyer in one of the largest firms, who is reputed to be making anywhere from $30,000 to $50,000 a year, told me that Chicago is the easiest place in the country to break into practice. So you can't tell. If you do make good here the returns are very large. But if you don't belong to that fortunate 2% you had better go somewhere else where the competition is less bitter.

Mr. Pirie, whom I saw this morning was very nice. Pushed a button and sent for the head credit man in the establishment and told him to inquire in all the firm's legal connections for possible vacancies. Said that he would do anything in the world for the woman who wrote the letter of introduction, and told me to come back tomorrow and he would see what had turned up. He is not in touch with many lawyers personally he said. This afternoon I go around to see Mr. Barton, former president of the Western Electric Company, who is Mrs. Calhoun's cousin. He seems to be a great man around these parts.

I don't suppose that letters of introduction to these people will do a tremendous amount of good, except that they have instilled in Harry Toller a proper amount of awe and respect for the Arnold family which may do him some good. I am sorry, but the presence of Harry leaves me emotionally cold. He has bought an automobile, about which he is not over-modest. It is a pleasure to hear him refer to it as "the car." However he has been more than kind to me, and done everything in the world for me. I really wish I could like him better.

I have learned from the Law School that I came thru my last examinations with a terrible wallop, getting one point better than an A average for the year (76%). This puts me with the first 10% of the class for the year. I am very much gratified with this, and it came as a complete surprise. I wish that I could have done it last year because it would have put me on the law review.[16] It came a little too late, but still it is a great personal satisfaction to me to know that I am not necessarily only a "B" man, and that some of the awe that I have wasted on various other lights of the law school has been misapplied. Without it my law school career would have been a complete disappointment to me. Mediocrity may be my lot, and has been in the law school up to this last year, but I can never be happy unless I get above it.

The strangest thing about it is that I did less work this year than any of the three, resorting to my old Princeton Method of cramming for the exam. Thus we see that virtue is ever unrewarded in this vale of tears.

I am not certain, but it looks as if I might not take my bar exams in July, but come home next week. Will let you know later.

*With love*

---

*To Mr. and Mrs. C.P. Arnold*

Chicago, Ill., Sept. 2, 1914

Dearest Mother and Father:

I have located temporarily at the Wilson Ave. YMCA, 1725 Wilson Ave. It is just 20 minutes from the loop. This is about as good as you can do temporarily. There is a swimming pool in the building and a good gym, which makes up for the exceedingly diminutive character of the rooms. It costs $13 per month for a room. I had to dig up $15 for membership in addition, but I think on the whole that is money well invested for one staying in the city.

The first night I was here I was intending to go out to Cousin Bessie's but Mr. Follansbee[17] invited me out to his home and I went there instead. He is an old bachelor living with his mother and father. They have a beautiful house out in the suburbs, opening on the back on a delightful formal garden. He is a royal host and hands out 25¢ cigars in profusion,[18] and I passed a very pleasant evening there.

The firm seems pretty blue about the business outlook. They had a whopping big year last year, and increased their force. The war however has put the kibash on everything, and Follansbee tells me that nothing new that looks good has come in. Adams told me that last year he made $40,000 gross out of his bonding business and this year will be lucky if he makes $5,000. They spend the time working on each others' shoulder. Follansbee says there aren't even domestic difficulties anymore in Chicago because everyone is too poor to get gay.

The establishment is a larger one than I thought. They maintain four young fellows in the office beside myself, four stenographers, one bookkeeper, an office man, a girl to run the telephone exchange, and one office boy.

So far I have done nothing but look over files of a few cases in the office that don't amount to much. Adams this evening however started me looking over abstracts of titles—a dull enough job.

Hunters passed thru here today and gave me a lunch. Was glad to see someone, as so far I have not had sufficient diversion in the way of companionship to make even Mrs. Hunter's line of conversation unacceptable.

I like the men in the firm very well. Mr. Follansbee is one of the most delightful men I have ever met. I hope they can rake up enough business this year to keep me busy.

*With lots of love*

---

## *To Mrs. C.P. Arnold*

Springfield, Ill., Oct. 6, 1914

Dearest Mother:

I am here in Springfield after spending a day taking bar exams. They are just half over, thank the Lord. I have a session tomorrow morning, and one tomorrow afternoon, and take a night train back to Chicago. They are not particularly hard, and I think that so far I got through all right.

The worst thing about them is that they are in the capitol building, an indescribable mid-Victorian architectural monstrosity with two mansard roofs surmounted by a huge dome.

The ceiling of the legislature hall where we take the exam, looks like a cubist painting of a scene of indescribable carnage. Every time I look up at it my nose begins to bleed. Never have I seen more incongruous colors placed in juxtaposition with more telling effect.

My co-examiners are mostly of Hebraic extraction, and seem from an exterior view, to show signs of a depressing lack of intelligence. If they get thru I ought to.

I had dinner this evening with a class mate of mine and his mother. He is going into the diplomatic service, and his mother follows him around from place to place while he takes his exams. She is a widow and he is apparently all she has. They appear to have wads of money however. They are very entertaining people and I enjoyed dinner very much.

I am very tired now after writing all day, so I must close.

*With lots and lots of love*

---

*To C.P. Arnold*

Chicago, Ill., Nov. 19, 1914

Dear Papa:

Acting on the advice of Mr. Follansbee I have joined the city club. The dues amount only to $20 per year, and it enables you to get in touch with all sorts of civic work. Besides that it is a very nice place.

This has been a rather busy week. Monday night I attended a banquet of the social service club, where social legislation, your pet aversion, was discussed. Tuesday night Cousin Bessie was in town, and Wednesday night is the night I teach a class of Italians at the Chicago Commons. They are trying to learn English, poor waifs, and seem vastly impressed by my feeble efforts to instruct them in the niceities of that tongue of which I am part master. No common linguistic meeting ground creates all sorts of difficulties. One has to explain words by waving one's arms and legs. It's all right when it comes to objects to which you can point, but the attempted explanation of the difference between "knew," and "new," last night, nearly dislocated my brain.

Mr. Moores, whose letter I enclose, attended the dinner of the bar association and learned by accident from Mr. Follansbee that I was here. He tried to look me up, but I was in a far-off suburb hunting witnesses. I wrote him that I was enclosing his letter to you, and that you would no doubt write him.

*With love to all*

---

*To C.P. Arnold*

Chicago, Ill., Jan. 7, 1915

Dear Father:

I have been so busy for the past week, both daytimes and evenings that I have not had a moment to write home. However I am feeling fine. I have used up all of mama's great catarrh remedy, and find, upon an attempt to procure more of the stuff, that there is no such thing in the Pharmacopia, or however you spell the encyclopedia of drugs, as cream of camphor, which throws such a dark and mysterious aspect over the wild tales of the mythical hired man as to lead me to suspect that some clever enemy is attempting to poison me. I am informed that there are about fifty patent catarrh preparations, all of them based on camphor, but with that caution which will some day land me at the head of the Chicago bar, I have decided to have nothing to do with any of them until I have had a secret and confidential interview with some competent nose hound who specialized in my ailment. The aroma of romance, and glad optimism, shed over this mysterious preparation by the combined enthusiasm of those emminent medical experts, Mama and Aunt Emma, has become faint and dissipated without the personal magnetism and appeal which lent such success of their campaign for the stuff while I was in Laramie, and I yearn for the advice of the hired expert. So I will repair to one, with the full realization that it was just such glad and open financial tactics which led to financial nonentity of so many of our distinguished relatives, but with my face set like a flint nevertheless.

The Latin class progresses at length, but I find that it is a prelegal class, and the students are not expected to get much law out of it, but to learn Latin. This they will be utterly unable to do, partly because the book is no good, partly because the time is too short, and partly because the young gentlemen in the class are slightly bored, and the young ladies, while interested, do not combine with their Diana-like grace, and Atalanta-like spring, the Minerva-like cranium necessary to the successful prosecution of this classical subject. However I have presented my ideas to the Dean of the school and my conscience is clear. If the hungry sheep look up and are not fed, it will be his soul that is damned for it and not mine.

Many evenings have been spent in earnest speculation with the other young lights of our prospective firm. Gavin of our office has been approached on the subject and seems favorable for a fourth partner. If he joins I will. I do not think that he is much of a business getter, that is at first because he has not the acquaintance, but I consider him a far abler lawyer than anyone in this firm except Adams. He has had five years experience, and with the addition of him, I would consider the new firm competent to handle any business that came to it, of however complicated a nature. And it is on ability in the long run that the success of a firm counts. If he joins in, I am going to take the gamble. If he doesn't, I may anyway for I think that the first year or so we would do about as much with him as without him. But with him in the firm I think that we would have a combination that would make good. I don't see why we couldn't make the thing a go. All of us have more ability, and two of us, O'Bryan[19] and Waite, have a much wider acquaintance than the average. The business is here waiting for us, if we can only get hold of it. The vista looms big if we do make good.

I wish you would make your trip to Chicago sure, and in the near future if possible. With your wayward and ambitious son about to stake a lot of money on a venture which may land all of the Arnolds, not only in this country but abroad on the tottering verge of bankruptcy, and destroy the last vestiges of their tattered reputation, and place a new stain on their escutcheon, it seems to me that you might be interested in sizing up his co-conspirators.

*With love*

---

## *To C.P. Arnold*

Oshkosh, Wis., May 5, 1915

Dear Father:

I have just made my initial appearance in this region of disordered nomenclature. Rather interesting business calls me here. The Paine Lumber Company, located here, is in the hands of a receiver. It is a huge corporation, the largest sash and door plant in the country, employing about 1200 men, and until recently having the best of credit. Last December Moseby & Co., a large Chicago commercial paper house wrote their regular letter to the Paine Lbr. Co. asking for some of their paper to discount. They received a reply to the effect that the company was in no need of funds and proposed to discount no more of its notes, but as a special favor they would let Moseby have $50,000 of their paper, which would probably be the last paper they would issue for a long time to come. They sent a report for January, 1914 which showed a very favorable financial condition. As a matter of fact the Company was in desperate need of funds and asked for $50,000 only because they thought it was about all they could get without extensive inquiry being made into their condition.

Mosby took the paper and discounted it at various banks subject to the 1915 statement of the company which was due in about a week. When the statement came out it showed such a shrinkage of assets of every kind, and increase of liabilities that the banker turned back all the paper to Moseby. On April 12th the Paine Lbr. Co. went into the hands of a receiver.

The question bothering the office therefore, is what had best be done. There is sufficient fraud to justify rescinding the notes, declaring the amount due, and throwing the company into bankruptcy. This of course is only a last resort. What Follansbee wants to do is to use it only as a threat and to get the company to furnish some good indorses on the paper. He does not want to spring this however till the receivership gets well under way and it looks as if the company were going to pull thru. Then those who are pushing it thru will get together and take care of the notes (which are not due yet), rather than see all their labors go for nothing by our rescinding and throwing them into bankruptcy.

For this reason it is essential that the firm keep out of it at present. I am up here representing another creditor (whose claim is only $42.10, but I take pains not to state the amount) as an independent attorney. There is an informal creditors' meeting today which I will attend, without undue ostentation, because of the size of my claim. I will also interview all of the receivers, and generally find out everything possible about the condition of the company, how they got there and their chances of pulling thru. If the Wisconsin Trust Co. of Milwaukee, one of the receivers, is not here, I will go to Milwaukee tonight to interview it.

Oshkosh is a very pretty town, as I have discovered from my walk. A perpetual Sunday atmosphere pervades its long shaded streets where the trees almost meet overhead. An occasional bell, rung from somewhere in the distance above the tree tops makes you think that it is always Sunday here, and the people are always good. Only in the downtown district, which is not large or particularly impressive, has Satan mobilized his forces in an occasional saloon, from whose open doors a stale smell stalks silently and carelessly like a long procession of spectres. Queer truncated street cars, with yellow stomachs like bumble bees, sound out their masquerade by making a pleasant peaceful buzz as they disappear down the long avenues. Picturesque they are, to the stranger, but the populace chooses to ignore them, trusting to their sturdy legs, and great-hearted little Fords—though an occasional passenger may be discerned peering from the dirty panes, his face wistful and hungry for human companionship. He has paid his nickle, and achieved, not speed, but only loneliness—wherefore his heart is heavy within him.

To while away the time before the meeting I have composed a triolet. Of course it is meaningless, but the neat form, with its trice repeated refrain, and ingenious rhyme scheme fascinates me. It is interesting to think that the 19th century which produced the complicated decorative form in architecture is also responsible for all the complicated decorative forms of verse.[20] Do younger civilizations care more for form than content or are their reflections all nonsense?

Triolet

So dainty are my triolets,
I swell with pride when I compose 'em.
Like elfin woodland violets
So dainty are my triolets—
They make the dearest mental pets,
As anyone will tell who knows 'em
So dainty are my triolets,
I swell with pride when I compose 'em.

*With love*

*To C.P. Arnold*

Chicago, Ill., June, 1915

Dear Father:

I got your last letter and enjoyed. Also noted what you had to say about coming home in advance of my guests. I have written them therefore, to put off their vacations for a week, which I guess they can do. I will start for home somewhere around the first.

The Kid[21] was through looking fine. He puts up quite a good appearance, and I was quite proud of him when I introduced him to Mr. Follansbee. I think that Princeton has done him a world of good in general appearance and personality, whether he has learned anything there or not, which is of course very doubtful. I might add that in passing he borrowed fifteen dollars of me, which I obtained only by drawing my salary away down in the dim future, and which he has not seen fit, at the present writing to remit me. He does not realize the bitter lot of one who lives from ten dollars to ten dollars, and would suggest that you remind him that there is an implied obligation on the part of the borrower to repay, and that this was not a time loan, but rather of the call variety, and from the above he may, not without a certain degree of correctness, infer a call. You might remind him of the bitter experience his previous dilatory financial tactics furnished him in connection with the University Store at Princeton, and how worried we all were about it at the time when things looked rather Stygian, and criminal prosecutions loomed darkly in the offing. This hint will, I think, convince him of the error of his present ways.

You might also suggest to him that unless he wants to use the key to our house here as a watch charm or earing, he might return it to me, as I labor under the impression that my closer proximity to the lock of which it is the necessary complement, gives me superior opportunities for utilizing it. The fact that if I have the key I may be able to get in without waking everyone up by ringing the door bell continuously for fifteen minutes, as has been my custom in the past week since he left, you may bring in as an added argument for his returning it, though it may be doubted that an appeal to his purely philanthropic instincts will be of much effect. All of the above however is subject to the exception and reservation that the key has not fallen out of his pocket, as it is well known from past experience with pocket knives, etc. that in those mysterious sartorial recesses the ordinary laws of gravitation do not operate.

I close now, and will write again when I learn when I am coming home. It will probably be about the first of July.

*With love*

*To Mrs. C.P. Arnold*

Chicago, Ill., Oct. 11, 1915

Dearest Mother:

I am still very busy indeed, my criminal cases not being disposed of. I have another client who was tried for bigamy, which change I got dismissed. They are trying by a series of prosecutions, all of them groundless, to keep him in jail. I don't know whether I told you about it, but it is so very complicated that I haven't the heart to tackle it this evening after a long day's work.

I wish you would send on the money that I paid out for those enlargements, which same is $7.00. When a person lives from hand to mouth the way I do, he misses chunks of money like that. I realize that you want other enlargements, but am totally unable to find out of what pictures, and how large. Carl had a list, but had lost it.

I am making a very fool move in loaning a young lawyer $100 on his personal note.[22] He started out to practice law, and made out fine for a couple of months, and then struck a dull time. However I can't see him kicked out of his office for not paying rent, and anyway I have great confidence in his ultimately making good. He is a fellow of lots of initiative and pep.

*With much love*

---

*To C.P. Arnold*

Chicago, Ill., Nov. 2, 1915

Dear Father:

Am waiting for a train to take me so will drop you a short line. Don't know whether I told you or not but the firm has raised my salary from the first of this month to the staggering amount of seventy per month.

I tried the last of my criminal cases the other day. It took most of the day to try it and it was a fairly hard fought case. The defendant whom I defended was convicted, but the judge called me up to the bench after the verdict and complimented me on the defense that I put up. Considering the fact that he was guilty, I guess that it came out as well as could be expected.

What is going to happen Christmas. I probably could get a week off and come home, or are you coming to Chicago. It is not such a very long time.

I am getting all excited in my childish notion of going over to France and driving an ambulance. I understand that it is a very safe way of seeing the war, as you do not get very near the front. I hate to be sticking around a law office in Chicago when history that will never be repeated is going on. I would like to find out the conduct of a nation like France in a time of great national trouble. I suppose that you will cast a gloom over the project, but you will have to admit that it is a temptation hard to resist when one is young and foot loose. A couple of months over there would be worth a couple of years anywhere else. I understand that ambulance jobs are going begging.

*With much love*

---

## *To Mrs. C.P. Arnold*

Chicago, Ill., Jan. 13, 1916

Dear Mother:

I was very glad to get your letter enclosing the one from Carl. He must have had a great time traveling around the country, and I for one consider that it is just as well for him to have it before settling down to a life of drudgery, such as all life is. My cousin Betty disagrees with me.

Business has been picking up since the first of the year.[23] A friend of mine, who was employed by Zane, Morse and McKinney, has deserted them for the position of general counsel of the Reo Automobile company. He has turned over to us all of his business due to the fact that he is very displeased with Papa's friend, Zane. There is a suit on an insurance policy which we just started for $5,000 which we should win, and a very important suit for $14,000 on a judgment in Montana against a corporation. The suit here is to enforce a director's liability on directors here in Chicago. It looks very good. Also some other smaller business. The trouble with these suits of course is that it will be about a year before they are reached and we can get no money until that time, and therefore the present financial stringency is not relieved. However we are getting business which will take care of us in the future. We also got an estate to handle which contains about $14,000.

Aside from that we are just about making office expenses and no more. Last month we ran $50 behind.

Would you mind sending me the interest on my note for the months of December and January.

Pat has just finished the trial of a very difficult murder case. I did not think that we had a chance in the world of getting any better than a manslaughter verdict. The trial lasted nine days, and I was never more surprised in my life when the jury brought in a verdict of acquittal. The accused had shot and killed a policeman, and the defense was accidental shooting and self defense. The State's attorney's office is very bitter over it, and the newspapers all published sarcastic comments about the soft-hearted jury. We got quite a reputation over it around the criminal court building. However there seems to be no money in it. We haven't been paid anything yet, and I don't see where anything is going to come from.

I spent the night with Bessie and Harry. Stanley is sick which irritates Bessie exceedingly.

*With love*

---

## *To C.P. Arnold*

Chicago, Ill., March 4, 1916

Dear Papa:

I was very glad to get your letter enclosing news from Riley and the ranch. The last two weeks have been, I think, about the busiest that I have ever spent. We have been going just four weeks. The first week we spent moving in, the second in starting out announcement lists with other work, and the last two we have been working all the time, evenings included. Most of our work has come from lawyers, Adams, Follansbee, Hawley and Shorey, Miller, Starr, Packard and Peckham, and another firm, Beckman, Cottrell and Phillips. We have charged a dollar an hour for our services, and have been swamped with work at that rate. Phillips of Beckman, Cottrell and Phillips, whom we assisted in the trial of a rather important case, which lasted for ten days, and which we succeeded in taking away from the jury, was much pleased with our work and turned over a death claim against the Street Car Company, which was on yesterday's trial call to us to handle. I went in and got two weeks extension of time to prepare the case on the ground of substitution of counsel, and we are going to have little enough time to get it ready and try it. If we recover there will be a thousand dollar fee of which we will get half, and if we lose we get nothing.

As I figure it up this evening, the first three weeks of our practice will net about two hundred dollars in fees, which will pay office expenses and show a profit right from the start. As I had expected that we would run in the hole for a few months, and was gloomily figuring out how long a thousand dollars would last when I had to pay office expenses as well as my living out of it, I feel rather good at the way things have been coming.

Of course I can't see at present just where the business for next month is coming from, but then at the beginning of this month there was not a thing in sight either.

Harry has a big bunch of collections at his disposal, and after talking largely for some time about turning over $1,200 of them over to us to handle, he wonders if he dare trust us with any more. He then calls up every day about the dumb thing, being apparently of the impression that the three of us ought to spend our undivided time on it. He also has the vague impression that as an incident to the collection of a thirty dollar claim we ought to write short briefs on points of law in connection with his business for nothing. And then when we have spent about five times the amount of time on it that the thing is worth, and have collected a staggering fee in the sum of three dollars, less sixty cents car fare and telephone calls, he thinks that he has made us a present of the money and genially refers to how he started us out in business. He means well, bless his heart, and honestly thinks that we are under tremendous obligations to him. However, if he decides to keep on sending the rest of his business to the pleasant, though ignorant Hebrew who has been doing it, I shall be just as well pleased. I had always heard of the old adage, "Never do business with relatives," and the excellent Dean Thayer[24] noted it in his humorous way in one of his talks with me, but I never realized its force until I was retained in the GREAT CASE of Sheldon School vs. Tapper.

I never think of Dean Thayer without a deep sense of sorrow and personal loss. I never hope to win the friendship of a finer man.

I was so busy this week that I had no time to think up anything in particular to say at my lecture.[25] I had barely time to arrange the slides. Thursday I had to get up some specifications of objection to a discharge in Bankruptcy which had to be filed Friday. Consequently I had no time for lunch. I worked until 6:15 on that, and had three sandwiches sent up which I consumed for supper while I was going over to the law school. I kidded the law Latin students along for a while in an endeavor to conceal from them the fact that I had not prepared the lesson, and dismissing them ten minutes early rushed down stairs and on to a car for the West side. The car was slow, and so I had to run three blocks with some heavy slides and got to the lecture hall all out of breath, just in time to throw off my coat and address an audience of about two hundred half-witted day laborers. I talked for about fifty minutes extemporaneously, giving the signal for a new slide every time that I ran out of things to say about the one on the screen. It was up hill work all right. Every time that I would make a peculiarly apt remark, and would pause for the roar of laughter which was due to rise and shake the building, peering through the gloom in order to see the audience rolling round on the floor, the buttons flying off their vests in paroxysms of laughter, like shrapnel from a machine gun, a dull heavy silence would greet me. I finally quit, disgusted with the lecture I had given. The *Daily News* Lecture Bureau man however seemed quite pleased and said that I had a quality of facetiousness rare among his lecturers. So I passed all right and am duly retained on the staff. This lecture that I gave was not a regular *Daily News* lecture, but given under a different name, and used by the bureau to try out their new stock and see if they can qualify. I give another next Friday night.

The pictures are colored very beautifully. The only one which brought any applause was the one of Papa, in a red shirt, holding up the five pound trout (which same I informed them was the family's sole and only claim to distinction, but intimated that their dull souls could little realize the honor attendant upon the capture of such a colossal monster).

I got home about eleven, so tired that I could not sleep the rest of the night. I am pretty much all in this week, but on the whole I enjoy being rushed to death, and have learned the great truth that there is nothing in the world so much fun as hard work, so long as you feel that it is leading you somewhere. I feel that I have gained one thing anyway out of my year and a half in Chicago, and that is confidence in myself. Without being conceited I honestly feel that I am as good as the average, and probably a bit better. A year ago I would have had a nervous headache at the mere thought of giving such a lecture, but now I am ready to tackle anything that comes along, without it bothering me overmuch. Self confidence has been my chief lack in the past, and when I left law school I felt that the only way I could ever attain it was to get away from home and start out asking no odds of anyone. In this my time here in Chicago has been far better spent than if I had been in Laramie. I am really astonished at the change that has taken place in myself during the year and a half that I have spent here.

*With much love*

P.S. Unless business lets up I don't know when we will get out our announcements. I am borrowing another two hundred and fifty from the bank at home. The first two hundred and fifty was spent in getting started and the office fixed up. I am making enough to live for another month or two but I have got to have a checking account in a down town bank. It is too undignified to run across the street with a savings book every time I want to pay anyone anything and makes a bad impression. To run a checking account requires about two hundred dollars balance, but I figure it is worth the interest I pay.

My clothes are coming all to pieces also, and I've got to spend about $60 for shoes, socks, underwear, shirts and a new suit.

Thanks to Mama for the night shirts.

---

## *To Mrs. C.P. Arnold*

Chicago, Ill., April 9, 1916

Dearest Mother:

The law school course is finished and as a result I have a little time to myself in the evenings. I am very glad of it, because when one doesn't have an evening to one's self all week it gets a trifle monotonous.

Our business at the office keeps up as well as ever. We balanced our books last month and found that we had taken in in cash just $300. We have $260 standing on our books already earned, the collection of which is sure, so our income for this month will exceed that of last month. I had thought I would have to borrow more money for living expenses, but find that I am paying office expenses and making a living without it, so I will not have to call on our friend Mr. Jones this month anyway.

I am going out so that I close hastily, enclosing a photo of myself published in the *Daily News.*

*With love*

---

## *To C.P. Arnold*

Chicago, Ill., June 7, 1916

Dear Father:

We have finally succeeded in avoiding a suit for negligence by our wild Irish client on promise of our giving a bond to indemnify the City Railways for any recovery which may be had against them and for other expenses upon appeal. The case has already been placed in the hands of other attorneys who are looking into it with the view to appealing. I do not consider from the way the evidence stands that there is one chance in a hundred of the judgment being reversed. However, if we did not fix up our record it is an absolute certainty that our client would sue us, which we could not afford to have her do. If we get the record fixed up I do not think she will take an appeal as I doubt that she can get anyone to handle it for her on a contingent basis. I will, therefore, tomorrow send you the bond which I hope you can sign. Through the kindness of John S. Miller who interceded for me with the General Counsel of the City Railways they have waived a bond by a surety company which would cost considerable money. Of course, they want other sureties than ourselves. Waite knows of no one he can ask but Pat is getting his mother to sign it, (his mother, I understand, is worth about a hundred thousand dollars), and I am sending it to you. We will all appreciate it very much if you sign it. It is needless to say that we will hold you harmless. The only actual expense if there is an appeal will be the attorney's fees and costs to the City Railways. I would be glad also, if you would get the First National Bank to write a letter to Mr. J.R. Guilliams, General Attorney for the Chicago Surface Lines, 600 Washington Blvd., Chicago, stating your financial responsibility.

We have just balanced our books for this month and find our gross income is showing a gradual increase. The first month we took in cash $293; the second month $197, and last month $301.85. So you see our business is increasing gradually. We have on our books $275 in earned fees which we can collect within the next three months. In addition to that we have $200 in stock in a company for the sale of a motor lock which looks to me to be a very fair proposition. The company is capitalized for $14,000 and there has been paid in $7,000 so the stock is possibly worth about fifty cents on the dollar—at least until they spend the $7,000.

Business is slow just at present but we are finding enough to keep us busy. Our expenses last month were $208. They ought to run $180 but there is always something special. Last month, however, is the first month that we showed a profit as our expenses of the announcements and stationery of the previous months were very heavy. Of course, this is a long way from making money, but there seems to be an increasing line of business which is our own, and the amount on our books in fees which we have not collected seems to gradually increase. We are getting quite a number of suits on the contingent basis. Last week we started two suits for $10,000, one a personal injury action, the other for libel. We also have some tax objections which involve about $1,700 and which we have on a contingent fee of one-sixth. None of these fees, however, will be coming in for about a year and one-half or two years.

*With much love*

---

## *To C.P. Arnold*

Chicago, Ill., June 14, 1916

Dear Father:

I have been doing all sorts of things during the past two weeks. Among them was a trip from Fort Sheridan to Chicago to take part in the big Parade they had here for preparedness. I have asked everyone I knew who was wild about preparedness, just what it was that they were preparing for. Nobody seemed to know, exactly. But I suppose that it must be all right because everyone gets so excited over it. They had about 130,000 in the Parade and it took twelve hours to pass. Our Battery, fully equipped and mounted rode in at about 7:00, between long lines of admiring spectators. It is quite a thing to be a soldier at times. We started from Fort Sheridan on Thursday, and camped on the road Thursday and Friday nights. Saturday night we camped on the open ground across the Illinois Central tracks opposite the Blackstone. We had a fine time in the three days we were gone.

My particular position is wheel driver of the caisson. Each driver rides the near horse and drives two horses.

If it is not too much trouble just now I wonder if you could get the bond in the Britt case signed. The sooner we get it fixed up the sooner we can write our client that she has just a certain amount of time in which to appeal. My military camp is the 15th of July. Shall I come home now, or in August?

*With love*

---

*To C.P. Arnold*

Chicago, Ill., June 17, 1916

Dear Father:

I received your letter today with the executed bond and I confess that upon thinking it over I find that I have not been definite enough in informing you. The trouble was that it has been on my mind so much, and I had written and received several letters from you and Mama about it that I sort of took it for granted that everyone understood about it. If I had been writing to a stranger of course I would have been more definite, but in my haste I always had the subconscious feeling that I had explained everything to you. We are all very grateful to you for signing it.

The facts are as follows. Through our negligence we had put our client in such a position that she could never take an appeal. We had also put Beckman, Cottrell and Phillips in a very embarrassing position. It is true that we were under no obligation to prosecute an appeal for our client, but still we had the unquestioned obligation to preserve her record so that she could get someone else to take an appeal if she wanted. I do not think that an appeal is worth anything whatever, and we have so informed our client. She will not believe us, nor will she believe anyone who tells her so. Since therefore she wants an appeal, and since we have deprived her of that right, Waite and I both feel that the only honorable course for us to pursue is to give it to her at whatever cost to ourselves. O'Bryan disagreed with us, but the firm stood two to one, and that determined our policy. Through the intervention of John S. Miller we got Mr. Busby, the

President of the City Railways, to stipulate that the judgment be vacated, a new motion for new trial made, and at that time we can ask for thirty days to preserve our bill of exceptions. The unfortunate part about it is that if we had succeeded in getting the matter arranged more quickly her time to appeal would already be up. We have been advised to tell her that it is up, which would be a very simple way of getting rid of her, but one which we would not consider taking for a moment.

So far she knows nothing about our slip. She is very sore because she thinks that railroad paid us for losing her case. She has taken her case to two attorneys in succession, who have called up, and after some discussion and consideration decided that there is nothing in the case for them to spend their time on. Yesterday we got a telephone message from a third. The old lady certainly keeps on the job, and the case has been an obsession with her for the past three years.

As for the liability on the bond: The suit is for ten thousand dollars, but any recovery more than three thousand dollars would be held excessive under the decisions in this state under similar facts, which we have examined very carefully. The likelihood of a recovery seems to be negligible. It takes about two years for a case to get through the Appellate Court, and two more years to come up again in the Superior Court if it would be remanded. Then it could be appealed again and another two years consumed. I don't see how the Appellate Court could reverse the trial court in this instance, and if they did, I am quite sure that the case would be taken from the jury again if the Railways put in their defense. Of course we will have to pay all the Street Railway's expenses. It is impossible to tell just what they will be. If the old lady gets an attorney who will spend the time on it under such a slim chance of recovery, they will turn it over to one of the offices that handle their work with the recommendation that they make their charge as low as possible because of professional courtesy. It may cost a couple of hundred dollars.

I am inclined to think that we have taken too serious a view as to the danger to ourselves. If the old lady should sue us I do not think she could get anywhere, nor that it would do us any substantial harm. But we have deprived her of a right that she wants, and so it is up to us to make it good, and I do not think that the question as to whether she could force us to do it or not should enter into it. I have made up my mind that we are pursuing the only honorable course, and have made my self disagreeable enough about it, and gone through so much argument about it that I am weary of discussing that phase of it. I am not entirely alone in that position because Mr. Guilliams, the General Attorney, took occasion to compliment me highly on the stand I was taking. He said that while he thought that there was no other course open, still he thought there were very few lawyers today who had a very serious idea of their obligations, and he was glad to see some of the younger members of the bar who, etc. etc.

That is about all there is to it, except that I am sure that we will be able to save you harmless from any liability on the bond. We could have accomplished the whole thing without a bond if it had not been for Mr. Busby, the President. He has the general reputation of being the meanest man in Chicago. However in this case, as a matter of business, it is hard to see how he could do any differently, inasmuch as there was no obligation on his part to do anything, and it simply means a lot of trouble for them.

I regret to report that we have not made any money this month, except a very few dollars, and that the prospects of taking any in are not bright. This does not mean that we are not busy. The office resembles Laramie in the old days when all the booms were on. We have organized the company for the sale of an automobile lock, which is a patented device and looks pretty good. We have $700 in stock and are doing quite a lot of work on it. There is also a wild scheme for a Subway that Pat is dabbling in with a lot of politicians. They have got Mr. Jones interested in it, who spent the greater part of yesterday afternoon up here in the office going over it. It has always sounded to me like the very worst sort of bunk, but Jones is the first responsible individual, or person with any semblance of responsibility who has yet appeared, so we may indirectly get a good deal of good out of it in the way of becoming known to various people. Mr. Jones is the head of the Guaranty Trust Company that Neil Roach and Sodergrey[26] belong to. He says he knows you quite well and that you are handling the Wyoming end of the matter. We are also organizing a company to control a patent electric sign, which is a wonderful thing if it is patentable. We have got to raise about seven hundred dollars on this to start it rolling. This means a lot more stock. The sign looks so good that we will have no trouble whatever in getting the money if we can give any sort of assurance as to the validity of the patent. It achieves the same effect as the big moving sign on Michigan Avenue. Words and letters move across its face. However we have no patent as yet, and the whole thing hinges on the validity of the patent. We are also trying to buy the Cleveland Baseball Club for another dreamer, who has no money that I can discover. To hear them talk you would think they were worth millions. So you see we have a lot of stuff, with people coming in and out of the office all the time. It looks very prosperous, but so far as real hard actual cash, the outlook this month is the worst yet. We will run in the hole unless something turns up in the next ten days. Pat loves the far-flung schemes with their rosy impossibilities but I would prefer just one good case, not on a contingent fee, where I could earn a dollar an hour, to the whole raft of them. However we take what comes. My experience is that it is no trick at all for a young lawyer to keep busy. The only rub comes in getting anything for his work.

I don't believe that I ever thanked you for the five dollars and letter you sent me. The letter was a masterpiece. I sent it to Harry and when I get it back I am going to send it to the Atlantic Monthly. I have not read anything for a long time that has got so much of the spirit of the plains in it.

*With much love*

---

## *To Mrs. C.P. Arnold*

Chicago, Ill., June 19, 1916

Dearest Mother:

I was going home this week but we have been called to mobilize to patrol the Mexican border, and there is no alternative but to go. I have received orders to be ready, but beyond that I know nothing.

We will only be sent down to patrol the border so there is nothing to be alarmed about.

I don't believe that I every thanked you for the five dollars you sent and the pajamas, and underwear. They came in very handy.

I have written on Saturday about everything I was doing.

Just got a telephone call to take first train to Ft. Sheridan.

*With love*

---

## *To C.P. Arnold*

Chicago, Ill., June 20, 1916

My dear Father:

My battery has been called out and is mobilizing at Fort Sheridan awaiting orders to leave Chicago. We may be there a few days and then will probably go to Springfield and from thence to the border after staying there three weeks. That is the probability but no one knows anything. I am down at the office on a few hours leave in my uniform ready to take the four o'clock train for Fort Sheridan. It is somewhat inconvenient for me to go, of course, but there is no alternative and it is a satisfaction to go with such a fine crowd of fellows. I can further consider myself very lucky in comparison with some who give up good positions and some who are married. To a few of them I know it means tremendous financial hardship so on a whole I may count myself lucky. It seems a rather wasteful method of patrolling the border with men who have an earning capacity of over $5,000 a year when it could be done as well by a standing army getting $2 a day. But that is the way they do things in this country.

You had better address any mail to this office until I can find out whether we are going to Springfield or to the border. My battery is Battery "C" First Field Artillery, Illinois National Guard.

I suppose Mama will not be very much pleased at the turn things have taken and neither am I. Still inspite of myself I cannot help a feeling of elation because there is so little adventure in life anyway that if any comes it is welcome. So long as we are going I hope that we will not have to stay at Springfield long.

My partners have very generously told me that the arrangement would go on the same no matter how long I was away. I have signed promissory notes for $250 which I have authorized them to send to the First National Bank and draw the money if the firm runs in a hole.

I am in town only for a few hours and so will not have time to sign this letter.[27]

Give my very best love to Mama and the folks.

*With love*

---

## *To Mrs. C.P. Arnold*

Fort Hood, Tex., July 12, 1916

Dearest Mother:

If you knew how hard it is to write you would not blame me for not acknowledging your $10 which I received. Thank you. I paid it all out to a dentist, so didn't get a very good time out of it.

We have been working very hard down here. Entirely too hard, in fact, and when a regular army colonel took charge of us yesterday it slowed up. Our routine has been 5:45 Revellie, feed horses, come back, get breakfast, drill 8 o'clock till 11, unhitch, groom, water. Mess at 12:30. In the afternoon we have dug ditches and loaded wood. All this is at a temperature of about 100° in the shade, or 105 degrees in the sun, or there isn't any shade within five miles of the camp. You can almost feel the sun hit you on the top of the head, and on all the heavy details you see men drop, thrash around a bit and then they bring the stretcher. However, they seem to be all right the next day. A few have died in the camp, but more as a result of sprees the night before than anything else. The nights, however, are very cool and delightful.

As for myself, I thrive on the heat. It never seems to give me the slightest trouble even when men are dropping around me. I have sweated off the last ounce of superfluous flesh and am beginning to take on some. I will be able to haul a gun around all by myself pretty soon.

The camp will be organized in a short time and the trench digging and plumbing will be over.

We are camped with about 12,000 troops on an elevated plateau, above and about four miles from the city. From every side you get a beautiful view of the country. The approaches to the camp are lined with mesquite trees—queer looking shrubbery from eight to ten feet high, shading nothing much but pear shaped cactus. Sunrise and sunset are wonderful. On the whole, I like the country very much.

I have no idea when we will get paid. I get $19 a month as a first class gunner—if I even get it. That is the reason I need cash. The government ration of corn beef, beans, crackers, bread and coffee—no butter or milk,—is an awful thing and an occasional meal in town is a great relief. The thing that bothers me most is the water. It comes out of the faucets, not warm, but actually hot. Of course you can't quench your thirst with hot water, so they put oat meal in it, which makes an awful mess which you hate to drink, but have to.

We eat our food in the blazing sun, as there is a rule that you can't eat in your tents. As a result, your only desire is to choke down what you have and get back to your tent and smoke—our only joy. I would like to have some money for an occasional cigar.

San Antonio is a very interesting place, but I have been in only once. It is a long way and the only way to get in and out is by auto. I have been in and out only once, as it comes rather high.

It looks, from the preparations, that we would be here at least six months. That is a trifle gloomy, but I am having a good time. So many funny things happen that we laugh from morning till night.

The trip out here wasn't half bad, even tho we did ride in ancient day coaches 3 to 2 seats, I spent most of my time on top of a box car, from which one gets a unique view of the surrounding country. I wish I could find pep to write an amusing letter, telling of the incidents that happen in camp, but it is too hot. I can only roll over and struggle weakly.

Occasionally some one gets bit by a scorpion. They fill him full of whiskey and let him rest for a few days and he is all right. They are not dangerous—only unpleasant. However, I haven't even seen one.[28]

I am sending two pictures taken in Springfield. The ladies are friends of Pat's who were very nice to me, giving me a party, automobile rides, etc. In the larger picture I am the wheel driver, the one next to the carriage. The two cannoneers on the front are just lifting the prop which holds up the pole as we start.

*With love*

LAW OFFICES
O'BRYAN, WAITE & ARNOLD
716 NEW YORK LIFE BLDG.
CHICAGO

EDWARD MACK O'BRYAN
RAYMOND WAITE
THURMAN W. ARNOLD

PHONE CENTRAL 2123

Dec. 24th, 1916

Dear Father:

Your Christmas check was much appreciated, though I am sorry I needed it ~~then~~ so much. $10 of it went for the earnest instruction in dancing, for which amusement I care but little. Still one cannot afford to be too different from one's fellow creatures.

No very rosy sunset closes the year with O'Bryan Waite and Arnold. Poverty still lurks in every corner. We made about $110 this month, but then we only made $51 in November ~~&~~ so that we show a substantial improvement.

Mama seems to think I want the insurance policy to borrow money on, but happily I have not spent all my money yet. I simply want it to keep with the rest of my papers.

## *To C.P. Arnold*

Chicago, Ill., Dec. 24, 1916

Dear Father:

Your Christmas check was much appreciated, though I am sorry I needed it so much. $10 of it went for the earnest instruction in dancing, for which amusement I care but little. Still one cannot afford to be too different from one's fellow creatures.

No very rosy sunset closes the year with O'Bryan, Waite and Arnold. Poverty still lurkes in every corner. We made about $110 this month, but then we only made $51 in November so that we show a substantial improvement.

Mama seems to think I want the insurance policy to borrow money on, but happily I have not spent all my money yet. I simply want it to keep with the rest of my papers.

I am perfectly enchanted with some of your poems. I suppose I must be partial, but there are one or two of them that I think are as beautiful as anything I ever read.

*With love*

P.S. I am going to spend Christmas Eve at the home of John Miller's father. They are having some sort of family party there. Christmas day I am going to spend with Ray Waite and on Christmas Night I am going out to Winnetka with Johnny Miller, Jr.

---

## *To Mrs. C.P. Arnold*

Chicago, Ill., Feb. 7, 1917

Dearest Mother:

I got the night shirts.
I got the night shirts.
I got the night shirts.

Thank you very much. They have been very comfortable these cold nights. I am sorry I did not speak of them before but I never happened to think of them until it was time to put them on and that was always too late to write.

Last night I had a rather funny time. A minister in some obscure corner of the city got hold of my name, somehow, thru the *Daily News*, I guess, and wanted me to come out and make a talk. I consented and went out last night. It was in the driving sleet, bitterly cold and the sidewalks were covered with ice. I finally struggled to the door of the church. The pastor was a kindly old man with only one arm. He welcomed me in and I found about twenty-five wet and bedraggled people who had braved the storm. (Was called away from this letter yesterday so I finish it now.) They opened the meeting with prayer and a hymn and then I delivered my somewhat facetious lecture. It seemed odd to be occupying the pulpit in a strange church on Sunday.

Harry was there looking tired and bored because Bessie had dragged him out of a cold Sunday evening. I spent the night with them.

*With much love*

P.S. Business has been picking up slightly this month and it looks as if we would show a small surplus over expenses.

---

## *To C.P. Arnold*

Chicago, Ill., March 26, 1917

Dear Father:

I got your letter and check for $66.17. I consider that I was somewhat overpaid for the work that I did in Laramie and Guernsey, however I am very glad to turn it in to the firm as my partners have been making all kinds of money during my absence. Altogether this month we will make all office expenses and take in about $125 apiece profit. Our gross income will be about $600. The bank in Iowa settled the case for $750.

Business for the future looks better than it ever did before. We have already fees lined up for next month to the amount of $350. We are very busy right now.

I congratulate you on your big verdict in the breach of promise case. It was a great victory whether you can sustain it or not. Next week sometime I will look up a little law on that instruction.

On Wednesday night they have the annual Princeton dinner at $4.00 per plate. I had decided not to go but I was called up and asked to make a humorous speech, which opportunity I accepted, tho I am half sorry I did. I have nothing whatever to talk about and am only supposed to be funny in a general sort of way, which is very hard to do. As yet I haven't an idea. They are having a couple of bright lights from the faculty to give all the heavy informative part of the program. However the opportunity of appearing in a position of prominence before the Princeton men of the city, many of whom are influential, is too good to be missed so I shall make a stab at it.

I have sent in my application for the Federal Reserve, and will be called up for examination soon. They have already called out some of the Illinois infantry and the military situation looks dark.

*With love*

---

*To C.P. Arnold*

Chicago, Ill., April 22, 1917

Dear Father:

I haven't been doing much else for the past month but studying military affairs, from one angle or another. I prepared for and passed a rather difficult examination on Field Artillery, and was recommended for a commission. Lately however much to my disgust they have let down all bars, and are admitting men to the officer's training camps which they are going to establish on the first of May, without any examination. They have also held up all commissions until the end of these training camps.

I felt a trifle disgusted with the officer's reserve for that reason, and also for the reason that no money has been appropriated for it. It looks as if we would have to pay our own expenses at the training camps, if we attend them. I just got a pamphlet to the effect that board at the camps would be fifty cents a day, and we would have to supply our own uniforms. I tried to get into the marine corps, but did not succeed in passing the physical examination. The physical examination is very severe indeed, and only about one man in ten gets by. My trouble is heart murmur after exercise, which surprised me very much because I have been examined physically quite a bit of late and no one ever mentioned it before. I understand that this is a slight defect, and may be functional or organic. If it is organic there is nothing that can be done. If it is functional, a month of diet and general sane living will get rid of it. I am going to have myself examined by a heart specialist and find out just which it is. If I can get into the Marines I consider that I would have more opportunities of advancement, better chances of seeing service, and a sure commission.

However it looks as if my choice lay in either staying with the militia where I am, or going in for the officer's training camp. In the militia I am a sergeant and would get thirty dollars a month, a clothing allowance, and all expenses. In the officer's training camps it would cost some money for a while, though I cannot believe that Congress will have the crust to leave them for very long to be supported at private expense. It is a disgrace that they should have to start that way. I am inclined to believe that I had better enroll for the training camp at Fort Sheridan, and at the end of three months my chances of getting a commission would be pretty good. Of course if I can get in the Marines I would do that, but my chances do not seem to be very good.

The finances of the firm are all right and business is pretty good, except that the war leaves all up in the air. We have, as you know, just signed a lease for another year which we had to sign or get out. Now Waite, after struggling with himself for about a month has decided that it is his duty to enlist, and nothing in the world can change when he once makes up his mind. That leaves Pat to support the whole thing all by himself. We have been making money for the last two months, but I do not feel that I can draw anything out, in view of the fact that Pat has the very heavy expense of this summer to meet with no one to help him. We have been trying to lease the office and take a smaller one, but the loop of Chicago is already about thirty-five percent over-built, and it is practically impossible to do this. We have succeeded however in leasing one of the offices for thirty-five dollars a month, which will be some help. It looks as if the whole thing would go to pot, though Pat may be able to keep it alive after a fashion.

I had hoped that I would be able to get along without drawing any more money, but after May first my income will stop, and I must buy a uniform and equipment. So if you will send me one hundred dollars I will be able to pay all the bills of this month and make a start on the training camp idea. At the end of the month I will have about one hundred dollars credit with the firm, but Ray and I have decided that it is not fair to Pat to draw it out. He may need it for office expenses later on.

We are moving out of our house on the first of May. The place cost us fifty dollars last month for room and breakfast, repairs and back bills. It looks like poor management on the part of George Lindblum, but there is nothing to do but pay it. I don't know just where I will live for the few days that I am in town after May first, but I probably can get a room somewhere.

*With much love*

---

## *To Mrs. C.P. Arnold*

Chicago, Ill., May 3, 1917

Dear Mother:

I just got a telegram from Carl that he was ordered to the camp at San Francisco. He says that he will be through here on Saturday. I look forward to seeing him as I have not seen him for over a year. I'm glad he's going into the thing as it seems to be about the only course of conduct for a young man of any spirit.

I suppose that the camp in California will be very pleasant, but all my friends will be at Fort Sheridan so that it will be very much better for me there. I expect to go there about the fifteenth of this month.

We have left our house on the first of May because the least expired. I was invited to stay at about four different places until the camp started but I preferred independence and a room about 12 blocks from the loop on Dearborn Street. Three of us have it, and it is not much of a place, but only costs $8 per week. I'm never there anyhow.

The house cost us about $50 a piece this month, due to breakage and back bills, aside from the expense of moving. This is irritating. I shipped all my books out to Cousin Betty's.

I am having my solid gold watch fixed up with a new monogram and I am going to send it to Papa. It will cost about $10 to do it but the watch is worth $75, and it should be put in running order.

Business is demoralized on account of the war and I can't do much because of the atmosphere of excitement. Ray Waite tried to enlist but was turned down on account of his eyes. He is very much disappointed, but his mother and sister are not.

I decided to get a specialist to examine my heart, as I did not want to go to the training camp and then get turned down later because of it. I selected a good one, thinking that the money would be well spent. He gave me a thorough examination and told me that I was perfectly sound. I asked him about smoking and he says that there is no reason why I should cut it out or change my habits in any way so far as my heart is considered. It is too late to apply for the marine corps now, however, because all the provisional lieutenancies are full.

The war is having a profound effect on all the younger men. It overshadows everything and takes all the zest out of every thing you do. It is impossible to look beyond it and lay plans for the future. Sometimes I think this is a great time to live in, and other times I don't. However we're in it anyway.

*With love*

---

## *To C.P. Arnold*

Chicago, Ill, May 7, 1917

Dear Father:

Carl has come and gone. I was very glad to see him, and tho he seems a bit young to have to go in the army, still I think it is the only thing for him to do.

I am leaving tomorrow to register at Fort Sheridan, but I do not know exactly when my active training starts. It will not be later than next week anyway. I expect to get my commission within the next month and then I may be ordered anywhere. I have been buying my outfit for the camp. It is rather expensive. No money has been appropriated for the camp as yet, and of course none will be for the coming months, if my past experience with the army is any criterion. If I can get hold of a commission however I will be self supporting and perhaps there may something develop out of the efforts to obtain $100 a month for the members of the training camps.

It is too bad that the sheep situation looks so bad, when there are so many other things.

I think your figure of speech on the hydrophobia of power is very striking and I will use it if I get a chance to make any more speeches just now.

*With love to everybody*

---

## *To Mrs. C.P. Arnold*

Ft. Sheridan, Ill., May 20, 1917

Dear Mother:

I have been at the training camp a week now. The work is not bad and not nearly so exhausting physically as the life on the border. We get very good food, and do not have to cook or wash dishes ourselves. Today is Sunday, which we have off, and I am in Chicago at the Waite's.

Our days are so full that I shall not attempt to write, except Sunday, but will get off a letter every week.

We get up at 5:15. Fall in at 5:30. 5:30 to 6:20–Wash and clean up barracks. 6:20 Breakfast. 7:00 to 12:00–Drill of various kinds. 12:00 to 1:00–Lunch. 1:00 to 4:00 P.M.–Drill or exercise etc. 4:00 to 5:00–Time off. Usually spent in study. 7:00 to 9:30–Study–Classes etc. 10:00–Bed.

I enclose a picture of the camp. Each line of four buildings represents a company of about 167 men. The first building to the right is the mess hall and kitchen. The next two are barracks. The last one, smaller than the rest, is the shower etc. We have electric lights and cold running water. We sleep on canvass cots, with mattress, two sheets, two blankets.

On the whole it is the height of luxury compared with our experience on the border, and the physical work nicely calculated to build us up without overstrain. But I don't know that I like it as well. There is such an air of deadly seriousness about the whole thing. Down at the border, life was one huge joke, and the army was the biggest joke of all. It was a great big ridiculous picnic. Here it is depressingly serious.

I have been acting Lieutenant of Company 12 for the last week, though the appointments are just temporary and the reserve officers are treated just like everyone else.

I don't care much for the infantry, which is all we are having for the first five weeks. Doubtless if they insist on having a war they have got to have infantry, but I will be glad when they start in on the artillery.

We had another physical exam the other day which I passed successfully and nothing said about heart murmur. Did I tell you that after my examination for the Marines I went to a specialist to find out just what was wrong with my heart and he said that there was nothing whatever wrong with it. This was a great blow to Cousin Bessie, who had looked upon the heart murmur as a divine proclamation of the evil of tobacco.

*With love*

---

## *To C.P. Arnold*

Chicago, Ill., July 22, 1917

Dear Father:

I spent the weekend with Waite at a cottage some friends of ours have up in Michigan, and am now waiting for the train back to Fort Sheridan.

The camp is getting to an end—only about a month more and I am hoping for a furlough at the end of that time. It's impossible to tell whether I will get one or not. The only fellows who are sure of one are those who will not get assignments to regiments, and I think I will miss that class.

The artillery work is very interesting though I never worked harder in my life. It is completely staggering the amount of technical knowledge a battery commander must have in the field today. All the old theories of speed without much accuracy have had to be discarded in Europe, because of the impossibility in war time of producing powder that will burn at a uniform rate. Corrections must now be made for different lots of powder, for temperature, and for barometric pressure, and when you are firing over the heads of your own troops and a mistake in one shot may cost the lives of fifty men, the responsibility is overwhelming. I have no desire for a Captaincy in the artillery, which I would have had a fair chance for had I stayed in the National Army. My hope is to get over to France which is the only place you can get real training in the science of Artillery, which they have developed to an extent that no other nation has equalled.

The English and American guns are unable to stand the constant firing that the French guns seem to survive. Their barrage fire is only 3 shots to the minute, compared with the French 5 or even 10 shots. And the odd thing about the French 75 mm. gun is that no nation can copy it. It has a system of recoil on the carriage by means of compressed air, while the British, American, and German guns have spring recoils. Germans have captured hundreds of French guns, taken them apart, and made others like them, only to find that they won't work.[29]

I haven't heard from Carl for a long time. I hope he applied for the aviation. It is the safest branch of the service, as shown by percentage of losses, and every day some new aspect of the terrible misery of the front line trenches is brought home to us.

However there is always a very good chance of the National Army never going over, or at least never getting into actual fighting. They will require about 3 months training in France, and it is my belief that the actual presence in France of a large American Army will end the war before they ever get up to the first line.

I am feeling very well indeed.

*With love to all*

---

## *To Mrs. C.P. Arnold*

New York, N.Y., August 30, 1917

Mother dear:

Just a line before I leave for Plattsburg. My sailing has been put off till the 8th of Sept.

I've been in a state of indecision as to whether to wire Frances to come and stay with the Calhouns for a few days.[30] Maybe I will.

*With love*

---

## *To C.P. Arnold*

Southampton, Eng., Oct. 4, 1917

Dear Father:

I have spent two days in England now, one in Liverpool, short night on the train, so crowded that we couldn't stretch out to sleep, and today in Southampton, very tired indeed. Tonight we go to France, and as the channel is very rough, and the trip 8 hours, and we have no staterooms, I expect to feel even worse tomorrow.

England seems scarcely recognizable to me. Everyone is in mourning, and a sort of grim unhappy determination hangs over the whole place. No regular trains run, railroad stations are deserted, and the hotels have an atmosphere of gloom. Everything in England begins and ends with the war, and the return of soldiers are a constant unhappy reminder of what it is costing. The convalescent hospitals here are by no means a pleasant sight.

America never can feel the war as England feels it now. It is too big. Never can America so exhaust her supply of young men as England has done, because there are not enough ships to get them all over.

They all seem to look to America to win the war, and they seem to leave none of the hope of peace that you hear of so much at home.

I hope you meet Frances sometime. It was wonderfully brave of her to come and meet me. She is a thoroughbred, a girl of proud and high spirit. She has courage and poise, and she has that indefinable grace of character and fineness, that makes her meet things and do things differently from most. You'll love her courage and her whimsical humor.

I must go to the boat now.

*With love*

---

*To Mrs. C.P. Arnold*

London, Dec. 2, 1917

Dear Mother:

Today came two letters, one from you mailed in Chicago on Nov. 5th, and one from Frances dated November 7th. Also a letter from Papa enclosed, which I was very glad to get because all of his letters to me have gone astray.

My carbuncle is about well now, which is a very great relief. I never had a more annoying thing in my life.

We had a wonderful dinner on Thanksgiving, which we had ordered weeks in advance—and eight of us, all from Ft. Sheridan gathered around the table at the hotel here. The censorship regulations are so strict about revealing names of places, but Frances writes that a couple of my letters were postmarked, so you know by this time where we are.

Next week we are going to give a Princeton dinner to Paul Van Dyke,[31] who is coming down from Paris. Papa will remember hearing him lecture in Princeton long before the war was ever thought of. (Those days at Princeton seem a long time away over here.) He is here in France helping out the Princeton men over here.

There go taps, and lights will go out in a minute.

*With love*

---

*To Mrs. C.P. Arnold*

London, Dec. 10, 1917

Dear Mother:

It's getting near Christmas time and you can tell it's not June around here, even without looking at the bare leafless trees and the white frost on the ground that crunches under our feet as we go out in the morning to the firing range. It's always dark when we start, and one's feet do get so very cold. I haven't heard from you since your letter written in Chicago just before you left. But I got a letter from Carl which he mailed to the London Bank, and a couple from you mailed there, just the other day. No doubt you have written me about Frances' finances, but I haven't gotten it, so please write again. I want her to get the income from my property, and to take care of the interest on my notes and pay my insurance herself. I would like to know that the matter was all fixed up. You know I lost my trunk with over $300 worth of stuff in it, most of which I have had to replace at great expense, so I have been able to send Frances only one month's salary, and I do want her to feel independent. So please write me about how the matters stand. I can't seem to get a word out of anybody on the subject.

Last Saturday night we had a big Princeton dinner. Paul Van Dyke came down from Paris, and Major General Menoher,[32] of the American Army, and a lot of French officers were there. I presided with some success. Sunday I spent with Paul Van Dyke. He gave a very eloquent talk on the war at the Y.M.C.A. I informed the French officers at the dinner that we had seen and marveled at their technical skill and ability, and that at first we could not understand how the Germans had withstood such a combination of courage, endurance, and efficiency. But exhaustive study had disclosed the reason. It was their barbarous custom of petit dejeuner, whose slender ration of chocolate and bread gave to every morning the tinge of the morning after. I assured them that if they would eat a good American breakfast in the morning they would scatter the Germans like chaff before the whirlwind.

If you should want to send anything please remember that the following are very welcome.

1. Cigars (Can't get good ones here.)
2. Heavy pajamas (Lost all I had.)
3. Woolen socks (Lost all I had.)
4. Milk Chocolate (Can't get it here.)
5. Smoking Tobacco (Terrible)

The School will be over on the 28th. Where we will go after that I have no idea.

Most of our time now is occupied with firing on the range, and we are busy as usual.

*With love*

P.S. I have a new address because they have now established an American Post Office here.

U.S. Post Office 718
Am. Exped. Forces
THURMAN W. ARNOLD, 1ST AT FA USA

*To C.P. Arnold*

South of Paris, Dec. 16, 1917

Dear Father:

Today I received from a Paris bank a letter which informs me that they have instructions to pay me $25. I suppose this is a Christmas present and that a letter is somewhere on the way. I appreciate very much and it will come in very handy as it strikes me at a time when I am very very broke. My equipment has cost me a great deal of money, and there seems little chance of getting anything for my lost trunk unless I take it up with the Court of Claims or with our beloved Congressman.

I sent Mama a lace something or other, which the vendor assured me was something very special and of a high order of merit. I hope that it has reached her over there. I haven't had any mail for a long time and am expecting a great load of it almost any day now.

School is about over, and we are all idly speculating on what they will do with us next. But not a glimmer of information comes from the dark mystery which surrounds the war office. There are rumors which place us all the way from the Russian to the Italian front, but they are of the defective verity that characterizes all rumors.

Yesterday we took a French Battery and had some drill in locating positions and establishing liason with the infantry and the observation post. We made a peculiar and remarkable mess of it. These things are not so easy as they seem. We have a rather unusual individual from one of the Southern Camps, who lives principally on alcohol in various forms. He was in good form yesterday, and lost the following articles—1 telephone, 1 reel of wire, 1 horse, saddle and bridle. He left the latter tied to a tree and came in by himself. The French are out hunting it, and our Southern friend is having an interview with the General.

The marks are being computed, and I am rather keenly disappointed to find that I am not one of the three recommended for battery commander out of our section. I had thought I would be, but you never can tell in the army.

Christmas is coming but we will only have one day vacation, and no leave after the school is over, thereby proving that the war is not such a joke as it is cracked up to be.[33]

If anybody has any intense desire to send me anything you might let the information seep out that pulverized coffee, condensed milk, sugar, sweet chocolate, and good cigars are not obtainable here for any price.

*With love*

---

*To Mrs. C.P. Arnold*

n.p., Jan. 10, 1918

Mother dear:

Today I got a package from Rev. Parasoe which is the only thing that has come thru. I haven't had any letters for three weeks, and am in a considerably heated state over the inexcusable handling of the mails over here. One has an even chance of getting a letter that has been sent, and that is all. The letters are sent to the wrong addresses about half the time and there they are lost. I've only had about eight letters from you since I have been over here and I know you write more than once a month. And only one letter from Papa. Then I've got none of the things you said you were sending. It seems that any post office system which loses half the mail it handles is inexcusable. There seems to be no improvement with time. I wish some decided protest would be made about it in America.

The note inside the Red Cross package sent by the Rev. Parasoe said that I was to give it to some boy who had not been remembered, I saw at once that the person referred to was myself, and at once appropriated its contents. It contained some of that elixir of life, tobacco, which is getting harder and harder to obtain over here. I will write a letter of thanks but it may never arrive, and you can thank him for me anyhow.

The work here is interesting, and would be pleasant if it were not so cold and muddy.[34] One sloshes around in the mud from morning till night. I did some firing yesterday, with deadly effect on some imaginary Germans. I suppose that those few words comprise about all I can tell of what I am doing. There is nothing very mysterious about my work however and the days pass quickly under the spell of the routine. I hope some of the cigars you spoke of sending come through, as I am dying for a good American weed to puff at. It would be preferable to much gold and fine raiment.

I wonder if Frances has visited you. I am very homesick for a letter from her, as I haven't had one since Christmas. When you write her please tell her to send me two pictures of herself, in separate packages, so done up that I can carry them around. If one is lost I may get the other. I have been writing for it ever since she came over, but she seems to ignore all requests, so I'm going to try to enfilade her by getting you to write. I'd also like to know about my money. What is she living on. Is she getting the income from my property. I sent her my October's pay but here it is January and I've heard nothing from it.

*With love*

*To Mr. and Mrs. C.P. Arnold*

n.p., March 4, 1918

Dear Mother and Father:

I'm afraid that I've been somewhat remiss in writing letters of late. There are two reasons. (1) I haven't been real warm or dry since I can remember. Mud and slush all the time, and no stoves. One can, of course go to bed, but one cannot write there. I haven't had my clothes off for weeks, and if you get a bath every two or three weeks you are lucky. But I digress. I was explaining why I didn't write. The second reason is Frances. She gets letters at all hazards, cold or wet, and when I have written her a long letter my hands are cold and I have to move around and when I get another chance she must be written to again. So you will have to glean news from her, till we are sent back from the front, and I get quarters where I can write.

For the past week, and until tomorrow, I have been in charge of a detachment of 14 officers, 14 privates—(orderlies), one non com.—(mess sergeant), and 29 horses—(1 apiece), at this little ruined village, about four miles behind the lines. We are getting instruction in the art of Artillery liason with the infantry—a pleasant enough job, except in time of attack. A liason officer is responsible to nobody and just wanders around the front line trenches to keep them in touch with the Artillery in the rear.

The school is instructed by a French Captain. He is very much bored with his job, and only instructs about two hours a day. The rest of the time we spend in waiting for meals, eating and sitting around and singing afterwards. And how we do eat. That is our principal occupation, and we do it as only men can do it who haven't had enough to eat for a month. Butter costs $1.20 per lb., Jam about 25 cents a bite, eggs 12 cents a piece—but hang the expense. We live on these articles, for Lord knows when we will see them again.

The only thing that is cheap and plentiful is champagne. We have it for supper, and some of the officers have it for breakfast and lunch too. However they have conducted themselves very well considering.

Personally I'm sick of it. (Champagne I mean) When it used to cost $5.00 a bottle I used to consider it very hot stuff. But I have learned that its only charm is in its former price, and when a quart of champagne costs less than a lb. of butter (butter is 7 fr. per lb. and champagne is 5 fr. a quart) I prefer the butter.

The last month has held many very interesting experiences. I have observed from the front line trenches, and seen the German trenches. I have passed along roads under shell fire, and seen the splinters drop a few feet ahead of me. I've been at the battery and watched dozens of airplane fights, and helped prepare barrages which we have fired. I've taken ammunition and supply trains up to the battery at night—and I've been in command of the supporting battery in rear of the lines. I've seen the candles bounced off the table by the force of the explosion from an air raid on a town almost half a mile away. Terrible things, these high explosive thin-walled air bombs. And for the past month every night I've been lulled to sleep by the booming of the big guns.

This war seems such an endless business. Both sides lodged in almost impregnable positions, shooting millions of dollars worth of ammunition, consuming incredible quantities of supplies, and accomplishing nothing—not even in a military way. Everyone seems so settled in the war. Seems normal method of existence almost. Except one gets so weary of the cold, the lack of civilized comforts, and the endless ruin everywhere.

It's almost incredible the ruin that the Germans have accomplished where they have withdrawn. What good was the endless labor of destroying these great stone buildings and leveling these endless walls? Such an aimless fury of destruction it seems.

I'm glad I don't have to live here after the war. I'm going to be completely domesticated when I get home and ever so content just to locate in one place and lead a comfortable sane existence.

I'm talking as if I'd been in the war six years instead of only one month. But it's the interminable prospect ahead that makes one very old in the service. Over here one can't find a glimmer of peace hope or peace talk. I'm always surprised when I get papers from home. However there is an end somewhere and home will be all the sweeter when I get back to it. And I'm coming back all right. You needn't worry about that. The danger is tremendously exaggerated, and estimates based on a few battles, particularly at the beginning of the war, are grossly misleading.

Frances wrote me a statement, and I notice that I am charged with $500 on Aug. 20th, as well as the $350 I drew when I was married. I lost drafts amounting to $200 I think, and payment was stopped on them. That money should still be in the bank. Will you please correct this in the statement. I am very pleased to get this straightened out, as I realize the tangled condition it was left in was entirely my fault. Please let me know about the drafts.

*With love*

*To C.P. Arnold*

n.p., March 14, 1918

Dear Father:

Just got a long Christmas letter from you written in Tacoma, a wonderful letter, which quite cheered me up. And I've had a perfect deluge of Christmas boxes, and best of all cigars. Got a box Mrs. Knight sent way back in October, a box that Mama sent with some sox and things, and three boxes that Frances sent. And it's one of the blessings of fate that they came when they did, because I was dying to smoke one, and very heavily indebted to one of my brother officers whose cigars I had been smoking for weeks.

And this very evening came a package from Mama with tobacco, night shirt, bouillon cubes, socks, etc., and a can of Washington coffee.

I'm on duty all night so you can figure out how pleasant it is to have coffee and bouillon and chocolate drop in out of the sky. I've got a cup of it in front of me to keep me awake, and am nibbling at the chocolate. I've had ten Christmas packages in the last week.

It's now just two A.M. I am sitting in the battery command post, dug into the side of a hill. The roof is composed of 6 feet of alternate layers of logs and sand bags which will stop anything smaller than 155 mm. shell. To my right a steep stairway leads down to a very small chamber 40 feet below the surface of the ground where we sleep. The air is very bad down there but it is absolutely bomb proof, and one is as safe there as he would be at home, from anything except gas. And safety against gas simply consists in having your mask always in reach. We have them hanging on us all day long, and sleep with them at night. The other day a stray shell lit on the roof of our dugout and blew out a hole 7 feet across and five feet deep, without even waking up an officer who was sleeping inside. So you have little need to worry about me here.

The whole thing is an abandoned German position. A German battery was here about 8 months ago, and the dugouts show their ceaseless labor and infinite care. It is a matter of months of labor for a hundred men to construct anything like this. And the best of it is that the place still looks like an abandoned position. You could wander all over it without seeing one of our guns, unless you ran into them, and the air photos show nothing at all. We have been busy for about a month, including Sundays, with picks and shovels and dynamite, and the Captain is quite proud of it. There is a French Battery near us that has been shelled frequently, and most of the shots fall on us. But if it were not for that I don't believe we would get anything.

Tonight has been a nerve-racking one. Orders came from Headquarters changing our barrage, just half an hour before the change went into effect.

Its quite a lot of work figuring out one of these barrages, when things like the powder lot, the weight of the shell, and the length of the fuse, the temperature, the barometric pressure, the speed of the wind, the altitude of your position all have to be figured in. And your barrage must always be ready. A lookout is posted waiting for the signal from the trenches, and if he gets it and the battery is not firing within one minute it may mean disaster for the infantry, and even if it makes no difference to the infantry, it certainly means disaster for the officer in charge. The barrage may not be called for for days and the signal may come the next minute.

I figured as fast as I could, and telephoned the data to the pieces. Then I checked up and found I had put it 50 meters to far to the right. The cold sweat formed on my forehead, and I nervously tore the receiver from the hook and rang the 1st piece. As always happens when you want it most, the phone wouldn't work. I rushed round to the pieces, seeing the signal go up in my mind every 30 seconds. When one of these barrages get started it is very difficult to change them, because the pieces are all separated, dug in the ground and covered, and connected only by muddy trenches, in which one is always tripping and falling down, particularly when there is any hurry. The noise makes it impossible to shout any commands. I got the change around, and went back and rechecked. Again the cold sweat. My figures showed I was shooting into a crest. Gosh what an awful feeling. But a moment later I found my mistake and saw the barrage was all right and I breathed again.

Its nervous work to figure these things in a hurry when a mistake of a few hundred meters will kill off a few of your own infantry.

Just now the German shells are bursting with great regularity on a road a few hundred meters away. They are trying to catch some supply train going to the front. All supplies have to come up at night, because the sky is dotted with Sausage balloons looking for them.

Yesterday the Captain told me that we had not fired our allowance of ammunition that week and I could use it up as I chose. I got in touch with the officer in the observing station and picked out a camp kitchen in a village across the lines, figured my data from the map and blazed away. What harm I did I don't know, but we probably bothered them some. Then the observer saw a working party on a hill, and we changed our deflection quickly and killed two of them, so he informed me over the telephone. (The observing station is in the front line, about a mile away.)

Such is life in a quiet sector. Not so bad, when it's dry and warm as it has been for the past week. But the last time I was up here, and the mud was ankle deep, and it was cold, and no fires possible because of the smoke and our feet were lumps of ice for 24 hours at a time, was a somewhat different story. I never was so glad to see the signs of Spring in my life.

Nobody really appreciates the difference between summer and winter unless he has to live out in the open thru them both.

The best part of the big guns is that you can always hear them coming about two seconds before they land, which gives you plenty of time to get out of the way if you are near a dugout or a shell hole—and you can't get more than ten feet away from a shell hole no matter how hard you try. This is a very famous part of the front that we are on, and the scene of some of the bitterest fighting of the war, and the whole place is just a series of holes. But when you first come up you will be standing talking and you will hear a long, indescribable whizz. It comes nearer and nearer, and finally you decide that its about on top of you, so you jump for shelter. Just as you jump you hear a boom, and everyone laughs. You look up, and away off in the sky, the winds are scattering a cloud of black smoke. Even as you look another ball appears, a moment later you hear another whizz, just like the first followed by a boom, and you realize that you have jumped out of the way for a shell which burst so far away that the smoke had almost cleared away before the sound reached you.

I visited the French Battery the other day, and found out that the best practice when you hear a shell coming is to pick out a good reliable Frenchman and keep him in the corner of your eye. If he is not disturbed you can keep your hands in your pockets, but if he jumps, you had better jump too.

When you are alone however, you might as well jump for everything you hear till you get the sounds classified. They say the Austrians have a gun of such muzzle velocity that you can't hear it coming. They call it the Whiz bang, which describes it. There doesn't seem to be any in this sector however.

At the beginning of the war, before the days of the deep dug outs and reinforced protection, these big shells carried heavy loses, but now thousands and thousands of them burst without hurting anybody.

The other night our barrage was called for, and I climbed up on the lookout. Thirty-two batteries were firing at once. Their flashes lit the horizon on every side, and the thunder and roar made the ground tremble. It was a stupendous spectacle. In front rockets were going up on all sides, and star shells, which illumined the terrain like great ark lamps.

Then in 15 minutes all was quiet except for the occasional shots you hear every minute or so, day and night.

Well, dawn will break in a little while, and I will get breakfast and go to bed for a few hours. I'm very tired, and very sleepy just now.

Have just received a flood of letters about my carbuncle. I created a wave of worry which extended from Chicago, thru Missouri, way out to Wyoming. I don't know what I said, but hereafter I shall be silent about my minor ailments.

I enclose some pictures, taken in the rear of the lines, in a village that had been shelled out of existence. It was far enough back so we didn't have to wear the heavy steel hat which is shown in the picture of my bunkie. We wear them all the time up here, and while they are a nuisance they are an absolute protection against fragments of shell. If they had had them at the beginning of the war, thousands of lives would have been saved.

Please send them on to Frances with a copy of this letter. I haven't the pep or the time to write another as long.

It's a stupendous struggle, this war. But it seems so fixed, so stationary. Progress seems impossible against the defenses they have nowadays.

However, *C'est la guerre,* (which phrase covers all troubles for the French.)

*With love*

---

## *To D.W. Cumming, Esq.*

Laramie, Wyo., Dec. 27, 1920

Dear Sir:

I went to Denver Thursday morning, December 24th, and found J.D. Clark,[35] General Counsel for the Midwest, in his office. I explained that I wanted to examine the Midwest title maps, so far as they were not confidential. He took me in and introduced me to the President of the Midwest, Mr. Blackmer,[36] who informed me that they had not kept title maps up to date for three years. They had however maps of some of the fields showing the titles up to the beginning of last year, and some of them later. They also had maps of the Midwest holdings in all of the fields. I was given a book of blue prints which they said contained everything that the Midwest had in the way of maps.

It appears that they are not attempting to make maps until the permits on the various fields have been granted. They have a large map of Salt Creek, with the numbers of all of the conflicting applications, but they asked me not to copy the application numbers, and told me that as soon as the leases were granted they would furnish me with a complete map of the holdings in the Salt Creek area. I therefore was not able to include Salt Creek in the maps which I am sending, but will be able to get one as soon as the leases are granted.

The book of maps which I was given was not at all complete as to titles, but contained full geological data on each field. I started to make notes of the geological data, when Clark stopped me and asked me to copy only the titles. I assured him that I would make no more notes on the geology, and therefore the maps I send are not complete in this respect.

Clark informed me that at any time I wanted any particular information on any field to write him and he would give it to me unless it was against the interest of the Midwest to do so.

McFadyen,[37] of the Ohio Oil Company wrote from Casper that he would have to refer my request for maps to the Vice President of the Company at Findlay, and would let me know within a week or so whether I could have blue prints of their maps. Inasmuch as the Midwest has no maps of the fields in which they are not interested, I would like very much to get the Ohio maps.

Under separate cover I am sending title map of the structure which Hay controls on the Wyoming-Utah line, south of Rock Springs. It is all government land except that which is noted on the map.

I saw John Hay[38] the other day, and he would like to know about when we expect to send a geologist to examine his structure. I told him that our geologist was on a vacation and that I would let him know after the first of the year. This will give you time to make a decision as to further investigation of this structure.

Clark informed me that there would be an opportunity for the National Exploration Company to make an offer to drill certain lands in Salt Creek which the Midwest could not handle under the leasing bill. He will let me know as soon as the leases on this land are granted. This is the same land that I wrote you about before which is controlled by a Syndicate of certain individuals.

I learn that A. Baker, State Land Commissioner, has been very industrious in collecting title maps of Wyoming structures, and in the near future I will run down to Cheyenne and get what information he has.

*Very truly yours*

---

Report

The structure is covered by four separate applications for prospecting permits, filed by Hay's friends, and there are nine hundred acres of title land in the center on which Hay has a lease. Hay has very able counsel, and therefore I do not doubt that his titles are all right.

I would therefore recommend that you send Allen to Rock Springs to look this structure over. There is a possibility of its being a very wonderful field, and Hay has not had the reputation of spending his money unless there was something rather substantial to spend it on. If you decided to send Allen, let me know, and I will get in touch with Hay. The weather conditions have been ideal down here for the past few weeks. If they continue good Hay will furnish a car for Allen, and send Hallett along to assist him and show him the ground. Hay will put a Pierce Arrow at their disposal, and will send a sheep wagon on the ground for them to live in for a day or so. Inasmuch as you have let Vernon and Carr go, if Allen thinks he needs any help carrying rods etc. I might arrange to go down with him.

Hay allowed me to look at his maps, but would not give me copies, and requested that I should not copy them, stating that he preferred to have our geologist approach the field without any preconceived notions. However I enclose a map drawn from memory which approximately covers the land in the structure. It is not accurate.

Please let me know as soon as possible your decision as to about four miles east of Rock Springs. I went over this structure in a car. It is very plainly visible. However there are gas wells on the south side, with 1800 lbs. pressure at the top of the Wall Creek, 2490 feet deep. Lowell, a geologist with Ralph Arnold of Salt Lake claims that there is a fault through the structure and the gas wells are on the wrong side. W.W. Hallett, Hay's geologist, would make no recommendation.

The second structure which Hay offers seems to be quite remarkable, if Hallett's maps are anyway near correct. It is just over the Wyoming line into Utah, about seventy miles south of Rock Springs by road. There is coal and water on the land. Hallett's map shows a close structure, cut off from the Uinta Mountains by a fault, and with a dip of from 4 to 62 degrees around the other sides. I enclose a plat showing the lands covered. According to the map, there is about 7000 to 8000 acres of possible productive land in the structure. The drilling will be 2500 to 3000 feet to the frontier.

The structure seems quite remarkable on paper. Hay told me that the Ohio were willing to go ahead and drill, but he is unwilling to give it all to any gas company. The Ohio are sending Harris, their geologist, to examine it in the near future, according to Hay. W.J. Hallett is quite enthusiastic about it, and he seems to be a very capable and rather conservative geologist. It is off the line of travel and practically no government work has been done on it since Powell's maps of the country in the '80s.

# II

# UNIVERSITY OF WEST VIRGINIA

# 1927 – 1930

---

## *To Philo Calhoun*

Morgantown, W. Va., Jan. 18, 1927

Dear Philo:

I am in receipt of two books for Christmas which I hereby acknowledge with thanks. As I stated some time ago your Christmas present consisted in the Seats for the P-Y-game which I procured with so much difficulty and not without a certain amount of perjury.

In regard to Christmas gifts, I have adopted a policy of acquiescence in a pleasant enough custom. I make it a rule never to look a Christmas gift in the mouth. For this reason you will never know, or even suspect, my feeling of horror when I found that with all the lovely things being printed, you selected a book by Bruce Barton. Gosh. Didn't you realize that he is the man who interviewed Coolidge? Didn't it occur to you that he wrote "The Man Nobody Knows," which every minister of my acquaintance has been trying to force me to read for the past two years? It stands to reason that the man must be soft somewhere or the evangelical clergy wouldn't fall for him. I gather from a cursory examination of the book that he is going to fix everything by having a priesthood composed of men whom everyone admires and loves. They will combine the qualities of the virile he man and the lonely aesthete. They will appreciate beautiful things, admire efficiency, and not be above sentiment. When he gets them ready he will turn them loose to worry and harass poor dubs like myself—because it is quite evident that neither Mr. Barton nor his contemplated priesthood has any use for what is generally termed by my charming wife as "shallow cynicism" or "half baked ideas."

God save us from such people. No doubt Mr. Barton's sane and conservative ideas whatever they are will have a soothing effect on many a troubled soul. But why should I have to read him?

The other book looks interesting, and starts out in a readable fashion.

It so happens that I seriously contemplate attending the justly celebrated Yale Law School this summer. I don't feel that I should loaf, and it may be that some ideas have been let loose in law school pedagogy since you and I went to Harvard. At any rate Yale looks interesting. It will also offer us an opportunity of getting together rather frequently because as I recall it, New Haven is about 20 miles only from Bridgeport.

Now what I want to find out is whether a cottage of some kind within striking distance from Yale Law School, furnished, can be obtained, and if so, for how much. Would it be too much trouble the next time you are in New Haven to inquire what the situation is from some real estate man? I don't suppose there is any such thing as little cottages on the beach within a half hour's drive. A preliminary report as to possibilities and prices would be appreciated.

*Affectionately yours*

---

## *To David C. Howard*[39]

Morgantown, W. Va., Dec. 20, 1927

Dear Dave:

Mr. Frank D. Saupp appears somewhat irritated at having your car around. He says that it destroys the reputation of his garage. An examination of the car will convince any reasonable man that you are doing a great wrong in foisting this disreputable wreck on him.

However it appears that, contrary to Dr. Hartley's statements, the man has a heart and he agreed to accept five dollars a month instead of ten. Your car is now going on its sixth month in the garage. He is particularly anxious that you take it away before nine months have elapsed. Why, he did not state. I enclose a copy of the letter which I sent to Doctor Saupp, with which I enclose your check, inasmuch as our final agreement was made over the telephone.

I have assured Dr. Saupp that you will do the following: Remove the car immediately or send on deposit of $25.00 to purchase wheels for same so that it can be removed under its own power. Dr. Saupp considers the storage of cars beneath his dignity, particularly such cars as this one, and it appears that the whole place is getting a black eye and a bad reputation among the profession.

In as much as I have been retained in this matter, I feel it is only fair that I should advise you that the best thing to do is to give away this car to some of your enemies as a Christmas present. Probably Dr. Trotter might like it. The most excruciating mental effort indulged in on my part without cessation since I got your letter has not revealed any way that the owner of this car can avoid more expense than the car is worth.

It appears that new licenses must be purchased shortly after the advent of the new year. In as much as I have been so successful in handling this commission as to the reduction of storage prices, may I be permitted to try my luck at persuading the state authorities to give you a license at half price? This would seem a difficult task to some, but I am sure that all I would have to do is to show them the car. Unless he has a heart of stone he will probably break into tears, and while under the influence of the emotion induced thereby I wouldn't be surprised if I couldn't get him to give you a license. Nor do I conceive it at all impossible to get gasoline at half price from the Salvation Army or other charitable institutions.

Please do not take anything I have said to mean that I am not enthusiastic over your car. I know how people feel about these things and I would not, for the world, hurt yours or Virginia's feelings. I think she must think the same of the car as you do.

I am rushing off to Wyoming to attend some odds and ends of jobs and then back to Chicago. Frances is going to New York. It rather breaks up my Christmas vacation but it can't be helped. One of my worst peeves is the fact that the *Law Quarterly* is not out. The proof has been in the hands of the Antioch Press since November first and we have been indulging in acrimonious letters, telephone calls and wires ever since. Nothing seems to move them. It is particularly irritating because we got the proof in unusually early and the net result is going to be that the *Quarterly* is going to come out unusually late. However we will not have them publish it again.

Wishing you and Virginia A Merry Christmas, Happy New Year and a Glorious Fourth of July, I remain

*Sincerely yours*

---

## *To John R. Turner*[40]

Morgantown, W. Va., May 29, 1928

Dear Doctor Turner:

In accordance with your suggestion I called on President Trotter[41] and asked to see the budget of the Law School. He did not show it to me but stated that everything was going in as it was last year. This, of course, is not what I want if it is possible to get anything more. Therefore I enclose a briefer list of recommendations which omits references to matters such as tuition of non-resident students included in my first draft sent you. I omit this since you apparently have a comprehensive plan in mind regarding tuition.

The thing I am most interested in is the summer work on research. As pointed out, only two men will be available for five weeks this summer, after summer school closes. The work which I intend having them do is annotating the work of the American Law Institute in their respective fields, with West Virginia cases, and an attempt to get this restatement of the law in some shape so that it will be useful for West Virginia lawyers and could be used as authority in a West Virginia court. A good start could be made on this in five weeks. It is a work which has not yet been done by any law school and there is an opportunity for at least two men doing a distinguished piece of work. It is a work which the American Law Institute is trying to get the law schools to do because if they do not it will be taken up by hack writers.

If at all possible I would like to have this work definitely planned for the summer after this. I have substituted it instead of a raise in salary, and therefore have increased the amount recommended. If it could be made a policy for the future everyone would be on their toes this year and we could get the Bar Association interested in the prospective problem to be worked on next summer.

Please understand that, while I am naturally enthusiastic about these recommendations, I also realize the problems you are up against and therefore all I ask is your respectful consideration. I know you are busy and therefore will suggest that you do not bother to answer this letter. I have perfect confidence that you will do what is possible for the Law School in respect to these recommendations, and I therefore do not want you to assume the burden of writing me further on the matter.

*Very truly yours*

---

## *To Leon Green*[42]

Morgantown, W. Va., Oct. 30, 1928

Dear Green:

I am delighted that you will be able to come here. Our second semester begins January 31st. Shortly after that will be the best time. In as much as you say it does not make any particular difference I will take a little further time to decide just what date to schedule these lectures and will write you further, or, better than that, talk it over with you in Chicago at the Association meeting.

While the remuneration which we are paying is inadequate, nevertheless I will give you a tip in part payment for your services which will be worth thousands of dollars if you handle it properly. The tip is this. Our friend Smith will be elected.

While it is probable that a court of equity would not approve the investment of trust funds in an election bet on Smith, nevertheless I believe that this is only another example of the blind conservatism of our courts. In West Virginia where not a cent of Smith money has been spent there is an undercurrent for Smith that is amazing. My secretary who lives in Pennsylvania informs me that the mining camps in Pennsylvania are going largely for Smith and that there is very little effort on the part of the mine owners to prevent this sentiment.

In West Virginia the mine owners, while all Republican, are not doing a thing to influence the miners for Hoover. Ordinarily they practically control the mine vote. This election they are allowing the miners to do as they please. I know of one instance where one of the superintendents got in considerable trouble by telling the negroes that they would have to vote for Hoover or lose their jobs. This would have been perfectly fair play in an ordinary election but in this instance he is in considerable trouble with his company. This is a rather extraordinary situation.

When the Republicians in West Virginia commence to get frightened in the face of the fact that not a Smith speaker has been in the state you may suspect that there is a very strong Smith undercurrent and that Hoover is not at all popular with his nominal supporters who could absolutely control the election if they wanted to.

I have advice from Wyoming that a similar undercurrent is taking place in that Republican stronghold. Neither Pennsylvania nor West Virginia are even counted in the doubtful column and if the same thing is happening in the doubtful states, as I have every reason to believe it is, Smith will certainly be elected.

I have always been a pessimist on elections heretofore but I have a strong hunch that the fourteen million new voters who are going to vote in this country are mostly for Smith. Regardless of how the election comes out however we will look for you sometime around about the first of February and I will talk to you about the date at Chicago, if you are going to be there. If not I will write you again.

*Very truly yours*

---

## *To Fred Nussbaum*[43]

Morgantown, W. Va., Feb. 2, 1929

Dear Fred:

I've just finished a letter to Margaret Brown—a hard task, and one that makes me feel very blue indeed. I tried to picture Doc Brown to her as I see him—a gallant figure with that self-assurance in the face of difficulties which would worry me to distraction which I would term courage—with a poetic strain as you term it—with a ready sympathy—with a gift for friendship. All in all a very lovely person and one whose equal we will not meet again. Loneliness often develops more affection than constant association—and I have been lonely here the past year. Out of the entire community I have not made one intimate friend. As a result I have become very sentimental indeed about my old friends in Laramie—of whom you, and Brown and the dear old Archdeacon[44] stand first. And Doc Brown's death has made a dull ache in my heart for a week—sometimes acute—at other times bothersome. Laramie—that we are always planning to return to soon—seems so different with him gone. That home party we had—that camping trip last summer at what do you call it glen—the night under the stars after our drunken party—the breakfast at Libby Lodge. The laughter—the criticism of everyone else. The lovely nonsense. Where will we find another Doc Brown? I stand with you Fred in silent memory of very, very happy times. What a nice thought it would be to believe that you and I and he would someday meet again somewhere—in hell maybe, because none of us could stand heaven. Look at any pleasant illusion too hard and it disappears and the unlovely reality left is no more real than the illusion was, but only less beautiful. And so I cling to my one last faith that there is something divine in that mystical human relationship known as friendship—and that if we are worthy of it, it will endure somehow beyond this life.

And now you and the Archdeacon are left—far away, but at least on this earth. We must meet somewhere again. I'm going to write to him tomorrow. In a world of promotion, hot air, and petty prudences—why can't we afford to be sentimental and make a few gestures toward the person we love, even if it costs money? We owe it to Doc Brown to meet and drink to his memory. If our relationship is an illusion it's better than most realities. If you get this letter in the cold hard daylight will you think that it's merely what Frances calls "mooning"—(a state of mind peculiarly obnoxious to her)? I hope not. I feel that need somehow of sitting with you and Balcom and drinking to the memory of dear old Doc Brown. And—maybe I'm getting old and imbalanced—but I can't help feeling that if we did somehow Doc would know. Is this what they call "wishful thinking" or "escape from reality?" I don't give a damn if it is. I choose to believe it, whether or no—nonsense or not—I'm writing to Balcom tomorrow—God bless him.

I'm glad you are working so hard. I have a feeling, amounting to a certainty, that in real mental ability you are the pick of the lot of us. Certainly you profoundly influenced my thinking, even tho your ideas underwent strange transformation in their passage thru my head. You gave me a new point of view.

As for me I have become a promoter. Scholarship does not seem particularly in my line. I'm too lazy. If you care to go to the law library and read the February number of the American Bar Association journal you will see a skit on what I am trying to do here. I'll be working by it in Yale this summer and we can meet this fall. I've got myself in a dangerous position with a lot of talk and nothing accomplished. There is much enthusiasm over the talk however. They raised my salary $1000 this year, instead of the $500 which was called for in my contract. The extra $500 was by private subscription among unknown members of the bar. Just why this curiously misguided charity I can't understand. Frances and I feel a bit uncomfortable. I don't know whether to consider myself like an orphan asylum or a community chest. There doesn't seem any way of giving it back however because I can't find out where it came from. I suspect that a crash is coming. Such enthusiasm goes in waves—and outside of a lot of talk, I don't seem actually to be accomplishing anything toward what I'm driving at.

Be sure to send me your new article as soon as it comes out. They probably won't have the publication in the damn library here. The new President is asking the legislature for $90,000 a year for the next two years to bring it into shape—but the legislature is unimpressed. He wants to establish a graduate school and is hot for research. There may be a chance here for you. I'll keep my ear to the ground and if there is anything doing I'll let you know.

I stop in order to write the Archdeacon an inquiry into the possibilities of our meeting for the purpose of making fitting tribute to the memory of old Doc Brown and renewing old ties. Give my love to Cecil. I close a bit sadly. The loveliest things in life somehow seem to pass so quickly— and the drudgery is with us always (Not an entirely new discovery I suspect.)

---

## *To Charles E. Clark* [45]

Morgantown, W. Va., Oct. 12, 1929

Dear Dean Clark:

You have asked me to write you concerning the possibilities which the summer session at Yale might offer in the development of legal investigation, which possibilities we have discussed at some length. I have a personal interest in the development of this kind of a summer session at Yale because it might be very useful to future plans for investigation of West Virginia problems which I am attempting to get under way.

### *Outline of General Plan*

I believe the future of law reform in this country is going to be greatly influenced by investigation work done by state and national law schools. Yale at present with its greater funds and opportunities appears to be taking the lead in such investigations among national law schools. If Yale wishes to make its work effective it must devise ways and means of getting its results to the law schools in the various states. State law schools cannot hope to duplicate that work but they can take advantage of it and bring it to the attention of their state bar associations. My hope therefore is that Yale will offer an opportunity in the summer time to members of the faculties of state law schools to work on particular problems of state importance, with the assistance of members of the Yale faculty. I believe that there is a great opportunity for the national law school which takes the lead in doing this kind of work in the summer time.

*Results of the cooperation between Yale and West Virginia last summer*

Yale has already tried this experiment with West Virginia and it has been an unqualified success. As you know, West Virginia Law School has made arrangements with the Bar Association by virtue of which the law school faculty acts as a research bureau, investigating problems which are of state-wide interest. The general scheme of liason between the State Bar Association and the Law School I have outlined in a short article published in the February issue of the *American Bar Association Journal.* Last summer we were engaged in making a report to the State Bar Association concerning pleading and practice in West Virginia. We spent much time at Yale and due to the advice and criticism we received there, rewrote our entire report. The advantages which West Virginia received from the assistance given by Yale in the summer may be summed up as follows:

(1) We felt more confidence in what we had done because of the critical examination which it had received.
(2) The fact that Yale gave a sort of quasi-endorsement to this report added greatly to its authority.
(3) We enjoyed our work much more because of the friendly contact with the Yale faculty and the interchange of ideas.

The advantages to Yale consisted in the fact that it received a great deal of favorable publicity in West Virginia and unquestionably extended the sphere of its influence in this state more effectively in this way than it could have by any other method. I attach hereto a few pages of clippings which are only collected at random. You already have other clippings of the same nature. Practically every paper in the state carried notices of the cooperative work and ideas but it occurs to me that one of the chief objects of any national law school should be to make its investigations of practical use in the various states. This has certainly been accomplished in West Virginia. Universities in the past have given a great deal of time and thought to advertising and to the various methods of spreading their spheres of influence. I can imagine no better way of doing this than by conducting this kind of work.

Of course your presence at the West Virginia Bar Association meeting was a great help and much of the publicity is due to that and to the statistical work which Yale is doing in West Virginia. Nevertheless these things are direct results of the work at Yale last summer. You had a concrete purpose in coming to West Virginia which would not have existed had we not had a report prepared under your direction to present to the Bar Association. A more effective way of spreading the results of any kind of legal investigation can scarcely be imagined. The statistical work now under way would not have been attempted if our faculty had not prepared this report at Yale.

West Virginia intends to investigate as many state problems in the future as is possible under the funds which the law school may obtain. Among these suggested are:

(1) Practice and procedure in West Virginia;
(2) The problem of automobile traffic regulation;
(3) The problem of water power regulation;
(4) The problem of interstate coal rates in West Virginia.

It is our hope, if Yale offers the opportunity in the future, for the faculty to do further work in New Haven during subsequent summers.

*Possibility of extending this kind of work to other schools*

Your decision on giving work of this kind must necessarily be influenced by the practical problem whether other law schools in addition to West Virginia will be interested. This is of course somewhat of a gamble. There are however the following indications that work of this kind is just beginning:

(1) The fact that bar associations are being stirred into activity by such publications as the *Journal of the American Judicature Society,* and are unable to accomplish anything concrete without reports laid before them by state law school faculties.
(2) The increasing popularity of the judicial council machine. Judicial councils which have lacked some paid organization for research work have been ineffective. The only answer to this need seems to be the state law school.
(3) The fact that already there are numerous members of other law schools who want to come to Yale in the summer time. Usually these men have nothing in particular they want to do. [It could be] suggested to them that they might become of real influence in their state by investigating more problems. I question if it is the degree of S.J.D. which brings them to Yale. It is probably the desire to become known to persons who have opportunities to recommend them to positions. They could acquire this advantage in this way,

and you would not be under the embarrassing necessity of refusing them degrees if their work was not satisfactory.

(4) The importance of legal investigation is in the air everywhere. Ambitious state law schools are casting about in every direction for some activity which is new and which will bring favorable publicity. If this kind of work is brought to the attention of some law school that wants to do something but doesn't quite know what it is to be, it might be gratefully adopted.

Finally, there is one consideration which makes this kind of work much less of a gamble than most projects. This is the fact that it will be known in advance just who is coming to do this kind of a summer school, how long they will be there, and just what they will do. Yale by some method which can be decided on, makes the offer to assist in legal investigation. If no one accepts the offer, there is obviously no contract, and the Yale faculty will have their summer free to do whatever it is their habit to do when not engaged in research. Personally I suspect that such a project would start from a small beginning and grow rapidly in importance. If this prediction however is incorrect the experiment would not cost anything in keeping numbers of you tied up for the summer.

I have the fear that so much advice given by one who knows very little about the problems of Yale may seem presumptuous. However I have two causes for offering it. First, that you have asked for my opinion, and second, that I am personally interested in Yale's doing work of this kind because West Virginia hopes to be one of the beneficiaries.

*Very truly yours*

---

## *To John R. Turner*

Morgantown, W. Va., Feb. 5, 1930

Dear Dr. Turner:

Confirming our telephone conversation I beg to report on the law regarding the rule suspending undergraduate students who marry while in college. There are a number of cases in which attempts have been made to compel college authorities to re-admit students whom they have suspended or to whom they refused admission on account of some rule. These cases run all the way from breaches of discipline to suspension on account of joining Greek letter fraternities. The statement of the rule of these cases is necessarily vague. The courts say that the authorities of a state college or high school may pass or enforce any reasonable rule or regulation.

The question in the cases, therefore, is always whether the particular rule invoked is reasonable. This allows a wide latitude for the courts if they desire to take it. Generally the courts will sustain the school authorities. However every now and then they do not do it. For example, most courts allow high school authorities to suspend a student who joins a Greek letter fraternity if such happens to be their rule. A few courts however say this rule is unreasonable and compel them to re-admit the student.

There is only one case on marriage of students. That is the case of *McLeod* v. *Trustees of Moss Point Public Schools,* a Mississippi case, found in 122 Southern 737. In that case the Trustees refused admission to a girl of fifteen years of age who was married but otherwise eligible under one of their rules. It was argued in support of the rule that such children were a bad influence on unmarried children, which seems, in view of experience, to be reasonable enough. The Court however indulged in the eulogy of marriage and gave as grounds to their decision the following remarkable statement: "The effect of marriage on the husband and wife is refining and elevating rather than demoralizing. Pupils associating in school with a child occupying such a relation it seems would be benefited instead of harmed" and more of the same kind of language.

It is quite obvious that there are many differences between this case and the case excluding students from college, one of the chief ones being that all children under sixteen years of age in Mississippi are compelled to go to school and this child was fifteen. However the courts seem to prefer to put it on the ground that marriage is a sacred institution.

I do not think that our court would take a similar view if it were presented to them, but of course it is impossible to give a certain answer. I further do not think that it would pay any student to bother with mandamus proceedings when there are other colleges open in the United States, but that again depends on the student.

I do not know whether the rule would operate as effectively if it applied only to marriages where one of the students was under age. If that were the case we would have the additional argument that our statute does not permit anyone under the age of twenty-one to marry without the consent of their parents. It could be then said that this rule was in accord with the policy of the statute, even though it went further than the statute and required notice to be given to the Dean of Men. However if the policy of the University would not be served by such a rule I believe that the chances are in favor of the court's sustaining the rule as it now stands.

I wish that I could state my conclusions more certainly but like most matters of this kind there can be no certainty until the court has actually spoken.

*Very truly yours*

---

*To Charles E. Clark*

Morgantown, W. Va., March 18, 1930

Dear Clark:

I feel very much flattered at your invitation to spend next year with you. Frankly I would like to avail myself of this opportunity. I tried to see President Turner yesterday before he left for Chicago but missed connections. He left last night and will be gone for about a week, so I have been unable to determine what his reaction would be toward giving me a leave until he returns.

The only other consideration which deters me in the slightest is a financial one. Unquestionably I will have to make some financial sacrifice to spend the year up there but I would like to get an idea of how much. I have two problems, (1) to dispose of a lease on a house here and (2) to ascertain how much a furnished apartment would cost in New Haven, because the expense of moving furniture would be prohibitive. My salary here is $7500, which I assume I would have to give up, unless the President would show more enthusiasm for my going than I expect him to. This, of course, cannot be ascertained until I see him. However I presume I can tell him in advance approximately what they ask for furnished apartments in New Haven. I could get along with a very average one. Someone has told me that furnished apartments there are very expensive. Would it be too much trouble for you to have Miss Hadley inquire of some forward-looking real estate agent and get an idea of how much I might reasonably spend to keep out of the rain?

I regret very much to introduce any sordid monetary note in the negotiations but my wife insists that we make out a tentative budget and know in advance about what it will cost us to accept your offer.

You do not indicate in your letter in how much of a hurry you are to know my decision. I assume however that you must know definitely within a reasonably short time. Therefore I will interview the President immediately upon his return and write you. In the meantime I would appreciate Miss Hadley writing me as to the cost of furnished apartments. If I come to Yale next summer I will have to operate on a rather careful budget, particularly if I am not able to sublease my house.

*Very truly yours*

---

*To Leon Green*

Morgantown, W. Va., April 12, 1930

Dear Green:

Thank you for the information over the long distance phone. It was rather unusual to call you up but as I told you it just so happens I am leaving for Yale to consider a man to take a one year's appointment in my place while I am visiting professor there. I thought I would be in a better position if I knew whether I was going to have one or two vacancies to fill. I am afraid Havinghurst[46] will accept the offer if made and I congratulate you on getting him. He is careful, accurate, hard-working and exceedingly intelligent. If I could conscientiously advise him to stay I would do anything in my power to keep him, but the trouble is I have so much confidence in your being able to do remarkable things at Northwestern that I am frank to say that I consider it a great opportunity for him.

If I ever get to Congress I am going to pass a law to the effect that law professors are fungible. In the event that any dean makes an offer to a professor in any other school the opposing dean may, at his option, substitute any other professor for the one selected, upon giving five days notice by registered mail and defraying all crating and shipping charges. In the event that the offering dean does not accept the professor tendered by the opposing dean the man shall be automatically transferred to the staff of the American Law Institute to work with Mr. Boston in attempting to restate the law of proximate cause. No human device has ever been discovered better adapted to keeping a man out of mischief than the task of annotating the Restatement of Laws.

I will see you in Washington in May and in the meantime hope to hear from you as to the substitute you are going to furnish me.

*Sincerely*

---

# III

# THE YALE LAW SCHOOL

## 1930 – 1936

---

*To John Roscoe Turner*

New Haven, Conn., Dec. 23, 1930

Dear President Turner:

It is with much regret that I have decided to resign from the Faculty of West Virginia. I have been about a month in making up my mind and have finally concluded that it is the only thing to do under the circumstances, which are as follows:

About a month ago an unforeseen vacancy occurred on the Yale Faculty. Dean Clark asked me to consider remaining here. This was a complete surprise as nothing of the sort had been contemplated when I first came here but the situation had altered meantime. The work will give me opportunity not only to teach but also to investigate procedure from a statistical point of view, with ample funds at my command, which would be impossible anywhere else.

I do not like the idea of giving up West Virginia as I have thoroughly enjoyed my associations there and am very appreciative of the consideration with which I have been treated. However, the salary which will be paid me here is so much larger than West Virginia can ever pay that I do not feel that in justice to my family I can very well decline the offer.

Unfortunately, I am not a man of any independent means and in view of the future expenses in the education of my children the matter of salary must loom up rather large in my decision.

I shall feel an obligation to assist you in finding a new Dean and I will come to Morgantown on the 4th of January to talk this matter over in more detail in order to see if I can be of any help to you. Meantime, I am not communicating the fact of my resignation to any one and will delay saying anything to any of the Faculty about it until I have seen you. I think that this may possibly avoid complications in deciding on the selection of someone to take my place. If the news gets about that I am not coming back the Faculty may be more or less upset over the selection of a Dean and half a dozen candidates will immediately bob up which would not help the situation any. I have several people in mind any one of whom would make a better Dean than myself.

Frankly, I do not think that it is disadvantageous to West Virginia to change Deans at this time. In many ways I have done everything to start certain projects and in doing so have made some enemies. A new man in carrying them on will not be handicapped by any ill-feeling that I have caused. The main body of the Faculty will not change insofar as the internal administration of the Law School is concerned and in the teaching and the curriculum, I think my absence will be scarcely noticed. So far as outside contacts are concerned, I think that a changing personnel at the head of the Law School will continually bring fresh enthusiasms to its aid and keep it more favorably known than if it continued under one man. The chief trouble with too many law schools in the Association today is that they have continued under the same leadership too long. I have been somewhat of an extremist in certain directions which has aroused a certain amount of resentment, evidenced by the fact that some of the recommendations in my report were voted on adversely at the last Bar Association meeting. A new man at this time can do more with them than I can.

I further believe that the general policy of retrenchment which probably will have to be followed in every state in these depressed times might be aided by the fact that I have in mind a man who probably can be obtained for less money than you were paying me. The man I am thinking of is Coates[47] of North Carolina. I came to West Virginia with the understanding that my salary would be $5000 the first year, $7000 the second, and $7500 the third. I believe that as a practical matter the ordinary man feels better with a salary scale that is increasing than if he had been paid the maximum at the start and gotten used to it. I therefore believe that it will be possible, in view of the opportunities which the deanship at West Virginia offers, to get a man at a less salary now by holding open hopes for the future.[48]

I will come to Morgantown on my way back from Chicago, and until I have seen you I will not disclose to anyone the fact that I have resigned. It is with great regret that I feel forced to leave West Virginia. I have been more than delighted with my work under you and will always feel the greatest appreciation for your consideration, expressed in so many ways.

*Sincerely yours*

---

## *To Roscoe Pound* [49]

New Haven, Conn., Jan. 23, 1931

Dear Dean Pound:

After thinking it over for a week since my delightful dinner and evening with you I have regretfully decided that I am not in a position to accept your very generous offer. Of course Dean Clark was gracious about it. He congratulated me on the recognition from my old school, and said of course he did not want my acceptance at Yale to influence my decision. He said however that while my remaining at Yale did not imply that I could not accept another position in the future, he did not think that he wanted me to stay if I had a definite obligation to leave at the end of another year. He wanted me to stay with the idea of becoming permanent unless after a year's trial I did not like the work. An acceptance of an offer now could mean that I would leave whether I liked it at Yale or not, and he naturally did not want me to remain under those conditions.

Under these circumstances I feel that I should decline. I am under a very great obligation to Dean Clark. He financed the work in West Virginia which gave me my first experience with the study of the trial courts. The opportunity which he offers me at Yale is to carry on the work with trial courts which [William] Douglas has been doing. It is adequately financed, and we will be able to determine just what can, and what cannot be done with statistics in this field. As you know, I have no very great faith in the revealing power of statistics, but I think that they may shed light upon certain predetermined problems, if the problem, and not the statistics are made the principle end of the study. If I leave Yale for Harvard at this time I would simply indicate that I am leaving a carefully planned project simply on account of the greater prestige which the Harvard Law School undoubtedly has, and doing it after a previous acceptance at Yale. The salary is the same and the opportunities are so nearly equal, that I am afraid that no other construction could be put upon it.

I cannot help having the feeling that declining an offer from Harvard is a good deal like refusing a position on the Supreme Court, as my friend Dave Howard wrote me yesterday. In the meantime I hope to be able to gain in experience and wisdom, so that if other opportunities arise in future, and I find that I do not fit into the Yale scheme I may be better able to take advantage of them.

May I say that the thought that I was capable of filling a place on your faculty will always fill me with pride. May I congratulate you on building a faculty which includes so many diverse points of view, just as your library contains so many different kinds of books. As for yourself, a rather significant incident came to my attention while reviewing Mr. Jerome Frank's book. You know that Frank attacks you as a conservative, though he is forced to admit that you are the best of the lot. Adler, in his counterattack on Frank in the *Columbia Law Review* puts you in his catalogue of radicals. If there is a higher tribute than being put in opposite camps by two able extremists, I do not know what it is.

I am unable to refrain from remarking how much I would like one of your photographs, and thus reminding you of your promise to send me one, if you have any available.

*With the best regards and most sincere appreciation*

---

## *To Wilson Clough*

New Haven, Conn., March 17, 1931

Dear Clough:

I was never more pleased with anything in my life than your appreciative comment on my review. Your description of the review is exactly what I hoped that the review was, put exactly as I would like to have expressed it. I have read it over and over again, and compared it to the review, wondering vaguely if what you said could really be true.

Your remarks on the state of the civilization in English Departments discourages me, because I recognize its truth. I have met intelligent persons who taught English but they always seemed to be in subordinate positions. The thick headedness at the top is always a new surprise. I suppose that the law, for all its medievalism is always refreshed by contact with actual situations, and the problems are very real and very fascinating—all the more so because the logical parade which accompanies (but does not determine) their solution is so inevitable. I am engaged here in a study of the American Trial Court, with busy little persons collecting statistics in all parts of the country, and equally busy ones counting them on huge machines here at Yale. All I have to do is to get a bright idea which I will proceed to prove with them. Statistics are a lot like judicial opinions. They can be used to prove all sorts of results just as logical arguments deduced from doctrine can be used. However, at present they give the freedom which any break with tradition can give.

I have had an exciting time the last three months. I fell in love with the Yale Law School—wanted desperately to stay, but did not even dream that I was competent to permanently associate myself with the group here. I was weighing in my mind whether I could afford to take an assistant or associate professorship if they offered it. I was therefore completely dumbfounded when they offered me one of their sacred full professorships at a salary of $8,000. I jumped at it like a hungry dog. About a week later Roscoe Pound telegraphed me from Washington to meet him in New York. He gave me a grand dinner at the Century Club, and offered me a professorship at Harvard at $10,000 with promised raises to $12,000. The idea was that I should take charge of their new project for the Study of the Trial Court which is what I am going to do at Yale. Harvard seems to feel a lack in comparison with Yale in this kind of thing. I know nothing about what should be done, and started to ask a few questions. This lead to the astronishing discovery that Pound didn't have the faintest idea as to what it was all about, but was quite sure that I knew just what should be done. I let it go at that. I could think of nothing more apt than Manuel in *Figures of Earth*,[50] with his white feather. Some one had presented me with a white feather, and I just couldn't convince them that it was just an ordinary feather, no matter how much I talked. (I'll admit that I didn't try very hard to convince them .)

When I reported this offer to the Yale group they were obviously impressed, and immediately met Harvard's offer so far as salary is concerned. Against the advice of all my friends I decided to stay at Yale, because I think there is vastly more freedom here than at Harvard. Now I sit here as a permanent officer of a great institution, with one of the ten or twelve best salaries in the entire place—and I am as completely at a loss to understand just how it happened as if I had suddenly been made king of England. Other people here, over whose heads I have been put, seem so much more competent, so much more learned.

The moral to all that is that the two most important things in life are contacts and luck. And now as to your situation. I have always felt very sincerely that the quality of your mind was superior to mine. If I could have written the poem which appeared in the *Literary Digest*,[51] I would feel much prouder of it than anything I have ever done. You have two handicaps: (1) You are a graduate of the University of Colorado. This does not put you in with the same crowd that my Harvard and Princeton associations give me. (2) You do not have this here now Ph.D. With an ordinary luck you ought to pull out from under both of them. I will be in a position here to get you one of these Sterling Fellowships *I think* (of course one never knows). I had dinner last night with Tucker Brook and Young of the English department, and while I thought Young was not highly original—I was quite struck with Tucker Brook. I suspect that he and I will get to be friends, because I think he liked me also. It appears that the two of them alternate as the heads of the graduate English Department. So you can file that away for future reference. I have the feeling that if you could ever get on here for a year you would make an impression. You seem to me to be so infinitely superior to most of the people whom they have hanging around.

Well anyhow—keep your fingers crossed—meet everybody you can—with the idea that if you ever happen to run across someone in the English Department anywhere with a point of view similar to mine they will grab you, just as I appear to have been grabbed by people who are sympathetic to my way of thinking. And it will all happen in an instant.

The Kahn something or other which runs a $5,000 fellowship for travel around the world asked me to recommend some one from the West. I sent in your name, and my brother's. I wonder if anything comes of that. Up to date my letters on your behalf have been singularly devoid of results, but now that I can write them on more impressive stationary they may go further.

*Best regards to Mrs. Clough and the little cluffs*

---

## *To Mr. and Mrs. C.P. Arnold*

New Haven, Conn., March 29, 1931

Dear Mother and Father:

Did Frances tell you that we had bought a house. It is a nice large place, without much lot, but very comfortable inside. On the outside it looks quite respectable, though not particularly beautiful. We will take a picture of it and send it to you when we get our camera from West Virginia. There is a central hall, with some kind of a living room on each side. Upstairs it has four bedrooms and two baths, one of the bedrooms being very large and comfortable. On the third floor there is a maid's room and bath. We got it for $16,000 in various kinds of papers which I signed. No cash passed hands, excepting that the attorneys told the seller to give me $3.11 for adjustment of the taxes. The reason of course is that the University loans me $12,800 at four and one half percent, which is paid to the seller. This is repaid in installments of $128 a month and amortizes in about fifteen years. This money makes it a great deal cheaper to buy than to rent for under one hundred and fifty to seventy-five dollars, and none of these places are as nice as the one we are moving into.

I got a letter from Glenn Frank, President of the University of Wisconsin,[52] urging on me the opportunities which the deanship of that school offers. He writes a very attractive letter, extremely informal, and not in the nature of the ordinary letter which that peculiar type of animal known as a college president usually writes. I rather liked it. He does not mention salary but asks me to give him my ideas on that and on what cooperation the University can offer me if I will only come out there and fill them with new ideas about legal education. Of course I was tremendously flattered. However I shall not consider it. The last dean got nine thousand dollars, (he died two years ago and they have been looking for his successor ever since) but even if they gave me ten thousand, the work of the deanship would be very distracting and would interfere with the reorganization of legal materials on the trial court, which will probably not amount to anything—but I think I will take a chance on being able to do something worth while on this line, rather than another job where I will have lots of speeches to make and contacts with everybody in the world to keep up. I have been very happy here this year, and do not miss the speech making and general dashing about which accompanies the dean's office a bit. In fact I feel tremendously relieved to be rid of it. Wisconsin has been flirting around with me for about a year, and I was convinced that a definite offer was in the offing, but I don't see any particular point in getting back into a state university. However big the buildings, a state university will always be dependent on the legislature for its funds, and there can be no development comparable with Yale. I'll get a big kick out of turning it down however.

I had a perfectly grand time last night, at the annual banquet of the *Yale Law Journal.* They asked me to be toastmaster, much to my surprise, and I spent a terrible nervous two days worrying about it. The speakers were President Angell of Yale, Elihu Root, Jr., the head of Root, Buckner & Clark, one of the largest law firms in the world, which employs about one hundred lawyers and occupies four floors of one of the office buildings on Broadway, Harold Laski, of London who was secretary to the round table conference between India and England, whose writings on this and that are quite famous, and who refused a peerage offered by the King about two years ago, and the incoming and outgoing editors in chief of the *Law Journal.* I felt very grand sitting with Angell on my right, and Elihu Root on my left, with the other fixtures removed a couple of seats down the table, though I can't say I really enjoyed it until it was all over. I had a lot of stuff thought up which I thought was very clever, but I kept having sinking doubts as to whether it wouldn't seem flat in comparison with the others. I haven't the faintest idea of what they had to eat, or whether I ate it. However when I once got to my feet my nervousness vanished, and I think I got by fairly well. There was enough heavy artillery on the program so that I decided to confine myself to plain nonsense which I had made up myself, without having to resort to stories. I started out by explaining the relative unimportance of the principle speakers to the toastmaster, going back into the history of toastmasters which was all made up, and ending with a proposal that principle speakers at banquets be abolished. Thereafter I treated each speaker as an interruption to the continuity of my discourse. It really went over very well indeed—and it was a trifle different because I roasted everybody, and didn't say a single nice thing about any speaker. Of course the speakers were so well known that the usual introduction saying what great people they were would have been entirely superfluous. By treating them as annoying interruptions to the grand entertainment that I had to offer if only they had not been on the program I think I gave them some real novelty. I'll bet that none of them ever got introduced that way before. My slogan was "Anybody can make speeches, and unfortunately always does." I introduced Laski as an internationally distinguished man as myself, but what with a large family to support and the various other things that kept crowding on my attention, I had never gotten around to it—and when all was said and done I couldn't see any particular point in being one. It doesn't seem to sound very funny when reduced to writing, but it seemed to go over in great shape, which is the main thing. There were about a hundred people at the banquet, from all over the East.

Well, its time to go to bed now, so I must close. I enclose a program. The speeches, Laski's in particular, were quite brilliant but it would take too long to go into them.

*Lots of love*

---

## *To Glenn Frank*

New Haven, Conn., April 18, 1931

Dear President Frank:

Since your long-distance call of last week, I have given the matter of the deanship of the Law School of the University of Wisconsin a great deal of thought, and have finally reached the conclusion that it would be impossible for me to accept within so short a time after having accepted a professorship at Yale. I hope that my delay in making the decision has not inconvenienced you. I was unable to make up my mind right away because the offer did tempt me very much indeed, even before I realized that the salary would be so generous. Under your leadership I consider it one of the major opportunities in the Law School world today and will certainly congratulate the fortunate individual whom you finally select.

In my own case, however, I have just started some very extensive and interesting work on the activities of the Trial Court which I do not think that I should leave within such a short time after I have undertaken them. I look forward with pleasure to meeting you sometime and expressing in person my appreciation of your confidence in me. With very best regards, I remain

*Sincerely yours*

---

## *To Arthur L. Goodhart, Esq.* [53]

New Haven, Conn., March 12, 1932

Dear Professor Goodhart:

I produce with triumph documentary proof that my review of your book has not misled readers into dismissing your arguments as curtly as I did. In the last issue of the *Columbia Law Review* on p. 393 (Vol. 32) Professor McLaughlin of Harvard has the following footnote:

> "See A.L. Goodhart, Essays in Jurisprudence and the Common Law. Mr. Goodhart's rationalization of this phenomenon has been criticised with more wit than balance. See a Book Review by Thurman Arnold in (1931) 41 Yale L.J.: 318. Reforms achieved chiefly by way of legislation render stare decisis more tolerable rather than negative its existence in England."

All of which leads me into the desire of further explaining my review and expressing my appreciation of your gracious letter concerning the misquotation. I do not know whether I can do this briefly or not. I tried to do it at some length, and my letter began to assume the proportions of a leading article without its intelligibility. Pressure of other work led me to lay it aside and when I reread the letter I tore it up. Hence my delay in not replying to your last letter inviting me to contribute to the *Law Quarterly Review.*

May I say at the outset that I think your rationalization is beyond attack once one admits certain assumptions. It goes beyond any other attempt to reduce stare decisis to a formula, and is really a very beautiful thing of its kind. Its introduction into this country as a method of judicial logic I would regard as unfortunate for the reason that it *really does* lay down a logical scheme which can be followed. The reason for this is expressed in the paradox that courts in this country, because they are actually trying to decide the main run of cases by the principles of stare decisis, must have a very loose expression of that doctrine. In England, where the appellate courts need speak only on occasion, they may have a more symetrical system of logic without interfering with the operation of the court as an institution for settling disputes. Your various methods of keeping questions away from appellate courts permit on the one hand great freedom in the trial court in deciding cases, and greater logical strictness in appellate courts. Logical strictness can be obtained only at the expense of ignoring matters which properly should be taken into account in the ordinary case.

I doubt if this is very clear, so I will try an illustration. My picture of the function of "substantive law" insofar as that word applies to general principles and processes of thought, is that it consists of an ideal of impartiality and uniformity. (I am not referring to "substantive law" insofar as it consists of definite directions such as the requirement of three incorporators to obtain a certificate, etc., etc.) This ideal justifies the existence of an independent judiciary. The appellate court opinion is the concrete expression of that ideal. The trial court may take its general attitude from that expression of the ideal, but it must be given freedom in detail.

I would therefore justify your rationalization of stare decisis, and even your caveat about the collection of records by law librarians, on the ground that it permitted (given the procedural system which did not demand constant interference by appellate courts) an expression of the ideal of impartiality and logical uniformity without which our courts would begin to appear more like "bureaus." I would not justify it, however, as an accurate description of what the courts are actually doing.

May we compare the decision of an appellate tribunal to a play, which is well acted, and which is accomplishing its purpose in moving the audience. To some in the audience the lines convey great moral lessons; to others definite directions which they think will help them in future situations which may be similar; to others it may only be great art. Most of the audience will swing from one of these positions to the other. A realist who bobs up constantly calling the attention of the audience to the fact that it is only a play, will spoil the performance, and should properly be ejected. The judges are the actors, and they have no business leaning over the footlights, and explaining in an aside that it is only a theatrical performance. However, I would place the scholars in the position of directors and critics. They should, in this function, not concern themselves with the fundamental truth of the lines, or they will ruin the play by insisting on Hamlet's soliloquy in a piece by Shaw on the ground that it expresses a fundamental unchanging principle. They derive certain dramatic effects, and the lines should be judged by their utility in expressing the ideals that the performance aims to get across the footlights. The litigant had no place in the drama staged by the appellate courts, because they are concerned, not with him, but the audience. He finances the play, but that is all. (My figure is not perfect here. However, the appellate court is more concerned with general expression of ideals and principles than the particular outcome of the litigation.)

If you will grant that the function of your appellate courts are even remotely expressed by the above illustration, I will grant that in the *English* play your rationalization of stare decisis may be good practical stage direction and that my criticism of it without pointing out this possibility is entirely unfair. On the other hand in America, where I suspect much of our trouble comes in treating stare decisis as a method of *deciding cases*, and not as a method of classifying ideals (I use this term because "principles" has so many meanings, and I am referring to those principles which determine general attitudes, such as contracts, torts, etc.) your stage directions would be very bad. (I have thrown this stuff into an article in the next *Harvard Law Review*.)

All this can be read into your book, and your very acute analysis justified in this way. I believe that we both dislike "Muristic realists." My own objections to them is that they think that some day we will "grow up" and will no longer feel the need of drama and ritual and ideals which can only be taken on faith. I do not believe that I would want this to happen. Just how far apart are we anyhow? My general attitude toward courts and substantive law is generally criticised as "cynical," but I do not intend it to be so. Drama and even melodrama are to me very effective instrumentation controlling human emotions and conduct.

I am willing to admit in any event that "dividing them by the number of opinions" is simply a meaningless wise crack. In the future I shall not attempt to be funny in discussing serious books. It is too easy a substitute for thoughtful discussion.

I hope that all the above has not bored you. I write it on the express condition that I shall not expect an answer to this letter unless the mood happens to strike you. Nothing is more annoying than invitations to argument by correspondence which I occasionally get and sometimes feel compelled to reply to. I have been put in that position so often that I want to make this clear.

We were delighted with Hanbury. [Walton] Hamilton and I will not rest content until we have procured him an invitation as visiting Professor. The budget this year is a bit thin, but times may get better, and if so we intend to start a movement toward inducing him to come over. He saved me hours of work on a brief article on martial law and I was very much impressed both with his analysis and also with his ease in shifting from a discussion of doctrine to a consideration of the courts as institutions. If you see him give him my regards and tell him that the article is finished and sent in, due to his assistance.

I will be delighted to submit an article for the *Law Quarterly Review* some time later if you will feel perfectly free to return it if it does not happen to suit your readers.

*Sincerely yours*

*To Carl Arnold*

New Haven, Conn., May 20, 1932

Dear Carl:

I answer your letter in haste because of its air mail stamp. I read over McGuire's recommendations and am rather skeptical about them for two reasons.

First, I rather doubt McGuire's judgment and I certainly have no confidence in Pound's. Very likely I reflect the bias of Frankfurter, Powell and Landis who are my best friends at Harvard but, be that as it may I am rather impressed with the fact that the young men that they have been taking on in the past two or three years at Harvard have been very colorless people—all of good grades in school—but as uninteresting a lot as you would care to pick up.[54] Reed Powell says this is because of the two factions on the faculty, the conservative faction being the stronger one. In any event I am not struck with their picking ability.

Second, we have been fighting for about six months in this faculty on the proposition of adding an additional instructor. Finally someone suggested that we look the Harvard bunch over. We got a list of their recommendations up there and curiously enough in their recommendations to us they did not include a single one of the men whom they had recommended to you. (We ended by taking one of our own men.) I suspect this indicates that they might be giving you a list of second choices.

Monday night Frankfurter, Powell and Landis are coming down to spend the night at my house in return for a visit which Roger Foster and I made up there spring vacation. I will ask them about this list. I have great confidence in their judgment and if they either do not like any of these men or do not know the men, I would be a little skeptical about them.

Harno's man Kurgis, I think, is very good indeed. Incidentally at the last faculty meeting we voted to offer him a teaching fellowship on Dean Clark's recommendation so that if you make him an offer you will have that to compete with. I happen to know the other two people, that Harno speaks of, personally. Heilman is a nice fellow—he got a raw deal at Kansas—and I like him. He has ability and you would be making no serious mistake in taking him. He is not, however, particularly popular with the students as a teacher and has a general slouchy appearance and will not impress people. With your peculiar needs of someone with an attractive personality I would question Heilman on these grounds alone. Anyone who knows him will like him but he will not go well in a crowd.

Payne is a total loss. Don't take him under any circumstances. He got a low C at Yale years ago and got in the teaching profession against our recommendation. He has been a white elephant on our hands ever since. Everybody feels awfully sorry for him because he has been on the verge of starvation for the last five years. Mississippi is unquestionably the place for him. He has a nice appearance and a good selling personality, but he is as dumb as an ox.

I have talked a little more around the faculty about Farley. Sturges has the same opinion of him that I have. Nelles concurs with me. Dorothy Thomas with whom he is taking statistical work thinks he is nice but a trifle dumb. I think that this is due to the fact that he is not interested in the course. Hamilton thinks he is a real spark but prefers Kenan' although he says that you would be making no mistake with Farley in view of your conditions.

Kenan is by all odds, in my opinion, the ablest man among our graduate students and I think you could get him for a few thousand. $2,700 would be enough for Farley. However, Kenan's ability consists in being able to dive in to a piece of work and make an excellent job out of it. His personality may possibly be a little aggressive. He has made a couple of enemies on the Yale faculty which is the only thing which prevents our taking him on here. I believe that if I were you I would take Farley at $2,700 rather than Kenan at $3,000 in spite of the fact that Kenan can write a better law review article than Farley. I say this because I am so certain that you will like Farley's personality and that he will fit into the bar association situation and be of real assistance there.

I really believe he is your best bet. If you can hold off I will write you next Tuesday the reactions of Frankfurter, Landis and Powell to the Harvard list. If you are interested in the Harvard list I would be glad to interview any of them for you. I would never pick anybody without somebody you know interviewing him. It is too dangerous.

*With best regards*

---

## *To Felix Frankfurter* [55]

New Haven, Conn., June 9, 1932

Dear Felix:

Charlie brought up a paper on Dickinson's[56] book which he said you had sent for comment. I have finished reading it a moment ago. It seems to me that the writer has done this for someone with whom he has talked the matter over. There is a certain verbal shorthand—a jump from one idea to another, which makes it difficult reading to turn to when one has not been thinking about the subject. I have a feeling that he may have ideas which I do not get—and I sympathize with him if this is so because I recall in my struggles to write my last article I would take the manuscript in to Harry Shulman who would tell me that he did not understand what

I was talking about. Hamilton would always understand, but this was not a fair test because I kept talking it over with him. In any event the paper is hard to read. However, unless my thinking about it clears up rapidly while this letter is being written, this letter will be just as hard to understand.

I wonder if the following restatement of the writer's position is fair: Administrative bodies are held in check by (1) our conception of a supremacy of law (which is found in the courts) (2) by the legislature (3) by ideals held by the administrative tribunals themselves. The last two seem to him to be sufficient to take care of the situations with which administrative tribunals deal. Courts cannot review administrative tribunals effectively unless they abandon their ordinary judicial technique. Therefore either administrative finality is indicated, or review by a higher administrative tribunal. The ideal of Supremacy of Law, insofar as it applies to *modern* as opposed to medieval times can better be expressed in this way than by a philosophy which requires "Judicial Review."

In other words, the Supreme Court of the United States and the Supreme Courts of the various states can jolly well keep their hands off rate matters and such like things, and here is a philosophy which will justify it in the very terms of the older conception that there is such a thing as "Supremacy of Law."

I agree that this is so. If one needs a philosophy to justify one administrative tribunal sitting over another, or a philosophy to justify administrative finality, the one in this paper is sufficient. But why bother with such a dilemma or even admit that they knew nothing about taxation. Constitutional law would totter on its throne.

When priesthood admits that the laity can preach sermons and baptize babies the church gets in a bad way.

But, argues your writer—at least they could let go of rates. Maybe they could—but if they do it must not be on the theory that somebody else can administer the sacrament of Supremacy of Law. It had better be by using loose terms which put discretion into the commission. It is astonishing how difficult it seems to be for an appellate tribunal to reverse for abuse of discretion—by the cases, and how easy for the misinterpretation of a rule.

However my opinion as we go to press is that if Brandeis says "administrative finality" the rest of the court will always answer "jurisdictional facts."

I would prefer to say "Of course courts must review." However what they review is a mere question of appellate procedure. The best appellate procedure is a discretionary review, based on whether the parties got a fair hearing. My guess is that such a formula would cut down court interference in administrative tribunals much more than any philosophy which attempted to deny their fundamental *right* to see that any and all times the "Law" was "Supreme."

I know perfectly well this is not clear. But blue books call. To make my point clear requires an article which I have in contemplation. Therefore take this hash for what it is worth. And the next time you write me, tell me why it is such a slow and laborious process to get even a simple idea on paper *rapidly*, and in intelligible form. *You* can do it. What is your secret process anyhow?

*Sincerely*

---

## *To Felix Frankfurter*

New Haven, Conn., June 14, 1932

Dear Felix:

How are naive persons like Wes Sturges and myself ever going to see through your devious ways? So what you were actually doing when you sent the note which provoked such painful thought was to boost Freund[57] for our faculty. It was not a case of being so anxious to get my opinion on Dickinson's administrative law notions that you could not get to your blue books till you had it! Well I'll be canned! All that effort wasted. Gosh. Well anyhow, remember that you have got to be frank and open with us Yale boys. We belong to the battle axe school of legal thought, and you must draw diagrams, and accompany them with pointers and shouts in the future.

Now that the issue is before me for the first time I will say that I like your new candidate. His paper is full of clever writing, and has as many ideas to the square inch as anything I have seen recently. I wish we had known of him before we appointed Tweedy, and I'll pass the paper around to persons here who will appreciate it. Maybe something may come of it.

As to your letter on the trial court, I am frankly disturbed at what I have done. I thought that even at Harvard *some* of the faculty realized that cases had a habit of being started in courts of first instance (sometimes referred to under that revolutionary phrase "trial courts," which is being discarded around here because of its Bolshevistic connotations). The notion that *Crowell* vs. *Benson* was really an instance where the appellate courts were reviewing the decision of a body of judges which for want of a better name I will refer to as a commission, and that therefore the word "appellate review" of the findings of that commission might in some remote way be descriptive, is of course a more difficult one to grasp. Even the Chief Justice seems to have thought that what he was really doing was putting that dangerous dragon "bureaucracy" in its place and reinstating "the supremacy of law." Nevertheless I was not aware that this notion could be hailed as a "discovery." I also recognized that most persons assumed for the purpose of dialectics that all cases were tried on stipulated statements of fact, or made up as *test* cases in order to get rulings from appellate courts as to what the "law" was. But I never thought that this was more than a convenient assumption—or that the idea that *most* cases were brought by persons who wanted to win that particular case would have shocked even Mr. Maitland.

And yet I suddenly wake up to find that I have made a "discovery" which completely ruins both Maitland and even perhaps Pound. (Though in the case of the latter I am sure I can find something which he has said which lets him out.)

If my idea that appellate courts review the decisions of trial courts (I beg your pardon—I mean courts of first instance) is going to reduce the appellate court to a mere footnote, by all means let us suppress the news before the public hears of it. In general appellate courts have a most convenient way of forgetting all about the particular case which they are reviewing, and if by calling their attention to it we destroy Maitland, by all means let us keep quiet.

I have therefore prepared the following questions and answers for my course next year.

Q. Professor, do please tell us how cases arise in Supreme Courts.

A. They are brought there upon stipulated statements of fact by persons who want to hear the Court lecture on the law. They are divided into two classes (1) important cases and (2) unimportant cases. The first class are the cases where the court is not deciding the case before it but other cases which it has thought up in its own head, or where it is directing those cases which it has thought up in its own head, or where it is directing those who will never read its opinions how to act. The second class, commonly known as the unimportant cases, are designed to support the West Publishing Company and you will find them in footnotes headed by the word "Accord."

Q. But Professor, might not an unimportant case be important to a litigant and might we not spend a little time studying the—

A. Get out of here you Bolshevick. You are dislocating the center of the sum total of the legal order.

. . . . . . . . . . . . . . . . . . . . . . . . .

Now that the disorder has quieted down, are there any more questions?

Q. Why do we study procedure, Professor?

A. (loud voice) IN ORDER THAT WE MAY KNOW THE METHOD BY WHICH SUBSTANTIVE LAW QUESTIONS ARE BROUGHT UP TO THE APPELLATE COURTS.

Q. Do all cases arise as test cases Professor?

A. No, not all. Many of them are based on records before the Supreme Court.

Q. How do the records get to the Supreme Court?

A. They are laid on its doorstep by the Stork. No one has ever discovered just where the Stork gets them.

Q. But I thought that the Stork brought *babies,* Professor.

A. They still think so at Harvard. But here, in our course on family law, we study that wonderful book by Mrs. Stopes, (whom we have recently appointed a research associate to this faculty), called *Married Love.* And when you study it you will discover how much more important it is for married people to know what she teaches than it is for them to be familiar with the traditional course on domestic relations.

Well, I'm just throwing this in temporarily until I get started on my paper—which you are going to have to criticise before I publish it.

*Sincerely*

---

## *To Frank P. Kenan*[58]

New Haven, Conn., Nov. 7, 1932

Dear Frank:

I am certainly ashamed of myself for not answering your letter. I have missed you every minute of the time since you left. In fact I never missed anybody more in my life. I have actually had to get down to work on these darn statistics myself with the net result that I got out about 200 pages. I then went in and intimated to the Dean that I thought the whole thing was pretty much the bunk and we had been kidding ourselves. This created a terrible amount of conversation and argument. Then a committee went over about 200 pages of junk which I had written on the statistics based almost entirely on your figures and they all said it had too many conclusions in it. Now I have got to rewrite the whole thing cutting out the conclusions which makes it look more like your figures than ever, only more of them. I am beginning to get an idea of the Hell which you must have gone through so patiently during the entire last year. I have made up my mind to one thing, however, as a result of this study and that is this: I have no particular objections to statistics but I personally am no statistician. When this study is finished I am going to let someone else do the counting. In any event the thing will eventually get done I suppose and will appear published by the American Law Institute. They will probably sell a lot of copies because I can't see how anyone can fail to be interested in these lovely, lovely figures.

How do you feel about statistics now? Do you believe in counting or don't you believe in counting? Do you prefer counting to arguments? Do you prefer counting to prayer? What are your favorite numbers? Do you like decimals better than fractions? What is your favorite percent? Do you have any preference as to counting? Personally I prefer to count telephone poles to trees because telephone poles occur at more regular intervals. I am told that really good statisticians prefer to count trees because they are harder to count.

I wonder if you would do a little counting for me out West? I don't care what you count so long as you count something and send me the totals. You did a grand job of these figures and its a shame to have you lose your knack at it. Try counting 150 jobs before you go to bed every night just to keep your hand in, and then send me the totals for the week. I am sure we can do something with them. When this Federal Study is done we will be running short of numbers around Yale and we must rely on our loyal alumni to keep us supplied with them. We want big numbers.

Best regards to your wife and my congratulations to you that you went through what you did last year and are still sane—or are you? Drop me a line when you can and I will answer it probably within a month or so from the time I get it.

*Sincerely yours*

P.S. This man Hicks that you recommended, I think is going to do a good job. I can't tell yet, but he looks very promising.

Thank you very much for your organ study. Send me everything that you can get your hands on with tables in it. I am getting so I don't like to read anything else.

---

## *To Stuart Chase*[59]

New Haven, Conn., Jan. 24, 1933

Dear Mr. Chase:

I hasten to write you to remedy any defects which may have existed in my technique of salesmanship last night.

The whole group is very anxious to form such association with you as may be possible. We have a distinct feeling that you can contribute more than any person outside of Yale of whom we have any knowledge. Your pamphlet on technocracy, for example, represents the kind of thinking to which we want to become more accustomed and also the kind of presentation which we would like to learn. May I, therefore, try to answer possible objections which may arise in your mind to hinder accepting.

(1) Regular attendance at Yale at stated periods is a hope and not a requirement. Our hope would be that we would make you want to come as often as your other engagements would permit. However, you need not feel bound to any visitorial program if you accept the invitation. Almost any attention which you could give us would be satisfactory.

(2) We do not wish to pin you down to any specific assignment of work. I thought we might start out with a general classification of human affairs with a general definition of aims which would accomplish two purposes. [1] It would limit the discussion of any given topic and [2] it would give a sort of unity to different things which different members of the group might be doing. The point of view of the group is so similar that I think that it will be entirely possible to develop a certain unified objective.

(3) We have a tremendous mine of energy in our best students which only needs a little direction. I know of several who would be delighted to work with you on any project in which you found interest. Such work as this could be done by correspondence as well as by visits, and it would be our hope that you would find students' work of real use to you. As far as the students here are concerned, assistance in any investigation you would undertake would be the very kind of "legal" training we would be interested in developing.

In other words, I am trying to make the acceptance of this thing appear to involve only those obligations which your own interest might create. I am trying to show it will involve no preferred demands upon your time whatever.

So far as ends and purposes are concerned we can always have the hope that we may be able to influence actual legislation. But we can have the complete certainty that we have made a step in breaking down those hard and fast categories which separate law in action from law in books, and governmental theory from politics. In such a task we all feel that we do not know of anyone who can quite fill your place.

If this letter does not induce you to sign on the dotted line, please indicate to me some other type of argumentative technique to which you would be susceptible.

With best regards from myself and the psychocrats.

*Sincerely yours*

P.S. I note from your Technocracy pamphlet that you require a chaser of psychology and anthropology with your energy economics. Isn't it possible that we can mix that chaser here?

## *To Bruce Bromley*[60]

New Haven, Conn., Feb. 14, 1933

Dear Mr. Bromley:

I presume I had better put in writing in more detail the general idea of the Research Associateship which we are very anxious to have you accept.

The Yale Law School has established a classification of Research Associates with the rank of full professor to be given to men of distinction in the legal profession who are sufficiently interested in legal education to desire to assist in making it a study of operations of institutions rather than Appellate Court doctrine. The purpose is to give us contact with the situations which arise in business affairs and offices.

The Research Associate is given a small honorarium sufficient to cover expenses. At this time I am unable to say whether it will be $300 or $400. The obligations of the Research Associate are necessarily of rather loose and indefinite character. A somewhat artificial standard is set of one hour a week. However, we recognize that regularity in attendance is impossible for anyone in practice and therefore the time can be arranged to suit the convenience of the Associate. The time is so arranged that Sunday would be as convenient as any other day, and the Associate may also spend a couple of days here at any time. Groups will be arranged to meet informally so that regular attendance will not be required. We also understand that pressure of business might require prolonged absence and therefore the obligation simply means an understanding that the Associate will come as often as he can.

The Research Associates for this year were Jerome Frank, of Chadbourne, Stanchfield & Levy, Edson Sunderland of the University of Michigan, and Mr. Bates, Assistant Dean of the Harvard Business School. For next year we are planning on yourself, Mr. Stuart Chase, Mr. George Soule, Editor of the *New Republic,* Mr. Jerome Frank, and some lawyer interested in taxation who has not yet been agreed upon.

The Distinguished Visitors Suite in the Sterling Law Quadrangle will be available without charge to both the Associates and their wives. This, we hope, will create stimulating and interesting weekends because several of the Associates will probably be here together.

The field in which we want you to work is, of course, the law from the point of view of the litigant. The material to be discussed will arise out of your trial experience and such records in your office as are not absolutely confidential. Formal lectures are not contemplated, but instead the analysis of trial situations on which the students can prepare in advance. So much for the benefits to the Yale Law School.

It is hoped that the Research Associate may derive some profit due to the fact that we have a great deal of unutilized energy in the student body which can be directed along the lines of assistance with the Associate in any particular project whether of reform or any intellectual interest which may appeal to him. This notion of publication by research associates however, is one which involves no obligation but merely a possible appeal.

It is hoped that Research Associates may be interested in some of the more general economic problems to be discussed with persons like Stuart Chase and George Soule. Rogers, the author of *America Weighs Her Gold*, and Sapir the distinguished anthropologist, and Robinson the psychologist are also much interested in the operation of legal institutions from their own points of view. I hope that you can accept our invitation along these very loose and flexible obligations and that we can count on you for next year commencing in the Fall. If this is possible I can have some conferences with you this Spring and during the Summer when we can better organize these somewhat nebulous ideas.

*Sincerely yours*

---

## *To Felix Frankfurter*

New Haven, Conn., Feb. 23, 1933

Dear Felix:

Your suggestion as to a round robin letter is, I believe, better than the form in which I originally planned the assault on the Governor.[61] However, I just received a letter from the Governor in the same mail as yours in which he thanks me for bolstering him up with eastern support and says the matter has been concluded by giving the University a small additional sum. I had a number of people, both from Yale and Princeton, write him and it seems to have helped. I don't know how large the addition recommended by the Ways and Means Committee is going to be, but apparently it is something. Therefore, no more letters are needed at this time.

What do you think about the statistical report on the Federal Courts? My own personal opinion is that it shows two things. (1) That statistical studies should be an incident in a general observational study which would be of great help in determining how much detail it is advisable to go after. I have labored long and earnestly in writing this draft, in fact have completely rewritten it at least once. Much of the material in it is unquestionably useless. Some of it is interesting. Nevertheless I feel that it is worth while because the limitation of this type of study is one of the things that had to be proven. We have made the most elaborate purely objective study of the courts which, I think, has ever been made, and it shows, among other things, that there is no particular object in counting anything until you have an idea what you want the information for.

It also shows that the census type of investigation should confine itself to totals involving less detail. For example, we are unable to get much interesting data out of the Attorney General's figures because they cover a long period of time. The three years we selected are approximately the same in general social conditions and there is not the opportunity for comparison which a sudden break like the depression or the war might have offered us. Therefore, in the future a very simple and not detailed set of figures should be kept by the Attorney General. We have already submitted a set of forms to him and the final chapter awaits his comments on them.

The conclusions of the report, it seems to me, should not materially differ from the conclusions drawn in my article in the *American Bar Association Journal* on the progress report. In other words, the picture given is that of a smoothly running system depending on guilty plea technique for its operation. Most of the pleading reforms now contemplated are therefore based on that point and the attention should be directed towards removing the guilty plea technique from natural criminal cases. Only by doing so can we ever achieve the combination of civil and criminal liability of the continental law.

These conclusions are not included in the report. Of course the one concerning the limitation of the statistical method is one which some of the people with whom I am working do not share. I personally suspect that frankness on this is desirable even though it includes the admission that the work is too detailed. The answer is that the statisticians would not have believed it until it had been tried out.

Do you mind keeping this letter strictly confidential, because as you have often told me, one must stick with his gang, and I do not wish to appear to be disloyal to the work in criticising its limitations. I would like, however, your advice as to whether this frank criticism is justified, and whether it should go into the conclusions.

*Sincerely yours*

---

## *To Harrison C. Dale* [62]

New Haven, Conn., March 17, 1933

Dear Dale:

The three most intelligent letters we have gotten so far on our farm loan plan have been yours, Charles A. Miller, President of the Reconstruction Finance Corporation, and Mordecai Ezekiel, Financial Adviser to the Secretary of Agriculture. All three of you seem to think along the same general lines. Ezekiel seems to think there is a possibility of using some of the ideas in the ensuing discussion in Congress and he has given us a list of other people to write to. He and Miller have been sitting in on all the conferences over the present farm bill and seem to regard the present bill as something which is all right to start with but not a final piece of legislation. In the meantime our correspondence has grown by leaps and bounds with all sorts of people all over the country and the Dean is wondering whether this is "law" or not. We assure him it is.

Regarding your own criticisms: (1) Your historical criticism I have turned over to Wallace Notstein of the History Department. Certainly I agree with you that the best solution would be to develop a happy and content peasantry. However, I doubt whether this is possible in our present cultural pattern. Just as soon as you get a bunch of Russians on farms they are sent to public school and then they become manufacturers instead of farmers when they go back. There is a big trend back to farms in Ohio, according to Mr. Notstein and that simply means more of a farm problem. I don't believe you will ever get a definite status of farmers as you have in the past with the radio, newspaper, and public school stirring them up all the time. I am somewhat copying the ideas of Max Handman of the University of Michigan, whom you may know, who happened to be here a few weeks ago. He was interested in developing the implication of what he called our "pecuniary culture." In any event, the only answer to your historical argument is that history will not repeat itself. However, this is hardly a point in issue between us if you look at the plan of emergency legislation.

(2) Unquestionably your criticism is sound about the dealing with unmortgaged farms. It may be politically impossible to do this by penalties. However, our credit stabilizing scheme would fit in just as well with the system of basis as it would with penalty. Personally, I am inclined to think that the present bill of leasing surplus land is even more impractical than our attempt at taxing it.

(3) I imagine that the states will be very glad to get government bonds for their farm loans. However, I have no data on this situation, nor does any seem to be immediately available.

(4) The administrative problems you point out regarding non-basic commodities do offer administrative difficulties. To attempt to regulate all kinds of produce is very dangerous. Walton Hamilton puts it this way: "I am convinced that your scheme for limitation of production will not work. I am also convinced that any scheme which does not attempt to limit production will work even worse." Under these circumstances, we figure that the next five or six years will see one emergency piece of legislation after another.

I wish we had thought about your final point; i.e., about the Secretary of Agriculture. Ezekiel, who is Financial Adviser to the Secretary of Agriculture, has written us the same thing. I believe we under-estimated the popularity of this department and its power in the farm situation. I do not think it will be content to take a back seat.

*Sincerely yours*

---

## *To Carl Arnold*

New Haven, Conn., March 20, 1933

Dear Carl:

I guess that we can get Maxwell in without the summer work. You are probably right that there are some nitwits around the place, but nevertheless we attempt to exercise supervision for advanced credit. Incidentally, I am interested in your statement about someone who had a Master degree from Yale not amounting to much. I am going to use it before the faculty because I always opposed granting these Master degrees. They indicate that a man has done graduate work here and failed, and such degrees should certainly not be tolerated. So I think you can assume that we can do something for Maxwell.

I hope the Law School gets along all right. These are certainly hard times. We were all comforted by an announcement from Harvard that under no circumstances will they cut salaries. This means, I suspect, that Yale will not get a cut either because they could not bear to get a horse laugh from Harvard.

Thank you for distributing the farm relief bill. The question as to how we are going to determine the fair value is the most frequently raised objection that we have to meet. The answer, however, is easy. Values of lands are appraised as they always have been at the best guess of the appraisers. There never has been, or never will be any other method. The fact that it cannot be formulated is just that much more in its favor. The scheme is in effect putting mortgaged farms through a composition in bankruptcy.

Your second objection that we are more interested in capital than we are in farmers is also frequently made. The answer is that purchasing power in this country depends upon the credit structure. The reason that the West is flat on its back is that there is eight billion dollars in frozen assets represented by farm mortgages. If these can be transferred into government obligations, there are several advantages: (1) The release of this enormous purchasing power, or a large percent of it; (2) the rehabilitation of the western banks, because under the recent banking bill they can obtain lawful money on government obligations; (3) there will be no interest charge accumulating on the part of the government as in the case of ordinary governmental loans; (4) it will not break the bond market because non-liquid assets are issued to purchase bonds.

The effect on the farm of restoring this purchasing power should be obvious. Most people are for currency inflation without realizing that our money today is entirely credit money. I will not discuss it more in detail because Sturges and I have about 300 letters from all parts of the country to take care of somehow. We have sold Harvey Rogers[63] who wrote *America Weighs Her Gold* and he is going to have a conference with Wallace on the scheme. He is tremendously interested in the credit stabilizing aspect which is the main part of the plan.

Our other chief backer is Miller, President of the Reconstruction Finance Corporation. We are going to Washington this week and will take it up with Borah and Norris. We are going to try to get our names off of it as soon as possible and dress it up so that it will appear to be some senator's idea.

*With best regards*

---

## *To Sheridan Downey* [64]

New Haven, Conn., March 26, 1934

Dear Sheridan:

I enjoyed your letter to Upton Sinclair very much and think it is an excellent piece of work. I intended to get George Soule[65] interested in your campaign the last time he was down. I hope you are going over in your gubernatorial contest although I cannot imagine how anyone with any ideas could get elected to anything in California. The difference between California and Connecticut, in my mind, is that in Connecticut there are a lot of intelligent people who never get elected to anything because they don't like to elect intelligent people to office in Connecticut. In California there are practically no intelligent people and therefore they cannot get elected to office, not only because the voters do not like them but also because there aren't any. Thus, there are two reasons why intelligent people are not elected in California and only one in Connecticut. However, I am tremendously interested in your getting by.

I gave George Soule of the *New Republic* a long talk about you and he said he would do something about it in his columns. Your letter will be a reminder to jog him up a bit. However, George is going pretty sour on the New Deal because he is such a born critic, also he doesn't like to write about any situation without sending a man out to look the ground over. Therefore, I am getting a little discouraged with the publicity I promised you.

Of course I was gratified about the Nebbia case because I had written a brief in it. However, I had very little question about how the case was coming out so therefore it was not a surprise.

I enclose an article on economic theory which I suspect is too objective for any political purposes. Also I am sending your letter to Jerome Frank,[66] General Counsel of the Agricultural Adjustment Administration, asking him to call it to the attention of the people in the department. Tugwell is now in Puerto Rico.

My reaction to the present situation is that times in terms of industrial activity are going to get better all over the world, somewhat slowly. I make this prediction based on a pure hunch. I do not think it makes very much difference what the government does about it, provided they are not stiff necked and will move gradually to the left. It is for this very reason that I think it is so important that a few people with decent humanitarian ideas are elected to office in the next year or so. You can have just as much industrial activity under Hitler as you can under anybody else, but it makes a lot of difference in the distribution of the national power and income.

*Sincerely yours*

---

*To Sam Bass Warner*[67]

New Haven, Conn., April 26, 1934

Dear Sam:

Thanks for your very understanding letter. Of course the two articles are based on exactly the same idea. Their only merit consists in the theory that if you adopt a psychological, or if you like an anthropological, point of view you can understand the system you are studying better. The point of view does, of course, not lead you to correct conclusions. It only prevents you from stating irrelevancies. If you once understand that human behavior is symbolic then you cease to look for the reality behind the symbols. You judge the symbols as good or bad on the basis of whether they lead to the type of society you like. You do not cling to them on general principles when they are leading in the wrong direction.

Therefore, if you think that the Supreme Court by clinging to a strategic position which an unplanned petition in judicial review gives them it is in a better position to take pot shots at experimental legislation without endangering their prestige, I can see that the position is entirely arguable.

As far as my article[68] was concerned I was not particularly interested in the conclusion but rather in the method of approach.

I distrust, however, your conclusion of the present political situation. In times of change I would rather trust the legislature than the court and would prefer to force the court[69] into a position of immediate approval so that the government can experiment. There is a lot of evidence that we are in the same position that the French Government was in forty years before the Revolution. We have a system that does not seem to be able to adjust itself to a new class which is rapidly coming into power, i.e., the employee class, big and little. This class must save in order to get security and must work in order to get purchasing power. Both savings and work intensify the problems of distribution. Savings can only be invested in capital goods industries. Work can only be used in general to produce. Over-production in terms of purchasing power puts the whole capitalistic system in reverse. This possibly may be a pipe dream yet our prevalent notion that history ended with the last page of the latest history book is a dangerous one. Worse things happen to societies because of failure to adjust than because of temporary misfortunes due to experimental adjustments. However, I see I have started on a book and I had better close. It was certainly nice of you to write.

*Sincerely yours*

---

## *To Felix Frankfurter*

New Haven, Conn., June 11, 1934

Dear Felix:

Your delightful letter is just at hand. You have put your finger on exactly what my article, in so far as it represents advocacy, was attempting to do.[70] Very few people have done this. I had thought that I had made it clear in the rest of the article that the reason why we should put the real problems up to the courts is that only by that method would we ever get rid of the incubus of "judicial" thinking on problems which require "administrative" thinking.

So long as the judicially minded are in the strategic position where they can take pot shots without assuming responsibility, I consider that the judicial symbol will penetrate into corners where it has no business. Only responsibility can create clear thinking.

I would prefer not to call this irony because I would prefer not to seem to be attacking the judicial way of going at things. Unquestionably it has its place just as great operas and great theatrical performances have their places in civilization. We cannot very well describe those verities which move you and me about and which we may call "values." If we analyze them they disappear. The best way that we can make them real is to write little plays and little poems about them. Constitutional law is the purest kind of poetry and this is no criticism of it either. However, poetry has its place and that place is not everywhere. What I am trying to do is exactly what you point out, i.e., to give to people the symbol of judicial power with an understanding of what it is, i.e., the symbol of individual rights which are dramatized by fighting. I would also give the courts who exercise that symbol enough responsibility for planned administration so that they would not feel that they had to conduct battles where none were necessary.

On one point I disagree with you, but that is only in the matter of protection. You seem to think that the thing would be accomplished by "popular revulsion and thus lead to the appropriate confinement of judicial power." Personally I would venture the hope that a judiciary which was permitted to face real problems would not again split into a double-headed system as it has done in the past and that it would assume different roles when the different occasions demanded it. Its talk would become looser and more practical. Its dialectic, where dialectic was required, would become more poetical and symbolic.

In Russia, of which I know very little excepting the outline of the courts, their four-story judicial systems seem to be set up along these lines. I am told today by people who have been there that inefficient as Russians are in economical and industrial techniques, they are marvelously efficient in avoiding the dialectic traps in governmental techniques. Maybe this is not so, but at least the thing is as plausible as any prediction and one is always entitled to indulge in wishful thinking when one is prophesying.

After all "judicial activity" is only a way of thinking. I would be the last to deny its usefulness where dramatization of an ideal is required. But a government which dramatizes itself too much goes the same way that an individual does when he dramatizes himself too much,—that is the way of the manic depressive subject to constant violent ups and downs and swings from right to left.

If you want to call this irony, I don't particularly mind, although it is not the term that I would use. My delight in your having been one of the very few to put your finger on the nub of the essay is so much that you can call it anything.

In the same way you have understood what I am trying to say about the declaratory judgment a lot better than Borchard[71] ever will. I am trying to tell Borchard that his declaratory judgment will never work so long as he attempts "judicial" thinking about everything. That way of thinking requires that inconvenient cases are shoveled off somehow. The declaratory judgment pushed to its logical conclusion means that the courts must plan for situations. Therefore, in situations where the court is acting "judicially" it will have to escape on the implications of the declaratory judgment through the medium of an elaborate and confused literature. If Eddie [Borchard] really believed in relief against peril and insecurity he would try to force the courts into a situation where they would have to plan. What he is actually doing is to give lip service to planning, and then letting them out through his declaratory judgment precedence in the same way that they ignored denying injunctions etc. Therefore the real believer in the principles of the declaratory judgment is one who attacks the judicial process itself where it is obviously inapplicable.

I would not remove the judicial process from everything. Neither would I make rules as to where it should be applied or where something more direct should be applied. I would only be for the social change which comes in satisfying conservatives that their own symbols are not being abandoned and at the same time forcing them to face real issues and plan where a symbolism only confuses.

I suspect that your understanding of the article is due to the fact that this is in effect the philosophical justification of your own writings. You have never denied the value of symbols. On the other hand you have always been intensely practical where you felt symbols should be short-circuited. Perhaps you might disagree that the best way to do this is by making a single body like the courts face all the problems involved in the human disputes at once rather than having two sets of people doing it. I give you the Catholic confessional at its best feature as a very successful method which another institution has adopted. There the priest is logical, mystical and practical at the same time. Critics are always pointing out that the three positions are inconsistent but in spite of this the method has great therapeutic value. I think that one set of priests advising on morals and another giving sympathy and practical plans would make a failure out of this system.

This idea was so hard to express that I cut it out of my article although I attempted it. I doubt very much if I have made it clear now. However, I send you these loose, vague thoughts in appreciation of your real understanding of what my purpose in the article was. I wish you would retract the word "ironic." I am trying to develop a Machiavellian phrase of my own. Machiavelli insisted that the world was run by knaves and therefore to be a good governor one must act like a knave. In this is a moral judgment which destroys the acceptability of his teaching. I would prefer to say that the world is run by very nice people of ordinary intelligence and therefore the governor must understand the limitations of nice people of ordinary intelligence and act accordingly. How about neo-positivistic-semi-realistic-post-Machiavellistic as a name to offer to Pound to express this point of view if he ever decides to include it in his jurisprudence?

*Affectionately*

*To Harold D. Lasswell* [72]

New Haven, Conn., Feb. 22, 1935

Dear Professor Lasswell:

I am delighted with the pamphlets you sent me. I think that the "Moral Vocation of the Middle Income Skill Group " is one of the best things you have ever done, in spite of the heavy title which might keep some people from reading it. Indeed, I would hope to apply the adjective "brilliant" to it. It seems to me a peculiarly penetrating analysis of present psychology. The other two, though not so interesting from a general point of view, are, I think, very significant experiments in studying political attitudes. As to the one in the *Psychoanalytical Review*, I am a little puzzled to know what you will do with this data, but that is not a real criticism. It is only one of the troublesome remarks which always confronts anyone who studies detailed phenomena. I suppose the answer is that no one ever knows in advance. In any event, I am very sympathetic to the general point of view indicated by all three papers. They represent the same attitude applied to a general education of group attitude based on the reading of literature and newspapers and more detailed scientific observation based on the reactions of individuals and a study half way between. I have a feeling that if we are ever going to get anywhere with a science of psychology that can be tied up with law and economics, it will be along the lines of your present effort. Therefore, I congratulate you on the three. The more general one, of course, is the more interesting, but that does not necessarily indicate that it is the most valuable.

*Sincerely*

---

*To Arthur Goodhart*

New Haven, Conn., March 9, 1935

Dear Goodhart:

After reading Karl Llewellyn's review[73] of your book I felt impelled to write the enclosed, which will be published in the *Columbia Law Review*,[74] because, fond as I am of Karl, I think he has missed the point of what you are trying to do. I do not take it that your book pretends to be a psychological study of human attitudes nor do I think that had you attempted such an enterprise the book would have been effective in persuading lawyers. Personally I was tremendously intrigued with the way you linked up the past to the present and evolved a doctrine which could be cited by any court without breaking their traditions. If you are lucky, this essay might go down as one of the land marks of the progress of the law. You have evolved just the formula which courts in this country need. The phrase "sociological jurisprudence" has a certain emotional appeal, but it is ineffective because it gets all tangled up with stare decisis. If we could only achieve a frank abandonment of precedent, such as you advocate, it would cut down our lengthy briefs and complicated analyses of cases in this country to an amazing extent. The trouble with us over here is that sometimes a court talks in terms of stare decisis and sometimes drags in all sorts of social and economic factors. Attorneys who are arguing for the Supreme Court of the United States never know which style to adopt in any particular case. They usually attempt both styles with the result that the brief looses punch and coherence. Our Supreme Court is constantly wavering between one position and the other. The trend of our law review talk is that courts should follow only those precedents which are of the type that ought to be followed. The American Law Institute has been caught on the horns of this dilemma and has achieved something which is neither a code nor a common law text book.

It seems to me that those who call themselves "progressives" in this country ought to get behind your formula rather than attempt to tear it down. It is perfectly unrealistic to assume that courts are going to use the language of the objective scientist. This does not mean that law cannot be cited realistically, but anyone who studies it should recognize the importance of the apt phrase. Realistic writing is good to write if one understands the human attitudes which make up the law. It is just as useless in court, however, as it is on the stage. Therefore, those who are anxious for more judicial freedom should be the last to attack a formula such as yours which is so skillfully phrased that it has every chance of working to the great practical advantage of the system. I only wish that we could have gotten behind this last essay of yours and pushed it across. You and Karl Llewellyn are really on the same side of the fence and it is a shame to see his influence used to tear down what I consider a very effective piece of work.

*Sincerely*

---

## *To Mr. Jerome Hall* [75]

New Haven, Conn., April 11, 1935

Dear Mr. Hall:

Thank you very much for your comment on my article. The article is the third chapter in the book and I have gone into the question you raise at greater length in other chapters. However if I attempted to answer your criticism very briefly it would be as follows:

I do not intend to reject theory. Indeed I attempt to show that it is probably the most important thing about any human institution and without it the institution loses its morale. People have got to believe before they will follow and in a rational climate of opinion they will inevitably give good livings to people who prove to them that their beliefs are rational. I lean neither for or against this phenomenon; it is simply the way group mind operates and I see no reason to believe it will operate differently in the future. As I point out in the last paragraph of my article, I do not think that a purely objective point of view is pragmatically useful in operating a human institution. Its use is limited to the person who finds out about an institution. There is no necessary connection in knowing how an institution works and actually operating it any more than there is in knowing how football is played and getting out and playing the game. I therefore do not attempt to justify my work on the ground that it will have any particular pragmatic usefulness to persons in positions of governmental power. I have, however, the vague faith that in the course of time the more we find out about any institution the better it will be operated according to humanitarian standards. This faith is based on human experience of the treatment of the human mind. We are not very far in the study of insanity and the most learned psychiatrist is often not the best at therapeutics. Nevertheless, I believe that we have advanced since fifty years ago. The only pragmatic utility therefore of dissecting the group mind and thinking about it as the psychologist thinks about the human mind is in the hope that the advancement of objective opinion will somehow or other aid us in solving problems of group psychology.

Therefore I do not think I can be said to "weaken my argument by not giving a different place to principle" because I am not making any argument. Such being my purposes I would never affirm nor deny your suggested notion that we make discoveries through the hypothesis route. I would simply say I am not dealing with how discoveries are made by individuals.

Perhaps you are thinking that "society" makes discoveries about themselves by accepting and rejecting theory. This does not seem to me to be true. Society furnishes a climate of opinion in which individuals make discoveries and discoveries are no doubt easier in some climates of opinion than in others. I have a hunch that social discoveries are easier in a climate of opinion which does not deal in theory at all. For example, I think that Henry Ford has added to our knowledge in the technique of an organization. The fact that he built up his enormous institution makes it easier for the next man to build up a similar institution. I do not believe, however, that Henry Ford went through any mental process which could be properly described tentative acceptance of hypothesis. However I do not know Mr. Ford and therefore I cannot be sure about that.

Although my article is not about how discoveries are made, I do have the feeling that the discoverers are not people who are trained in the application of logocal principles. I suspect that Henry Ford would never have built the Ford Plant had he been well grounded in the theory of his time. I was his complete inability to think in a theoretical way which enabled him to take the chance which resulted in success. However, when I make a statement like that, I recognize that it is a very naive explanation of the psychological processes and probably just as naive as the hypothesis notion. I suppose that the hypothesis notion which you seem to prefer should properly be regarded as neither true nor false but simply an inadequate description of a type of human behavior which results in discovery.

However I recognize the emotional necessity for anyone dealing with theory to prove that his work is contributing to progress and not simply to maintenance of status quo. For such people who feel that need, I suspect the hypothesis notion gives them greater freedom than the notion of fundamental truth of theories and to the extent that it sets them free probably does contribute to their thinking.

I do not know whether I have made myself clear. Probably not, because words are very tricky when you are using them to describe what words do to thinking. However, I like to talk and write about such mystical matters as you present and therefore would be interested to know if this explanation seems adequate.

*Sincerely yours*

---

## *To Mrs. T.W. Arnold*

New Haven, Conn., Aug. 12, 1935

Dear Frances:

I have such a pile of correspondence that I am going to dictate a letter. In the first place, I noted that a letter sent to Millbrook, Wyoming,[76] had been returned because there is no such post office. I only point out that I told you so. You had better get your stationery changed. I also enclose postcards.

I had a very pleasant trip, landing in New York at 11 o'clock in the morning instead of 9 because the conductor took my whole ticket to Los Angeles and return instead of giving me back the unused portions. When I got my ticket back at Chicago I found this out. The train was an hour late and I had to go to the downtown office and so could not catch the 11 o'clock train to Chicago. I caught the one at 2:30 but did not see anybody in town because I was too busy.

I had a leisurely luncheon in New York and took a 2 o'clock train out. As I was sitting in the coach Sunday afternoon I heard the conductor call out South Norwalk and it occurred to me it would be a grand idea to stop off and have a swim with Luke. I thereupon got off the train, called up Luke and found no one there. I then called Frank and Susie Wells and found they were out. I consulted the time table and found out that no trains stopped in South Norwalk until 7, some four hours away. In desperation I called up Bridgeport. Philo [Calhoun] was out but Doris [Calhoun] answered the phone. I told her to get into the car and come down and get me. She showed no enthusiasm whatever, although it is only one-half hour from South Norwalk. I pled with her and she said the car had just been washed and it was raining and also that Philo had some people coming in and would be sore at her if she were out when they came. I don't know why it is I have no more success with women than I do and I don't suppose I have any right to be sore at Doris because after all why should she drive a half hour to pick me up. However, I think that she rather enjoyed getting even with me for leaving her on the front porch and going to dinner with another woman three weeks ago. It certainly was a grand triumph for her. I sat in Norwalk for nearly four hours, waiting for the train, and I bet she enjoyed every minute. I finally got here at about 8 o'clock Sunday evening and Bill [Douglas] called up. He had some people named the Geisers who were awfully nice coming into his house about 11 o'clock. I asked if they were related to the Yellowstone geisers which I thought at the time was a pretty good joke. Bill said, however, he was tired of it because everybody else thought of the same joke when the Geisers were mentioned. Anyhow Bill and I sat around doing some mild drinking until they arrived. They added sufficient gaiety to the party then we started out for Savin Rock about 12. We discovered a big dance hall with a little place over the water where you danced and I was just feeling in the right mood to get into the spirit of the thing. I amazed everyone by the speed, grace and proficiency of my dancing. I taught them the tumble weed. It made a great hit. Finally they started putting chairs on tables. We ignored that for a while until they pushed us out. We then went home and I got to bed about 3 o'clock. This morning I am down bright and early dictating answers to all my mail, but Bill is still comparatively in bed. He is a younger man than I am but he can't take it. Aren't you proud of your husband?

*Love*

---

*To Frank Murphy* [77]

New Haven, Conn., Sept. 3, 1935

Dear Governor Murphy:

On my return from Washington I find your very welcome note which I appreciated. The excerpts from the papers are most interesting and it must be a great satisfaction to you to retire from such a difficult job with so much good will. Needless to say, I concur enthusiastically. I believe you will enjoy your High Commissionership even more than the Governorship because it will contain great opportunities for service and you may be relieved of the heavy care that complete executive office always brings. However, predictions are difficult in the world today and the situation in the Philippines may require even more tact and finesse from the High Commissioner than it did from the Governor General.

I am sending a copy of your letter to President Angell[78] who will be very pleased indeed, and I am asking him to send you a copy of his address.

I have had an interesting summer, As you know, my best friend, Jerome Frank, was purged out of the Department of Agriculture at the time Roosevelt was attempting to line up business support.[79] The move was political and without bitterness and I was asked to become a special counsel for the Securities & Exchange Commission since my position in the Department of Agriculture was no longer tenable after Frank had left. We have been investigating corporate reorganizations this summer and I have found the work quite fascinating, although the partners of the great law firms who are called on the stand to be examined are quite irritated at times at the idea of being asked questions about the advice they gave to clients. The whole picture of corporate reorganization in this country is one of anarchy but I am not quite prepared at this moment to say just what can be done about it.

I had one disappointment. Secretary Perkins asked me to become a member of the new National Labor Relations Board, a position which I was extremely anxious to accept because of my interest in those problems. However, President Angell opposed the matter of giving me a leave so that I could not take it. So much for my personal affairs.

The political situation, as I see it in this country, may interest you. My personal conviction is that the country as a whole wants inflation. I believe that Borah if nominated might beat Roosevelt. I have been to the coast for the Securities & Exchange Commission and talked with a great many people in Wyoming and Nebraska. The West is wildly enthusiastic about Borah. He gets all the radicals and at the same time will collect all the votes of those who are disgruntled with the present administration. The vote in Rhode Island clearly indicates the situation. The Soldiers' Bonus was endorsed and a large sum for relief was voted and all the work relief projects were voted down. Borah stands for both a managed currency and the Soldiers' Bonus. He is at present the strongest Republican candidate in the field.

My personal guess, however, is that Borah will not be nominated. The people I know in the East who have influence are almost as bitter against him as they are against Roosevelt. They will use every effort to stop his nomination. If they succeed in stopping his nomination they will, in my opinion, beat the Republican Party. I personally believe that Roosevelt is the only hope for sensible conservatives if they could see it that way. It is tragic that they should be so convinced that the clock could be turned back to 1929 that they do irreparable damage to a sane, conservative position by moving to positions on the extreme right. However, it is difficult to talk to them. All they can say is Bureaucracy and Constitution. I do not think the Constitution as a political issue is worth anything. It is just another way of calling the New Deal names and wins no one over who is not already bitter about present policies. That is the situation as I see it at the present time. However, I suspect that Roosevelt is gaining strength on his own account every week. Even the *New York Herald Tribune* of the last few days is running out of invectives and conservative newspapers are gradually getting tired of calling him names. The height of the uprising against Roosevelt came a year too soon, and if I were betting, I would bet on a gradual rise of his power. There is a good deal of evidence of this and the astonishing reversal of form in Congress which finally surrendered on the Holding Company Bill. The fact is that Congressmen began to get frightened as to the results of their opposition to Roosevelt and many of them sensed the fact that the wave was at its peak and was about to recede.

There is probably nothing in any of these political guesses and the future will probably prove, as it has in the past, that I am entirely wrong. However, it is fun to make them and I set them out on the theory that you might be interested in the observations of a somewhat biased observer. Personally I still prefer Roosevelt to anyone else in the field in spite of the fact that he swings back and forth and from right to left. However, I think that is all one can do in a political office in these confused times.

With very best regards and hoping to see you when you again return to this country, I remain

*Sincerely yours*

---

## *To Frank W. Wozencraft*[80]

New Haven, Conn., Nov. 14, 1935

Dear Mr. Wozencraft:

I was much interested in your letter and very much pleased at the confidence which you have in the Yale Law School. I am rather doubtful about my judgment on the education of the young. However, since I have the same problem myself, I am glad to give you the benefits of my own cogitation on it. Personally I believe that boys should go to a small prep school and a big college. The larger prep schools like Andover and Exeter are pretty tough propositions for a youngster. The fraternity system is in full swing at those schools and I am doubtful if boys of that age should be put up against such social discriminations. For that reason, I decided against them for my own son. However, if a boy has gone to a small prep school, there is no reason to send him to a small college. The eastern prep schools develop social characteristics so that a boy can handle himself in a larger place. The only advantage of small colleges that I see is that a boy is not so apt to get lost. However, there are a great many disadvantages. In the first place the faculty is usually less distinguished. In the second place, and more important, they turn out men according to a pattern. That is my objection to Williams. It is very social in its atmosphere and not much opportunity to develop individuality. There is not enough variety of groups with which a boy can associate himself. If a boy had not had the advantage of a prep school it is possible that a smaller college would be a good thing for him. However, he will get enough of that sort of life in a good eastern prep school so that four years more of it would be too much of a continuation of the same thing. A third reason why I prefer a larger college is the advantages which contact with the alumni offer wherever he settles. If he graduates from Yale, Harvard or Princeton he cannot go anywhere in the country where he does not find someone, usually among the people he wants to know, who is an alumnus. All things else being equal, therefore, I would not think of sending my own son anywhere else than these three. Dartmouth is not national enough in its scope to suit me. As long as you have to spend four years in college, you might as well get as much prestige and advantage as you can and I think that the prestige value of the big three does amount to something.

As between Yale, Harvard and Princeton, it is difficult to choose. If I were to characterize those three colleges I would say that Harvard offers more opportunity for a boy to develop intellectual interests than any other university and yet from a social angle it is the least desirable place to send a boy. From that side it is very cold blooded and not at all as companionable a place as Yale or Princeton.

Princeton, I might prefer to Yale were it not for the advantages which Yale offers in the House Plan. I like very much the present method of dividing Yale into groups of about 150 with their own athletic teams, their own dining halls, etc. Princeton suffers because of a system of upper class clubs which is, to my mind, a very unfortunate social hierarchy.

Why don't you drop down here some weekend and I will put you up in a Distinguished Visitor's Suite at the Yale Law School and you can look over the House Plan. I am quite sure that you would enjoy looking Yale over and I am in a position to offer you the facilities of the Law School without any inconveneince or expense to myself so that you may feel perfectly free to come down at any time. You also might be interested in looking the Law School over and talking to the faculty.

I would certainly not select a college on the theory of what law school your son is going to, for the reason that no one knows what any law school in the country will be like in seven years. Personally, I am quite conscientious in liking Yale better than any other today but what it will be in seven years, no one can say. Further than that, if he happens to choose Yale Law School, I do not consider it very significant that he spend seven years in New Haven. Cambridge and New Haven are so much alike in general culture and atmosphere that it almost seems to me like the difference between moving from Park Avenue to Fifth Avenue in order to get a different climate of opinion. In any event, you might not like the Yale Law School in seven years as well as you do now and I would certainly leave that matter open and not consider it in selecting a college.

As far as prep schools are concerned, my own son is going to Hotchkiss. I rather like it because it keeps the boys busy, gives them a rather severe discipline and at the same time a very good time. I suppose, however, there is very little to choose between most of the better prep schools in New England. Deerfield would be my second choice and Choate my third. I have personally investigated Andover, Exeter, Deerfield, Hotchkiss and Choate. As to the others, I know them only by reputation. Whether they are better or worse than the ones I know, I have no knowledge.

I don't know why I should set myself up as a guide in the education of anybody but this letter represents my offhand reaction. In any event, I hope that you will plan to drop down here sometime. In as much as we can arrange for your accommodation at the Distinguished Visitors' Suites, please feel perfectly free to make the trip at any time. It will be a great pleasure to see you and no trouble to anyone. Your wife may also be accommodated at the suite. I would suggest that you do not come on a football day because the place is in such a turmoil that you cannot see anything or anybody. With very best wishes and hoping to see you soon, I remain

*Sincerely yours*

---

## *To Arthur E. Sutherland, Jr.*[81]

New Haven, Conn., Dec. 1, 1935

Dear Sutherland:

Your letter is on my desk on my return this morning and I make haste to answer it because I suppose that the time must be getting short. I like your general notion of outlining the constitutional powers which are in dispute today. It seems to me to be necessary as a basis for a discussion which necessarily will have to be very general. Personally, on the basis of close reasoning which is part of a good brief, I am never able to argue any more than one case at a time. When we are compelled by the limitations of our subject to argue the constitutionality of a number of acts at the same time I suspect that we will be compelled to discuss generalities and attitudes rather than closely reasoned legal arguments.

I take it from your letter that you regard an extension of the commerce power to matters which go beyond what may be included in transportation as doubtful both as a matter of law and of policy. You also think that this power should not be extended by indirection through the device of taxation. In other words your general position is that if an industry cannot be directly regulated through the commerce power, you would think it unfortunate if regulation were actually effected through taxation. Taxation, in general, should have for its primary purpose, revenue and not regulation,—as I get your view.

My thought is that the commerce power should be extended to all areas where, as a matter of fact, regulation by the states is impossible. I decline to accept Robert's opinion in the Pension case as final, in view of Hugh's dissent. I do not yet admit that the Schechter case[82] settles the issue if another case arises where there is proof that the particular regulation of chickens is necessary in order to conduct a general interstate business in chickens, provided that a showing can be made that local regulation is not feasible to meet the particular situation. I would agree with you that the use of the taxing power to regulate is a somewhat hypocritical manner of extending the commerce power. It has the disadvantage that there is no logical stopping place. However, on this point I would take the position that if the commerce power is so narrowly restricted that effective regulation is impossible, it then becomes necessary to utilize the taxing power to fill the gap. My general test of whether it had reached its limit or not would be the same test which I would apply to the taxing power, i.e. do we have a situation before us where the only regulation possible is federal regulation?

This brings us to the chief difference between our points of view. You would like to see a number of areas where no regulation was possible, because of your desire to keep government out of business. This I suppose is based on a general attitude that economic situations work out best when left alone, and that the possibility of government interference has its dangers in bureaucracy, unfortunate social planning, regimentation, etc. etc. I would prefer to admit frankly the power to regulate and limit only by the somewhat vague notions of due process, which would never be directed at stopping future legislation, but only at preventing certain arbitrary effects of the particular legislation before the court.

On the actual results of the decisions there would not be so much difference between us. You would admit that Hughes's dissenting opinion had at least a chance of survival. I would admit that the language in the Schechter case was very broad and that the case would have to be distinguished on its facts. Yet you on the other hand would probably admit in return that while the language is broad, it is still subject to a lot of possible qualifications.

So far as guessing on the actual results, I would prefer to avoid that, because there are too many personal factors. Have you heard the hot dope now current in Washington about the present feud between Roberts and Hughes on account of the railway pension case? I don't know how much there is in it, though the source quoted seems to be unimpeachable. However, a prominent New York attorney gave me odds that the A.A.A. was unconstitutional because of that supposed feud. The odds against the Guffey bill are quoted at four to one. Therefore, on the basis of guessing you have all the betting odds in your favor. On the holding company bill, attorneys that I know give the government a better chance, although just why they do so is not at all clear to me. In any event I prefer to avoid predictions, and at the same time it will be impossible to go much into detail about particular bills. Therefore, I suggest the attached as something which might go to the printer.

I don't know whether we want the explanation or not. If it ties you down too much, either reformulate it or throw it away.

Don't hesitate to change the wording of the principal question. All we want is freedom to develop our points of view.

Please give me your reaction.

*Very sincerely yours*

---

*To Sheridan Downey, Esq.*

New Haven, Conn., Dec. 4, 1935

Dear Sheridan:

As I remember the Townsend Plan it consists in a sales tax which is used to pay off pensions for old people. My personal opinion is that there would be nothing unconstitutional about the scheme unless the court held that this was an illegitimate use of the taxing power in order to regulate industry or to further some ulterior motive following the Child Labor Tax case. If the pensions were paid out of general revenue and the taxation provision introduced as a separate measure, it would be safer from an argumentative constitutional angle. However, I do not know the details of the scheme and therefore it may be that there is something about the tax itself which might put it under the heading of a direct tax rather than an excise tax. Offhand, however, I can't see just why the federal government can't levy a sales tax and then spend the money any way it pleased. I note that you think it is unconstitutional and perhaps you have something in mind which does not at the moment occur to me. You asked for my offhand opinion and that is, of course, what you are getting.

I also believe that the present Social Security Act is constitutional on the same basis. However when opinions are coming down like Roberts' majority opinion in the Railway Pension case which I think is unjustified from any constitutional law I ever knew, one cannot be dogmatic about constitutional matters.

I will look forward with great pleasure to your book.[83] Don't send it to me but let me know when it comes out and I will buy it. The reason I suggest this is that I have just finished a book of my own and developed a hardboiled principle that I am not sending it to anybody. Therefore, being a man of principle, I would rather buy yours. My own book is entitled *Symbols of Government* and is published by the Yale Press. It has been out a month but I do not know whether it has gotten to the coast yet. There has not been time for any reviews to come out on it.

Personally I am not sold on the Townsend Plan as a method. However, I do not think we should be too critical about methods in times like these. The main point at present is to get American people to recognize an obligation. Methods will eventually take care of themselves. However, I might change my mind as to the methodology of the plan after I read your book. At present my position is that I am glad that Townsend is pushing the pension idea in spite of the fact that I have grave doubts as to the particular means he advocates. More power to you. I am glad that there are a few people in the world that are willing to spend their time on liberal causes.

*Sincerely yours*

---

## *To Rev. William G. Gehri* [84]

New Haven, Conn., Jan. 9, 1936

Dear Gehri:

I am delighted that you are writing a book of your sermons and am very much flattered that you should think of me in connection with the foreword. I would like very much to read the book. I do not know whether you quite realize the depth of my skeptical position however and perhaps I will not be able to conscientiously write a foreword which would fit the book. My own feeling is that man was born to be harnessed by priests and that this is one of the crosses which he must bear. However a realistic appreciation of this fact is like the physician's appreciation of the fact that he has certain physical limitations and a social diagnosis would require that his need in this direction be ministered to. Therefore I will make a distinction between useful and useless priests from the standpoint of humanitarian values. Yet to my way of thinking, you are a useful priest and I took great delight in your sermons because I felt that they filled a need for people who might otherwise be more intolerant and more bigoted if you had not preached. The Supreme Court of the United States is my idea of a collection of useless priests and their preaching fills me with melancholy in spite of the realization of how inevitable it is. For my own purposes, I do not find much comfort in personifying my ideals and connecting them up with an individuality like Christ. I am very happy, however, when I see someone else like yourself making of the personification of ideals a less intolerant thing than it would have been had you not spoken.

Therefore I do not promise to write a foreword even though I may like the book. However I will be delighted to see it.

With very best regards to Mrs. Gehri,

*Sincerely yours*

---

## *To Harold J. Laski* [85]

New Haven, Conn., Jan. 9, 1936

Dear Harold:

I can think of no one else in the world from whom praise is more welcome and more heart warming than yourself. Therefore to say that I was delighted with your letter is putting it very mildly. I also appreciate the fact that you took the time and trouble to write. It is one of my faults that I always intend to write such letters but never seem to get around to it. Your recent articles in *Harpers*[86] have filled me with enthusiasm and yet when I mention them after your letter it seems like an anti climax. Your statement that the book will make its way slowly is encouraging.[87] Even my best friends are unwilling to accept the position taken in the book and insist that the real criticism is the fact that they cannot tell when I am being satirical and when I am being serious. When I tell them that I am serious throughout the book they think that this is just another satirical statement.

Like yourself, I believe that philosophies are the most important thing in the world. When I first heard you lecture I was entranced with the beauty of a skeptical position. I recall telling you that while I admired the first lecture I heard from you at Yale I disagreed with everything in it. That was because I thought that the man of intellectual integrity should scorn all formulae. I have now, as you know, come to believe that a completely skeptical position means only a futility,—that a sincere humanitarian must formulate a philosophy in words if he is to move people about or even maintain his own morale and that leadership consists in skill in formulating such a philosophy and getting people to respond to it. I can see now as I could not see then that this is what you are doing and I am convinced that you do it as well as anyone in the world today. When young men cannot listen to you without becoming intensely moved and when the only result of Walter Wheeler Cook[88] is to make them extremely hardboiled, I began to see what was wrong with the realist's position. And so I tried to express a philosophy which permitted an idealistic use of the opinion which can only be obtained in a skeptical frame of mind. In it was, I am aware, all the inconsistency between the position of an observer and the position of a reformer but I have, so far as my own spiritual comfort is concerned, been able to jump from one platform to another without feeling logically inconsistent. I have only been able to do so however by considering logic itself as just another one of the conflicting ideals which I cherish.

Therefore I would have been very much grieved if you had not understood what I was driving at and am tremendously pleased by your appreciation.

Your criticisms are certainly well taken. I am aware of the lacks in the book which you point out. However, your suspicion that I know of this as fully as you do is not quite correct. I know the book would be better if I related the various current theories to the class in power and if I showed how they were evolved by the intellectual slaves of the conquered. If I could relate with the facility which you do, I would certainly have put it in the book. Your Storrs lectures however did that job so beautifully that I despair of imitation.

The history of the social sciences in the 19th century is another topic on which I agree with your conclusion but for the discussion of which my acquaintance with the literature is all too brief. However, these are only excuses. I now wish that you had read the book in manuscript instead of in print. I feel that even with the second-hand knowldge I could have made these points clear and your criticism gives me the feeling of a person who has handed in an examination paper and then realizes that he has forgotten to discuss one of the important points.

I hope when you come this way you can stay long enough so that your friends do not have to content themselves with a single hurried evening with you. This means a long time in New Haven because your circle is so large here and so diverse that if everyone who wants to see you is to get a chance, it will take months of your time. However, please make it as long as you can.

*Affectionately*

---

## *To Harry Elmer Barnes*[89]

New Haven, Conn., Jan. 27, 1936

Dear Dr. Barnes:

Although I am a reader of your column, I missed seeing your comments on my recent book until today when somebody handed me the clipping. Needless to say, I was tremendously pleased at your exceedingly generous statements. Being familiar with nearly all of your writing I would have been surprised if you had not agreed with the point of view. Nevertheless you were more generous than I had any right to expect. It has seemed to me that your own writing on government, particularly at the time when anti-German prejudice was the strongest, indicates that you had adopted this same point of view long before it was a part of my own mental equipment.

I recall very distinctly, when I was practicing law in Wyoming, how your writings on the World War were the first breath of fresh air which I had had. It completely changed my own point of view because I had been caught, as most other people had, in the war psychology. In view of my indebtedness to you therefore, I am particularly pleased at a compliment coming from you.

*Sincerely yours*

---

## *To Judge V.J. Tidball* [90]

New Haven, Conn., Feb. 13, 1936

Dear Judge Tidball:

Thanks for your letter and questionnaire.

You were right about the fact that this is no time for liberals on the Constitution to stick their heads out of the storm cellar. The discussion is much more virulent in the East than it is in the West. I recently conducted a debate before the New York Bar Association in which I mildly suggested that possibly Mr. Justice Stone was not connected with Russia. I have never spoken before a more hostile audience and my opponent got by with a perfectly asinine speech. The debate was followed by a broadcast from John W. Davis who occupies the same position in New York that Lacey[91] used to occupy in Cheyenne. Davis talked for an hour and a half about bureaucracy. Nothing he said made any sense whatever and yet he was received with tremendous applause. I had dinner with Davis just before the speaking and was quite astonished to note the extreme similarity between all of his attitudes and those of Lacey. He is also very much of the same type, excepting he is a lot better looking and more impressive, which is the only explanation for the relative prominence of the two men. He patted me on the back and patronized me as a bright young man just as Lacey used to do. His general attitude toward the arguments of my speech was that while they were clever and permissible in a country where free speech must be tolerated, nevertheless I would know better when I grew up.

However, I am much encouraged at the violence of the reaction in the East. I think that the situation is not unlike what it was in prohibition and we have got to go through this period. I have a letter from Mr. Justice Stone. Pardon me for bragging but I have become acquainted with Stone and he is the only real man on the bench and he feels the same way. He has conviction that his opinion will finally survive and I am inclined to agree with him. He is a great guy with a lot of nerve. Cardozo and Brandeis are good but I do not think they have his force at present. With Brandeis it is simply a case of advancing age and ill health; with Cardozo it is the difference between a fighter and an essentially literary character.

The bitterness on the Supreme Court is now very intense. I hear all sorts of rumors about the terrible time they are having with the T.V.A. These rumors originate from chance remarks made by secretaries and I don't know how reliable they are but they would indicate that the liberals and the conservatives scarcely speak to one another.

With very best regards, I am

*Sincerely yours*

---

## *To Arthur E. Sutherland, Jr.*

New Haven, Conn., Feb. 21, 1936

Dear Sutherland:

I had just dictated a letter this morning when your letter came. Can you select a date between the 1st and the 16th of March which is not on Friday or Saturday? We will make our schedule conform to your convenience. As I told you, the moot courts[92] run for six weeks and we are particularly interested in getting outsiders in as judges because of the prestige it gives the moot court work. It is easy to get outsiders for the finals but my whole effort is to make the regular work in moot court as important as possible. By doing so I get a condition of nervous strain and activity in preparation which is not dissimilar to a real court. My own experience at Harvard was that the moot courts were fairly offhand affairs until the finals were reached and I am trying to avoid that.

You may or may not get a good argument, but I am sure you will be interested in looking the School over and I think we can show you a good time. We shall put you and your wife up in a Distinguished Visitors' Suite if she can come with you. Unfortunately we have no money for expenses but we can take care of you while you are here. Perhaps Mrs. Sutherland might enjoy the experience of staying in the Law School quadrangle and being kept awake late at night and early in the morning by the students. We have rather attractive suites for this purpose.

Much as I hate to disappoint you, I do not believe there is much new love for the Supreme Court as a result of the T.V.A. decision.[93] I have just returned from Washington and there are many who feel that the real issue was dodged and the decision is simply preliminary to a greal deal more litigation. The Court seems to have put itself in a position where the government cannot find out until after a dam is completed whether it is going to be able to use it or not and that all activity must be conditioned on possible injunctions in lower courts. It may be that the government should stay out of business entirely but I believe that you would agree with me that if it is to go into business that is no way to conduct business efficiently.

Publicly of course those connected with the T.V.A. assume expressions of great delight because they cannot afford to do anything else. But most of the people I know hoped that the Supreme Court would either clarify the issue by deciding against the T.V.A. or else indicate more clearly just how far the government could go. The *Wall Street Journal* says the suits are about to be started on the Norris Dam which is much more important than the Wilson Dam and so the whole thing will have to be gone through with again. Frankly, is this your idea of judicial review at its best or do you have some lingering doubts?

Incidentally, what has become of Roberts' coercion in the A.A.A. case? Isn't the government using its power to handle its own property in such a way as to coerce the utilities just as it used its spending power to coerce farmers? I am all mixed up.

*Sincerely yours*

---

## *To Leon Green*

New Haven, Conn., Feb. 25, 1936

Dear Leon:

I have several good men in mind whom I think would work out very well. They are good enough so that I would vote for any one of them at Yale.

First, as to men without experience. *Ferdinand Stone*[94] is now working for Charles Clark on the Supreme Court rules. He is an Oxford man and got a S.J.D. degree from us last year. He has done work with Douglas in corporate reorganization. He has an extremely nice personality and would fit in well any place you wanted to put him. My guess is that he is just as good a man as Spaeth though of course it is always difficult to know how a young man will develop. I do not mean that he will be as good when he comes to you as Spaeth was, because Spaeth has more experience and maturity, but I should think he would develop into Spaeth's calibre.

Now as to men with more experience. The prize of the whole lot and one of the best men that ever graduated from the Yale Law School is *Abe Fortas,* now on our faculty. We appointed him and he resigned to go to the A.A.A., where he made a brilliant record. Starting as a sub-counsel, in eight months' time he was managing the whole peach industry negotiations in California and the Citrus Fruit negotiations in Florida. He was one of Jerome Frank's most trusted assistants. He can take any responsibility. He was Bill's right-hand man in the Protective Committee Study. No job he has ever undertaken has been slurred over and his performance is uniformly brilliant. He is a splendid teacher and the students here are flocking into his Corporate Reorganizations courses. You will immediately want to know why he should leave Yale. He won't leave Yale if I can help it, and if you make him an offer, I will do everything I can to compete with you. However, he is under a handicap here because he is a Jew and they are paying him a miserable salary. Frankly, I would like to see him get an offer from somewhere else. I suspect that if we could not raise his salary he might go to Northwestern. He is married to a Gentile, a most attractive girl who will fit in anywhere. He is not Jewish in appearance and if his name were not *Abe* Fortas, I do not think anyone would know he was a Jew.

I hesitate to recommend my brother because of personal reasons but, on the other hand, do not see any really valid reason why I should not. He is, as you know, Dean of the University of Wyoming. For the last year he has been on leave as Assistant General Counsel to the Federal Communications Commission. This has given him a wide experience with business organization of telephone, telegraph and radio. They seem to think very highly of him. He is about forty years old and I think extremely competent. His background and practical experience is probably greater than any other man you could get for the price. He is a very popular teacher. As Dean of the University of Wyoming he gets only $4,000 a year. As Assistant General Counsel he gets $7,500 but he does not want to give up teaching and expects to resign from his Washington job next fall. Of course I am probably biased in my recommendations of my own brother, and if you are interested would suggest that you write to F.W. Wozencraft, General Soliciter of R.C.A. I don't know what Wozencraft will think of him, but inasmuch as he has been on the opposite side of the fence from Carl in a good many matters before the Commission, his opinion ought to have no bias whatever. I give you his name because he comes from Texas and says he knows you and purports to admire you greatly.

If you could pay nine or ten thousand, I could not recommend anybody more highly than *Sam Clark,*[95] the Dean's brother, who has been Bill Douglas' assistant in the Protective Committee Study. It would take a large salary to get Sam Clark, however. He is now with the Securities & Exchange Commission.

*Kenneth Rush*[96] of Chadbourne, Stanchfield & Levy, is a man I can back very highly. He wants to go into teaching. He graduated from here three years ago and has done very well in the firm and I think is getting about $4,500 now. He was on the *Law Journal* here. He has had wide experience in reorganization work with that firm.

I am also impressed with another Oxford man, *H.H. Wasson,* who is in my seminar this year and has done a good deal of work for Douglas.

Of the men recommended, Fortas is unquestionably the pick of the lot. In fact he is a man in a thousand. I hope you go after him strong and that it creates enough interest here so that we will be able to keep him.

However, I think I ought to be frank and warn you that I am recommending him because I feel I ought to for his own advantage and that if you decide to go after him I hope you will be unsuccessful.

I was talking to some people in New York who purported to know all about the Chicago judgeship. They said there was a prominent Jew who had given heavily to the Democratic Campaign Committee who was balling up the works and standing in your light because he wanted the job himself. My informant told me the Jew was not a good man for the position and hoped that you would get it, and was doing everything he could for you. I have forgotten the Jew's name, but you very likely will know. Maybe you can guess who my informant was. He was a prominent lawyer from Chicago and apparently a very strong supporter of yours.

*Sincerely yours*

---

## *To Willmott Lewis*[97]

New Haven, Conn., Feb. 27, 1936

Dear Sir Willmott:

You certainly are a valuable ally. I would be very much interested in Mencken's reaction to the book. I would be interested because my prediction is that he would believe that it is a betrayal of his cardinal principles of intellectual integrity, which gives his writing so much of its force. I do not see how anyone can write with the vehemence of Mencken without very profound, deep-seated and unexamined principles.

May I have one of your speeches or articles where you develop the meaning of the phrase "legal state vs. welfare state"? This seems to me so completely satisfactory and distinctive that I want to use it in a short article which I am preparing, and therefore would like something which has been published which I can cite to show where I got it. Robinson and I have both adopted it to fill a long felt want. My own theory is that if you ever define a term carefully, it loses all meaning and the very clumsy contrast between "moral-rational" and "practical-humanitarian" which we have been using, appears to be an attempt at definition. The only thing that we have done so far with these two terms is to confuse people. I have tried your terms out and they seem to click. Therefore, we are both anxious to get hold of something which expresses them in your language which we can quote. I suppose I could find them myself by hunting, but if it is not too much trouble it would save me labor if I could get a few citations from you. Thanking you, I remain

*Sincerely yours*

---

## *To Harold J. Laski*

New Haven, Conn., Feb. 28, 1936

Dear Harold:

As you probably might expect, I was delighted with your review.[98] You were very generous with your praise and your criticism seems both thoughtful and well taken.

The trouble with the last chapter is the fact that I have as yet been unable to find words to properly express a science *about* law and government. I make a distinction in my own mind of a science *of* law and a science *about* law. I will agree with you that we can understand the history of the Supreme Court of the United States or the Napoleonic code better through an appreciation of government as an expression of class relation than we can through the eyes of any conventional governmental theory. And yet I distrust this explanation of society. It seems to be an admirable tool for reform but not quite a platform for observation. As a prophet, I see politicians always running the government. I am therefore looking for symbols to put a different class of politicians in power. Not a set of brighter or more intellectual politicians, because I doubt the efficacy of reason in political action, but a set of people with a different kind of objective. In order to put that crowd in power I must work out a non-intellectual philosophy for them since they are opportunists and philosophy must justify opportunism of a little different sort. The trouble with a long range view as a slogan for such people is that it enables them to dismiss practical humanitarian objects directed at meeting the problem of the American. Thus many of my most liberal friends in this country think that the best way to raise wages in the long run is to destroy labor unions and lower them for the present. If I could make these people look only at the present and forget the future and the past, I think perhaps we might have a better government. I was impressed by the fact that comparatively stupid people were doing a wonderful job in the Philippines, from a humanitarian point of view. A better job than the same people could do in America. This isn't any better than my last chapter and therefore I shall not accept your invitation to comment on your review. In the first place, I like the review too much as it stands to want to create an anti-climax. In the second place, in my present state of thinking, I am completely unable to express in words the answer which I rather generally feel.

To your sentence "given a Marxist approach to the issues confronting American law today and a fruitful analysis of their outcome can be made the basis of confident prediction," I can only reply that I very sincerely hope that you are right and that I am wrong. However, my purely political judgment is that in this country we will fumble gradually toward a better distribution of government under a less reasonable set of symbols.

I have read no other review which had the double effect of making me happy and pleased and at the same time compelling me to examine critically my own assumptions. Therefore, I give you my very heartfelt thanks for it.

*Sincerely yours*

---

## *To Mr. and Mrs. C.P. Arnold*

New Haven, Conn., April 6, 1936

Dear Father and Mother:

It has been a long time since I have written and I have been working day and night trying to finish a casebook which went off to the West Publishing Company[99] the day before yesterday. The labor on an affair of that kind is very tedious and endless. I got a colleague of mine, Mr. Fleming James,[100] to share the authorship with me and the labor, but even then it was hard to get it out on time. The vacation is ended and I am feeling somewhat tired but glad the thing is done. I now have the chore in front of me of proof reading about 1000 cases, checking citations, etc., but there is some respite for awhile.

I was in Washington a week ago Sunday and Monday and had quite a talk with Carl. He has nothing whatever to worry about except for the fact that a row in the Commission has unloaded a case on his shoulders without competent assistance. A bunch of timid people who are helping him out have filled him full of a lot of bogies which, in my opinion, amount to very little. The Hearst outfit, with a bunch of attorneys very much like Anderson, have started a publicity suit, as you know. I think the suit is ridiculous. Carl is afraid of Judge Wheat but I can't see whether it makes much difference whether they win it or lose it. All that is needed is a good speech at the trial and Carl has a real opportunity. His record is completely in the clear because he shows a written warning to the Commission about disclosing telegrams. My own opinion is that it is the duty of the Federal Communications Commission to disclose telegrams to the Senate and I would be delighted to argue that publicly. I would not care in the least what the judge said. However, the Commission is a bunch of very timid and incompetent people and Hearst has them frightened in the same way that Anderson has succeeded in scaring people in Laramie. The General Counsel is dodging the whole affair and unloading it on Carl. If Carl would simply get the idea that the case is a cinch and that the Commission had done right, and that no one would be harmed by an adverse decision, except possibly Senator Black, he will do fine. I think I cheered him up.

The type of attorneys he is getting, however, is terrible. There are two very cautious young men who look up rules of pleading and think of more things to worry about. They had Carl all bothered on a lot of very piffling stuff and I tried to tell him that all he needed on that type of objection was just a loud voice. If the court ever decided the case on the kind of piffle that these young men had dug up for him, he would make himself ridiculous. However, I sympathize a lot with Carl because he does not realize the situation in a trial court and has been under a very intense nervous strain. It is a great opportunity for him to get that experience with a lot of people around. Nothing can possibly happen if he makes a good speech and I am sure he will. He seemed to have some fear that he might have made a mistake somewhere but I went over everything he had done carefully and all I can say is that I would have been much less cautious than he has been and still would not have worried in the slightest. It is a great experience for him and he is lucky to have the responsibility. I think that I did him some good, although I got him a little out of patience with me because I kept insisting that the case was so easy from his point of view that he need not give it a thought. This irritated him a little but I believe that it was the right attack. The only thing to do in a case of this kind is not to give a damn whether you win or not. Nothing hangs on the decision except publicity and there is no possible way that they can get at Carl other than the general slams which are inevitable when anyone is in public life and dealing with a complete scoundrel such as Hearst.

I am therefore unable to take the situation very seriously other than to sympathize with the nervous strain which being the center of such a public controversy throws on Carl.

I went down to Washington to see the Solicitor General, Stanley Reed,[101] at his request. I had not met him before but found him to be a very nice person and had lunch with him in his private dining room in the new Supreme Court Building which is magnificent. No one in the world is done up in any grander style than in this magnificent building. The Solicitor General has a suite of offices which make Louis XIV look like a piker. He wants me to get a leave from Yale and present cases to the Supreme Court next year. The work is killing them and as you probably read in the papers, he collapsed during the A.A.A. argument. There are only three now who are presenting cases: Reed, Jackson and John Dickinson; they need help badly. I am entitled to a sabbatical leave at half pay, and they can give me $7,500, so I could make the grade financially. Reed talked to me in terms of a great opportunity,—said that even a lawyer in a large firm would not argue more than one or two cases before the Supreme Court in a lifetime and that they would give them to me to present just as fast as I could prepare them. I asked him where the biggest jam was and he said in tax cases. I told him that I knew nothing whatever about tax law and he replied that they had plenty of experts but very few who could give a competent oral presentation and that I need not be worried about preparation. I stated that I would not take a leave to do brief work because I would rather write articles than books but he told me I would not be asked to do anything of that sort and that preparation of that type would be taken off my shoulders. They appeared to have been impressed with my ability to present cases orally because of the speech at the New York Bar Association which they heard. That was the only sample of my work which they knew about and it went over pretty well. They intimated vague possibilities during the next four years rising out of such an assignment, but as to that I am not particularly interested as I have no desire to leave Yale. The chief fly in the ointment, of course, is the fact that if Roosevelt is not re-elected, I would be through January first with six months' leave on my hands and only half pay to live on. Inasmuch as more than half of my pay is taken up by life insurance, obligations on the house and tuition, that would leave me with precisely nothing to live on and I would have to borrow three or four thousand unless I got something to do for the rest of the year. However, the Republicans appear to be demoralized just at present and most of the people in Washington have no doubt of Roosevelt's re-election.

Well, anyhow, that is the situation, and I have been stewing about it for a week without being able to make up my mind. Every lawyer would like the idea of arguing before the Supreme Court and I hate to die without that experience. It is amazing how terrorized most of the lawyers are due principally to mean questions by McReynolds and Butler who are perfectly vicious. I have seen a couple of lawyers collapse under the fire because the Justices looked so big in their great robes and the atmosphere is like a funeral, excepting that there are nine corpses and all of them sitting around the grave. Bob Jackson, who is Assistant Attorney General, tells me that it is the most depressing atmosphere to argue in that he has ever encountered. He says it is like a cold, wet hand pressing on the back of your spine continuously throughout the performance. However, this makes me only the more anxious to try it to see what I could do. So I have decided to ask for a leave, although with some misgivings.

I am trying to finish another book for the Yale Press by the middle of the summer, composed of the stories in the corporate reorganizations, some of which I told you last summer. It would make a great book in the middle of the campaign and would not be worth anything afterward. This would take me to Washington the last of August and make even a short vacation out of the question. However, the Yale Press tells me that it is imperative that I get this second book out because one book sells another and you can't get anywhere with just a single book. On the whole, therefore, I believe I will apply for a leave. They refused to give me a leave for the Labor Board but that was largely because they regarded the Labor Board as something pretty radical. Arguing cases before the Supreme Court is sufficiently respectable so that I have a pretty fair chance. In addition to that, next year will be my sabbatical year and this year was not.

My book seems to be going fairly well. It is required reading in Dartmouth and I have a certain amount of boosters who are helping out, most of whom I did not know before. One of my most enthusiastic ones is Sir Willmott Lewis who is American correspondent for the *London Times.* I met him in Washington after some correspondence about the book. Curiously enough, Alice Longworth is much impressed and wants Sir Willmott Lewis to bring me around to dinner. I also got a grist of letters from lawyers in various parts of the country. I send you some of my letters that I have been getting and reviews. I would appreciate your returning the letters. You may keep the reviews if you want them.

Frances left for Missouri because her Uncle died leaving her Aunt, who is eighty, without any friends, all by herself, and the situation has to be ironed out. She will be gone about a week.

I took Turno back to Hotchkiss yesterday leaving George and one of his buddies who was visiting him all by themselves. When I was gone they decided they would go to New York for a lark and took a train, spending the afternoon and evening in New York and getting in about 2:30 in the morning, leaving a note telling me not to worry. I did not worry particularly and did not wake them up this morning, but when I get home this evening I am going to have a lot to say. However, the whole thing rather tickles me, although I presume I should be angry.

That is about all the news. I hope I am not foolish in applying for leave to go to Washington as the thing will be quite a nervous strain, but I don't believe I would ever be satisfied if I turned it down. Therefore, I think I will get it out of my system if the University lets me. In any event, if I go through with it, I will know more about the Supreme Court than most lawyers no matter how long they practice.

*With lots of love*

*To Max Radin*[102]

New Haven, Conn., June 5, 1936

Dear Max:

I liked your book review in the last *Harvard* very much.[103] I think that you bring out the general thesis of my book with more clarity than any other reviewer so far. However, I would still insist that the fact that a man can't make a common sense observation in public about government shows a great deal of uneasiness and a great deal of spiritual trouble. In physics it is entirely possible to make observations of any kind in public. In medicine it is more possible than in social science, although there are some lingering intellectual symbolic conflicts here.

The areas where uneasiness has disappeared are better illustrated in the field of sports. It is perfectly possible to make a common sense observation about a baseball game in public to the most ardent fan without dampening either his enthusiasm or ardor for the game. The game is symbolic of the greatness of his city and a number of other things, but he does not feel any worry about it. In government today there is great uneasiness. When a man says "democracy is a failure" or when an Italian says that "the country needs Mussolini, but I reject Fascism" he is just expressing a mental worry. The terms democracy and fascism are both reifications of a very complicated situation. Nor do I think that the symbols of the law are mnemonic devices. You haven't been attending meetings of the American Law Institute or the American Bankers Association. They may be such devices for you but they are loaded with very heavy connotations for practically everyone operating in the system. The term "mother" is a mere classification of women who have children, just as the term "trust" is the classification of cases. I quote you a typical reaction of that forward-looking group of men headed by Dean Clark who are making up federal rules so that trials will be less like a game. Clark had decided to include under the term "pleadings" all motions. The committee voted him down on the ground that motions really were not pleadings. Clark said "they will be pleadings if we call them so," and the committee said "no, you can't change a fact by manipulating language." This was in the year 1936 and occurred in a group of pleading reformers, most of whom claim to be realists. I don't believe it would have been possible to select a committee of prominent people of the Board who would not have done the same thing.

I hate to destroy your illusions about lawyers because you have so few of them left. However, I wish you would give me a list of legal terms that are mere mnemonic devices. I will give you ten cents apiece for any one that can be said to be only that.

However, there is no real disagreement here. My observation of the scene in front of me is only slightly different from yours. I believe the law is a much more primitive ritual than you seem to think it and I think it has little chance of being anything else. Possibly living in the enlightened State of California, where men do not react to taboos, has given you a wrong impression of the rest of the country. Enough of such argument. Your review delighted me because of its sympathetic understanding, and God alone knows who is right about such detailed observations as I have just discussed.

*Sincerely yours*

---

## *To Oliver M. Thomason*[104]

New Haven, Conn., June 19, 1936

Dear Mr. Thomason:

Your letter is a most interesting document. The reason that I subscribed for the *Industrial Democrat* was that it seemed a very extraordinary publication for a Louisiana town, or for any colony with which I had ever been acquainted. It was written mostly by you with a clear moving style and full of penetrating ideas. My own experience with both colonies and Louisiana was such that I was completely amazed at the ideas and the literary sophistication. Apparently, however, this is the product of an industrial accident which put a man like yourself into such a colony and does not reflect the intellectual level of the place. Your own experiences are most interesting. It seems to me that you have a great biography which is crying to be written. Not knowing you, my guess is that the reason that you are not a reporter for a prosperous newspaper is the fact that you are too much of an artist. The short piece on your highest ambition is beautifully done. It seems to me, therefore, that anyone with your power of expression and your objective point of view ought to write a biography. I can think of no more effective way of picturing the social system in which we live than to describe your wanderings in the newspaper world. We have been living in a typically medieval period—the dark ages of political thought—since the war. An industrial feudalism has been full of doubts and timidity. Such times are hell on the artist because people who would ordinarily support it feel too insecure to tolerate anything but a solution of their ancient taboo. There are signs of change however. You have a unique biography to write in that transition period. Your letter is sufficiently interesting to expand into a book.

Sherwood Anderson did a pretty good job in "Puzzled America"[105] but one has to go through the experiences which you have gone through in the depression to really picture the situation. Sherwood Anderson has been so successful that his best work is based on experiences of an earlier day.

Major Douglas's "Social Credit" is interesting.[106] Of course there is no hole in it other than the fact that no social philosophy is worth anything unless it becomes part of the folklore of the people. My own prediction is that it will not become part of the folklore of the American people because it is too well articulated. Articulated philosophies achieve their greatest sharpness in a period of revolution and I do not think we are going to have any. Security only comes through a mass of contradictory notions. I do not feel called upon, however, to write the folklore of the America which may finally emerge. When we solve our problems, instead of the social bookkeeping which will follow, we will necessarily be unexamined and inarticulate as is that of Sweden of the present day. Therefore I think Douglas's "Social Credit" is most useful as a force to make people demand things which they might just as well have. I doubt if it is as effective as Townsend who I think is responsible for the recognition of the Old Age Pension in the present Republican platform. However I do not judge governmental philosophies by their intellectual content because I think that that is, from a practical point of view, immaterial. I judge them only from their effectiveness in creating public demands which have to be recognized.

*Sincerely yours*

---

## *To Epaphroditus Peck*[107]

New Haven, Conn., July 13, 1936

Dear Mr. Peck:

I enjoy getting letters about my book and it was very kind of you to write me. May I say, however, that I am trying to avoid doing what Mencken has done and assuming that the human race are boobs. The point of view I try to take, although at times unsuccessful, is that of a naturalist observing a bunch of sheep. He does not either criticize sheep or defend them. He simply observes them and that sort of person makes the best sheep breeder. I am aware that such observations about one culture do look a little like cynicism. In other words you can talk about Philippine customs and taboos and their effect upon the Filipinos without being accused of being cynical about Filipinos. However, many people have accused me of cynicism in reviewing this book. Perhaps that is my own fault but insofar as I have been able to I have simply written down what I have observed.

I would not want to be doctrinaire about your observation as to the practicality and effectiveness of state control of child labor. How federal control can work out is of course a political guess and you and I could very reasonably differ on that guess. I did not use the illustration in my book for the purpose of discussing child labor but only to illustrate the effect of the symbolic type of argument. All of the literature which I have received and read on child labor has been a battle of symbols. Very few took the point of view which you do. In addition to that I think that most people who read my book might agree that federal control was more efficient. Therefore, I could use the illustration and it would click with the greatest number of people. As you no doubt realize, I am using it for the purpose of illustrating the typical type of argumentation. In regard to the merits of my belief that federal control is more efficient I can only say that I do not think that states are economic units and therefore the control of labor by state laws simply creates opportunities for selfish states to take advantage of a general situation. If it is true that the southern states are as emotionally opposed to child labor as they were to prohibition, I would certainly say that you were right in the last part of your letter. You cannot control a settled habit or attitude with people from the outside. My own impression, however, is that child labor in the south exists only because of political control of the few interested people. A thing like this is difficult to prove but nevertheless it is the result of my own observation. In any event I like the tone of your letter because you argue the case on its merits rather than bringing in the bogies which most of the literature on child labor consists of.

In regard to your observation about page 181 I do not believe that there is any real difference between us. Apparently I had not made clear the particular issue which was appealed. It was only a question of which judge should be the Receiver. The same question had been decided in the 90's in the Northern Pacific R.R. receivership in a perfectly informal way by the Supreme Court of the U.S. There were a number of federal judges who claimed to have appointed the domiciliary receiver. The Supreme Court simply administered the thing by means of an informal conference. It seems to me that matters of the selection of judges to sit on cases should be a part of judicial administration and not of judicial decision. I do not, therefore, intend to take the extreme position indicated in your letter. I use the incident only to illustrate how the ideal of trial by combat extends to simple administrative matters.

Thanking you again for writing me about my book, I remain

*Sincerely yours*

# IV

# WASHINGTON & ANTITRUST

# 1936 – 1942

---

*To Mrs. C.P. Arnold*

Washington, D.C., Oct. 23, 1936

Dear Mother:

This is Saturday afternoon and I am at the office working, but wishing I had time to be out because it is such a beautiful fall day. However my new job is very exacting indeed because it involves getting a background on all sorts of complicated problems with which I never had had any experience. So I have to put in Saturdays and Sundays as usual. I had been putting some time in on my new book which I had hoped to have finished by the first of November. I have it about two thirds done, but for the last three weeks I have not had a moment to put on it.

We were all very glad that father had decided to go to Rochester to the Mayo clinic. I am sure that it will do him a lot of good, and we will be very much interested in learning of the diagnosis. Please send me his address so that I can write to him.

I suppose that you will be interested in my experiences. I argued my first case before the Supreme Court of the United States last Friday. I think that I won it. In any event the Court did not bother me with questions which I could not answer, and when it came time for my opponents to talk (they were a firm of attorneys from Chicago) the members of the Court gave them a perfectly miserable time, asking them about the arguments which I had advanced. However one never can tell how these things are coming out till the opinion comes down. I would like to win my first case however just for the sentiment.

You would be interested in the whole ceremony. The Court sits in a magnificent room, which must be at least fifty feet high, with great marble pillars, which have heavy red velvet curtains hung down between them from the ceiling. The bench is about forty feet long which they sit behind, and raised above the floor on a base of black marble. There is a long table at which the attorneys arguing cases sit, and in the middle there is a sort of pulpit on which you can put your papers while you are speaking. The bench is so long, and the acoustics are so poor that you have to talk quite loud. Some of the attorneys do not realize this and their voices are lost in the big room.

On the stroke of twelve a buzzer sounds, and everyone rises. Then the curtains in the back part, and in file the nine justices wearing long black robes and looking very formidable indeed. Then the clerk intones in a deep base voice "Hear ye, hear ye, hear ye, the Honorable Supreme Court of the United States is now sitting. All ye who have business before this court draw nigh and give attention. God save the Government of the United States and this Honorable Court." Professor Corwin of Princeton who is retained to consult with me on the social security case brief was with me when court opened the other day. He says that they ought to change the invocation from "God save the Government of the United States *and* this Honorable Court", to "God save the Government of the United States *or* this Honorable Court." He insists that God can't possibly do both, and he should not be asked even to try. He should be given his choice and let it go at that.

In any event, after the invocation is over, everyone sits down, and the Court calls the cases. They call ten cases ahead, and make the attorneys in all the cases attend, because perhaps some of them will be submitted without argument, in which case the next case might go on quite unexpectedly. I had to attend and be ready for argument for two days before my case was finally reached.

There is a rule that attorneys representing the government must appear in cutaway coats with long tails, grey striped trousers, grey ties, etc. Why the Court wants to see them rigged up in this way I do not know. However now that I have purchased my outfit I quite fancy myself in it. It makes me look very mature and dignified. Attorneys who do not represent the government do not dress up as a matter of requirement. However most of them appear in cutaways anyhow.

I was quite nervous before my case was called, because the whole atmosphere of the place is as if some one were pressing a heavy weight on top of your head. However after the first few sentences were out it wore off. The Court asks a lot of questions, so it is impossible to prepare any set speech in advance. Attorneys who do this invariably get all balled up. I was particularly impressed with how scared most of the attorneys were. You see ordinarily an attorney will not argue before the Supreme Court more than once in a life time, and when they do they appear very nervous indeed. It is an entirely different experience from the homey informal atmosphere of a State Supreme Court.

My next case comes up around November 16th. It is a much more complicated case than the first one. The government is trying to collect nine million dollars from an oil company on account of a reorganization in 1919. The printed testimony and exhibits are all of 2500 pages and I have got to get so familiar with the whole record that I can answer any question about it instantly, and tell the Court the page I am referring to.

The transactions are most complicated and involve figures that are positively astronomical, because the property which the oil company acquired was valued by them at one hundred and eighty seven million dollars. It seems odd to roll these huge sums off one's tongue after the litigation which I used to try in Wyoming.

The thing however which makes the case most exciting is that John W. Davis will argue against me. I don't consider that John W. Davis is any smarter than I am, but he is a whole lot more impressive looking. I think that the case for the government can be won if I can only get the facts before the Court within the time allotted, and make them clear. I can do it all right if the Court does not interrupt me too much with details, which they sometimes do, in which case the hour is gone before you know it. The whole trick of the case is to get the record boiled down so that the facts can be stated simply. Therefore I am working night and day for the next three weeks. The department is fine about furnishing all the assistance that I can use, and I am trying to do nothing but live and think and talk and dream about this case during all the time that remains. It looks as if it would be quite a strain, but gosh it will feel fine when it is all over, and I am glad to have an opportunity to oppose an expresidential candidate in my second case.

After this case is over I have another which comes up on December 7th, but this looks like an easy one with a small record.

In view of the complexities of this litigation the trip to California is out of the question. That would have made a nice trip because the case before the Circuit Court of Appeals that I was going to argue was an easy one. However as soon as I get time I'll pick another case in San Francisco and come out and see the family. One of the conditions of my coming here was the idea of taking a few trips, and they will assign me a case anywhere I want, whenever I want it,—therefore you ought to see me about Christmas.

Any spare time I have had has been spent in consulting about the brief the government will file on the constitutionality of the Social Security Act.

So you can see that I am having an exciting time. However I am so busy that one day slides into another, and weeks pass without my knowing where they have gone. I'm afraid I am not much comfort to my family, but Frances is making calls on the Embassies, and is already getting a round of tea invitations, so she is well occupied. George is doing well at the Friends School, and likes it very much. Most of the children from the embassies go there, and so he will get an acquaintance of a different kind than any he has had yet. He likes the son of the Mexican ambassador very much indeed. Says he is a queer chap, who has spent most of his time in Paris. I think that the contact with a group entirely differently brought up than any he has known before will be very good for him.

I see Carl about every week. He and Olga are having an interesting time, and he seems very busy.

*Lots of Love*

P.S. When you sit down at the counsel table in front of the Supreme Court bench you find in front of you a pad of paper to take notes on and an old fashioned quill pen crossed on the pad. This is an ancient custom which goes back to the days before steel pens were used. Of course you don't take notes with the quill pen. You put it in your pocket for a souvenir. I am sending you the pen that I got when I argued the case last week. Please don't lose it because it is an interesting sort of a memento. It will come in a box as soon as I can find one and get it properly wrapped.

---

## *To George Parmly Day*[108]

Washington, D.C., Nov. 4, 1936

Dear George:

Your letter was so good and I was so busy that I did not dare answer it before election. I think I would have had to admit that it presented an unanswerable case.

The psychology of any political campaign is that everyone should vote for one party or the other. Practically, of course, it would be most unfortunate if all the good people were on one side and all the bad people on the other. You cannot run a democratic government without an opposition party and the Republican Party needs its liberals. I am quite willing to agree with your definition of yourself as a liberal and, also, some, though not all, of the specific criticisms you make are well taken.

However, political arguments are cold hash after an election. The result was a complete surprise to most of us here, who were convinced we would win but had no idea of the swing. Farley kept insisting that Landon would get no more than two states, but no one believed him. I am somewhat in doubt whether this complete crushing in the opposition is a good thing. A center of opposition must gather itself together again and the result of the last election will be fortunate for the country only if it means that the reactionary element of the Republican Party is definitely out and people like yourself are in.

In the meantime, I will make a pledge that if four years from now they put you on the Republican brain trust, I will vote for the Republican candidate.

I am terribly busy, with three cases to argue in succession at the next session of the Court on December 7th.

Give my love to Wilhelmina. With best regards

*Sincerely*

---

## *To George Parmly Day*

Washington, D.C., Nov. 21, 1936

Dear George:

The pressure of three cases which I must argue before the Supreme Court soon prevents me from answering at length your very good letter written after the election.

I am all for your idea of constructive criticism, except that with the present American press I don't think it is possible, since corporate newspaper writers, including editorial writers, are not permitted to say what they think. The majority of the editorial writers of the *New York Herald Tribune,* for example, were for Roosevelt and were compelled to write against their own convictions. The editorial staff of the *Washington Post* conducted a war against Eugene Meyer and did get some concessions from him, but as a newspaper publisher Eugene Meyer is more liberal than most. In a situation where 60% of the electorate have nothing but cheap and poorly edited newspapers to express their point of view no rational debate can be hoped for.

I don't know whose fault this is, but it is a fact. The cynicism of the newspaper writers I have met in Washington is amazing. Further than that, it has become clear that no one any longer believes that newspapers are attempting to give an unbiased account. Most of the instances, such as the vilification of Farley and Tugwell, which have been written against the beliefs of the reporters, you would not believe, so I won't go into them. One of them, however, you might believe. The election of Roosevelt was a foregone conclusion for at least two months. There were literally no newspaper correspondents in Washington, Republican or Democrat, who thought Landon would get more than 100 votes. This news had to be kept from the public in order to get campaign contributions for the Republican Party and it was kept from the public. David Lawrence, although he talked Landon in his column, refused to make any predictions when specifically asked by a *New York Times* reporter. The poll at the Press Club here showed an overwhelming majority, giving Landon less than 100 votes. It was won by Willmott Lewis, correspondent of the *London Times,* who gave him eight votes, which is exactly what he got.

The point I am making is this: When newspapers feel compelled to misrepresent news because of partisan motives, it is impossible to expect any kind of fair or constructive criticism.

Of course, I would not make such a criticism if the newspaper reporters had guessed wrong. Anyone is liable to do that. I am only making the criticism because they were not permitted to publish their actual opinions by the owners. The net result of the false optimism created has been the unnecessary wreckage of the Republican Party.

A party is an organization. It is not seventeen million voters. No party can live which uses its small professional group who are in offices in cities, counties and states and in Congress. The Democratic Party kept alive during the sad days of Davis and Cox by sacrificing its presidential candidates to the end that its professional soldiers should not be annihilated. I have been a machine politician myself and know exactly why and how this is done. In a losing campaign a party must have an eye to the future if it is to live. The Republicans, encouraged by a press which did not publish the real facts, have destroyed all their pivotal organizations everywhere in the United States. It will be twenty-five years before they get back into power, and don't let any soft-headed literary lady like Dorothy Thomas kid you about this. This, I think, is regrettable, but it was an inevitable result of the kind of campaign which was conducted. Whether the Republican Party has gone the way of the Federalist or not is, of course, anybody's guess. Maybe they can rebuilt their organization, but if they do it has got to be in towns and counties, and that is a slow job. It is easy to get fooled by thinking that unorganized voters constitute a political party. That is not true in any country in the world, but it is less true in America because of its four-year elections and the fact that there is never any chance to take issues with people at appropriate times when they will not be hopelessly confused.

So go ahead with your constructive criticism idea. I am all for it and also for building up the Republican Party. However, don't get the idea that you can do it by redistricting voters. Voters are too fickle. Shock troops always win against amateurs. There is no right or wrong about it. It is simply one of the laws of thermodynamics.

I enclose proof of a wire which I sent to *The Nation* on request, which will appear next week. I hope that you don't disapprove of the sentiment expressed therein.

With best regards

*Sincerely*

---

*To Philo C. Calhoun*

Washington, D.C., Nov. 24, 1936

Dear Phil:

I got off a letter to Moe, copy of which I enclose. Don't let anybody see it. I did the very best I could for Hugh, and even then strained my conscience. I know of nothing in the world more completely sterile than his project. It started out fairly well, but it has gotten more and more abstract until it is completely useless. We have enough abstract theologians translated anyhow without going back to pre-revolutionary Russia. However, I have written a disingenuous letter in which I indicate that there might be some possible good in it and refer them to my book, which they will probably never read, in order to protect myself from the letter being a boomerang.

You need not worry about starting a new party yet. The fight is still on. New cases against the Social Security Act are bobbing up weekly and we may have as many as four thousand of them before January. We have a board of strategy which meets once a week on the Social Security cases alone and later we may meet every day. It is rather interesting.

In addition to that I have three cases coming up before the Supreme Court, two of them in the December session and one in the January session. One of them is against our old friend John W. Davis. My record with the Court so far is perfect, having argued one case and won one.

In the meantime, I am trying to get a little time on my new book, which was supposed to be in the hands of the printers the first of this month. I have now promised it for spring and don't know whether I can make the grade or not. I have about three hundred pages of it done, but most of it has to be rewritten.

Frances and I are having a grand time in Washington and I am very glad I came down. The work is very exciting and it is fun to be with a crowd of liberals again instead of with a bunch who suspect you of being bright but irresponsible.

Incidentally, I had tea with Mr. Justice Butler[109] yesterday afternoon and found the old gentlemen quite charming somewhat to my surprise, because he acts so mean on the bench. He knew all about Wyoming and Judge Lacey and Bill and me, etc. He is a very companionable sort of guy.

With best regards

*Sincerely*

## *To H.L. Mencken*

Washington, D.C., Dec. 17, 1936

Dear Mr. Mencken:

I just ran into your mention of my book as one of three in the *Herald Tribune* of December 6. I write to express my extreme pleasure and appreciation. The reason that selection by you is particularly gratifying is the fact that I have followed your writing since the early days when I was practicing law in Wyoming and you were awarding custard pies. I have forgotten now whether it was *Munsey's* or the *Smart Set,* but I used to get the magazine regularly for your column. Your writing at that time was a breath of fresh air in a very stuffy atmosphere and I developed a tremendous admiration for both your style and ideas. I was one of the original subscribers to the *Mercury* and have religiously read all of your books, up to and including "The American Language." In fact, you and Cabel were my favorite authors for a long time. In view of this long literary companionship, nothing had pleased me so much for a long time as your selection.

I am on sabbatical leave from Yale arguing cases for the Government before the Supreme Court of the United States and am located in the Department of Justice, as you will note. I am, incidentally, in the middle of a new book, which may or may not be called "Symbols of Finance."

I am quite struck with certain analogies which can be made between the development of governmental formulae and the development of language which had never occurred to me until I read "The American Language." Of course, political theory is nothing more than a vocabulary with which men talk about governmental organizations. It is at times flamboyant, at other times it partakes of the argot of the criminal classes and at other times it is staid, grammatical and precise. You show that development in "The American Language" in your quotations from the West in about the 80's and 90's. I probably have not made the idea clear in this letter, but I would appreciate a chance to talk it over with you. I have your book on my desk at home and have already started the chapter from which I am trying to develop the similarity between language and political theory.

I am wondering, therefore, if some time in January it would be possible to have a talk with you. I could very easily drive over to Baltimore on some day that you are at leisure. Or, if you happen to be in Washington, I would very much like to have lunch with you. I am closely occupied with cases in the Supreme Court until about the 15th of January, after which time I hope to get time for my new book.

With very best regards and appreciation, I remain

*Sincerely yours*

---

## *To H.L. Mencken*

Washington, D.C., Jan. 7, 1937

Dear Mr. Mencken:

I can sympathize with your affliction since I went out to Chicago between Christmas and New Year and went to bed for a week myself without having planned the affair in advance.

However, I am going to be here until next September and so there will be plenty of time to get together.

I am particularly anxious to discuss the implication of your book on American language[110] on the study of political theory. It seems to me that the book is extraordinarily valuable for that purpose. I have always considered political theory as a polite and grammatical language gradually built up and refreshed by the argot of people tied up with political organizations. I never realized until I read your book how closely the type of political theory follows the type of language currently used. I don't know whether you have thought of these implications or not, but any accurate descriptive piece of work such as you have done is bound to have reverberations far beyond the intention of the author. That is the great merit of accurate descriptive writing.

Looking forward, therefore, to seeing you when you return, I remain

*Sincerely yours*

---

## *To C.P. Arnold*

Washington, D.C., Feb. 4, 1937

Dear Father:

The reargument of the Tex-Penn case started on Monday and finished Tuesday. The Court gave us an extension of time and Davis and I each had an hour and a half, all of which we took.

I had drawn up some charts to illustrate my argument and I send you a copy. They will be completely unintelligible and will not interest you, except for II and III, which may be of interest to show how I illustrated my argument that this transaction was not a reorganization.

The highlight of the case was this. In 1918 an act was passed exempting from taxation profits on exchanges of assets "in connection with reorganizations." This act was liberalized and extended by Andrew Mellon until it became one of the great tax-dodging devices for large corporate interests and actually operated to confer a bonus on the sale to large corporations. It is an interesting commentary on the antitrust laws. While they were operating in one direction, the tax laws, which no one knew anything about, were operating in the other. The reorganization provisions are so tremendously complicated that I can't give you an accurate picture, but I can illustrate the kind of thing by the following example, which, incidentally, is not quite correct as a matter of law but it gives the background.

Suppose you had started a store in 1913. In 1925 you have been successful in business and the store is worth $300,000. You want to retire and live on your earnings. If you sell the store to me, you will have to pay an enormous income tax because your gain will be assessed in that year. It may amount to $50,000 or $60,000 on that amount of money. The A & P comes to you and says: "Our stock is just as good as cash. It will pay you dividends. You can get money on the stock exchange as quickly as cashing a check. It will support you in your old age. If you exchange stock in your business for stock in the A & P you can call it a reorganization and escape $50,000 in taxation. Of course, you sell to the A & P.

This reorganization provision had been ingeniously used by very skillful attorneys until many people were able to get rid of their taxes by working out complicated reorganization schemes. This particular case was a stock promotion scheme. Five people owned some oil leases in Texas. They gave a 5/8ths interest in these leases to Tex-Penn Oil Company simply as a protection against suits for drilling. Tex-Penn operated the field. They kept a 5/8ths interest for themselves, as appears on Chart I. Two of them, Benedum and Parriott,[111] who are the taxpayers in this case, conceived the grandiose scheme of taking those leases and of putting them together with a lot of other companies of doubtful value, and on the basis of the whole thing selling stock to the public. They actually sold about $30,000,000 of this stock, raising about $9,000,000 for the new company and a great deal of cash for themselves.

In order to escape taxation they did it all through the Tex-Penn Oil Company and called it a reorganization. They made one mistake, however. The reorganization requirements of 1918 provide that the exchange must be of securities for securities and there must be no cash in the deal in order that it be exempt. They exchanged the assets of Tex-Penn (which were worthless) for 1,000,000 shares of stock on the new corporation, the Transcontinental, for which they had created a market of from $40 to $60 a share.

$50,000,000 out of thin air. Of course, the tax is not based on these market values. The Board of Tax Appeals found $7 a share to be the value at the time and that is what they are being taxed for.

Since the cash spoiled the exemption, all the parties testified that it was a mistake. As Davis said, it was a tragic blunder on the part of the attorney and there was no intention that cash be paid to Tex-Penn. The Board found that cash was quite a consideration. The Circuit Court of Appeals found that it was not and the question of whether the Board had substantial evidence behind it was the principal argument in the case.

On this basis the case looked pretty technical. Certainly, the parties could have done it in another way and it seemed too bad to charge them $10,000,000 for such a mistake. Therefore, I conceived the idea that this was not a reorganization at all, even though it conformed with the strict letter of the act. My argument was that the only purpose of the reorganization exemption was to permit corporations to recapitalize and readjust *existing* assets; that Congress passed it because it did not wish to put heavy penalties upon the use of the corporate device for more efficient organizations. However, there was no intention to exempt from taxation something in the form of a reorganization but which really was a sale for profit or, in this case, a pure stock promotion scheme. This was not a recapitalization or readjustment of existing assets. In other words, if you have a railroad and I have a railroad and we put them together, that is a reorganization and they will not tax us as a sale because it is presumed that the resulting organization will be more efficient and they do not wish to penalize us. However, if we each have a railroad before the reorganization and then come out with eight railraods and a kitchen stove, the profit is made on the transaction itself and is not a readjustment of existing assets. In this case it was worse than that because it was simply a scheme to sell stock to the public.

I am quite confident of the merits of this argument. However, I had a very serious difficulty. The case had been in court since 1926 and the argument had never been advanced before. It was tried before the Board on the theory that cash had been part of the consideration and only on that theory. That was the only theory argued before the Circuit Court of Appeals. Davis' answer to the argument was that it was too fantastic to need a reply and that since the point had not been raised on petition for certiorari or any time previously it could not be heard now.

I developed a theory which I will not detail here and which I think permitted me to raise the point. I was not so much interested in getting them to decide on that point as I was to take the curse off the case, since without this argument it looked like an exceedingly technical case.

On the reargument Hughes questioned me very closely on the matter of whether the point could be raised. I was somewhat encouraged by the following remark. He said: "Your argument on this point is very interesting, but can we consider it here?" I explained my reasons for thinking they could and they did not stop me. However, I don't care whether they decide the case on this point or not. Davis made a very plausible plea of injustice and as long as I could put this forward I think I answered that quite completely, although in an indirect way.

I have no cases to support me on this reorganization argument. It is the first time it has ever been raised in any case. However, I think that it is obviously sound.

On reargument I had a copy of the chart which I enclose before each Justice, not as part of a brief but to illustrate the oral argument. The first chart shows the assets that went into the reorganization and the assets that went out. The squares are only half filled because Tex-Penn owned only half of the stock of Transcontinental. The first chart is not drawn to scale. Then I had Chart III drawn up to show the difference in value Tex-Penn gave and what they got. The Court looked at this chart, except McReynolds, who refused to even open his. I think the rest of the others got the idea, however, better than on my first argument. It is a lot easier to explain it in a letter than it is before the Court because the actual facts are very much more complicated than I have stated in here. The rest of the chart has to do with other points in the case which I will not bother you with because they relate to burden of proof and require a certain tax law background to explain. As to these charts Davis stated they were full of inaccuracies regarding the position taken by the taxpayer. He got through his argument without pointing any of these out, so I was able to call the attention of the Court to the fact that if there were inaccuracies they should not be very important or he would have called the Court's attention to them.

The argument was much more heated than the first one. I also felt much easier and more at home because not having thought about anything else or read anything else than this record for two weeks I was pretty familiar with it.

The Court appeared to have the most difficulty with the fact that when these parties took the stock in 1919 they agreed not to sell it while the syndicate was distributing stock to the public and making a market for it. In other words, they agreed not to sell it during that year. Cardozo and McReynolds seemed bothered about this. In insisting that a restrictive agreement did not deprive the stock of value any more than if I got a diamond from my grandmother and promised not to sell it would make the diamond valueless in my hands. Butler said: "Isn't the test of whether the stock had value in 1919 the test of how much the state would have to pay for it if it took it on some such process as eminent domain?"

Here I muffed them all. Butler was giving me just the argument I needed, but I was over-cautious. In the last case I argued he tried to lead me into a trap. His method sometimes is to get you to answer a harmless question and then say, "Well, then, if that is so, you must admit so and so," leaving you in a hole. I was cagey and said: "I think so, your Honor, but I am not sure of all the implications around the words 'eminent domain.'" He then developed the argument a little more for the Bench until I thought it went my way completely. However, McReynolds, by his questions, still seemed inconvinced. All this, however, has nothing to do with the reorganization argument but with Davis' defense that there could be no tax in 1919 because the stock had no value then. Of course, on all other years the statute of limitations had run.

Davis closed his argument in quite an oratorical fashion. He said: "Not since Caesar sent his legions to collect taxes from the suffering and conquered people has a tax so utterly unreasonable and arbitrary as this ever been exacted by any government." This gave me an opportunity, I thought, to be less respectful and in my rebuttal I kidded him somewhat. Frances thinks that I got by with it all right.

Well, the case is over and nothing more can be done. I enclose the opinion of the Circuit Court of Appeals that I am seeking to have reversed.

In addition to the Tex-Penn case I argued two cases the first part of January, which were fairly easy. I won one of them and lost the other. During the argument of the one in which the opinion finally came down in my favor, I was trying to prove that a case in the Circuit Court of Appeals which was against me was wrong. I pointed out that the court had treated the loan of a "position" on the Cotton Exchange like the loan of a horse, when it was really a complicated set of relationships between the brokers, customers and clearing house. I concluded by saying that this was simply a naive reification. After the argument I went out to tea at the house of Mr. Justice Roberts. The minute I came into the room Roberts came up to me and the following amusing colloquy took place.

Says he: "You had the Court stumped this afternoon." Says I: "How is that?" Says he: "You used the word 'reification' and none of us knew what it meant." Says I (quick as a flash and putting him in his place): "If the Supreme Court of the United States does not know what the word means, then in the eye of the law there is no such word." Says he (struggling to get on his feet again after the impact of the blow): "Oh, yes, there is such a word now. Sutherland looked it up in a little dictionary and couldn't find it, but we got a big dictionary and looked it up and now we all know what it means." Says I (knocking him on the ropes a second time): "Apparently, then, I was in error in assuming too much learning on the part of the Court." Says he (coming back rapidly and winning a round): "No, I don't think you were. We don't mind learning new things from you fellows, provided you don't ask us to learn too many of them."

*With Love*

---

## *To Richard Joyce Smith*[112]

Washington, D.C., Feb. 19, 1937

Dear Dick:

I was so deeply moved by your defense of Sheila that I am dropping everything to answer your letter immediately. It illustrated all the saint-like characteristics for which some day you will be canonized. Those who know you best have always realized that no matter how unreasonable Sheila's conduct may be you always defend it and that no word of criticism has ever issued from your lips during your married life. It is this outstanding and undisputable fact which makes Sheila envied by all other women whose husbands are unable to live up to the standards which you have set for them.

However, in this case you have gone too far and for Sheila's good I must protest. I have no doubt that when she saw you lying on the floor the wave of tenderness to which you referred surged in approximately the manner and form which you described in your letter. Nevertheless, I think that you missed the point. My criticism of Sheila's conduct is based on the fact that her attitude was that of a mother toward a erring child and not that of an able and sacrificing woman toward a fallen hero. What she should have done was to have stood up with flashing eyes and said "I am proud of my husband for what he has done this day. He alone of this group has not allowed petty consideration of vanity and personal dignity to interfere with the great purpose of giving my sister's wedding the inebriate appearance without which no wedding connected with the Smith family would be legal. Were it not for his supreme sacrifice this party would have had almost a sober appearance." And then she should have turned to the slackers who always disgrace such gatherings and, pointing them out one by one with the finger of scorn, should have continued thus: "What have you—and you—and you (pointing out the conspicuous examples of sobriety)—done to make this party a success, you cowardly underdrinkers." Only after making the rest of the group realize the craven character of their conduct should she have permitted the tender emotions, which I admit are entirely appropriate in their place, to take possession of her. She should have disposed of the remains of the departed in a dignified manner, in which sorrow, of course, would be present but not unmixed with pride.

She did not do this and therefore, much as I love her, I think that she should be made to realize the error of her ways. Of course, it is noble of you to stand up for her. Nevertheless I understand your blindness to all of Sheila's faults which makes you rush to her defense. However I think that every wife's husband should remember that a word of criticism at the right time is sometimes necessary. Since you refused to perform this duty, painful as it is, I shall have to do it myself. Please read this letter to Sheila. I have no doubt of her reaction. Fundamentally she is sound and I think that all that is needed is to point out to her the way to truth and light and she will follow.

With best regards

*Sincerely*

---

## *To Eugene Davidson*[113]

Washington, D.C., April 30, 1937

Dear Gene:

Thanks for your copy of Borchard's book.[114] I think you are doing some good advertising for it. I hope that this represents a new burst of energy on the part of the Yale Press which will be carried on in my next book. As you know, I always had an uneasy feeling that "Symbols" was not being pushed with the vigor which my vanity as an author considered essential. The leaflet sent out was linked with books which I considered excessively dull. I note you have taken a new attack with Borchard's book in sending out several leaflets. May I inquire if you are going to do the same for me?

I haven't got the book[115] finished yet because of the press of a lot of other things. I have seven chapters, however, in pretty good shape. Will this be enough for the dummy if I send them on to you during the next week? Let me know and I will get the necessary stenographic changes made in a hurry. The last two chapters, in the present rush of business, will have to wait until the first of June.

Now that we are approaching an actual contract, I would like to clear up a few things in connection with the forthcoming volume. Since Mencken and a few others took up "Symbols" a number of publishers have been pursuing me with all sorts of blandishments, explaining just why the Yale Press did not sell ten to fifteen thousand copies of my last book and telling me how much better they could have done it had it not been in your hands. This stuff, of course, I realize is mostly selling talk. I know that the question of how hard to push a book is one of judgment. At the time "Symbols" was written I had no other publishers on the string and was delighted that the Yale Press was willing to take a chance. However, now that I am being pursued, I would like to straighten a few things out before the book goes to press. I will list them.

First, "Symbols" was not launched with any such fanfare as you have given Borchard's book. It was linked in the statements with several other books which I personally considered rather dull affairs. This, your competitors tell me, was one of the things that injured the book. In the case of the new book, are you willing to do approximately what you have done for Borchard's "Neutrality"? The leaflet you sent out sounds pretty good and it is directed at the particular book. It is much better stuff than anything you did for "Symbols."

In the second place, Mencken and Fred Kelly and a couple of other people who do not wish their names mentioned say that the format of "Symbols" is not suitable for selling purposes. Mencken tells me that it looks entirely too much like a textbook; that people like fatter books with thicker paper and that the new book should be gotten up on entirely different lines. I know that you have done this for Borchard. Are you intending to put out my new book in the same format or not? I didn't think at the time, but I am inclined to believe that Mencken is right. If you go into any book store, you don't see any popular sellers dressed up the way "Symbols" was. I don't mean to sound a critical note because I am very grateful for the treatment I have gotten from the Yale Press. Were I not, I would not give you the new book. However, I have been so bombarded by people who tell me that if I want to drop the Yale Press I will make lots of money, that I cannot help being impressed with some of the criticisms as to the handling of "Symbols." I am not recounting them here as personal criticisms of the way you have handled "Symbols." There was no particular reason at the time to think that any considerable expenditure on "Symbols" would be justified and I hope that you don't take this letter in that light. However, I will only feel more comfortable if these things are thrashed out in advance.

The third criticism which I hear again frequently is the fact that you are alleged to be unable to get your books in the leading book stores. One gentleman offered to bet me that I couldn't buy it at Brentano's in Washington. We called up and sure enough he was right. They had sold out all their copies and they had not replaced them. He claimed that his house would not have permitted such a thing to have occurred. I suspect this is pretty much hokum, but I will always recall the shock of going into the Yale Coop with three of my friends last June and finding that they did not have one copy of the book. They are still kidding me about it.

Being somewhat hard up, I would like to make a little money out of this book if it is possible and therefore send on the line which has been handed to me in the past month or so about the Yale Press' method of distribution for what it's worth. This letter is particularly for your own ears. I don't want any critical letter regarding the Yale Press to have general circulation among the group because I like everybody connected with the institution too much. Please let me know as soon as possible if the first seven chapters will do you until the first of June.

Finally, I would like to get this committee business all straightened out somehow or other. Two years ago when the committee was fussing with my book and I was not sure it was going to be published, I took the matter up with the Norton Press, who were willing to publish it if you wouldn't. This time I would like to have definite assurance when I send the book in. I know that the committee mess was not your fault, but still it is a hurdle which might delay the publication, particularly in view of the fact that I am going to be terribly pressed for time to finish it by the first of June.

With very best regards

*Sincerely*

---

## *To Barton Leach*[116]

Washington, D.C., May 17, 1937

Dear Bart:

Thanks for taking the trouble to write about my *Bar Association Journal* article.[117]

I have been spending a good deal of time reading, first, medical history and, second, development of psychological techniques. I am personally convinced that taking a moral attitude toward any organization, whether it be composed of cells or human beings, the arguments run in exactly the same pattern. I have literally hundreds of illustrations like the quinine one. In each instance the arguments run along the same line. Personally I think that once a moral attitude is adopted, there is no other way in which a man can talk or think. Of course, similarity is inevitable.

I have no objection to this way of talking and thinking for the purpose of developing a moral atmosphere, which I confess I like to live in as well as you do. I only claim that it is an awfully poor way of talking for purposes of diagnosis. You get the same kind of diagnosis of a social situation using this platform that an old-fashioned Protestant preacher gives you when he makes a rational analysis of the sinner. It may be a good way of keeping up the Church, but it has nothing to do with accurate description. Therefore, I would regard it as certain that anyone who took a moral attitude toward the constitutional crisis would insist that the quinine analogy was crap. Personally, I don't believe it is.

Anyhow, I regard a compliment from you as very worth while and I appreciate your sending it.

*Sincerely*

---

## *To Fred S. Caldwell, Esq.*[118]

Washington, D.C., May 17, 1937

Dear Mr. Caldwell:

It was most thoughtful of you to write me about my article in the *American Bar Association Journal,* since kind words are the only payment one gets for writing for this particular publication. I assure you yours are most appreciated.

Incidentally the whole controversy is becoming uproariously funny to me the longer it goes. Roosevelt has already accomplished his objectives and we are rewriting all our briefs in the Department of Justice in terms of the new definition of the commerce power. The question now seems to boil down to whether he will get two justices or six. I think it makes very little difference. However, many of us feel here that we cannot take the position of advocating less than six. The reason is that this is a permanent law based on age qualifications and would apply to another court in the future. Two justices will be a measure directed at this particular court and therefore the historian will call it "packing."[119] With this in view, it is better if the administration can get two justices to be beaten on the issue of six so that their record will be clear.

Personally, I am not a sentimentalist and this argument arouses me neither one way nor the other. However, there are a large number of people who feel quite strongly about this.

As the smoke clears away, one cannot help admire the uncanny political genius of Roosevelt. Needing an opposition very badly, he selected the battle ground. He has lined up against himself absolutely irreconcilable elements in our political life which cannot be held together for ten minutes on the kind of sentimental issue which he is peculiarly skillful at handling. The opposition of the American Bar Association is one of the most valuable things any popular leader can have. The opposition of conservative newspapers is also helpful just now. Truly, politics has fallen into a strange way in these times of change.

Nevertheless, I think that these are the facts and every time I think about it, I get another laugh at the way the crowd rolls to the bait.

*Sincerely yours*

---

## *To Norman Donaldson*[120]

Washington, D.C., June 2, 1937

Dear Norman:

The only trouble with the contract is the possible difficulty which may ensue because of the delay in action on the part of your committee. As I read it, if the committee doesn't approve, I pay you back the money advanced and look elsewhere for a publisher. This, of course, is perfectly reasonable.

However, when "Symbols of Government" was published, I found that the procedure was for the committee to send the book out to a critic, who took a couple of months. Then it was suggested that I conform the book to the views of the critic, which took me some time. Then, much to my surprise, I found that approval could not be given until the book, as changed, had been sent to another critic. As a result, late in August I found myself in New York looking for another publisher because I felt that had the second critic made more suggestions, the same thing would have happened all over again. I was unable to deal with the other publisher directly because I could not act until the Yale Press had definitely turned me down.

Under the circumstances, therefore, don't you think the best thing to do is not to sign any contract at all until you can let me know if you are going to publish the book?

You know a good deal about the book already. You know that I am perfectly reasonable in making changes or deleting objectionable matter. Therefore, I should think that you should be able to enter into a more definite contract or else that I should be left free to pay you back the money if you cannot give me definite assurances very shortly after the manuscript is submitted.

I have just about decided that "The Folklore of Capitalism" is the best title. I have tried it out on a number of people, including Stuart Chase, George Soule, Curtice Hitchcock and Robert Lynd of "Middletown" fame, and they all like it. I don't believe "The Symbols of Finance" will do under the circumstances. I am informed that "Feudal America" has already been used.

*Sincerely*

---

*To Francis W. Coker*[121]

Washington, D.C., June 4, 1937

Dear Frank:

I am very much ashamed of myself for not answering your letter. The reason I didn't do this is that every available minute of my time is occupied in trying to finish my book, which is due July 1.

All I can say is that like most liberals you misunderstand the situation. You seem to think that the court bill is the objective of the Administration. You don't quite understand the advantages of a flank attack. What is happening is just this. A bunch of people of completely irreconcilable views have been forced into opposition to the President by virtue of pendency of this bill. This opposition cannot get together on anything and is therefore not considered in the least dangerous. Most of us here in Washington think that the attack on the President was due anyhow and therefore it's good political strategy to get it over with in between congressional elections. Some day it may dawn on students of government that the fact that the Roosevelt opposition is highest between elections rather than at the time of elections is not a mere accident. There is always a reaction from attacks such as the present attack on the court bill. You can say Fascism so many times and pretty soon get tired.

Had this attack been made on the court bill it would have been made on the wages and hours and power projects. However, when people are screaming about the destruction of liberty involved in the packing of the court, they have got to be liberal on other matters. The wages and hours bill would not have had a chance without the pendency of the court proposal.

From a political point of view, it would have been entirely impossible to have won the court proposal had it been forced through immediately. However, the present rage would then be venting itself on the legislation which is being prepared. This legislation is being carefully timed.

You will note that today Roosevelt has revived the proposal again in a compromise form. This will again unite the opposition and compel them to be more liberal toward the other legislation.

If you don't believe this, look at the *Herald Tribune* the day that the wages and hours legislation was announced. In one editorial it bitterly denounced Roosevelt for continuing the court plan; in another it headed the wages and hours proposal with the title, "A Note of Reasonableness." The only thing that the opposition can consolidate on is little petty gestures like cutting Hopkins' salary and earmarking work relief funds. This is absurd and easy to beat.

This man Roosevelt is a political genius. He knows how to utilize opposition. He knows the tricks of the matador, who gets the bull to charge at a cape. The game on the inside is fascinating. It has its objective—the weeding of reactionaries out of the Democratic Party and the passage of progressive legislation. That legislation will be directed at getting new ideas accepted. It will be drawn with full knowledge that it requires amendment as soon as the ideas are accepted. Therefore, cheer up about this man Roosevelt.

Do you remember how you and I used to get together and point out his political mistakes, which would cause him to be reelected by such a reduced majority? Let's not do this anymore. He plays the political game as a general fights a war. His objectives against the names are always masked. He has a fine sense of humanitarian values and is playing for a place in history. The court bill is a mere incident to a large purpose. It is being used admirably. Now it has been dragged out again simply to get the opposition to shouting once more during the debates on the wages and hours. My personal opinion is that it will not be forced through because it is more useful as a threat. This is just a guess.

I don't know whether I have made myself clear, but time presses and I cannot explain in good literary form the brilliant political tactics by which the court has been put to flight. The historian of the future, however, will recognize that the progressive legislation was given a start, the Republican Party completely silenced, because they were afraid to bring out their big guns, and the reactionary Democrats worried because they needed no longer be considered as party members, except on sufferance of the Administration.

Of course, it may not work out with complete success. Nevertheless, look at it so far from the point of view of hindsight. A situation was created where the court had to break or else the bill would be passed. The court broke. The bill was continued in order to prevent any coherent opposition forming and in order to make the opposition a bunch of irreconcilables. This has succeeded. The highest point of hostility toward Roosevelt is being attained in between two elections, instead of at the election. The Republican Party has lost ten months because they have been afraid to open their mouths.

You may start to worry about Roosevelt whenever you find opposition in the Senate which can follow a leader.

With best regards

*Sincerely*

---

*To George Parmly Day*

Washington, D.C., June 8, 1937

Dear George:

The family are well. The weather is hot but not unbearable. Roosevelt is still President. The Yale Corporation has not yet fired me, so I feel very cheerful indeed this morning.

There is only one little cloud on the horizon. This fellow George Day, of whom I have written you before, has started in making political predictions as to the waning popularity of Roosevelt. Now, just between ourselves, George Day as a political prophet isn't so hot. He made some guesses about the last election which were almost incredible. Personally, I didn't think any the less of him for that and would not dream of calling those predictions to his attention. Now he has started in making more.

However, a friend of mine named Arnold insists on doing it. I have talked to him about the matter and told him that on the principle of the pendulum if anyone was as wrong as he was before the last election on his prognosis, he must be right now because the pendulum must be near the end of the swing by this time. Arnold says that political predictions are more like a golf game and anyone who makes a lot of bum drives is apt to repeat them. I cannot seem to do anything with Arnold and I suspect that there is no way of keeping him from recalling Day's last experiment as a political prophet in answer to his present remarks.

Suppose you get to work on Day and tell him that political predictions, particularly positive ones, are very apt to be boomerangs. In the meantime, I will see Arnold again and tell him that the "I told you so" argument is a mean argument and not at all fair. I do not have much hope, however, that these negotiations will be successful, because both Arnold and Day are a hard pair to do anything with.

*Sincerely*

---

*To Robert Lynd*[122]

Washington, D.C., June 14, 1937

Dear Lynd:

I am delighted at your expression of interest in the seminar. You can have all the time you want to decide because I haven't tackled the Dean as to finances yet and don't know what arrangements can be made.

So far as work is concerned, I am thinking in these terms. I will do all the work. All you have to do is come down and give us the benefit of your comments on the students' papers. What we will try to do is to throw an objective point of view on the various studies which graduate students are making in the law school. I will expect you to reflect your studies of "Middletown" in your comment and discussion of the papers of these men.

The first part of the seminar will be an attempt to inoculate law students with an objective point of view. Then the balance will be a discussion of the work which they do from that point of view. It will be a small informal group. No preparation of any kind on your part will be necessary. The objective of the seminar, so far as you and I are concerned, will be to make an outline of a more orderly organization for the next year. I will undertake to make the organization for this year in view of your having commitments. If you could get down there once every two weeks, it would be sufficient.

I hope that we can get together and at least start something, even if your participation is not as heavy as I hope it will be in the future.

*Sincerely yours*

---

*To Mr. and Mrs. C.P. Arnold*

Washington, D.C., July 1, 1937

Dear Father and Mother:

It's a long time since you heard from me. I have been so busy that I have not had enough energy to write. However, there is a lull this morning and I am going to dictate a chronicle of my doings for the past couple of months.

You last heard from me in Chicago when I debated with Senator Burke. I had several other engagements on the court plan. I had a debate with Senator Van Nuys scheduled before the American Judicature Society in Washington. Senator Van Nuys didn't show up because of a previous engagement, so that was a one-sided affair. However, the audience was sufficiently hostile so that he really was not needed. I was also one of the joint speakers at the annual banquet of Temple University in Philadelphia. The other speaker was President Stinchfield of the American Bar Association. He gave a very lugubrious talk about the state of the nation and I tried to kid him a little bit in my reply. I had a very good time and was entertained royally in Philadelphia. I also made a speech at Duke University. In fact, I got so many speaking engagements that it became somewhat tiresome.

My experience with the *American Bar Association Journal* may interest you. In the April issue eight articles were printed against the President's plan. They were so extreme that my friend George Morris, who is a prominent attorney in Washington and who happens to be President of the House of Delegates of the American Bar Association and also on the Editorial Board of the *Journal,* called me up and asked me if I would write an article in reply. I told him that I would not because I didn't see that there was any use in writing for that audience and that I was too busy. He wouldn't take no for an answer, but I held my position. Finally, he went to the Attorney General with his problem and said that the time was short and that as a member of the Editorial Board he felt that there ought to be something from the other side. The Attorney General intimated that I would be a good man to do the job, and with this pressure I cancelled plans for a short week-end vacation and wrote the article.

When I got halfway done I called up George Morris and told him that I didn't think they would like the article I was writing and that I thought we had better call the whole thing off. He said he couldn't do that and that I had better go ahead. I recite all this because it has a bearing on what follows. The article, which you may have read, took a somewhat satirical vein. The Attorney General read it in manuscript and was delighted. He called me up in the evening and asked me to take a copy to his house so that he could give it to the President, who was leaving for the South. Naturally it pleased me very much.

I heard nothing about it for a couple of days. Then the Attorney General called me up to his office. He told me that my article had been turned down by the *American Bar Association Journal* in Chicago and that Major Tolman had dropped in to see him about it. He was chuckling and wanted to tell me what he had just told Major Tolman. The conversation ran about as follows. Major Tolman stated the situation—that the article had been turned down—in order to get the Attorney General's reaction. He leaned back in his chair and said: "Well, Major, there are two Homer Cummings. One of them still has a little respect for the American Bar Association—not much, but a little. That Homer Cummings hopes that you publish the article. The other Homer Cummings has no respect for the American Bar Association and he hopes that you don't publish it. However, he feels that it is only fair to warn you that if you don't publish it, it will become a national issue and published from coast to coast as the article the American Bar Association refused to publish." He then told me that he insisted that he did not want me to change a line or a sentence in the article and we would see what happened. There followed one of the greatest struggles in the history of the Association. Hundreds of dollars in long distance calls were spent. They called up Chicago and New York and finally had a meeting of the Executive Committee. The Executive Committee decided that they had better publish the article under the circumstances. They pushed it back as far as they could and wrote an editorial that it did not express their views. However, it struck a responsive chord apparently with many lawyers because I have been simply overwhelmed with letters from all over the country about it.

George Morris says that he will not tell me the whole story about the fight over the article until I have resigned from both Yale and the Department of Justice. Some of the people whom I satirized were pretty sore. However, I had lunch with George Wharton Pepper and he seemed quite good humored about it. He is a very nice person and used to giving and taking. I send you the article in case you have not seen it.

In the meantime, I was forced to take a couple of days off to write a tribute to Professor Robinson for the *Yale Law Journal,*[123] which I also enclose. All this time I was trying to keep up with my new book which had to get to the Yale Press. Several other publishers wrote me about the book and I tried to get it away from the Yale Press, but they insisted upon publishing it themselves. Things got so bad that I asked Bob Jackson if I could have a couple of weeks and do nothing but my book. Finally I got the book finished and off to the press about two weeks ago by putting in all available time, including Sundays.

It was lucky I did because on the 15th Bob Jackson called me and said that they were in a jam over at the Treasury because they were being forced in with the tax investigation which they thought they would have several months to prepare for. The President wanted to call the rich tax dodgers as witnesses and conduct a sort of Pecora hearing like the one a couple of years ago when they called in the bankers. Bill Douglas had recommended me as counsel for those hearings. However, when the committee got together, they decided that they did not want to handle it that way. They simply wanted the Treasury to make a lot of prepared statements. He asked me if I would go over to the Treasury and look over the stuff and help them out in getting their material for presentation. This was Tuesday afternoon. I went over to the Treasury and saw Magill, the Undersecretary. He turned me loose with a couple of people to work the data up and I got up a sort of plan of presentation. Magill then called in Morganthau and I explained my plan, which Morganthau approved. Then Morganthau, Jackson, Magill, myself and Senator Harrison[124] had a half hour conference with the President.

This was the first small conference I had ever had with the President and it was very interesting indeed. The President sits in a little oval office which is quite small and unpretentious. The furniture is somewhat shabby and the whole atmosphere is very informal and democratic. You can hear the tourists visiting the White House going up and down on the outside with the guides talking to them. The President's desk is covered with little animals—elephants, horses, dinosaurs, etc.—very much like the ones which father has on the piano. His desk is clear of all papers. He started out the conference with a friendly word to everyone and laughed about the attacks because of his own personal income tax. He said that he had forgotten to put in $5.00 he had won at poker last year and he supposed they would be after him on that account. He then sketched what he wanted done at the hearing, which was a bold, vigorous attack upon the rich tax dodgers. I suggested that we call a number of New York attorneys who were getting up these fantastic schemes for the Morgans and the du Ponts. He agreed with me that this would be an excellent idea, and when the conference ended it looked as though that was what we were going to do. However, Morganthau, who is a very cautious man, suddenly decided not to call them. I thought at the time, and still think, that this was a very bad mistake. I would have liked to see John W. Davis on the stand explaining the ethics of his advice to his clients to use a Bahama corporation as a method of dodging taxes.

When I went back and got to work, there was a committee who helped me, but we started at 7:00 P.M. and the Secretary of the Treasury and the Undersecretary were due to go on in just about thirty hours. There was not a line of anything written. I got rid of the committee at about 10:00 o'clock because they were simply in the way and wrote until 3:00 in the morning. I then got up again at 5:00 and by 2:00 in the afternoon had the Secretary's statement all done. The Secretary in the meantime was occupied with the crisis in France and could not give it any attention at all. However, the speech seemed to click very well and he was very appreciative. In fact, at a meeting of the Treasury officials the next afternoon at which I was present, he came in and made a very extended statement of his appreciation. This, I thought, was very generous of Morganthau because ordinarily when you do ghost writing in Washington the person who uses your stuff never reveals who wrote it. His willingness to acknowledge before that number of people the fact that I had written the speech is quite an unusual thing here and I thought it was most generous of him. He scarcely changed a word of it.

However, that did not end my labors. The Undersecretary's speech had to be done for the same hearing and so I was up until 2:00 the next morning with that. Then came Irey's[125] description of the Bahama corporations. Irey is the head of the Investigation Department of the Bureau of Internal Revenue and he is a grand detective. However, he is unable to put anything in good English and so he and I sat up all night the next night getting his stuff in form so that it could be read. The next night was a repetition of this on the foreign insurance companies. White,[126] one of Charles Hughes' partners, had used this fraudulent device and he was our big sensation for that next day. Hughes dissolved the firm on account of the publicity. So the thing went on without my getting any sleep at all. By Saturday morning I was completely exhausted and they were trying to get in some people to help. Sunday we got in five other people and the work was distributed so that I managed to get a little sleep. However, it has been quite absorbing up to date. Today, however, we are sufficiently ahead with our statements that there is quite a breathing spell. I am now engaged in writing the final statement to be made by Oliphant,[127] who is the General Counsel for the Treasury. I have a lot of assistance on that and expect to get it done tomorrow.

I send the speeches which I wrote myself thinking they may interest you. The Secretary's speech, I admit, seems pretty good when I read it over, for having been written in such short notice.

The hearing should be over by July 6. Then I have a terrific job in getting my manuscript in final shape. It has to go to the printer on the 15th of July and there is a good deal of rewriting to do. So between July 6 and July 15 I expect that I will have another fifteen-hour schedule to keep up. However, I am feeling very well. I wish I were not in quite so much of a jam, but one thing seems to follow another so fast that it is impossible to get in breathing spaces. I don't see any chance of taking any vacation at all this summer because whenever I get to work on my official duties I get behind on my book.

I send you a copy of the cover which they got up for the dummy. The book will appear in the fall.

Just one more thing that you might be interested in. I was tremendously impressed with the confidence and cheerfulness with which Roosevelt acted. Here he was on the spot. The whole Eastern press was on his neck. Congress was forcing the investigation before they were prepared. He had, of course, the situation in France, the strike situation and everything else piling in on him. He was not in the least worried about anything. The Treasury officials went into the conference all bothered and in quite a stew. They came out feeling calm and confident. Roosevelt's power is easy to understand when you see how he conducts himself in a conference like this. He simply doesn't worry. He never gets excited. He makes his decisions fast and if they don't come out all right he is just as cheerful as if they did. He simply radiates confidence. He takes the position that half of the things that are done are apt to turn out wrong and if a good enough proportion turns out right it's enough. In any event, there is no use stewing and if everyone does the best they can, you have a feeling that he is satisfied. It's this power of instilling confidence in others and not fussing or lying awake nights which gives him his leadership and also his charm. He calls everybody by their first name. He called me by my first name after two minutes of the conference.

Another interesting thing which has happened is my experience with literary people. I gave a lunch for Mencken some weeks ago with Bob

Jackson and Jim Landis[128] as guests. Mencken was most entertaining and everybody had a fine time. Then Mencken gave a return lunch for me in Baltimore, inviting the editors-in-chief of the *Morning Sun* and the *Evening Sun.* The lunch was magnificent. I have never tasted such food or such wine. We spent most of the afternoon talking about the affairs of the world and I had a marvelous time.

The other literary adventure was in New York. I was invited as joint guest of honor with Robert Lynd, who wrote the two famous books on Middletown, to address a group of editors and writers. Among them were George Soule of the *New Republic,* Bruce Bliven of the *New Republic,* Stuart Chase, John T. Flynn, Walter Millis, who wrote "The Road to War" and "The Martial Spirit," and a number of other editors and columnists. I took the night train back to Washington after having had a most enjoyable evening.

This covers the highlights of my doings during the last two or three months. You won't hear from me again until after I am over the hump and my book is safely in the printers' hands, because I have a lot of night and day work to put in until then.

With lots of love to both of you,

*Affectionately*

---

## *To Eugene Davidson*

Washington, D.C., July 23, 1937

Dear Gene:

Nothing could induce me to work on that book prior to the return of the galleys. I have good reasons besides my disinclination. (1) You have the only corrected copy in existence; (2) in order to check such things as you have in your letter the whole manuscript would have to be gone over. Since it has got to be gone over anyhow in the galleys, why do it twice?

It would be a lot of help if, instead of looking up spellings or locations such as you have in your letter, you would just put a question mark so that I can check it. Or if the matter is not clear from the text, put a sign suggesting a footnote.

The principal checking I have to do is on the Securities and Exchange material. I wrote most of that out from memory and I know there must be some minor errors. I assume, however, that I can do that in the galley, too. I would rather pay for the changes than go over the manuscript.

Therefore, the only thing in issue is time. How much time will you give me on the galleys after you get them back? I have no schedule.

The President having overplayed his hand on the court bill and gotten soundly walloped does me out of my trip to Denver. I had to call up and cancel my part of the debate in spite of the fact that radio time and everything else had been engaged. The Administration has made an agreement that it will lay off the court bill for the rest of the session and therefore no one from the Department of Justice can start whooping it up just now. This does me out of my week in the mountains but it gives me a week on the book so get the galleys back as soon as you can and I'll start in on them.

To change the subject away from the book, I think that the President made a very serious mistake in ever compromising. He should have allowed himself to be defeated on the original bill without compromise and left it hanging over the court's head. At present the other side has the ball and there is going to be a lot of line bucking and forward passing for a while. You can see the results already. Tammany Hall, which was going to defeat Copeland,[129] has now voted 2 to 1 for him to run for mayor. Wheeler[130] thinks he is the greatest man in the world and is going to write some kind of a judiciary reform bill which he thinks will make him famous. They have overridden the President's veto on farm credits. There is going to be a lot of shouting and insurgency for a while which the Administration has simply got to sit and take in as good grace as it can.

However, I am not in the least downhearted because of my absolute and complete confidence that the opposing team can't get together on anything. There is no question in the world but that it is going to make a complete mess out of things. They are already getting very uncomfortable. O'Mahoney is sore at Wheeler because he is grabbing all the credit. Burke is sore at O'Mahoney because O'Mahoney criticized Burke. All three of them are sore at Copeland because they think Copeland is a poor fish and hate to see themselves tied up with him and Tammany. There isn't an ounce of leadership in the lot. In addition to that the Republican anti-Roosevelt forces are getting a little worried. I had lunch with Eugene Meyer who was somewhat concerned about the ascendancy of Wheeler.

Those opponents of the bill who do not know what it is all about are quite jubilant and think that the power of Roosevelt is broken. They are going to be the most badly fooled bunch in the world because there are two sides to this power business. First, you have got to break the power of the President, which they have done very nicely. Then you have got to put something into the vacuum which is created. This they are completely unable to do. Even George Day, who had been sending me copies of Wheeler's and Copeland's speeches, is going to get awfully tired of supporting these two. Therefore, I make this prediction which you can file away for future reference: There is going to be a period of confusion and Roosevelt will be back stronger than ever in a year. Good, bad or indifferent, he is the only leadership there is and things are moving too fast for chaos.

This guess is predicted on one assumption which may be wrong. My own belief is that the problems of unemployment relief, agriculture, farm tenancy, public health and administrative organization will not be solved within the next year and will require attention. In other words, I believe that there is sufficient discontent in this country, as illustrated by Gallup's poll income which shows two-thirds of the people don't think they are getting enough money to live decently. Now, it is not important what they are getting. The only important thing is whether they think they are getting enough. So long as they don't you are going to see no pressure to get back to normalcy. A change to a contented attitude on the part of the American people would upset all my calculations about Roosevelt's comeback. A building boom, for example, would knock my prediction into a cocked hat. I personally, however, don't see one in the absence of heavy governmental interference.

You are certainly a lucky bird to get the benefit of all this advice for nothing. If you want to send me five dollars for all the trouble I have taken educating you in this letter it would be gratefully appreciated. However, I don't suppose you ever will. That is the way of the world; there just simply isn't any justice.

With best regards,

*Sincerely yours*

P.S. Give me a time schedule on checking and I'll live up to it with the guarantee there will not be more than an average of two mistakes per page after I have read them through and maybe there won't be that many. I only made one mis-statement of fact in symbols in my last book which was never noticed by anybody and which I didn't find out until just the other day or I would have changed it in the second printing.

---

## *To C.P. Arnold*

Washington, D.C., Aug. 6, 1937

Dear Father:

You may enjoy the speech which I wrote at the request of the Attorney General, which is an attack on the emasculated Court bill which our friend Joe O'Mahoney, Burke and Wheeler drew up to meet the demand for procedural reform. Under the compromise it was agreed that the procedural reforms advocated by the President should be passed with only the Supreme Court eliminated. Instead of fulfilling the terms of that compromise, the committee emasculated the President's procedural proposals.

I see no excuse whatever for Joe O'Mahoney's conduct in this matter, even granting his sincerity in opposing the Court bill. He might at least have gone as far as the American Bar Association was willing to go with respect to reform.

This speech is now in Barkley's hands, who will assign it to someone or other. Therefore, you must not let this draft out because it isn't supposed to be known that I wrote it. However I was very much pleased with the fact that the Attorney General liked it well enough to send a copy to the President. I enclose a copy of the Attorney General's letter to the President about the speech.

*Love to you and Mother*

---

## *To Porter Sargent*[131]

Washington, D.C., Aug. 6, 1937

Dear Mr. Sargent:

I was delighted with your pages on perpetuating stupidity and keeping teachers timid. It is a beautiful job and one that ought to have a lot of influence.

I have your book on the list of things I must read as soon as I get a moment. I am now spending all my time in finishing a book of my own called "The Folklore of Capitalism" which will be out in the fall. This, with my official duties, keeps me entirely too much occupied for anything else.

The answer to your question "Who are the coming American economists?" depends on a guess as to what will be the governmental and educational philosophy of the future. My own guess, therefore, is that you yourself are one of the coming American economists. However, that is probably not the kind of an answer which your questioner expects. Therefore I give you the names of Max Lerner of the *Nation,* Arthur Krock of the *New York Times,* Walter Millis of the *Herald Tribune,* T.V. Smith of the University of Chicago, Irving Brant of the *St. Louis Times,* Mordecai Ezekiel of the Department of Agriculture, Ben Cohen of the Department of the Interior, William O. Douglas of the Securities Exchange Commission, and Assistant Attorney General Robert H. Jackson.

These are all friends of mine with economic philosophies which I think are inevitable. I believe that the economists in colleges are too far out of touch with governmental affairs to have the grasp on the problems which these men have. However, only a couple of them have economic training so I don't suppose this will answer your question either.

With very best regards, I remain

*Sincerely yours*

---

## *To C.P. Arnold*

Washington, D.C., Sept. 9, 1937

Dear Father:

I liked your poem a lot and am saving it with the things I collected on the trip. It's in your very best vein.

We had a great time. The boat was 41 feet long and contained a galley with a stove, plus somewhat crowded sleeping quarters for six. We left North Falmouth on Cape Cod and were gone about 11 days. Most of the time we put up in the harbors at night but several times we sailed all night. The life of these fishing villages from the harbors is very interesting and there is just enough to do on board a sail boat to keep one busy. There were five us us: Jim Landis, of whom you know; Allen Troop, who is general counsel for the Securities and Exchange Commission; Gerald Swope, who is the son of the president of General Electric; and Stuart Guthrie, who is in charge of the public utilities for the Securities and Exchange Commission, and myself. We had no crew but did all our own work. Landis, Swope and Troop knew how to sail a boat; Guthrie and I never having been on one before. There is a great deal of skill in sailing and it requires constantly taking down and putting up sails. We had an auxiliary motor which broke down the last day, leaving us out to sail all night, but the wind finally took us in.

The coast of Maine is a good deal like the Snowy Range country, all covered with spruces and white rocks which appear to be the same formation. It is dotted with islands. The prettiest place was Mount Desert,[132] which jutted out of the ocean about 1,500 feet and it is completely pine covered.

I have been back about eight days, spending all my time in an endeavor to get my book finished. I finally finished it yesterday and for the first time this year I have practically nothing to do. It will be out in about a month.

*Lots of love*

---

*To Mr. and Mrs. C.P. Arnold*

Washington, D.C., Sept. 18, 1937

Dear Father and Mother:

The President has just offered me the unexpired term of Jim Landis on the Securities and Exchange Commission. Douglas is to be Chairman.

I am leaving tonight for New Haven to see if I can get a year's leave from Yale. The Securities and Exchange Commission is probably the most important in Washington just now and the work will be extremely interesting if I can only get the Yale authorities to see it my way. The difficulties, of course, are financial. The salary is $10,000 but it will be practically impossible for me to live on that in Washington next year with the boys at school. It is more expensive than New Haven and I always get a chance to pick up a little money in the summer, which I can't do in the Commission. However, the chance of being one of a rather select official family in these very interesting times is, I think, probably worth going slightly in debt over.

I am leaving for New Haven tonight to try to get hold of President Seymour. I expect a rather chilly reception but am hoping for the best.

Although the term is five years, I don't believe that I would resign from Yale in order to take it, so everything depends on their being willing to let me go for another year.

This must be kept very confidential.

*With lots of love*

---

*To Homer S. Cummings*

Washington, D.C., Sept. 25, 1937

My dear Mr. Attorney General:

I am resigning effective October 18, 1937, which is the expiration of my annual leave. I am leaving Washington at the end of this month.

May I express my appreciation of the consideration with which I have been treated and the opportunities which have been given me in the Department. I have enjoyed my experience thoroughly and consider it well worth while. I am deeply indebted to you for my year in Washington.

*Respectfully*

---

*To Charles W. Street*[133]

New Haven, Conn., Dec. 1, 1937

Dear Charlie:

I was much touched in receiving your wire on Armistice Day. It hit me, however, at a time when I was so busy I could not think of an appropriate reply and the answer has dragged on until today. I still am unable to be properly humourous because I am so sentimental about the old group and the fun we used to have. I can only sing snatches of "That Old Gang of Mine" and light up another cigar looking out into space. The pleasures of getting up your own plays and acting in them is something which is reserved for the small town. It is the kind of thing they apparently do not do in New Haven, and the loss of this creative amusement is one of the things I have missed most since I left Wyoming.

It certainly makes me happy to hear that Joe Peberdy and Bessie Koch have finally been elected. Peberdy is essentially a tragic character and will make a great Hamlet. Bessie Koch is the very picture of Ophelia. If you don't happen to like Hamlet, Joe Peberdy would make an almost perfect Romeo and Bessie Koch as Juliet. If you don't like Romeo and Juliet, Joe would make a marvelous Damon with Bessie Koch as Pythias. And even if none of these possibilities appeal to the young intellectuals of the Club, no better actor to take the part of David, with Bessie Koch acting as Goliath, can be found than our old standby, Joe Peberdy. With this pair the Jesters ought to enter into a new era. There is hardly any combination that you cannot fit them into. Joe is a perfect St. George with Bessie playing the part of the dragon. Bessie would make a marvelous Santa Claus with Joe acting as a reindeer. If you want to do some creative and whimsical bit of ancient mythology, Bessie would make a wonderful Diana and Joe a perfect Apollo. And what a Jeanne d'Arc Bessie would make, with Joe acting all the other characters in succession.

All you need with this pair to make a successful year for the Jesters is to train the rest of the Club into scene shifters, directors, and peanuts, popcorn, chewing gun, and candy vendors.

Of course, if you really want to do something in a big way that would make you famous, I would suggest that you dramatize my last book, "The Folklore of Capitalism," with Bessie taking the part of Folklore and Joe, the part of Capitalism. If you did this, you would achieve what the French call *succes d'estime.*

With very best regards and very real appreciation in sentiment at your thinking of me on your first meeting, I am

*As ever*

*To Edward H. Levi*

New Haven, Conn., Dec. 11, 1937

Dear Levi:

Just finished reading over your article.[134] It is a beautiful job of very clear cut reasoning. I liked it very much indeed. I cannot tell you whether I agree with it or not, but you know I am pretty much at a loss whenever I hit the formulation of a general philosophy of anything. You will recall our old discussions. I am constantly caught into a belief that a purely mechanistic view of society, under which there is no free will, is the best for diagnosis and that is the point of view from which I try to write most of the time. This involves no philosophy in law whatever anymore than a child looking at a display of fireworks has a philosophy of fireworks. When I am compelled to state my philosophy I am apt to retreat to the New Testament which, as you know, is nothing but a bunch of parables. However, I can point at it and thus avoid the labor of dialectic analysis. A workable philosophy, it seems to me, is necessarily a maze of contradictions so hung together that the contradictions are either not apparent or else are reconciled by a mystical ritual. Your article makes me believe that this is pretty much the old natural law idea. In other words, the term "natural law" is a better way of describing the result than in other static terms. I have a more dynamic conception of society in the back of my head, but I cannot quite get the words to express it. It seems to me that the Russian ballet theory of law adds just the moving element to the natural law concept necessary for my comfort. In other words, the unity and rhythm of an institution requires people dancing in different directions and alternately coming together and apart. If anyone dances apart, he is out of the way. Words are very cumbersome tools, however, to describe the difference between a good and a bad ballet. I have never tried a constructive article on jurisprudence. Maybe I will some day. In the meantime, your effort is most interesting. I disagree with nothing in it. It does not quite convey to me the Russian ballet idea and yet, since I am utterly unable to express this notion myself, I can scarcely call that a criticism of the article.

I only hope that my natural vanity at seeing my philosophy discussed seriously does not give me a bias in favor of this piece of work because I consider it a beautiful job. However, in evaluating this compliment you should remember that personally, I enjoyed association with you more than with any other graduate student I can remember for a long time.

Best regards.

*Sincerely yours*

## *To Homer Cummings*

New Haven, Conn., March 4, 1938

Dear Mr. Attorney General:

To my great gratification President Seymour has recommended a leave. It will not be granted until sometime later, but his recommendation is, I think, sufficient.

I look forward with the greatest of pleasure to my association with you. I can say frankly that I can think of no one for whom I would rather work and I will endeavor to give you every ounce of service and cooperation of which I am capable.

As you will recall, I requested that the announcement be held up as long as was convenient to your office. Now that President Seymour has acted I see no reason for any delay, so far as I am concerned. You may, therefore, consult your own convenience without any further thought of my position in this matter.

With kindest personal regards and appreciation, I remain,

*Sincerely yours*

---

## *To William Borah*

New Haven, Conn., March 16, 1938

My dear Senator:

I understand that my appointment has been confirmed by the Senate and, therefore, I think it is not improper to write you about my extreme regret at the reference to yourself in my book.[135] Of course, I felt that I could not do this before confirmation since it might appear to be an attempt to gain your vote. I do it now, not because I think you are particularly concerned, but simply to satisfy my own conscience.

I believe that my chapter in the main is an accurate description of what has happened to the Anti-Trust Laws. In seeking an illustration I naturally associated your name with them. I was not writing about your career at all. The center of my attention was on what had actually happened under the laws. The result was to make the paragraph seem to blame you for a condition which arises out of very complex facts.

I had forgotten that it was in the book and was, therefore, shocked when I first saw the reference to you in the *New York Times.* However, since you were on the Judiciary Committee, I felt I could not explain until after the vote was passed.

I believe, of course, that my chapter is a reasonably accurate description of what has happened. Taken as a whole, I do not think the reader should get the impression that I am holding you responsible. Taken out of the context, the paragraph unquestionably does give that impression. I regret this particularly because of my tremendous admiration for your career. I only wish that I stood with you when the war first broke out and I was fooled into believing that we were going to make the world safe for democracy. Perhaps that was a futile stand, too, from the point of view of results. Nevertheless, it was a magnificent one and will go down in history as such. I also believe that even though the antitrust laws, as at present administered, may be imperfect, it would be fatal not to do the utmost we can with them since that is the only instrument we have. I doubt, therefore, if there is any real disagreement between us, although I have never, of course, talked with you about what I consider the chief defects. In any event, I trust that you will forgive me for a phrase which simply does not do you justice.

May I say, therefore, that your attitude towards me during the hearing showed unusual tolerance and fairness. Of course, I did not expect you to publicly take exception to what I had said. However, as you know there are many other ways in which, had you been a man of less tolerance, you could have made me uncomfortable because of my somewhat unguarded utterance. The fact that you declined to do this and kept the entire hearing on a very high plane shows conclusively that you regard public questions as being more important than any personal consideration.

With deep appreciation for your fairness and in the very sincere hope that your doubts about my attitude may be satisfied by my future actions, I remain,

*Sincerely yours*

---

*To Thomas Reed Powell*

New Haven, Conn., March 30, 1938

Dear Reed:

Thanks for your letter.

I think I am going to get a leave from Yale all right. President Seymour has been a peach about the whole thing and he has assured me that he will get it through in spite of some opposition on the part of the corporation. He told me to go ahead and for me not to worry. With this assurance I accepted the job.

I am quite anxious not to cut my ties with Yale since I am not at all sure I could get back, and I am not ambitious to go into practice. An academic seat on the Atlantic Seaboard at a decent salary is more to my liking than anything else I can possibly think of, and I have no illusions about the possibility of my election to any place other than Yale, at least, just at present.

It may have been foolish for me to accept the appointment because it was quite expensive. However, I never would have been quite satisfied with myself if I had not, so here I am.

I note your reactions to the Hazlitt[136] letter. In fact, you did not need to advise me because I could have predicted them. Felix Frankfurter and a number of my other high class friends all tell me I was wrong. All my low class friends tell me I was right. These matters of taste are hard to judge. Personally, however, I have no regrets about the letter. In order to understand this you have to remember my background. I have been a member of the Benevolent Protective Order of Elks and this is just the way us Elks act. We can't help it.

I intend to get up to the *Law Review* Dinner even if it wrecks the New Deal.

*Sincerely yours*

---

## *To Jerome Frank*

Washington, D.C., May 27, 1938

Dear Jerome:

You will recall in a conversation the other evening you stated that the *New York Times* had a conscience, and I agreed with you.

There was considerable discussion among those present as to alleged violations of fair reporting on the part of the *Times* and some thought that the *New York Times* was slipping gradually into the position of a paper that colored its news. You and I both denied this and you stated that if an instance occurred in which the *New York Times* appeared to be coloring its news you would see that the matter was presented to the management of the *Times.* I am going to take you up on that offer because I think no greater tragedy could occur to American journalism than for the *Times* to give an impression of unfair reporting. I have an instance which not only looks unfair but almost like a positive misrepresentation.

There were two criminal prosecutions brought against substantially the same corporations and individuals in the Mid-Continent field for violation of the antitrust law. One case was tried and most of the defendants found guilty. It was in fact a major victory for the government. The *New York Times* was among the leaders of the many newspapers in the United States which charged the Department of Justice with bad faith and inequitable dealing in bringing that prosecution. Positive statements were made (all of them untrue) that the oil companies were simply following governmental direction in the activities which were charged against them as violations. Not even the instructions of the Judge and the verdict of the jury were sufficient. It became an attack not only upon the Department of Justice but on the effectiveness of the judicial process. Later a protest was mailed to the *Times* tending to correct some of the things we observed. The impression was given generally throughout the country that this particular suit, even though it resulted in a victory, was unjust and unethical.

Such representations always put the prosecutor in a difficult position, particularly with respect to the antitrust laws. There is really no way of correcting them because the evidence in an antitrust suit is unlike that in a murder case and can not be briefly and succinctly summarized, and the evidence before the grand jury is of course secret. Such stories undermine public confidence in the administration of justice and in the courts. If a deliberate attempt were being made to sabotage the antitrust laws no better way could be found than this. However, the Department was not particularly concerned because the evidence in our possession seemed so conclusive. In addition to that there was another prosecution pending where we believed the evidence to be even stronger. Shortly before May 26 the defendants, who were substantially the same group as in the first suit, capitulated in the second one. They pleaded nolo contendere which is substantially the plea of guilty, and agreed, subject to the approval of the court, to submit themselves to maximum fines. This suit was important because it completely vindicated the Department's policy in prosecuting these oil companies. Of course the charge could still be made that the oil companies, with their vast resources and unlimited supply of attorneys, had been terrorized by the smaller and younger staff of the Department. Yet this would seem so absurd on the face of it that we were not concerned.

The story was released on May 26 and printed with various abbreviations in all the newspapers. I wish to analyze how three different newspapers treated it.

1. The *Baltimore Sun* published the story on the front page and the headline was "Fourteen Oil Concerns Will Pay U.S. $400,000 *Fines*."

2. The *Herald-Tribune* published the story on the 14th page but gave a correct headline, i.e., "Fourteen Oil Firms to Pay $400,000 Antitrust *Fines*."

3. The *New York Times* put the story on the first financial page but completely misrepresented in the headline both the character of the proceeding and the nature of the penalities. The headline was: "Fourteen Oil Companies Not to Fight *Suit*." The subheading was: "*Costs* to reach $400,000." Actually the costs were $25,000.

In other words when the *Times* was attacking the Department of Justice for what it called an unethical prosecution it called it by its proper name—a criminal prosecution. Few of the previous attacks on the Department of Justice by the *Times* have taken view of the fact that the headline carefully avoids mentioning either fines or criminal prosecutions while the release contains nothing which would justify this has given the men who spent long and unselfish hours an attitude of cynicism towards what I have always regarded as our greatest newspaper.

Frankly, all those intimately connected with the case have completely lost faith in the impartiality of the *Times* due to these incidents. Personally, I do not agree with them. I therefore stated that I would write to you confidentially and find out what explanation there was for these particular headlines. I enclose the clippings from the three papers containing the same story and showing the different headlines. I have no desire at present to make any public protest about this, so please regard this letter as a confidential communication. Nevertheless, I regard the matter as of some public importance. If there is to be fair and vigorous prosecution of the antitrust laws there must be fair reporting on the part of at least our most influential newspapers. Headlines are often more important than the small print which follows them, particularly in this case.

*Sincerely yours*

---

## *To Eugene Meyer* [137]

Washington, D.C., Aug. 5, 1938

Dear Mr. Meyer:

I do not write you for publication, but only to call your attention to what seems to be a somewhat serious misinterpretation of the Department's position with respect to its grand jury investigation of medical practices. I do not wish to object to the *Post's* criticism of these proceedings, but would appreciate it if in the future the criticism is based upon the actual position taken by the Department instead of misinterpreted variation of it.

I refer particularly to the following paragraph in your editorial:

> The statement by the Department of Justice "interprets the law as prohibiting combinations which prevent others from competing for services as well as for goods." Under this broad interpretation it might be said that any move of organized medicine to debar quacks is potentially illegal. And it might further be suggested that the entire program of the National Labor Relations Board, founded

on recognition of majority labor unions for collective bargaining, is perilously close to violating the Sherman Act. An Administration, which lays great stress on the right of labor to organize, should be doubly careful in suggesting that similar action by professional men may be open to legal question.

This paragraph is in error in the following particulars. It is impossible under the interpretation of the Department of Justice to declare that any efforts of organized medicine to debar quacks are illegal, potentially or otherwise. In the first place there is a specific statement to that effect in the Department's present release. In the second place, under the Sherman Act, reasonable regulations to improve the standards of any trade are not in violation of law. In the third place, there are specific laws relating to the medical profession. There are no grounds whatever for the statement that the present prosecution may lead to lowering standards, either by precedent or any other manner.

The statement in your editorial that in some way this proceeding makes the National Labor Relations Board in violation of the Sherman Act is equally absurd. The National Labor Relations Board is created and limited by the provisions of the National Labor Relations Act. The National Labor Relations Act, being passed subsequent to the antitrust act, controls. If the National Labor Relations Board goes beyond the National Labor Relations Act, it exceeds its jurisdiction. There are of course many acts which limit the application of the antitrust law. Nothing which this Department can do under the Sherman Act can in any way affect the subsequent acts.

The editorial seems to be an attempt to make the Department appear (a) as possibly lowering the standards of medicine and (b) as possibly interfering with the National Labor Relations Board. I am surprised that the *Post* should attempt to drag two such extremely red herrings across the path of this investigation. Both are highly prejudicial inferences and neither can by any stretch of the imagination have any bearing on the case.

I was also amazed by your statement that if the local hospitals open their doors to Group Health Association staff, it would be under circumstances which would give the staff "little confidence," in using the institutions. This is a charge which I think no responsible person should make against the staff of these hospitals. I assume you mean that in retaliation against the Group Health Association, the local hospitals would neglect to take care of sick people whom they had admitted. That the local hospitals would retaliate on sick people in this way is incredible. Further than that, I can authoritatively inform you that the Group Health Association will renew its application to be admitted to local hospitals without any fear that if they are admitted their patients will be treated with any form of sabotage.

With respect to the inference that this proceeding is novel and unusual, I would like to call your attention to the fact that as early as 1793 an English court held that the business of a surgeon, apothecary and man-midwife was such a business as was covered by the principles involved in "restraint of trade." About ten years ago in England it was held that similar efforts on the part of the English Medical Society were conspiracy and restraint of trade. Of course you are right in the statement that the case is unusual in this country.

It has been our custom to prosecute similar practices when conducted by labor unions. In fact, we have an office in New York which does nothing else and has met with quite extraordinary success. To subject doctors to the same standards as labor organizers I recognize is a shock to many people. One of the principal defenses in this suit will be that medicine is not a trade. I personally see no justification for this defense either in law or in conscience. However, there are thousands who feel quite strongly about it and the issue must be met.

*Sincerely yours*

---

## *To Hamilton Owens* [138]

Washington, D.C., Sept. 30, 1938

Dear Mr. Owens:

I regret not answering your letter and your editorial correcting the statement that I desire to put Dr. Fishbein[139] in jail.

Much as I hate to look a gift horse in the mouth, I think I should call your attention to three more misrepresentations which occurred in the correcting editorial. May I explain by citing a typical instance? Since it is part of the sort of thing we have to prove in court, it is not for publication.

A physician had a contract with a large corporation to take care of its employees.[140] He was an enthusiastic member of the local medical association. No objection was raised. Indeed, this type of practice is widely applauded. An excellent example of it is found in the Hershey service in Pennsylvania.

The physician referred to above, out of pure enthusiasm for his calling, signed a contract with a labor union which was identical in every respect with the contract he already had with the corporation. Immediately after the second contract became known, the following thing happened: (1) He was expelled from his medical association; (2) The medical association demanded that the hospitals exclude him; (3) It did not succeed in excluding him from one of the hospitals, thereby giving him limited opportunity to continue his practice; (4) The medical association then brought direct pressure to bear on the insurance companies on which he had liability policies. As a result of his efforts all of his policies were cancelled.

This man is a fighter. He thinks that this is a free country and that views on the methods of medical care should not determine the right of a physician to practice who conforms to the standards which a medical association has the unquestioned right to guard (under the rule of reason). Therefore, he is continuing his group practice at a great financial loss. He has to insure in Lloyds at a much higher rate. With respect to this sort of coercion, do you think it correct to say:

> Indeed it is even conceivable that in some technical fashion it (The American Medical Association) may have acted in violation of the law.

It is difficult for me to understand how you can call the prevention of secondary boycott a mere technicality as a matter of ethics or good government. So far as the *law* is concerned, it might interest you to know (a) that physicians have been liable for conspiracy in restraint of trade since as early as 1793; (b) that the English courts in the last twenty years determined identical practices of the British Medical Society to be conspiracy in restraint of trade; (c) that we are now prosecuting labor organizations for similar practices.

You further state with respect to this practice that the American Medical Association has "merely established a rule against cooperation with Group Health." This statement comes from the assumption that most editors allow the public to make, that the editor knows the evidence which the Department is going to present to the grand jury. Since grand jury proceedings are secret, the Department is helpless against this sort of attack. This, however, is not a justification.

Finally you state that the net result of all recent activities of the Department is the case against the doctors. The facts are, out of ninety men in my division, there are only two in charge of the medical suit. We are carrying on more antitrust activities than ever before, and are attempting to go elaborately into our prosecution policy by public statements. All of our statements have been received by the *Sun,* but little attention has been given to them except the one in the medical suit.

In view of these misstatements, is it an imposition for me to ask you to send a representative to the Department so that I can personally explain some of the policies we are trying to put into effect? Your editorials show a complete lack of understanding of these policies, and I think there is a public interest in making them clear. The *Herald-Tribune* was good enough to spend some time finding out what they were. I would appreciate the opportunity of explaining them to some editorial representative of the *Sun.* If this proposition interests you, I would be more than glad to go into our policies in some detail.

*Sincerely*

---

## *To Gordon Dean*[141]

Washington, D.C., Oct. 15, 1938

Dear Gordon:

With respect to our conversation regarding Wile's column,[142] which announced that I am only appointing Yale, Harvard and Columbia men, the following are the facts:

Sixty-nine men have been appointed by me on either the Monopoly or Antitrust payrolls increasing the roll or filling certain vacancies caused by resignations, in the old staff. The lawyers come from twenty-three scattered law schools from coast to coast. The economists and experts come from six different colleges. Yale leads with twelve men appointed. The reason for this is that having taught at Yale for the last eight years, I know, personally, hundreds of men from that institution, and, therefore, felt in a better position to judge their capabilities. For the same reason more men were rejected from Yale than from any other institution. They all know me and Yale applications exceeded all others.

George Washington University was second in the number of attorneys selected with eight. Harvard was third with five. Texas and Montana tied for fourth place with three each. Columbia, to which Mr. Wile ascribed preferred treatment, tied with National University, Nebraska, Chicago, Florida, Michigan, California, the University of Washington, and men with office training only for fifth place with two lawyers each. (One economist also came from Columbia.) Institutions with one representative are: Columbus, Wyoming, Wisconsin, Ohio, John Marshall, Georgetown, Virginia, Oxford, Oklahoma, Northwestern, Notre Dame, New York University, City College of New York and Southern California University. In selecting my men I had not the faintest notion of confining myself to Yale, Harvard and Columbia Law Schools, as appears from the appointments made. I attach a list of schools and the number selected from each, also a list of the names of the new men and the schools from which they came.

The method of selection of the men was as follows. I appointed a committee composed of the heads of my sections: Mr. Berge, a Michigan Law School man, Mr. Cox, an Oxford Rhodes Scholar, Mr. Avery from the University of North Carolina, and Mr. Abt of the University of Chicago

Law School. The appointment of this committee was necessary because for a while the applicants came in at the rate of twenty or thirty a day. It was utterly impossible for me to see them all. This committee did not appoint the men. It was a "sifting" committee, and sent in to me those who were considered worthy of consideration. In addition to those sent in by the committee I saw other men who were sent in by Senators or Congressmen or who specially desired audience. I do not know what percentage of the men I saw, but it was a comparatively small percentage of those who originally came in. Had I seen them all I would have had time for nothing else.

The unjustified statement of Mr. Wile's is damaging for three reasons. (1) It creates a feeling of justified indignation on the part of hundreds of applicants we have turned down. Some of these people are in tragic circumstances. Many of them came to Washington at a considerable personal expense. Mr. Wile's announcement to these men that I was only fooling when they were interviewed because of policy of restriction to Yale, Harvard and Columbia, will make enemies for the department in literally hundreds of communities. You can picture for yourself how they must feel about their expenditures of time and effort after reading his column. (2) The article will have unfortunate political effects. For example only this afternoon (Saturday) a Senator called me with some indignation to ask me if Mr. Wile was correct in the reason his candidate had been rejected. I managed to convince him of the complete unreliability of Mr. Wile's statement, but a number of other Senators and Congressmen are not going to get in touch with me and an ill feeling is bound to result. (3) The column is bound to have an unfortunate result upon further applications to the Department. I am hoping for an increase in my staff, and for that reason am keeping files of a large number of men so that I can be prepared for that increase. I got a letter this afternoon from one man withdrawing his application on account of the column. Others will undoubtedly follow. (4) I am a member of an association of Law Professors who come from all over the country. I am now on leave from Yale. The story depicts me as an educational snob. As a member of the bar I dislike being put in such a position toward my colleagues who have come from other schools.

Mr. Wile's statement is untrue even in minor particulars. For example, Allan Hart is not my assistant. He is a member of the Trial Staff and on a minor salary. The Number 2 man in the Division, Wendell Berge, is not a Harvard Law man. He graduated from Michigan. I am not a "one time Professor at New Haven." I have been granted a leave.

When I first read the story I assumed it was written maliciously for the sole purpose of causing me trouble. My reason for making that assumption was that the correct information would have been so easy to obtain from my secretary and only at the expense of a phone call. You tell me, however, that you are convinced that Mr. Wile was not malicious in publishing the story because he is not that kind of a person. I would, therefore, appreciate your taking it up with him, personally.

I confess I am in somewhat of a dilemma whether to let it ride or attempt to correct it. I dislike disputes with columnists, but this particular misrepresentation has most embarrassing consequences.

I think I know Mr. Wile's informant because I recall talking about Yale, Harvard and Columbia to only one man. He was from Notre Dame. In the course of a general conversation I remember telling this man that I had special confidence in Yale and Harvard law review men. This is true. However, it was tactless to tell him so and I should not have done it. A natural enthusiasm for your own school is apt to lead you astray when talking casually. I appointed Mr. Leddy from Notre Dame because he particularly impressed me, which should be sufficient proof that Notre Dame is not on any black list.

The man had gotten into my office as a special favor on a very busy day. He apparently took advantage of my hospitality by running to the press. The story probably arose from these careless remarks.

You may tell Mr. Wile that the particular man from whom the story arose seemed a nice follow, but I gathered from the interview a distinct impression of inaccuracy and unreliability. That was the reason he was rejected. I do not suspect him of intentional falsehood. His account to Mr. Wile was, no doubt, the result of hurt feelings which cannot be avoided when men are turned down. Since you know Mr. Wile I would appreciate your taking up the situation with him. It may be I attach too much importance to it, but I do not recall any story which has appeared reflecting on my character as an administrator which is so completely unjustified or on which the actual facts were so readily available.

If you think it worth while you may show this letter to Mr. Wile. The facts and list of names are all public property, except, of course, the statement about Mr. Hart's salary.

*Sincerely*

---

## *To Helen Rogers Reid* [143]

Washington, D.C., Dec. 2, 1938

Dear Mrs. Reid:

I hope that you will have luncheon with me the next time you are in Washington. It will not only be a pleasure, but will give me further opportunity to talk about a non-political antitrust policy and the possibility of getting support for it.

The fact that the Ford and Chrysler decree[144] involved a concerted action on advertising was unavoidable hard luck. We knew, of course, that we would bring down the wrath of the newspapers on our heads, but saw no way of avoiding it since the decree is actually a very reasonable solution of the problem.

I confess that I was greatly disappointed that the *Herald-Tribune* should sabotage a policy designed to give businessmen a precedent as to the kind of concerted action which they could safely undertake. I expected it from the press in general because I was aware that Ford and Chrysler were attacking a very sensitive pocketbook nerve. I had supposed that the *Herald-Tribune* would understand the difference between regulating advertising and the approval of the voluntary combination with respect to advertising which is inherently reasonable and beneficial.

Confidentially, the irony of the whole situation is that the first plan submitted by Ford and Chrysler demanded the right to cancel franchises of dealers who would not conform to what Ford and Chrysler considered to be reasonable financing methods. This would have eliminated any advertising whatever. This, the Department declined to approve. The plan which we did approve requires a great deal of advertising. Nevertheless, the *Herald-Tribune* misrepresents it as a plan to control advertising and drags in the old dead cat, "freedom of the press." This is exactly what my staff prophesied your editorial would say. I told them I had explained to your editorial board my policy and they understood the difference between a decision involving the reasonableness of a voluntary combination and a plan for direct regulation. They replied that your editor would understand the idea, all right, but that he would attack the advertising angle as an outrage on a free people. They were right. The editorial in question closed with, "It is as crazy a bit of delusive scheming—to call it 'thinking' is to over dignify it—as has come out of Washington in several years." The editorial made no mention of our trying to control collection methods.

You asked me my views on advertising. I haven't any in particular. Obviously, advertising, like any other form of spending money, is sometimes beneficial; is sometimes merely wasteful; and is sometimes positively harmful. This is also true of architecture which I have no desire to regulate either. I would prosecute a group of architects who restricted the type of building in a given area so as to exclude competitors. On the other hand, I would approve a zoning plan which was in a reasonable restraint of trade, provided that the matter was presented to me as a solution of a pending litigation.

This seems to be a reasonably simple idea to me. However, I don't suppose I'll ever get it across. Meantime, I will look forward to having lunch with you at the first opportunity.

*Sincerely*

---

## *To Raymond Moley* [145]

Washington, D.C., Dec. 3, 1938

Dear Mr. Moley:

In the *Newsweek* of November 28 you state, "It seems that Mr. Arnold was just letting people know, if they were interested, what he thought about advertising. Assistant Attorneys General used to be hired to tell us what the law was. Under the new dispensation it seems to be their job to tell us what the law isn't."

This is a complete misrepresentation of Department policy which I trust you will be anxious to correct. My release was a statement of the reasons why I was willing to recommend to Judge Slick in Indiana approval of a decree voluntarily offered by Ford and Chrysler authorizing them to take certain concerted action with respect to advertising. Judge Slick, after giving the matter most thorough consideration for over a week, signed the decree.

Consent decrees are not a new thing in antitrust law. I think I have made no modification on the policy of the Department *other than to state publicly the reasons why the decrees are proposed to the court by the Department*. The aim of making such public statements is to act as a guide to businessmen in similar situations. As you no doubt know, the Sherman Act does not prohibit all combinations—it only prohibits unreasonable combinations. A constant exercise of judgment, first on the part of the Department, and second on the part of the court, is required to determine whether under any given set of circumstances concerted action is unreasonable.

The lack of definiteness in the antitrust laws has always caused great pressure on the Department to inform businessmen as to what they *can* do as well as *cannot* do. There is no way of giving them any degree of security except by submission of a decree to a court. This was what was done in the Ford and Chrysler cases.

In other words, the Department took the position that concerted action to advertise the most economical plan of financing and to avoid certain harsh collection practices was not unreasonable. The court agreed. This is in no way regulation of advertising or anything else. It is simply a precedent as to the type of combinations under particular circumstances which will not be prosecuted.

It is difficult for me to believe that you would assert that businessmen may not combine in a method of advertising which is fair both to the consumer and to competitors. That is the only issue raised in the Ford and Chrysler case. You have completely misrepresented it. I enclose my release and my letter to the advertising publication for your further information.

This letter is not for publication as it is the Department's policy not to argue with editorial commentators.

*Sincerely*

---

## *To Jack T. Graham*[146]

Washington, D.C., Dec. 5, 1938

Dear Jack:

What a pleasure it was to get your letter. I have thought of you frequently. I don't think I ever had a happier time than the days in Laramie when we used to have time actually to live. Since then I have been engaged in such feverish activity without any possibility of vacations and under such constant strain that all I seem to get out of it is nervous indigestion. However, there is a certain excitement in being in a position where a single misstep will bring down a pile of bricks on one's head.

I am struck with the advantage of being a critic. All you have to do is to wait until somebody else does something and you can be quite logical and reasonable in showing the errors.

I told the Attorney General the other day that if I could only read the editorials about my statements with respect to the antitrust policy before I wrote them, I could write much better statements.

I have been yearning to come out to Laramie for two years now, and never seem to get any time off. There is always something that has to be finished, whether it's a book or a case or something else.

However, I still have a tremendous sentiment for the old gang. I certainly have never associated with a better bunch since that time.

I think you are right about "Symbols" being a better book than "Folklore." The test of this is that "Symbols" never sold more than 25 copies a week while "Folklore" at one time mounted up to 2,000 and was on the national best-seller list. This ought to prove that there was something wrong with it by any critical standing. However, "Folklore" was a curious accident. What I was writing was an account of a large number of corporate reorganizations. Out of this came a book of about 800 pages which no one would publish. I therefore had to cut out all the details and get back to a general philosophy and the net result was a repetition of "Symbols" with different illustrative material.

Best regards to you and please remember me to your daughter and Harry Thompson.

*Sincerely*

---

*To Russell Wilbur*

Washington, D.C., Dec. 21, 1938

Dear Reverend Wilbur:

Thank you for writing me so cordially about the misinterpretation of my remarks before the *Herald-Tribune* forum.[147] I used "church" as a figure of speech in a way which I had not thought would be misunderstood.[148] All my remarks are subject to the careful scrutiny of a number of persons who are supposed to be familiar with press relation, and they did not catch it either. Therefore, I am disposed to regard the whole thing as one of those accidents which cannot be avoided.

I am not disturbed by the attacks which the members of the Catholic Church are now making on me, in fact, it seems rather amusing that well intentioned people can be so stupid. They only thing that I do not like is the support I am getting. Articles of this character have been so widespread all over the United States that requests for my speech are pouring in from all over the country. The anti-Catholics are now looking on me as their saviour. Letters come in asking for the speech, they then read it and write me back asking me to join with them in the movement to keep Catholics out of office.

It is odd, but at various times in my life I have been involved in the same kind of a controversy. When I was Mayor of Laramie I insisted on appointing a Catholic as Chief of Police just at the time the Ku Klux Klan movement was sweeping over the country. I stood by my appointment in the face of bitter opposition, even though, I confess, it caused my defeat as Prosecuting Attorney the next term. However, I did not want the office very much anyway.

When I was Dean of the West Virginia Law School I supported Al Smith. The Klan was very strong in Morgantown at the time, and they burned a cross and set dynamite near my house, evidently as some sort of warning. Therefore I have gotten into plenty of hot water.

With these experiences behind me you can realize the nation-wide response from anti-Catholics to the publicity that certain Catholic journals are giving to my speech. It is most unfortunate that Catholics do not realize that attacks of this kind make prejudice flame up against them. It seems almost axiomatic that you cannot start a fight without having someone else fight back, and I am being thrown by a ludicrous accident into the position of a champion of an anti-Catholic movement. It is a position I do not like.

The articles in the Catholic periodicals bothered me very little, but the flood of letters acclaiming me as a new Protestant champion are most distressing.

In the last election in Maryland a ballot was distributed all over the state marking all the Catholic candidates for the information of the voters. It had an enormous influence in the election. Why is it that the Catholics do not realize that this is a very dangerous phenomenon? Their attack on me is not hurting me in the least, but it is unquestionably hurting their cause. Probably the figure of speech was unfortunate although I did not realize it at the time. I am, however, very much bothered at the harm they are doing themselves in anti-Catholic circles. Reverend White who is Dean of the Law School here in Washington has been one of the chief agitators in advertising my speech. He is as sincere a man as I know, and I think there is nothing whatever can be done about it.

In any event, I appreciate your writing me.

*Sincerely*

---

## *To James A. McLaughlin* [149]

Washington, D.C., April 3, 1939

Dear McLaughlin:

I will certainly give consideration to Mr. Maxwell S. Isenbergh. Tell him to send in an application so that his name will not get lost in the shuffle. I have, now, about 2500 applications, but of course most of them are not of law review caliber. If the additional appropriation goes through which I am seeking, there may be a very good chance of using him.

Changing the subject, I am interested in figuring out how more procedure can be introduced into courses like yours. The antitrust law is a tool which needs correlation with the practical problem it attacks and with other departments of the Government. This correlation must be entirely procedural, as I find that most students, for instance, (I do not have in mind any graduates of your own course) who have taken anti-trust work in law school, have no imagination whatever as to the use of the various procedures at hand. We have to run our own law school here in the Department for entering men. They know little about business structures. They seem to have very little notion of how to build up a case through examination of documents. They know nothing about psychological devices like request subpoenas or methods before sitting grand juries. They have no notion as to the actual workings of a special grand jury. They have no notion of the impact of an antitrust suit upon an industry, in fact they are only good at preparing the memorandum where a record has already been made up and the case is on appeal.

Since all this procedure has got to be learned anyway, and since the appellate end of it is much simpler than the investigation and trial end, I have better luck with men with business school background than those who know the antitrust cases. I am informed by counsel on the other side that they have the same difficulty with young lawyers in antitrust work.

I suspect that the union between a business school and a law school is an unnatural one, but do you have any ideas about training men so that they would be better prepared to assume responsibilities in a division such as mine? Maybe it is something that just can't be done. Nevertheless, a Government career is a very necessary, and I think, important function in modern society, and the problem deserves consideration.

I enclose a copy of my report which you probably won't like but nevertheless I would appreciate your reaction. I would also like to get your opinion on whether a course in antitrust laws might not start out with ten major cases pending in the Department of Justice and follow them through which would at least give a survey to the application of the rather simple formula of applying the antitrust laws to particular situations. Do you think that such pedagogic endeavor would be possible?

*Sincerely*

---

## *To William L. Chenery* [150]

Washington, D.C., May 5, 1939

Dear Mr. Chenery:

Thank you for your letter about my article. The first paragraph puzzles me. I do not know what situation at Washington you have in mind, which is holding up the article.

If you are thinking about possible amendments to the antitrust laws, I can tell you now there is practically no chance of any. Any proposed amendment is caught between the extreme trust busters and the extreme appeasers, and nothing ever happens. This has been true for forty years and will continue to be true. Amendments will follow enforcement and not precede it. Effective procedures will result out of the necessities of working them out. Nothing makes this clearer than the fact that even at the height of public interest in the monopoly problem I could get no attention paid to amendments which I myself drew up. I could get no reaction at all—not even a hostile one.

It is for this reason that I am also not interested in the critics who say that federal courts are not the best agency to handle civil decrees. In a vacuum I can imagine an administrative agency so formed as to do it better. However, business men are so enamored of judicial protection that there is but the remotest possibility of any change occurring. The only effect, that of the talk of amendments and the worry about whether federal courts are the best agency of control, is to postpone actual enforcement. There are tons of literature on the subject. People have used the better antitrust law in the future as an excuse for not doing anything under the present antitrust law.

John T. Flynn thinks that I invented the civil decree. Actually what I have done is to use criminal procedures to an extent never before known in antitrust enforcement. I continuously refuse to make the office NRA settlements out of which the movie and aluminum monopolies grew. I am trying to bring the civil process into the open. I decline to accept responsibility for its inauguration.

Therefore in my article I will be more interested in discussing *present* possibilities of enforcement than *amendments*—though of course I have no objection to explaining the possibilities of amendment.

If this clears up what you call in your letter the "situation in Washington" please let me know if you are still interested in the article. If I am to write the article I would prefer to use housing as my principal illustration in spite of John Flynn, because the construction industry will be one of the chief concerns of the Division next year.

*Sincerely*

---

## *To Kernan Robson*[151]

Washington, D.C., June 5, 1939

Dear Mr. Robson:

I have your letter enclosing what purports to be a memorandum of the conversation which took place early in the morning when you called me at the Bohemian Club. My own recollection of the conversation is as follows: You woke me up out of a sound sleep and immediately attempted to argue with me about the Giannini case.[152] I attempted to explain to you why it was not proper for me to see you or to have any interviews about the Giannini case because of my public position. You will recall that I declined to see you. I attempted to avoid getting into an argument with you and did make a number of answers to leading questions on your part, the exact phrasing of which I have no recollection of. However, I am certain that these answers were not as stated in your letter.

For example, it is absurd to say that I am acting as attorney for the SEC the same as I would for a private party, and of course I realize the Bank of America does not sell its stock directly. Therefore you are not authorized to use this memorandum as expressing any of my views.

I am, of course, familiar with the device which many people use of calling a public official on the telephone and then making an ex parte summary of the evidence of what he said in connection with litigation. To protect myself against that sort of thing I have all conversations with people whom I do not know taken down in shorthand by my secretary. In your case, however, I assumed that you were calling up as a personal friend. I had met you through the auspices of Sheridan Downey who is a close personal friend of mine and, therefore, never dreamed that this was the same trick of attempting to get admissions by a casual conversation. To say that I am surprised that this was what you were doing is putting it mildly. Indeed, I can scarcely believe it even now such has been my opinion of your high character and good faith. Therefore until I learn to the contrary, I will assume that the memorandum which you have sent me is not to be used.

All I care to say at the present is, I am not in a position as a public official to discuss the Giannini case with you for purposes of making any record whatever.

*Yours very truly*

---

## *To Frank Knox* [153]

Washington, D.C., July 6, 1939

Dear Colonel Knox:

I appreciate very much your support, especially since I realize its disinterested character. The administration of the Antitrust Acts is a matter of too vital an importance to industry and to the public to be made a matter of party politics. For that very reason I have refused to make a political speech of any character since I came into the Department.

Your interest prompts me to send you a copy of a bill which, at my request, Senator O'Mahoney has just introduced in Congress. The enforcement of the Antitrust Acts must be just, effective and constructive. As matters go now, business men get caught in situations in which a too scrupulous regard for the requirements of the law is a luxury they cannot afford. I know of instances in which illegal payments have been made to walking delegates by contractors in desperation to have their work go forward. In the heavy goods industries—in which recovery still lags—

price-fixing arrangements are often entered into as the only possible answer to aggressive tactics.

My great bother is the cumbersomeness of the remedies at my disposal. The private suit for damages is utterly inadequate to police industry. The confiscation of goods shipped in violation of the Antitrust Acts is virtually a dead letter. The resort to equity, and the use of the injunction, has little value as a deterrent. A business man, however questionable his activities, is in little danger until a suit is begun. Then he has months in which to avoid, limit, restrict, or deflect the prohibitions which the Government seeks to impose upon him. The criminal process which, for want of anything better, the Department has been forced to use in the ordinary case has serious shortcomings. The real question is the legality of some course of business activity; the issue in court is the criminal guilt of the corporation and individuals whose conduct is under review. The very antithesis is unfair alike to the Government and the persons under indictment. It forces the Government to put an industrial picture together under all the ponderous and time-consuming ceremonial of a criminal process. It is unfair to the defendants, for it is the indictment, carrying the taint of crime, which the business executive most fears—and the indictment is returned before the man is tried. And even if the courts fail to convict, or suspend the sentence, the stigma remains.

It is this situation, attested by scores of cases, which suggests the new remedy. The Department should have at its disposal a civil suit with civil penalties. The O'Mahoney Bill makes a restraint of trade a kind of wrong against the State. It simplifies procedure, and robs the antitrust suit of its imputation of crime to the business man. Its penalties may on first blush appear to be severe; but they are at the discretion of the court. It moderates, clarifies and revises the penalties in the Act as it stands, where now the sky is the limit. Instead of stiffening the exactions of the law, it makes them more humane. It creates no new offenses; it broadens in no way the exposures of business activity to the law. It merely creates for public policy a readier, more flexible, more usable weapon.

If I can get the bill through, I can waive the criminal process, yet retain the hazard to a violation of the Antitrust Acts. You may have seen the editorials in the *New York Times* and the *Washington Post* which, probably written hurriedly and without study of its intent and provisions, mistake the character of the bill. I can not otherwise account for the utterances, for the expressed views of both papers rather accord with the objectives of the bill.

I hope I can interest you in this. I am sending along with the bill, a copy of a memorandum which states the reasons which prompt it.

*Sincerely*

---

## *To Felix Morley* [154]

Washington, D.C., Aug. 14, 1939

Dear Mr. Morley:

I was much disappointed with the position you took in your letter of August 3 concerning the explanation of the misrepresentations of fact in the *Post* editorial.[155] You state that "when the Government brings a criminal suit for combination and conspiracy in violation of the antitrust laws, the natural assumption is that the offending organization, if found guilty, will be dissolved. The natural assumption is that if the American Medical Association and the Medical Society of the District of Columbia had been found guilty of criminal conspiracy they would have been dissolved."

It is difficult to believe that you do not yourself realize that no such assumption can possibly be made. Dissolution and criminal penalty rest upon entirely different grounds. If the *Washington Post* enters a conspiracy to violate the antitrust laws it does not mean the *Washington Post* will be dissolved. May I list the reasons why an informed person could not make your assumption:

1. The Department of Justice is on record that it has no intention of dissolving the American Medical Association. The *Washington Post* has no right to assume that our statements are dishonest without some basis for it.

2. The assumption is particularly incredible in this case because there is no conceivable theory which anyone can spin out of the wildest use of antitrust precedents which would give us a leg to stand on in dissolving the American Medical Association. It is established beyond question that such organizations as medical associations, bar associations and trade associations, where they keep within legitimate activities, are not illegal.

The Department is often falsely charged with dragooning and coercing business to adopt its particular schemes. Such charges are without any foundation whatever. We do have a policy involving the concurrent use of civil and criminal procedure which we have explained at great length in speeches, releases and public statements, none of which you have apparently done us the honor of reading. In carrying out that policy we never under any circumstances make suggestions of any kind. We made no suggestions to the medical society. However, if any consent decree should come out of this it should be along the lines of strengthening the American Medical Association in order to permit it to maintain higher standards instead of the inadequate ones which now govern the admission of physicians to Washington hospitals.

With a sense of disillusionment I realize that the *Post* is not going to correct its obvious and positive misrepresentations which have done much to confuse the issue in the medical case. This disappointment is shared by many members of the staff who had had a different opinion of your policy. For the benefit of the record, however, I will state unequivocally the following:

A. We do not have and never have had the slightest intention of dissolving the American Medical Association.

B. Such a suit would be absurd under the antitrust laws.

C. We believe that the American Medical Association is of great value.

D. We hope the American Medical Association becomes more influential along lines which have to do with the dissemination of medical information and the maintenance of standards.

This is only a hope. We have no desire or power to control the standards of the American Medical Association. If they do not have adequate standards we will be sorry, just as we are sorry about the present editorial standards of the *Post* as evidenced by your recent letter. However, we will take no action.

Finally, as we have stated over and over again, in this case the purpose of the suit is to prevent physicians from running an economic boycott for the purpose of imposing their own peculiar ideas on hospitals and other doctors.

I would not have the slightest objection to your calling our motives silly, our law ridiculous, or to your praising Judge Proctor to the skies. I do resent, however, your positive misrepresentation of our policy toward the medical association and your unwarranted assumption that we are trying to dissolve the American Medical Association.

There is little object in continuing our correspondence further. The balance of your letter regards matters on which our opinions differ. As you know, I am not willing to dismiss any prosecution simply because the offenders have stopped the practices complained of. This would, in my mind, be a commendation of the offense and an abandonment of antitrust enforcement. You are entitled to attack this policy and refer to it as "silly" if you want to provided you do not misrepresent the purpose of the proceeding.

Your second point is that you are confused about how the practice of medicine can be a profession and still be within the provisions of the antitrust laws. Our position is that the professional status of physicians makes concerted action along certain lines entirely reasonable. That concerted action, however, does not include coercion and boycotting of experimental methods by admittedly competent physicians. As I read Judge Proctor's opinion the boycott of Borden's Milk which occurred some years ago would be legal because of the learned character of the boycotters.

It is legitimate for you to argue about this all you please provided the issue is clear.

Experience has taught me that it is a waste of time to write to a newspaper editor. I am sorry I did not follow this with the *Post* because I am afraid that our correspondence has gotten neither of us anywhere.

With kind personal regards,

*Sincerely*

---

## *To Max Radin*

Washington, D.C., Aug. 4, 1939

Dear Max:

I do not know to what extent radical connections are a handicap in Government departments. That depends a lot on the temperament of the person in charge. However, I do not think that the blame can fairly be put on Mr. Hoover's investigation. He is instructed to go into all a man's connections, the type of people he associates with, clubs and other activities. This is very useful information. So far as I know, however, Mr. Hoover never has made any suggestions whatever on whether the man should be hired or rejected.

Let me give you an example. A young man from your school was taken on by the Antitrust Division. Mr. Hoover's investigation showed that he had been connected with a number of clubs and individuals who, in California parlance, might be termed left-wing or radical. It also showed that a number of people in Berkeley considered him a Communist, although it did not appear that he ever had any connection with the Communist Party. The report was thorough and accurate.

We thought this young man was competent and took him on. At the time there was considerable publicity and worry about Communists in the Government. Mr. Hoover's report enabled us to protect ourselves against such charges by securing letters in advance from responsible people. The young man is doing excellent work. We like him. We are prepared in the event anybody makes any ill-founded charges against us. If Mr. Hoover had not investigated all the student activities of this young man we would be unprepared. Therefore, in my own experience, Hoover's investigations of radical activities have been a help.

It may be that in the case you mentioned the connections of Mr. Robert Willard prevented him from getting a job. However, I am sure that Mr. Hoover himself never offers any advice to the particular department in regard to hiring the man. Therefore, if there is a fault, I do not think it could be laid with the Federal Bureau of Investigation.

With regard to Mr. Hoover's attitude on the radical question, I frankly never heard him express himself one way or another. He has been quite meticulous in not using any influence to induce me either to reject or approve an application. He simply sends the reports and I use my own judgment.

How much association with labor or radical movements affect different agencies in the Government, I do not know. However, I believe this is a problem entirely apart from Mr. Hoover's investigations which are confined to transmission of the actual reports.

*Sincerely*

---

## *To Arthur Sulzberger* [156]

Washington, D.C., Aug. 25, 1939

Dear Mr. Sulzberger:

At the very pleasant luncheon I had with you and your staff I got the very distinct impression that you approved of the prosecutions of unreasonable labor practices in the building trades. Indeed, the only criticism I got at the luncheon was my failure to devote more space to denouncing them under the antitrust laws.

I was, therefore, very much surprised this morning when certain persons opposing my prosecutions in the building trades came in with your editorial "Government 'By Definition' "[157] and stated that it would be made the spearhead of an attack on the unfairness of the proceedings before grand juries which I now am undertaking.

I have just read the editorial. It takes a portion of a personal letter which I had written to Mr. Crider, one of your staff, without any intention of having it published. Out of this letter it draws the inferences (1) that I do not wish the antitrust laws clarified, (2) that prosecutions of labor restrictions are unfair for that reason. It is a variation of the old argument "Don't enforce the antitrust laws until you have codified them." The specific example which is used to prove this is the prosecutions in the building trades.

I expect that the unions are going to be able to make very good use of this. I think it is a very fair question, therefore, to ask you why I was misled into believing that at least the *Times* would not attack my efforts to clear away the ridiculous restraints in labor. As you know, I am in for a tough fight from elements both within the administration and without. As you also know, the chief weapon against me is that the antitrust laws are too uncertain to admit of any fair enforcement thereof. Is it a fair question to ask why your editorial staff should criticize me for not denouncing labor more vigorously, and at the same time write editorials showing how unfair it is to use the present antitrust laws against them at all?

The editorial, of course, is a complete misrepresentation of my policy. I am not opposed to clarification. There are, however, two ways of obtaining it. One, by codification in advance which is following the continental model. The other, by the common law method of reasoning from precedents which are publicly stated. The first is roughly represented by the NRA, the second by my own policy. I have gone so far as to attempt to clarify prosecution policy through the precedent method in order to make it more consistent. In my published statement to the Attorney General last year you will find the following:

> The Function of Public Statements of Prosecution Policy:—
> In consequence, on May 18, 1938, the policy was adopted of publishing explanatory statements in connection with each important step taken in the administration of the antitrust laws. *These statements are intended cumulatively to formulate a consistent antitrust policy through the development of a body of explicit departmental precedents. It is hoped that a dual effect will thereby be achieved: to furnish a guide to business men; and to enable successive administrations to adhere to a consistent though evolving policy.*
>
> The statements which have been issued to date are set forth at the end of this report, since the report represents at present the only means by which the statements may be gathered together and given general circulation among lawyers and others who are advising business men.

The completeness of your editorial misrepresentation of my policy is illustrated in the following sentence which I quote: "The various law-enforcing administrators would then make their own personal decisions concerning what was or was not in the public interest and *each judge would decide each case in accordance with his own opinion.*" This is nonsense. Who ever heard of a Federal judge deciding a case except on precedent and principle? What right has your editor to characterize our common law case by case method as a series of arbitrary personal opinions? Your editor is using the old antibureaucracy argument against the common law process. In answer I quote again from my printed report to the Attorney General.

> The necessity of the case method of development and clarification is in accordance with our judicial tradition. It has peculiar utility with respect to the Sherman Antitrust Act because in every new

> case it is necessary to seek the judgment of the court on at least one of two questions. The first is this—Does a particular type of organization go beyond the necessities of efficient mass production and become an instrument of arbitrary price control? The second question is—Does a particular combination among organizations tend toward the creation of orderly marketing conditions which facilitate the distribution of goods, or is it an instrument to maintain rigid prices? The answer to these questions for the benefit of American industry can only be obtained by presenting factual situations to the courts, in a sufficient number of cases to cover our industrial problems. The laws will never be clarified before they are enforced—they will only become clarified afterwards. Not only judicial policy but prosecution policy must be developed by precedent and on publicly stated grounds if it is to clarify the law. Indeed, prosecution policy in a sense takes in a larger area than judicial policy. It must consider economic factors which cannot be stated in the narrow issues of a case drafted according to the necessary requirements of legal strategy. Business men are entitled to know what kinds of situations will lead to prosecution, because prosecution itself is a most important business hazard regardless of whether the Government succeeds in proving its case.

I have said these things over and over again in speeches, many of which have been published in the *Times.*

I would consider it perfectly legitimate for the *Times* to argue the inadequacy of the common law method of clarification as opposed to clarification. I do not consider it legitimate for the *Times* to represent my policy as being opposed to *any* clarification. If you want codes in every industry you should say so. You should not misrepresent the alternative which is the traditional precedent method of the common law through which most of our law developed.

Having spent a large portion of my efforts in attempting to clarify the antitrust laws through statements of reason in particular cases, and having only opposed the general clarification of everything at once represented by the NRA, I think I am entitled to a more informed treatment in your editorial columns.

The editorials on antitrust policy in the *New York Times* have consistently shown a lack of background. There is no evidence that your editor ever read the reports of the Attorney General. Therefore, I do not think that the misrepresentation of my policy contained in your editorial is deliberate.

This, of course, is generally true about lay writing on the antitrust laws and would not ordinarily call for a letter to a newspaper. However, your editorial staff in private conference not only expressed approval of my drive to clean up restraints in the building trade unions but also criticized me specifically for not making them stronger. That attitude, I think, makes it a fair question for me to ask why it is the *New York Times* is taking the lead in sabotaging my building prosecutions by throwing over them these two red herrings— (1) that I am opposed to any clarification at all, and (2) that prior to codification prosecutions are unfair.

The closing sentence in the next to the last paragraph of your article reads as follows: "To repeal all such laws and regulations on the ground that they were 'complicated,' and to put the whole matter in the discretion of administrators, would open the doors not merely to administrative abuses but to chaos." I ask you in all decency and candor if this is a fair representation of what I am trying to do in the building trades—if this is a fair review of the report of the Attorney General, copy of which I enclose.

Incidentally the last paragraph does not correctly state the purposes of the O'Mahoney Bill. In the first place, it is not the principal recommendation of the Committee. The Department of Justice drew up a number of specific patent recommendations which were based upon an elaborate investigation of facts and we certainly do go in the lines of specificness which your editorial writer desires. In the second place, the purposes of the O'Mahoney Bill are not to impose additional penalties but rather to avoid using the indictment process. However, this letter is long enough, and I don't want to argue that since you never gave me any impression that you approved of the Bill.

*Sincerely*

---

## *To Mr. and Mrs. Dexter Keezer* [158]

Washington, D.C., Oct. 26, 1939

Dear Dexter and Ann:

I have no reasonable excuse for failing to write you since I got home. I have kept putting it off with the idea that I might say something clever if I thought hard enough. In addition to that I have been to Detroit, New York and Chicago and had two cases to prepare for the Supreme Court.

I don't recall ever having had a better time than while in Portland. The fishing was perfect, like everything was perfect. It is the first mountain outing I have had for years.

I am embarrassed about the $20 which my secretary just informed me has been added to my account. She had no business cashing the check, but having done so I don't suppose there is any use in my sending a check back. I am going to have to figure some other way of getting even. Anyhow, it was a very generous gesture and one which makes my own

Dutch treat philosophy which I consistently follow in Washington look parsimonious. These glad-hand, liberal spenders, these gay butterflies who scatter money to the wind certainly are attractive people until winter comes and they find themselves on relief. The trouble with our country is that thrifty people save their money and the spenders spend it. If we could just get the spenders to save and the thrifty to spend; if the parsimonious could become extravagant and the extravagant parsimonious; if the virtuous would only slip a little from time to time and the wicked would only become good, many of our most perplexing problems would be solved and the influence of the home would again become one of those great consolidated factors which might save us from bureaucracy, communism, and the totalitarian state. A realization of this profound truth is the result of your sending the $20. I am going to preach it from now on so that your money will not be misspent. In a confused world it is important to have a clear objective.

*Affectionately*

---

*To Dorothy Thompson* [159]

Washington, D.C., Nov. 27, 1939

My dear Miss Thompson:

May I express my appreciation of your support with respect to my letter to the Central Labor Union of Indianapolis.

This letter is not for publication or quotation, nor is it written with the idea that your very helpful column needs any correction. I write this in the hope that you will have the patience to read it and understand some of our difficulties.

The Antitrust Division cannot act except in a case where there is a direct effect on interstate commerce. This limits us quite severely in prosecuting the practices you point out in the theatrical union. In the building trades we are usually able to prove a very substantial stoppage of the flow of goods between the states. For example, we contend that a labor restriction limiting the paint brush that can be used to 4½ inches stops the flow of paint from the factory to the house. We think we are on solid ground here, although we have to face the gamut of the Federal courts before this is established. On such questions, however, we are willing to take a chance.

However, it is practically impossible to spell out sufficient restriction on the flow of goods in interstate commerce to do anything about the theatrical unions in New York. We have stepped into theatrical strikes in the moving picture industry. I give you an example of the kind of dispute in the theatrical industry where we feel we have jurisdiction: The IATSE[160] were picketing the largest independent moving picture chain in Brooklyn because they had been organized by the Empire State Union. The IATSE demanded that the contract with the Empire State be broken and only that IATSE employees be hired. This went on for about a year and the Antitrust Division took no action because we could see no interference with interstate commerce. Finally the IATSE threatened to pull out of the operators of the film exchanges if the major producers did not refuse films to the Brooklyn independent. Had the IATSE pulled their operators from the film exchanges they would have closed every theater in New York City in an attempt to force the independent union to its knees. Here was a clear interference with interstate commerce which could not be justified as furthering a reasonable labor objective. We therefore informed the IATSE that if they closed the film exchanges criminal prosecution would immediately follow. They suggested fighting the thing out on the civil side but we declined to accede. The net result was that the unions settled their differences somehow and no major dislocation of the industry followed. Had we taken a different stand a serious strike over an illegal objective would have been the result.

You can see, however, that we are powerless *until a very substantial stoppage of goods in interstate commerce occurs*. What is the answer? Obviously it is close cooperation between the Department of Justice and the local officials who should enforce the *State* antitrust laws. If we could work together whenever someone said "intra-state commerce" a local man could step forward, and whenever someone said "interstate commerce" the Department could act. It is the only effective way of handling the situation. To put it specifically, if Mr. Dewey, who has a much higher paid personnel than we have and who has nearly as many men for New York City alone as we have for the entire country, would join forces with us we could clean up the situation which you outline in your column in no time. Without his cooperation we cannot handle this particular type of problem.

Obviously we are not going to get very much from state officials' cooperation. The political issues are too hot. So far as I am personally concerned I have no political ambitions whatever and therefore this kind of pressure cannot be put upon me. However, you can understand why local prosecutors refuse to step into the labor picture. Note Mr. Epstein's letter in Sunday's *New York Times* of November 26 attacking my labor policy. It has been a tough proposition for the administration to run the chances of alienating such a large section of voters. However, the administration has stood by me. The natural tactics of the opposition will be to take advantage of the situation by claiming that they are the real friends of labor. Therefore, it is not likely that we will get intrastate cooperation.

I am not going to publicly comment on this lack of cooperation. The reason is obvious. If I charge the other side with failing to do their duty it will have the tendency to throw the Antitrust Division into politics. So far I have succeeded in keeping it out of politics by declining to make any political speeches whatever. Our effectiveness depends upon continuing this attitude.

In the meantime I am going ahead with my own efforts in the building line to the fullest extent that funds are granted to me by Congress. I intend to ask for more funds at the next session and am convinced that correcting the situation is solely a question of adequate funds and personnel. This all depends on whether I win any cases when I get to court. I am confident I will win them. However, if I lose them, prosecution itself can do much to clarify the situation. I am hopeful that if my own program succeeds, the pressure on certain state officials to follow will increase and thus local situations such as you describe in your column will become ameliorated.

*Sincerely*

---

## *To Max Lerner* [161]

Washington, D.C., Dec. 9, 1939

Dear Max:

Sorry I neglected to acknowledge your book.[162] The reason is that I have been under too much pressure to get a chance to read it. I intend to get at it during Christmas vacation, however.

I am weeks behind in all of my personal correspondence and I am answering this letter late Saturday afternoon without time or energy to discuss anything.

I am sure that I will like your book in spite of the fact that I think ideas are not real weapons—they are opiates. People who deal exclusively with ideas necessarily live in a dream world. I don't say that you are living in a dream world, and I haven't read this new book. Nevertheless, we do part company somewhere along these lines.

I enclose copy of my testimony before the TNEC and also copy of my letter to the labor union. I think I can make a dent in the building situation if I can get funds and personnel. I think that these are more important than sermons or abstract principles of the present confused situation.

In the meantime, the Supreme Court of the United States is gradually manufacturing a new set of slogans, which, I trust, will be less of a hindrance to someone who is trying to do something than the old ones were. However, they are still hovering over the situation like a cloud and creating confusion whenever they speak. Witness their refusal to decide in the medical case and their recent refusal to declare themselves on whether a labor union is subject to the antitrust laws, in the case where a labor union had been indicted in Chicago and was trying to find out whether it had to be tried. Their refusal to decide this question is going to cause endless fighting and confusion for another year. However, that is in the nature of judicial institutions, and I would be the last to complain if the Supreme Court is more interested in maintaining its own prestige than it is in doing anything practical.

Now that Stalin has shown that he is a practical man rather than an idealist, what have you to say about the Socialist form of government as represented jointly and severally by Germany and Russia? Have the differences in ideas between the two forms of government made any great difference in the form of their conduct under the present pressures?

*Sincerely*

---

## *To Freda Kirchwey* [163]

Washington, D.C., Dec. 14, 1939

Dear Miss Kirchwey:

It is a pleasure to send you a testimonial of the high regard in which I hold your publication. I sometimes regret your tendency to pop off without any information whatever or any adequate understanding of the practical subject matter as you did with respect to the antitrust laws and labor conspiracies which have nothing to do with labor objectives. In other words I wish you were a little less like the under-dog's *New York Herald Tribune.* I can put my point more specifically by getting down to specific cases.

A number of poor students attempted to run a cooperative boarding house in the University of Chicago. They got their milk in quantities from an independent distributor. The milk wagon drivers union is part of the conspiracy between the Pure Milk Association and the large distributors, aimed at perpetuating a luxury system of distribution upon the poor. They told the students to stop buying from the independents. The students refused, whereupon the milk drivers union went to the Teamsters Union and shut off all food deliveries to the boarding house. The students decided to fight it out, whereupon the Teamsters Union succeeded in cutting off the collection of garbage and the students capitulated as all the little stores have capitulated. Again, only kitchen cabinets of one manufacturer can be installed in a house in Chicago. Again, the Pittsburgh labor unions have established a protective tariff raising costs tremendously to local builders by boycotting materials which come from large areas of the United States.

The point you make is that we should prosecute the distributors of milk in the first place and leave the labor unions out. The answer is simple. We would not get a conviction, and even if we did we wouldn't do any good. The *Herald-Tribune* praises us for our labor prosecution and condemns us when we prosecute the doctors for doing exactly the same thing because they love the doctors. You praise us for going after the doctors and condemn us for going after the labor unions.

I don't think there is the slightest chance of changing either your opinion or the *Herald-Tribune's*, but it is the failure to recognize the practical problem involved in the application of liberal slogans which constitutes your greatest weakness. However, I don't want to say this publicly. The *Nation* itself is faced with a practical problem. It needs support from all liberals and not criticism, and therefore any praise I can give you I regard as a real opportunity.

*Sincerely*

---

## *To Max Lerner*

Washington, D.C., Dec. 20, 1939

Dear Max:

I am distressed to learn that the issues on which we part company are broader than I think. This leads me to worry that you are going to end up as a pure and simple preacher like my grandfather. I hope this is not so, in spite of the evidence of a certain blindness to the way human organizations work which I have detected in some of your observations about the Antitrust Division.

There is a great future for preachers in America, and prestige and esteem. The best way to get attention is by advocating some unpopular cause and then they ride to glory later in life, after the fashion of the prodigal son theory. It takes a tough mind to resist this temptation. Looking into a crystal I see the grave possibility of that future for yourself. I hope you repent before it becomes too late. You have an easy style, a brilliant gift for epigrams and an ability to pound the ground. Don't let these gifts destroy you as a student and observer of human institutions. For example, you are about to discuss the TNEC before your class. You are going to look at that work through reports. I will bet you 10-1 that you don't know anything about it. I will talk to you about what you think its function and effect is when you come to Washington and I am hoping against hope that I will lose my bet.

*Best regards*

---

## *To Dorothy Thompson*

Washington, D.C., Jan. 4, 1940

Dear Miss Thompson:

Your column[164] on the Musicians Union is going to be most helpful to my coming battle with the Appropriations Committee. I am having some conferences with the counsel for the musicians but I do not think that the conferences without positive action will do any good. They seldom do.

I agree with you that we have here something that is within interstate commerce and also something which needs to be cleaned up. About five men and one jury would do the job. At present I haven't an available man to put on it and have so informed the numerous complainants.

At present my plight is pretty bad. I have no further travelling expenses and my men out in the field are paying their own hotel bills. This is an imposition on them because some of the salaries are as low as $2000. They are a good bunch of soldiers and their morale is excellent but I can't ask them to keep this up forever. They can't afford it.

I am convinced that we can establish free trade in this country. Fifty men, for example, could clean up the barriers and protective tariffs now obstructing free trade which are operating under the guise of inspection laws, etc.

At the risk of boring you, I am sending you a copy of my testimony before the Temporary National Economic Committee. In the meantime, public demand for action such as you have issued in your column is most helpful.

With kind regards,

*Sincerely*

---

## *To Robert H. Jackson*

Washington, D.C., Jan. 23, 1940

Dear Bob:

I read Essary's[165] column yesterday and later on saw Wendell Willkie and [Russell] Davenport, the Editor of *Fortune,* with a group at the Carleton. They were all full of the idea that you were about to sabotage the antitrust laws. I denied it with some heat. They said that the rumor was all over New York and that they understood from very reliable sources that I was resigning because of your appointment. I denied this also.

I doubt if any serious consideration should be given to this kind of stuff. However, for my own satisfaction I would like to put in writing for your files, and for any use that you might care to make of it, a letter setting out frankly, the facts. It is true that I was contemplating resigning from the Department, but that was because of possible conflict with Mr. Murphy. When I learned that you were to be appointed I reconsidered and decided to stay.

I actually did make plans to resign from the Department some time ago. The reason for those plans was the fact that Mr. Murphy was acting in a perfectly unpredictable way with respect to antitrust prosecutions.[166] At the beginning when he first came in he held practically all of our new cases up for a month for no intelligible reason. I could not get in to see him and when I did I got no satisfactory conclusions. The rumor that cases were being held up by the Attorney General became current among the staff of the Antitrust Division in spite of all I could do to keep it quiet. Then, suddenly, he approved all of the prosecutions which were then pending, although he expressed a good deal of dissatisfaction about my methods which he thought at the time were too drastic and particularly complained about the fertilizer investigation and the automobile prosecutions. His relations with me were always pleasant, however, and while I was somewhat alarmed at times at not receiving cooperative backing I could not put my finger on any breach between us.

When the war broke out Mr. Murphy expressed his lack of faith in the antitrust laws as a method of price control and formed a committee to study an anti-profiteering law, announcing it in the press without informing the Antitrust Division. This was somewhat disquieting and bothered the members of the Division not a little. No member of the committee which he formed, although it was engaged in studying a problem which concerned the antitrust laws, ever consulted with the Antitrust Division.

Finally the building investigation, the plans for which he had laid during Mr. Cummings' administration, got under way. Mr. Murphy became very much alarmed at the fact that labor was likely to be prosecuted. I took the position that it was impossible to leave labor out and that if we did we might as well drop the whole building investigation. The issue finally came up with the indictment of Mr. Hutcheson in St. Louis. For a week I was unable to get any decision from Mr. Murphy as to this indictment. Finally, I called him up and told him the indictment could be no longer delayed. He told me he disapproved. The indictment came out the next day.

Faced with that apparent split in policy, I felt in my own self-interest I would have to think of where I would go if I were compelled to resign. I, therefore, set in motion inquiries in New York which I limited to as few people as possible and asked that complete confidence be observed. Three firms became interested and I suppose that as many as twenty people must have known of my possible resignation. I also took up with the authorities at Yale the possibility of my returning and found that there was no way which I could get back next Fall. I suppose the entire faculty at Yale knew that I was contemplating resigning, and, as you know, it is difficult to keep a secret under those circumstances. The rumor of my resignation must have leaked out from some of these sources. I could see, however, nothing else to do under the circumstances, because I did not know from day to day whether my policy would be supported or not. Indeed, it appeared at the time to have definitely met the disapproval of the Attorney General.

At a later date the pressure of the labor group became so great that I felt it necessary to end it by making a public statement of policy. I submitted a letter substantially in the terms of my letter to the Central Labor Union for the joint signature of the Attorney General and myself. He refused to approve the letter. When I insisted that some sort of a letter had to go out he told me that all reference to the Department of Justice or the Attorney General must be eliminated and that it must go out on my own responsibility as my personal views. At that time I again felt I might be compelled to resign and went so far as to make a quasi-commitment to a New York firm, explaining to them that I could not tell whether I would have to resign or not and asking them to leave the matter open on that contingency. They agreed to this.

After my letter had been favorably received by the press, Mr. Murphy upheld my position in a letter which went further than my own statement of prosecution policy in that it seemed to be based on the majority opinion of the Bedford Stone Case, whereas my letter was based on the dissenting opinion. I was somewhat embarrassed by the inconsistency between the letters but finally developed a theory by which they could be reconciled. However, the difference between the two letters left me in a somewhat uncomfortable position. After your appointment was announced I had lunch with the senior member of the New York firm that I was contemplating joining and definitely told him that I was not resigning from the Department. My reason for telling him this was the fact that I knew that the difficulties of the character which I have described above would be over the moment you took office. I knew of no one more interested in the enforcement of the antitrust laws than yourself.

In the meantime the rumors, apparently based on the fact that I was contemplating resignation under Mr. Murphy, began to leak out with the astonishing interpretation that the reason for my dissatisfaction was the fact that Mr. Murphy was leaving and that you were coming in. I do not know where they came from, but they were helped along by numerous statements from Mr. Padway[167] to other labor leaders to the effect that you were going to reverse Mr. Murphy's policy. One of the prominent labor leaders, who happened to be in sympathy with my policy, came to me in some alarm and said that Padway had informed him to that effect. Padway made a speech in which he stated that Jackson was "going to curb the wild antics of Thurman Arnold" which was broadcast in the press. This, tied up with the other rumors, no doubt has lead to these stories.

As I said at the outset, I don't know what to do about it. It seems impossible to state the facts without appearing to attack my former Chief. The only thing I can see to do is to deny the rumors that I am going to resign and let it go at that. However, I am sufficiently distressed about the whole affair that I would like to have this letter in your confidential files. It will probably be of no use to you, but nevertheless you are privileged to use it if at any time it will do any good.

I believe that the whole thing will blow over, but in the meantime this contemporary record will remain in case the question is raised in the future.

*Sincerely*

---

## *To Arthur Sulzberger*

Washington, D.C., Jan. 25, 1940

Dear Mr. Sulzberger:

Thank you very much for your friendly editorial on the indictment of the International Longshoremen's Association which appeared in the *Times* of January 25.[168] The editorial is entirely correct in all its statements but it does not emphasize a point which I would like to get more emphasis on in comments on my labor policy. The point is this:

I am not conducting a campaign to police labor unions. I am attempting to break down simultaneously all the barriers which stand in the way of low-cost housing. The reason that the International Longshoremen's Association were indicted is that they tied up lumber and prevented it from being moved off the docks. Their action increased the cost of the house and impeded the distribution of goods in interstate commerce.

The reason I want this point emphasized is that it is important for the public to understand what the antitrust laws can do for the consumer. It is important for antitrust prosecutions to center upon the distribution of a product. When I investigate building, labor practices come in as one of the restraints on building materials. When I investigate milk in Chicago, labor restraints must be prosecuted as one of the methods used to prevent low-cost store delivery and fixed prices.

If I keep production and distribution of a product as the central goal of all my investigations, I am going to get some economic effect. If, on the other hand, I have policing unions as the objective, people are going to ask why the Antitrust Division should be entrusted with that task. I am getting hundreds of complaints against labor unions which could occupy the entire time of my force if I took them as the central problem. Taking the distribution of a particular product as the central problem, however, my prosecution policy has a fair chance of succeeding because in some cities the effect of the simultaneous attack on all the restraints has been magical.

We have not had such startling results in New York as we have had in a town like Pittsburgh because five men can make a bigger dent on a city the size of Pittsburgh than New York. I really need an additional fifteen or twenty men to handle the New York situation properly, in which case I believe I would get much more substantial results than I am getting now. However, the principle of both investigations is the same. We are not investigating unions, we are investigating distribution of houses. We are not prosecuting the unions because we feel it is our duty to discipline them, we are prosecuting them because they keep lumber tied up on the docks over a dispute which the employer who is anxious to distribute the lumber is helpless to solve. Free trade within the borders of the United States is my aim. There are lots of vicious practices and all sorts of organizations. They are investigated by the Antitrust Division only when they hold up the distribution of goods for unjustifiable reasons.

Of course, your editorial is entirely correct and requires no amending or elaboration. I write this letter only to emphasize a point which I would like to see treated if your editorial staff ever has the occasion to write on the subject again. I would, therefore, appreciate it if you would give this letter to the writer of the editorial on restraints by unions.

With best regards and many thanks for your most helpful support.

*Sincerely*

---

*To Robert H. Jackson*

Washington, D.C., May 18, 1940

Dear Bob:

To give you a specific illustration of the type of thing which the Government is going to be up against in the purchase of war materials, I will recite what happened with respect to the contracts between Bausch & Lomb Optical Company and the Navy.

Some time ago the Antitrust Division discovered price fixing agreements between Bausch & Lomb and Zeiss, which have unquestionably cost the Army and Navy a great deal of money during the past ten years. They have done more than that, they have affected the prices of camera lenses and other lenses to American consumers. They have made naval equipment more expensive to local ship building concerns than building vessels in South America because of the cartel arrangements with Zeiss.

Excerpts from two letters will show the type of thing Bausch & Lomb are doing. In a letter from Carl Bausch to one of his subordinates the following appears:

> A great many of the patents that we are operating under are very weak and if we wished to, we could break them ourselves and not pay royalities, but good business judgment, I believe, justifies the idea of paying royalties even on weak patents in order to maintain a price control picture that is helpful.

In a letter dated February 24, 1932, from Bausch & Lomb to Zeiss, appears the following quotation:

> In order not to divulge to the Navy Dept. that we earn a commission of 10% on this transaction, it will be necessary that the consular invoice and export declarations which you will have to make out be higher in this particular case than your net invoice prices to us.

With evidence of this general character the Government appeared to have an open and shut case. Bausch & Lomb and its officers are indicted but the trial date has not been set.

Bausch & Lomb made no intimation to the Department of Justice that the trial would delay their manufacturing operations; they made no attempt to negotiate with us as to the most convenient date for trial. Instead of that, they attached a letter to their bid to the Navy Department for rangefinders on two cruisers in which they said that because of the trial they would have to extend delivery date on rangefinder equipment for about six months "beyond the time which ordinarily would be required." They also insisted that liquidated damage provisions be deleted from the contract.

It is difficult to conceive of how the trial can interfere with the manufacturing operations of this very large company because only two witnesses connected with production have been subpoenaed. Their time on the witness stand may be arranged. They will only be needed about two days apiece, their testimony will be limited to the identification of correspondence.

The force behind this threat consisted of the fact that the Bausch & Lomb Optical Company is the only source for rangefinders. The reason that it is the only source is that years ago leading manufacturers of lenses agreed not to compete and to divide up the field between them. Bausch & Lomb, through the oppressive use of patents, obtained this concession and is now the only large scale manufacturer of lenses. This sort of thing is typical of the kind of coercion by which cost plus contracts were obtained during the time of war by firms which dominated the market.

The procedure for handling this kind of a case is simple. We immediately called up Bausch & Lomb and stated that in our opinion their representations as to necessary delays because of the suit were false, and informed them that we would publish excerpts from letters in our possession indicating their practices in the past. We stated we would add to the publication the threat which they made not to complete rangefinders on time for the Navy, and that we would ask for Congressional investigation. We finally added that we considered their representations to the Navy proper to present to the court in the event of conviction as a basis for the imposition of jail sentences rather than the fines which are ordinarily imposed.

Bausch & Lomb immediately collapsed. They agreed that they would furnish the material on time. They are pleading guilty in the antitrust prosecution.

The incident was quickly handled without publicity. This solution was possible, however, only because the Antitrust Division had a grand jury actually in operation in New York. This illustrates the necessity of having investigations of this character in all the restricted fields in which the Government must buy its military equipment.

*Sincerely*

---

## *To Westbrook Pegler* [169]

Washington, D.C., June 9, 1940

Dear Pegler:

You have been so effective with labor unions that they are beginning to wake up. Out in Chicago on Monday, the first international union, the Bricklayers, Masons and Plasterers International Union of America, is agreeing to sign a decree taking responsibility for policing their locals.

The situation is this. Local unions affiliated with the Bricklayers, Masons and Plasterers International Union of America were among the defendants in Chicago, Detroit and St. Louis in indictments obtained by the Antitrust Division. (The indictments were for price fixing, driving independent contractors out of business, etc.) The cases against them were pretty clear. The *international* union was not indicted nor were there any charges against it. As a matter of fact, the president, Harry C. Bates, and the secretary, Richard Gray, are two of the most responsible people in the A.F. of L.

These men came to the office after these indictments were brought and wanted to know what the international union could do. After a series of conferences a decree was drawn up in which the international union voluntarily became a party. The terms of that decree are not important for your purposes. It is enough to say that it prohibits all of the conduct for which the locals were indicted and gives the international union the responsibility (which can be enforced in court) in disciplining recalcitrant locals. If this decree is carried out in good faith, and I hope it will be, we should have little further difficulty with the situation. If it is not carried out, the government has the weapons to attack the trouble quickly.

The trouble in the past has been that the best type of labor leaders have had no power whatever over local outrages. This setup gives them that power. I believe it will work.

Bates and Gray forced this decree down the throats of the locals. Of course, it could not have been done if we had not had an indictment. However, there is necessarily some hard feeling because Bates and Gray have, according to some at least, sold out to the Department of Justice. In addition to that, considerable bitterness may develop between Bates and Gray and other national A.F. of L. officials that are still keeping up the fight. The Apex decision has made it perfectly clear that labor has no exemption, so the thing is settled as a matter of law with respect to all the government prosecutions. (The government does not prosecute attempts to enforce a closed shop which was the reason for the Apex strike.) The job of getting the unions to accept the Apex case is still to be done, but Bates and Gray have made a good start. I think we ought to hold up their hands.

For these reasons, if you should care to comment upon the release which I enclose, and give the bricklayer's international union a hand in your column, it would be most helpful. I think this letter and the release gives you all the story that you need.

With best regards,

*Sincerely*

---

## *To Richardson Wood*[170]

Washington, D.C., Oct. 19, 1940

Dear Mr. Wood:

Thanks for your letter. You asked for suggestions and there are two particularly important ones:

First: after returning from the Coast, I am convinced that the agricultural price fixing is in about the same situation today as the NRA was before that bubble burst. There is commotion among the farmers because the only situations where marketing orders can be obtained are in closely organized situations such as milk, asparagus, peaches, etc. The marketing orders do not help general farm purchasing power. They work only for the benefit of large producers in a few products. An example of this is found in the New York milk situation where there is a threatened strike of 53,000 farmers. You can get the data on this really exciting story by contacting Maurice L.A. Gellis of the Antitrust Division office in New York City, 301 Federal Building. In the New York milk area an annual fund of $12,000,000 is collected from low income groups, 80% of which is distributed to three large companies, as a reward for diverting fluid milk through less essential uses. The consumers are sore, the farmers are sore; nobody appears to like it. It is a beautiful example of the kind of thing I would like to see your article take up. Corwin Edwards[171] can give you the data on an equally absurd situation in canned peaches.

My second suggestion is that you study some of the recent activities of the Teamsters' Union on which we have a good deal of information. The Teamsters were a small union in 1933. They now have over six hundred thousand members. They are getting a complete strangle hold on the entire transportation system by coercive practices of the rawest character. Example: In Richmond, traffic is being paralyzed by the refusal of Teamsters' Union carriers to handle goods from non-union carriers and also from carriers organized by the CIO in Virginia and West Virginia. In Pittsburgh all independent carriers are being forced out of business. In Detroit a hoodlum wastepaper wholesaler has made a deal with the Teamsters to put four of the better wholesale paper dealers out of existence. After the union gets in power, it then enters into a combination to raise prices and in exchange then forces the employment of unnecessary labor. Various types of boycotts which raise the price of food can be found all over the United States due to Teamster activity. We are rapidly drifting into a situation where the entire trucking transportation of the United States is going to be controlled by a few big companies, which in turn are controlled by the Teamsters' Union. The Teamsters' Union is not a real labor movement because labor does not have free opportunity to join it. Example: Colored men are excluded from driving trucks in Detroit, except for a few who are specially selected.

In the meantime, independent trucking companies are being forced to merge into a competing association. The Horton Lines have taken the lead on this. Our information is still incomplete on this but everything we have points to trouble, and it offers a most interesting subject for your investigation.

*Best regards*

---

## *To Frederick Roe*[172]

Washington, D.C., Jan. 3, 1941

Dear Mr. Roe:

I have your letter of December 18 concerning the recent round table conference sponsored by the *Savings Bank Journal.*[173]

The statement to which you refer in your letter was part of a general informal discussion about the effect of the fear of domestic inflation on capital investment. There were some who had the idea that this was a psychological factor which was stopping business expansion. It was my opinion that restraints of trade were a much more important factor and that a period of high prices and low turnover automatically dumps business abroad.

To illustrate that theory I referred generally to typical correspondence of large concerns which has turned up in our grand jury investigation which expressed confidence in Germany and Italy. It would have been obviously unfair to name the companies involved because the correspondence had been obtained through grand jury investigation.

Large investment of one of the plumbing companies, however, was a matter of common knowledge and therefore, I felt that I could use it as an illustration since references to its position had already appeared in print. For example, the March 1940 issue of *Fortune* contains an article on the American Radiator and Standard Sanitary Corporation in which it is stated that "American Radiator and Standard Sanitary Corporation has a $50,000,000 stake in European civilization." This article was approved by Mr. Reed, President of the American Radiator and Standard Sanitary Corporation, before publication.

Plumbing is, however, only one of the instances of this sort of thing. Incidentally, legislative schemes to dump agricultural products abroad are a part of the same kind of phenomena. If you want to examine the Protective Committee studies made by SEC in 1936 you will find the same force operating in order to create enormous loans in South American countries, the bonds of which were sold to the American public. I treated this phenomenon at some length in my book, "The Folklore of Capitalism."

There is, of course, a discrepancy between the *Fortune* article and the statement of the American Radiator Company. However, both could be easily correct because there are so many different ways of keeping books and in figuring out capital investment. We run across many instances where companies claim that earnings plowed back in a corporation represent investment. There is the other extreme, which is to call the investment only the amount of the original capital contributed. I have no information as to the basis on which the American Radiator keeps its books or the reason as to the wide variation between *Fortune* figures and their consolidated statement. For the purposes of using American Radiator investment as an illustration of American money going abroad, however, I do not think that the difference is important.

*Sincerely yours*

---

## *To Hugh Johnson*[174]

Washington, D.C., Feb. 7, 1941

Dear General:

In your excellent column of February 7[175] on the lumber industry, you speak about the need for me to have a little talk with Leon [Henderson]. May I assure you that we are together on this thing and that at the time that he made his speech we were prosecuting lumber industries on the West Coast and in New Orleans. The moment the grand jury assembled, lumber, which had been jumping five and six points a week on the West Coast, stopped its rise. We sent one of our investigators to New Orleans and he hadn't been there two days when there was an actual drop in Southern pine. Yesterday the Western Pine Association entered a plea of nolo and paid $81,000 in fines. They also accepted a decree against themselves which should alleviate the situation in the future.

We have not as yet had enough men to get into the retail price situation, but we believe they are being illegally pyramided. We will get to them when we can.

Leon and I are planning to coordinate our efforts as closely as we can. We are not curing everything, but we are at least achieving some results. In the meantime, columns such as you wrote today are most helpful.

Now, with respect to your statement as regards the antitrust laws, don't you ever get tired of misrepresenting my position? Since you have once compared me to an idiot in a powder mill, may I use equally strong language. You seem to know nothing about the decisions of the Supreme Court of the United States with relation to the combinations necessary to national defense which we are trying to follow. It is all nonsense to say that there is any conflict between the Defense Commission and the Antitrust Division. It is also complete nonsense to say that a group of industries which obeys the directions of the Defense Commission or the Office of Production Management are guilty of a conspiracy. It would be impossible to prosecute anyone for so doing. I do not know about the correspondence of McReynolds and Baruch but suspect you have it balled up somehow.

A long time ago I suggested that you come over and have a talk with me to give me an opportunity to explain the function of the antitrust laws as a remedy for consumers. You said you were going to but never did. In the meantime you continue to blithely misstate the position of the Antitrust Division.

The invitation is still open if you care to accept it. If you do not care to accept it I will send you a copy of my book[176] at my own expense, (although my income is much less than yours), if you will promise faithfully to read the chapter on "A Free Market in Time of National Emergency or War."

I do not mind in the least your criticisms of me but it would be a lot more fun if you would criticize me for the ideas which I actually have instead of those which I do not have.

With best regards,

*Sincerely*

---

*To Edward A. Evans*[177]

Washington, D.C., Feb. 17, 1941

Dear Evans:

I am sending you the analysis of the labor cases we will still prosecute which I prepared for the TNEC.

As a matter of fact, I think that the Hutcheson case[178] throws doubt over all of our labor prosecutions excepting those where labor has combined with employers, but I do not want to admit this. I should think that the Supreme Court would hesitate, for example, in compelling a small trucking concern to do business with a certified CIO union and then allow the A. F. of L. the privilege of destroying the CIO union because it obeyed the law. I don't know just how the Supreme Court would wiggle out of this situation, but when they are writing decisions which give "hospitable scope" to legislative policy introspectively arrived at they have almost any latitude that they want to give themselves.

We are also going to take the position that labor has no exemption merely because it acts alone. This is essential, for example, in the plumbing case where we are charging a combination of labor and employers to keep out cheaper plumbing.[179] If labor had an exemption, provided it acted alone, it wouldn't do any good to win the plumbing case. The next time the conspiracy appeared it would not be an agreement but rather a demand on the part of the labor union to which the employer acceded. You can't enforce the Sherman Act where one party to the conspiracy is exempt because the exempt party will always be the one that takes the initiative. I hope this clears up the questions which you ask in your letter.

The real trouble with the Hutcheson case is that win, lose, or draw the labor law is going to be in a good deal of confusion so that we are not going to get the enforcement effect out of bringing these cases which we got before. This is a tremendous loss. Prior to the Hutcheson case, the mere calling of a grand jury was enough to stop a vicious labor practice. I suspect that labor is going to be pretty cocky and not pay much attention to it. However, all that remains for the future to decide. We certainly are not going to give up the fight and we don't admit that we are beaten yet.

This letter is not for publication as I have not had it released.

*Best regards*

---

## *To Robert H. Jackson*

Washington, D.C., Feb. 21, 1941

Dear Bob:

You asked me for a hasty memorandum concerning the legislative problems which may be raised by the Hutcheson decision. The following, I think, will give you the highlights. A more comprehensive memorandum is being prepared which I hope to have ready within a week.

The decision in the Hutcheson case, which in effect allows one union to destroy another regardless of the wishes or free choice of the employees and regardless of the willingness of the employer to be fair to organized labor, has raised problems which not only concern defense but also the distribution of food and housing to low income groups. They may be discussed under two headings:

1. The protection of the employer from retaliatory action when he deals with a legitimate union.
2. The protection of the right of collective bargaining of the workman himself from exploitation by labor dictators who charge him for his right to work.
3. The effect of such activities on national defense.

We will discuss these problems in that order.

1. *The protection of the employer from retaliatory action when he deals with a legitimate union.*

The problem may be illustrated by a typical case. In New York 60% of the retail lumber yards had been organized by the CIO. The A. F. of L. gave a charter to ten persons, which in effect prevented any free elections in that union. Before that union had any members it entered into wage contracts with 40% of the lumber yards less advantageous to the workers than the CIO contract. The workmen were then forced unwillingly to join this union.

Thereupon this conscripted union joined with the teamsters and other longshoremen's unions to crush the lumber yards employing CIO labor by preventing lumber from being delivered to them from the docks.

Local lumber yards are in an impossible situation. They are faced with a labor war whichever choice they make between the two unions. They are small and many of them will be unable to survive.

The situation is found all over the country both in controversies between CIO and A. F. of L. unions and in controversies between two unions both of which are affiliated with the A. F. of L. It harasses large businesses, but it ruins small ones. For example, Anheuser Busch had its sales cut down in Florida by 20% because of false statements that it was unfair to organized labor in St. Louis. It can survive this, but the little lumber yards in New York will have to close entirely. There is already set up machinery to settle such disputes without ruining the employer. Where the employment is permanent the NLRB may decide between the two unions. Where employment is not permanent, as in the case of building trades or the distribution of food, there is plenty of arbitration machinery which could settle these disputes. The reason it is not used is that the losing union if it is strong enough to combine with the teamsters, or exhort to a nationwide boycott, does not pay any attention to the award.

The remedy for this situation is not difficult. All that is necessary to protect the employer when he deals fairly with a legitimate labor union is to restore the criminal penalty under the antitrust laws.

The *language* of the Norris-LaGuardia Act need not be changed. It takes away from private individuals the right of injunction in such cases. This is as it should be because private law enforcement is always accompanied by injustice. It would be desirable to increase the protection of labor from private suits by abolishing the right to employers to collect triple damages from unions in such cases. The Government alone should have power to deal with such cases.

2. *The protection of the workmen from exploitations by labor dictators who deprive him of the right to work.*

This situation may be illustrated by a complaint which came from Fort Riley. Only 20 members of the glaziers' unions are available there to put in the glass in the steel windows. The reason for this small number is that the dues of the Glaziers' Union runs about $1500. The Glaziers' Union has issued temporary permits to work to 170 non-union men and charges each of them $2 a day for the privilege. These men are outside the union only because they cannot afford to join. They are paying tribute of nearly $2000 a week. If they refuse the employer will be forced to discharge them. If the contractor should protest he would be immediately attacked not only at the camp but wherever he does business.

Such problems are not isolated evils. It is notorious that the carpenters' union charges poor people for the right to work and denies them the privilege of belonging to the union. The Hod Carriers' Union furnishes one of the most pathetic of these cases. On a single project at Kingston, New York, $600,000 has been collected from the hod carriers in two years. There is no accounting for the funds. There has been no election for 29 years. There is at present only $2000 in the union's treasury.

With reference to accounting we have a constant succession of complaints from working men whose cards have been taken away and who have been blacklisted all over the country because they were too inquisitive about the expenditure of union funds. The men have not even received effective protection for their money. Union officials have failed to insist upon the observance of safety regulations at the Kingston project. As a result 85 men have been killed on this project in the last two years.

Such evils bid fair to become a national scandal. Many legislative remedies could be devised by way of regulation of union dues, etc. However, the simplist remedy would be to protect the workmen themselves who form an independent union. In every situation that we have investigated we believe that an independent union would be immediately formed by workmen themselves if it did not run the hazard of being immediately crushed with subsequent retaliation against those who formed the union and the employer who dealt with them. There is no chance for any new union representing the free choice of the employees to get started under these circumstances. The democratic right of unions to organize could be easily protected by application of the antitrust laws. Other legislation might also be necessary, but this single change would go far to remedy the situation.

We are preparing a lengthy summary of our complaints of this character which should be done in three or four days' time. The total picture is shocking. Though very few labor unions are engaged in these practices, millions of laborers are affected. This may be illustrated by the Teamsters strike in Washington, where 15,000 men were thrown out of work because of a jurisdictional strike between the engineers and the Teamsters. These practices affect particularly two industries: (1) the distribution of food, and (2) the building industry. For example, in the lower Manhattan market it costs $112 more to get a car of fruits and vegatables from the pier to the retailer than elsewhere in New York, largely because of rackets which are protected by the kind of union activity we have outlined here. In New York relief milk is being sold at 8¢. Dealers have offered to sell it to low income groups at the same price without a subsidy. They have been prevented from doing this by the Teamsters' Union. The reason why the Teamsters have so much power in this situation is because they control transportation. Second to the Teamsters are the unions, such as the carpenters and glaziers, which stand immediately between the consumer and the materials he wants to buy.

3. *The effect of such activities on national defense.*

Illustrations of this problem may be found in a letter to Mr. Sidney Hillman, a copy of which is attached. We ask you to note particularly the last illustration which deals with stoppage of the production of zinc.

---

## *To Reed Powell*

Washington, D.C., Feb. 21, 1941

Dear Reed:

Your letter was a joy to the entire Antitrust Division. I was very much shocked myself at the decision although not surprised. We were familiar with these two quotations, but only used one of them in our brief—the one from Frankfurter and Green in the labor injunction. My own belief was that I would lose the case by some refinement of the Apex case. I never dreamed that the Norris-LaGuardia Act would be interpreted to take away the criminal remedy. Now the question in front of us is how far the decision goes. I appeared before the TNEC[180] and the Judiciary Committee of the House, stating the cases we still thought we were entitled to prosecute. One of the first cases I am going to get up is an indictment from

New Orleans where the union is certified by the NLRB[181] and at the same time the employer is being forced to go out of business because he bargains with it. So long as the court is talking about legislative policy, it seems that that kind of a case might make them stop and think because the Wagner Labor Relations Act was passed subsequent to the Norris-LaGuardia Act. However, when the court starts to give hospitable scope to acts of Congress which they determine introspective I am at a loss to know what they can do next.

In the hope you will be interested I am enclosing copy of my testimony before the TNEC. I expect to dump the cases which I have outlined on the court's doorstep as quickly as I can provided I am permitted to do so. I think I will be because there is enormous indignation about the Hutcheson case.

There are some interesting situations developing. The Greif Clothing Company, for example, has developed a conveyor-belt system of making clothes which makes them no longer dependent on the Amalgamated Clothing workers in the lofts in the cities. They have twelve factories all in rural areas. They pay very good wages for unskilled labor and make excellent clothes. So successful have they been that today they are practically the only clothing concern in the United States of any size which is making any money. Hart, Schaffner & Marx, for example, are broke. [Sidney] Hillman has never been able to organize the Greif Clothing Company plants because the workers are afraid he would try to close them down in favor of the loft workers of New York and elsewhere. In other words, Hillman's interests are against the introduction of new methods of making clothes when they might displace his own workers. Therefore, they organized their own unions. These unions were attacked as company unions but the Circuit Court of Appeals held finally that they were the free choice of the workers and the NLRB did not appeal from that decision. Thus, as the record stands, the Greif unions are not company unions.

Now Hillman is striking against the Circuit Court of Appeals' decision in the following way: He finds out the jobbers who are handling Greif clothes and writes them a letter threatening various kinds of organized retaliation if they do not boycott all Greif factories. The letter is on the union's stationary, but of course Hillman is credited with the power to control vast Government orders because of his position on the National Defense Council. Therefore the jobbers are getting badly frightened. (This paragraph is strictly confidential.)

If Ed Stettinius had kept his Chairmanship with U.S. Steel and written threatening letters to everyone who dealt with Bethlehem Steel you would have a similar situation.

One of the interesting things about this situation is that Hillman has been compelled to loan money to the clothing industry in order to keep it on its feet and employ his workers. This is an added incentive to keep more efficient methods of making clothes in rural areas out of the picture.

We are getting wires and letters from all over the United States. The thing which creates the most indignation is the fact that the A. F. of L. unions aided by the Teamsters' are permitting small, closed unions to levy tribute on non-union men by giving them licenses to work. For example, at Fort Riley, 300,000 panes of glass must be put in. There are only twenty glaziers available. The reason that there are only twenty glaziers is that the initiation fee of the Glaziers' Union is $1500. 170 non-union men are permitted by the union to work provided the union collects $2 a day from each one of them for that permission. In one cantonment I estimate the Carpenters' Union will collect $500,000 toll from non-union men. All of this would be impossible if it were not for the cooperation of the Teamsters who control the transportation. In the meantime, hundreds of poor devils are flooding my office with complaints that they are being charged $25-$50 for temporary permits to work and then being fired so they show a net loss at the end of their period of employment. It is simply fantastic.

This is the kind of stuff on which the Supreme Court has set its seal of approval by permitting a few powerful unions to break any attempt of the poor devils who are temporarily employed to form a union of their own choice.

Public indignation is rising in all parts of the country. However, I am getting the support of everybody except a few so-called liberal papers. The trouble with liberals today is that they are unable to see any individuals. They see unions and they see labor movements. When individuals are crushed they think no more of it than Mr. Hitler does who is also working for an ideal system in which there is a place for everyone and everyone has a place.

It is very easy to become pretty bitter about this sort of thing when you come in contact with the victims like I do. If you stay away from the victims you can write swell abstract theology about it.

With best regards and affection to you and Mollie,

*Sincerely*

*To Reed Powell*

Washington, D.C., April 19, 1941

Dear Reed:

I enjoyed reading your opinion and I am circulating it around the Division so that others may enjoy it too. I think it is a fine critique on the methods adopted by the Court.

Personally, however, I am glad that the Hutcheson case was written as it is. It is getting a terrific hammering from all quarters and the fact that apologists for the result, like Hart, are compelled to re-write the opinion is most helpful to my own cause.

In the meantime, I have practically abandoned hope of the Court and am trying to see what I can do with Congress. One of the great difficulties here is to keep the extremists out of the picture. The Administration apparently does not want to tackle the problem at all. However, small business groups are getting pretty bitter. Only last week the Teamsters in Washington demanded that retail stores which were selling an oversize loaf raise the price of the loaf 40% or they would cut off deliveries. This was engineered by price fixing bakers in the following way: They put on long faces and told the Teamsters that they were afraid if that kind of competition kept up sooner or later wages would go down. That was all the Teamsters needed.

I talked to about four hundred small businessmen in Cleveland on Wednesday. They told me that the unions were practically ruining their businesses. They were particularly bitter about the fact that the unions will not allow paint to be put on with spray guns. Brushes must be used of the size specified. They said that with all this talk about price ceilings and extra taxes the Government ought to be willing to let them cut down their expenses and not compel them to boost prices at the request of the labor unions. There is an undercurrent of bitterness about the thing which is not good at all.

Last week I was in Denver where we have indicted a large number of cement and lumber firms. The Denver citizens are having meetings and are determined to disunionize the town. They haven't got much of a foothold in Denver and the businessmen are not going to let them. This is a typical result of uncurbed labor power.

I enclose an article which has just been accepted by the *Reader's Digest*[182] which, as you know, has a circulation of four and a half million. I have tried to keep criticism of the Court out of it and paint the problem with a series of incidents. I wish you would show it to Hart and have him write an opinion in the Hodcarrier's case. I would be very much interested in the Hodcarrier's case. I would be very much interested which way he would write it, assuming that the facts in my article are correct.

I am very sorry you feel that you should not publish your opinion. Personally I think it ought to be published, and I am not impressed by your argument that licked lawyers should not kick about cases they have lost. It seems to me that we do not have that kind of a situation here. There is either a real public issue of importance, or there isn't. If there is, we ought to keep on fighting, win, lose or draw.

The world certainly moves fast. At Yale during the Remington Rand strikes I was considered a radical because I insisted that a labor union ought to be uncurbed by Federal law for as long as they pursued the legitimate objects of a union. Now, in the same position I have become a labor baiter.

An interesting incident occurred day before yesterday. A friend of Senator Norris', running a small radio station, is being put out of business by exorbitant demands on the part of Petrillo for payment of unnecessary musicians. I was about to indict Petrillo but have given that enterprise up. I told him that his only remedy was to see his Senator. He went to see Senator Norris who said that he must be mistaken about the law, that there was nothing in the Norris-LaGuardia Act, or any other act, permitting Petrillo to make that sort of demand. He called me up and I saw Senator Norris. Senator Norris told me that he was shocked and grieved that the Act which he had sponsored had been so misinterpreted by the Court. He will support an amendment to reenact the Clayton Act, with due emphasis on Section 6, but says he is simply too sick a man to take the burden of introducing it. He thinks that should be up to the Administration.

I have put in a requisition for $500 to cover your expenses and per diem. You will get it in due course. I hope you spend some of it in coming down to see us.

*Affectionately*

---

## *To Robert H. Jackson*

Washington, D.C., May 17, 1941

Dear Bob:

On my return Hugh Cox showed me an excellent letter you prepared to Leon Henderson. The policy of the letter is fine, but the practical carrying out of this policy depends on enough personnel really to do an effective job. For example, Henderson's efforts in Denver to keep the price of lumber out of bounds is ineffective so long as the distribution of lumber is controlled by a small ring of wholesale dealers. His efforts on food in Connecticut will be ineffective so long as the retail groceries in conspiracy with chain stores are raising mark-ups so that the standard becomes that of the less efficient distributors. It will be ineffective in necessities like meat and cheese under present systems of distribution. In steel, we have evidence on the Pacific Coast of a conspiracy to block new production. Our work assisting Leon is going to put substantial additional burdens on our staff. He has already sent us one case which he wants us to investigate, and I have no doubts others will follow promptly.

It is difficult to estimate the cumulative effect of all these restraints because there are no statistics on matters which can be uncovered only by grand juries. I think, however, it is enormous. If this is overstatement, it still remains true that the known existence of this sort of thing is becoming a scandal. Farm organizations and small businessmen's organizations have a feeling of injustice, and the sincerity of our efforts may be questioned.

As you know, our $750,000 appropriation has been eliminated in the Senate Committee. The matter was left to the last, and no hearing was given. Joe O'Mahoney tells me that one of the reasons was a feeling that the Administration was not particularly interested in view of the fact that the amount given us by the House exceeded the Administration budget. A word from the Administration, therefore I think, will clarify the situation.

I regard the situation as very serious, and I wish you would carefully consider what can be done.

*Sincerely*

P.S. I enclose copy of letter I wrote to the President, which of course he may never see.

---

## *To Franklin D. Roosevelt*

Washington, D.C., May 17, 1941

Dear Mr. President:

I have never addressed a communication to you before on behalf of the Antitrust Division because I felt that your time was too much occupied. However, today a matter has arisen which may impair our usefulness to the Government, so serious that I ask the privilege of calling it to your attention.

The burden on the Division has increased tremendously on account of the war. We are attempting to extend our activities to prevent restrictions of production, particularly conspiracies which are blocking the defense effort. A poll conducted by *Fortune* Magazine among business executives last year showed that our program is supported by business. We are also attempting to clean up restraints which block the distribution of necessities, such as food and housing. Here we have the cooperation of the farmer and small business.

Due to that support, the House Appropriations Committee gave us an additional $750,000. It has now been taken away by the Senate Appropriations Committee without any hearing, for reasons which we do not understand.

A few scattered examples will show the kind of enforcement we will have to drop:

1. The investigation which we are now conducting in the drug and chemical industries which, we believe, will help us eliminate restrictions which hamper our defense program and which prevent us from competing on equal terms with the Germans in South America. Drugs are an outstanding example of this.
2. Strategically located processors depress prices paid to farmers for raw materials and artificially raise prices to consumers in food, clothing and war materials.
3. In Chicago, commission men shake dice to see which particular pens of sheep are allocated to the winner, and the sole privilege of bidding is allocated to the winner.
4. In 27 states, retail grocers are raising the price of food by an illegal use of the Unfair Practices Acts.
5. In North Carolina, the price of potatoes is being affected adversely to the farmer and the consumer.
6. The distribution of cheese is a scandal; so are the practices in the packing industry.
7. In building, in nearly all large centers, oppressive practices, especially to small business men, are widespread.

Our complaints are increasing by leaps and bounds. For example, in Denver, cement and lumber are higher than anywhere else in the country due to a tightly controlled method of allowing only certain wholesalers to sell them.

We feel that our activities are indispensible if Mr. Henderson's efforts at putting a ceiling on prices are to be successful. In cases where there are combinations to raise prices, or to maintain artificially high prices, or to disregard Mr. Henderson's request, the antitrust laws provide the only legal remedy which is now available. We have just worked out the details of an arrangement with Mr. Henderson under which our staff is to deal with all problems of this kind which threaten to block the success of Mr. Henderson's efforts. I think everyone realizes that there is little advantage in putting a ceiling on prices if the existing prices are artifically high.

Mr. Henderson deals with the general economic problem. He needs the assistance of the Antitrust Division to make his efforts effective. If we have to let these things go for want of more men to take care of them, we believe the accumulation of these restraints will have a bad economic effect. Statistics cannot be compiled on this if it is an over-statement. Nevertheless, we feel the psychological effect of the known existence of these restraints of trade will militate against the entire policy of attempting to put a ceiling over prices.

Therefore, we feel that the necessity for having this additional $750,000 is so imperative that I take the liberty of calling it to your attention. It is my belief that one of the reasons for the elimination of the increase by the Senate is the fact that they felt that they should stick to the Administration's appropriation. Therefore, I feel that all that is needed to correct it is a word from you.

*Respectfully*

---

## *To Kenneth W. Payne*[183]

Washington, D.C., Aug. 2, 1941

Dear Mr. Payne:

The letter which the Aluminum Company sent you would be a surprising document from any other company than this one. It is a highly argumentative attempt to confuse. They ask you to interview their representative. If you do so, may we ask you also to send a man to Washington and examine our own voluminous records. Some of the material we have is startling in its implications. We believe we will convince you that the article is an extreme understatement of the facts which we have.

However, there is nothing in the letter which indicates any necessity of going into the voluminous material which bears on this highly technical matter. I will briefly review the points made.

1. The letter claims that according to the Bureau of Mines my statement that Germany is far ahead of the United States in aluminum production is incorrect.

The last *official* figures of the Bureau of Mines are in 1938. They show the United States with 130,129 tons and Germany with 175,000 tons. Since 1938, German production has been a military secret. However, the Bureau of Mines in its 1940 yearbook, on Page 653, states as follows:

> Aluminum Production. . . . Germany is believed to have remained the principal producer, accounting for an *output twenty-one percent greater than that of the United States.*

Our figures derive from sources close to the British Intelligence and indicate a greater disparity than that. On Pages 2 and 3 of the Truman Committee Report you will find a set of figures which I believe to be reliable and which indicate even greater disparity between German production and American production of aluminum. They were established at a hearing in which the Aluminum Company was present and had an opportunity to present its case if it wished. You will note that this Committee is highly critical of OPM and points out that OPM had been misled by the Aluminum Company.

Outside of these reports, it would seem that the mere fact that we are trying to collect pots and pans in order to bring our airplane production up to that of Germany's is sufficient evidence of what has been happening.

2. The second point of the letter is that Aluminum Limited was not formed to prevent world surpluses.

This is refuted by the admission in the letter at the bottom of Page 3 which specifically states:

> The members of the cartel (which included Aluminum Limited) were concerned with preventing the dumping of surpluses into one another's markets.

They were also concerned with the limitation of production and fixing of world prices, although the letter appears to ignore this fact. The Bureau of Mines figures from 1931 show the results of the cartel's activities in limiting production. The year the cartel has formed (1931) the United States produced 80,534 tons and Germany produced 27,100 tons. The cartel agreed to cut production to half of capacity. The next year we find the United States, following that agreement, was producing 47,577 tons, with Germany producing 19,200 tons. At the beginning of Hitler's regime the United States had reduced its production to 38,614 tons, and Germany had decreased its production to 18,900 tons. After Hitler had been in power one year, Germany was producing 37,200 tons, while the United States had dropped to 33,647 tons. In 1938 Germany had risen to 175,000 tons, while the United States was producing 130,127 tons.

It is true that in condensing my article I give the impression that Aluminum Limited was incorporated in 1931. There is no question about the figure of 1928. Therefore the paragraph on Page 2 of the letter should read:

> Well, in 1931 there was a growing world surplus of aluminum which threatened to invade American markets and disturb the monopoly control and price structure of the Aluminum Company of America. So that company *used a Canadian affiliate, previously formed for this purpose,* thinking that it could escape the antitrust laws, etc.

The fact that Aluminium Limited of Canada was formed for this purpose is admitted in the record by E.K. Davis, its president. In fact it is admitted in Mr. Carr's letter to you where he speaks of the concern of the members of the cartel to eliminate foreign competition. The evidence that Aluminium Limited was formed to escape the antitrust laws is uncontroverted in the record.

You will note the letter on Page 3 states:

> Great advantage could be gained by incorporating within the British Empire and specializing in foreign markets.

The only advantage was this imagined freedom from the antitrust laws. The record shows that the other advantages set out were pure hokum.

3. The Aluminum Company of America denies that it was a member of the world cartel and states that it "has no way of knowing whether production in European countries was limited by the cartel."

This is simply a red herring. Aluminium Limited, the affiliate of the Aluminum Company, owned by the identical people, (its president was the brother of the president of the Aluminum Company), admits that it was a member of the cartel. The Aluminum Company of America then asserts that it has no way of knowing what its affiliate was doing. Frankly, I consider such arguments childish.

4. On Page 3, the letter infers that aluminum prices were not fixed within the United States.

Of course they were fixed, because the Aluminum Company of America had a complete monopoly. The way they were fixed was by eliminating world production and putting a floor under world prices through the Aluminum Company's Canadian affiliate. This is admitted by the next paragraph which we pointed out before.

5. Objection is made to our statement that "even the collapse of France failed to wake up the aluminum industry to the dangerous shortage."

One answer to that is that the Antitrust Division has been proved to be right and the Aluminum Company wrong. The excuse given by the Aluminum Company in their letter is that it was not their function to know anything about aluminum and advise OPM. With respect to this claim, we are in a position to show that the Aluminum Company constantly tried to influence reports and recommendations about aluminum. However, it is a sufficient answer simply to refer to the paragraph on Page 3 of Senator Truman's Report.

6. The next point of the letter attempts to excuse the Aluminum Company for entering into an illegal patent pool with the German Dye Trust.

They say that they were trying to sell magnesium to the military authorities and that they did their utmost to develop the use of magnesium. Why then did they enter into an illegal arrangement with the German Dye Trust limiting American production to 4,000 tons? The obvious purpose of this was to keep magnesium one-third above aluminum. It is not a real competitor of aluminum at this price.

7. The next point of the letter is that the Aluminum Company was merely one of thirty or more fabricators.

As a matter of fact, by a price differential controlled by the illegal use of the patent pool, the Aluminum Company maintained a complete monopoly control over every one of the fabricators. It could put any one of them out of business at an instant's notice.

8. The next point of the letter is that the *illegal patent pool* made available valuable fabricating patents to American manufacturers.

On the contrary, the patent pool prevented any fabricator from having an independent existence. It controlled his price policies and his production.

9. The next point made is that Germany was producing 18,000 tons instead of from 25,000 to 50,000 tons.

Our own information, derived from sources close to British Intelligence, is that the figure is close to 50,000. 25,000 is conservative.

Frankly, I consider the arguments flimsy and patently against the established facts. I can see nothing in this letter which is worth going into in any detail. However, if you wish to do so, we would be delighted to spend any amount of time with you. There are half a dozen more startling stories that can be written on the Aluminum Company than the one we now have. One of the most interesting ones is their failure to cooperate in national defense and their attempts to keep Reynolds from getting started, which I did not go into in my article at all.

*Sincerely*

---

## *To Rockwell Kent* [184]

Washington, D.C., Sept. 4, 1941

Dear Rockwell:

I am glad to be able to help you out with H.T. Tsiang,[185] but I must confess that I do not have the same sympathy in the case of Earl Browder.[186]

In the first place, he was convicted after a fair trial and I do not see why anyone should receive immunity from the criminal law because he is a Communist. You mention the Communists' support of the

Administration. I personally think that the less we have of it, the better. They are an unmitigated nuisance.

With best regards and hoping that everything is going well with you,

*Sincerely*

---

## *To Miss C. Warriner*

Washington, D.C., April 28, 1942

Dear Miss Warriner:

You have an excellent article.[187] I only have time to comment on one part of it which I think in the interest of honesty you should leave out.

On page 14 you say, "There isn't much to the pother that the utilities of incandescent lamp manufacturers have tried to sidetrack fluorescent lighting, though until recently it might have been said that some utilities didn't want to see it move too rapidly."

We have evidence prior to that time that we consider conclusive that General Electric for at least two years, which is as far as our documents go and probably prove, has been attempting to get control of fluorescent lighting and develop it in such a way that it would not interfere with the Mazda lamp business. Had it not been for Hy-Grade Sylvania and several others they would have succeeded in completely stopping the fluorescent lamp business at least until their machinery for the other lamps had become obsolete or until they were assured of sufficient control so that they could maintain fixed prices. They are even now suing Hy-Grade Sylvania for patent infringement.

This attempt to control fluorescent lighting in the interests of electric light production is not a matter of circumstantial evidence, but is supported by documents. Today General Electric is using every effort through the War Department to prevent the trial of our lamp suit which would have the effect of freeing the market in the fluorescent field. Their machinations in Washington to prevent the trial of this suit and to prevent this evidence from coming out have been notorious. It is probable that if they succeed in stopping this suit the Bone Committee will go into the matter, and we will get our evidence out through that channel.

Your minimizing the efforts of the utilities to stop fluorescent lighting is also incorrect. It was not some utility but the principal utility that entered into an active conspiracy to slow down the exploitation of fluorescent lighting in order to increase their wattage. We have, for instance, the Edison Electric Institute (I am writing this in a hurry and do not know whether I have the name exactly correct), which had a committee who met with General Electric frequently over a period of years to discuss a policy to which the word "sabotage" of fluorescent lighting can properly be applied. This again is not a question of hearsay. We have the documents.

I can understand why *Fortune* may not want to make a positive statement without examining these documents or before this story is told publicly. However, I would be shocked beyond all measure, since I know *Fortune's* stand upon production, if they attempted to butter General Electric by any such statement as you have in your article.

May I urge you, since the article does not permit you to go into the entire situation, simply to leave the statement out. I think that you would desire to do this because I expect within the next two or three months I will be in a position to make public my documentary evidence.

The story on fluorescent light is definitely one of our very worst cartel pictures. In addition to the domestic picture, there was an international cartel rigidly allocating world markets which eliminated any new developments by independents. That cartel was amended in 1940. During the national emergency agreements were made with companies in Japan and Germany to include fluorescent lighting within the former electric lamp cartel. This, of course, is not exactly side-tracking fluorescent lighting. However, it gave the control of fluorescent lighting to dominant companies tied up with utilities whose interest lay in not permitting fluorescent lighting to interfere with their dividends on obsolete lighting or their relations with public utilities. There is no question in my mind that this international cartel had an enormous effect in slowing down the progress of fluorescent lighting. I confess, however, that this is a guess based upon the inevitable tendencies of such cartels.

We do not have the figures on foreign countries, and, of course, we have no competitive figures on what would have happened in the United States had fluorescent lighting been free. We do know, however, that a continuous effort was made to stop independent production in this country which was successful to a very large degree. To the fact that it was not completely successful, we owe the present status of the industry which is advancing rapidly.

Our attack on General Electric's control was started by investigation in 1939. From the first time after our public announcement in that year General Electric and Westinghouse began to expand their own production. We have figures which show that exploitation of fluorescent lighting did not occur to any substantial effect before our proceedings were instituted. If you look at the figures, you will have little doubt about this. Since our attack it is true they have attempted to expand their own production. They have increased their activities, however, to prevent others from producing. Their only licenses have been to

Westinghouse and Consolidated Electric Lamp Company. Consolidated Electric was put on a quota basis with restricted production. Westinghouse is not only on a quota basis but also on a price basis.

To this sabotage of production of fluorescent lighting it should be added that through an illegal arrangement Corning has become the only supplier of glass tubes for fluorescent lighting. Corning works hand in glove with General Electric, and production is at the mercy of these two companies.

I don't expect you to develop this in your very excellent article which is on another subject. However, I sincerely hope that you will not go out of your way to throw perfume on this particular cesspool.

*Very truly yours*

P.S. I dictated this in a great hurry and have no time to rewrite it. I did not intend to be critical of your grand article. The word is used unintentionally.

---

## *To George H. Adams* [188]

Washington, D.C., July 13, 1942

Dear Mr. Adams:

Thank you for your vigorous editorials and stories about the milk situation in Minneapolis. The distribution of milk is so fantastic as to defy intelligent comment.[189] It is a combination of dairy interests, labor unions, and milk companies, all attempting to keep the price at levels which during the depression prevented the sale of milk and which during the present emergency will keep prices unnecessarily high at a time when the Government ought to be trying to get them down. I was interested in the contention of the union that the only way to create employment is to keep prices up, by force, if necessary. This is a strange doctrine at a time when fifty per cent of our National Economy is to be diverted to the War effort and the Government is trying to keep down prices.

So long as the Supreme Court decisions exempting labor unions from penalties for combinations in restraint of trade stand, there is very little we can do about the milk situation. The remedy is to get labor unions back under the Sherman Act, define their objectives, and indict them when they pursue objectives which are not legitimate. The bills introduced in Congress for that purpose have been ignored. We need some sort of force to get this kind of legislation passed.

More power to your "editorial arm"!

With best wishes,

*Sincerely*

---

## *To Evans Clark*[190]

Washington, D.C., July 13, 1942

Dear Clark:

I just got a chance to read Stuart Chase's manuscript "Goals for America." It is a brilliantly written job and I am in accord with his objectives, particularly public works.

I wish he wouldn't put so much emphasis on what he conceives to be a revolution. For instance, on page 102 he says "The prime motive of industry should now be to supply the community with the goods it needs. Men first, money second. Consumers first, producers second. That is what the revolution seems to be all about." The trouble with this atmosphere is that it scares people and makes Stuart Chase's objective—to wit: sensible public works for utilitarian purposes—more difficult.

Personally I do not see any such revolution in human motivation nor do I think that private industry is capable of doing anything more than pursuing short-run profits. When an industry gets so large that competition is impossible, government ownership is probably the only answer. Government regulation without government ownership leads to things like the fiasco of railroad regulations, the present radio monopoly, the absurd price fixing tactics of General Electric, et cetera. Such monopolies have in the past and will continue in the future to dominate the market, restrict production and fix prices. They will be strong enough in the future, as they have in the past, to prevent any public works which interfere with them.

The monopoly problem has got to be attacked on two fronts: *first,* freeing of industry to competitive forces where that is possible; *second,* government ownership where it is not possible.

To trust in a revolution in human motivation to accomplish these things, and to expect a political government to be able to engage in public works which interfered with uncontrolled entrenched monopoly, is entirely Utopian.

My criticism of Stuart Chase's book, therefore, is that he ignores the central problem which interferes with the objective which he seeks.

Of course the antitrust laws are not the only instrument which deal with the monopoly problem. It is equally true that there may be many solutions of this central monopoly problem. Nevertheless, the monopoly problem cannot be ignored if the Twentieth Century Fund is really interested in post-war planning.

If the monopoly problem is taken up and studied you will find that it has one great advantage. It will get your research confined to specific cases and thus keep its feet on the ground. The monopoly problem in steel is different from trade associations. All these various things cumulatively have an enormous effect on our economy. They have got to be studied, one case at a time, and research which directs itself to such case studies may be very practical indeed.

*Sincerely*

---

## *To Robert H. Jackson*

Washington, D.C., Sept. 9, 1942

Dear Mr. Attorney General:

I appreciated Mr. Donald Nelson's[191] candor in sending me a copy of his letter to you protesting against the activities of the Antitrust Division. In view of this fact, I would like to get permission to send a copy of this reply to him. In a situation like this, candor is essential to a full understanding.

Mr. Nelson claims that he is not referring to our legitimate law enforcement activities. Obviously, the antitrust laws have not been abrogated. It is our duty and responsibility to curb monopoly evils, and *it is particularly our task to see to it that those monopoly interests do not abuse or misuse the war emergency as a cloak or a disguise for extension of monopoly domination and the evils attendant thereon.*

At the very outset, let me state, without reserve or qualification, that both in formulating and carrying through our antitrust policy the record will bear me out that we have not only shown a scrupulous regard for the war effort of WPB,[192] but have actually leaned backward almost to the breaking point. The record will show the following:

1. Every request for exemption from the antitrust laws under Section 6 of the Smaller War Plants Corporation law has been consented to, and that with a reasonable dispatch after the request was made. This in spite of the fact that as to some of those requests we entertained grave doubt.

2. In every situation in which the Army or the Navy has requested us to postpone an antitrust proceeding, we have either acceded to such request or worked out some arrangement satisfactory to the Army and the Navy. This despite the fact that recently members of a Congressional committee questioned the propriety of making some of those requests.

3. Although the Division has been literally flooded with numerous complaints to the effect that monopoly interests, having representation in WPB through dollar-a-year men who were drawing substantial salaries from their institutions, had violated the antitrust laws with the connivance of those representatives, not a single such suit has been started, either civil or criminal, and we have taken the pains to make it clear to both Mr. O'Brian[193] and Mr. Nelson that it is not our policy to commence any such action without first presenting the facts to WPB for such correction or remedies it may see fit to take.

4. Every request of WPB as to the conduct or postponement of suits or investigations has been honored.

5. Mr. O'Brian has referred to the Antitrust Division numerous cases in which he as asked us to institute court proceedings, and in some of which he has asked us to conduct investigations. These references began in February with the steel priorities cases. In that regard, we have at all times attempted to extend our full cooperation, and certainly we have had no complaints from the Legal Division of WPB about our handling of those cases.

6. We have taken the pains repeatedly to advise Mr. Nelson and Mr. O'Brian that it is our intense desire to avoid any possible friction and to cooperate in every possible way. As late as Friday, September 4, Mr. Podell stated to Mr. Weinberg, at a luncheon meeting, that if there was the slightest friction to notify him immediately, because it was the desire of the Antitrust Division to offer every cooperation and to avoid friction.

In the face of this record, which is readily provable by documents on file with both Departments, and which I believe will not be denied or disputed, I cannot conceive how, short of abandoning our responsibility under the antitrust laws, folding up our office, and allowing monopoly to run riot not only in the war effort but in the nation's business, we can offer any further cooperation.

I cannot believe that Mr. Nelson was aware of the foregoing record when he allowed the letter to be written containing these vague and intemperate charges and reflections.

Mr. Nelson appears to be chiefly worried about the criticisms which have arisen from the fact that many men connected with monopoly interests are found on the staff of WPB. He seems to think that this criticism arises from the Antitrust Division. However, if we take, as an example, Mr. Amory Houghton[194] who resigned from WPB, with a press release to the effect that his resignation was on account of antitrust activities, we may get a relevant illustration. The criticism of Mr. Houghton because of his monopoly activities stemmed from a monopoly investigation made by the TNEC long prior to the war. The criticism was inevitable, because it is difficult for anyone to defend the practices of Mr. Houghton's company. Mr. Houghton, in the face of criminal charges, pleaded nolo contendere and was fined in one case which was open and shut. In another civil suit, commenced long before there was any WPB, and contested for years, the Court found his company guilty of conduct so outrageous that the Court criticized the Department of Justice for not bringing a criminal prosecution. It was immediately after this decision that Mr. Houghton resigned. We never directly criticized Mr. Houghton. Criticism, however, was inevitable in view of his record, particularly at a time when independent business men felt themselves discriminated against by monopoly groups attempting to dominate the war effort.

It is true that the Antitrust Division has been handling and investigating complaints which come to us from independent industries large and small, from such men as Houdry, Kaiser and Higgins down to the smallest businessman who feels himself discriminated against by what he thinks is the influence of the monopoly group. But these men would complain even though there were no Antitrust Division. Houdry, Kaiser and Higgins complained to the press before they ever came in to see us. We believe that our influence in analyzing their complaints was constructive and did not add to the criticism. Certainly sensitivity to the criticism that dominant groups are keeping such people out of war production should not lead WPB into adopting the policy of stifling that criticism by stifling an antitrust program.

We have endeavored not to bring prosecutions against the wishes of WPB. For example, when we discovered plain evidence of a conspiracy to escape Federal jurisdiction in the failure to build inter-connecting power lines between electrical power pools in New York, we first submitted the situation to WPB. We were asked not to bring a case. In spite of the fact that the situation looked serious to us, we did not bring a case. This is a typical example.

We believe it is essential that we investigate well founded complaints that independent enterprise is being crushed by monopoly groups. There is evidence of monopoly control in practically all of the basic materials essential to the war effort. We think we are of service in calling the attention of WPB to that sort of control, especially when it results in curtailment of production. Certainly we are of service to the cause of increasing production, because that is going to require the maximum use of independent productive capacity. If WPB thinks that we have investigated any case beyond the preliminary stage which does not represent a monopoly problem or a war fraud, we believe that case should be called specifically to our attention.

The tenor of Mr. Nelson's letter would seem to indicate that he not only does not want cases brought, but he does not want the situations called to the attention of WPB, because he considers this sort of activity as "unjustified and burdensome intrusions." Certainly he cannot have it both ways. If he wishes us to pursue our way independently of his office, he should not be complaining about our not giving him the prima facie evidence under which we ordinarily start a criminal investigation. If he wishes us to inform him of what appear to be substantial complaints prior to the time that investigation has either established them or disproved them, he should not call such activity an unjustified intrusion.

Perhaps some of the general charges in the letter about "unjustified instrusions" may be based on attempts I have made to acquaint WPB, in advance, of prosecutions or investigations which might involve WPB officials. I have passed such information on to members of Mr. Nelson's staff, including Messrs. Coonley and Weinberg, particularly in connection with possible involvement of Messrs. Philip Reed,[195] Zay Jeffries[196] and Amory Houghton. It seems inconceivable to me that it is not to the advantage of WPB to receive such information in advance. However, again, I do not see how they can have it both ways. They cannot complain about our informing them confidentially about a possible fraud in cables on the part of General Electric and then, at the same time, complain about the case itself.

Of course, investigations of monopoly control do annoy those who are engaged in an attempt to perpetuate it during and after the war. This was true during the depression, it was true prior to the war, it is true today. Prominent leaders of industry will always make the charge that our activities are directed at unsubstantial technicalities. Mr. Nelson's letter, in which he selects as one of the unjustified cases the palpable fraud upon the Government committed by General Electric, General Cable Company, and others, shows how he has been misled by this sort of rumor among business men. As a matter of fact, you will recall that General Electric was willing to plead to an antitrust charge if it could escape the fraud indictment. This was the same company that had written to the War Department, using Mr. Philip Reed's services on the War Production Board as an excuse for continuing another antitrust case. They have fought their cases bitterly through every channel both within and without the courts. It is scarcely likely that they would make this kind of compromise if the fraud case had been of the character Mr. Nelson claims.

The statement that it is impossible for the War Production Board to obtain the services of able and seasoned industrial personnel because of antitrust investigations, if true, would amount to saying that only persons engaged in criminal monopoly practices are capable of conducting the defense program. Actually our experience since the war in Europe started has shown a progressive series of failures by this very group. The shortages which now exist are most acute as the result of monopoly activities of American industry in the past. The failure to expand is a result of the judgment of men who desired to perpetuate their domination of industry after the war. We believe that antitrust investigations have been a stimulus to production. We are convinced that without such activity present production will be concentrated in a few hands to the detriment of war production and with disastrous effects on our post-war economy.

We emphasize these broad objectives because as a matter of fact the sum and substance of Mr. Nelson's letter is an attack on them. I assume Mr. Nelson did not personally write this letter, and therefore it is no disrespect to him to say that its writer apparently does not believe in actually curbing the evils of monopoly. The attitude of the letter is one of resentfulness against any effective antimonopoly campaign—even against the prosecution of large concerns for actual fraud. When the letter refers to specific instances, every single charge is inaccurate with the possible exception of a few trivial violations of an artificial and inconvenient system of liaison designed rather to slow down cooperation than to promote it, and of two insignificant preliminary inquiries which were based on a misunderstanding. These minor inquiries by two subordinates based on preliminary complaints are the sole basis for this mountain of accusation. I cannot escape the conclusions that the real complaint of the letter is that large industry is being curbed in its effort to dominate the present and the post-war markets.

*Sincerely*

---

## *To Robert H. Jackson*

Washington, D.C., Sept. 10, 1942

Dear Sir:

Henry J. Kaiser came to me today, in an extremely discouraged frame of mind, to complain of his treatment by WPB, which he believes is due largely to the influence of the sales executives of the major steel companies which run WPB's Iron & Steel Branch. He has just been subjected to an experience which, he says, is not an isolated case, but is typical of the treatment that he and others have been receiving for many months from WPB. For this kind of thing to happen once would be sufficient to create a major scandal. When a man of Kaiser's reputation and standing says that it is a typical and usual occurrence, I feel that the situation is so serious that it should be brought to the attention of the President.

The story concerns the incomprehensible refusal of WPB to give Kaiser's company permission to buy less than *50 tons* of steel, which is available in a warehouse for immediate delivery and apparently not needed by either the Army or the Navy, when that refusal of that small tonnage will cost the war effort at least *60,000 tons* of urgently needed steel.

Kaiser Company, Inc., is building a blast furnace and steel plant at Fontana, California, which will produce 350,000 tons of steel plate annually. The blast furnace is scheduled to go into production early this December.

Late last month, the company was notified by Bethlehem Steel Corporation that an order for 57.8 tons of structural shapes, scheduled for delivery by September 15, and having a super rating of AA-3, had been displaced from Bethlehem's rolling schedule by an emergency Navy order, and that the Kaiser Company will not be able to obtain this steel from the mill before October or November at the earliest. The Kaiser Company must have this steel on time or have construction on its steel plant stopped to wait for it, and if the company relies on the mill for this order, the blast furnace will not go into production until at least two months behind schedule.

Mr. Kaiser immediately put all his branch offices to work trying to find an alternative source for this steel, and finally located a warehouse in Houston, Texas, which had it in stock and could give him immediate delivery on the entire order. However, under OPA rulings, Kaiser could not buy this amount of steel from a warehouse without a certificate from the Iron & Steel Branch of WPB. Therefore, on September 1, Kaiser Company began its efforts to secure such a certificate from WPB, which, if issued, would permit OPA to adjust the price on this quantity of steel so that the warehouse would be able and willing to sell it. The total order for the 57.8 tons would amount to less than $3500, and the impact of a small price differential on this non-consumer item would be extremely remote in its inflationary effect.

Mr. Kaiser put four men on the job of obtaining the certificate from WPB, including his General Counsel and his Project Manager, who is as familiar as one could be, after many months' experience, with WPB procedures. The story of their attempts to get this certificate from WPB would be ludicrous, if its implications were not so tragic.

At least two of Kaiser's men were continuously on the job at WPB every day for 9 days. They interviewed at least 14 different officials, some of them several times. They first went to the Warehouse Unit of the Iron & Steel Branch, where, they had been assured by OPA, they could get quick relief in this kind of emergency. They finally succeeded in reaching the head of the Warehouse Unit, who said he had no authority to act, and then they were successful in reaching the Acting Chief of the

Iron & Steel Branch, Mr. David Austin, Vice-President in Charge of Sales of Carnegie-Illinois Steel Corporation, the author and administrator of a company system of dealing with priorities which stymied WPB regulations and resulted in a suit against his company, on the recommendation of John Lord O'Brian, General Counsel of WPB, for extensive priorities violations. Mr. Austin referred Kaiser's men to D.N. Watkins, in charge of the Iron & Steel Branch's Plant Facilities Section, President of Steel Publications, Inc., of Pittsburgh, to whom Kaiser was told to write another application setting forth all details of his needs and from whom Kaiser was to obtain a letter signifying Watkins' concurrence as to the pertinent facts. This carried Kaiser's efforts to September 2.

On September 3, Kaiser submitted the requested application to Watkins and obtained from him the requested covering letter, which he was told required approval by Austin and J.R. Stuart, the head of the Warehouse Unit of the Iron & Steel Branch. Stuart refused to sign, stating he had no jurisdiction over priority ratings. Kaiser then went back to Stuart's chief, Austin, who approved and signed the letter. However, when the letter was taken back to Stuart, Stuart said that he must have a different form of application before he could approve the letter.

After this experience, Kaiser was referred to E.B. Mason, Chief Priority Specialist of the Iron & Steel Branch, a market analyst for United States Steel Corporation. But Mason advised Kaiser that neither he nor Austin could give Kaiser his certificate, but that he must obtain it from Frank Connally of WPB's Emergency Rating Section, which is outside the Iron & Steel Branch. Kaiser then obtained some more forms from Elmer Purdy, of another section of the Iron & Steel Branch, to whom he was referred, and filled them out and delivered them as his fourth form of application, to Mason for presentation to Connally. This was on September 3.

On September 4, Purdy advised Kaiser that the forms were not made out in the proper manner. They were changed and returned. Further conferences were held with other members of the Iron & Steel Branch that day, and Kaiser was informed that he would probably get the necessary certificate.

On September 5, Kaiser was advised that his revised form had reached A.E. Spence of the Emergency Rating Section in the Railroad Retirement Building. When he went to Spence, he was advised that it had been referred to the Army and Navy Munitions Board. Then, after several calls on Spence, Kaiser was told that the only kind of a rating which would permit the release of the steel was a rating reserved for the Army and the Navy, and that the place to get a release was back in the Warehouse Unit of the Iron & Steel Branch of WPB, where Kaiser had started five days before. Kaiser was able to learn from Spence, however, that as far as Spence could find out, the steel which Kaiser had located which was waiting and unused in the warehouse in Houston, was not wanted by the Army or the Navy, and that neither the Army nor the Navy had any intention of using that steel at a later date. The steel is still there.

Finally, on September 9, the Iron & Steel Branch advised Kaiser that his request had been finally turned down.

Kaiser feels, as stated in a letter of complaint written to me today, that there may be

> a definite and deliberate attempt of someone or of certain interests to delay the completion of our steel project. Since this 58 tons of steel is on hand in the warehouse at Houston, Texas, it does not seem possible that incompetency and bureaucracy alone can account for the delay and final denial of our request for this steel. Therefore, I feel that this matter should be brought to your attention.

As you know, there are, at present, no steel plants on the West Coast, and United States Steel Corporation has a distributing subsidiary on the West Coast, Columbia Steel Corporation, which is the most profitable unit in the United States Steel Corporation family.

It should be noted that Kaiser's need to go to a warehouse for this 58 tons of steel was not the result of poor planning, but arose from an emergency beyond his control. His blast furnace, if he gets this steel, will, he assures us, be in production early this December, and will be producing 1200 tons of badly needed pig iron daily. The original steel plant project was finally approved by Mr. Nelson after long delays and after every obstruction had been placed in Mr. Kaiser's way by the large steel companies who run WPB's Iron & Steel Branch. Every day of delay in obtaining this 58 tons of steel means another 1200 tons, or almost half a Liberty Ship. If Kaiser waits for mill delivery on this steel (and he must do this now that WPB denies him a certificate), his blast furnace cannot get into operation before next February at the earliest, and a minimum of 60,000 tons of steel will be lost to the war.

You may be interested to know, also, in this connection, that Mr. Kaiser's presently approved steel plant will make only steel plates, but that he has been trying desperately to expand it to make other steel products, which will make the West Coast, which has no steel mills, independent of steel shipments from the East, and which will greatly relieve the serious transportation situation which now requires the shipment of all West Coast steel either by rail or by boat. With 6,000 tons of steel a month for the next five months for this plant expansion, Kaiser says he can guarantee an additional steel output on the West Coast, over and above the plant he is now constructing, of 600,000 tons a year beginning not later than nine months from today. Judging by the 111,000,000 pounds of copper which a survey published today has shown to be in excess inventories, and with the data in the memoranda I have already given you on the steel crisis, it is perfectly obvious that far more steel than these 30,000 tons is lying idle in excess inventories and in warehouses, wholly apart from the hundreds of thousands of tons going to other destinations without the close control which is imperative. Of course, this is a question of strategy, but it is hard to believe that nine months from now the West Coast will not have the most urgent kind of need for 600,000 tons of steel a year.

*Sincerely*

---

## *To Hugh Cox*

Washington, D.C., Dec. 15, 1942

Dear Hugh:

Your letter arrived and I scattered the news about the Division that you were well and happy. Then the thing lay on my desk and I am ashamed to see that I have failed to give you sooner the important information which you requested.

As you know, there were already signs of disintegration about the Horsehead story when you left.[197] Western stories should not have so much water in them. The hero and the girl, after a series of miraculous escapes where they were banged and battered among the rocks in the yawning chasm, finally were cast up on a small neck of land. Precipitous cliffs rose behind them, unscalable even by a human fly. It was pretty cold. The cold drew them together and she spent the night with her head on his shoulder. Needless to say, however, there was no improper thought on the part of either of them, only a vast tenderness and companionship.

The next day they bound some logs together with string and wrapping paper and set forth down the canyon once more. The logs all broke apart. But through some unexpected miracle they were saved and cast ashore at the ranch of the old bozo who was introduced at the beginning of the story. They were resuscitated with coffee and grog.

In the meantime, however, everybody had been killing everybody else off. Trumbold quarreled with the father of the girl who jumped in the boat, whose name I have forgotten. Then this bozo hung all of the Horsehead men. Then he turned on Trumbold and tried to shoot him. Trumbold was quicker and shot him. This left everyone dead excepting Trumbold and the hero. Trumbold realized that he must kill the hero in order to solidify his dominance of the entire valley. He learned that the hero had been rescued out of the river. Therefore, with infinite stealth he approached the ranch where the hero was standing by a corral hardly recovered from his perilous trip down the river. It looked as if it was all up with the hero. However, he was watching out of the corner of his eye. Trumbold made a move and the hero shot him. This left the hero and the two girls as the only important figures.

The only problem which remained was to get the hero to marry the right girl. You remember the girl who drank and smoked. She saw the hero one evening at a party. The blood throbbed in his veins at the sense of her nearness. It looked as if it were all up with the heroine when suddenly something clicked in his mind and he realized that this young woman who drank and smoked was appealing to his baser instincts whereas the other young woman (whose name again I have forgotten but who was the daughter of the villain who had started all the trouble in the first place) was really a pure young woman who would give him those qualities which the hero of a Western most desired. Therefore he pushed aside the young woman who drank and smoked, feeling very sorry for her, of course. She took her rejection with great sadness but still realizing that he was doing the right thing, and the story closed with the hero and the girl who did not drink and smoke vis-a-vis, as the great mystic George Nebolsine would put it.

I hope that this is the information that you desire. I was thinking of putting it before a grand jury but the War Department sent me a letter saying that it would take time from the war effort, and the Attorney General refused to appeal to the President.

As you know, plans are on foot for getting you back to the Department in an important capacity, and I am using every effort to push them along.

With kind personal regards,

*Sincerely*

---

## *To Corwin Edwards*

Washington, D.C., December 15, 1942

Dear Corwin:

I congratulate you upon the very apparent progress you are making in South America; although it is with a heavy heart that we extend your leave, you know of course that we will give you such leave as you may require from time to time. You need not concern yourself about this at all. We hope that things will work out so that you can come back to us.

Of course South America is a tempting adventure but if I were you, thinking of your own future, I would pass it up. Don't let your interest in a foreign country get you out of the current of things here. If you go down to South America and then come back you will always be one of the world's greatest experts on South America and when the next important job relating to that country bobs up you will be Johnny-on-the-spot. If you stay down in South America you will be working for some tyro who was in Washington and got the important job. I have seen this happen too often with some of my very able friends in the economic service which Hoover set up some years ago. Remember Commerce sent out economists to all the various countries? Some of them did marvelous jobs. My friend Hester in the Philippine Islands became a real expert on the Orient. However, he never got anywhere. He was always writing memoranda to various commissions which came over, and now he's back in the State Department working for far less able men.

I may not know much about economics but I do know something about careers in Government. If you are too far from the Court of Versailles you get no patents of nobility. The colonial service is always dangerous. It is alright to dash in and out of it. But you have a real career with the Government if you are in Washington and have the actual contacts with the men who run the show.

With your peculiar talents you are much better off in the Antitrust Division where your contacts make you available for all sorts of interesting things. If you ever actually marry one of these jobs then you are liable to grow old in it. I know you haven't solicited my advice. Nevertheless I think that you are on the threshold of a great career. You are just getting your contacts. You have become recognized in the last year all over Washington. Don't be off in a foreign country while the real policies are dictated during the peace in Washington.

With best regards,

*Sincerely*

# V

# CIRCUIT COURT OF APPEALS

## 1943 – 1945

---

*To Franklin D. Roosevelt*

Washington, D.C., Jan. 16, 1943

My dear Mr. President:

I deeply appreciate the honor of being appointed to the Circuit Court of Appeals for the District of Columbia and I will do my best in that office to justify your confidence.

I am particularly grateful for your taking the time, in the midst of affairs of such overwhelming importance, to write me a letter so full of understanding of what I have been trying to do in the Antitrust Division in the past four years.[198] Whatever has been accomplished has been due to your support of our prosecutions at times when it would have been far easier and a matter of political expediency to postpone them. Due to your support the staff of the Antitrust Division was increased four-fold. This support has enabled this administration to attack the monopoly problem on a scale that was not possible in any former administration. We have tried to make our prosecutions fit in with the economic policy which you expressed with such directness and force in your monopoly message of 1938.

I am grateful for the opportunity you gave me in the Department of Justice. My dearest hope is that in the future some opportunity to follow under your leadership will again arise.

*Sincerely yours*

---

*To Erwin D. Canham*[199]

Washington, D.C., Feb. 6, 1943

Dear Sir:

A number of people have sent me copies of an article appearing in the *Christian Science Monitor* of January 26th by Harold Fleming entitled "Business Sees Arnold After Scalps Rather Than Justice." The article contains a number of misrepresentations, one of which is so important that I feel justified in asking for a correction.

The general theme of the article is that I am misusing the power of my office in seven ways. The particular abuses written up in this installment appear to be (1) choice of venue; (2) indictments of individuals who were following established Supreme Court precedents; and (3) prejudicial appeals to juries.

These general charges are untrue but I am not writing about any general statement, which can properly come under the head of opinion. I am concerned only with the specific false statements which appear to have aroused indignation against the Department of Justice. Of these the most important is the representation that the General Electric Company was indicted for following practices approved by the Supreme Court in the General Electric case of 1926. The article states that this was done in the hope of reversing the case. The writer then goes on to say that every other corporation which has followed this Supreme Court decision is in danger of being indicted and punished.

It is a very serious thing in my opinion to mislead the public and misrepresent to businessmen the operation of any law. This is particularly true about the antitrust law. The statement in your article is inexcusable because the most superficial examination of our records and public announcements would have shown its falsity.

The facts are as follows:

(1) The Department has never either during my tenure of office or before brought indictments under these circumstances.

(2) Because the question was raised when I first took office I made a public announcement that no indictments would be brought where defendants were following precedents which gave them apparent justification.

(3) All our suits which can be said to develop new law of any kind have been civil proceedings in which no penalty of any kind can be imposed.

(4) The two specific cases which involved the General Electric decision were the Masonite case (316 U.S. 265) and the Univis case (316 U.S. 241). Both were civil cases which I lost below on account of the General Electric case, and won in the Supreme Court.

(5) The only proceedings against General Electric for practices which could conceivably be justified under the 1926 decision are civil cases. General Electric has been indicted in two cases—one for a cartel arrangement with a German firm and the other for making fraudulent claims against the United States Government. There are no disputed questions of law in these cases. The sole issues are issues of fact.

(6) The hypothetical possibility of a criminal case brought under the circumstances you set out exists in the administration of any law. However, in a case dealing with an entirely different law the Supreme Court has

indicated that there is not even a hypothetical possibility of such an indefinite method of proceeding.

The consequence of your misrepresentations is to arouse fear and confusion on the part of businessmen. It is evidenced by the correspondence which I have been receiving. I think, therefore, it is important that you make a full and clear correction of this part of your article.

The other misrepresentations in your article have more to do with me personally and are not so serious from a public point of view. They are, nevertheless, misstatements which I should think a paper of your reputation would desire to correct and so I call your attention to them.

In attempting to prove that I have taken advantage of class prejudice appeals to juries you cite the only antitrust case that I know of in which the court below the Court of Appeals took exception to the remarks of trial counsel—the Madison Oil case.

This trial, as any conscientious reporter could have found out by checking the dates, occurred before I took office and while I was a professor at Yale. The attorney who made the remarks was a local counsel employed by my predecessor on a part-time basis. After I came into office I did not re-employ him. My only part in this case was the argument before the Supreme Court of the United States, long after the trial when the record was made up.

Your third set of misrepresentations concerns the choice of venue. My policy in choosing venue is ordinarily to bring a case in the jurisdiction where the principal overt acts of oppression of independent business or price fixing, et cetera, have occurred. Sometimes this policy must be changed on account of crowded dockets, particularly in New York and Chicago.

This policy is based upon the familiar principle of criminal law that a crime should be prosecuted where it was committed. Of course you may criticize that policy if you want to. Your article uses as an illustration a choice of venue which occurred before I took office. This case was no doubt selected because the venue was criticized in a Congressional hearing which received a good deal of publicity. Therefore, it makes a better weapon against me. Your report refers to the original proceedings against the automobile financing companies brought in Milwaukee, Wisconsin. That proceeding was dismissed before I got into office. When the case came up again after I took office the venue selected was not Milwaukee but South Bend, Indiana (incidentally before a Republican Judge).

Of these misstatements of fact in your first installment, only the one I have mentioned is of importance. The others are merely an attempt to bolster up a general attack by false illustrations.

I would appreciate your giving attention to this matter and letting me know what corrections you are willing to make.

*Very truly yours*

---

## *To Charles E. Clark*

Washington, D.C., Feb. 18, 1943

Dear Charlie:

Thanks for your letter. As you say, the opportunity of becoming the prop and support in the declining years of a man like Judge Groner[200] is the kind of a chance that occurs only a few times in centuries. It was an opportunity like this that made Boswell famous. And so I am entirely satisfied with the job provided the Senate is.

I note your nostalgia for the cluster of giants at Yale, of which you were the shining and resplendent Fuhrer. Whether these boys have gone up or down since those great days is a question which can only be decided by a philosopher. A very plausible brief could be written upholding the contention that none of them would ever see better days again. Whether the Supreme Court would agree with this or not, at least it is true the boys made a certain amount of noise at Yale. Even Glenn Saxon was at least a Chinese firecracker. The boys at Harvard, on the other hand, have only remained precious.

Therefore, I think it would be a tactful and useful thing to get up a Round Robin to be signed by yourself, and Bill Douglas, and Abe Fortas, and me, and Charles Ulysses Samenow. This Round Robin would be directed to the attention of that great and good man, Charles Seymour. It would tell him frankly that Yale Law School would soon go to the dogs unless he rapidly recruited another bunch as near like us as could be found. The memorandum would point out that we had never been sufficiently appreciated while we were at Yale; it would show the terrible consequences of the failure to realize what great men we were.

Anyway, those were great days and I don't think any of us will ever see any better.

*Sincerely*

---

## *To Francis Biddle*

Washington, D.C., March 3, 1943

Dear Francis:

When you take up with the President the matter of sending Mr. Tom Clark's name to the Senate as Assistant Attorney General in charge of the Antitrust Division, I would appreciate your telling him that I think he is the only man, under the present circumstances, who can carry on without any loss of momentum the work in the Division.

As you know, I first suggested the name of Mr. Hugh Cox, who had been my first assistant almost from the beginning and whose brilliant work was largely responsible for the job the Antitrust Division has done. Circumstances have so changed since this suggestion, however, that I am fully in accord with your idea that Mr. Cox would find a better field in the War Policies Division, for which I understand you are suggesting his name.

Mr. Clark has worked up from a minor place to the position as Chief Assistant. He has also made a great record in the War Frauds Unit, which as you know is largely composed of Antitrust Division men. Everyone in the Division knows him and has confidence in him. His appointment will be a guarantee that there is going to be no change in policies. Within the last few days practically all of the heads of sections have been in to see me asking that I use every influence towards getting Tom Clark as head of the Division. I am sure that if he is appointed there will be renewed confidence in all of our offices throughout the country. If anyone else is appointed, under the present circumstances, there will be a period of confusion which will materially interfere with the work of the Division.

Since I am tremendously interested in the future success of the Division I am writing this letter which you may show to the President if you think it appropriate.

*Sincerely*

---

## *To Homer Cummings*

Washington, D.C., March 20, 1943

Dear Homer:

Thanks a lot for writing me. I appreciate particularly a letter from you because if it hadn't been for your understanding of what the Antitrust Division was trying to do, we would never have gotten off the ground.

I was tremendously flattered that you should come to the banquet[201] because you have the distinction of being the only Attorney General who was never worried about my activities.[202]

With affectionate regards to you and Mrs. Cummings,

*Sincerely*

---

## *To Mrs. Eleanor Patterson*[203]

Washington, D.C., April 16, 1943

Dear Cissie:

Here's my translation of your friend Cal's[204] letter.

Cal won his suit and got the water right adjudicated in his favor. However, the law of Idaho gives a man a right only to the water which he has actually used in the past. If he does not beneficially use the water he loses his right and it goes to the person who does use it. I gather that a man named Woods sometime in the past had turned water in his ditch out of Cal's head gate, and to the extent of that diversion Cal has lost his water right.

He is not satisfied with his attorneys because he thinks they sold out to Woods, which, of course, is nonsense but in any event he appears to have gotten all the water now which he used in the past, which should satisfy him but probably won't. After his attorneys have won the suit he has decided if it comes up again to get another attorney that they can't buy off.

I gather that the exact amount of water Woods can take from Cal's ditch has not been adjudicated but has been left to the water master to determine. If the determination of the water master is not satisfactory to Cal, he has the right under the law to bring another suit and have this decided.

Cal thinks that it was only my lack of faith in him which prevented me from getting on a train and settling the suit myself without so much expense. He is worried for fear the attorneys will send you a bill to collect additional money to which they are not entitled.

Thanks for letting me see the letter. It was very amusing indeed.

*Sincerely*

---

*To Joseph Hergsheimer* [205]

Laramie, Wyo., July 12, 1943

Dear Joe:

I was very much entertained by your letter. The only difference between us is that what you call hypocrisy I regard as the inevitable conflict between idealism and common sense. It is a psychological necessity for every human being to put on a silk hat and watch himself go by. He has to adopt a lot of different roles and, of course, they are inconsistent. However, if while he is playing one of them he does a good job of it I am not distressed because at other periods in his life he has to play an entirely different part.

I enjoyed the quotations from Dr. Johnson. However, I suspect that he is reflecting the inborn snobbery of the time rather than the truth. I think Thackeray in "The Virginians" draws a better picture of the aristocracy of Johnson's time than Johnson does.

With kind personal regards,

*Sincerely*

---

*To Mr. and Mrs. William Allen White* [206]

Washington, D.C., Sept. 9, 1943

Dear Mr. and Mrs. White:

I woke up this morning with the distressing realization that I had not written you my appreciation for the delightful weekend in Estes Park. It really was an event for both Frances and myself.

I expect you have little realization of how you have caught the imagination of that peculiar brand of liberal who comes from the Middle West and who believes in the simple philosophy that our institutions are fundamentally sound and, therefore, all we need to do is to attack entrenched special privileges. The economic planners are always too complicated for me. They were bound to get in power during a period of frustration when people were afraid to face a world in which they had to take a chance on the success or failure of their own efforts. But now, in spite of all the reactionary influences, I begin to feel a new spirit rising in this country. I believe that men like Henry Kaiser, whom I got to know very well in my efforts to prosecute the steel companies for preventing him from getting into production on the Pacific Coast, are going to get strong enough through this war so that they cannot be stopped. If they do, liberalism in this country is going to change from faith in Government bureaucracy to the sort of thing that you have represented for many years.

I am taking the liberty of sending you an article, containing a quotation from your speech, which is being published in some fool collection of essays someone at Columbia is getting out. The thing doesn't satisfy me and so I am going to have to completely do it over before it appears in a book I am trying to write.

Also, I am sending you a memorandum on the transportation problem in which I would like to enlist your interest, though I realize the vast mass of material you have to read.

Frances and I both think that *Queens Die Proudly*[207] is the most dramatic and moving piece of war writing we have yet read.

With kind regards and appreciation for the opportunity to meet you both, I remain

*Sincerely*

---

## *To Reed Powell*

Washington, D.C., Nov. 8, 1943

Dear Reed:

It was a pleasure to get your letter. Frances and I have missed you and have been wondering why the Government has been neglecting you of late. We have gotten to counting on your coming to Washington at regular intervals for some mission or other, and I was rather expecting the new railroad strike vote might require the assistance of your analytical mind. I can't imagine that Washington will be able to get along without you much longer. Its present failure to avail itself of your services is creating all kinds of social and economic difficulties.

Frances and I spent the summer in Wyoming, which was very fortunate because my father died shortly after our return, and Frances and I went back to the funeral. It was a real loss but I am comforted by the fact that he was in excellent health when he died at the age of eighty-four and had no serious illness except a slight touch of influenza. He simply did not wake up one morning.

Thurman, Jr., has had a couple of promotions and is now a full Lieutenant in the Navy about to sail for England on some mysterious mission which he cannot explain to us. George has had some tough luck. He was among the some fifty percent of his group which was dropped out of Officer's Training Camp in the Marines. It appears they are over-officered and the college training plan is just coming to its height so only about half get through. However, naturally, I could not see much sense to their selections. They emphasize "aggressive personality" rather than the tests in which George did very well. The net result seemed to me that only officers with loud voices got by. Be that as it may, he chose to re-enlist as a private and is now engaged in drudgery which I hope will be good for his character. However, he took it very well and is reasonably contented and happy.

Frances and I are now living at 120 South Lee Street in Alexandria, Virginia. I like my work on the Bench although I am having some difficulty in keeping from getting lazy now that the pressure is off. We have sufficient work so that it is a full time job and I haven't had much energy to do anything else excepting for a short article in *Cosmopolitan* Magazine[208] which was published last month. I started to write a book but found I was re-writing *Bottlenecks of Business* and so I dropped the whole thing until I could get a new idea. I now have the new idea but as yet none of it is on paper.

Somebody put me on the Board of Visitors of the law school (I think that is what it is called). The duties are not at all clear. In fact, I got the general impression that we were not supposed to come up there and run the school but simply to be entertained at dinner and show a polite interest. I have determined to change all that and when the meeting is called I expect to make it a rapid inspection trip which will enable me to write a minority report indicating that whatever you are doing must be immediately changed. So when you see a headline "Arnold recommends complete reorganization of Harvard Law School from top to bottom" you will know what I am up to.

Best regards and affection, in which Frances joins,

*Sincerely*

---

## *To Preston Slosson*

Washington, D.C., Nov. 23, 1943

Dear Preston:

My reason for such a long delay in answering your welcome letter of October 27th is that I wanted to write you a considerable history and discussion of the things that you mention in your letter. But with one thing then another, however, I kept putting it off.

Father died early in October. Frances and I were out to Laramie for the funeral. It was very sad to lose him. However, we have the consolation that he had no protracted illness at the end. He died at the age of nearly eighty-five, still vigorous and with very few of his faculties impaired. Mother is still living in the old house. She didn't want to move to Washington and I think her decision was a wise one.

Frances and I are living in Alexandria, about twenty-five minutes from my office in Washington. It is a quaint old place and I have rather gotten to like it although the houses are flush with the street and pretty much huddled together. Our house is about 200 years old and is one of a row. It has two little postage stamp gardens. Frances and I are continually hoping that you and your wife will come to Washington. It would be grand to have one of our old arguments.

As always, I was interested in your political views. I can't see much to quarrel with them. So far as isolationism is concerned, I do not think that after this war there will be much left of it in any party. However, if I interpret Russia correctly (which I probably don't) there isn't going to be anything possible which looks very much like a League of Nations. I can't imagine Russia trusting her own foreign policy to such a League.

To my mind the greatest danger after the war is commercial imperialism. England is going to put up a hard struggle to maintain the international cartel arrangements which caused so much trouble in the past and which, I think, were directly responsible for the Munich appeasement policy. The present industrial bureaucracy of Great Britain, combined as it is with our own monopoly group, is a real threat to any form of stable world organization. I am certainly discouraged with the Democratic party meeting that threat. There is a lot of talk about international cartels coming from the Republicans but I suspect Republican backing. I am all for a League of Nations but not one dominated by du Ponts and the Imperial Chemical Company and the steel crowd, as the last one was. I am afraid that any cooperative international league would be so dominated, and so I look upon what I think is Russia's attitude with more complacence than I would if the business situation were different internationally.

The great difficulty about educating the public on international cartels is the fact that one can't get the story told in the press adequately. The historian has difficulty getting hold of it because practically all of it is grand jury records and the historian sources are usually books. The difficulties with the press are illustrated by a recent experience. I wrote an article for the *Cosmopolitan* Magazine on Labor. They were delighted and paid me a good sum of money for it. They wanted more articles. I suggested that the most exciting story which is not told to the public yet is the story of the transportation monopoly in this country and abroad. After a meeting of the directors, *Cosmopolitan* decided it would be unwise to publish it.

Give my very best to your delightful wife.

With best regards,

*Sincerely*

---

*To J.R. Sullivan*

Washington, D.C., Nov. 24, 1943

Dear Joe:

Thanks a lot for your letter. I return herewith the claim against the estate, which I have signed. If it is convenient I could use the money now as I have over a thousand dollars in insurance premiums to pay this month, coupled with a very heavy income tax. Ain't it hell! It seems to me that there is too much sympathy going out to refugees and people in occupied countries while the sufferings of the Federal judiciary go unnoticed. If you don't mind dropping a couple of tears for me I would appreciate it and you can add it on to your bill.

I read the appraised values with interest. I am inclined to agree that they are too high but I suspect that the point as to future income tax is well taken. Mother writes that she is very much interested in the estate and I am happy that you are consulting her and keeping that interest alive. It's doing her a lot of good.

Walter Davis is doing a lot of work in connection with fixing up the barn and helping Mother out. I wish you would call him in and give him a little cash for his services. Tell him that it is out of the estate but send the bill to me of the amount you pay him and I will take care of it promptly.

Incidentally, if a payment on account of your fee would be convenient at this time I will be very glad to write to the court giving my consent. I would advise against it because you will probably spend the money for liquor at the prevailing prices, and when your creditors got around to collecting it would be all gone. I would suggest keeping it where it can be garnished. However, this is only a suggestion made because I love creditors as a class and think that eternal vigilance is necessary for their protection, particularly in the cases of persons like you and me.

An ominous silence with respect to the Taylor grazing lease is all I get from the Sphinx who sits in the spider web above the Albany bank. I am worried because I am afraid that the fumes arising from the mouldy negotiable papers stored in that institution may have seeped through the floor and asphyxiated him. Has he been seen on the streets lately or do you have any other evidence which would be admissible to prove that he is still alive?

With best regards,

*Sincerely*

## *To V.J. Tidball*

Washington, D.C., Dec. 18, 1943

Dear Judge Tidball:

I will be very happy to consent to any reasonable payment to Joe Sullivan on account of attorney's fees in my father's estate. There is a delicate problem here which will require all your judicial training. On the one hand, we must keep Joe reasonably contented and supplied with liquor; on the other hand, we must not spoil him. This requires a balancing of the equities on available evidence and facts of which you feel you can take judicial notice.

It is a troublesome and difficult problem but it is just such problems as these which have induced the taxpayers of Wyoming to pay you the top-heavy salary which enables you and your wife to throw money around like drunken sailors. I feel that you should earn that salary in this case and hence make no other suggestion excepting that something should be done for the Sullivans in order to keep them alive and happy during the war and give them courage to face the problems of the post-war world.

With kind regards,

*Sincerely*

---

## *To Eugene Meyer*

Washington, D.C., June 9, 1944

Dear Eugene:

On my return from Florida I found the box of magnificent cigars such as I haven't had since the last time I dined at your house. There is nothing in the world that has given me more pleasure. Indeed, I have a theory that one of the reasons for the excellence of the *Washington Post* is that you are a cigar smoker.

Through long years of experience I have observed that cigarette smokers are flighty and unstable people, even though at times they may be brilliant. Any Republican will admit that all of the troubles of the New Deal would have been eliminated if we had refused to put in office persons who smoked cigarettes. Pipe smokers are a more dependable lot but they are only good for cogitative and ruminative work. They are not men of decision and action. They cannot manage things and push forward an aggressive policy. Cigar smokers are the dependable men in every community and the hope of our democracy. One the one hand, they are a progressive force counteracting the indecisiveness of the ruminative pipe smokers. On the other hand, they are a bulwark against the flighty action of the cigarette smokers.

The trouble with most cigar smokers is that they are not refined. It has been demonstrated by modern science that lack of refinement comes from smoking cheap cigars. Men like yourself who have the vision to smoke and distribute fine Havana cigars are, I believe, our only hope for wise leadership in the post-war world.

I suspect that Mrs. Meyer smokes these cigars on the sly; otherwise she couldn't do such good writing.

With heartfelt thanks and appreciation,

*Sincerely*

---

*To Thomas Reed Powell*

Washington, D.C., Nov. 4, 1944

Dear Reed:

After many years of friendship during which I have said nothing but nice things about your work I trust you will not be angry at a critical comment.

I have just finished your article on insurance.[209] It deals, as you know, with a case I started some years ago after the kind of examination of both the law and the facts necessary to convince Attorney General Biddle (who is usually meticulous in this regard) that the case was legally sound and that its prosecution was economically imperative. You, therefore, can understand how I feel about an article which at the end insinuates an illegitimate design in bringing the case.

I will not attempt to argue with your analysis. After composing seventy pages of logic chopping you must be too fatigued to argue any more. I realize that you have convinced yourself that you have fabricated a ten-ton logical blockbuster. Instead of arguing, therefore, I would like to comment on the new T.R. Powell who seems to be emerging at the head of a new Liberty League. The object of your new Liberty League is the same as the former one, i.e., to remove ancient cast-iron dicta from their setting and set them up in new areas in order to protect uneconomic special privileges and to sabotage reform. The main theme of your new league is the same—the notion that the rule of logic and law, the division of powers and respect for the Supreme Court are alike undermined unless the Court approves of business abuses which these dicta may be used to support. The evasion of the real issue, i.e., the purpose of the Constitution and the statute, is the same as in the old Liberty League. And finally, the tone of arrogance which inpugns the intellectual sincerity of your opponents is the same.

You will undoubtedly get applause from our contemporary James M. Becks. Some of my friends in the Senate tell me that the Insurance lobby is going to use your reputation as a spearhead in a new attempt to get their boycotts and conspiracies legitimized by Congress. Governor Bricker last night referred to the case as an example of the New Deal tearing down the Constitution all over again. I predict that the article will give you great kudos among that section of the Bar which used to view you with alarm in the old days.

But you are, nevertheless, in error in your last observation that the Bar as a whole is shocked by the decision. I recall a conference with a prominent Republican attorney who has held high office in the American Bar Association. He was urging the necessity of the insurance suit. When I asked why he could not come out publicly in its support he said that it would endanger the interests of his clients whose products were already being discriminated against by insurance companies in favor of other manufactured products which went into housing. Such power is implicit in an insurance exemption from the Antitrust Laws and the fire insurance ring does not play marbles for fun as Senator Pepper found out in Florida and Senator O'Mahoney found out in Wyoming. I am no Gallup Poll and neither are you. But I happen to know that many responsible members of the Bar who know a great deal about fire insurance will resent the assertion with which you close your article.

I have no doubt you believe that the ability to carry on boycotts through interstate conspiracies is part of the legitimate growth of the insurance business and that they grew up in reliance on the dicta which you support. When I first took up the case with insurance companies they denied all of the conspiracies charged. They still deny them. But your article shows no evidence of any investigation of the implied assumption that the insurance business will be injured by the decision.

You will, of course, answer that your logic chopping is irrefutable and I have no doubt that it seems so to you. The passage of time, however, has a way of making the kind of logic which supports rackets as necessary to observance of the great principle of the rule of law appear full of holes. And, therefore, I predict that when the temporary applause for your new Liberty League has died away it will begin to look just like the old one does today. For that reason I am terribly sorry you joined it. You don't really belong in it any more than Al Smith did.

Hoping that these comments do not offend you, I am

*Affectionately*

---

*To J.R. Sullivan*

Washington, D.C., Nov. 17, 1944

Dear Joe:

I wish you would give me your fatherly advice on a problem about which I have been unable to make up my mind, and the necessity of making a decision is nearly driving me crazy.

Bob Woodruff, president of the Coca-Cola Company, recently came to me and told me that if I would set up an independent office in Washington the Coca-Cola Company would sign a contract for $25,000 a year retainer for five years, as a backlog. I would not be in a position of general counsel so my time would be perfectly free to take all the outside business I desired. Coca-Cola would pay me additional fees for any litigation on which my services were required. The net effect of this would be to set me up in business on a very secure basis and I would make a good deal of money, at least for a while. I would also be back in the stream of things, which would permit me to advocate my pet crusade and take advantage of such opportunities in public life as chance would offer. Coca-Cola is a highly competitive concern and completely free from the kind of practices which I do not care to defend.

The necessity of taking antitrust cases against the government was the reason that I finally decided to turn down the New York firm when I went on the Bench. I could not feel comfortable in a big business practice. But the present offer seems to give me a complete opportunity to pick and choose.

It is the kind of a thing that doesn't happen very often so that if I turn it down I would not expect to get anything else like it. Therefore, it is a major decision. These are the advantages.

The disadvantages are equally obvious. I like it on the Bench, I like to be called "Judge," I like the long vacations and the complete security in old age. I don't, however, like the feeling that I am on the shelf and that I will probably go to seed through the lack of contact with everything (a thing which has happened to every Federal judge that I know who has stuck to the Bench for a long time). I hate to give up a $12,500 a year pension.

Another disadvantage that is somewhat nebulous. I can't understand why Coca-Cola wants to pay me so much money simply for the right to call on me for advice. These big businessmen are simple-minded people and I am afraid Coca-Cola has gotten the idea that I have some kind of magic in the postwar world problems at home and abroad, and that they will be very sadly disappointed. It is one thing to write books and make lectures where you are dealing with abstract problems. It is an entirely different thing to translate that advice into concrete guesses as to policies in domestic and foreign markets. I am very much afraid that Coca-Cola thinks that I have got something on the ball which isn't there and will find themselves disappointed. Of course, a five-year contract is considerable protection but still the risk of disappointing a client is one to be considered.

I am only a country boy and never have understood these large city fees. Lawyers around here certainly do get money for nothing if they get in the inner circle, but the whole apparatus of a city practice is as unfamiliar to me as it is to you. I actually don't feel that I know anything about it.

I wish you would cogitate on this and give me your advice, which I will value very highly. Of course, you don't know very much about it but neither do I. At present, every time I decide I want to stay on the Bench I become completely dissatisfied, and vice versa. I am completely up in the air.

Please keep this strictly confidential and don't mention it to Mother because any kind of decision making worries her. I would appreciate hearing from you within the next ten days what you think.

With best wishes,

*Sincerely*

---

## *To R.W. Woodruff* [210]

Washington, D.C., Dec. 16, 1944

Dear Bob:

Frances and I are deeply indebted to you for arranging such a pleasant trip. We had a wonderful time.

I was tremendously impressed with my glimpse of the vast merchandising operations of Coca-Cola. I take it that what you are driving at is to make Coca-Cola an American institution of permanence and character. To use an analogy from another field, you want it like the *New York Times* and not like the Hearst Press because the *Times* has a place in American thinking and achievement which will outlast any temporary journalistic success based on a short-run policy. A company can get to the top by all sorts of methods. In order to remain at the top it must anticipate long-time economic trends in changing government policies all over the world.

The thing that makes your company even more interesting is my belief that American influence in the world is more dependent upon business enterprises which distribute real goods than it is on programs and plans which distribute only ideas. In other words, domestic and foreign policy depends entirely on business policy. It is either the reflection of business activities or else it is a curb on them.

Frances and I are looking forward to seeing you any time you get to Washington, and again thanking you for your marvelous hospitality,

*Sincerely*

---

## *To Joseph R. Sullivan*

Washington, D.C., Dec. 21, 1944

Dear Joe:

I appreciate your letter about the Coca-Cola matter, but I am still up in the air. I was invited last week down to Atlanta, Georgia, as the house guest of Governor Arnall[211] who is quite a fellow. He is the man who is starting the freight rate suit in the Supreme Court. Frances went with me and we had a wonderful time and a round of lavish entertainment. I spent a good deal of time with the officials of Coca-Cola.

Their principal problem after the war is going to be the organization of their business in foreign countries, which is going to be in terrific confusion. It certainly is a fascinating problem, with law and economics split about fifty-fifty. They are making thirty million dollars a year so money doesn't mean very much to them. So far as security is concerned, they will give me everything I want and I have no doubt I can get protection for life from them. I can make a good deal of additional money in Washington, at least while the Roosevelt Administration is in power, although I would not take the offer on account of the money.

It is a hard choice because I am not sure that I want to stay on the Bench the rest of my life. The thing that fascinates me is that it is something new and something I have never tried before. In any event, I told them that I would let them know in six months.

Bill Douglas advised me very much against it unless they offered me at least $150,000 a year. I am not so sure about the wisdom in this. $25,000 a year gives me absolute independence and no obligation other than consultation and no strings on whether my advice is acceptable to them or not. I also like its long-run feature as they indicated a willingness to give me permanent security. In any event, that's the way the thing stands. I have a feeling that if I don't take it I will never get anything else like it. Bill Douglas tells me that I can get off the Bench any time and make a good deal of money. However, I am somewhat skeptical about that. The way things go in this world is that everybody wants you or else nobody wants you. For example, I was just offered $25,000 a year to become an officer of a large publishing house, and my old firm in New York still would like to have me. I am afraid that when one of the parties starts losing interest they will all lose interest at the same time, and that my present choice is whether I want to stay on the Bench the rest of my life, or whether I don't.

With kindest personal regards,

*Sincerely*

---

## *To Jerome N. Frank*

Washington, D.C., June 18, 1945

Dear Jerome:

I can well understand why you should worry about my review of your book[212] in the light of your chapter on the inevitability of vast integrated corporations, which is contrary to the fundamental thesis in which I live and have my being. Also, I had a hard time adjusting myself to your emphasis on writers, economists and philosophers as motivating forces in the development of social organization. Personally, I think that they have very little to do with it and you would have just as much socialism if Karl Marx had never lived as you have today. You know the thesis of my *Folklore of Capitalism.*

Nevertheless, from the point of view which you have written the book it is an extraordinarily interesting and stimulating job and anybody who says to the contrary is just simply not interested in the subject. Congratulations, and I hope you like the review. I would have preferred to have not criticized it in any detail but I had to preserve my own position which as you know is slightly different from yours.

With best regards,

*Sincerely*

---

## *To J.R. Sullivan*

Washington, D.C., June 26, 1945

Dear Joe:

This letter is personal and confidential. I am going to see President Truman on the 2nd or 3rd of July and tender him my resignation at that time. Then I am going to start a firm in Washington, taking in some very able younger men to do the work. I will start out with a $25,000 retainer from the Coca-Cola Company, which you know about, a $12,500 retainer from the Chesapeake & Ohio Railway Company, and a $12,500 retainer from Otis & Company (not the elevator people but a large banking house in

Cleveland). Curiously enough, both the railroad people and Otis & Company came to see me about retainers out of a clear sky because they had read the book *Justice in Transportation*[213] to which I had written an introduction. The book is an attack on monopoly rates and it is along the lines that both the Chesapeake & Ohio Railway Company and Otis & Company are trying to work. So when they read the book they immediately took the train down to see me. I am taking in partnership Arne Wiprud, who used to be the chief of my Transportation section and who wrote the book. He knows more about the railroad problem than anybody else in America and he will be very necessary.

According to the plans of Otis & Company and the Chesapeake & Ohio Railway Company, over a period of a couple of years there is the likelihood of about $100,000 in fees from these two sources, and I have no doubt I am going to get more business than I can possibly handle. However, the $50,000 backlog is quite a comfort.

Now, the point of this letter is this. I spoke to you briefly about forming a firm with you in Wyoming. I would expect no share in your business but the connection would be valuable to me. I have in mind—and this is very confidential indeed—the possibility that I might get a chance to run for the Senate. Whether this would work out or not is hard to tell but I want to have an anchor out that way. My theory is that if I can get a firm started, with a substantial business and some young men to carry it on, I will be in a financial position so that I can make the race, if things worked out in a couple of years. I couldn't do it from the Bench first, because my connection with Wyoming is too tenuous, and second, because I could never afford to gamble on the Senatorship. Don't breathe a word of this to anybody, even my Mother, because if it didn't work out I would look foolish. But, in any event, you can see the advantage to me of having a position in a Wyoming firm.[214]

The advantages to you are somewhat speculative but, on the other hand, they might turn out to be substantial. It is probable that with the connections I make in Washington some substantial Wyoming business might develop. And then, on the other hand, you might well profit after the war with a Washington connection. Almost everything is going to be centered here and Washington lawyers are going to be very expensive. I expect to be an expensive lawyer myself, but so far as you are concerned we would get the work done on a basis which would be profitable to you.

As you know, I would prefer to have a connection with you than anyone else in Wyoming. Please write me your reaction.

Give my love to Aimee.

*Sincerely*

---

*To Harry S. Truman*

Washington, D.C., July 3, 1945

My dear Mr. President:

I hereby present my resignation as an Associate Justice of the United States Court of Appeals for the District of Columbia, to take effect on the 10th of July, 1945, when my work for the present term will be completed. I leave this important and honorable post with great reluctance. My reason for returning to private practice is my desire to further the cause which was my chief interest in the Department of Justice.

I believe that economic forces are moving toward freedom of business opportunity and a truly competitive economy in the postwar world. Industrial invention and a new age of transportation have created industrial opportunities for all sections of this country which never existed before. Full production after the war, and the elasticity of our economy, depend on the release of new and independent initiative in industry. This, I think, must be the direction of a successful liberal movement in America.

Your own public life has been an outstanding contribution to that movement. I believe that sort of liberalism in business can be effectively advanced from within the business world.

Permit me to assure you, Mr. President, of my continued support in the difficult task which you have so well begun.

*Sincerely*

---

# VI

# WASHINGTON PRACTICE

# 1945 – 1950

---

*To Maury Maverick*[215]

Washington, D.C., July 11, 1945

Dear Maury:

Thanks for the picture.

I am certainly glad I got to swear you in before getting off the Bench. It was a hard decision to make, but some clients showed up who were interested in my economic ideas and willing to pay me substantially for pushing them if I got off the Bench. So I really believe that I can not only make a living, but also do something for independent business in this country. The most fascinating job I have at the start is in connection with railroad rate bureaus, and my clients want the thing pushed along the line of Wiprud's book. I am going to try to avoid cases which involve defending people for violation of the antitrust laws. It was the necessity of handling that type of case which led me to turn down a New York firm when I went on the Bench. Now I will be independent and I think sufficiently prosperous and I will not have to take that kind of business.

Best regards.

*Sincerely*

---

*To J.R. Sullivan*

Washington, D.C., July 25, 1945

Dear Joe:

I have been so busy since getting off the Bench that I neglected answering your letter of July 3, 1945. I will briefly account my adventures.

We were very lucky in getting offices. For a while it looked as if we would have to take desk space in somebody's anteroom as there isn't a cranny here in Washington that isn't filled up. However, at the last moment through mutual friends we moved into General Donovan's old offices which he was giving up. They are all furnished, with leather chairs, books, typewriters—in fact, everything we need. We are buying the furniture, lock, stock and barrel, at an evaluation which will be put on it by appraisers. The building is air cooled and is the best law building in Washington. We consider ourselves very lucky. Also, the rent is reasonable for Washington, $3600 per year.

As you know, we started in with the Coca-Cola business and the railroad business. There were a few immediate things to take care of for Coca-Cola but the railroad clients presented some very important immediate problems, particularly with respect to buying the Pullman Company. They are going to be very interesting. In addition, in the first two weeks I am afraid I have accepted more other retainers than I can take care of. I am a babe of the woods in this respect. I keep remembering the old days in Laramie and have got to learn to turn down fees when they are offered—otherwise I will get swamped.

Now, with respect to our arrangement. It seems to me that you should make such announcement as you deem appropriate in your graceful style to the effect that we have formed an association for the practice of law in Wyoming and Washington. It seems to me also that it might be well to have an announcement engraved and mailed. This would be, of course, entirely at my expense. Anything else that you think of go ahead and do.

I would appreciate your writing me about how Bob Gietz is getting along. I have the most disquieting news about his illness and it worries me.

I expect to get out to Wyoming in August or September if there is any transportation available. The situation as I get it from my railroad clients, however, is going to get very bad indeed and travel is going to be almost impossible. However, I will cross that bridge when I come to it.

With kind personal regards,

*Sincerely*

---

## *To Westbrook Pegler*

Washington, D.C., Sept. 18, 1945

Dear Westbrook:

I hasten to answer your letter of September 13 because I believe that when you are acquainted with the facts you no longer will have doubt as to the propriety of my representation of the Young group in connection with the proposed purchase of The Pullman Company. It also gives me an opportunity to interest you in what I think is one of the many important stories current in the development of the railroad industry.

I started the Pullman suit about five years ago. The reason was that the Pullman interests were preventing the railroads from purchasing and using sleeping cars except those manufactured by The Pullman Company. Independent car manufacturers were, because of the monopoly position of the Pullman interests, unable to get into the market. Thus, the Pullman interests were able to keep obsolete cars in service for as long as thirty to forty years. The present Pullman fleet of about 6800 sleeping cars has an average age of twenty-five years. They are completely obsolete in design. They carry 2½ tons dead weight per passenger when fully loaded and 8 tons per passenger on their average load prior to the war. (Airplanes carry about 1500 pounds per passenger.) The purpose of the suit was to introduce competition into the sleeping car business.

The Government won its case. A decree was entered compelling Pullman, Inc., the holding company, either to sell its sleeping car company or to sell its manufacturing company. The decree provided further that agreements between the new owners of the sleeping car service and the railroad should not contain any "exclusive dealing clauses" and that the railroads or anyone else could enter into the business of furnishing or servicing sleeping cars. Thus the Court insured that a monopoly of the sleeping car service could not be restored. The Pullman interests did not appeal and the decree became final about two years ago.

The Pullman interests elected to sell its sleeping car service. It offered to sell the service to the railroads as a group but they refused to buy. Nothing else was done. There are now no new sleeping cars on order. The whole policy and purpose of the court's decree seemed to be frustrated. The railroads are faced with a keen competition from the airlines and bus lines and without modern passenger equipment.

It was this situation which caused Young to take action. He controls the Chesapeake and Ohio Railway Company on which the passenger demand is highly seasonal. He saw no way of competing with the airlines with the dangerously obsolete equipment in the present Pullman pool.[216] Therefore, he decided that the future position of the railroads required immediate action. He has offered to buy the Pullman Company at the same price which the Pullman interests have previously offered to sell that company to the railroads. This offer apparently was not communicated to the railroads at the time that their committees met a few weeks ago and decided that they would ask the court for further delay because no purchaser of the Pullman service could be found.

In acting for Young in this matter I am fighting for the same principles which I stood for in public life, namely competition in industry including the transportation industry. As applied to this case, I am continuing the same effort which I made at the Department, to carry out the purposes and policies of the decree. Unless an independent group, competitively minded, enters this picture, all the public benefits which can be derived from the decree will be dissipated in inaction. This means that control will again drift back to the same old crowd which has monopolized the sleeping car business in the past.

Upon filing of the petition of Otis and Company and the Young-Kirby group in Court (I enclose a copy for your information), we discussed the matter informally with the Court at its suggestion. While, of course, the Court expressed no opinion as to its future action, it was exceedingly interested and cordial. The reason for its interest was the fact that the Pullman interests took the position during the suit that it was impossible to sell The Pullman Company (that is, the service company) because it was a dying business. Therefore, they argued that even though they had been guilty of illegal acts in the past, there was no use entering a decree which would do not good and simply hamper passenger transportation. Naturally the Court was interested that the decree was going to work out to give far reaching benefits to the railroad industry and to the Nation.

They were interested to learn that under Young's offer the present obsolete Pullman fleet would be completely replaced by modern equipment at a cost in excess of $500,000,000.

I might state parenthetically that, of course, the Court found no objection to my appearance in this case since the purpose is to further the objectives and policies of the decree which the government was instrumental in obtaining.

The dramatic side of this story is that Young sees in the passenger transportation of the future the same unexplored field that was before Henry Ford. Young, with independent and fresh ideas is going to explore the low cost market in passenger travel. With the new sources of power which are going to be available, it may be that this is going to be one of the chief sources of revenue to the railroads of the future. I would appreciate very much if you would read the enclosed petition, which we filed with the Court. I think it tells a most interesting story about the possibilities of effective competition in the transportation field.

With best regards,

*Sincerely*

---

## *To Edward H. Levi*

Washington, D.C., Oct. 11, 1945

Dear Ed:

Norman Cousins says he wants my article but he wants me to do some more writing and redrafting of it. In the meantime, I send you my check in the sum of $150.61 in full payment of the following account:

*EDWARD H. LEVI—THURMAN ARNOLD, Debtor*

Appraised depreciated book value of Levi material considered as a literary gem . . . $2,500.00

Appraised depreciated book value of Levi material considered in the light of its contribution to current economics . . . . $2,500.00

Total due by Thurman Arnold to Edward H. Levi on account of his extraordinary production . . . . . . . . . . . . . . . . . . . . $5,000.00

*THURMAN ARNOLD—EDWARD H. LEVI, Debtor*

Fee for expert services of Thurman Arnold, distinguished author, in connection with appraisal of Levi material as a literary gem . . . . . . . . . . . . . . . . . . . . . . . . $2,400.00

Fee due Thurman Arnold, distinguished economist, for services in appraising Levi material as an economic contribution. . . . . . . . . . . . . . . . . . . $2,445.00

Expense—entertaining Levi at luncheon at Mayflower Hotel . . . . . . . . . . . . . . . . . . . 4.39

Total Due by Edward H. Levi to Thurman Arnold . . . . $4,849.39

Due Edward Levi by Thurman Arnold. . . . . . . . . . . $150.61

*Sincerely*

---

## *To Joseph Hergsheimer*

Washington, D.C., Oct. 17, 1945

Dear Joe:

I am probably the worst correspondent in the world but I have an excuse. Since I got off the Bench life has been so hectic that I have not had an opportunity even to take Sundays off. We have had a great deal of business to take care of, it has been impossible to obtain stenographic help or build up an organization, or answer my correspondence. Anyway, this is the best excuse I can offer for not returning your book.

Frances has been doing over a two-hundred-year-old house, of very modest dimensions compared with your famous project. However, during the process of living with the plasterers I have reread *From an Old House*[217] and thought of how much fun I would get out of it if I only had your temperament. Unfortunately I was brought up in the West and lack the reverence of the past which I should have.[218] And so, I would rather read *From An Old House* than follow its program.

Last night I started to reread *Balisand*[219] and got as far as the end of Part I before I went to sleep. It seems to have even more charm and vigor and aroma than when I read it first. I don't know anything finer in literature than that first part. Tomorrow night I am going to start in on the second part and I will probably like it just as well.

I may neglect my duties in answering correspondence and returning books, but I am still one of those who consider you our greatest novelist. If anyone challenges this assertion in my presence it will lead to hostilities, which will not be called off even if all the lovely women in America fall down all the stairwells simultaneously.

*Affectionately*

---

## *To Matthew Josephson*[220]

Washington, D.C., Oct. 17, 1945

Dear Mr. Josephson:

Your interesting letter of August 11, 1945, has been on my desk for weeks. Since I resigned from the Court and entered private practice matters have been so hectic, stenographic assistance so hard to obtain, and my time so limited that I simply gave up on correspondence.

I enjoyed your article on Young, particularly in view of the fact that he is one of my principal clients.

I do not fear, however, the philosophical difficulties you raise in your letter. Of course competitive doctrine is a kind of folklore but so is every other economic theory. In my view it is the only one that we can operate under. It is part of our cultural pattern and no nation can change that pattern.

Of course, it is true that every economy in action will be inconsistent with its ideas. Russia will go capitalistic and independent enterprise will start up in a cartel system in spite of hell and high water, et cetera.

It is equally true that even in a competitive sport like prize fighting a man who gets the heavyweight championship will think that he has worked hard enough for his title, that he has a great investment in it and that he ought not to be compelled continuously to fight newcomers.

All of these forces are always present in every economy. Nevertheless, America can only survive under a competitive philosophy and a strong antitrust enforcement. Lacking that, it will become a subsidiary of some other dominant country. This was proved by the fact that prior to the war we had become an economic subsidiary of England and, to a certain extent, of Germany. We couldn't run the cartel system. It is too foreign to our habits of thought. For that reason Germany made suckers out of our businessmen.

I can put it another way. When we reach a frame of mind where we can make Owen D. Young the Earl of General Electric and put him in some kind of a governmental House of Lords we will have one of the minimum essentials to a noncompetitive big business bureaucracy which will work at least as well as it works. So long as we can't do that the operation of monopolies in this country will create only confusion, bitterness, and the constant backing and filling which went on during the years of the New Deal.

We are not going to pull out of the present mess without a great deal of confusion. On the other hand, we are not going to get any feeling of economic comfort until our predominant ideal has at least a semblance of reality.

I enclose a copy of a recent pamphlet I wrote which confuses the subject even more than this letter does.

With kind personal regards and congratulations on your splendid articles on Young,

*Sincerely*

---

## *To J.R. Sullivan*

Washington, D.C., Nov. 30, 1945

Dear Joe:

I think that the announcements you sent out were fine. I haven't received the bill for them, and this is an expense I want to bear myself.

Please send on a bill for your services in connection with the Pullman case which Mr. Young appreciates very much. I know very well why we didn't succeed. The railroads have been following me all over the United States. They did everything they could to get California to change her position and failed. They succeeded in getting Colorado to file an amended intervention which didn't do much harm but confused the issue somewhat. I have no doubt that they worked on Hunt in Wyoming. However, we surprised them at the last minute by getting the State of Georgia to intervene on our behalf.

California sent a special deputy all the way to Philadelphia to argue the case. He made a beautiful job of it. George Wharton Pepper, representing the Pullman Company, had referred to the intervention of California and Wyoming as a "fresh breeze from the West." He added that their intervention did nothing but confuse the issue. Linn of California made a very clever reply. He said that he was glad to be referred to as a fresh breeze from the West, and he also came bringing a warm breeze from the South. Whereupon he filed the petition of Governor Arnall of Georgia supporting our position. He then went on to say that he agreed completely with George Wharton Pepper that the entrance of the states was confusing to the issue because the public interest was always confusing to monopolies. In fact he made a vigorous and bang-up argument and struck to his guns all the way through. The hearing lasted a couple of days. We had a beautiful record. The only thing against us is pressure and influence. Every general counsel of every major railroad in the United States was jammed into the courtroom, and all opposed the expansion of the Pullman business.

I am enclosing a copy of our brief which may interest you. The argument is set for December 10 and will last several days.

I suggest that you charge at the rate of $150 a day for your time in this matter.

I expect to get out to Wyoming as soon as the Pullman hearing is over and I can catch up with a few other affairs in the office.

I am also enclosing the deeds which Frances and I have executed.

*Best regards*

---

## *To John C. Hamm* [221]

Washington, D.C., March 1, 1946

Dear John:

It was a great pleasure to hear from you again but I was distressed to learn that you have been an invalid. I hope that this letter finds you well and happy. I am sure your heart will last a long time, even on two cylinders, if you take care of yourself and don't put it to any strain.

The new generation of Arnolds is out of the Navy and the Marines, respectively, and starting separate establishments. Thurman got married in New York on February 2nd to the step-daughter of a New York lawyer of whom I am very fond. They had a big wedding with all the trimmings. The only thing I missed were some clowns and a calliope but apparently they don't have these in wedding parades. I went through the thing with fortitude and think I behaved myself very well. However, I couldn't help but think about the complete difference between my children's experience and mine. Out in Wyoming in the old days this wedding would have been regarded as an absolutely sinful waste of money and Father would have foamed at the mouth for the next two weeks if he had attended. Life has certainly changed and I am still so much of a country boy that I can't get used to it.

On the 16th of March my other son, George, who is just out of the Marines, is getting married to Ellen Pearson, the daughter of Drew Pearson the columnist. I am happy about this also. I am fond of both of my new daughters-in-law and also delighted with my new in-laws. There is going to be another big wedding in Washington and I am going to have to go through the whole thing again.

I would much rather try a law suit. In the case of a law suit you get fees and in the case of one of these big weddings they pay you nothing. However, thank the Lord, according to custom in these parts the cost of the wedding is on the bride's parents.

Both of my sons are going to be lawyers. George is attending the Law School at the University of Chicago. He has gotten an apartment there and is taking his bride to Chicago just after the honeymoon. Thurman is already ensconced as a student at Yale Law School. After they get through they will probably come into my office or some office in New York. But here again I think they will miss something by not going through the country practice. The trouble with the country practice today is that the monopolies have drained the small towns of all their independent industry, leaving only collections and divorces for the lawyers. And so I suppose it's wise for the boys to go to the cities. I am hopeful that the new technical revolution is going to have a decentralizing effect and make the small independent community grow up again.

I enclose a copy of a pamphlet I wrote for the Public Affairs Committee entitled "Cartels or Free Enterprise," in which you may be interested.

I am having to leave for New York in an hour and so I will ask my secretary to sign this letter for me.

*Affectionately*

---

## *To Edward S. Corwin*[222]

Washington, D.C., Jan. 7, 1947

Dear Corwin:

Thanks for your letter. I appreciate your comment on my talk.

Frankly, I am not hopeful about my case against the Rankin Committee but I, nevertheless, intend to carry it to the Supreme Court because I am convinced that the activities of the Rankin Committee are a dangerous threat to civil liberties. I only wish that the case came at a time when there was less anti-communistic feeling.

My point, as you apparently understand, is that no committee or administrative tribunal or court may seize the private papers of an individual on the sole ground that they consider that his activities may be found to be "subversive and un-American." It seems to me that the term "subversive and un-American" can only mean what the particular person likes or dislikes. For example, I would call anyone who advocated any form of cartel organization "subversive and un-American." Yet, that would scarcely justify a tribunal investigating people who had opinions contrary to mine, if such investigation went to the point of seizing private papers.

There are some difficult distinctions which I must make. For example, I would permit the investigation of any form of organized political activity, Democratic, Republican or Communist, because political organizations is a subject matter for legislation. I would further permit the subpoena of papers from any financial organization on the ground that finance is a subject of legislation. However, where a group of individuals is engaged in distributing relief to Spanish refugees and has conformed to all the requirements of the State Department regarding the collection and distribution of the money, there is no ground for seizing their papers on the charge that many of their members are communists.

The position of the Rankin Committee appears to be that if a group is suspected of Communism, their relationships with their friends and their charitable contributions may be investigated on that ground alone. They go so far as to say that since Communism is a dangerous philosophy, all persons suspected of Communism are subject to search and seizure.

I must distingush between this and the investigation of the political activities of communists. Certainly they should show all their contributions to such organized activities, but because the opinions of a group happen to be regarded as "subversive and un-American" should not give jurisdiction for investigating their activities unless they are shown to have some connection with political or financial organizations.

The difficulty, of course, is the fixed belief that whatever communists do is a dangerous thing and all of them must be up to something. If this be a principle in American law it means that a Congressional Committee can select any group of opinion which it considers un-American and segregate those who hold such opinion out for special investigation to which other Americans are not subject. This is a dangerous threat to civil liberties whether the Supreme Court sustains my position or not.

Best regards,

*Sincerely*

*To Mrs. C.P. Arnold*

Washington, D.C., April 22, 1947

Dear Mother:

Here is your monthly check.

The news of Walter's death was a terrible shock to us. We were very fond of him indeed. I hope you and the Davises are getting along without him but you must miss him a lot. Frances and I are anxious for you to come on to Washington this spring with the Davises. Frances tells me that she has written to Mom and Pop. I hope that you feel like doing it.

I have been trying to get out West. There always seems to be something around here or in some other town that has to be taken care of. We are very busy right now with a lot of court cases and you know how hard it is to get away when you have engagements in court.

We lost the Pullman case by a 4 to 4 vote in the Supreme Court of the United States which was a great disappointment. However, that is the fortunes of war. We continue to be very prosperous and fees seem to be coming in just the way they did last year.

You may be interested to know that Paul Porter, who was formerly head of OPA and Ambassador to Greece, is joining our firm the 15th of May. We have grown so fast that we no longer have office space but we are renting much larger offices in a new building which will be ready on the 15th of August, we hope. This will be a very comfortable change. The only drawback is that our rent will jump from $5,000 to $14,000 a year, which is a lot of money. However, as long as business keeps up the Government will have to pay most of it.

On the 1st of May I am going on "Town Hall of the Air" with Rebecca West, an English novelist and political writer; Louis Lochner, who has written some books about the German problem; and William L. Shirer who wrote the best seller about conditions in Germany before the war. The topic is "What Should We Do About Germany Now?" This is one of the things I never should have taken because I don't know what to do with Germany. However, nobody else seems to, so I guess I will get along alright. The broadcast will be at 8:30 P.M. our time on the 1st of May, which would be 6:30 P.M. your time. However, you can look it up in the radio list. It is "Town Hall of the Air."

I got a letter this morning from R.R. Hamilton of the University about Father's library. I thought we had given it to the University. I told him that that was our intention and that we would sign any papers that were necessary. This is not a particularly generous thing to do because the library is so out-of-date that it is hardly worth moving.

I do hope you can come on to Washington. We are having beautiful weather and the trees are all out. This is the time to leave Wyoming if you can.

*Lots of love*

---

## *To Mrs. Elisabeth Schmidt Ranke* [223]

Washington, D.C., June 7, 1947

Dear Betty:

Your are a most excellent correspondent, much better than I am. I have been intending to write you for about a year but have never gotten around to it until I received your interesting letter today. I hear a great deal about the distressing conditions in Germany from my friends who have gone over there on various government missions. I am hoping for gradual improvement in the future.

First I will tell you a little about myself. I resigned from the United States Court of Appeals in Washington, D.C., about two years ago because I found the work of a Judge much duller than that of an advocate. I think I might have liked the trial court but on the appellate court we sat in groups of three and all we did was to listen to argument and write opinions. I felt that a more active life was more to my taste, and so after much indecision I finally resigned and went into practice with Mr. Abe Fortas, who had just resigned as Under Secretary of the Interior, which is a Cabinet office. Recently Mr. Paul Porter, who was head of the Office of Price Administration and later a special Ambassador to Greece on an economic mission, has joined our firm. We have five younger lawyers with us, as you can see from this stationery.

Frances and I live in Alexandria, Virginia, which is just twenty minutes from Washington, in a house on top of a hill with about three acres of ground. It is a nice place and Frances likes to raise chickens.

I suppose Betty has written to you that my sons are both married and going to Law School—one at Yale University and the other at the University of Chicago.

My Mother is about eighty-seven years old and is very well. She lives by herself in Laramie, Wyoming. We have tried to induce her to come to Washington and stay with us but she says that she is just too old to pull up roots and prefers to stay in Wyoming, although that is over 2,000 miles from Washington. However, I get out to see her occasionally.

I read your husband's speech with great interest and I think it is excellent. Tell him I am having copies made and sending it to some of my friends here in Washington.

I am very much interested in the work of your daughter in the Russian Sector of Berlin. It sounds very hard but still a great humanitarian effort on her part.

I remember so clearly the last time I saw you in 1910. It seems hard to believe that that was 37 years ago. I remember getting off the train in Breslau and getting to your house early in the morning, too early to get in. I remember how well you played the piano and how charming and lovely you were.

We are very lucky here in America to be comparatively untouched by the two great wars that swept over Europe. I was in France in the Field Artillery in the first war and both of my boys were in this war. The older one was in the Navy, in Europe; the younger one was in the Marines and saw action in the Pacific. Neither one of them was hurt.

Today in America many people are afraid of another war, this time with Russia. However, I am optimistic. I don't believe that anyone is going to be able to plan our ways through the 20th century but I do believe that it is going to be like the 19th century, a century of tremendous progress. The very fact that everyone is afraid of another war is a hopeful sign to me. Wars do not occur when all the world fears them.

The times remind me of what I read about the Reformation when the cement seemed to fall out of social institutions and the world was in confusion for a long time while new institutions were building up. I firmly believe that they are going to build up the same way in the next century.

All this is of little comfort, however, to someone who has to live the next five years in Germany. However, you have my best wishes and sympathy.

Frances sends her very best.

*Your cousin*

---

## *To Leon Henderson*[224]

Washington, D.C., Sept. 15, 1947

Dear Leon:

I wonder if you or your associates have considered the possibility of Senator Joe O'Mahoney of Wyoming as a candidate for Vice President. I have not spoken to him and he knows nothing about this letter. I am writing solely in the interests of the party.

I need not tell you about O'Mahoney's great liberal record in the Senate. It is just the kind of a liberal record that we need. It has no tinge of radicalism, it is in line with every established American tradition. Nor need I speak of O'Mahoney's brilliance as a speaker. He has real magnetism and power.

What to my mind makes him particularly important in adding strength to the ticket is his influence in the West. He would unquestionably carry Wyoming because he has the support of responsible people in both parties there. I recognize that Wyoming is a small state. However, O'Mahoney is known throughout the entire West. He has come to occupy a place very much like that which Borah once had. His influence would be felt in every state across the Mississippi River.

I wish you and your associates would give some thought to the possibility of O'Mahoney for Vice President.

With kind regards,

*Sincerely*

---

## *To James F. Byrnes*[225]

Washington, D.C., Oct. 4, 1947

Dear Mr. Secretary:

We are addressing to you this appeal on behalf of seven employees of the Department of State whom this office represents to ascertain whether you have had the opportunity to review the action of the Department before we give further advice to these aggrieved individuals.[226]

We have today received a letter from Mr. Peurifoy in which he states that of the eight persons whom this office represents, and who were summarily dismissed on June 23 by the Department, only one will be permitted to resign without prejudice. As to the others, Mr. Peurifoy transmits the recommendation of the Personnel Security Board that none of the remainder "be now permitted to resign without prejudice" and states "that the Department proposes to take no further action with respect to the employees concerned."

We respectfully call your attention to the fact that there were transmitted to Mr. Peurifoy on July 9, 1947, the affidavits of five employees and subsequently the statements of two others were submitted. We have been in communication with Mr. Peurifoy from time to time on these matters. On August 6, 1947, this office submitted a petition to the Department of State Loyalty Committee asking for an immediate hearing on behalf of these individuals and no response has been received from that petition except the mere acknowledgment of its receipt.

The Department's own statement on its security principles (Departmental Announcement 765) has been completely ignored in these cases in the following particulars:

(1) No charges have been submitted to these individuals or to this office as their counsel even though we have requested that the charges against them be made definite and specific.

(2) No hearing has been given any of these individuals in the accepted sense that a hearing means an opportunity to appear and submit evidence in response to charges.

(3) No response has been made to the affidavits submitted by these employees denying the general and vague accusations that they were suspected of associating "directly or indirectly" with representatives of foreign powers.

In short, these individuals have been convicted in an ex parte proceeding, their reputations destroyed and their opportunity for future employment severely impaired, if not permanently eliminated.

We have represented to Mr. Peurifoy on repeated occasions that if it could be established that any of these individuals had made a material misrepresentation of fact to us as their counsel or had concealed a material fact, we would no longer represent them. To be specific, we wrote Mr. Peurifoy to that effect on September 2, 1947, and requested that he furnish us with any evidence of disloyalty of these employees or any other data which the Department has which raises any question as to the accuracy or completeness of the affidavits which they submitted affirming their loyalty to their country and to the Department. No such information has been submitted to us, or so far as we are advised, to the employees themselves.

We submit that the procedure followed with respect to these employees is unfair and un-American. On their behalf we have asked that they be permitted to resign without prejudice in order that their economic future would not be jeopardized by the stigma of disloyalty or in the alternative that they be provided with charges and an opportunity to confront their accusers and rebut such charges. This we feel is their fundamental and simple right as American citizens and to deny any or all of them this basic privilege of the Bill of Rights constitutes an unwarranted enfringement of such rights.

In fact, the procedure that has been followed is tragically analogous to the tactics employed in the police states dominated by communists and fascists and has no place in the American system where standards of civil liberties, fair play and the inalienable principles of the Bill of Rights are the privilege of the humblest without regard to race, color or creed.

We have heard it said that you think your Department is justified, for reasons of administration and to prevent revealing sources of information, in ridding itself of any employee without charges or a hearing.

We consider that a dangerous principle. But that principle is not in issue here. We do not ask you to keep these men in the State Department. They wish to resign and relieve you of their unwelcome presence. In our opinion they should not be allowed to do this if they are in fact disloyal. But if they are not demonstrably disloyal—if all that the State Department has is dislike of these people or vague uneasiness about them, they should be allowed to resign. If they are not demonstrably disloyal, why should the Department wish relentlessly to pursue these men into civilian life with vague charges that make it impossible for them to get employment? If the Department believes that this severe penalty should follow these men into civil life, what justification is there for refusing to give them an opportunity to be heard in their own defense?

We would not have undertaken the representation of these individuals if we did not feel deeply about the principles involved. These persons came to this office last June and submitted their cases. As lawyers we felt it our obligation to represent them because it is a special duty of members of the bar to undertake to protect the basic rights of all citizens. But it is also your personal responsibility to determine whether these individuals will be given the opportunity to have their cases resolved in accordance with established principles of American justice.

We think it appropriate to direct your attention to the Fact that this government is sponsoring through the "Freedom Train" a program designed to the rededication of all citizens to our basic American principles. On that train there is under guard the priceless document which includes our cherished Bill of Rights. The guard is there presumably to prevent its physical defacement. But in the cases of the individuals whom we represent its meaning and spirit have been summarily defamed. Indeed it is no exaggeration to describe these individuals as displaced persons who have not had a decent opportunity to invoke the basic principles of due process that our system is designed to make available even to the lowest criminal.

We cannot believe that you have had the time or the opportunity with the tremendous pressures which are upon you to give personal consideration to the injustice that is here involved. There is more at stake than merely the personal welfare of these employees, as important as that is to them. The integrity of this government is in issue. We cannot believe that you will permit it to be degraded and therefore we must make this appeal to you for a personal conference in order that we may lay before you the serious nature of the injustices that are here involved.

*Sincerely*

*To Geoffrey Parsons*[227]

Washington, D.C., Oct. 23, 1947

Dear Mr. Parsons:

I appreciated your interest in our unfortunate clients who are not permitted to resign from the State Department. I enclose a copy of the only hearing they have been given. I have permission to use this if the name of the individual is deleted. I think you will share my indignation about the way these people have been treated if you will read this hearing. The particular man who is the subject matter of the hearing I send you was an instructor at Columbia. Of course, he has lost his job and can't get any other.

The only thing we can do is to protest.

I am wondering if you would send one of your expert reporters around to our office to satisfy himself that all the facts which we have represented to you are correct. If you are interested, I would appreciate your advice as to how to handle this matter. Needless to say, we are getting no fee out of it and have taken it up purely as a matter which we consider in the public interest. I am afraid that if procedures like this are not stopped widespread suffering may be caused in Washington.

As I told you, this is not a case where we are asking the State Department to keep anyone. We are only asking that they do not pursue them into civil life with charges against which they have no defense, because they do not even know what they are.

Thanking you for your interest.

Best regards,

*Sincerely*

---

*To Tracy S. McCraken*

Washington, D.C., Dec. 12, 1947

Dear Tracy:

Your editor Joseph Ray has asked me about current rumors in Wyoming to the effect that I am considering becoming a candidate for the United States Senate. Before replying I would like to get your confidential advice.

I had nothing to do with the rumors starting, but as a matter of fact I would like to take a try at the Senate if Hunt does not decide to run. If he does decide to run I would forget about it completely.

The weakness of my position is obvious. I have an office with Joe in Laramie, I own a ranch there, I pay my real estate taxes in Wyoming and vote in Wyoming. I spend such time there as I can.

However, there is no use concealing the fact that my principal income comes from my office in Washington, D.C., and that it would be financially impossible for me to give up that office and spend most of my time in Wyoming except during the Senate race. I would like confidentially to know what chance you think I would have under these circumstances in the event that Hunt does not run.

Best regards.

*Sincerely*

---

*To Wesley A. Sturges*

Washington, D.C., Jan. 12, 1948

Dear Wes:

Thanks for your note and I appreciate your interest in my welfare.

You asked for suggestions. I would like, if it can be arranged, to have a brass band at the station and a parade of the Governor's footguard or whatever you call it preceding me to the Law School. I would like to have the faculty lined up outside the Law School in appropriate robes and a large and expensive present, to which the faculty should contribute pro rata based on their salaries, given to me with a speech by yourself and papers with footnotes and citations by other members of the faculty.

As to my stay, I hope that you will enforce rigorously the rule that there is to be no liquor served in the dormitories.

With best regards,

*Sincerely*

---

*To the Editor* [228]
*New York Times*

Washington, D.C., Feb. 12, 1948

Dear Sir:

If you are planning at any future time to become a government employee, you would do well to obey the following ten commandments for pure conduct of Government Employees if you want to be safe. These commandments are in no way farcical or exaggerated. For in the effort to uncover the few men and women in government ranks whose loyalty is genuinely suspected, individual dossiers are now being collected on *all* federal employees—whether or not they work in areas of the government where secrets important to the national defense are guarded—and inevitably a large number of men and women are compelled to submit to formal hearings because of charges against them based on irrational gossip, hearsay, or rumor. As a lawyer practicing in Washington, I have come in contact with many government employees thus accused; and I can testify that each of the commandments set down here is based on actual cases either in my office or observed by me.

*Ten Commandments for Pure Conduct of Government Employees*

1. Do not attend any social gathering, no matter how large, at which a "subversive" may also be present. This includes dances.

2. Never talk, even to your neighbors or at social gatherings, about controversial issues. If your views offend someone, they may show up in a report in a distorted fashion and you will never even know who gave the information.

3. Do not subscribe to the *New Republic* or the *Nation,* or any other liberal publication. Maybe it's communist and you don't know it. Don't read any books about Russia even out of curiosity, because you can never prove that it was only curiosity. You will be safer if you can honestly swear that you do not know where Russia is or what it is like.

4. If anyone sends you as a gift a publication of the sort described in the foregoing Commandment, cancel it at once, with an indignant letter. Otherwise it may be taken to mean you have communist friends.

5. Do not ever attend the large annual reception at the Russian Embassy. How can you prove that you merely wanted to see what the Russians look like and to eat caviar? I recently advised a friend of mine not to attend a party at the Polish consulate in New York City.

6. Do not contribute any money for the legal defense of some old acquaintance or college classmate charged with disloyalty, for even if he is found innocent, you may be charged because of your contribution.

7. Do not marry anyone who, however many years before, had radical associations in college. Avoid if you can marriage with any girl who has ever visited Russia, read Karl Marx or contributed to war relief drives for the Spanish loyalists.

8. Be particularly careful never to ride in an automobile in which a "subversive" may be another rider. The car pool is a favorite object of suspicion.

9. Do not yourself be unduly critical of Fascists or Nazis, and carefully avoid the company of those who have been outspoken on these subjects.

10. If any relative of yours, no matter how distant and no matter how much you disagree with him, has ever been a "radical," do not take a government position at all. The salary can't possibly be worth the effort it may take to defend yourself.

The conduct required by the above Commandments will not, by itself, keep you out of trouble. There are cases pending before loyalty boards in which, for example, a person is charged with an association which may lead to divulging secrets, where the alleged associate is dead; or where a person has been charged with activities sympathetic to communism in a certain year and in a certain city in which he never set foot in the year in question; or where a person is charged with desertion from the army during World War I at a time when he was nine years old. So nothing will keep you entirely in the clear, but these Ten Commandments will help.

Such pressures paralyze independent thought and action in government today. Walter Lippmann may safely argue that due to blunders in connection with the Berlin crisis, Russia today has much logic on her side and we must beat a diplomatic retreat. But if an employee of the State Department presented the same sort of a memorandum for consideration he would in my opinion be undergoing a serious risk. True, most of those charged in my Ten Commandment cases were cleared, but only after worry and strain exceedingly unpleasant for sensitive people.

Twelve million dollars is being spent on collecting gossip as to the thoughts, private lives, associations, reading, political opinion, and social views of government employees. Everyone expects sooner or later to be investigated. Given the assurance of secrecy and complete anonymity your enemies may fill your file with gossip and innuendo. You will never see the evidence against you, or know who your accuser is. It will be your word against an unknown. If that unknown is believed, your job will be lost, your career ruined, and your chance of finding a good job elsewhere scant.

Most of the people charged can't afford a lawyer. Preparation of the cases is long and difficult, particularly because the charges are hopelessly vague. The hearings are long, the appeals endless. The result is humiliation and mental torture. The public and the press do not seem to care. They assume, as in all witch hunts, that an accused employee must be guilty or he wouldn't be accused. And why should anybody object to proving his innocence?

This attack on government employees is a poor way of fighting a cold war against Russia, and as counter espionage it is sheer nonsense. Secret investigations of private lives, opinions and associations can never strengthen a democracy. Instead, they bleed it white of those corpuscles of independent thought which are essential to the character of democratic government. Independence of thought and action is the safety of our country. It is not difficult to drive such independence out of government.

True, not many are hit by the lightning that flashes over the heads of government servants today. But only the most hardy spirits can avoid fright from the thunder, and they are usually those who will not choose to serve a government that subjects them to wild suspicions. They are the kind who can get jobs elsewhere, and they are leaving. The trouble with government service is its tendency to develop a type usually called "bureaucrats." These are timid people, afraid to take a chance, relying on the most absurd technicalities because inaction is always safer than action. They want their pension at the end. Their chief purpose in life is not to do anything to disturb security. The Thomas Committee is turning the government over to that kind of bureaucrat.

I recall that in the Sixteenth Century Elizabeth of England was conducting a cold war against Philip of Spain, not entirely unlike the cold war that Stalin is conducting against us. Elizabeth used every art of deception. Like Stalin, she was too weak to precipitate a war. She commissioned men like Drake and Hawkins to capture Philip's ships and sack his towns in the new world, all the while denying responsibility for these acts. Philip thought he knew the answer. The English were heretics. The real danger, therefore, was that heresy would sap the foundations of the Church that was the cornerstone of the Spanish way of life. And so when Elizabeth sank ships Philip investigated heresy in Spain and burned Spaniards whose thoughts and associations were suspected. He succeeded in bleeding Spain white. He destroyed independence and initiative in his empire.

Today many Americans think that the same sort of purge, conducted of course on more civilized lines, is useful to protect our own government. And many others who consider such an undertaking suicidal nonsense are afraid to speak out lest they themselves be accused.

It might be well also to remember what our blind preoccupation with the problem of spies and internal sabotage at the expense of examination of the real danger cost us at Pearl Harbor. We had broken the Japanese code. We might have deduced from that information where the Japanese fleet was, and what it was doing. Instead, generals in the War Department cabled Kimmel and Short to take measures against internal sabotage. The planes at Pearl Harbor were bunched together in response to that fear. They never got off the ground. If we had given Japanese spies free passports they could not have served their country as well as did this obsession that the real danger was from within and not from without.

*Sincerely*

---

## *To L.E. Aylesworth*[229]

Washington, D.C., April 28, 1948

Dear Professor Aylesworth:

I am very happy to answer your letter of April 22, 1948, although my experience has been that it is useless to argue with members of the American Medical Association. I suppose they are no different than any other association such as the dairymen when they attack oleomargarine, or the Southerners on civil rights, or the National Manufacturers Association on a protective tariff, or John L. Lewis on coal. However, I myself have always been a little more irritated with them because the problem of health is involved.

In answer to your first question, of course I warned the American Medical Association and the local medical association and tried to induce them to stop their boycott. They sent their attorneys to me who threatened dire consequences in the event any proceedings were taken against them. They declined to make any change in their practices. During the progress of the suit they conducted a campaign of misrepresentation of the purpose of the suit. Thousands of letters poured into the White House and also to the Attorney General to stop the proceedings. Pressure was also put on the medical schools. For example, two professors at a prominent medical school had urged the commencement of the action. When I called on them to testify they said that they did not dare, that it might hurt their school and their positions in the school.

In answer to your second question, of course no one in his right mind expected that the American Medical Association would not fight the Wagner Bill. In so far as there was intimidation it was the other way. There were numerous threats against the Administration and some people in the government were successfully intimidated by the Association so that they attempted to stop the suit. Fortunately, however, the President did not listen to them.

I never had any question about the illegality of the restraint of trade in the American Medical Association case. The Association relied on a statement of Holmes' in the *Baseball case* to the effect that medicine was a profession and not a trade and tried to build up from this their right to boycott organizations which did not follow their code. Apparently they were sincere in the belief that the court would hold their way and, as you remember, they did get a lower court to dismiss the indictment. After the Court of Appeals had reversed the case I am inclined to doubt whether the attorneys themselves thought they had much chance except through jury oratory. They retained my friend Bill Leahy, who is one of the best jury lawyers in the United States, and he did get the individual doctors off by pleading with the jury not to convict "your doctors and my doctors." The verdict was illogical in that the jury found that the Medical Association had violated the Sherman Act but that no human being had had a hand in that violation. However, it is the function of a jury to be illogical and Bill Leahy certainly did make a magnificent speech to them.

Finally, in the Supreme Court the American Medical Association contended that it was a labor union and could, therefore, act like Mr. Petrillo. The Supreme Court rejected that contention. Since most of the doctors that I come in contact with were very bitter about the activities of labor unions it was very amusing to find them relying on the labor cases as a last resort.

I wish you luck in your argument with your Medical Association friend. However, I will give you 2-1 that no form of argument makes any impression on him whatever. It has been my experience that any group, whether from labor or industry or the profession, which gets itself in a position where it thinks it has special privilieges will fight for them with complete intolerance and that John L. Lewis and Dr. Fishbein are brothers under the skin. This has been true, however, for 6,000 years so there is no point in being concerned about it.

With best regards,

*Sincerely*

---

## *To Andrew Heiskell* [230]

Washington, D.C., May 25, 1948

Dear Mr. Heiskell:

You recall that at your Round Table I protested against the shocking pictures which appeared in *Life* desecrating the memory of my friend Evalyn Walsh McLean. However, when I talked to you I blamed the auctioneers. I had not realized that your photographers had obtained the pictures through misrepresentation.

On my return to Washington I had one of my associates take the statements of everyone involved. I found that the auctioneers had been victims of a trick; that their only negligence was in trusting the good faith of *Life's* representatives. As you probably know by this time, the *Life* photographers entered the house with the authority to take dignified pictures. They were given the same treatment as the rest of the press. In doing so they became acquainted with subordinate members of the staff who were working on the premises. One evening, when Bradley Delehanty and Stanley Solon, the owners of Meredith Galleries, were away your representatives entered the house with the avowed purpose of completing their work. They got Jack Berman, a furniture mover, to step up on the table and assume the posture which appeared in the magazine. When members of the staff protested the *Life* photographer assured the group that the pictures then being taken would not be published. He said that it was only a souvenir for Berman. *Life* knew that Berman was a furniture mover. Yet in its caption it falsely represented him to be one of the auctioneers. The other pictures were taken under the same misrepresentations and false statements were made in *Life* about an allegedly "boisterous" party going on at the time. *Life* discarded all the dignified pictures which they apparently were using only as a means of throwing the staff off guard. They published the pictures which were taken on the promise they were not to be used.

The reaction in Washington was one of amazement and disgust. I enclose a copy of a typical letter, addressed to me.

You recall the two days of the Round Table given by *Life* in which the responsibilities of magazines were discussed and at which the *Life* representative carefully explained the high purpose of your publication. Mr. Luce will recall the number of times he was a guest of Evalyn McLean.

The damage done by *Life's* extraordinary combination of bad taste and deception is irreparable. For example, an outstanding auctioneer in New York will never get another commission in Washington. The general impression is that the auctioneers were drunk though, as you well know, your photographers staged the scenes portrayed, and no party was going on. For example, I have a letter referring to the "drunken auctioneers." This, of course, reflects on my competence as an executor in employing drunken auctioneers, and many people have told me so. The principal fault of the staff was that they trusted a representative of your magazine.

What action I shall take awaits consultation with the other trustees (Father Walsh is in Washington but Monsignor Sheen is still abroad). In the meantime, I am writing to find out whether the pious sentiments expressed at your Round Table about the responsibility of *Life* magazine to rise above the level of malicious gossip are pure hypocrisy. I will know the answer to this question when you tell me what you propose to do about this disgraceful incident. I shall expect an immediate reply.

*Very truly yours*

## *To Philo Calhoun*

Washington, D.C., Feb. 15, 1949

Dear Phil:

I got your letter with the enclosure which I promptly turned over to Mr. Justice Black as you suggested. He has been in the hospital ever since.

I think it is a little early for you to expect me to be writing thank you notes for Christmas presents. I usually try to get these things attended to by June, but February is out of the question. However, since you have raised the issue, I am authorized to inform you that the ashtray came. I find it the most wonderful ashtray I have ever had. I have no doubt that it cost a small fortune, but it is well worth it. I do not agree with you that it does not look like an ashtray. Both my wife and I spotted it for what it was almost instantly. Visitors who come into the house point at it and say, "That's an ashtray, isn't it?" and I say, "Yes, it's an ashtray." The thing in the middle is to knock the ashes out of your pipe without injuring the delicate adjustment of the complicated smoking tool.

Thanks over and over and over and over and over again for the wonderful ashtray which you sent me on Christmas and which I have received with gratitude and have enjoyed every moment since its arrival.

Thank you for your thoughtfulness. Thank you for your generosity. Thank you for your discrimination in selecting the one gift which I like more than any other gift I got this Christmas and which, indeed, I like better than any other gift which I got at any other Christmas during my life and which to sum up, I like better than anybody ever liked any gift given to them anywhere or any time.

*Affectionately*

---

# VII

# THE McCARTHY YEARS

# 1949 – 1955

*Statement*[231]
*Philadelphia Bulletin Forum*
*March 22, 1949*

Theoretically I suppose it would be possible to conduct a Congressional hearing on Communism in the public interest. Practically, however, every such hearing always and inevitably degenerates into an un-American inquisition. Starting from the narrow base of investigating Communists, such hearings inevitably spread to investigating every idea which the Committee does not like. Starting with the idea of tracking down and exposing subversive ideas such hearings inevitably end by creating a sense of insecurity throughout the land and making American citizens fear for the stability of their political institutions. Starting with the idea of protecting government from subversive employees such hearings inevitably result in destroying freedom of speech and association of all government employees. Today a situation has been created where the independence, thought, action and association of every government employee is now in danger.

This has been the course of the Thomas Committee. It has likewise been the course of every such hearing of that kind throughout history. The Puritans thought that the Quakers with their peculiar ideas were undermining the power of New England theocracy and so they tried to drive out Quaker heresy. Philip of Spain engaged in a cold war with Elizabeth of England and thought that the answer was to drive heresy out of Spain because Elizabeth was a heretic. And so whenever Elizabeth sank ships Philip intensified the investigation of heresy in Spain. He succeeded in destroying only initiative and independence throughout his government.

Today Senator Mundt is telling you that the same sort of a purge conducted, of course, on more civilized lines is necessary to protect our own government. He has succeeded in spreading fear, insecurity and hysteria to such an extent that it is dangerous to contradict him. I assert that any government employee who made the speech that I am making tonight would do so not only at the risk of his job but of his future career. We are discharging men and women today with the public brand of disloyalty which ruins their careers on records which do not contain a line of derogatory evidence. The evidence against the accused on which conviction is made is kept secret. If you can convict a man on secret evidence it means you can convict him on no evidence. To adopt such a procedure is to spread terror throughout the Government in an un-American way.

Let's not blame Senator Mundt and his colleagues. They are doing the best they can considering the pressures and hysteria that surround their enterprise. How can you run such hearings without publicity if you are going to get appropriations? How can you avoid the necessity of constantly providing the public with thrills if the Committee is to have the power it wants? The trouble is not with the Committee but in the idea that freedom of speech and association is dangerous if it happens to be something you don't like. We are engaged in a cold war with Russia. Russia is trying to undermine our institutions and ideals. It is trying to make us believe that they can be pushed over like a house of cards by the machinations of an insignificant minority. Nothing promotes the Russian purpose more than the reverberations in Government and industry which a hearing on un-American activities inevitably creates.

They say they are getting a few disloyal individuals. That may be true. It is equally true that if you turned a machine gun loose on Times Square you would get a few pickpockets.

---

## *To John Haynes Holmes*[232]

Washington, D.C., Nov. 30, 1949

Dear Mr. Holmes:

The career that Roger Baldwin chose for himself was a most difficult one. It involved giving up the luxury and security which a man of his ability could so easily have had. It involved great hazards. As Hughes, in *Tom Brown at Rugby,* so succinctly stated:

> If the angel Gabriel were to come down from heaven and head a successful rise against the most abominable and unrighteous vested interest which this poor old world groans under, he would most certainly lose his character for many years, probably for centuries, not only with upholders of said vested interest but with the respectable mass of people whom he had delivered.

Yet Roger Baldwin took the risk. He devoted himself to a principle supposed to be at the root of American democracy but too often honored in the breach. I am proud to have known him and to be asked to write this testimonial of my admiration and affection for a truly great American.

*Sincerely*

---

## *To George K. Gardner*[233]

Washington, D.C., April 19, 1950

Dear George:

I have been engaged in the trial of a case and hence have not answered your letters. I enclose a copy of the petition for a writ of certiorari in the Dorothy Bailey case.[234]

I can't tell you how much I appreciate your interest in the case. Your court-martial analogy is I think a very good one. The unconstitutional character of the proceeding lies in the fact that it is in every realistic sense a punishment just as a dishonorable discharge is a punishment. The only difference between the two is that the finding of disloyalty is much more serious.

No conceivable necessity exists for conducting a proceeding in this way. In fact, half of the loyalty boards refuse to do it. The point apparently troubled Prettyman because he struck out the three-year ban on competitive examinations. In doing so, however, he did not in any way relieve Dorothy Bailey. The right of an ineligible person to take a competitive examination is no right at all.

To my mind the easiest way of disposing of the case is to insist that the President did not mean to set up this kind of procedure when he spoke of "equal protection of the accused" and "all the evidence." Prettyman is making what seems to me a hypocritical distortion of the order when he says that it allows a conviction on suppressed evidence. The order does permit the suppression of "information." This information is contained in FBI files and is given to the department heads to determine whether loyalty proceedings should be instituted. The only place that the word "evidence" is used is in connection with the standards which support a finding of reasonable doubt as to disloyalty. The proceeding is not unlike a grand jury which can indict on secret information. However, this does not mean that the case can be tried on the grand jury minutes. Government counsel was asked during the trial whether ever in the history of this country the term "evidence" had been used to include secret information. Government counsel was forced to admit that this was the first time such a construction had been put upon the word. Prettyman[235] conceals this in his opinion and gives you the misleading impression you got in your letter.

The Nuremberg case can be distinguished but it is a distinction which the government was ashamed to make. Therefore, neither in the briefs nor the oral arguments has the inconsistency been even mentioned. Perlman is worried about the case and so is McGrath. I had a long conference with them. The only result, however, was to have them send an underling to argue it instead of the head of the Claims Division who argued it before Proctor.

Washington today is in a state of hysteria which you wouldn't believe unless you were here. The fantastic cloak and dagger intrigue, the bribery which we suspect surrounds the Lattimore case, is unthinkable. It is getting so attorneys are afraid to handle these cases for fear of losing respectable clients. The senators will tell you privately what they think of it but don't dare come out publicly, with rare exceptions. And the tragedy of it all is that I have very good grounds to believe that it is the communists themselves who are turning in to the FBI and the Congressional committees accusations against persons who are in their way. There are positive indications that this is what happened in the Bailey case. Dorothy Bailey was attempting to take a non-communist position in a situation where the communists in the union were trying to get control. Everybody in the union knows who the FBI agent is. She attends all the secret meetings with a notebook. She is a very naive person who makes a wonderful conduit through which the communists can get rid of people they don't want, using the government agencies as a weapon.

The communists are able today to paralyze our thinking about foreign policy. It takes about six months for anyone to be cleared for the State Department. If he ever had an original idea or was interested in the problems of communism they are afraid to use his services. Thus they are pursuing their stupid policy with respect to China partly because they were afraid to agree with Lattimore who is the world's greatest expert on the subject. This reaches down into all the minor posts. All government affairs are becoming a dark secret. Government personnel is deteriorating to an alarming extent.

I hope the Supreme Court will have the courage to act, but I am not encouraged by their past record in certiorari cases of this character. However, this case does give them an out. All they need to do is to interpret the President's order according to its plain intent and they can disregard the constitutionality of the loyalty program. This in itself would do a lot of good. The extent of the fear is indicated by a very nice government official of long standing whom I met for the first time at dinner. A lady asked him about the Lattimore case. He flushed and said "I have no comment to make on it either way."

In the face of this atmosphere Edgerton[236] is showing real courage. He is liable at any time to be subject to a speech in the Senate investigating communism on the Bench, and he knows it. The un-American Activities committee is already extending its investigations to communist influences in the District of Columbia. It recently summoned a business man of liberal leanings whom I represented. He was cleared or at least not questioned again. But the fact that he was called became known and his business suffered. His summons before the committee was like a summons before the Spanish Inquisition except that their methods go only to the destruction of the business and reputation of the victims.

In this situation I can't tell you how much we appreciate your interest. Have you ever considered whether it is possible to get a substantial group of professors to file a brief amicus curiae in the Dorothy Bailey case? So far we haven't had any luck. Turn this over in your mind and let me know of anything that might come up.

With best regards,

*Sincerely*

---

## *To Orrin Keepnews* [237]

Washington, D.C., April 20, 1950

Dear Mr. Keepnews:

Your letter of March 23, 1950, with the carbon copy of Mr. Colefax's communication, should have been answered sooner. But I have been literally swamped with very important matters, and have just gotten around to it.

The plain truth is that I am fed up on Mr. Colefax's[238] unctuous affectation of innocence. He recites not one word of the long story of American Potash & Chemical's long defiance of the antitrust laws. He insists that by presumption it must be maintained that his company represents the epitome of righteousness.

The facts in respect to past conduct are beyond dispute. American Potash & Chemical, sporting a charter from a state of the Union, for long years was owned and controlled by citizens of the Third Reich. For a period of decades it was in combination with Borax Consolidated to make the world market for borax and its products their exclusive dominion. The two companies concealed their iniquitous conspiracy against their independent competitors and against the public from 1929 and on so successfully that, had not American Potash & Chemical been seized by the United States as enemy owned, documents establishing the guilt of the conspirators might never have been found. And, only after a complaint had been drawn, reciting the facts of their long course of law breaking, did American Potash & Chemical consent to a decree written against it. All of this is well known to Mr. Colefax, who in his communications to you has exhibited no passion for the whole truth.

The borax trust is affected with a public interest; and its behavior, past and present, is of course subject to "fair comment." Because of my years of experience with the public control of business—as a teacher of law, as head of the Antitrust Division, as a judge on the Federal Circuit Court, and as a practitioner of law—I have had occasion to witness in numerous instances the attempts of the government to restore industries to the competitive pattern marked out by the law. And, on the basis of wide experience, I repeat, as a matter of fair comment on a matter of grave public interest, that I am not naive enough to believe that a change in ownership plus a decree which American Potash & Chemical accepted rather than subject its long course of wrongdoing to the judgment of the courts are enough to insure that the company has experienced a genuine and thorough conversion.

The great bother with Mr. Colefax's position is that it is self-contradictory. He invents the strange rule that fair comment should be limited to what has been proved in court. Yet the thing to which he is most opposed is meeting the issues on the merits. In the two cases to which he refers, the strategy was to secure the dismissal of the suits on technicalities. And in his first letter to you he protests that, because of my article, his company may be put "to the heavy expense"—not, mind you, of meeting suits on their merits—but "of incurring counsel fees and other expenses to attain their dismissal."

The detail of Mr. Colefax's second letter demands little attention. Aside from formal signatures, he digs up one person at the Department of Justice who had been somewhat active in the case. It is not challenged that Justice formally participated in the consent decree; the matter was technically before it and it had to take formal action. He does not deny that the pressure came from the military. Nor does he deny a current concert of action between American Potash & Chemical; he merely repeats his former statement that no "contact" now exists between them. And he admits that the two companies are "the dominant American producers of borax." But I shall not bother further to point out what Mr. Colefax says and what he goes to great pains to avoid.

It is understandable that, in loyalty to his company, he tries to make "the worse appear the better reason." But, frankly, I have had quite enough of such hypocrisy.

*Sincerely*

---

*To George K. Gardner*

Washington, D.C., April 29, 1950

Dear George:

I would appreciate it if you and such other men of good will around Harvard who would care to do so would join on a brief amicus curiae in the Bailey case in support of certiorari, emphasizing principally the importance of the question. I have no fear of losing the case if the Supreme Court takes it. I do have considerable anxiety about their taking it since they have consistently refused on so many other cases to consider cases involving the civil liberties of ordinary citizens. Criminals and Jehovah's Witnesses get much better treatment. However, I hope that I am wrong about this and that these remarks about the Court are unjustified.

It is of no consequence to me that the Court may deny your motion to file a brief amicus. That is what they customarily do but they can't help seeing the brief when they deny the right to file it, and I do happen to know that they read short briefs the filing of which is denied. The CIO is coming in with a brief in support of certiorari which may or may not be a good thing. That is one of the reasons I would like to get a couple of professors of high standing like yourself.

With respect to your letter of the 24th, I am not concerned about the point you make that "if the plan has not been executed as the commander intended that it should be, no one but the commander can complain." The authorities on this point are all our way. The ordinary executive order is not like a military command and may be enforced by legal proceedings. This was not even questioned by the government either in the lower court or the Court of Appeals.

I note that you characterize Prettyman's opinion as "excellent." I may be blinded by partisanship but it seems to me that it is pure dialectic hogwash. He arrives at a result only by ignoring the realities, which are that Dorothy Bailey is being tried for an offense akin to treason and has not had due process. Of course, if you want to kid yourself and say that this is only the ordinary discharge from a government job, you may be able to come out where Prettyman does. Personally I think that this is a distortion of the facts and a failure to adapt the Constitution to a situation which requires its protection even more than in a case where the criminal laws are being enforced.

With best regards, and hoping that you will see fit to ask leave to file a brief amicus curiae to which motion a short brief will be attached, I remain

*Sincerely*

---

*To Cecil Nussbaum*

Washington, D.C., Sept. 2, 1950

Dear Cecil:

September 9th would be a grand date and Frances and I would be horribly disappointed if you did not come. It may be 500 miles from Boston to Washington, but I doubt if it's five hundred additional to Laramie. Tell Fred that he ain't that old yet, and to buck up and take some vitamins and a quart of whisky and nothing can stop him. Tell him to read a poem by Henry Wadsworth Tennyson (the great Scotch songbird) called "Ulysses" which contains a lot of important observations regarding the advisability of old goats like Fred getting off their fannies and stepping out in a high wide and handsome manner. Tennyson puts this idea in more expansive work but I think I have accurately given you the substance. Tell Fred that there is no way of getting the moss off a stone unless you keep it rolling. Tell him that Washington needs his presence to affect the Communists who are infiltrating here by the thousands. One trip by Fred should convince Stalin that Washington means business. If Fred stays away it will be a clear indication that American Scholars are unconcerned with their nation's government, and therefore can't be relied on to drop atom bombs in case a shortage of atom bomb droppers develops.

In addition, I have valuable information to impart. I got back recently from a business trip that included Switzerland, Luxumberg, Heidelberg, the Russian sector of Berlin, Frankfurt, Rotterdam, Amsterdam, Brussels, Paris and London. I'm an expert on all these countries and a most valuable source of information to a historian.

And as for you, who are interested in art, I have lots of information "aussie" (that's a French word. It means "aha").

Hope you can come.

*Sincerely*

---

*To Philo C. Calhoun*

Washington, D.C., Nov. 29, 1950

Dear Phil:

How in hell would I know John Horton who lives on George Mason Drive in Arlington? It's at least ten miles from my house and there are at least 100,000 people in that particular suburb. My secretary lives there and she says she used to know a John Horton when she was a little girl in South Carolina, only his name was George and not John, and he died when he was fifteen years old. If this helps you any, you are welcome to the information.

In return, may I ask you if you know a man named George Comminger Krystophlis who lives in one of the suburbs of Greenwich about two and one-half miles southeast of the residence of Norris Pierson, as the crow flies? I don't happen to remember the street. If you don't know him, to hell with it. Just forget it.

Why don't we get together sometime before Christmas. I am going to California in the next two weeks but will be back shortly before Christmas. I am terribly sorry to hear of the death of Otis Bradley.

The Supreme Court turned down our petition for certiorari in the Bank of America case. We have just petitioned for a rehearing. I tried to get associate counsel to agree that the enclosed would be the last paragraph of our petition. Unfortunately it was left out of the petition so I send it on to you as an example of effective legal draftsmanship. The case is the Federal Reserve Board against the Bank of America. Townsend is general counsel for the Federal Reserve Board and Evans is the member who presided.

Thanks for delivering the documents.

With kind personal regards,

*Sincerely*

---

## *To Arthur Krock*

Washington, D.C., Dec. 20, 1950

Dear Arthur:

I promised you this letter sometime ago and then was suddenly called to the West Coast for a trial and forgot it in the rush of getting away.

You wanted to know the background of the colloquy between Justice Jackson and the Solicitor General. The *Lovett case* (*United States* v. *Lovett,* 328 U.S. 303) held that a declaration of ineligibility for government service was a punishment. This being so, if it were done by act of Congress it would be a bill of attainder. If it were done by a court or a government agency without a fair hearing it would be a violation of due process. No one claimed that Dorothy Bailey had a fair hearing. We therefore asked that the action of the Loyalty Board be set aside under the Due Process Clause.

The government claimed that the Loyalty Board had not made Dorothy Bailey ineligible since Judge Prettyman had set aside the portion of the Loyalty Board's order declaring her ineligible to take competitive examinations. Mr. Perlman said therefore that all that was involved was the discharge of Dorothy Bailey from a job and no one has a property right in a government job.

In answer we had argued in our brief that making Dorothy Bailey eligible to take competitive examinations did not make her eligible for a government position. This is because it is the clear intent of the President's order to make all persons whose loyalty is subject to a reasonable doubt permanently ineligible so long as that doubt exists. Justice Frankfurter had questioned Paul Porter on this point and Paul had answered to the above effect.

When Perlman was arguing he asserted that Dorothy Bailey was eligible. Justice Jackson interrupted him and said "I don't mind being amused but I don't want to be made a laughing stock of. Do you mean that Dorothy Bailey can get a job?" Perlman admitted that she couldn't as a practical matter get a job again in the government, but as a theoretical and technical matter she was not ineligible. Jackson said, "Does the government actually wish to win this case on that point?" Perlman said, "No, we have other points."

Personally I do not see how the Court can support the Board without in effect reversing the Lovett case.

Another colloquy occurred between Frankfurter, Black and Perlman. Perlman was arguing that the high and distinguished character of the members of the Loyalty panel constituted a guarantee of a fair hearing. Frankfurter said [of course I can't remember his exact language], "I appreciate their high character but under the circumstances of this case I don't see how you claim that they exercised any judgment of their own." Black continued from there about as follows:

"Did any member of the Loyalty Board ever interview the informer against Dorothy Bailey?" Perlman answered, "No." Black then asked, "Did any member of the Loyalty Board ever see or interview the F.B.I. agent who interviewed the informer?" Perlman again answered, "No." Black's final question was, "Did any member of the Loyalty Board ever see or interview the F.B.I. agent who certified that the unknown informer was reliable?" Perlman again said, "No."

This was encouraging because it seemed a complete destruction of Perlman's argument that there was some guarantee of a fair hearing on account of the distinguished character of the Board. It was obvious from the government's admissions that the only person who evaluated the testimony was the F.B.I. Of course the F.B.I. claims that it does not evaluate any of the evidence. This is a somewhat Pickwickian position. They do evaluate the reliability of the informer. Therefore, if the information given by the informer is damaging it becomes conclusive against the accused and the Board has no option except to accept the F.B.I. evaluation.

A third colloquy was between Justice Frankfurter and Perlman. Justice Frankfurter in effect said that much of the general background in the government's brief and argument was irrelevant. This background consisted of what happened under Wilson's Administration, the Hiss case, the Fuchs case and so on. Perlman got quite annoyed with Frankfurter on account of this suggestion.

I enclose copy of our brief in case you have not seen it. We don't have an extra copy of the Government's brief but of course you can get it from the Department of Justice.

With best regards, and thanks for your letter to the Metropolitan Club,

*Sincerely*

---

## *To Hugh Cox*

Washington, D.C., Feb. 24, 1951

Dear Hugh:

I congratulate you and also the bar of the District of Columbia on your new partnership. I hail this announcement as the most important advance in local legal standards since our distinguished brother, James J. Laughlin, was acquitted of abortion by a jury and thus restored to continued service in our midst.

I am also profoundly moved by the mellifluous quality of the new firm name, Covington & Burling, but in this connection, one thing disturbs me. I seriously question the wisdom of dropping all three of those heavy names at once. While I know of no case which is precisely analogous, I am informed by my doctor that if you take weight off too rapidly, you upset your metabolism. Furthermore, eminent balloonists whom I have consulted advise me that when all the ballast is suddenly thrown out of a balloon, it shoots up with such incredible speed as to endanger the occupants. Had I been consulted, I would, for a reasonable fee, have pointed out that this danger could have been eliminated by removing the names one at a time over a period of about three weeks. Since I was not consulted, in the event you experience dizzy spells, ringing in the ears, and perhaps the bends (which unfortunately are extremely painful) I can accept no other responsibility than to point out that in the future I or some other member of my firm will always be available and that we give day and night service.[239]

*Sincerely*

---

## *To J.N. Pew, Jr.* [240]

Washington, D.C., May 31, 1951

Dear Joe:

I send you the enclosed article appearing in the *Atlantic Monthly*[241] just to show you how I spend the extra time your retainer gives me.

I was very much pleased at the action of the Sun Oil Company with respect to Governor Mennen Williams' price fixing scheme. This shows that the N.R.A. still lingers in the hearts of the old New Dealers. I knew Mennen Williams intimately when he was Murphy's assistant in the Department of Justice. He is a very nice fellow but I believe will always be committed to the notion that Government should call businessmen into meetings and impose its will on them by threat of political action. This is happening over and over again in Washington today under the guise of price stabilization. As a result it is my belief that price controls are going to raise more prices than they lower. However, most people won't know that.

I am still fascinated with what you told me about corporations like the United States Steel losing money while their books are showing high profits. The end result it seems to me would be the inability of companies like United States Steel to replace their equipment. This would mean operation with patched-up and obsolete equipment and plants. This would, in turn, force large companies to form international cartels and divide the market because they could not compete on an efficiency basis.

When I was investigating the British cartels the ideas which you now suggest had not occurred to me. Today it is a most interesting problem. To me it presents a convincing argument for a position I have held for a long time, i.e., that corporation taxes should be abolished. However, this is a purely academic position so long as corporate books show profits. To change corporate bookkeeping so that they reflected the situation as you showed it to me would be so revolutionary as to be impossible. No board of directors would wish to face the situation that frankly, and if they did the Government probably wouldn't let them on the theory that honesty in bookkeeping was tax dodging.

So we come back to the necessity of somehow or other achieving a stable dollar. Your idea is extraordinarily interesting. I do not recall ever having seen it written up and analyzed. Certainly none of the economists around here that I know have even discussed it. As you point out, they are all talking about the consumer's dollar and about inflation as it affects housewives. The long run destruction of plant efficiency has not been considered.

This leads me to attempt an article on the subject if I can get my thoughts in any kind of order. Certainly we can't run the economy on Government spending forever.

In any event, it was a fascinating afternoon I spent with you and I appreciate it very much. I came back full of new ideas.

Please don't bother to answer this letter because I know how busy you are.

With warm regards,

*Sincerely*

---

*To Eugene Davidson*

Washington, D.C., Aug. 20, 1951

Dear Gene:

I learn that my friend, Dick Field at Harvard, is getting up a compendium of the sayings of great men for the use of Harvard students; and that pages 172-174, 178 and 183-185 have been selected from that monolithic work "Symbols of Government," the copyright to which in a misguided moment I assigned to Yale Press. I am also informed that the Yale Press has adopted an intransigent attitude and is attempting to frustrate the development of scholarship at Harvard by demanding payment of $30 for the use of these excerpts.

It occurs to me that the Yale Press ought to pay Dick Field for the privilege of having one of its publications mentioned at Harvard. I am therefore surprised that an appeal for reconsideration of the $30 payment has gone unanswered.

I have told Field to go ahead and publish the excerpts and in the event you do not desire to participate gratis in his effort to stop the spread of Communism at Harvard by republishing my remarks, you may bill me for the $30 and I will promptly remit with the hope that it chokes you.

Hoping that this letter will cause the light of reason to infiltrate into the murky atmosphere that surrounds your mouldy institution, I remain

*Sincerely*

---

*To Elizabeth Toll* [242]

Washington, D.C., March 17, 1952

Dear Betty:

I intended to write you a long personal letter in my own hand this Saturday afternoon, but the pile of correspondence took so long to get through that I simply haven't the time to do it and get home to supper, so I will dictate a letter instead.

I appreciated your notes and am sorry that I am so negligent in answering them. It is awfully hard for a person who is not a habitual correspondent to change his ways, and I have been very busy and under considerable strain for the past two months. Christmas week was spoiled because I had to prepare a case in the Supreme Court of the United States, which I argued on January 2. I represented Fritz von Opel, the son of the German automobile manufacturer, in an attempt to get about $3,000,000 of property back which the Alien Property Custodian stole from him. I hope the Supreme Court takes the same view.

At the conclusion of my argument, I flew to Denver, where I tried a jury case against the motion picture companies on behalf of an independent theater. I had expected this case to last about three weeks. Instead, it lasted eight and a half weeks. This is because the Judge could not make up his mind, would not rule from the bench, would dismiss the jury for days while we argued and handed him briefs on every little point. It was one of these mean bitter trials, with about ten attorneys on the other side calling our clients perjurers and subjecting them to days and days of harassing cross examination. They did succeed in getting them all mixed up, and at the end of the trial I was very worried about the result. There were five men and seven women on the jury, none of them getting more than $3,000 or $4,000 a year. You can imagine the thrill I got when, after being out about twelve hours, the jury came in with a verdict for us for $300,000 which is the biggest jury verdict that has ever been handed down in Denver.[243]

I flew back to Washington, where Abe was suffering in the Lattimore hearings. He had to go to Puerto Rico, and so I took up where he left off. Never in my life have I seen anything more vicious or contemptible than the way the Committee is trying to break Lattimore. They are crookedly and dishonestly attempting to spring traps on him. So far they have not succeeded, in spite of day after day of constant hammering by at least four or five people. McCarran threatened to throw Abe out of the hearing room. He also threatened to throw me out for attempting to protect our client against this sort of unfair questioning. They let Lattimore go on Friday, to be called back again. There seems to be no end to it.

I have just come back from the Pacific Coast, spending only two days. Saw Thurman and Janie. Frances has been out there. She flew there from Denver after the trial was over, and I came back to Washington.

Now I have to prepare for a trial in New York, and that's the way it goes. I don't know whether my peregrinations interest you or not, but at least I have been too busy to get into trouble, as I almost did in Paris—you remember the last long letter I wrote you.

*Lots of love*

---

## *To R.W. Woodruff*

Washington, D.C., Nov. 20, 1952

Dear Bob:

Sometime ago you talked with me about a proposal for encouraging private investment abroad, in the form of the construction and operation of plants and productive facilities. I thought then that your idea was sound and constructive. I now think that the time has come to put some push behind it, because I think that the new Administration will be receptive to it; that the need for investment of American capital in other free countries, including those of Western Europe, is even more acute; and that unless a plan such as yours is adopted, the flow of dollars into these countries will diminish, instead of increasing as they should if we are to maintain world stability and our own level of productive activity.

As you know, the dollar gap is widening, not diminishing; and the economic position of our allies, with the dubious exception of West Germany, is deteriorating. If we merely sit by, the results may be disastrous to those countries, and, if there is a general retrenchment on government spending, particularly for defense and foreign aid, the consequences to our own economy may be very serious.

I should think that your plan would, in these circumstances, have great appeal to the Eisenhower Administration. It does not involve direct government spending; it practically avoids the political difficulties of governmental diversion of capacity and output from civilian purposes to foreign governments; it presents a way of enlisting American business ingenuity to aid in the progress of foreign countries; and it affords a method for increased productivity and opportunity to our economy.

I think we could well afford to go even further than your plan contemplated, as I remember it. For example, we might do something along these lines:

1. Any project for construction and operation by private U.S. groups or companies of facilities in a foreign country which was approved in certain respects by that government and by ours, would be guaranteed by our government against loss of invested capital (with or without interest) for any reason whatever. Working this out in detail would be complex, but not too difficult.

2. Convertibility of proceeds of operations—dividends, interest, proceeds of lease or sale—would be guaranteed at a given rate of exchange.

Abe and I are thinking that we might get together a small group including some staunch supporters of Eisenhower such as Fred Lazarus, Jr., who is a friend of Abe's, and perhaps Paul Mazur. I am writing to find out if you are still interested in your idea and whether you have any suggestions.

With kind regards,

*Sincerely*

---

## *To Will Shafroth*[244]

Washington, D.C., Dec. 30, 1952

Dear Will:

Abe, Paul and I were very much touched, more than we can tell you, by your check for Lattimore. It is a depressing thing to think that in America a man can be indicted for perjury in denying that he sympathized with or promoted Communism. It is just as if I said under oath that I was sympathetic to labor unions. Then I am indicted for perjury and the jury is given my labor prosecutions to prove I was a liar. If men can be tried for opinions of that kind we have come to the end of the road.

The other counts of the indictment are trifling and the trial will be easy. On the first count, however, the Government can keep on presenting evidence to the jury for as many months as it wants to.

Again thanking you on behalf of myself and my partners, I remain

*Sincerely*

---

## *To Arthur M. Schlesinger, Jr.*[245]

Washington, D.C., March 9, 1953

Dear Mr. Schlesinger:

Your column in the *New York Post* for December 21 about Lattimore has just been called to my attention. You say:

> Now Lattimore was certainly for many years a notorious and unabashed fellow-traveler. Sens. McCarthy and McCarran, however, have accused him of worse things than fellow-traveling. It would be much easier to defend Lattimore against these probably unwarranted and certainly unproved charges if he would at least

> be candid enough to admit that he went through a long period of infatuation with the Soviet Union. But he has chosen to pitch his defense on the disingenuous ground that he has been a stout anti-totalitarian from the word go.

The principal count in the indictment against Lattimore is that he perjured himself when he denied that he had "promoted or sympathized" with Communist interests. The lapses of memory are minor counts. You are therefore accusing him of the same "perjury" as the indictment charges if the words "disingenuous" and "unabashed" mean anything.

It is difficult for me to understand how a responsible historian could have made the statement you did. As you know, you yourself have been subjected to similar charges. Only a few days ago I was present in a group which claimed you were one of the worst fellow-travelers in the Stevenson campaign. It may also interest you to know that in the *Washington Post* on March 3 you and Lattimore and Fairbank were mentioned among the authors whose books might possibly be removed from foreign libraries supported by the United States because of charges against the three of you.

However, I am not writing this letter to quarrel with you but rather to ask you to assist me in finding out what it is about Lattimore's actions or writings which led to the charge of sympathy with Communist interest. Neither my partners nor I have been able to discover it after careful study, and certainly the Committee has given us no hint of what they are talking about. In preparing our defense to the first count of the indictment we do not know just what we have to get.

It would be, therefore, very helpful if you would list precisely what writings, policies, or activities of Lattimore have led you to the conclusion that he was an unabashed fellow-traveler and that he was disingenuous in denying it. Certainly you must have had some specific things in mind when you wrote your column. I think, in view of the amount of injury your column has done to Lattimore in connection with the first count and the fact that you, as a so-called liberal, are being quoted extensively against Lattimore and may even be used as part of the argument in court in answer to our motion to dismiss, you owe it to Lattimore to give us this bill of particulars.

For your enlightenment as to what we are up against in this respect if the first count is sustained as a matter of law, I enclose a copy of our motion to dismiss.

Senator O'Mahoney, who is a Catholic and a former member of the Judiciary Committee and who before taking the case made an extensive investigation of Lattimore's opinions, is at a loss to understand your statement. As you know, it is particularly hurtful because it comes from a person who is regarded, in some quarters at least, as a sort of fellow-traveler himself. You have great influence with the persons who ought to be on our side.

I would appreciate hearing from you as soon as you can formulate a basis for your statement.

*Sincerely*

---

## *To C.R. Smith* [246]

Washington, D.C., April 8, 1953

Dear Mr. Smith:

In a folder which you distribute to passengers I note you say

> We are never entirely satisfied with our service, each day and each week we endeavor to make it better. It may be that you can give us suggestions how further to improve the service, in the air or on the ground.

The suggestions I am about to make are based on the following circumstances. Yesterday, April 7, 1953, I and my partner, Norman Diamond, were in Chattanooga. It was important that we get back to Washington last night. We discovered that by paying extra we could take an Eastern Airlines plane to Nashville and have about one-half an hour to catch your Flight 2 which is non-stop to Washington. The Eastern Airlines plane was late (as usual) but still it looked as if we could make it. We instructed the girl at the Eastern Airlines office in Chattanooga to wire that we were trying to connect with your Flight 2. Whether the wire arrived or not we do not know.

When we got to Nashville we observed with relief that your Flight 2 had not departed. The door was open, the ramp was in place. We ran over to the plane and attempted to board it saying that we had tickets to Washington and were making connection from Eastern Airlines which was late. We were informed by the man at the ramp that there were seats available on the plane. However, he said he had no authority to let us board the plane without the O.K. of the ticket office. He did not call the ticket office although he could easily have done so. Instead he slammed the door in our faces and moved the ramp away.

We ran at top speed to the ticket office. We asked the man behind the desk to hold the plane until we could get aboard. He flatly declined to do so and instead spoke into a little box. What he said I do not know but in any event the plane departed without us.

We were quite angry and expressed ourselves somewhat violently for not being allowed to board the plane. The ticket officer was most courteous but also very firm. He said that he had no authority to let us aboard at the last minute unless our space was confirmed. He did not know about any wires from Eastern. He told us that the reason for the rule was that somebody else might have space confirmed at an intervening point and the fact that there were seats at Nashville, therefore, was unimportant. In reply we pointed out that it was a non-stop flight from Nashville to Washington and that the likelihood of anyone with a prior reservation boarding the plane in mid-air was not great. We believe we scored a point on him here, but it was the only one.

We proceeded to Nashville. All the hotels were filled but we finally managed to get a room in a small hotel. We took your Flight 12 out at 6:30 o'clock this morning, April 8th, arriving in Washington at 10:30—just twelve hours late.

We estimate that it would have taken about sixty seconds to have gotten us aboard the plane. We saw the captain of Flight 12 who said that two or three minutes difference in a non-stop flight would have made no difference whatever in landing in Washington.

On the basis of these facts we respectfully offer two suggestions:

1. That you join with us in obtaining a little competition with American between Nashville and Washington. This we think would improve your service tremendously.

2. In the event that you reject this idea we suggest that if the regulations be as stated by your employee you change them to permit passengers from connecting planes, who arrive while the door of your plane is still open and the ramp in place, to board the plane provided there is space for them. We are not experts in air transportation but we cannot believe that this problem is so difficult that it cannot be solved by your trained technical staff. If you will study the practice of other airlines we think that you will find that they have situations like this under better control. Mr. Diamond coming up from Miami to Chattanooga on Sunday, April 5th, boarded an Eastern Airlines plane under precisely the same circumstances in Atlanta. His connecting flight was late and he was permitted to get on the plane without going to the ticket office. Although Eastern is a competitor of yours we are sure that if you have one of your officials call them up they will explain to you how this difficult feat can be accomplished and you can incorporate it in your own procedure.

Our hotel bills and taxicabs because of our enforced stay in Nashville amounted to $12.50 in case this is of any interest to you.

This firm spends approximately $15,000 annually on air travel, most of which has heretofore gone to American Airlines, and this firm has one of your credit cards.

Hoping the above suggestions will be of value, I remain

*Sincerely*

---

## *To George K. Gardner*

Washington, D.C., July 27, 1953

Dear George:

Pardon my belated acknowledgment of your excellent article in the *Boston University Law Review* which everyone in the office read with interest and pleasure.

Incidentally, if we could ever give our much abused civil servants the dignity and privileges of commissioned officers in the Army, it would be a real civic achievement. However, I suspect that the prevailing American attitude which existed as long as I can remember is to treat civil servants as leeches, bleeding the taxpayer.

The tragedies of Eisenhower's new policy of discharge can be observed everywhere in Washington. People of long experience who thought they had some sort of career protection are being thrown out in the street by the thousands, not because of any loyalty reasons but in the interests of balancing the budget. The whole saving is infinitesimal. The effect on the morale of the civil servants is great. I have never known it to be so low.

*Sincerely*

---

## *To Murray Seasongood*[247]

Washington, D.C., Oct. 12, 1953

Dear Murray:

Thank you for your letter of October 6th. If your friend sends me a letter giving me what he thinks is the relevant data I will be glad to call on his Department as a favor to you without charge. Frankly, however, I think the situation is hopeless. All the departments are under pressure to get rid of people. If they can get rid of them for cause, then they don't have to bounce someone else.

Washington is full of disconsolate wrecks who thought they had security and are now wandering around from door to door seeking employment. Not a day passes but some displaced lawyer comes in. I sympathize with them but that's about all I can do. It is cruel treatment and in my judgment not worth the money that is saved, but it seems to be popular with most people to take a certain sadistic pleasure in seeing Government bureaucrats kicked around.

It is possible that I can get your friend a hearing, but under present pressures they would kick him out anyway. There are no real standards and there can be no review of such a hearing. It is certainly not worth his paying a fee to anyone. In my judgment all you can do is to see the head of the Department once, which won't take much time. Further visits would be useless. In any event, it won't do any harm for me to make the call and maybe it would help your friend's morale to think that he had obtained some legal representation.

Best regards,

*Sincerely*

---

## *To Patrick Henry Malin* [248]

Washington, D.C., Oct. 30, 1953

Dear Mr. Malin:

I was somewhat disturbed by reading in your recent report that upon motion by Mr. Seymour, the Due Process Committee is about to formulate a statement of its position in the Lattimore case. You, of course, know the reason for my concern.

Our dispute arose out of the fact that the Due Process Committee did not consider that any civil liberties issue arose out of the Lattimore indictment standing by itself. The position of the committee was, and it was also your position, that the only proper action was to ask for a bill of particulars and that the question of whether the indictment should be dismissed would be dependent upon a bill of particulars.

We, of course, filed a bill of particulars and argued it and we also filed a motion to dismiss. The Court ordered the bill of particulars on three of the counts but on four dismissed on the ground of the First and Sixth Amendments without considering the bill of particulars. Your position, therefore, is contrary to that of Judge Youngdahl's and, of course, is contrary to the argument we are going to make in the Court of Appeals to sustain Judge Youngdahl. I think it would be most unfortunate if the ACLU took a position contrary to Judge Youngdahl's opinion and, according to my latest information, your position is still contrary.

It does not seem to me that ACLU, by any public statement, would desire to throw difficulties in our way or to bolster up the position that the indictment should not have been dismissed before its scope was determined by a bill of particulars.

Under these circumstances, I hope you will refrain from making a statement unless it be a brief one that you have not intervened because you thought counsel competent and that you agreed with Judge Youngdahl's decision.

If you decide to make a statement, I think you should allow Senator O'Mahoney and myself to be heard. But I hope the time and expense will be spared us.

Since it may be that the matter is not clearly understood by your Board, I am sending six copies of our brief which I wish you would distribute to any one who desires to read it. It seems to me that the position taken in the brief should be in accord with that of the American Civil Liberties Union. If it is not, I do not think it should be the function of the Union to make the defense difficult by taking a different position.

*Sincerely yours*

---

## *To Charles Fahy*[249]

Washington, D.C., Dec. 3, 1953

Dear Charlie:

My congratulations on your dissent in the Wheeler case. I have no interest in the case whatever but of late I have become very much concerned with the failure of Courts of Appeal all over the United States to put any curb upon deliberate violations of the rule by prosecutors. Your dissent and Judge Hand's dissent in the Remington case I hope are the beginning of a trend the other way.

I could give you instances from the criminal cases I have personally tried and from those that I know about where the prosecution I think deliberately paid no attention to established rules of law, firm in the belief that the prejudicial error doctrine would take care of that. For instance, in a recent criminal case where I represented the defendant a grand jury was called three days before the trial. All my witnesses were held for days before the grand jury and subjected to a ruthless grueling. They were frightened to death when they went on the stand. The law seems to be clear that a grand jury cannot be called for purpose of preparation for trial and extensive examination of the defendant's witnesses. The Department of Justice attorney was quite cynical about it and he was right. His argument that there was no prejudicial error prevailed. Things like this are a dirty business. He also on his closing argument made a deliberate misstatement of the record. At the end of the argument I asked for a chance to set the jury right. This was refused and I am now on appeal but again I have little hope because of prejudicial error.

Prejudicial error means today that if the appellate court thinks that the defendant is probably guilty it will ignore any and all instances of unfair tactics on the part of the prosecutor. The idea that Holmes once had that there are certain trial tactics which appellate courts will not tolerate seems to have gone by the board. In this situation your dissent is a ray of light.

As Judge Hand says in the Remington case: "The postulate on which the exclusion of such testimony depends, must be that only by upsetting convictions so obtained can the ardor of prosecuting officials be kept within legal bounds and justice be secured; for in modern times all prosecution is in the hands of officials."

*Sincerely*

---

## *To William D. Neary*[250]

Washington, D.C., May 3, 1954

Dear Mr. Neary:

I read with interest your note on the Lattimore case.[251] It seems to me that you have overlooked a couple of points. For example, you seem unable to distinguish the Barsky and Lawson cases from the Lattimore indictment because these cases hold that Congress has the power to inquire whether a person is a believer in Communism. The Lattimore indictment, however, is for perjury because Lattimore said he never sympathized with "Communism or Communist interests." Communism is a philosophy with fairly sharp outlines. Communist interests, however, are utterly impossible to define.

I cannot agree with you that an inquiry into a person's religious or political beliefs is a proper subject for investigation, particularly where, as in this case, they deal with Lattimore's activities as editor of *Pacific Affairs.* In this connection I think you should read *United States* v. *Rumely.*

The Lawson case gives superficial support for your conclusion but I would still hope that inquiry should be restricted to activities. If not, freedom of opinion is gone. For example, the doctrine of Communism comes from Karl Marx. Socialism is very difficult to distinguish from Communism and certainly a Socialist would have to believe in a good deal of the Communist doctrine. If he said he did not sympathize with Communism a prima facie case could be made against him, and in these troublesome times any Socialist who happened to be indicted would be almost sure to be convicted. If the Supreme Court gives the Lawson case the scope which you say it has the First Amendment has no meaning left.

Thank you for sending the Note to me.

*Sincerely*

---

## *To Philip L. Graham*[252]

Washington, D.C., Oct. 29, 1954

Dear Phil:

I have always spoken in terms of greatest admiration for the *Post.* With that in mind perhaps you might accept a little criticism. Of all the principal papers which I read the *Post* reporting of the Lattimore indictment was the worst. There was a superficial analysis of Rover's[253] pleadings, there was no analysis of ours whatever. If you will compare your report with that of the *Washington Star* or the *Baltimore Sun* you will see what I mean.

Perhaps it was this bad reporting which led you to miss the point when your editorial writer criticized Judge Youngdahl for dismissing the affidavit as scandalous. Such an affidavit filed by a private litigant would unquestionably have led to a fine for contempt of the court. Youngdahl was charged with bias, among other things, because he expressed a serious doubt as to the materiality of the trivia which were the basis for perjury in the minor counts of the indictment. In reply, I pointed out that four judges of the Court of Appeals had held categorically that the indictment on its face showed the immateriality of these counts. In his reply to me Rover intimated that if he had a statute permitting him to do so he would have sworn the four judges off the Court of Appeals. The Attorney General had publicly associated himself with Rover's position, another point your paper failed to get. Why I do not know.

To permit the Attorney General of the United States to intimidate judges in a cause celebre by saying that their opinions are so bad that they could not be the product of a judicial mind is completely shocking. Yet the *Post* appeared to think that it was the duty of the judge not to follow the plain mandate of the law and that he should not have stricken the affidavit as scandalous. He should, according to the position of your paper, have said "Thank you, Mr. Rover. I am sorry you think I am biased. I am sorry you don't like my opinions. I still think I am unbiased."

I know you had nothing to do with the editorial and I know that you probably do not understand the case. I am, therefore, sending for your personal attention a copy of our Motion to Dismiss the indictment which was so poorly reported in your paper of today, October 29th.

With best regards,

*Sincerely*

---

## *To Herbert Monte Levy*

Washington, D.C., Oct. 29, 1954

Dear Mr. Levy:

Apparently I have not made my position clear to you in connection with the American Civil Liberties Union's participation in the Lattimore case. In the first full paragraph on page 2 of your letter of October 28th, you state that your Committee considered whether American Civil Liberties Union could join in a motion to dismiss the new Lattimore indictment on First Amendment grounds, as amicus curiae.

I am a member of your national committee. I have in the past supported the American Civil Liberties Union. I don't want you in the Lattimore case. If the American Civil Liberties Union attempts to participate in the case as amicus curiae or otherwise, I will object strenuously. I repeat, I want the American Civil Liberties Union to stay out of this case.

I thought that the position that you took with respect to the first count of the old indictment, insisting that the correct procedure was to demand a bill of particulars in lieu of filing a motion to dismiss, was wrong and was an unwarranted attempt to interfere with the conduct of the case by Senator O'Mahoney and this office. I was confirmed in my opinion as to the strategy of the case by the District Judge and by eight judges to one in the Court of Appeals and by the Solicitor General, who refused to apply for certiorari. But whether we were right or wrong, in our judgment the threat that the American Civil Liberties Union might interfere was highly objectionable.

I have seen some of the letters that have emanated from American Civil Liberties Union's office about the Lattimore indictment. I don't like them.

Your present letter is a resumption of the kind of quibbling debate which ignores the fundamental legal and constitutional issues, and violates the fundamental civil liberties values that are concerned. I have no patience with your approach, and no time to devote to dealing with it.

If the American Civil Liberties Union management does not realize that the new indictment of Owen Lattimore is a fundamental assault upon civil liberties, it will certainly be beyond my capacity to demonstrate the point. Beyond this, the technical questions of law and the questions of legal procedure should, I suggest, he left to me, Abe Fortas, Paul Porter and our partners and associates—and to Senator O'Mahoney when he returns to participate as co-counsel in the case.

At your request, I send you under separate cover a copy of our Motion to Dismiss. I have no doubt that you will disagree with it as you did with the Motion to Dismiss the old indictment, but I have no intention this time to engage in a debate with you. The only thing I want is for the American Civil Liberties Union to stay out of this case.

*Sincerely*

---

## *To Earl Godwin*

Washington, D.C., Nov. 24, 1954

Dear Mr. Godwin:

I am one of your faithful listeners and admirers. May I take advantage of that status to suggest that your comments on the Lattimore case are not based upon full appreciation of the facts.

Never before in the history of the American judiciary has a judge been sworn off the bench because he wrote an opinion against the government. It has been recognized as contemptuous conduct when the Communist Party has tried to use this ground. But the Communist Party attorneys are by definition irresponsible. When the Attorney General of the United States certifies the good faith of an affidavit on this ground, he puts the ordinary judge in a difficult position. If he follows his opinion, the affidavit will be renewed. If he gets off the bench, the second judge is under pressure not to follow the opinion which is alleged to be the result of bias. Remember that the Attorney General initially determines whether a judge is to be promoted. How would you like to try a case before a judge under these circumstances? The Judge did the only thing he could do.[254]

If there had been a shadow of an excuse for the filing of the affidavit, the government should have appealed. Their failure to appeal shows that they do not actually believe they have a substantial question. This is true because I think that under Judge Youngdahl's former opinion he will necessarily have to dismiss the new indictment.

But the government did more than this. After deciding not to appeal, the United States Attorney reiterated the charges in the affidavit.

It seemed to be the impression that those who criticize the course of the Department of Justice are being soft on Communism. I can understand how you can get that impression from the press.

Lattimore has been charged with perjury in that he denied "following the Communist line." That is certainly a definite enough charge standing by itself because the phrase has been defined by the House Un-American Activities Committee and is generally understood to mean the shifting of an individual's opinion with certain shifts in Soviet policy listed by the House Un-American Activities Committee, such as the Hitler-Stalin Pact. But I wish you would note the new definition which the government is going to attempt to prove. I submit that as a rational man you will have to admit that this is an inquiry into opinion.

I enclose a copy of our Motion to Dismiss. I would appreciate your reading this.

This letter, of course, is not for quotation or publication.

*Sincerely*

---

## *To John P. Peters* [255]

Washington, D.C., Dec. 6, 1954

Dear Dr. Peters:

I am sorry for the delay in answering your letter of November 16.

I may have been over-anxious about the interview. However, your case hangs in a very delicate balance. Certiorari takes four votes. Jackson, who was with us before, had died and I thought that meant the end of our case. I doubt very much if Minton, Reed, Clark or Burton will change the views they had on the Bailey case. That means that we must have gotten Warren on our side to make up our four, i.e., Frankfurter, Black, Douglas and Warren. (Clark did not sit on the Bailey case but he prosecuted Bailey.) This means that winning the case depends on how the new Justice Harlan votes. They tell me he is a pretty good man. On the other hand, he will be indebted to Eisenhower and winning your case would make a big dent in Eisenhower's present loyalty program.

Well, anyway, that's the way it looks from here, as the great humanitarian philosopher Fulton Lewis puts it.

You might be interested to know that we have had numerous requests from various government agencies for copies of our petition for certiorari in your case.

Best regards.

*Sincerely*

---

## *To William M. Oman*[256]

Washington, D.C., Jan. 7, 1955

Dear Mr. Oman:

I am sorry to be so long reporting on Gerhart's[257] biography of Mr. Justice Jackson. Unfortunately several briefs came due at the time I expected to read it which delayed me.

First, as to the merits of the book. It is well written, it catches the spirit of Bob Jackson, it is easy to read. By all means it should be published.

Second, as to the book's demerits. Jackson was a great advocate; in fact, the greatest lawyer I have ever known. The book says so over and over again. But it does not in any way explain why he was a great advocate. It does not analyze his technique as a lawyer. In the chapter about Jackson as Solicitor General there is no adequate explanation of the character of his arguments or of the techniques he employed or of the results he achieved. If the author is not a lawyer this may be hard to do. But if there is adequate time to examine the briefs and arguments which Jackson made from the technical lawyer's point of view, the analysis of why he succeeded. as an advocate would make a much more complete picture of the man.

A more important defect or perhaps the principal defect in the book is the attempt to justify Jackson when he was plainly wrong. This occurs in the chapter on the Jackson-Black controversy. Here the writer abandons all pretense of impartiality and objectivity. He makes Black a creature of expediency whose political stock in trade was race hatred, until he went to the Court, at which time he shifted to a more human scheme. Nothing could be greater nonsense. He then argues that Jackson betrays no confidence because Black had previously betrayed a confidence. He uses a column of Doris Fleeson as circumstantial evidence of this. He shows that he knows nothing of the relations between Black and Crampton Harris. Nevertheless he insists that Black could not properly sit in the case. He accepts as true all Jackson's statements in his letter from Nuremberg. He quotes a revision of the statutes with respect to judicial disqualification as if it prohibited Black from sitting in a case where Harris was involved which it does not do.

The chapter is very bad indeed and should be entirely omitted in the interests of both the publisher and the author. Here we have a good book about a man of great qualities. It is not critical or objective but still it is very good. Then in the middle of the book we have a chapter which is extremely vulnerable. It is so controversial that all the reviewers, many of whom are Black's friends, will concentrate on that chapter. The good parts of the book will be ignored. The fact is that Jackson was a great man but a born scrapper. When he got into a fight he was always sincere but about as reliable as Harold Ickes under similar circumstances. I know enough about the facts to tell you that this chapter in its present form is dangerous to the reputation of the entire book. It will bring down tons of criticism. It will obscure everything else in the book. In my own opinion it is entirely inaccurate.

There are other less important incidents in the book which should be deleted. For instance, we are told that when Jackson took over the Attorney-Generalship he found the Department of Justice in a "mess." This again is nonsense. Murphy had his faults as an administrator but in some respects he was a stronger Attorney General than Jackson, particularly with respect to his willingness to enforce the antitrust laws. Jackson, an old NRA advocate, never really believed in them. But anyway, why build up Jackson at the expense of Murphy. They were both great figures of strikingly different qualities. What does it add to the book to bring down the wrath of the Murphy admirers, of whom I am one? Why not say something about Jackson the administrator, as he was a very good one indeed. Why not analyze the way he administered the Department. All the book does is to say Jackson was a great administrator and Murphy was a mess.

This is a single instance. The book, however, should be gone over carefully for other instances of this kind. It's a good book but I think it would be a better one with the corrections I suggest.

The manuscript is being returned to you by Railway Express.

*Sincerely*

---

## *To B.M. McKelway*

Washington, D.C., Feb. 4, 1955

Dear Mr. McKelway:

I appreciate your spending so much time answering my letter. Our difference seems to be a different set of values with respect to the First Amendment. Prior to the Lattimore case I would never have thought that almost anybody would have agreed that the sincerity of a man's appraisal of his own views—his opinion whether or not they were unduly sympathetic with Russia—could be the basis of a perjury charge. If they could there would be an end to opinion testimony. Hypocritical opinions are expressed at every hearing. Hypocritical speeches are made in every campaign, and few newspapers are able to avoid coloring their expressions of opinion to fit the financial situation in which the paper finds itself. Should they be asked whether they are sincere and put to a jury trial on this issue?

May I put it this way. If the First Amendment does not protect a man who gives an economic or political opinion from indictment on the ground that he was insincere the right of free speech is clearly in danger. For example, I was charged with bringing antitrust indictments for political purposes. I denied it under oath. Even if I had been insincere it would be far better to let it go than subject me to indictment. Take your own letter. Had you given it under oath, men who agreed with me that your observations about Judge Youngdahl were unreasonably critical would have convicted you for perjury if the prosecutor whipped them up into disliking you or distrusting you. And of course today in the present state of hysteria the hardest man to defend is one who has been accused of Communist sympathy. Juries have believed the ridiculous tales of professional perjurers like Matusow in this kind of a case.

And so when you say that Judge Youngdahl was on shaky ground in applying the First Amendment I am profoundly shocked. And the fact that the Court of Appeals who applied the First Amendment in the Rumely case did not apply it to Lattimore does not reassure me.

Again, when you criticized Judge Youngdahl for his condemnation of the United States Attorney in the affidavit of bias and prejudice I was also shocked. Never before has a responsible government official filed an affidavit which stated that the official written opinion of a judge can be used to show bias and prejudice. If such affidavits can be filed by the Department of Justice without reprimand the pressure on Federal judges would become unsupportable. I have a clipping service and have been reading the editorials commenting on Youngdahl's dismissal of the indictment. There are many like the *New York Daily News* with millions in circulation which was editorially demanded that Youngdahl get off the bench and take his seat with the defense. These pour into our office. Large numbers of people actually believe the United States Attorney is right and that Youngdahl's decision in favor of Lattimore is a dishonest one. In all conscience how can the *Star* support this kind of tactics on the part of the prosecution? Why should we be compelled to try a case with a judge under that kind of pressure? Why should not such tactics be reprimanded?

Well, anyway the *Star's* recommendation has been accepted and the Government has decided to appeal. The five years of persecution go on. The appeal probably will not be heard until next Fall. Lattimore, once a prosperous citizen consulting large corporations on Eastern affaris, making money out of his writings, is excluded from the Johns Hopkins campus. His capital is dwindling. His reputation is still good abroad. He has been invited to speak at an international conference in Rome. He probably can't get a passport. He has been offered a small position in Baltimore which might make him a living. They are unwilling to take him, however, until the criminal proceedings are ended. Meantime the struggle goes on to get funds to meet the costs of this litigation.

Fortunately he does not have to worry about attorney's fees. There aren't going to be any. And your paper has editorially stated that it is fitting and right that this continue another year.

Will you pardon me, therefore, if I express my disappointment and shock that the *Star* should have lent its support to keeping Lattimore on the grill and expressed the opinion that he should be forced to trial for the utter impertinent trivia which remain.

I know that you are an honest and sincere man. And the *Star* is unquestionably a great paper. That is why my disappointment is so keen.

*Sincerely*

# VIII

# ADVOCATE & AUTHOR

# 1955 – 1969

---

*To Warren P. Hill* [258]

Washington, D.C., March 29, 1955

Dear Professor Hill:

I have been so busy that this is the first opportunity I have had to comment on your article.[259] I am, as you may suspect, immensely pleased with it. In fact, it is the best article I have ever read on the subject. If you think I am biased because you have made me the subject of the article I can inform you that everyone else in the office, including those who worked on the Durham case, is most enthusiastic.

I have no quarrel with anything that you say in the article. Our chief difference appears to be on the practical consequences of the new rule. For example, you seem to think, though I am not at all sure of this, that there are certain practical consequences involved apart from public respect and deference to our trial procedure as a symbol. For example, you state in footnote 40 that "the probable effect of the new rule will be to increase the number of criminal defendants who are admitted under indefinite stay to the already overcrowded mental hospitals of the District."

My experience as a jury lawyer convinces me that the new rule will have no effect whatever in this respect. I predicted that Durham would be as quickly convicted under the new rule as he was under the old, which proved to be true. And I will give you any odds you ask that the Court of Appeals will not reverse the conviction in spite of the fact that the evidence as I view it shows an almost conclusive case. They would, I guess, have recourse to reasoning such as I used in the Fisher case. Durham, though unquestionably insane, is a menace to the community. Nothing could do more harm to the cause of those who advocate the new rule than to have him turned loose and commit some more crimes which he probably would do. It is unlikely that the Court of Appeals would put the rule to such a strain. (This of course is not the kind of an argument you advance in a law review article. It is, however, a practical consequence which means the new rule will not turn loose more criminals than the old.)

Indeed, I suspect that the new rule will make it *more difficult* to acquit, at least in cases of some emotional crimes, than the old one. I recall a cause celebre a few years ago in Washington where I.G. Miller, a prominent criminal lawyer with autographed photographs of the President and Cabinet members in his office (one of them was mine), caught his wife having an affair with a psychiatrist at St. Elizabeths. He waited until they came out of Woodward & Lothrop's and promptly shot the psychiatrist. He was acquitted under the right and wrong test on the theory that he was so emotionally disturbed during that brief period that he could not tell right from wrong. Nobody in Washington seemed to mind particularly. At least no hue and cry was raised about criminals getting loose on the right and wrong test. I point out it would have been much more difficult to have acquitted him under the new rule. A long line of emotional disturbances would have had to be produced and I doubt if there were any in his life. Though I am confident that a good psychiatrist properly enthused about the case could have produced some, still it would have been a tough assignment.

There was never any difficulty in getting psychiatrists under the old rule to testify for a fee. You suggest (top of page 385) that I seem to be saying that it might be socially disastrous to let the jury know that the criminal was not a breed apart. But under the old rule, as you will note from the Holloway and Fisher cases, all of the symptoms of the accused were given to the jury.

Bazelon owes the opportunity to write this decision to the attempt of Judge Holtzoff to make the old rule, which was very elastic indeed, into a hard and fast dogma to be strictly applied. Judge Bazelon took the offered opportunity and his decision may well be a landmark in the gradual change of our attitude towards crime. It is claimed that the new rule will permit a better class of psychiatrists to appear in court than those now willing to testify about right and wrong. This I doubt. Under our trial system no attorney for the defense is going to pay a psychiatrist fees for testifying unless he is going to be pretty positive and doctrinaire. Neither will the prosecution hire him unless they are equally positive on the other side. It is the law of supply and demand which will exclude the more objective men.

Your article shows that you realize that the criminal trial is a symbolic battle in which the state is protecting its citizens from their enemies and at the same time being just to them. Men simply cannot be objective if they take part in any public contest on which they must choose sides. Psychiatrists are no exception. I argued with my psychiatric friends about the denazification proceeding in Germany which violated every concept of due process. It was as bad as the worst Congressional investigation. Their instinctive reaction was that I must be some kind of a Nazi.

So long as the issue to be tried is whether defendant is to be *blamed* for his conduct and tried in a society which will not pay for the care of delinquents we are not going to get much difference in results. The great advance which the opinion will make lies in the fact that a priestlike tribunal has formally recognized mental disease as the controlling factor in an insanity case rather than sin.

You indicate that perhaps judges would be better than juries. In my view they would be much worse. The fantastic difference in treatment of criminals between one judge and another with respect to sentences is shocking. Judges are much more under pressure than juries because juries have comparative anonymity. They are fearful of criticism. Indeed there are very few like Bazelon. He was extremely fortunate in having an opportunity given by the trial court who tried to narrow the former loose and easy application of the right and wrong test. By making it too tough he made it impractical.

He was also fortunate in having two colleagues willing to embark on a course that might be criticized as judicial legislation. I was surprised at the lack of criticism although the *Washington Star* did go after him pretty hard. But in general the decision was accepted as sensible.

The practical effect of Bazelon's decision is to provide the escape which used to be provided by the phrase "irrestible impulse." This term was offensive both to those who wanted the criminal trial to represent the punishment of sin and those who wanted to apply the point of view of psychiatry. Psychiatrists cannot talk in such terms. They have the further disadvantage of making possible purely inflammatory appeals. The complicated words of psychiatry give a calmer and more rational appearance to a trial.

You may well ask since I am so enthusiastic about Bazelon's opinion why I did not write one to the same effect. The reason was, as you make clear from your article, that I thought that the right and wrong test was more necessary to a public sense of justice than it appears to be now.

My opinion at least had the advantage of arousing the psychiatrists. They liked parts of it, they hated the conclusion. I have appeared at least six times before groups of psychiatrists and once before the national convention in Atlantic City to explain my opinion. The more they talked the more determined they were to obtain a more dignified place in criminal procedure than was possible under my analysis. I, therefore, should be credited with an assist to Bazelon and am flattered that he used parts of the opinion which were acceptable to psychiatry as a stepping-stone to his radical and, I think, proper change.

The problem will never be solved until the sentencing power now exercised by federal judges with a shocking inconsistency is transferred to a competent board not operating under the glare of publicity. That time is a long way off but it will come sooner because of the opinion in the Durham case.

*Sincerely*

P.S. On re-reading this letter I am somewhat doubtful about the precise applicability of the Miller case. I am not taking the time to look it up but I think that Miller did not plead insanity. However, the result would have been the same and even more certain had a psychiatrist testified that Miller was so disturbed at the time he did not know right from wrong.

---

## *To Eugene Davidson*

Washington, D.C., March 31, 1955

Dear Gene:

Thanks for your letter. *Symbols* is suggested reading in quite a number of colleges. Apparently the only trouble with this is that the little bastards don't seem to want to buy it. They take it out of the libraries instead. Can't you do something about it?

You will find an entire article on *Symbols* in the *University of Chicago Law Review*, Volume 22, No. 2, Winter 1955, under the title of "The Psychological Realism of Thurman Arnold." If you were an enterprising press you would all get off your fannies and sell a lot of books by using this article. If the sales don't go up soon I am going to hire an attorney and sue you.

You ask me who is going to be the next dean of the Law School. I can tell you quite confidentially that Griswold has been calling me frequently over the telephone. His position is that unless I accept the deanship the law school will go to pot. I keep telling him No but it doesn't seem to do any good. He called me last night at ten P.M. and I refused. He called again at three in the morning, saying that he couldn't sleep thinking about what would happen to the law school if I continued my adamant position and he hoped I would not mind his waking me up to reconsider. I have my two young grandchildren with me. The phone waked them up and they started crying. Frances is not feeling her best and she couldn't get to sleep the rest of the night.

Of course I am flattered by these calls, still there is a limit. Can you think of some tactful way to convey to him that I prefer to be called while I am at my office. I realize the urgency of the situation and the need of the Yale Law School. Nevertheless, I must get some privacy, so ask him to confine his calls to office hours.

Please keep this entirely confidential because the Faculty would be very much upset if they thought there was any chance of my becoming the Dean. If I accept Griswold's offer it should be released with a bang and not with a whimper!

*Affectionately*

---

## *To Alexander T. Schenck*[260]

Washington, D.C., May 24, 1955

Dear Alex:

Thanks for sending me "The Case of John Peters: Test of Security Program." The thing makes me mad because it is not a correct statement of the facts. It omits to say that Dr. Peters was on the identical evidence acquitted twice. It states: "What Dr. Peters told the Loyalty Review Board in reply to the charges against him cannot be learned, since only he can make public the transcript of the hearing, and he has not chosen to do so." As the record shows, on behalf of Dr. Peters we offered the transcript for public record in the Supreme Court. The Supreme Court after a brief consultation declined to accept it saying it was not necessary. Under these circumstances we thought it quite inappropriate to publish it.

It is apparent from the article that the Department of Justice has shown the record to the representative of the magazine. It contains everything in the record except Dr. Peters' explanation which was in effect that he was not aware at the time that these organizations were Communist dominated. It would have been utterly impossible for any reporter to have collected these organizations without access to the record. It's like the Yalta papers. The Attorney General is leaking the record to anyone who will agree not to tell that he saw it. Had the reporter really studied the case he would have discovered as part of the public record the fact that Peters offered the record to the Supreme Court.

With best personal regards,

*Sincerely*

---

## *To Norman V. Donaldson*

Washington, D.C., Dec. 5, 1955

Dear Norman:

I am delighted that *Symbols* is going to be translated into Japanese but I wish to protest against the tone of your letter. You seem to infer that the book will not have great sales in Japan. This means one of two things—(a) that you do not have confidence in the intelligence of the Japanese people, or (b) that you do not have confidence in my book!

If the first assumption is correct it is an insult to a nation with which we are trying to have friendly relations and to save from Communism. The repercussions if your letter becomes known to the Japanese government will unquestionably be serious and you will have done a great disservice to our foreign policy.

If the second assumption is correct you certainly are not in the frame of mind which will enable you to promote my Japanese sales. There are over 80 million people in Japan. Assume half of them buy the book; that will be 40 million copies which is more of any book than you have ever sold in the history of the Press. But let's be conservative and assume that sales fall down to 10%. That amounts to 8 million copies which most publishers would be delighted with.

I suggest that you make immediate efforts to put the book in the hands of the Geisha girls so that they can read it to their patrons. That's the way you get things started in Japan. They are very intelligent girls, they have great influence. (I know this only from reading books.) Once you get them started the sales will go up like wildfire.

I suggest that you finance a trip for me to Japan this spring and I will personally see to it that the first copies go to the prettiest girls. If you're not willing to engage in this promotion you will force me to sue you for gross neglect of the terms and spirit of our publishing contract.

If you want to go over with me as an assistant I would be delighted. Under my guidance you will find it a most interesting experience!

With kind regards,

*Sincerely*

---

## *To Joseph J. Daniels*[261]

Washington, D.C., April 27, 1956

Dear Joe:

As I have degrees from Yale, Harvard, and Princeton, and also one from Wyoming, you can imagine how many letters I get such as the one you last wrote me. However, old age is approaching and I am struggling to get into a position—against the income tax—where my wife will not have to scrub floors. When I got off the Bench I was in debt.

Nevertheless, with utter disregard to the future security of my loved ones, I enclose a check for $100 which you may credit to the Fund provided by the time you have finished reading this letter you do not feel so sorry for me that you will refuse to take anything.

With kind personal regards and hoping to see you soon,

*Sincerely*

---

*To Frank C. Waldrop*[262]

Washington, D.C., Oct. 30, 1957

Dear Frank:

It was good to hear from you again, but at the same time quite a surprise. I never had any idea you read *The Progressive* since I don't happen to take it myself.

I had a hard time with Rodell's review.[263] He is a close friend of mine and is really a most interesting person. I like him because he irritates people like Felix Frankfurter which I believe is a virtue sufficient to overcome his other faults.

I tried to get out of writing the review but couldn't without offending him. I agree with you that his thesis is nonsense but the book at the time did start a lot of people thinking.

May I ask why you get in such a stew because people in general can't get along without a sharply defined philosophy of government and fall in love with ritual, etc. That's been true for some twenty-five thousand years and it's hard for me to see how organized society can be held together without it. When we get in the state where we don't have to fight over ritual we'll eat without tablecloths and use our fingers instead of silverware. The fact which you do not seem to realize is that the most important social values in the world are the things that make no sense.

As for F.D.R., why don't you read Schlesinger's latest book. It's excellent and if you go over it carefully it may clear up your present state of utter confusion. In the meantime, if you want to improve your mind without the expenditure of any capital, read the reprint of a very great article on Jerome Frank which I enclose. Don't throw it away because it will be only a short time that the demand for it will be so great that it will be a collector's item.

I note that you do not say anthing about integration. That would seem to indicate that you have not yet become a true Southerner. Referring to this subject, I was talking to my friend Charles Pickett, the great-nephew of Pickett's Charge. I told him that I was completely in accord with Governor Byrd's plan to deny funds to any school which was integrated under a court order. I told him, however, that in my opinion it did not go far enough. He said, "Well I'm glad that at least you're coming to your senses." "Yes," I said, "I have concluded that any funds spent on the education of Virginians are a waste of the taxpayers' money. It has been conclusively demonstrated that education does Virginians no good. So, I think all the schools should be closed, not just the integrated ones." The more I think of this the sounder idea it seems to be.

With best regards and affectionate greetings from Frances to you and your family, I remain

*Sincerely*

---

## *To Arthur Krock*

Washington, D.C., Feb. 27, 1958

Dear Arthur:

Thank you for your letter.[264] My comment on George Lodge's letter is as follows:

Labor unions are the only organizations which are exempt from the antitrust laws. Even railroads are liable in spite of the Interstate Commerce Commission. Farm cooperatives are liable in spite of their power to control the supply and fix prices. Labor is the only type of organization which has achieved complete exemption.

Of course, like farm cooperatives labor must be exempt to the extent of fixing the price of labor if it can be collective action. But where the concerted action of labor unions goes beyond collective bargaining for wages, hours, better conditions of work, etc., there is absolutely no excuse for not making them fully liable under the Sherman Act.

The exemption of labor has actually worked to the detriment of unions like Walter Reuther's and to the enhancement of power of unions like the Teamsters. The Teamsters union is the fastest growing union in the United States. They get their power by their control of transportation. They can hot-cargo any employer. They use this power of hot cargo to expand their organizational power.

Under the Taft-Hartley Act, to refuse to deliver goods to any business concern with whom the Teamsters do not have a direct relationship of employer and employee is an unfair labor practice. But in actual operation this is meaningless. The only way of enforcing the unfair labor practice is through the National Labor Relations Board. That Board has been so sympathetically inclined to labor that the cases where it will ask for an injunction are very rare indeed. Hence the Teamsters are able to use the secondary boycott with impunity.

But even if we had a labor board willing and anxious to stamp out the abuse of the secondary boycott, they couldn't possibly police the entire United States. Congress would never appropriate that amount of money. The best and most continuous type of enforcement of the antitrust laws is, of course, the private suit for injunction or damages. As the law is at present, the private individual can find himself cut off from supplies by the Teamsters and he can do nothing about it.

It is true, of course, that the Act does allow a suit for damages but he would be out of business before such a suit pursued its weary way through the trial and appellate courts. So, there are practically no suits for damages against unions for secondary boycott.

The Supreme Court of the United States has added to the difficulties by holding that when the Taft-Hartley Act was passed it vested in the Labor Relations Board complete jurisdiction over all illegal practices of unions. The case of *Gus* v. *Utah* shows the extreme to which that doctrine has gone. In that case a small manufacturer with a business of about $100,000 a year was the victim of an illegal secondary boycott. He appealed to the National Labor Relations Board. The National Labor Relations Board answered that they would not intervene and ask for an injunction because the interstate commerce involved was not sufficient, although there was some. Whereupon, the employer sought and obtained an injunction from the Labor Board of the State of Utah. The Supreme Court reversed on the ground that the entire jurisdiction was in the Labor Board and the State of Utah was excluded from giving the employer relief. It was pointed out to the Court that the employer was in a bad situation. His business was being destroyed by an illegal act and all rights to protect it were taken away. The Supreme Court said in effect that that was too bad, it was the intent of Congress to strip him of his property by denying him legal protection.

How your friend George Lodge can defend this practice I do not know. His letter is a bunch of generalities. He wants to regulate instead of leaving the matter to the courts where it belongs. It is a typical example of regulation-minded government officials and these people are just as wrong-headed whether they are in the New Deal or in the Eisenhower Administration.

We recently took a case up to the Supreme Court of the United States from Tennessee. There, two businesses were involved and they were in the same building. The employees in one business struck. The Teamsters threw up a picket line which of course was a secondary boycott and illegal, thereby depriving both concerns of supplies.

Both manufacturers sought an injunction against the common carrier, a trucking company, under state law for not delivering goods. The common carrier answered that it couldn't deliver goods because of their employees' refusal. Thereupon the court enjoined the Teamsters Union from interfering with its order against the common carrier. Some of the Teamsters were fined for interference with the court order. This was affirmed by the Supreme Court of Tennessee. The Supreme Court of the United States granted certiorari and reversed the Supreme Court of Tennessee.

Curiously enough, these secondary boycotts do nobody any good except the Teamsters. Reuther couldn't effectively use a secondary boycott.

The responsibility for the power of Hoffa and Beck is directly on people who think like your friend Lodge.

If you will look back in the *Reader's Digest*[265] you will find two articles on how I think the antitrust laws should be applied to labor. I think they were in the year 1943.

With best regards, in which Frances joins,

*Sincerely*

---

## *To David L. Bazelon*[266]

Washington, D.C., Dec. 8, 1958

Dear Dave:

I was very much interested in your opinion in the case of *Drivers, Chauffeurs and Helpers Local Union No. 639, International Brotherhood of Teamsters, Chauffeurs, Warehousemen and Helpers of America* v. *National Labor Relations Board.* I thought that you in turn might be interested in the impact of your decision on an actual case, particularly since your opinion states that the issue "presents implications of serious and far reaching consequences."

Before your decision I was consulted by a small manufacturer in a midwest city. The Teamsters, under the claim that they wanted to organize his clerical help, had thrown a picket line around his plant and threatened to hot cargo his shipments. The NLRB informed him that there wasn't enough interstate commerce involved to justify their seeking an injunction—though the Board did appear to believe at that time that they had the power to do so.

The clerical force, no doubt misled by misrepresentations of the McClellan Committee, refused to join the Teamsters. Worse than that, like white collar workers generally, they did not want to join any union. My client solved the problem and got rid of the picket line by paying dues to the Teamsters out of his own pocket for his unorganized workers.

I told him that such payments to a labor leader might be construed as a violation of the Taft-Hartley Act. He replied "What the hell am I supposed to do—go out of business?" According to my present information he is still making these payments. Such disrespect for law I find most shocking, but it is unfortunately a characteristic of small business men when caught in this kind of a jam.

The obvious solution is to get rid of these small business men, and the Teamsters are a more effective instrument for that purpose that any other union because of their power over transportation. These small businesses are difficult to organize because they establish personal relationships with their employees who do not want to accept union discipline. Furthermore small businesses, unable to pass on a wage increase through administered prices, are apt to fight wage increases, particularly when they are going broke. All in all, they are a thorn in the side of the labor movement which should be removed.

Your opinion, while it does not completely solve the small business v. labor problem, is at least a step in the right direction. My client now knows that if he stops paying dues on behalf of his unorganized employees, there is no use going to the Labor Board and asking for an injunction against the picket line that will immediately follow his refusal to contribute. Your opinion will go a long way in teaching him the facts of life.

With these considerations in mind it is difficult for me to understand the basis for the dissent of my friend Judge Miller. I hate to say it, but he must be an old labor-baiter at heart.

*Sincerely*

---

## *To David Ginsburg* [267]

Washington, D.C., April 24, 1959

Dear Dave:

Enclosed find a copy of my speech at Bill's [Douglas] party. The first part of it is accurate and the last part of it is the best I can remember, since I had no notes except for the first part.

With kind personal regards,

*Sincerely*

Two score years and seven hours ago (give or take an hour) our guest of honor Mr. Justice William O. Douglas took his seat on the Supreme Court of the United States. We are here tonight in solemn conclave assembled to commemorate that historic occasion.

I was present and the scene is etched in the tablet of my memory. The Crier of the Supreme Court was obviously harrassed and disturbed. I remember him saying immediately after Justice Douglas took his seat "God save the United States and this honorable Court."

He had been saying the same thing long before the appointment of Justice Douglas but in those early days it was only part of a routine. When Justice Douglas took his seat, the Crier for the first time seemed to realize the tremendous difficulty of the task which he was imposing on divine Providence. There were anxiety and supplication in his voice when he petitioned that both the Court with Mr. Justice Douglas on it and the

Nation be saved at the same time. He was conscious of the drastic character of the equitable relief contained in that prayer.

But he was a man of courage. He did not amend his petition in the light of the newly discovered evidence that Bill had become a member of the Court. A lesser man would have modified his prayer to make the relief demanded appear more reasonable. He would have said "In the event that both of the following objectives seem impossible of accomplishment in the light of our new appointment, God save the United States *or* this honorable Court," thus giving Providence its choice.

But the Crier did not waiver. He did not compromise. He did not surrender to any policy of appeasement. He decided to go for broke asking divine Providence to save both the Court and the Nation simultaneously.

Now twenty years have passed and have demonstrated the wisdom of the Crier's courageous decision. I am happy to report to you this evening that the Ship of State though buffetted and tossed by storms is still sailing proudly on, and the Supreme Court, though slightly sea-sick is still huddled in her prow, their faces set like flints Zionward and their black robes flapping in the gale.

It is strange how little incidents like this may alter the fate of nations.

Now that twenty years have passed I think it most appropriate to review the issues paramount in the troubled times when Justice Douglas accepted his appointment. It is doubly important because such a review will show the kind of problems which Justice Douglas must have known he would have to face if he decided to go on the Court. I have therefore taken the trouble, in preparing this address, to have a thorough and exhaustive research made in *Time* Magazine of the problems facing the nation twenty years ago. Time will not permit me to give a complete picture, but the following illustrations will be sufficient to show the outlines of the picture.

In the same month that Justice Douglas took his seat Tommy Manville married his fifth wife. And even more significant, it was in that very month that *Time* reported the story of a man in New York who stepped out of a bathtub, reached for his towel, stepped on a bar of soap, skidded through the kitchen, crashed through the kitchen window and to the street five floors below. This sounds even more improbable than the appointment of Justice Douglas sounded to the venerable leaders of the New York bar but it must be true or it wouldn't be in *Time*.

Again, it was in the month of the Douglas appointment when the Secretary of the United States Brewers Association predicted that prohibition would be back again by 2247 A.D. All this appears in that fountain of truth and objective reporting known as *Time* magazine.

Nor is this all. *Time* reports that during that same month an undercover FBI man and also an agent of the Post Office Department was delegated the important task of investigating harlotry and white slavery. After extensive research he recommended the restoration of red light districts. And strange to say, the Post Office Department repudiated his entire report and refused to follow his recommendation. In the light of experience of twenty years, you may conclude that the Post Office Department was blind and short-sighted. But such was the climate of opinion of those troubled times of twenty years ago.

It was in the same month, according to *Time* Magazine, that Senator Ellender's sub-committee began an investigation of why pretty girls in the civil service got promotions faster than homely girls. Simultaneously with Senator Ellender's investigation, though not necessarily connected with it, was England's promise to support Poland against Germany.

No doubt as a result of these and other disturbing events, *Time* Magazine reported that students had started to eat goldfish at Harvard in the very month of Bill's appointment. The habit spread to other colleges. At the week's end, a Northwestern man had eater 36 at one sitting. An M.I.T. man ate 42. Clark University set the week's record when a student ate 89 live goldfish.

Rising to this public emergency a Senator in the Massachusetts' state legislature introduced a bill to "preserve the fish from cruel and wanton consumption." The president of the Boston Animal Rescue League was sufficiently alive and responsive to the duties of that high office that he threatened to send agents to arrest the students who were eating the goldfish. And finally, the U.S. Public Health Service warned the students about the tapeworms which were probably in the goldfish which they ate.

Nor is this all. During the very month when our guest of honor took his seat on the Court, Carol Lombard was invited to a Hollywood party and asked to come in something white. She arrived at the party in a white ambulance, lying on a white stretcher, carried by three attendants dressed in white. *Time* reports that she danced all night with Clark Gable. Later Carol sent Gable the ambulance with red hearts painted on its white exterior. Gable reciprocated by sending her a fire engine. As a result of all this, they promptly got married.

And finally, it is most significant to record that during the year of Mr. Justice Douglas' appointment, the Washington baseball team failed to win the pennant.

I do not suggest that this is a complete picture of the times twenty years ago when Mr. Justice Douglas took office. There were no doubt other things happening at the same time, though I have forgotten exactly what they were. I have simply tried to give you a sample of the more significant events which bear most directly on the kind of perplexing problems which Justice Douglas knew he must face and solve if he decided to go on the Court. Justice Douglas did not falter. He did not hesitate.

He knew that if he went on the Court, he would be on the horns of a long dilemma that had no turning. Nevertheless, he crossed the Rubicon, cut the Gordian Knot, he burned his dams behind him. And all the events which have followed during the past twenty years are now water over the bridge.

Perhaps after all these years it is now safe to disclose the hitherto untold story of how Justice Douglas came to be selected for his high post. It happened in this way. Shortly before his appointment, Madrid had fallen and Franco was established as dictator in Spain. This event alarmed prominent leaders in the South. They reasoned that if Franco could become dictator in Spain, Bill Douglas might become dictator in the United States. They forgot that a dictatorship in America is impossible because not enough competent stenographers can be found in this country who can take dictation. But they reasoned rightly that if Bill ever *did* become dictator, he would enforce segregation on the solid South by force and arms. They figured, and events have proved them right, that while it is impossible to massively resist a dictator, massive resistance to a Supreme Court opinion is a lot of fun and can safely be carried on for years. It was on this theory that the appointment of Bill Douglas to the Court was urged and approved by the entire Southern bloc. Now that massive resistance has become an accomplished fact in the South, everybody is having a wonderful time, except perhaps Lyndon Johnson, and the wisdom of the Southern selection of Bill Douglas as Justice of the Supreme Court has been confirmed.

So much for the thrilling story of how Justice Douglas got on the Supreme Court of the United States. Before I close I would like to give a brief sketch of his earlier life and time.

I first met Bill when I was appointed on the Yale Law Faculty in 1930. He was then engaged in research for the Committee on Law Observance and Enforcement, commonly called the Wickersham Committee. The principal objective of that Committee was the study of the prohibition laws, but Bill was not considered a safe man to report on the moral problem involved in that noble experiment. Instead, he was delegated the task of collecting judicial statistics which were supposed to reveal how the courts were working. I worked under him in that endeavor. We counted divorce cases; we counted demurrers; we counted pleas in abatements and motions to quash. We counted everything that was capable of being counted in and about the courtrooms under observation. By dint of our industry and the consumption of midnight oil and pre-war beverages, we got hundreds of thousands of figures. These figures were transferred to cards which could be run through computing machines which would sort them out and tell us how many there was of anything that we wanted to know how many there was of. Then we proceeded to write our report. The only trouble was that we never could think of any intelligible thing to say about the figures or what to do with them. They are still around somewhere, probably in the Government archives waiting for someone who can think of a purpose to which they can be put.

However, I am convinced that this devoted effort on Bill's part laid the foundation for nearly all of the vast programs of economic and social research that are going on today. To our guest of honor, we owe the existence of that tremendous body of unintelligible and unreadable literature, the collection of which is contributing so much to the problem of unemployment.

Bill was a prodigious worker in those early days before he became a world traveler. But when he took time off, as he occasionally did, he could only find happiness in doing good for someone else. He was a pure philanthropist. He was always trying to make his friends happy and contented. I will give you a couple of examples of that unselfish kind of endeavor.

I had been in San Francisco on some intellectual mission or other, and had been fortunate enough to have been entertained at several large parties. About a week afterwards, I found in my mail box a note signed by a girl, whose last name I forget but I do remember her first name was Yvonne. She told me that she had met me at a party in San Francisco and admired me extravagantly. She thought I was one of the coming leaders in the intellectual world. She was bold enough to suggest that it would be a tremendous privilege if I would call up a number which she gave and arrange to have cocktails with her.

Of course I hesitated, being a man with strict regard for the proprieties. But I thought this would be unfair to the little girl. It would seem aloof and unresponsive and priggish. I therefore called the number she gave. I asked for Yvonne; the voice on the other end said "Who?" and I said "Yvonne," giving her last name. He said "What the hell are you talking about; this is the morgue."

I recall again that I was making a speech at one of the Yale Colleges. On the same evening my colleague, Wesley A. Sturges, was making a speech before the Bridgeport Bar Association. Just before I got up to speak a telegram was delivered to me. It said "Please mention me in your speech tonight if you can possibly do so. Signed Wesley A. Sturges." I was puzzled but I did mention Wesley's name, dragging him in by the heels somehow or other. The next day I went to Wesley's office with the telegram in my hand and said "I mentioned your name, Wes, but what the hell were you up to." He looked at me queerly and reached in a drawer and handed me a telegram to him which read as follows: "Dear

Wes I would appreciate it very much if you would mention my name in your speech before the Bridgeport Bar Association tonight. Signed Thurman Arnold."

That was Bill for you—always trying to do something for somebody regardless of his own inconvenience and his busy life. And he was modest about it too; he would never claim credit for any of these generous efforts to do something for his friends.

Bill, your friends are gathered from over the nation, partly because of their admiration for you but more than that because of their affection, at a party which I hope is a surprise. I have done the best I can with these prefatory remarks, inadequate as they are, to portray your real character. And now I am going to call on Senator Lyndon Johnson, a great Senator and perhaps the next President of the United States. If he can succeed in pulling this party out of the mud under these trying circumstances, and after this inadequate foreword, his nomination will be assured.

---

## *To Oliver Jensen*[268]

Washington, D.C., June 10, 1959

Dear Mr. Jensen:

I have read your letter and agree to your principal suggestions.[269] Certainly the introduction can be stepped up and the final paragraph should be the flight of the antitrust laws to Europe, and the new sort of competitive economy which is being built up in the Coal and Steel Community and the common market. For example, we are in an era of mergers and consolidations and the antitrust laws are not being enforced, partly due to an indifferent Department of Justice and partly due to the fact that the Court with the appointment of Potter Stewart has gone conservative. Warren no longer has his five members, as is evidenced from the recent Baremblatt case. However, in Europe the Coal and Steel Authority has enacted the Sherman Act.

One section of the treaty on coal and steel forbids any agreement of concerted practices to prevent the normal operation of competition, and in particular agreements or concerted practices are forbidden which fix or determine prices, restrict and control production and allocate markets. This is pretty much our Sherman Act.

With respect to mergers and consolidations the Coal and Steel Community goes beyond the Sherman Act and requires that no merger be permitted unless it is authorized in advance. A substantial body of jurisprudence is building up in the common market and in the Coal and Steel Community which appears to be, for the present at least, stricter in its competitive standards than our present antitrust policy. The interesting thing is that all of these decartelization agreements were drawn up by Americans and forced on the puzzled Europeans. Now they have gotten to like them and they are growing in strength and popularity. I would like to close on that note with the ironic contrast between the common market in Europe and the steadily growing concentration of economic power in the United States. The impact of the antitrust formula imposed by the decartelization about eight years ago has been terrific in its effect upon the present common market organizations in Europe. This is what I want to close with.

You say that I should mention my own prosecutions. Unless I can have an entire paragraph I could not explain the somewhat novel policy which I imposed upon the Department of Justice and which has not been followed subsequently. If you give me a paragraph I can do that. With respect to your minor criticisms. Unquestionably most of the holding companies were in violation of the Sherman Act as construed by Teddy Roosevelt and his five-man majority on the Supreme Court. In the period prior to the depression, however, no one paid any attention to the Act. Few prosecutions were brought. The holding company device grew to such gigantic proportions that a special act had to be passed and the Securities and Exchange Commission organized in order to deal with the problem. It would have taken fifty years of litigation to have dissolved these holding companies through the operation of the Sherman Act itself. The holding company legislation is, however, firmly based upon the Sherman Act. Of course not all holding companies are illegal, only those which substantially lessen competition.

With respect to your suggestion that it is not the concentration in steel but the rise in labor costs that is driving up steel prices: this argument made by the steel companies is nonsense. Careful studies have shown that from the Korean war to the recession steel profits were increasing at a far greater rate than wages were going up, and that was true at the time of the last rise in steel prices.

On a full production basis American labor costs in concentrated industries are probably the lowest in the world, although the steel figures are based upon the productivity of labor at the break-even point which is about 50% capacity. There have been many studies on this but I do not see how I can go into such a complicated picture. However, I can supply you with the information to answer letters which put forward this argument.

I am leaving for Europe for a month. May I suggest that you shorten the article all you can and then tell me how much space is left for my new beginning and new end. I will take it up immediately when I return.

*Sincerely*

---

*To John Cowles*[270]

Washington, D.C., Nov. 9, 1959

Dear John:

It is difficult to make an adequate response to your letter of October 27 about the turkeys. As I recall it, you first started sending me a turkey in 1940, which my accountant tells me is 19 years ago. At 20 pounds per turkey this amounts to nearly 400 pounds. At $1 a pound, which is a low figure for these wonderful birds, I am in your debt for $400.

In advertising value, which consists of being able to tell my friends who are not on your list that I am eating one of your turkeys, thus associating me with reflected glory and giving me a link to your great enterprises, I would say that the sum of $5,000 would be a low appraisal.

My accountant tells me that in the light of these figures and on the basis of life expectancy I can now deduct about $7,500 this year as a capital loss, which is an added bonus. If a value could be put on my appreciation of your thoughtfulness and deducted, I would not have any income tax to pay at all.

With appreciation and best regards,

*Sincerely*

---

*To A. James Casner*[271]

Washington, D.C., Nov. 9, 1959

Dear Mr. Casner:

Answering your communication about the most valuable and least valuable aspects of my experience in the Harvard Law School, I would say that it all depended upon the personality of the teacher rather than the subject matter, and I do not see how legal education can be evaluated in any other terms.

So far as recent graduates are concerned we have representatives of a number of law schools, all of them excellent. In my practice I have never been able to detect the difference between an able man trained at Harvard and an able man trained at any other school of good standing.[272]

*Sincerely*

---

## *To J.D. Hyman*[273]

Washington, D.C., April 21, 1960

Dear Dean Hyman:

Thank you for your letter of April 19, and being a born pedagogue I would be flattered to have my article used in your class. It will be published in May but in the meantime I send you four copies of the mimeographed sets. There are some corrections and tightening up of phraseology in the printed article but nothing substantial enough to make any real difference to the reader.

In the light of your interest in Hart's article[274] I also enclose an article which Justice Douglas has written which, I believe, destroys the myth that the Court is overworked.[275] I see a good deal of the Justices and the fact is that, compared with my own practice, they lead comparatively leisurely lives. As Bill points out, they are not doing as much work as they did in 1945. Nothing is more deceiving than statistical proof that you are overworked, as Mr. Parkinson has so ably demonstrated. Indeed, my former colleague and friend, Judge Stephens, proved by statistics that my own court was overworked and increased it to nine. He got up the figures and believed them in spite of the fact that my own experience with the Court of Appeals was that it was too leisurely a job to be a satisfactory career.

With best regards and hoping you will drop in to see me if you ever get to Washington,

*Sincerely*

---

## *To Eustace Seligman*[276]

Washington, D.C., May 27, 1960

Dear Mr. Seligman:

Your letter about my article is most interesting and you make your point entirely clear. It is based upon the premise that in a case involving the review of an unfair trial where a state court rested its decision on a state procedural ground, the Supreme Court has no right to look at the entire record and conclude that the state court did not mean what it said. If one accepts this premise, the conclusion follows that the majority opinion in *Irvin* v. *Dowd* is indefensible.

I proceed from a different premise. I interpret the Constitution to mean that if a state court condemns a man to death without a fair trial, it is the plain duty of a Federal court to reverse the conviction regardless of what ground the state court chose to rest it on. If this premise is to be accepted, some former decisions of the Supreme Court on this issue are wrong in principle. One who accepted this premise would approve of the majority decision in *Irvin* v. *Dowd* as a step in the right direction. The net effect of *Irvin* v. *Dowd* is to declare that where the state ground is palpably flimsy (as I think it was in *Irvin* v. *Dowd)* the Supreme Court is entitled to come to the conclusion that it was not the real ground of the state decision. This seems to me sensible, even though it may be a departure from precedent.

However, in spite of our differences as to the proper judicial method of getting Mr. Dowd a fair trial, I would not consider them an indication that the firm of Sullivan and Cromwell was lacking in professional skill. The reason I wrote the article was because I thought that Professor Hart had done a great deal of unintentional harm in encouraging extremist attacks upon the Court by his generalizations about the competence of its members.

*Sincerely yours*

---

*To Sergius M. Boikan* [277]

Washington, D.C., June 22, 1960

Dear Mr. Boikan:

Your letter of June 16 is most interesting and it is quite clear that you understand thoroughly the point of view which I tried to advance in my book, my articles and teaching. Senator Taft, who was a good friend of mine and a trustee at Yale, used to tell me that he thought it was a good thing to have one fellow like myself on the Yale Law Faculty but he certainly wouldn't want many more of them. There is some truth in what he said. The paradox is that I doubt if any law school as an institution can ever maintain an objective point of view as to the law. It would be like asking the Catholic Church to write an objective history of Catholicism.

Therefore, law schools all over the world gravitate into theology. The realistic law schools build up a theology of their own. If you read Professor McDougal[278] of Yale, who writes frequently, you will see this process. He was a student of mine and was a convert to my point of view. Now he is caught in the throes of a new jurisprudence which I am unable to understand. My own way of expressing the paradox is to say that if people generally agreed with what I said, nothing I said would be any longer true.

You may be interested in the enclosed reply I got from Mr. Justice Brennan to whom I sent your letter.

With best regards and hoping that when you come to Washington you will drop in to see me, I remain

*Sincerely*

---

## *To John R. Glenn*[279]

Washington, D.C., June 22, 1960

Dear Mr. Glenn:

Thank you for your letter of June 15. It was a real pleasure to read such an enthusiastic though undeserved tribute, and it is gratifying to know that something one has written has stimulated someone else to think along the same lines.

My anthropological point of view may be useful in understanding human institutions. It will never, however, be an inspirational force. In the concluding chapter of *The Symbols of Government* I express the opinion that the psychiatric viewpoint I have adopted might in the future make society more realistic, practical and humanitarian. Years have passed and I now find the point of view expressed in my book adopted by Madison Avenue. They recognize that people are motivated by symbols and can be manipulated by them. Having reached this position Madison Avenue thinks it knows how to lead people not only on the advertising front but on the political front. They are successful in inducing businessmen to pay large sums of money to create the proper "image" in the public mind. So far as public influence is concerned, however, Madison Avenue is an absolute failure. Their objective philosophy is too completely materialistic.

The paradox was best expressed by my friend Harry Sullivan whom I invited to give a course of lectures at Yale to a seminar group. He spent three lectures, full of apt illustrations, convincing the students that they should become adult and rise above their infantilisms. He described the necessary process of adjustment. At the end of the last lecture he paused and said, "Now, young gentlemen, when you have lost your desire for adventure, when you have forgotten romance, when the only things worthwhile to you are prestige and income, then you have grown up, then you have become an adult." The students left the lecture in utter confusion, but I know of no better way of expressing the reason why it is impossible for any society to become truly objective.

I have read your very able article in the *Indiana Law Journal*[280] and have given it to Mr. Fortas. It is a superb analysis and one of the most interesting that I have ever read.

With best regards and hoping that you will drop in to see me if you ever come to Washington,

*Sincerely*

---

## *To Fred H. Blume*

Washington, D.C., Sept. 27, 1960

Dear Fred:

Thank you for your letter. I appreciate it very much indeed. I can't tell you how much I enjoyed coming back to Wyoming.[281] I knew a lot of people, like yourself; a lot more people knew my father and the younger crowd all knew my brother, so it was a heart warming experience.

Further than that, I enjoyed coming into contact with lawyers who represent individual clients with personal law suits. That is what I miss in my present practice which makes it seem a business rather than a profession. Because of this, it seemed to me that the Wyoming lawyers were so much more human, so much more a part of their communities, that it was more pleasant to visit with them than with the stuffed shirts at an American Bar Association convention. The trouble with the corporate bar is that business-getting rather than legal ability is the touchstone of success. They practice under dead men's names to get the benefit of the going concern value of their organization which does not seem to me to fit the real traditions of law. For instance, in the largest firms in New York there is usually not a single lawyer in the firm's name who is alive. In Cravath, Swaine & Moore there is no Cravath, no Swaine, no Moore. In Sullivan & Cromwell there is no Sullivan or Cromwell. Nobody ever heard of Colonel Hartfield, and yet he is the senior partner in White & Case. He never argues a case in court; he couldn't write a brief if he tried; yet I suppose he has one of the largest incomes of any lawyer in New York.

I felt when I attended the Wyoming Bar Association meeting that I was among lawyers and not businessmen. That's what made me enjoy it so much. I intend to come out next year and every other year that I can, and certainly when I retire I will come back to Wyoming. It is a grief both to Frances and to me that because of a series of accidents there will be no next generation Arnold in the state. Both my sons are practicing in California.

I have a particular regard for you. You were on the Bench when I argued my first case in an appellate court. You have given learning, dignity and character to that Court. You spoke about retiring before your term expires. Personally, I hope you stay on.

*Affectionately*

---

## *To Alfred Friendly*[282]

Washington, D.C., Aug. 9, 1961

Dear Mr. Friendly:

Your first two questions read as follows:

1. To the layman, antitrust cases seem to have only two purposes. One is to bring down prices (price-fixing cases); the other is to keep businesses small (anti-merger, anti-monopoly). The layman needs to be reminded again why the antitrust laws were written, what kinds of business activity they are designed to control, how they exercise that control, and why certain kinds of business activity are bad.

2. The antitrust laws seem to have an internal contradiction. Those parts which are aimed at price-fixing seem designed to protect the old capitalistic society in which the most efficient producer is rewarded. Those parts which aim at mergers and monopolies seem designed to protect the little businessman at the expense of efficiency. Is there a contradiction? If not, why not? If there is, how can the nation operate successfully with it?

The purpose of the antitrust laws is to insure freedom of business opportunity. They are not designed to protect small business from larger and more efficient competitors. They are not designed to prevent the growth of nationwide business enterprises so long as that growth is a product of industrial efficiency. Even if, through greater efficiency in operation and distribution, a corporation achieved a monopoly, that in itself would not violate the Sherman Act. But this has never yet happened. Monopolies have been built up by using financial strength to buy out competitors or to force them out of business. It is this sort of growth and only this sort that the antitrust laws are designed to penalize.

Take, for example, the prohibition against mergers. If a nationwide concern which dominated the market in a single product should choose to diversify and purchase a corporation which makes some other product, there would not be the substantial lessening of competition required to make the merger illegal. Thus Coca-Cola recently acquired the business of Minute Maid without objection from the Department of Justice. This was because the Department of Justice did not believe that in any real sense orange juice, predominantly a breakfast drink, competed with Coca-

Cola. Had Coca-Cola acquired Pepsi-Cola it is certain that the merger would have been attacked.

Thus the anti-merger provisions are not designed to protect the small businessman at the expense of efficiency. Instead, they are to prevent the inevitable inefficiency which occurs in a big business which has taken over all or most of its competitors.

Two of the most commonly occurring violations of the antitrust laws, apart from mergers, are the following: (1) conspiracies to fix prices; (2) the use of a dominant position in the market for one product to destroy local business which depends upon that product for its existence. The second is illustrated by the motion picture cases prosecuted before the last war. The major producers who controlled the feature films would not supply those films to independent theatres. Thus they got control over the purely local business of motion picture exhibitions. This process repeated in industry after industry during the period between the first World War and the depression created a system of absentee ownership of local industries which made industrial colonies out of the West and South, prevented the accumulation of local capital and siphoned the consumers' dollars to a few industrial centers like New York and Chicago. This happened because enforcement of the antitrust laws during the big business government of Harding, Coolidge and Hoover was notoriously ineffective.

When big business is not restrained by antitrust enforcement it expands not through efficiency but through the ruthless use of financial power. It wants to sell without buying; it thus destroys the purchasing power of its own customers. This absentee ownership of local industry was certainly one of the causes of the great depression.

In Europe the result of the lack of an antitrust policy was the complete cartelization of industry. The markets were divided by international cartels. Hitler was able to manipulate the cartel system to his own advantage while the same system sapped the industrial vitality of England and France. Even in America during the period of non-enforcement of the Twenties many of our great industrial concerns joined international cartels. An example of how this hurt us can be taken from the rubber industry. One of our great oil companies entered into an agreement with our German cartels that it would not manufacture rubber if the German cartel would not compete in oil and gasoline. As a result, America entered the war far behind Germany in the production of a synthetic rubber.

The antitrust laws are not directly concerned with the lowering of consumers' prices. Their purpose is to permit new enterprise freely to enter any field of production and distribution and to succeed if they are more efficient than those already in the industry. This in the long run tends to give the consumer a better deal but it does not protect inefficient small business. It was the cartel system that protected the small businesses already in the market by assuring them of the continuance of their limited share.

Concentration of economic power achieved by putting artificial restraints on new business, or by the purchase of competitors, or by division of the market, draws the vigor out of the industrial system. The excuse of the cartel system is always that it protects respectable industry from so-called ruinous competition. The United States has adopted that policy only once and that was in the days of the N.R.A. and that did not last long.

To illustrate what happens in any field where the principles of the antitrust laws are abandoned one needs only to look at Jimmy Hoffa and his Teamsters' Union. Hoffa is able to control the bottleneck of transportation without effective deterrents from anyone. The result is what could have been expected in advance when labor was first freed by an unfortunate decision of the Supreme Court from any restrictions under the Sherman Act.

Your third question is:

3. In the last six months, there have been a half-dozen criminal indictments involving consumer goods price fixing. Will these actions have any effect on the prices which the consumer pays? Have there been many past cases in which the government attacked price fixing in the consumer goods market? If there have been few such cases (and it seems so to me) why has the government avoided this field? How can prices be identical if they are not fixed? How deeply should the government involve itself in pricing?

There have been probably more price-fixing cases than any other type of prosecution under the antitrust laws. Those prosecutions, however, have not prevented the administration of prices by large corporations through the device of price leadership in such commodities as steel. The difficulty may be illustrated by the following example: When I was a member of President Roosevelt's Temporary National Economic Committee we were examining an industry in which the prices were almost always identical. One of the presidents of a smaller concern was on the stand. I asked him why he invariably followed the prices of the large company in the field. He explained that Mr. X of the large company had been to M.I.T. He had studied economics, he had vast experience in prices. "Therefore," said the president of the smaller company, "I have confidence in him and believe that the price he fixes after study is the price that I should use."

When the hearing was over I took him to one side and asked him what would happen if he didn't follow the price of the large company. "That, Mr. Arnold," he said, "is something which I never expect to learn from actual experience."

In such a situation there need be no conspiracy in order to establish identical prices. The great problem of administered prices today in the United States is to this extent beyond the reach of the present antitrust laws. And for this reason we can observe that in many of our great industries prices remain the same or are even raised when demand is falling off.

Your fourth question is:

4. Do we need a wholesale revision of the antitrust laws? They were designed for a 19th-century economy far different from the existing one. Are they still valid?

If by "wholesale revision of the antitrust laws" you mean the abandonment of the principle of the Act in favor of what is often called rationalized production and distribution, such an effort would be an unmitigated evil. It is not true that the Sherman Act was designed for a 19th-century economy. It did not become effective in the United States until the 20th century. Today the principal policy of antitrust is spreading all over the world. Erhard, the German Minister of Finance, has a vigorous antitrust policy which succeeded because during the Occupation the great German combinations that existed before the war were broken up by the American decartelization program. In the long run we have only two choices, either the curbing of restraints of trade and monopoly power or the recreation of the cartel system the evils of which are today belatedly recognized even in Europe.

*Sincerely*

---

## *To Paul R. Ignatius*[283]

Washington, D.C., Nov. 1, 1961

Dear Mr. Ignatius:

Since I have joined the practice of the law I am delighted at any advertising you can give me. The story is true except for a minor amendment. It was not the Encyclopedia Britannica. At the time, in the Twenties, there was another Encyclopedia, practically unknown, which was sold through traveling salesmen. The gimmick was this: The salesman told my wife that she had been selected out of the prominent women in Wyoming to be the recipient of a gift of the Encyclopedia in order to advertise it;

all she had to pay was some small sum, $10.00 or so, and she would get these magnificent books. She granted to the Encyclopedia the right to use her name. She fell for it and signed a contract. The contract in fine print provided that she was to pay $150 for the loose-leaf supplements which came out every month or so. They started to send the supplements and billed her for $150. I informed the Encyclopedia that I was not going to pay it. From then on the story is entirely correct.[284]

Another incident may amuse you which occurred during my Wyoming practice. At that time a number of companies were sending out merchandise which you could either accept and send a check or return. A doctor friend of mine received three neckties with the instructions that he could either send $3 or mail them back. He wore the ties and did not remit the $3. When they started dunning him he came to me for advice. I told him that while he could have thrown the ties away, since he had worn them he was unquestionably liable. I then prepared a letter for him which stated that he was delighted with the ties and enjoyed wearing them and they were extraordinary bargains, in fact they were such good bargains that he felt he should do more than simply send the $3. Instead of cash he enclosed in the letter three pills, describing their therapeutic value in enthusiastic terms. These pills, he said, were a bargain at $2 apiece. He suggested that the tie merchant either send back the pills or send him $3, which was the difference between the price of the pills and the ties.

Believe it or not, he got back the pills with an indignant letter demanding the $3 since he had worn the ties. This time I got him to write a letter saying that he would be delighted to return the ties but unfortunately the local medical association required him to charge $5 for every call; he had consulted the local committee and had learned that a call at the post office was at the same rate as any other call. Therefore, if the company desired the ties back he would mail them on receipt of $2 cash. We never heard from them again.

With best regards and hoping to meet you soon, I am

*Sincerely*

---

## *To Charles A. Reich*[285]

Washington, D.C., May 24, 1962

Dear Charlie:

I was late in reading your article in the *New Republic*[286] on United States Steel because I do not take the magazine and non-current copies are hard to come by. It gave me a nostalgic feeling for the old days when Roosevelt delivered his outrageous monopoly message in 1938 announcing a witch hunting joint committee of the House and Senate to legislate against big business. I recall the time when I insisted on stating the industry-wide economic objectives of each grand jury investigation. I also recall the articles like yours written when after advance warning I criminally indicted the American Medical Association and its president in the face of a wise dictum of Justice Holmes which made them immune.

Since I was the target of articles so like yours that you might almost be accused of plagiarism, I think I am such a qualified expert on the cliches in this field that my comments may be of value.

Your point that any attack which impugns the motives and destroys the good will of big business ends finally in the sacrifice of individual freedom of thought compares favorably in force and logic with the articles expressing the same view written in 1938-1939. I further like the restraint with which it is expressed. For example, when the *Chicago Tribune* in 1939—after making the same point—ended with the statement that I was an idiot in a powder mill I personally thought it was going too far. You make the point more politely.

Your questions at the end—Will business now come crawling to government to seek its pleasure? And, what is more important, will individual citizens fear to disagree with "national policy"?—sum up the dangers inherent in the situation in a nutshell. These same questions were asked in the Roosevelt Administration. And I well remember that both business and individual citizens did become so terrorized during that period that practically no one dared criticize Roosevelt's "national policy" while he was still alive. Such a situation is unhealthy.

You also explain with great clarity why an antitrust enforcement policy should either have no economic objective or if it does that objective should not be publicized. The enforcement of the Sherman Act should be conducted in whispers without mentioning any economic purpose. This is because, as you point out, "A hint of criminal prosecution could be fatal." Indeed, it was just such hints in 1938 which so injured General Motors, Ford and Chrysler that they lost practically all their business to smaller competitors. It is also true that my publicly announced but unsuccessful policy of criminally prosecuting labor unions so damaged the good will of the unions that not even Jimmy Hoffa has been able to restore it.

You say "The description of the defeated Mr. Blough, calling on the President to find out what the steel industry should do next, is an ominous picture of the future." This point would be more forcefully made if you had added "just as ominous as when the great J.P. Morgan felt forced to call on Theodore Roosevelt when the prosecution of the Northern Securities case was announced." But this is a minor criticism.

And so I was all prepared to give you an A on your article until I came to the last sentence and found that you had omitted one of the most important cliches in the entire field. You say "President Kennedy's victory may have advanced peace and plenty, but it did no service to freedom." To concede that the victory could possibly have a good economic effect is dangerous. Many foolish citizens might be willing to give up their future individual freedom in exchange for a present materialistic advantage of having their automobiles cost less. Had you properly done your research and examined the writings of the great evangelists who preceded you, you would have had the answer right at hand. Didn't you realize that threatened antitrust proceedings create a loss of business confidence which in turn brings on a depression?

I regret that your failure to utilize this important cliche compels me to give you a B on your otherwise excellent article instead of an A.

With kind personal regards,

*Sincerely*

---

## *To David T. Bazelon*

Washington, D.C., June 11, 1962

Dear Mr. Bazelon:

I have read your book.[287] I found it most stimulating and interesting. I agree with most of the things you say. Your style has drive and arresting quality. Further than that, the book is a mine of statistics and information which would be useful to any other writer on American economics. I congratulate you on it.

If you want my criticism I would first say that the book is far too long. I believe you could get rid of 200 pages without omitting any of your points. However, I am not sure I am right on that. The same observation was made about my *Folklore of Capitalism.* One friend of mine who read it, at my request, said it was the most repetitious book he had ever read. I did not take his advice and it worked out all right.

However, I still think that the book should be condensed by at least a third. And certainly the first chapter would be better put in ten pages. For example, pages 34, 35 and 36 are about all you need for getting into your subject. There is nothing in the rest of the introduction that you do not say later and less abstractly. However, I'll bet you two to one that you do not take this advice and you may prove to be right.

As for the content of the book my chief objection is your belief in some kind of a managerial revolution. We had planned management from 1920 to 1929 by our very best business men. The idea grew out of our schools of business administration. Business school graduates were specially trained for that important task. The antitrust laws were just a pain in the neck which interfered with them by depriving industrial combinations of a sense of security. As long as the antitrust laws were on the books somebody might come along and interfere with their planning. They were not selfish men like the old robber barons. They had the interest of the public at heart. Now you suggest that these same kind of people be endowed with governmental powers. I say, God forbid.

It is, of course, true that the antitrust laws have not done what they were supposed to do. They are also unpopular and untidy which is disturbing to economists. Yet they saved the American economy from the utter stagnation of the cartel system. For example, you note the Aluminum Company was not dissolved due to new competition having come in when the suit was pending. How on earth did you imagine that the new competition got in? The suit was started because complaints were made to the Department of Justice by Reynolds who was being forced out of business by the Aluminum Company. If it had not been for the antitrust suit neither Reynolds nor Kaiser would be in the aluminum business today.

You seem to infer that the antitrust laws are not capable of dealing with an administered price system like steel. This is nonsense. If Roger Blough[288] had written to the president of Bethlehem asking him if he would follow his prices up it would have been an obvious conspiracy in restraint of trade. Instead of doing that Homer[289] testified about a year ago before the Kefauver Committee that he always followed steel prices up because it was good business. He said the same thing in interviews with the *Wall Street Journal.* Blough could be completely confident that Bethlehem would follow him. Inland Steel, with the most modern plant in the United States, was operating about 100% capacity. It couldn't possibly have filled the demand. In my view the reason Blough surrendered was the fact that his lawyers must have told him that if he persisted there was grave danger of both criminal indictment and dissolution of United States Steel. The situation was very similar to the one where the tobacco companies were convicted.

In 1940 I had a grand jury investigating United States Steel expecting to get an indictment. The pressure on the Administration was such that the Attorney General dismissed the grand jury. The same pressures will exist whatever planning gimmick you put in, assuming you have an independent planning commission. But it's ten to one the planning commission will not be independent. If Kennedy were to appoint it, it certainly would be composed of people like Dillon.

The Kennedy Administration has adopted a policy of nonenforcement of the antitrust laws. The Department has done absolutely nothing except prosecute cases of no economic significance. Nevertheless, the very fact that the antitrust laws are there is a factor of great consequence. If they hadn't been Kennedy would have lost his fight with steel.

I suggest that you study the Common Market antitrust laws. This is an amazing development. Three or four years ago I attended a conference on coal and steel and the European Community. At that time I was convinced that neither one of them would come into being. There was no use reducing tariffs if a cartel system could immediately raise prices. The English, French and Italian economists and lawyers read papers almost identical with your chapter on the antitrust laws. Only Erhard of Germany advocated the total abolition of cartels.

Now look what's happened. The Common Market has a super government and a super court. They have passed a series of antitrust regulations which are tougher than ours so far as language is concerned. For example, price leadership is an offense on the Common Market antitrust laws. The United States Steel could have been immediately fined one million dollars under these regulations. Of course, any antitrust law is necessarily vague and it will be interesting to observe what happens in the Common Market. Only one case has been handed down. This single decision is certainly not encouraging to those who oppose antitrust enforcement in the Common Market.

In other words, I still believe that in the private sector of the economy the ideal of the antitrust laws is the only workable solution. That is why it was finally adopted by the Common Market.

I think that the function of Government is to engage in the vast task of removing water pollution from our streams and so on through a long list of necessities. Leon Keyserling's idea of balancing the economic budget, i.e. spending money not on pump priming but rather public necessities which do not have a dollar value once the idea is digested, is our only way out. The only planning necessary is to see that Government demands on goods and services do not exceed the productive capacity.

Certainly this has been Erhard's philosophy from the very start. The first thing he did was to abolish price control in Germany. Throughout his regime he has been constantly attacking cartels. He put in something similar to an Antitrust Division but without the power of our Department of Justice. You could have said most of the things about Dr. Guenther's Antitrust Department in Germany that you say about our own antitrust enforcement. Yet in spite of their combinations and mergers in Germany there is far more competitive spirit among German business men than there is in the United States.

I agree with you when you say that Alexander Hamilton was an economic planner. Yet the only successful thing that he did was to redeem state bonds for the benefit of people who had paid only a fraction of their value. There were 4 million people in the United States and only 12 million specie. By one stroke of the pen Hamilton multiplied the available purchasing power of the country by about 800 per cent. Then, like Harry Hopkins, he went around saying that a public debt was a public blessing. This worked.

But Hamilton's planning was to be done by experts in the Bank of the United States. The Bank failed for many reasons, some of them political, some of them due to a distrust of giving that much power to the Federal Government. But the thing which finally pushed the Bank over was the fact that it was too conservatively run by Biddle to provide for the needs of growing industrial expansion in New York. This I think was inevitable, knowing the banking fraternity. It is fortunate that Hamilton's planning agency failed. I believe we owe our expansion to the currency printed by the wildcat banks which allowed for unlimited issues. By and large these banks did a pretty good job despite a number of notorious scandals. It is my view that the private sector of the economy should be let alone to print its own paper money curbed by the Sherman Act to such extent as those curbs are politically possible. But, as you clearly point out in your book, they can't print enough to keep up with the tremendous industrial plant of the Twentieth Century. That has been true ever since 1930. It is, therefore, the function of the Government to make all the public expenditures that the productive capacity can stand without excess demands.

I am not convinced that we are as far apart as this letter indicates. Certainly the antitrust laws are not in themselves an economic program, and certainly some kind of planning by somebody is necessary in our modern economy. For example, agriculture is subsidized in both the United States and Europe. Some kinds of credit mechanisms to get agricultural products to starving people are urgently required. However, the dominant idea of the Western world today is leaning towards free markets with antitrust curbs. In our Alliance for Progress we have the same basic idea. By various practical methods such as withholding of funds we are attacking monopolies and oligarchies in Latin America. By your emphasis on the failure of the antitrust laws to do what they were supposed to do, and your implications that you think the future lies in a planned economy, it seems to me you are going counter to the developments of our times. We are going to be forced to join the Common Market by sheer economic necessity. Yet some portions of your book seem to indicate that America's future will be that of an independent economy.

Apart from these criticisms I greatly admire your book and congratulate you on it.

*Sincerely*

---

## *To Hugh B. Cox*

Washington, D.C., July 4, 1962

Dear Hugh:

There seems to be something wrong with the system of smoke signals and jungle drums which, prior to the Kennedy Administration, used to keep us members of the underground informed as to each other. In any event, the first time I learned about your illness was last Friday at Hugh Black's when Justice Harlan told me. His information, though not precise, was distinctly on the gloomy side. I got the impression that St. Peter had already checked your record and set your case down for an early hearing on charges that during your career you had been contumacious towards Holy men and resigned to Hell. Frances and I, therefore, hurried out to buy a couple of candles, motivated by the same impulse that makes a drowning man grasp a straw.

Monday, I called up Howard Westwood and he told me that the hearing had been postponed indefinitely and that you were expected soon to arise from your bed and resume your godless ways. I can't tell you how much of a relief that was.

I can understand Ethelyn's feeling that the Supreme Court of the United States is the only appropriate agency to convey news concerning a man of your legal achievements. I would suggest to her, however, that in cases of this kind the Supreme Court is not adequate as a news dispensing agency. In the first place, the Court is overburdened with work, as Henry Hart points out. In the second place, a proper communications system requires speed in transmission and clarity of expression—neither one of which qualities the Supreme Court possesses in any marked degree.

So instead of buying candles, Frances and I have bought two big firecrackers which we will set off on this glorious Fourth of July in the year of our Lord Nineteen Hundred Sixty-two in celebration of your recovery.

Anyway, now that it's over, I'm glad that Frances and I did not learn about your danger. It would have worried us to death.

*Affectionately*

---

## *To John E.F. Wood*[290]

Washington, D.C., Nov. 23, 1962

Dear John:

I have your letter demanding 55¢ on account of the bet we made at Jackson Hole as to the respective distances from North Platte on the Arnold and Wood routes. It has a plausible sound and I was about to send you 55¢. Since the sum involved, however, is not inconsiderable in view of my present financial condition I thought I had better re-check the evidence.

The first sentence of your letter reads as follows: "A few days ago I was throwing away *old* road maps used in our trip last summer and was reminded to check the mileages concerning which we have an unresolved wager." This would appear to be a clear admission on your part that you were trying to collect money on the basis of obsolete maps and that you have now destroyed these maps.

My own calculations last summer were based on new road maps. I have no doubt that it is true that it used to be longer to go from Jenny Lake to North Platte by the way of Rock Springs than by way of Casper. Indeed, when I was practicing law in Wyoming the only road into Jackson was over Towgotee Pass. At a later time you had to go from Jackson down the Snake River and into Utah to get to Rock Springs. I have no doubt these were the old maps which you used. The fact that you have now destroyed these maps creates a clear inference that this statement is correct. If you had been using up-to-date maps in making your calculations you would have kept them in order to back up your statements with competent evidence. I don't know what the rule is in New York but in the District of Columbia, where you have to sue me, our Court of Appeals has held that a plaintiff who destroys evidence necessary to prove his case is presumed to be a very unreliable fellow indeed.

The best evidence, of course, of the distance would be a comparison of your speedometer with my speedometer. I strongly suspect that the reason you do not use this as a basis for your claim is that you have not kept the figures. If I am wrong, why do you withhold this vital information from me?

Since there is always one chance in a thousand that I am wrong in making these inferences I will withhold my decision on this matter until you give me an explanation of why in making these calculations you did not use up-to-date maps instead of old ones.

With best regards, and hoping that I am not doing you an injustice, I remain

*Sincerely*

---

## *To Frank C. Waldrop*

Washington, D.C., June 13, 1963

Dear Frank:

The only time that I saw Colonel McCormick, apart from incidental contacts at large parties, was in connection with the prosecution of the

Associated Press. I had attempted to bring this prosecution for some time. Cissy Patterson had complained with great indignation about her being unable to get an Associated Press franchise, and I had recommended antitrust action to the Attorney General. At first the suit was regarded as extremely dangerous because it would be treated by newspapers as an assault on freedom of the press by the New Deal. Finally, however, Marshall Field started his own newspaper and was denied press services. He had enough influence to swing the Administration to my side. Curiously enough, the minute he came into the picture Cissy Patterson changed sides. She no longer wanted anything to do with an antitrust prosecution of the Associated Press.

Having gotten clearance for the proceeding I sent FBI agents hither and yon. Among the places they visited was the *Chicago Tribune* which caused a great outcry. I have forgotten whether the *Tribune* mentioned it in editorial pages but other newspapers did.

Shortly after this publicity somebody called me from Chicago, whose name I have forgotten, and asked me if I would consider talking to the Colonel about the suit; if so he would come to Washington. I immediately called him up and told him I was going to be in Chicago the next week visiting my regional office and that I would be glad to call on him. We fixed the time and he said that he would have a car come for me at the Antitrust Division offices.

When the day arrived, a 7-passenger limousine with a chauffeur rolled up and took me to the *Tribune.* A red carpet was rolled out for me and I was taken over the entire Tribune plant by some courteous editor whose name escapes me. Finally, after a pleasant hour I was escorted to the Colonel's office in the Gothic Lantern.

There was an armed policeman outside the door. When the Colonel was informed I was present he walked out to greet me. The door had a brass panel at the bottom which the Colonel would kick instead of turning a knob. We shook hands and the Colonel led me into the office. The only persons present were the Colonel and myself and a large handsome dog. I think he was a police dog but my memory is not entirely clear; anyway, he was a big dog.

We sat down and the Colonel asked me what I was up to anyway. I told him that he had better get a new set of editors, his present ones were too flabby and too unused to the adequate utilization of invective to cover the situation which I hoped I could develop. I told the Colonel that they had called me an idiot in a powder mill but such mild terms would not meet the needs of the day when I would have him indicted. I told him that that was the purpose of the FBI investigation. I explained to him that I did not consider him a bad man, that I had no doubt he was sincere but that my policy was to prosecute criminally wherever I could.

He told me that he didn't think I could possibly get the Attorney General to approve an indictment of any newspaper. I replied that that might be true but at least I was going to try. He said he liked my frankness and appreciated my coming to see him. We chatted for fifteen or twenty minutes more and then I left.

The curious thing about it all was that from then on the *Chicago Tribune* quit jumping on me personally. It continued to attack the Department of Justice but never called me names any longer. Whether the Colonel had anything to do with that I do not know.

I don't see how anybody could hate the Colonel. He was an extraordinarily attractive and able man. He also had more prejudices than anyone I have ever heard of, although that is the impression I got from the newspaper rather than my one brief interview with him. In that interview he seemed tolerant, humorous and friendly.

With kind regards,

*Sincerely*

---

## *To Carl Bode*[291]

Washington, D.C., July 9, 1963

Dear Professor Bode:

My secretary reminded me that I had promised to write you about my acquaintance with H.L. Mencken.

When my book *The Symbols of Government* came out in 1933 Mencken gave it very favorable mention in the *American Mercury.* Then when I came to Washington as head of the Antitrust Division of the Department of Justice he invited me over for dinner at his home in Baltimore. I have forgotten who else was there. I do recall Mencken taking us out into the garden and showing us a brick wall which he had built with his own hands. After explaining how he did it he said, "This wall will be standing when Baltimore is dust." I am told that that was a regular ritual when he had people in for dinner. Anyway, it was very funny indeed.

I have never known Mencken's equal as a stimulating, provocative and witty conversationalist. He would start out on a subject and continue in a half-serious, half-satirical vein, giving new points of view and new facets to whatever he talked about. His only weakness of a thinker was his belief in the superiority of American Businessmen as thinkers and economists over the so-called liberals of his day.

I remember a squib which appeared in the *American Mercury* with respect to Roscoe Pound, which I think is so funny that I will recite it from memory since you may otherwise miss it. The Wickersham Report on Prohibition had just appeared. Pound was on the Commission. Mencken wrote that the Report showed that it was unsafe to trust a liberal in any position of public responsibility. He spoke of the great reputation of Roscoe Pound and the public confidence in him which was unhampered until they put him on the Wickersham Commission "whereupon he blew up with a loud bang, emitting suffocating fumes."

When I got on the Bench I wrote the opinion, copy of which I enclose, in the *Esquire* case. You will note the underlined sentence on page 7. After the opinion came out I got a letter from Mencken which I can almost recite from memory though the letter appears to have been lost. Mencken wrote:

> My dear Mr. Justice:
>
> If it is not an indecorum I would like to express my appreciation of your judicial certificate of decency. When my pastor heard of it he went on a roaring sacerdotal drunk and had to be knee-haltered. The Maryland Club, on the other hand, was so delighted at your endorsement of my character that they hung out the Confederate flag and reduced the price of all 15 cents cigars to 25 cents.
>
> Yours in Christ,
> H.L. Mencken

I recall another letter which he wrote to Dorothy Hergsheimer on an occasion when we were invited to Stone Harbor[292] and Mencken was to join us. For some reason he couldn't come. The conclusion of his letter to Dorothy explaining his disappointment ran something like the following (this was during the war):

> Things are in bad shape in Baltimore. The houses are crumbling and falling into the street. There is no decent food and we have to subsist on a liquid diet. Fortunately, however, I was able to fashion a bow and arrow out of an old fishing pole and two neckties and have just shot two policemen.
>
> Yours in Christ,
> H.L. Mencken

Joe Hergsheimer told me that Mencken was always shooting policemen at the end of his letters.

Mencken was very much annoyed at me for my prosecution of the American Medical Association. I really shouldn't say "annoyed" because I don't think that he translated his extreme views into any personal indignation. However, he thought that Dr. Fishbein (the then head of the AMA) was a very great man indeed, and in my investigation of the AMA files during the prosecution I found a note from Mencken urging Fishbein not to be intimidated by these New Deal "goons."

I remember also his comment on another prosecution which I conducted against the Associated Press. It was while I was on the Bench and Mencken had invited me over to dinner at the Maryland Club. Among the guests was Owens, of the *Baltimore Sun* (I can't remember which Owens it was). Owens started criticizing the prosecution, though in a friendly way. Mencken took up the cudgels and made one of the wittiest and most brilliant denunciations of the prosecution I have ever heard. I didn't mind because it was amusing and there was no malice whatever in it. At the conclusion of his comment, however, he turned to Owens and said "As a matter of fact, Owens, you and I both know Arnold was right." Owens was disconcerted and I was immensely pleased.

I wish you luck with your book, and suggest that you telephone me and we will have lunch together at some convenient time.

With best wishes,

*Sincerely*

---

## *To Robert W. Woodruff*

Washington, D.C., Jan. 10, 1964

Dear Bob:

The cigars arrived and I am enjoying them very much. When I had my coronary the doctor said I couldn't smoke any more but, having a legal mind, I decided that what he meant was that I shouldn't smoke in his presence. So far smoking has done me no harm because I am tested every two weeks.

By the same token he said I could only have two ounces of liquor a day. I applied my legal mind to interpreting this advice. I concluded that since I was an important person he couldn't have meant ordinary ounces but must have meant imperial ounces. I checked up with the weights and measures system of Great Britain and found there are two imperial ounces in each Fifth of whisky so I am well under my doctor's allowance, and feeling fine.

I enclose a clipping to show what an important man Abe has become. The rest of us are shining with reflected glory.[293]

With best wishes for the New Year,

*Sincerely*

---

*To The Editor*
*The* Washington Post

Washington, D.C., Feb. 27, 1964

Dear Sir:

Your editorial of February 26, 1964,[294] indicates your belief that public humiliation of a witness before a Senate Committee by asking repeated questions which the Committee knows he will lawfully decline to answer is an essential part of the legislative process. Certainly no God-fearing man would dispute a moral judgment made by your great pietistic journal. However, there are certain defects in the present procedure which often make it almost as humiliating to the Committee as it is to the witness.

For example, in the hearing to which your editorial referred the witness declined to answer 120 times. The Committee began with the hope that the law of averages would surely result in at least a few answers to so many questions. Certainly after 50 refusals the 51st question should bring down the jackpot. When it didn't, the look of pained incredulity on the noble faces of the interrogating Solons was painful to observe. It was encouraging to note that in spite of this they kept on. But when the 120th question elicited the same refusal any lingering hope indulged in by the Committee gave way to despair. At that point they became so groggy that, like Sonny Liston, they were unable to come out of their corner. Now this is not a spectacle that one of my admiring faith in Congressional investigations likes to see.

So my suggestion is this: The witness should be permitted to exercise his right to refuse to answer 1,000 questions. But if the Committee has the dogged persistence to ask question 1,001, the witness must answer. The theory behind this is that at that point the witness had enjoyed all the constitutional protection he deserves. Therefore, the Bill of Rights should be allowed to take a breather, and the members of the Committee should be permitted a brief moment in the sun to restore their injured dignity. This new constitutional doctrine should be named "The Filibuster in Reverse."

Yours of sin,

*Sincerely*

---

*To Livingston Hall*[295]

Washington, D.C., July 24, 1964

Dear Professor Hall:

I enclose my answer to your very interesting questionnaire. The difficulty with the practice of criminal law is that criminals ordinarily do not have any money. For that reason we have not handled many criminal cases and those that we have handled are either by court appointment or cases involving what we thought were important principles of justice and for which we did not charge any fee. The distressing fact is that only in rare cases—such as my friend Ed Williams, whose reputation is such that he attracts wealthy people who have been indicted—can a lawyer have a satisfactory career practicing criminal law.

Another handicap, even for the successful criminal lawyer such as Williams, is that corporate clients shy away from lawyers with criminal practices. Therefore, it is the custom of most firms not to take criminal cases even if they are remunerative.

The reform that I would advocate is to adopt the English practice where no lawyer has the right to refuse to represent anyone in a criminal case if a reasonable fee is offered. This, I think, would make a big difference in criminal practice and prevent it from becoming what it is today—a somewhat exclusive specialty.

*Sincerely*

---

*To Mrs. Paul Porter*[296]

Washington, D.C., March 22, 1965

Dear Kay:

I have read your book up to and through the big ball given by Josiah Ching. I am entranced by it and find difficulty in putting it down.

If I were to write a review of the book it would be something like this:

This book is a breath of fresh air in what seems to me to be the murkiest literary atmosphere of the present century. In the days when H.L. Mencken was assaulting literary critics who could not appreciate writers like Willa Cather, Hergsheimer, Dreiser, and Conrad, I joined in his parade and read extensively from his selected list. I found them interesting books about interesting characters which the reader could identify himself with and become interested in what happened to them.

Today our bright young people profess to admire writers like Salinger and books like *Ship of Fools.* I have bought some of these books and never was able to finish any of them. In fact, I have forgotten most of the titles and the authors' names. How anybody can get interested in the disagreeable characters of Katherine Anne Porter, or the psychiatric troubles of the hero in *Catcher in the Rye* (if that's the name of the damn thing), is beyond me.

Literary criticism today is as bad as it was when I was in college and William Dean Howells was the greatest writer the nation had yet produced and Mark Twain's *Huckleberry Finn* was a piece of low comedy without literary merit. The difference is that in those days sugar and water represented the standard of excellence and today we must all subsist on a diet of vinegar. We need another H.L. Mencken to put dynamite bombs in the leading places of contemporary critics and blow them to smithereens.

It is, of course, true that anyone who admired Salinger would not admire this book. But the public will like it and sooner or later (I hope sooner) it will be hailed as a great contemporary novel.

I reached the above conclusion after only a little over one hundred pages. Probably when I have finished the book I will hire one of these great mechanical scoops so frequently seen in the construction industry, get you to stand under it, and completely drown you in apple sauce or whatever other form of enthusiastic appreciation you prefer.

*Sincerely*

---

*To The Editor*
*The* New York Times

Washington, D.C., May 3, 1965

Dear Sir:

Late Saturday night I finished Kathleen Winsor's new novel, *Wanderers Eastward, Wanderers West.*[297] It is a long book but I was entranced and interested all the way through. I, at least, found it hard to put down because I wanted to find out what was going to happen next. I was a boy in Wyoming during the 1890s and the descriptions of the Western characters made those old times come alive. To sum up, I think it is a hell of a good book.

Sunday morning I read a review of the book in the *Times* written by a character with the highly improbable name of Knickerbocker. I was surprised and thought for a while that he was reviewing some other book than the one I had just read. On re-reading the review carefully, however, I was amazed to find that he was talking about the same book. I gathered from his review that he found the book very boring indeed and that the incidents and characters which I found so vivid and true to life lacked any historical insight with respect to the times or characters of the period.

The review makes it clear that I would not like the books which Mr. Knickerbocker likes and he would not like the books which I like. No one should complain about such differences of opinion. What depressed me was Mr. Knickerbocker's conviction that if I liked the book I must be some sort of a moron. He seemed very sad because he is afraid that the public is going to buy the book in spite of anything he can do about it. The notion that the paperback rights had been sold for $500,000 makes him particularly unhappy. His conclusion is that something is wrong with the American reading public. This conclusion inevitably follows from the fact that he is convinced there can be nothing possibly wrong with Mr. Knickerbocker or his books which, unfortunately, I never heard of before and do not now intend to read.

This letter is not to complain about Mr. Knickerbocker's review. It is simply to ask the question—why so many reviewers think that the art of story telling, which Miss Winsor has to an unexampled degree and which the majority of the public finds so entertaining, is a symptom of mental frailty on the part of both the author and the readers? I don't suppose you can answer this question but I wish you would try. It has puzzled me since I was a boy and my grandfather caught me reading *Huckleberry Finn* written by a clown, popular in those days, named Mark Twain. He took it away from me and said it was trash and gave me a novel by William D. Howells. Mr. Knickerbocker reminds me of my grandfather.

I happen to be the kind of a fellow who loves an intellectual treat and who is constantly trying to improve his mind. I also have a profound respect for the intellectuals like Mr. Knickerbocker who not only review books but write them. I would, therefore, deeply appreciate your obtaining from Mr. Knickerbocker a list of good books that I can read without his accusing me of wasting my time. He may, of course, omit the titles of his own books because I am afraid that in appraising them he might lose the fine sense of objectivity which appears so clearly when he writes about other people's books.

*Sincerely*

---

## *To Willard M. Kiplinger*[298]

Washington, D.C., July 29, 1965

Dear Kip:

I am so pleased and flattered at the warmth and humor in your letter[299] that I have been reading it over every morning and subsequently walking on air.

I immediately had the letter Xeroxed and distributed it to the forty lawyers who now make up the working force of our firm. All of them are law review editors and all have minds like steel traps. I was unable to make the law review because my mind is more like a sponge. Since distributing your letter I have noted a new tinge of respect in the attitude of tolerance with which they heretofore regarded me. It is even possible that one of them may be induced to read my book. I owe an obligation to you on account of my increased prestige in my firm.

You are perfectly correct in what you say about the ethics of journalism being better than that of the law. This is because lawyers, as you say, are not interested in people. Instead, they are interested only in clients whom they have to defend regardless of the merits of the case. In addition, you belong to that top hierarchy of journalists known as editors. A good editor has to be interested in people because he has to have some instinct for knowing what people in general like to read. The success of your *Letters* is due to this somewhat rare instinct which you possess.

With appreciation and gratitude,

*Sincerely*

---

## *To Joseph Featherstone*[300]

Washington, D.C., Aug. 11, 1965

Dear Mr. Featherstone:

Needless to say, your book review flattered and pleased me immensely. You express my general philosophy of government with great clarity and more briefly than I would have been able to do. You seem to have packed everything in it.

You asked what I think of Kenneth Galbraith's lack of enthusiasm for the antitrust laws. I am a great admirer of Galbraith. A case can be made that in actual practice the antitrust laws give little attention to economic factors involved in such things as mergers. The staff is inclined to be rigid and doctrinaire. At present they are taking up annoying little cases and not attacking the larger issues involved. On the other hand, sporadic as antitrust enforcement is apt to be, has been in the past, and will be in the future, if the concept were abandoned the last impediment to concentration of economic power would be gone.

It is interesting to note that this small Division of perhaps 250 lawyers makes more of an imprint in American thinking about concentration than other regulatory departments of many thousands of men.

I recall Homer Cummings calling me to his office when I had close to one thousand people under indictment to ask me what good I thought these cases would do. "Well," I said, "they have done at least this much good, the American businessmen are answering their mail better than before the cases were started."

With much appreciation,

*Sincerely*

---

*To Francis Biddle*

Washington, D.C., Sept. 20, 1965

Dear Francis:

Thank you for your letter about my book.[301] I am sorry to hear about the illness of Katherine and your daughter-in-law, but it sounds as if everything is coming out all right.

You refer to my error in substituting Anthony for Nicholas Biddle as a slight one. I wish it was, but I don't know how many readers have written me about it, most of them thinking I am an ignoramus. Actually I knew it was Nicholas all along, and I think I would have caught it if I had proofread the book myself but, being a lazy man, I left that to Harcourt, Brace.

The book has been criticized, and I think justly so, for being poorly organized and not really biography. At the insistence of my publishers I tried to put some biography in. I had a couple of chapters about you and other people I was in contact with in Washington. My publishers said they were stiff and uninteresting, and I finally gave it up. I do not have your gift for true biographical writing.

*With affectionate regards*

---

*To J. Russell Wiggins*[302]

Washington, D.C., April 19, 1966

Dear Sir:

I understand the *Post* has received a number of letters from writers who apparently believe that Professor Monroe Freedman[303] of the George Washington Law School should be disciplined because he expressed his views on the professional responsibility of a defense lawyer in a criminal case.

I read Professor Freedman's remarks. They are a responsible and thoughtful discussion of a defense attorney's obligation not to reveal facts disclosed to him by a client which indicate that the client is guilty. The real issues which Professor Freedman presented is whether a lawyer who learns of his client's guilt has an obligation either to tell the Court or to keep the defendant from testifying on his own behalf.

The answer to these questions is found in the Bill of Rights of the United States Constitution. Every criminal, no matter how guilty, is entitled to representation by counsel. An attorney who accepts the defense of a criminal defendant must use every legitimate effort to get his client acquitted. That means that if the client desires to take the stand the attorney, even though he knows he is guilty, must permit him to do so. He has no responsibility for seeing to it that his client is punished for the crime that he committed. His sole responsibility is to the client.

Of course, he must avoid making any positive misrepresentations to the Court with respect to his client's guilt or innocence. If he gave any personal opinion to the Court as to the truth of his client's story, he would not be acting as an attorney, but as some kind of witness. No attorney is permitted to be a witness of any kind, direct or indirect, in a case in which he is trial counsel. Therefore the Code of Ethics of the American Bar Association forbids the attorney from expressing his own personal view with respect to the guilt or innocence of a criminal whom he is defending. This does not mean either that he is lying to the Court when he puts the defendant on the stand or that he is guilty of concealing evidence when he does not tell the Court about the evidence against his client. That is in essence the position Professor Freedman took.

One might think that the commendable action of the Bar Association Committee dismissing the complaint against Freedman would have put the matter to rest. Since it hasn't, I write this letter in support of the dismissal of the charges against Professor Freedman.

*Very truly yours*

---

## *To T.A. Larson*[304]

Washington, D.C., June 6, 1966

Dear Doctor Larson:

I have been reading your book[305] with great pleasure. It is very interesting and well written. I am learning a lot about Wyoming.

I am annoyed with Cecil Nussbaum for telling you about my casual remark at a cocktail party with respect to your error in reporting my antitrust cases. I told her I had no intention of calling it to your attention. It is an infinitesimal part of a 600-page book. Furthermore, your history would not be improved by a tangential study of the impact of the antitrust laws on the nation's economy. So I decided not to write you on such an inconsequential matter.

However, since Cecil has written you and you have written to Cecil quoting authorities, and she has relayed your letter to me, this affair, like Viet Nam, has become escalated to the point that I must explain the basis of my casual remark, which I would not otherwise do.

On page 450 you say, referring to me:

> He failed in cases involving the more vital problems of medicine, milk, and oil.

It just so happens that I won all the cases which reached the Supreme Court in these three fields. In medicine the doctors were boycotting any physician who engaged in any organized medical care. They were relying on a dictum by Mr. Justice Holmes in the Baseball case where he said that the antitrust laws did not apply to professions. I lost in the lower court. The physicians relied on the Holmes dictum and also on the claim that they were a labor union and exempt for that reason. The Supreme Court reversed. It is now established that physicians are engaged in commerce and cannot boycott organized medical care of any sort. Without this decision the AMA would be in the same position with respect to the doctors as Jimmy Hoffa was with respect to the teamsters.

In oil, the Supreme Court also sustained me in the so-called Madison Oil case and in the Esso case against Standard Oil of New Jersey. We succeeded in breaking up the international cartels which were operating prior to the war and also the system of rebates given by oil companies to pipelines under the guise of rates. Those were all new precedents. We were equally successful in breaking up price-fixing arrangements in milk conducted by the big dairy companies.

With respect to the general observations which you quote as to the lack of significance of Roosevelt's shift from an NRA philosophy to anti-trust enforcement, I have this comment. Roosevelt began to realize in 1938 that the country was drifting into a European cartel system. Big business was dividing the markets of the world, as well as those in the United States. This was justified generally by a philosophy implicit in the NRA and later expressed in a popular best seller, *The Managerial Revolution,* by Burnham. The theory was that a rationalized and efficient economy could be built up through the cooperation of skilled business managers. It was argued that such restraints were "reasonable," on the ground that they protected small business, and made economics possible in big business. This view was accepted by most academic economists. It was the entire basis of the NRA. Had Roosevelt not decided to attack such combinations, or had the Supreme Court not held that the so-called "rule of reason" did not apply, we would have ended up in a few years with a legally approved cartel system.

Roosevelt shifted to antitrust as a major economic measure in spite of the opposition of men like Rexford Tugwell. More prosecutions were brought under his administration than in the half century which preceded. The result was a series of decisions which put a new arsenal of weapons in the hands of the Government. All of these decisions came as a shock to the business community. The Associated Press case was regarded by every newspaper as an unconstitutional attack on the freedom of the press. The aluminum case was denounced in a series of articles in *The New Yorker*. Roosevelt's antitrust program resulted in a change of those attitudes. And more practically a series of Supreme Court decisions, though generally by a divided court, changed the rules of the game and created hazards for big business which did not exist before.

The war suspended antitrust prosecutions because prices were fixed by the Government. There was no opportunity for price conspiracies. However, it in no way impaired the long run effect of Roosevelt's crusade to restore competition in our economy. After the war, big business was confronted with a new set of precedents with respect to antitrust, and an entirely different attitude on the part of the lower courts and the business community. For example when, before the war, I convicted General Electric for fixing prices, the Court imposed insignificant fines. After the war General Electric officials went to jail.

The authorities you quote seem completely ignorant about the purpose of the Sherman Act. It was never intended to prevent the growth of great nationwide corporations, nor do I think in the light of modern industrial techniques that is a desirable objective. It does not protect small business from what used to be called "ruinous competition" based on efficiency. Protection of small business is more efficiently given by fair trade acts such as your liquor laws in Wyoming. Small liquor stores in Wyoming make money—but you pay 40% more for good bourbon that I do in Washington, D.C. It takes a special exemption from the Sherman Act to justify that result. It didn't in the period from 1920 to 1938. No prosecution was ever brought based on the size of the defendants alone.

The historians whom you quote seem to think (1) that the antitrust laws are designed to prevent the growth of great industrial empires. This they were never intended to do. Their only purpose is to see that corporate growth results from efficiency—not the elimination of competition by aggression or merger. The only purpose of the present antitrust laws is to make great industrial empires behave. This they are doing, since the war, better than they have ever done before.

(2) Your historians think that in enforcing the antitrust laws I was off on some frolic of my own. This is not true. Roosevelt laid out the plan and stuck to it in spite of bitter business criticism.

(3) Your historians seem to infer that as a result of the failure of Roosevelt's antitrust program the antitrust laws and current practices today are the same as they were from 1920 to 1938 when the entire trend was toward a European cartel system. Actually the Sherman Act is as different in its application, interpretation and public policy today from what it was before Roosevelt, as the Constitution is different since Roosevelt.

Roosevelt did not solve any economic problems. It took the war to get us out of the Depression. His accomplishment was to change the attitude of the Supreme Court and of the American people on the issue of the function of a central government in meeting social problems. Not the least of his accomplishments was a new set of rules curbing the use of power by industrial empires. We came out of the war with a different attitude toward competition than England did. England revived its old business cartels and lapsed into its former industrial inefficiency. We became the most efficient competitive economy in the world.

The influence of Roosevelt's antitrust policy spread into Europe after the war, starting with Germany. Under the leadership of American antitrust lawyers, many of whom were formerly with me, the German cartels were completely dismembered, over the opposition of German businessmen. Germany emerged as a competitive economy. I talked to Erhard, in 1960, when he was Economic Minister. He gave credit to the decartelization of German industry for Germany's recovery. One of the first measures taken by the Common Market was the passage of an international antitrust law—something unheard of in Europe before the war. The reverberations of Roosevelt's shift from the encouragement of businessmen to cooperate with each other, to the revival of the antitrust ideal, are still being felt in the European Common Market.

I suppose that the reason why books by economic historians are uniformly so bad (Joseph Dorfman and Bray Hammon are exceptions) is that they think that economic history and political history are separate subjects. They like to paint with a broad brush. They hate detail. For example, I could point out the many errors in your quotation made by Howard Smith but that would take too much time. They show that Smith never read the cases he refers to. He does not know the relief the government was seeking. He has no idea of how these precedents made Wall Street attorneys change the advice they had formerly given to their clients or how they affect the competitive picture today.

Equally silly is Smith's dismissal of Teddy Roosevelt. It is apparent that he never read the Northern Securities case, Teddy Roosevelt's greatest contribution to our present competitive structures. The decision, which was 5 to 4, shows the bitterness of the conflict between two economic philosophies. Holmes believed in the beneficence of big business leaders like Morgan. He almost prevailed. Had he prevailed, our economy would have developed after the European pattern. It is true that Theodore Roosevelt, once he had established his precedent in the face of opposition from the entire business community, was satisfied to let it go at that. But Smith's appraisal of Teddy Roosevelt is like saying "The Magna Charta had no significant effect on British institutions. It was repudiated after it was signed, and though reenacted from time to time the powers of the King remained the same for nearly four hundred years," without mentioning what Lord Coke did with it in 1628. If you are interested in Teddy Roosevelt's contribution you might read Chapter XIV of my last book. Franklin Roosevelt was the first man to put teeth into the precedent, so courageously obtained by his predecessor, and those teeth still remain. It required a complete shift of attitude on his part, and a break with his former economic advisers like Tugwell, and my friend, Harry Hopkins.

I had not intended to write such a long letter. But after I started I became imbued with my grandfather's missionary zeal. If I can dissuade you from reading the kind of superficial economic literature which you quote, it may help to preserve your integrity as a historian in this world, and save your immortal soul in the next.

Anyway, I think you have written a hell of a good book.

*Sincerely*

---

## *To Melvin Wulf*[306]

Washington, D.C., Aug. 30, 1966

Dear Mr. Wulf:

I have just received a copy of the memorandum from Jack Pemberton with respect to proceedings which the American Civil Liberties Union is taking in the District Court. I thoroughly agree with the defense of Mr. Kinoy.[307] I am, however, very much concerned at the attempt of the ACLU to enjoin a Congressional hearing even though it is conceded that the Committee is overstepping its constitutional power.

The only way that such injunction could be enforced would be to arrest the Committee members and the chairman for contempt. This is a dangerous proposal and it puts the ACLU in a very disadvantageous public position.

Before publicly disassociating myself with the ACLU's position I would appreciate your explaining just how an injunction against Congressman

Pool's holding a hearing could be enforced. I agree with Mr. Pemberton as to the unconstitutional character of the proceedings. However, if you succeeded in putting Congressman Pool in jail you would make such a hero out of him as to insure his election for a long time to come and also insure the perpetuation of the Committee. I and other members of the ACLU feel so strongly about this that we contemplate filing a brief amicus curiae against your proposed injunction. I have no doubt that the ACLU will lose on the injunction issue. Nevertheless I hate to see it put in a ridiculous position while the proceeding is going on.

However, there may be some justification for what seems to me an ill-considered proceeding which has not occurred to me and I would appreciate hearing what it is. Mr. Pemberton in his memorandum avoids discussing the consequences of an attempt to put a Congressman in jail because of a sincere but misguided effort to save his country from an imaginary peril.

*Sincerely*

---

## *To John de J. Pemberton, Jr.*[308]

Washington, D.C., Sept. 7, 1966

Dear Mr. Pemberton:

I have your letters of September 1, 1966. I will go half way with you. I will not express any public dissent from the ACLU's position with respect to the injunction suit. At the same time, however, I will not sign your brief for Kinoy. I feel I could not do so without repudiating your position in the suit against the Congressman. The two proceedings are identified as one in the public mind. The net result of my endorsement and dissent would do the ACLU more harm than good.

I have read your letter with respect to the suit against the Congressman. I understand that you do not intend to put any Congressman in jail and that your purpose is only to sharpen the issues in public debate and obtain a greater precision of public understanding. I can think of no worse way of obtaining public understanding of ACLU purposes than by suing individual Congressmen, whether you ultimately intend to penalize them individually or not. I know of no Congressman who would support the proposition that he could be sued for any action taken in what he considered his Congressional duties. Your suit, therefore, makes the position of your supporters in Congress much more difficult, and the position of the HUAC[309] much stronger.

Your notion that the Supreme Court would engage in a knockdown fight with Congress by declaring that Congressmen could be sued personally for their official actions in committee proceedings seems fantastic. If they did they would be faced with a bill limiting the jurisdiction of the Court.

I am not talking about your theoretical argument on separation of powers. I am only concerned about the damage the ACLU is doing to itself and to its friends in Congress by its claiming that a Congressman is subject to suit for doing what he claims in his duty.

I urge you to dismiss the injunction proceeding at once.[310]

*Sincerely*

---

## *To Alpheus Thomas Mason* [311]

Washington, D.C., May 3, 1967

Dear Professor Mason:

I have your letter of April 26.

So far as preparation for law school is concerned, I doubt if it makes much difference what the students take in their undergraduate courses. The thing they must acquire to get good grades is the art of writing clearly and succinctly and the art of speaking persuasively. How these abilities are acquired I do not know but I suspect that almost any course in college which requires the student to write precisely rather than poetically, and in which he gets good criticism of his writing, would be helpful. So far as speaking persuasively is concerned, Oxford and Cambridge do a much better job than American universities. By and large, the British barrister is superior to the American trial lawyer in oral presentation.

Therefore, the issue is not what will best prepare a student for law school but what he ought to know to be a broad-minded lawyer. The worst courses in law school are courses in constitutional law. The tendency is to analyze and criticize the phraseology of the decisions rather than to put them in their historical setting. An understanding of Roosevelt's Court fight and the results he got is far more important than an analysis of the decisions from which a completely new constitution has been evolved and gradually accepted since 1934. Such a course will probably be much better taught in college than in law school where too much emphasis is put on the language and mechanism of the decisions. Having read some of your books I would certainly think you were much more competent to teach constitutional law than anyone at the Harvard or Yale law schools. I know of no book on the Constitution which has any merit which has come from the faculties of our American law schools. I would think that an undergraduate course in constitutional law would be of the greatest importance to a lawyer because probably the only place he will ever learn about the Constitution is in an undergraduate college.

You mention philosophy, psychology, economics and political science. Certainly these names would seem intimately related to a lawyer's education. The question, of course, is who teaches them. I know of no psychologist who understands the psychology of political institutions and I believe most economic courses contain only theology. An economic course should be a history of the effect of economic ideas and slogans on society. Most economic courses are an evaluation of the soundness of one economic theory as compared to another. I do not know how economics is taught at Princeton but if it does not include such books as Bray Hammond's *Banks and Politics,* published by the Princeton University Press, the student will never understand the actual effect of monetary theory on a changing economy. The economic courses at Yale in the 1930s, when I was on the faculty, were noteworthy for their lack of comprehension of what was going on in our economy. The only economic courses with which I am familiar today are those given by my friend Galbraith at Harvard, which is splendid, and the fantastic nonsense they teach at Chicago.

As I look back on my own experience at Princeton in the Class of 1911 the course I got the most out of was Corwin's course in the Constitution. Next to that was Hibben's course in philosophy.

So I wind up with the conclusion that the most important undergraduate course for a lawyer is constitutional law.

*Sincerely*

---

## *To Frank Serri* [312]

Washington, D.C., May 15, 1967

Dear Frank:

I am familiar with the arguments you make in your letter of May 10th. I disagree with all of them. I think they are unrealistic.

1. It would have been politically impossible to have admitted China years ago. If we had she would not have changed. It is equally impossible to admit her today because we would have to abandon Taiwan.

2. The world is too small to allow China and/or Russia a free and open road in Asia. There is also no way to obtain a peaceful modus vivendi with either China or Russia except by the use of military power.

You are quite right about the wisdom of failing to intervene in Hungary. Russia had an overwhelming force already in action. We couldn't win. We had no commitment to Hungary other than the foolish encouragement of a war of liberation which Hungary was supposed to do for herself. We have a commitment in Vietnam. We are bound to win the war in the long run if we have the resolution to apply the necessary force—and I think we have.

3. Your suggestion that if we had stopped the bombing Hanoi would have been more cooperative seems to me nonsense. Any North Vietnam general who failed to take advantage of it would be court-martialed. So far as world opinion is concerned, the more we try to court it the less we will get in our favor.

4. If the President is defeated, as he well may be, he will go down as one of our greatest Presidents.

Your idea that by making concessions Johnson will be a great peacemaker seems to me also unrealistic. Think of the concessions we made to Russia and how much peace did we get out of them?

Anyway, this is my judgment.

With best regards and hoping you will call me up the next time you get to Washington,

*Sincerely*

---

## *To Rexford G. Tugwell*

Washington, D.C., May 26, 1967

Dear Rex:

I appreciate very much your writing to me about my speech,[313] particularly for the reason that you seem to me to stand head and shoulders above all the other "intellectuals" in the New Deal.

Although my speech has been so interpreted, I never intended to attack intellectuals as such, or to claim that they were always wrong or always alienated. The phrase came from one of Walter Lippman's columns in which he said that Johnson had alienated all of the intellectuals in the country and that he therefore would unquestionably come to some sort of a bad end. Then Professor Feurer of the University of Toronto wrote an article entitled "Alienated Intellectuals' Elite"[314] so I thought the phrase was a good one to cover the group of people who were downgrading the United States today.

So far as intellectuals are concerned, I claim to be one myself, and I did not realize I gave the impression of attacking "intellectuals." I was only attacking the particular intellectuals who happen to disagree with me.

However, your interpretation of the speech as a general attack on intellectuals is the one which most people got. I received a lot of letters of congratulations from the radical right.

When I wrote the speech I had no notion that anybody was going to pay any attention to it. Without my knowledge, somebody sent a copy to somebody in the State Department and the President used it in his news conference. And so it got wide comment, to my complete surprise.

Now to answer your question as to whether intellectuals are emotional and always wrong. I suppose the answer is that everybody commenting on current affairs is always "wrong" except the complete cynic. He is always "right" but what an intolerable and ineffective nuisance he is.

I do not think that the terms "right" or "wrong" should apply to the expressions of social ideals. As an advocate I am in favor of attacking all pacifists. As a philosopher, I would feel the world would be greatly disadvantaged if it weren't for the continued expression of pacifists' ideals. You can easily prove Karl Marx was wrong but what a tremendous contribution he made to the world as we know it today.

From the point of view of "right" or "wrong" I suppose you would say this about the Russian Revolution: "The Russian Revolution was the right thing for the Russian people in order to end the tyranny of the Czars. The Czars had been wrong in creating conditions which made the revolution inevitable. However, the Revolutionists were wrong in going to extremes that ended in a tyranny almost as bad as what they had before. It would have been much better if the Czars had been more reasonable or, failing that, if their successor intellectuals had been more reasonable. We conclude, therefore, that though the Russian aristocracy was wrong, the intellectuals who succeeded it were also wrong, and it might have been better if the Revolution had not taken place at all."

The trouble with this is that it confuses the point of view of an advocate with the point of view of a historian. An advocate is always wrong in that he must oversimplify in order to convince people and gain a following. Yet, if he wrote about social movements objectively, as an anthropologist writes about the customs of a primitive tribe, he would exercise no leadership and wouldn't inspire anyone in the society he is writing about.

The inconsistency between the point of view of the advocate and the objective seeker of truth is one that never bothered me. In arguing cases I almost always convince myself that I am right. If I didn't I would not be able to argue them persuasively. For example, I was completely convinced that the NRA was morally and economically wrong. Looking back at it, I now realize that it was due to the NRA that the labor movement achieved the place it has in the American economy.

In addition, I now think that parades in favor of the Blue Eagle were instrumental in restoring national morale, absurd as they seemed to me at the time.

On the other hand, largely influenced by your own views, it seemed to me at the time that the AAA was morally and economically right, because in spite of the absurdity of killing little pigs in a hungry country, it was a step toward national planning as opposed to the surrender of that function to big business represented by the NRA.

The agricultural laws today are a sorry but probably inevitable compromise. But the thing that has survived from your administration is that national planning is recognized as a necessary objective. Out of the original AAA has emerged the present war on poverty.

Finally, I was convinced that national planning was impossible without strict enforcement of the antitrust laws, because without those laws we would wind up in a system of domestic and international cartels. Based on that idea, I wrote a book, *The Bottlenecks of Business*, which in effect asserted that if the antitrust laws were enforced all our economic ills would be remedied. It can be argued that this extreme faith in the Sherman Act is nonsense, but there seemed no other way of explaining the antitrust laws to businessmen who had been evading them for over twenty years.

From a philosophical point of view, I believe that stable social organization must be like a ballet in which all sorts of characters, representing different ideas, dance in some sort of balance. These ideas are necessarily the product of intellectuals. Without intellectuals we have barbarism.

Within that ballet, I feel my function as an advocate is to cuss the pacifists and to advocate wars would seem to me to be promoting the enforcement of an international law.

As to your anticipation of a world nation. This is a character in the ballet which I think is most important even though I have little faith that it will ever be achieved. But without that anticipation, strongly advocated by groups like yours, we would probably never achieve any sort of world stability.

This idea of a stable society as a set of contradictory ideas in some sort of balance has no utility in the public forum. It has no inspirational quality. Yet the public is becoming dimly aware of it as is evidenced by frequent use of the term "image" in political life. It is becoming the duty of the political leader to constantly improve his "image," rather than to rely on the assertion of "sound principles." He advocates principles, but both he and the public know that they are selected not because he believes in them but because they improve his "image."

Well, anyway, I do not think I have made myself clear. But since I have gone to all of this trouble, I would like to have your comments as to "soundness" and whether I am either "right" or "wrong" in the opinions in the enclosed taken from *Dun's Review.* I also enclose a copy of my speech.

*With warm regards*

---

## *To Ernest Gruening*[315]

Washington, D.C., June 27, 1967

Dear Senator:

Thank you for your letter about my small contribution to your campaign.

May I say that much as I disagree with you about the war in Vietnam I admire your courage in refusing to sign the statement of Fulbright, Morse, et al., that we were going to keep our troops in Vietnam regardless of their previous criticism of the war. It seems to me that there is only one issue. We should either surrender or prosecute the war vigorously. The position that we should surrender is arguable. There will be certain loss of prestige involved, but Russia and France have survived similar losses of prestige when they backed down from previous commitments. Personally I am convinced that surrender would be disastrous and that we are fortunate to have an army in Asia because otherwise Russia or Japan could go straight down the coast to Singapore.

However, I recognize that there is another side to the debate. But if you once decide to keep an army in Vietnam there is no possible way of avoiding escalation. One side has three regiments, the other gets four, the first side puts in five, and it goes on up. I have no patience with the people who want to keep the army there and think there is a possibility of not escalating. Therefore, I admire your courage in taking the unpopular side and refusing to go along with the message to Hanoi that we were going to keep our troops there, accompanied by criticism of the administration as to our military tactics.

As a tribute to your courage I would like to contribute another $50 to your campaign.

*Sincerely yours*

---

## *To Rexford G. Tugwell*

Washington, D.C., Aug. 22, 1967

Dear Rex:

Mrs. Arnold and I are leaving for Europe this evening to celebrate our Golden Wedding Anniversary (50 years of married life with never a blow struck with intent to kill). Before I go I want to make some comment on your letter of June 14th concerning decision-making in a democracy. Many of my friends are worried about the problem. I have subscribed to an organization headed by Senator Paul Douglas (I can't even think of the name right now)[316] which is making an intensive study about distortions in the news. I hope they come up with something but I doubt it.

In any event, I am tremendously optimistic about the present process of change in our society. Spurred on by the Negro problem architects are planning cities. Housing is being studied. Sociologists for the first time in history are making meaningful studies. The necessity of international leadership by the United States was tacitly admitted when Fulbright and his crew notified Vietnam that we are *not* going to get out of the war. The population explosion is being seriously studied. And, best of all, the vital ideal that there must be a war on poverty is being accepted even by Republican conservatives. The progress in the betterment of Negroes, while it has not advanced as quickly as it should, has nevertheless been startling. Real work is being done on every pressing American problem. Riots are a temporary phenomenon, and not nearly as serious as many people think. Indeed, I suspect they have their uses in making people face the urban problems. We have at least gotten rid of that precious group of Harvard idolaters and namby-pambies who surrounded President Kennedy.

We have still to recognize the necessity of national planning and the futility of State governments. That's going to take another ten or fifteen years of the kind of yapping and yammering which accompanied your own efforts to plan in the Roosevelt Administration. But all of Roosevelt's ideas have now become commonplace after the Goldwater defeat.

The intellectuals in the "great thinker" category are, of course, very unhappy. They are moralists, not realists. They would like to surrender in Vietnam but don't have the nerve to say so. Fulbright is writing articles about how sick our society is. But, compared with any other society in the world it is making extraordinary achievements. The Vietnam war is going to end sometime, like all wars do. And America is going to come out on top, as it did in Korea.

I disagree with you about the Supreme Court being an inadequate instrument for social change. I think it is most useful because it never presents a controversial issue in a way that requires any immediate action. It moves along from case to case as it has in the Apportionment cases and on the racial question. You remember it changed under Roosevelt's attack. By this method the reactionary groups gradually wear themselves out, like a big fish struggling against a line with thirty pounds pressure.

It is my own belief that once a problem is presented to the American people it's going to be solved gradually. The American people are beginning to be aware of the nature of the problems. Architects, sociologists and civic leaders are making real technological progress. The opposition to national planning is gradually being eroded away.

It may be that the Fulbrights and the Galbraiths and Luther Kings and Wallaces (The Governor, not Henry) will succeed in defeating Johnson and will elect Nixon. I would regret this, but Nixon is a changed man too.

As for the lawyers and the economists, they are hopeless. The lawyers believe that the remedy for everything is the enforcement of traditional law. The economists refuse to recognize that the real wealth of the nation is its productive capacity. They think of national wealth in terms of money. They are unable to imagine a planned distribution of national production. They are as worried today about inflation as they were in the depths of the depression in the 1930s. Everything they do creates more inflation, as I suspect will be the result of Johnson's present tax program.

But lawyers and economists have always been a frustrating force in American society. There is no more possibility of getting rid of them than a dog has of getting rid of fleas.

Anyhow, I'm not agreeing with the thesis that the United States is a sick society. It is today the most vital instrument for progress in the world.

*Sincerely*

---

## *To Otis L. Graham, Jr.* [317]

Washington, D.C., Nov. 20, 1967

Dear Professor Graham:

Thank you for your letter of November 14. Liberalism in the era of F.D.R. is certainly an interesting topic. I would be delighted to talk to you about it. All of my unpublished manuscripts during my New Deal days, such as speeches, etc., are in the archive of the University of Wyoming.

In answer to your question I would say that American liberals, unlike British liberals in the nineteenth century, have no sense of political reality as may be noted in their alienation from the Government today. They are essentially critics, they are hard to get along with and also impossible to get along without. I do recall how they were consistently disappointed with Roosevelt for various reasons depending upon the particular conviction of one group or another. Walter Lippmann, you may recall, came out for Landon and never had much use for Roosevelt. Today we are getting the same reaction of liberals against Johnson. Roosevelt's genius consisted in the fact that he had no definite economic program and at the same time had the ability to shift from one position to another.

Your question about the gap between what was possible and what was achieved and how things might have worked out if positions had been altered seems to me like an inquiry as to how the French Revolution could have been avoided. History does not give any answers to such alternatives.

*Sincerely*

---

## *To Alexander Holtzoff* [318]

Washington, D.C., Nov. 29, 1967

My dear Judge Holtzoff:

I learn from an editorial in today's *Washington Post* that you have decided to retire. I want to express my deep regret. In my opinion, the Bench will lose its most effective judge.

I think your outstanding merit has been the fact that all your decisions have presented a sharp issue which could be appealed. Too many Federal judges fuzz the issues and try to avoid reversal on appeal in that way. This you have never done and this clarity in presenting issues, which your opinions always exemplify, has speeded up the judicial process. For example, I recently represented a client in a Federal court for a period of two years during which the judge refused to dismiss on an issue which clearly required prompt action. At the end of two years, after building up a huge file, the case was dismissed.

The burden on judicial time of this kind of evasion of the issues by the lower Federal courts all over the country is one of the reasons the dockets got so far behind. It is not too important whether a judge decided a case right or wrong, it is much more important that he decide it.

I have always told my clients that if we could only get Judge Holtzoff the litigation would at least have a foreseeable end and we would not have to spend endless time on motions in a case where the issues were apparent at the outset.

I personally consider you one of the greatest trial judges in the United States. I hope that in your retirement you will continue to accept at least a large number of cases.

*Sincerely, and with great admiration*

---

## *To John de J. Pemberton, Jr.*

Washington, D.C., April 11, 1968

Dear Mr. Pemberton:

I have been a member of the American Civil Liberties Union for at least twenty years. I regretfully hand in my resignation.

I was first shocked at your release stating that Attorney General Ramsey Clark was suppressing freedom of speech.[319] Finally, your proceeding in the District Court against the handling of the arrests I considered an outrageous insult to an organization which had been handling an emergency problem in a thoroughly admirable way.

I resign with great regret but I do not wish to be connected with an organization which appears so utterly irresponsible and unrealistic as yours is today.

Please remove my name from your mailing list.

*Sincerely*

---

## *To Ernest Angell*[320]

Washington, D.C., May 27, 1968

Dear Mr. Angell:

I have your letter of May 21st about my resignation from the American Civil Liberties Union. I was sorry to have to part company with the Union after so many years, going back to Roger Baldwin. However, a succession of recent cases convinced me that I should sever my connections.

One of these was the defense of Lynd[321] in his trouble with Roosevelt University in Chicago. This action seemed to me subversive of all college discipline. Lynd in my view was unfit to be a professor anywhere but, whether I am right or wrong, I could not go along with the idea that the ACLU should try to force on any college a professor whom they did not think met their requirements. And certainly only an extreme leftist would defend Lynd as a historian or sociologist.

Another case was the defense of the Army captain who was not a pacifist but refused to obey orders because he didn't like the war in Vietnam. I spent three years in the Army during the First World War. I can't imagine how an effective military organization can exist if a captain does not choose to obey an order. The comparison between Johnson and Hitler which some people have made seems to me fantastically ridiculous.

A third case was the defense of Spock and Coffin.[322] Certainly anyone can be opposed to the Vietnam war and say so. But to say that the collection of draft cards, the presentation of them to the Attorney General, and the actual request of Coffin that he be prosecuted for what he admitted was an offense, goes far beyond free speech. I do not see how Ramsey Clark could possibly have ignored such a public challenge when the country was at war. But the ACLU did more than defend Spock and Coffin, it issued a press release saying that the Government in issuing the indictment was interfering with freedom of speech in the United States. This was too much for me to take.

And finally, your action in bringing a suit without legal foundation attacking the courts here because in the emergency some of them may have not followed the proper requirements with respect to bail seemed to me completely irresponsible.

You ask what the alternatives were before your Board when it took the actions of which I disapprove. At the time when I thought the ACLU was of the greatest utility was during the McCarthy era when men like Lattimore were attacked because of their opinions on China, when university professors' courses were examined to discover subversive opinions, and Robert Kennedy was actively engaged in this kind of witch hunt and J.F. Kennedy approved, when university presidents were not protecting their professors from scurrilous attacks, when anyone accused in the State Department of subversive opinions was brought before a loyalty board and his career ruined. I recall the Dorothy Bailey case, which this firm defended and lost, where a career was ruined on evidence which was not disclosed to the accused; the Fort Monmouth spy case where scientists were discharged on secret evidence, which this firm defended and finally won, but not until the careers of twenty-six scientists had been irretrievably damaged. In those days noisy people like Dr. Spock and Chaplain Coffin were entirely silent. It was impossible to raise among college professors a fund to defend Lattimore. Arthur Schlesinger, Jr., who was accused of being soft on Communism on the floor of Congress, was sufficiently frightened to prove his virtue by writing a column attacking Lattimore. In those days the ACLU although constantly being charged with subversion stood up to its guns and I was proud of it.

Today we do have freedom of speech in the sense that anyone can hire a hall or teach a course in a university or express views in Government without danger to his career. In other words, the battle for civil liberties in the sense of free expression of opinion has now been won.

It is regrettable that the ACLU should now be pushing the cause of civil liberties into what, in my view, amounts to a defense of civil disobedience. Interference with discipline in colleges, interference with discipline in the Army, defense of individuals who admit they are banded together to impede the draft in time of war and publicly dare the Attorney General to prosecute them—such activities are now being justified by the ACLU on the ground that a civil rights issue is involved.

I intend to make no public issue of this. I resign privately and with regret and without any desire to cause you any more trouble than you already have with an organization which seems to be going further and further toward the extreme left.

*Sincerely*

---

## *To Edward H. Levi*

Washington, D.C., Dec. 11, 1968

Dear Ed:

I wouldn't have missed your Inauguration if I had had to have gone on a stretcher. I got great vicarious satisfaction out of it. I hired myself a limousine and chauffeur to take me around while I was in Chicago. Frances, who is a born name-dropper, explained to the driver that we were intimate friends of the new President. He was so impressed that he raised the rates by twenty per cent.

I thought your Inauguration speech was superb. You did not make the mistake Bob Hutchins made when he promised a speedy reform of the University to conform to a lot of generalizations which were impossible to achieve and only alienated the University community.

I was particularly pleased with the enthusiasm with which your appointment was greeted by the press and by everybody that I talked to. You entered your term of office in an atmosphere of great confidence. Everyone seems to respect your judgment and to expect great things of you.

You have one of the most important jobs in the United States. It requires tact and a good deal of walking on eggs. You've got to get teamwork out of your faculty and this is very difficult in a group where all the professors hold life jobs by virtue of the institution of tenure, which I suppose is a necessary evil in any educational institution, however much of a nuisance it may be. The difficulty, of course, with the job of being a university president is that no university faculty can reform itself because it will cling to vested privileges like any other institution. I read somewhere that university scholarships should be given not to the university itself but directly to the students through the government or some other outside agency. Then they could buy the kind of education they wanted in a competitive educational market and pick the place they wanted most to go to. Instead of rioting they could move to some other institution they liked better. It is an attractive idea but like most such ideas it probably wouldn't work. In fact, you would be well advised not to write any controversial books on the nature of higher education in the abstract. The nature of your task is summed up in Tennyson's "Ulysses," where he speaks of the duty of his son Telemicus (however you spell it) "by patience to make mild a savage people and by soft degrees subdue them to the useful and the good."

In any event, you started out with the loyalty and confidence of your faculty, according to my spies and paid agents who had cased the place, to an extent which very few university presidents now have. A large part of the confidence in you is, I believe, due to the fact that you worked up from a mere professor to the dizzy eminence which you now occupy, and you ought to know how to handle professors and students through a long experience which very few university presidents possess. There is a great advantage of being considered by the people I talked to not as someone who has been selected from the outside to run the university but as an integral part of the university.

I suppose that copies of your speech will eventually be published; when they are I wish you would send one to me through the mail. I would like to read it more carefully to be sure I didn't miss anything.

As for myself, since my last heart attack I have been taking things very easy at the office, becoming incorrigibly lazy. It's a pleasant enough life being on a semi-retired status if you can get rid of the guilty feeling that you ought to be up and doing, which is difficult to do.

We left Chicago for New York with the intention of attending the banquet on the occasion of the unveiling of Abe Fortas' portrait at Yale. However, the next morning I suffered some kind of relapse and couldn't get up to New Haven. When we got back to Washington Frances found your beautiful flowers, and sends her love and appreciation. Frances also sends her regards to your wife and wants me to inform you how much we enjoyed your three sons.

*Affectionately*

---

## *To William O. Douglas*

Washington, D.C., March 27, 1969

Dear Bill:

Your letter suggesting the dissolution of the Hunt Club[323] came as such a shock that I was unable to answer it immediately. It is of course true, as you point out, that over a period of thirty years the Hunt Club has never found any new member worthy of admission. Indeed, applications for membership have been negligible in the last ten years. Our last application, as you probably remember, was from the Reverend Abernathy who seemed to be under the impression that membership in the Hunt Club would assist him in his poverty march on Washington. As you recall, we turned him down. Since that time we have had no further applications.

Pursuant to your suggestion as to dissolution, I examined the assets of the Hunt Club which are stored in a shack in New Haven. The mattresses are somewhat discolored because of a leaky roof, but they still have preserved their bounce. This renders them useless for any purpose except for use by the Club. Any movement on one of these bouncy mattresses would throw you about five feet in the air, and whether you land again on the mattress is a matter of luck. The flashlights are in good condition except the batteries are worn out. These, however, could be replaced at an expense of about $15. All in all, I do not think that a sale of the Hunt Club assets would realize more than $150. These considerations support your idea of dissolution.

However, I do not think you have adequately considered the international repercussions which an announcement of the Hunt Club's dissolution would create. I understand that Russia now has sixteen hunt clubs deployed around each of its ABM installations. We have only one. The national interest would clearly indicate that we should deploy at least one hunt club around the site of every new ABM missile. This would be expensive but it might be a valuable bargaining factor in negotiations with Russia which are soon to take place.

Secretary Laird informs me that an announced dissolution of the Hunt Club might destroy our bargaining position with Russia. He asked me to hold off the Hunt Club dissolution for at least six months to give the Nixon Administration a better chance to negotiate.

Personally, I think the time has come not to think about what our country can do for us but what we can do for our country.

*Sincerely*

---

## *To Abraham Ribicoff*[324]

Washington, D.C., April 3, 1969

Dear Senator:

Thank you for your letter of April 1, 1969, enclosing a copy of the *Statement of Ralph Nader* before your Subcommittee on March 20, 1969, on S. 860.[325] In your letter you call my attention to the paragraph on Page 7 in which this firm, together with two others of high reputation, is charged with "cutting down consumer programs in their incipiency or undermining them if they mature." What particular activities on our part, or on the part of other legal counsel whom he mentions, he refers to we have no idea. We suspect, however, that what Mr. Nader is really objecting to is any adequate legal representation before Congress or before administrative tribunals of the interest of any organization which does not meet with his approval. Such representation, he thinks, would result in "greasing of the corporate wheels and the softening of the bureaucrats' will." By this he means that it might be possible for counsel to persuade the bureaucrat in question that there was some merit in his client's case and thus his "bureaucrat's will" would become softened.

Perhaps a rule that counsel should not make any representation on behalf of his client without the prior approval of Mr. Nader would satisfy him. The necessity of hearing representatives of both sides of a case, even if one of them happens to be General Motors, may slow down many of Mr. Nader's praiseworthy objectives. But it is the only course consistent with the constitutional idea that adverse interests are entitled to have their claims presented by counsel of their choice.

Mr. Nader has every right to attack the claims and arguments of any group which he thinks opposes the consumers' interests. He has no right, however, to attack such a group for *presenting* its claims and arguments (however wrong they may be in his eyes) to the men who must make the decisions. That, of course, is what he is doing in the paragraph criticizing legal counsel to which you have referred us. He is saying to your Committee that we should get rid of skilled advocates because they confuse the court.

*Sincerely*

---

## *To Nathan M. Pusey* [326]

Washington, D.C., April 14, 1969

Dear Mr. Pusey:

As an alumnus of Harvard (LL.B. 1914) I want to assure you of my emphatic support of your position on the recent student uprising. I was shocked at the failure of the Faculty to give you the support you deserve. I am sure that the alumni will agree with you in overwhelming numbers. The only difficulty is going to be that they are unorganized.

I wish it was feasible to circularize the alumini on this issue.

What particularly annoys me about the Harvard Faculty's failure to support your position is the fact that you alone, of all the university presidents, stood out against the attacks made by Senator McCarthy on academic freedom. During that period this firm represented Owen Lattimore who was indicated at the insistence of Senator McCarthy. We represented Professor Edward Condon whose security clearance was denied. We also represented a number of professors who were called before the Committee. In none of these cases could we get any support, financial or otherwise, from faculty members of our great institutions. They were all literally scared to death. During that period you were the only President I can recall who took a firm and courageous step to protect his faculty.

Now that the heat is off members of your Faculty have been making irresponsible attacks against your administration. They feel protected by tenure, they seek the approval of a vociferous minority of rebellious students, they create the very situation which you have been compelled to meet.

As the vote of the Harvard Faculty shows, a faculty organization protected by tenure, and under pressure to yield to irresponsible demands, is incompetent to take leadership in the management of a great university. It may be that some university administrations have failed to keep up with the times. That certainly is not true of your administration at Harvard. I feel that it is necessary in the interests of university education that you do not yield to the irresponsible faculty pressure to which you have been subjected.

*Sincerely*

---

## *To Julian M. Sturtevant* [327]

Washington, D.C., July 1, 1969

Dear Professor Sturtevant:

I was distressed by your letter of June 26, 1969. You inform me that the fact that this firm represents some tobacco companies has deprived you of "hope for achieving a decent society in this country."

I was myself a professor at Yale for eight happy years. I know from experience some of the consequences when a professor gives up hope for a decent society. He becomes morose and irritable. He exhibits a tendency to thumb his nose at people with whom he disagrees under the delusion that this will put them in their place and make them ashamed of themselves. His point of view becomes narrow and even may affect his teaching. I feel, therefore, an obligation to Yale to give you such mental therapy as I can; hence this letter.

One of the great achievements of American constitutional law is the fact that every litigant either before a court or before Congress is entitled to be represented by an attorney. The duty of an attorney is not towards society but towards his client. An attorney is not ethically permitted when presenting his client's case to give his own opinion as to the merits. His duty is solely to make the best presentation he can. The tobacco companies are as much entitled to representation by counsel as the lowest criminal is. The duty of an attorney is to act as an advocate, not as a judge. The theory of American constitutional law is that better results are obtained from a system which requires each side to be represented by counsel of his own choice. When he is too ignorant to make that choice an attorney is appointed by the court.

Your position seems to be that a litigant has no moral right to adequate representation by counsel if he represents a cause in which you do not believe. That idea has been repudiated in American constitutional law. The great advance made by the Warren Court has been to insure adequate representation for the poor as well as for the rich, for the guilty as well as for the innocent.

This firm is retained by a large number of corporate clients. We have lost some cases and won others. Our function is solely to make adequate presentation of the evidence supporting our client's case. The responsibility of producing adverse evidence is on the other side. On the other hand, a very considerable part of our practice has been representing clients with unpopular causes who have no money to pay fees. We have represented people like Owen Lattimore whose ordeal before the courts and Congress lasted over five years. We represented Dr. Peters of Yale; we have represented a host of University professors charged with communist leanings. We have represented scientists laboring under the same charges. We represented the scientists who were discharged from Fort Monmouth because the Administration was afraid of McCarthy. We were responsible for the Durham decision which abolished the right and wrong test of criminal insanity. Durham, incidentally, was later convicted under this new definition. We were responsible for the Gideon case that no man however guilty should be of inadequate representation by counsel at any stage of proceedings. We have represented persons charged with homosexuality. We have even represented the head of the Ku Klux Klan. In all of these cases we have attempted not to judge the merits, but to do our duty as advocates to present the best case we could for the persons we represent.

During the course of these cases we have been subjected to hundreds of comments like yours. How can a reputable firm justify representing such despicable people? We have refrained from replying to such comments because the people who make them show such a lack of understanding of our judicial system that it is useless. The only successful riposte to charges of this kind was made some years ago by my partner Paul Porter at the Burning Tree Club. A prominent individual approached him and said with the same bitterness as you exhibit in your letter: "Paul, I understand that your firm is principally engaged in defending Communists and homosexuals." Paul replied: "Yes, that's correct. What can we do for you?" However, as you immediately recognize, this reply did not really meet the issue.

However, of the hundreds of letters that we have received, yours and Ralph Nader's are the only ones which have suggested that tobacco companies and General Motors are not entitled to adequate representation. Ralph Nader's charges are more general than yours so we attach a letter in which we replied to him.

Whatever be the ultimate solution of the cigarette problem it will not be furthered by establishing the principle that in any sort of legal controversy either side should be deprived of the services of the best counsel he can obtain. Your idea is a dangerous doctrine. Once established, it will sap the very foundations of the American ideal of a fair trial.

Letters like yours which attack the theory of adequate representation by counsel on both sides without judgment as to the merits represent a dangerous tendency which reached its height in the McCarthy era when even University presidents refused to support professors in their right to a fair hearing.

I doubt very much if this letter has any therapeutic effect in curing you of your present abandonment of "hope for achieving a decent society" if a tobacco company is given the right to be represented by counsel. Nevertheless, it is the best I can do. I suggest that you read it over at least twice, then take a couple of aspirins and see if that doesn't make you feel better about the role of a fair trial in American jurisprudence.

*Sincerely*

---

## *To Alan D. Harper*

Washington, D.C., Feb. 5, 1970

Dear Mr. Harper:

Several weeks ago, after his death, I removed from Judge Arnold's desk your letter to him of May 30, 1969, xerox of which I enclose.

I am sure you must have heard by now that Judge Arnold died in his sleep in the early morning hours of November 7, 1969. Up until his death he was able to come into the office a few days each week. I have been unable to find the enclosure in your letter of May 30, 1969, and it may be that he returned it to you.

If not, I am sorry that your letter was not answered.

*Sincerely,*

*Marguerite O'Brien*

---

# Notes to Introduction

1. William McGovern, Interview, July 21, 1971.
2. *U.S.* v. *Pullman Co. et al.* 50 F. Supp. 123 (1943).
3. William McGovern, Interview, July 21, 1971.
4. *Ibid.*
5. *Ibid.*
6. *Ibid.*
7. *Ibid.*
8. Wilson O. Clough, *A History of the University of Wyoming, 1887–1964* (Laramie, Wyo., 1965), 38.
9. Thurman Arnold, *Fair Fights and Foul* (New York, 1965), 3. Hereafter cited *Fair Fights and Foul.*
10. U.S. House *Reports*, 1st Session, 52nd Cong. (Washington, 1894).
11. *Fair Fights and Foul*, 9.
12. Laramie *Boomerang*, January 27, 1960; Laramie *Life*, December 5, 1952.
13. G. R. Hebard File, Western History Research Center, University of Wyoming, Laramie.
14. Thurman Arnold, *Transcript*, Registrar's Office, Wabash College.
15. *Fair Fights and Foul*, 16.
16. Thurman Arnold, *Transcript*, Registrar's Office, Princeton University.
17. *Fair Fights and Foul*, 16.
18. *Ibid.*, 20.
19. Thurman Arnold, *Transcript*, Office of Registrar, Harvard University.
20. T. W. Arnold to Mrs. C. P. Arnold, June 1911. T. W. Arnold Collection, Archive of Contemporary History, University of Wyoming. Hereafter cited Arnold Coll.
21. T. W. Arnold to Mr. and Mrs. C. P. Arnold, January 7, 1913. *Ibid.*
22. *Ibid.*
23. T. W. Arnold to Mrs. C. P. Arnold, November 24, 1913. *Ibid.*
24. T. W. Arnold to C. P. Arnold, February 15, 1914. *Ibid.*
25. *Ibid.*, September 2, 1914.
26. *Ibid.*, May 5, 1915.
27. *Ibid.*, January 7, 1915.
28. *Ibid.*

29. *Ibid.*, June 20, 1916.

30. *Ibid.*, December 24, 1916.

31. *Ibid.*

32. *Ibid.*

33. *Ibid.*, August 24, 1917.

34. Mrs. T. W. Arnold, Interview, July 21, 1971.

35. *Ibid.*

36. *Fair Fights and Foul*, 28.

37. T. W. Arnold to Mr. and Mrs. C. P. Arnold, March 4, 1918. *Ibid.*

38. *Ibid.*, December 10, 1917.

39. Laramie population, in 1930, declined 37 souls, from 1890 to 1,853 U.S. Census, 1920, Part 1 (Washington, D.C.), 319.

40. Laramie *Republican*, August 28, 1920; August 3, 20, 31, September 24, October 20, November 19, 1921; December 20, 1922.

41. *Ibid.*, December 22, 1921.

42. *Ibid.*, November 2, 1921.

43. Mrs. Carl Arnold, Interview, July 27, 1971.
Laramie *Republican* and *Boomerang*, February 5, 1925. As a new arrival in Laramie, Professor Wilson Clough, describing his first few months in Laramie, wrote of the Arnold's winter picnic, "We were invited yesterday to the Arnold picnic on a ranch on the Little Laramie [river] , west of town. This is a very generous gesture on the part of the C. P. Arnolds, whom we scarcely know. A lot of people were there, and though it was February, the weather was mild. A huge fire of fenceposts stood in tipi fashion warmed the area for the chilly. Some hiked out over snow banks and fields. I met a number of faculty, and particularly liked Dr. Knight and Mrs. Knight. Dr. Nelson made a speech about the willow as Wyoming's state tree, to which Mr. Arnold replied in amusing fashion, with pretended objections, and references to the 'weeping willow,' and other lugubrious associations values, he said rendered the tree most inappropriate for Wyoming. Smith says that such is Arnold's manner. He is a lawyer and wit." Wilson O. Clough, "Fragments From a Journal, Laramie, Wyo., 1924–1925," (unpublished manuscript, Western History Research Center).

44. Interviews with Mrs. T. W. Arnold, July 21, 1971; Mrs. Carl Arnold, July 27,1971; Paul Porter, April 5, 1971; Miss Marguerite O'Brien, July 23, 1971; George Arnold, March 8, 1973.

45. William McGovern, Interview, July 21, 1971.

46. George Arnold, Interview, March 8, 1973.

47. *Fair Fights and Foul*, 34; T.W. Arnold, "Roosevelt's Contribution to the American Competitive Ideal," *The Centennial Review*, IX (Spring 1965), 194.

48. Laramie *Republican*, November 3, 1920.

49. Many are the variations in phraseology of that fateful morn, but only one paper deemed it necessary to note the historic incident, and that notation was horribly antiseptic. Laramie *Boomerang*, January 11, 1921 ; Interviews with Mrs. T. W. Arnold, July 21, 1971; Mrs. Carl W. Arnold, July 27, 1971; T. W. Arnold, November 16, 1965, and *Fair Fights and Foul*, 32–33.

50. Laramie *Boomerang*, February 2, 1921.

51. *Ibid.*

52. *Ibid.*, February 9, 1921.

53. Laramie *Boomerang*, February 17, 18, 1921.

54. William McGovern, Interview, July 21, 1971.

55. *Wyoming Session Laws*, Ch. 87, 121–24.

56. Laramie *Boomerang*, February 18, 1921.

57. Arnold, 1,215; Blair, 1,171 votes. Laramie *Republican*, November 8, 1922.

58. *Ibid.*, November 4, 1922.

59. *Ibid.*, October 31, 1922.

60. *Ibid.*, October 28, 1922.

61. *Ibid.*

62. Laramie *Boomerang*, December 22, 1922.

63. *Ibid.*, January 3, 1923.

64. *Ibid.*

65. M. Cullen, "New Ideas in Town Improvement," *Country Life* XXXVII (November 19, 1921), 84–86; C. P. Gilman, "Making Town Fit to Live In," CII *Century* (July 1921), 361–66; C. Montoliv, "Fairhope," *American City* XXIV (April 1921), 355–59.

66. Laramie *Republican*, June 6, August 8, 1923; Laramie *Boomerang*, October 8, 1924.

67. Laramie *Boomerang*, August 13, 1923.

68. Laramie *Republican* and *Boomerang*, July 18, 1924.

69. S. C. Downey (R), 609; F. K. Dukes (R), 464; C. V. Garnett (D), 433; T.W. Arnold (D), 288. *Ibid.*, August 26, 1924.

70. Mrs. T. W. Arnold, Interview, July 21, 1971.

71. Laramie *Republican* and *Boomerang*, January 3, 1925.

72. George Arnold, Interview, March 8, 1973.

73. Mrs. T. W. Arnold, Interview, July 21, 1971.

74. Hugh Cox, Interview, July 15, 1971.

75. *Fair Fights and Foul*, 32.

76. Mrs. T. W. Arnold, Interview, July 21, 1971.

77. *Ibid.*

78. *Ibid.*

79. Laramie *Republican* and *Boomerang*, July 2, 7, 1927.

80. *Ibid.*, July 30; August 8, 16, 1927.

81. *Fair Fights and Foul*, 35.

82. Mrs. T. W. Arnold, Interview, July 21, 1971.

83. Douglas Ayer, "Quest of Efficiency: The Ideological Journey of Thurman Arnold in the Interwar Period," *Stanford Law Review*, XXIII (June 1971), 1049–86.

84. William McGovern, Interview, July 27, 1971.

85. Thurman Arnold, "Judicial Councils," *West Virginia Law Quarterly and the Bar*, XXXV (April 1929), 193–238.

86. T. W. Arnold to C. E. Clark, October 12, 1929. Arnold Coll.

87. *Ibid.*

88. Thurman Arnold, "Review of the Work of the College of Law," *West Virginia Law Quarterly and the Bar* XXXVI (June 1930), 319–29.

89. Thurman Arnold to David Howard, February 9, 1928. Arnold Coll.

90. T. W. Arnold to Fred Nussbaum, February 2, 1929. *Ibid.*

91. Mrs. T. W. Arnold, Interview, July 21, 1971.

92. Mrs. Yolande M. Gehri to Gene M. Gressley, June 15, August 1, 28, 1972.

93. Mrs. Carl Arnold, Interview, July 27, 1971.

94. Abe Krash, Interview, July 27, 1971.

95. *Fair Fights and Foul*, 63.

96. *Ibid.*, 35.

97. T. W. Arnold to Wilson Clough, March 17, 1931. Arnold Coll.

98. T. W. Arnold to Glenn Frank, April 18, 1931. *Ibid.*

99. T. W. Arnold, Interview, November 15, 1964.

100. Abe Fortas, Interview, July 19, 1971.

101. Karl Lewellyn, "A Realistic Jurisprudence—the Next Step," *Columbia Law Review* XXX (April 1930), 431–65; *The Bramble Bush or our Law and Its Study* (New York, 1951).

102. One of the most incisive and comprehensive treatments of legal realism is Wilfred E. Rumble, Jr.'s *American Legal Realism* (Ithaca, 1968). Other discussions, some of profit, are: Roscoe Pound, *An Introduction to the Philosophy of Law* (New Haven, 1922); Jerome Frank, *Law and the Modern*

*Mind* (New York, 1930); Benjamin Cardozo, *The Growth of Law* (New Haven, 1924); Edward S. Robinson, *Law and Lawyers* (New York, 1935); "Jerome Frank, Memorial Issue," *Yale Law Journal* LXVI (May 1957), 817–93; Max Radin, "Legal Realism," *Columbia Law Review* XXXI (May 1931), 824–28; and Underhill Moore and Sussman Gilbert, "The Lawyer's Law," *Yale Law Journal,* XLI (Feb. 1932), 566–76.

103. Gerald G. Gold, "Legal Realism at Yale" (unpublished Bachelor of Arts thesis, Yale University, 1963).

104. Sullivan and his theories of adolescent behavior are currently enjoying a startling renaissance. David Elkind, "'Good Me' or 'Bad Me'—the Sullivan Approach to Personality," New York *Times Magazine*, September 24, 1972, 18, 19, 99–110.

105. *Fair Fights and Foul*, 61–62.

106. *Ibid.*, 62.

107. Myres MacDougall, Interview, October 12, 1972.

108. William McGovern, Interview, July 21, 1971.

109. *Ibid.*

110. T.W. Arnold, *Symbols of Government* (New Haven, 1935), 34. Hereafter cited *Symbols of Government*.

111. *Ibid.*, 37–38.

112. Thurman Arnold, "Judge Jerome Frank," *The University of Chicago Law Review*, XXIV (Summer 1957), 633–42.

113. *Ibid.*, 635.

114. *Symbols of Government*, iv.

115. *Ibid.*, 44.

116. For Arnold's sons, George and Thurman, Jr., *Folklore* made a lasting impression as providing the "endowment" for their college education. George Arnold, Interview, March 8, 1973.

117. Most reviewers evinced a degree of enchantment with *Folklore*; a few found something to regurgitate, as for instance, Fred Rodell, "Fun in Fundamentals," *New Republic*, XCIII (December 15, 1937), 175.

118. Edward H. Levi, "Thurman Arnold," *The Yale Law Journal* LXXIX (May 1970), 983.

119. Hugh Cox, Interview, July 15, 1971.

120. Interviews with: Mrs. T.W. Arnold, July 21; and Mrs. Carl Arnold, July 27, 1971.

121. *Ibid.*, Mrs. Carl Arnold.

122. Paul Porter, Interview, April 5, 1972.

123. *Fair Fights and Foul*, 133.

124. *Ibid.*, 134.

125. "The Nomination of Thurman Arnold to be Assistant Attorney General, March 11, 1938," *Hearings*, before a Subcommittee of the Committee on the Judiciary, U.S. Senate, 75 Cong., 3rd. Sess., 1–11.

126. *Fair Fights and Foul*, 130.

127. "The Nomination of Thurman Arnold . . .," *Hearings*, 6.

128. *Forklore of Capitalism*, 217.

129. Ellis Hawley, in his brilliant *New Deal and the Problem of Monopoly*, has vividly portrayed the evolution of Roosevelt's thought on antitrust.

130. Hans B. Thorelli, *The Federal Antitrust Policy* (Baltimore, 1955), provides the best analysis of the origins of antitrust legislation. The following discussion of Arnold's antitrust period is an incorporation and a revision of the editor's essay in the *Business History Review* XXXVIII (Summer 1964), 214–31.

131. Statement to the Press, Homer Cummings, July 6, 1933, Franklin D. Roosevelt Papers, Franklin Delano Roosevelt Library, Hyde Park, New York. Hereafter cited Roosevelt Papers.

132. Harry M. Stephens, assistant attorney general in charge of the Antitrust Division, vigorously protested against the approval by the petroleum administrator of a marketing agreement of several Pacific Coast oil companies, led by Standard Oil Company of California. Stephens claimed that the agreement constituted a cartel, the same agreement for which the companies had already been defendants under an antitrust decree of 1930. Harry M. Stephens to Franklin D. Roosevelt, February 24, 1934. Roosevelt Papers.

133. A graphic description of oil marketing in the Rockies during the NRA period is given in the testimony of Pierre LaFleiche and W.H. Ferguson before the Temporary National Economic Committee (TNEC). *Investigation of the Concentration of Economic Power, Senate Reports,* 76 Cong., 2 Sess., No. 35, Pt. 20, pp. 9376–89; 10897–10916.

134. For the impact of the trade-association movement on Roosevelt, note Daniel R. Fusfeld, *The Economic Thought of Franklin D. Roosevelt and the Origins of the New Deal* (New York, 1956), pp. 56–57, 101. For a different interpretation see Frank Freidel, *Franklin D. Roosevelt: The Ordeal* (Boston, 1954), 138–59.

135. Among the more influential volumes were: Adolph Berle and Gardner C. Means, *The Modern Corporation and Private Property* (New York, 1933); Harold G. Mouton, *The Formation of Capital* (Washington, 1935); John Maynard Keynes, *General Theory of Employment, Interest, and Money* (New York, 1936).

136. Western senators recognized the political implications of the monopoly issue, but were divided as to what legislative measures should be taken. Joseph C. O'Mahoney to Burton K. Wheeler, September 9, 1937, Joseph C. O'Mahoney Papers, Archive of Contemporary History. Hereafter cited O'Mahoney Papers.

137. In a brilliant essay on the New Deal, Frank Freidel has written, "There are some indications, however, that the anti-monopoly program that he launched in the Department of Justice through the urbane Thurman Arnold was intended less to bust trusts than to forestall too drastic legislation in the Congress." Frank Freidel, *The New Deal in Historical Perspective* (Washington, 1959), 18–19.

138. Franklin D. Roosevelt to Robert Jackson, October 22, 1937. Roosevelt Papers.

139. The text of Roosevelt's address is in Samuel I. Rosenmann (ed.), *The Public Papers and Addresses of Franklin D. Roosevelt: The Continuing Struggle for Liberalism, 1938* (New York, 1941), 305–20.

140. Donald R. Richberg to Franklin D. Roosevelt, April 23, 1938. Roosevelt Papers.

141. *United States News*, June 6, 1938; Professor Freidel concludes that the antitrust program was more of a negative NRA than it was in direct disagreement. *America in the Twentieth Century* (New York, 1960), 348–49.

142. Two years after Richberg wrote to Roosevelt, he sent a cordial note to Arnold, which has more than casual interest in the light of his previous comments to the president. "You are certainly a persuasive cuss! I have just been reading your address to the American Farm Bureau Federation, and I agree with so much of your purpose and efforts that I wish I could be enthusiastic about the whole program. What holds me back is a feeling that a distinction must be made between cooperation in gauging the public and cooperation which is actually in the public interest. The plain need is for the setting of standards and creation of administrative machinery for their enforcement. In a way you are trying to act as lawmaker, administrator and prosecutor, which is not only a tough assignment, but one which should not be intrusted to that abstract individual, a 'public official,' who, in the concrete, may be as smart and well-meaning as you or as dumb and devious as ——— (you fill in any name that occurs to you)." Donald Richberg to Thurman Arnold, December 14, 1940. Arnold Coll.

143. *Ibid.*

144. On "preachers" Arnold wrote, "The chief difficulty is that there are too many people who believe that economic distress can be cured by preaching and too few who are willing to take practical measures industry by industry." *The Bottlenecks of Business* (New York, 1940), 282.

145. Thurman Arnold to Charles Seymour, July 4, 1939. Arnold Coll.

146. An excellent summary of the legal evolution of the Sherman Act is in Milton Handler, *Antitrust in Perspective: The Complementary Roles of Rule and Discretion* (New York, 1957).

147. "Free Trade Within the Borders of the United States," Address before the South Carolina Bar Association, Columbia, April 11, 1940, unpublished manuscript. Arnold Coll.

148. In the annual report of the assistant attorney general it was noted that the work of the Antitrust Division was usually regarded as devoted to three major acts: the Sherman Act, the Clayton Act, and the Federal Trade Commission Act. Less appreciated was the fact that the Division was responsible for the enforcement of thirty-one other acts. Attorney General, *Annual Report* (Washington, 1940), 54–55.

149. "Fair and Effective Use of our Present Antitrust Procedure," Address before the Trade and Commerce Bar Association of New York, New York City, April 28, 1938, unpublished manuscript. Arnold Coll.

150. William L. Baldwin, "Changing Concepts of the Large Firm and Antitrust

Enforcement" (Ph.D. dissertation, Princeton University, 1958).

151. H. L. Mencken to Thurman Arnold, August 24, 1938. Arnold Coll.

152. An excellent description of the use and abuse of the consent decree is in *Bottlenecks of Business*, 144–62.

153. "How Far Should Government Control Business?" Address before the Economic Club of New York, February 2, 1939, unpublished manuscript. Arnold Coll.

154. *Ibid.*

155. Joseph C. O'Mahoney to Thurman Arnold, July 9, 1939. O'Mahoney Papers.

156. "What is Monopoly?" Address before the Advertising Federation of America, Detroit, June 15, 1938, unpublished manuscript. Arnold Coll.

157. Joseph Alsop and Robert D. Kinter, "Trust Buster–The Folklore of Thurman Arnold," *Saturday Evening Post* CCXII (August 12, 1939), 7.

158. Regarding the merits of the case by case approach, Arnold wrote the editor of the *Saturday Evening Post*, "I contend that the case by case method of handling present problems when they arise and not before is the essence of a free economy. Instances where the antitrust laws are inadequate I contend we had better legislate case by case rather than attempt to pass sweeping generalities that only end in confusion." Actually, Arnold never did achieve a legal staff of the size sufficient to prosecute on a "case by case" approach. However, he did amass a sizable enough legal force to initiate prototype cases aimed specifically at the distribution level in the economic structure. Thurman W. Arnold to Wesley Stout, August 25, 1939. Arnold Coll.

159. "National Defense and Restraints of Trade," manuscript draft of an article in *New Republic*, May 19, 1941. Arnold Coll.

160. The Antitrust Division during Arnold's regime was primarily interested in monopoly in business. However, Arnold was not unmindful of the problems in agriculture. In a letter to Colonel Knox, Arnold stated, "At the outset I wish to emphasize that in my opinion there is no basic inconsistency between this special agricultural legislation and the antitrust laws. Whatever privileges may be conferred upon farmers by this legislation, the Department of Justice stands ready to prevent those privileges from being abused in the special interest of a small and aggressive group. Far from being inconsistent with this legislation the antitrust laws are absolutely necessary if the privileges conferred are not to be pushed far beyond their proper limitation and the real purpose of Congress defeated." Thurman W. Arnold to Frank Knox, December 19, 1939. Arnold Coll.

161. *Bottlenecks of Business* (New York, 1940), 277.

162. The pressure for the TNEC proceedings issued from diverse sources. Emmanuel Cellar, congressman from New York, wrote Roosevelt on March 31, 1938, advocating a revision of antitrust laws. Emmanuel Cellar to Franklin D. Roosevelt, March 31, 1938. Roosevelt Papers. The president of the American Federation of Labor wrote Roosevelt a year to the day before the monopoly message endorsing the attorney general's recommendations for an overhauling of the legislation on antitrust. William Green to Franklin D. Roosevelt, April 29, 1937. Roosevelt Papers.

163. Leon Henderson to Franklin D. Roosevelt, September 3, 1939. Roosevelt Papers.

164. David Lynch presents an adequate account of the history of the Temporary National Economic Committee in *The Concentration of Economic Power* (New York, 1946).

165. Thurman Arnold to John T. Flynn, July 6, 1940. Arnold Coll.

166. Francis Biddle to Franklin D. Roosevelt, March 20, 1942. Roosevelt Papers.

167. Published as *Democracy and Free Enterprise* (Norman, 1942).

168. Thurman Arnold, "Must 1929 Repeat Itself?" *Harvard Business Review* XXVI (January 1948), 43.

169. Hugh Cox, Interview, July 15, 1971.

170. Victor Kramer suggests that many heads of labor unions simply refused to believe what Arnold said. Victor Kramer, Interview, July 14, 1971.

171. T.W. Arnold to Robert H. Jackson, February 21, 1941. Arnold Coll.

172. T.W. Arnold to Reed Powell, February 21, 1941. *Ibid.*

173. T.W. Arnold to Arthur Krock, February 27, 1958. *Ibid.*

174. "Arnold on Conspiracy, " *Business Week*, May 21, 1949, 76.

175. Thurman Arnold to Benjamin Hibbs, October 1, 1942. Arnold Coll.

176. Arnold never arrived at the place the venerable progressive partisan, Amos Pinchot, did in 1937. Pinchot in a letter to Harry Elmer Barnes asserted, "I am trying to do what seems to be right. I think the President has enough power for all legitimate purposes already, and I really fear we are in great danger of losing our democratic standing—which has been pretty amateur anyhow during the last few years.

"I don't feel that everything that is labeled 'labor' is necessarily in the interest of labor. Nor that things called 'Progressive' or 'Left' necessarily make for progress.

"Also, I do not believe in collectivism. I do believe in the profit system as a means of increasing production and raising the standard of living. I think we ought to have our natural monopolies all owned by the Government, and I don't see any tendency in the present Administration to fight monopoly or privilege or to go much beyond a very surface kind of reform." Amos R.E. Pinchot to Harry E. Barnes, April 1, 1937. Harry Elmer Barnes Papers, Archive of Contemporary History.

177. Thurman Arnold to William Allen White, September 9, 1943. Arnold Coll. The writer is indebted to Robert O'Neil, Indiana University, for bringing to his attention this significant letter.

178. "The War on Monopoly," Address before the Oregon Bar Association, Gearhart, Oregon, September 29, 1939, unpublished manuscript. Arnold Coll.

179. The newspapers were strangely silent in reporting Arnold's emphasis on the consumer. In the extensive clipping file in the Arnold Coll., a search of thirty notebooks revealed only eight clippings devoted to Arnold's interest in the consumer.

180. Abe Fortas, "A Memorial Service for Thurman Arnold (1891–1969), Thursday, November 20, 1969," (Washington, D.C., 1969), 20.

181. *Fair Fights and Foul*, 158.

182. *Ibid.*, 159.

183. I am indebted to Victor Kramer for calling my attention to this provocative analysis of Arnold's court experience. Paul Albert, "Thurman Arnold, A Legal Realist Takes the Bench" (unpublished seminar paper, Georgetown School of Law, 1971).

184. *Holloway* v. *U.S.*, 148 F. 2d., 665–67.

185. *Fisher* v. *U.S.*, 149 F. 2d., 29.

186. Warren Hill offers a searching examination of these two opinions in "Psychological Realism of Thurman Arnold," *University of Chicago Law Review* XXII (Winter 1955), 378–91. If readers wish to compare, they will note that the editor is somewhat at variance in interpretation with Mr. Hill's analysis.

187. *Durham* v. *U.S.*, 215 F. 2d., 862–76.

188. Abe Fortas, Interview, July 27, 1951.

189. Thurman Arnold, *The Criminal Trial as a Symbol of Public Morality* (Charlottesville, Va., 1965), 149. For an incisive analysis of another aspect of this subject, see Abe Fortas, "The Case Against Capital Punishment," *New York Times Magazine*, January 23, 1977, pp. 8, 9, 24, 26, 28, 29.

190. Interviews with: William McGovern, Abe Krash, July 26, 1971; Carolyn Agger Fortas, July 14, 1971; Milton Freeman, July 19, 1971; Paul Porter, April 5, 1972; Hugh Cox, July 15, 1971.

191. Milton Freeman, Interview, July 19, 1971.

192. *Ibid.*

193. *Esquire, Inc.* v. *Walker*, 151 F. 2d. 1–8 (D.C. Cir., 1945).

194. *State of Vermont* v. *Verham News Corporation*, Supreme Court of Vermont, No. 1305.

195. *Esquire, Inc.* v. *Walker*, 151 F. 2d. 1 (D.C. Cir., 1945).

196. *Ibid.*, 3.

197. *Ibid.*

198. *Ibid.*, 3–4.

199. *Ibid.*, 4.

200. *Ibid.*, 5.

201. *Ibid.*, 8.

202. William McGovern, Interview, July 26, 1971.

203. *State of Vermont* v. *Verham News Corporation*, Supreme Court of Vermont, No. 1305.

204. *Ibid.*, 10–11.

205. *Ibid.*, 21.

206. *Ibid.*

207. T.W. Arnold to C.P. Arnold, November 3, 1938. Arnold Coll.

208. T.W. Arnold to Joseph Sullivan, June 26, 1945. *Ibid.*

209. Arne Wiprud, *Justice in Transportation* (New York, 1945).

210. T.W. Arnold to Joseph Sullivan, June 26, 1945. Arnold Coll.

211. *Ibid.*, July 25, 1945.

212. William McGovern, Interview, July 26, 1971.

213. *U.S.* v. *Pullman Co.*, 64 F. Supp. 108 (E.D. Penn., 1945), affirmed by a divided court 330 U.S. 806 (1947).

214. *Fair Fights and Foul*, 190.

215. Victor Kramer, Interview, July 14, 1971.

216. *Fair Fights and Foul*, 1901.

217. "A Memorial Service for Thurman Arnold (1891–1969), Thursday, November 20, 1969," (Washington, 1970), 21.

218. July 21, 1947.

219. Interviews with: Victor Kramer, July 14, 1971; Abe Fortas July 19, 1971; Carolyn Agger Fortas, July 14, 1971; William McGovern, July 26, 1971; Paul Porter, April 5, 1972; and Abe Krash, July 26, 1971.

220. Abe Fortas, Interview, July 19, 1971.

221. William McGovern, Interview, July 26, 1971.

222. Victor Kramer, Interview, July 14, 1971.

223. Abe Fortas, Interview, July 19, 1971.

224. Interviews with: Abe Krash, July 26, 1971; Victor Kramer, July 14, 1971.

225. Interviews with: Hugh Cox, July 15, 1971; Victor Kramer, July 14, 1971.

226. Interviews with: Hugh Cox, July 15, 1971; William McGovern, July 21, 1971; Abe Fortas, July 19, 1971 and Milton Freeman, July 19, 1971.

227. Victor Kramer, Interview, July 14, 1971.

228. Carolyn Agger Fortas (like many other of Arnold's friends and acquaintances) emphasized Arnold's perpetual boyish enthusiasm and optimism. Carolyn Agger Fortas, Interview, July 14, 1971.

229. "I like Big Business," *Liberty* (July 18, 1942), 34–36.

230. T.W. Arnold to Julian M. Sturtevant, July 1, 1969. Arnold Coll.

231. Mrs. Carl Arnold, Interview, July 27, 1971.

232. The emotionality of the McCarthy era and dispassionate history have been intertwined in thousands of pages of text. Nothing brings back the paranoia of the age quite like the reading of the House Un-American Activities *Hearings*.

The following tomes, by participants, historians, and observers, self-evidently reflect the prejudices, biases, subjectivity and objectivity of the authors: Alan D. Harper, *The Politics of Loyalty* (Westport, Conn., 1969); Robert K. Carr, *The House Committee on Un-American Activities, 1945–1950* (Ithaca, 1952); C. Herman Pritchett, *Civil Liberties and the Vinson Court* (Chicago, 1954); Ralph S. Brown, Jr., *Loyalty and Security* (New Haven, 1955); Earl Latham, *The Communist Controversy in Washington* (Cambridge, 1966); Frank S. Meyer, *The Moulding of Communists* (New York, 1961); Whittaker Chambers, *Witness* (New York, 1952); Alger Hiss, *In the Court of Public Opinion* (New York, 1957); Alistair Cooke, *Generation on Trial* (New York, 1950); William F. Buckley and L. Brent Bozell, *McCarthy and his Enemies* (Chicago, 1954); Richard Rovere, *Senator Joe McCarthy* (New York, 1959); Owen Lattimore, *Ordeal by Slander* (Boston, 1950); Eleanor Bontecu, *The Federal Loyalty-Security Program* (Ithaca, 1953); Richard M. Freeland, *The Truman Doctrine and the Origins of McCarthyism* (New York, 1972); Michael P. Rogin, *The Intellectuals and McCarthy The Radical Specter* (Cambridge, 1967); Lately Thomas, *When Angels Wept* (New York, 1973); Robert Griffith, *The Politics of Fear: Joseph M. McCarthy and the Senate* (Lexington, 1970); Charles C. Alexander, *Holding the Line, The Eisenhower Era, 1952–1961* (Bloomington, 1975); O. Edmund Chubb, *The Witness and I* (New York, 1974); William Hellman, *Scoundrel Time* (Boston, 1976). A fine historiographic survey of the literature of the McCarthy era can be found in Thomas C. Reeves, *McCarthyism: Interpretations Since Hofstadter* LX (Autumn 1976): pp. 42–54.

233. "A Memorial Service for Thurman Arnold (1891–1969) Thursday, November 20, 1969," (Washington, D.C., 1970), 21.

234. *Friedman* v. *Schwellenback,*159 F. 2d., 23 (D.C. Cir., 1946).

235. *Ibid.*, 25.

236. *Fair Fights and Foul*, 205.

237. *Friedman* v. *Schwellenbach*, cert. denied, 330 U.S., 838, 1947.

238. Paul Murphy discusses judicial restraint, with historical perspective, in his extremely incisive volume, *The Constitution in Crisis Times, 1913–1969* (New York, 1972).

239. Paul Porter, Interview, April 5, 1972.

240. Milton Freeman, Interview, July 19, 1971.

241. Abe Fortas, Interview, July 19, 1971.

242. George K. Gardner, "*Bailey* v. *Richardson* and the Constitution of the United States," *Boston University Law Review* XXXIII (April 1953), 176–203.

243. Milton Freeman, Interview, July 19, 1971.

244. *Bailey* v. *Richardson*, 182 F. 2d. 55 (D.C. Cir., 1950).

245. *Ibid.*, 66.

246. *Ibid.*, 73.

247. *Ibid.*, 74.

248. *Bailey* v. *Richardson*, 339 U.S. 977, 70 St. 1019, 94 L. Ed., 1382 (1950).

249. T.W. Arnold to Arthur Krock, December 20, 1950. Arnold Coll.

250. T.W. Arnold, "Due Process in Trials," *The Annals* CCC (July 1955), 128.

251. Hugh Cox, especially, recalls numerous conversations in which Arnold gave vent to his extreme disgust at the destruction of the individual in the McCarthy era. Hugh Cox, Interview, July 15, 1971.

252. *Peters* v. *Hobby*, 349 U.S. 331 (1954).

253. *Ibid.*, 333.

254. *Fair Fights and Foul*, 209–10.

255. *Peters* v. *Hobby*, 349 U.S. 35 351 (1954).

256. *Fair Fights and Foul*, 211.

257. Milton Freeman, Interview, July 19, 1971.

258. *Ibid.*

259. Owen Lattimore relates his reaction to the Tydings Committee in *Ordeal by Slander* (Boston, 1950).

260. "A Resolution to Investigate Whether there are Employees in the State Department Disloyal to the United States," 81st Cong., 2nd Sess., U.S. Senate, Subcommittee of the Committee on Foreign Relations, *Hearings* (Washington, 1950) 50. Hereafter cited as the Tydings Committee.

261. *Ibid.*, 160.

262. T.W. Arnold to George K. Gardner, April 19, 1950. Arnold Coll.

263. "Hearings on the Institute of Pacific Relations," 82nd Cong., 2nd Sess., U.S. Senate, Committee on the Judiciary: Subcommittee to Investigate the Administration of the Internal Security Act and other Security Law (Washington, D.C., 1952). Hereafter cited as the McCarran Committee.

264. Loyalty probes in the early fifties were very agrarian-oriented, as investigators found themselves in "punkin patches" in Maryland and in barns in rural New England.

265. McCarran Committee, 3525–27.

266. *Ibid.*, 2935.

267. *Ibid.*, 3096.

268. *Ibid.*, 2999.

269. *Ibid.*, 3674.

270. *Report of the Committee on the Judiciary*, 82nd. Cong., 2nd. Sess. (1952), 224.

271. *U.S.* v. *Lattimore*, 112 F. Supp. 507, 511 (1953).

272. *Ibid.*, 516–20.

273. *U.S.* v. *Lattimore*, 215 F. 2d 853–61 (D.C. Cir., 1954).

274. *U.S.* v. *Lattimore*, 125 F. Supp. 295–96 (1954).

275. *Ibid.*, 296.

276. *U.S.* v. *Lattimore*, 127 F. Supp. 405, 412 (1955).

277. William McGovern, Interview, July 26, 1971.

278. T.W. Arnold to Ernest Angell, May 27, 1968. Arnold Coll.

279. Henry M. Hart, Jr., "The Supreme Court 1958 Term Foreword: The Time Chart of the Justices," *Harvard Law Review* LXXII (November 1959), 92–125. For an amplification and a different perspective on the Arnold-Hart contretemps readers will want to read J.S. Auerbach's brilliant and provocative volume, *Unequal Justice: Lawyers and Social Change in Modern America* (New York, 1976), 260–61.

280. *Ibid.*, 100.

281. T.W. Arnold, "Professor Hart's Theology," *Harvard Law Review* LXXIII (May 1960), 1298–1314.

282. *Ibid.*, 1314.

283. *Ibid.*

284. Hugh Cox, Interview, July 15, 1971.

285. George Arnold holds the firm conviction that his father's friendship with Abe Fortas and Lyndon Johnson provides the raison d'etre behind Thurman Arnold's stand on Vietnam. However, some close friends of Arnold insist that he would not have been swayed by friendship on so vital an issue.

286. Victor Kramer, Interview, July 14, 1971.

287. T.W. Arnold to Ernest Angell, May 27, 1968. Arnold Coll.

288. Thurman Arnold, "The Growth of Awareness: Our Nation's Law and Law Among Nations," *International Lawyer* I (July 1967), 534–47.

289. Lewis C. Feur, "The Elite of the Alienated," New York *Times Magazine* (March 26, 1967), 22–23; 74–77.

290. Thurman Arnold, "The Growth of Awareness: Our Nation's Law and Law Among Nations," *International Lawyer* I (July 1967), 544.

291. *Ibid.*

292. Rexford G. Tugwell to T.W. Arnold, May 17, 1967. Arnold Coll.

293. T.W. Arnold to Rexford G. Tugwell, May 26, 1967. *Ibid.*

294. *Ibid.*, August 22, 1967.

# Notes to Letters

1. Thurman spent a few weeks in the summer of 1910 in Europe. This student holiday left him with mixed emotions, although he retained his affection for his German relatives and his empathy for Germanic traditions and culture his entire life.

2. Thurman spent from September 27, 1911, to June 18, 1914, at Harvard, leaving with an LL. B. and a deep impression on one Roscoe Pound.

3. A Harvard Law School classmate.

4. At one time possessing the largest beach in New England, the town of Revere has been billed as the "city beside a beach."

5. A community of 1,300 souls in 1910, Stafford Springs was specifically renowned to Thurman as the home of his chum, Dick Valentine.

6. A life long and avid leader in the Democratic party, C.P. Arnold participated in a series of Wyoming political campaigns; this one was on behalf of John B. Kendrick. Seeking to unseat Senator Francis E. Warren, Kendrick was defeated, but in 1916 was elected to the United States Senate, where he stayed until his death on November 3, 1933.

7. The Red Sox played the Giants and won the series four to three behind the phenomenal pitching of "Smoky" Joe Wood.

8. Thurman did not care for sports, regardless of the shape of the ball.

9. As far as Thurman was concerned Bridgeport was notable chiefly as the home of his close friend Philo Calhoun (1889–1964). After graduating from Williams College in 1910 and the Harvard Law School in 1913, Calhoun practiced law in Connecticut until his death. A widely known bibliophile, Calhoun amassed one of the significant Charles Dickens collections in the United States. New York *Times*, December 20, 1964.

10. A sunset-and-lilac-style writer, William F. De Morgan (1837–1917) was an extremely popular novelist at the turn of the century. *Joseph Vance*, a melodramatic tale of a middle-class executive of the 1850s, received high critical acclaim when it appeared in 1906. Some reviewers insisted on comparing De Morgan to Ibsen and Dickens. *Independent* LXI (November 15, 1906), 1161.

11. Onetime professor of chemistry at the University of Wyoming, E.E. Slosson (1865–1929) achieved fame as the author of eighteen books and some 2,000 articles. As a literary popularizer of scientific subjects, Slosson was unrivalled. Slosson came to the faculty of the University of Wyoming in 1891, having received his bachelor of arts degree from the University of Kansas in 1890. He stayed in Laramie for the next thirteen years; in the meantime he obtained his doctorate from the University of Chicago in 1902. From 1904 to 1920, Slosson held the editorship of the *Independent*. In 1920, he moved from New

York to Washington, D.C., where he became director of the Science Service Company, a position he held at his death. Wilson Clough, in his dashing history of the University of Wyoming, characterizes Slosson thus, "Slosson's work at Wyoming was extremely valuable because of his very versatile interests and talents. An excellent teacher, he was also in great demand as a lecturer on almost any subject associated with science, chemistry, physics, psychology, and even literature and history. At his death, he ranked as perhaps the outstanding interpreter of science to the general public, and had published numerous books, most famous of which were his *Creative Chemistry* (1919); *Easy Lessons in Einstein* (1925); and *Sermons of a Chemist* (1925)." Wilson O. Clough, *A History of the University of Wyoming, 1887–1964* (Laramie, 1965), 66. Laramie *Boomerang*, October 16, 1929; Laramie *Republican-Boomerang*, June 9, 1930.

12. Son of E.E. Slosson, Preston Slosson achieved eminence as a historian on the faculty of the University of Michigan.

13. Carl Arnold, Thurman's brother.

14. Sherman L. Whipple (1862–1930) practiced in Boston from 1885 to his death. His chief fame came as a trial lawyer. During the First World War he served briefly as general counsel for the U.S. Shipping Board and Emergency Fleet Corporation.

15. A pioneer ranch about fifteen miles west of Laramie. R.H. Burns to Gene M. Gressley, February 12, 1973.

16. In later years, Thurman changed his mind about the value of the editorship of a law journal to legal education. In attempting to sway his young protege, William McGovern, to take over the moot court at Yale, Arnold scorned law journals. He told McGovern, in typical "Arnoldese," "You make a mistake going in for this law journal stuff; it will absolutely kill you; it's no damn good; it's an absolute waste of time; law journals are no use whatsoever. They are just a bunch of God damn pundits putting forth a lot of nonsense that no one ever reads; it's all footnotes anyway. Besides, you will ruin your eyes!" William McGovern, Interview, July 21, 1971.

17. George A. Follansbee (1843–1920), upon graduating from Harvard Law School in 1867 returned to Chicago and practiced corporate law there the rest of his life.

18. While Thurman would never go so far as to say that the quality of the cigar in a man's humidor indicated the quality of the man, a fine cigar dangling from an acquaintance's mouth was as good a recommendation as a man could have.

19. Edward Mac K. O'Bryan and Raymond Waite, later partners of Arnold in O'Bryan, Waite and Arnold.

20. A typical "Arnoldism," the comparison of the gingerbread architecture with florid verse.

21. Carl Arnold.

22. This was neither the first or last time Thurman would make a loan to friends. He was a notoriously easy touch to the "needy" or to those who thought they were.

23. In late winter of 1915, Arnold decided to leave Adams, Follansbee, Hawley & Shorey to establish O'Bryan, Waite & Arnold.

24. An admirer of Greek and English classics, Ezra R. Thayer (1866–1915) practiced law in Boston, was a member of the committee of the American Bar Association that drafted a national code of legal ethics; and in 1910 reluctantly agreed to become dean of the Harvard Law School. Overwork and extreme conscientiousness brought his suicide at the opening of the fall term in 1915.

25. To make life easier financially Thurman taught night school for the better part of a year, but finally decided "the students were not as bright as the teacher, and therefore the whole process was very boring." Thurman Arnold to Mrs. C.P. Arnold, November 17, 1916. C.P. Arnold Coll., Western History Research Center, University of Wyoming, Laramie.

26. Neal Roach and Oscar Sodergren were local Laramie entrepreneurs involved, á la frontier fashion, in a number of enterprises including banking, lumber and ranching. In the 1940s Neal Roach built an imposing but unattractive home on Laramie's Grand Avenue, the prime arterial street. When Thurman passed the new Roach home, horrified by the architecture he exclaimed, "Good Lord, has he seen it yet?"

27. The next day his friend and law partner wrote a long, masterful letter to Thurman's parents, explaining the glories of their son's patriotism, his good physical condition, ending the missive with the reassuring sentiments, "I can imagine how you feel about T.W. having to go to Mexico, but I am sure he will come back safe and sound, and it will certainly be a great benefit to him, as the battery he is with is made up of a fine crowd of men." Edward Mac K. O'Bryan to C.P. Arnold, June 21, 1916. C.P. Arnold Coll.

28. Arnold's emotions and thoughts on the Pershing punitive expedition are typical of the general "doughboy" reaction. Freezing nights, blazing hot days, uncertain supplies, shortage of water, intolerable delays and a seemingly elusive enemy combined to make this "Mexican adventure" less than appealing to thousands of troops. Clarence C. Clendenen, *Blood on the Border* (New York, 1969), 213–84.

29. A comparison of French, British and American artillery can be found in Barbara W. Tuchman, *The Guns of August* (New York, 1962), 207.

30. Wire her he did. Frances Arnold recalls most vividly the moment that she received that wire: "He [Thurman] thought it would be much better if we got married before he went over, I said, no, that wouldn't do; but I felt awfully bad after I said that, really terrible. I should have married him before he left. Then I got this telegram saying, 'Won't you please come on?' We were having lunch at the Blackstone Hotel, Sister and I, and some friends from Sedalia [Missouri]. Sister said to them, 'Wouldn't you all like to drive along the lake, and come out and have tea with me this afternoon?' They said they would love to, and Sister said, 'Well, Sister, if you're not too tired, you can drive us can't you?' And I said, "No, I can't, because I just made up my mind. . . .I am going to go on to New York, and get married,' at which Sister said 'Well you can't do that.' I said, 'Why can't I?' If she had just kept still, I probably never would have married him. Well, one thing led to another, and Sister said, 'Well, Mama would never get over it; you can't do that kind of thing; you know you can't run away like that, and none of the family being with you; you know I can't

leave and go to New York with you.' 'Have you any money?' I said. 'Well, not much,' and she said, 'I can get plenty over at Marshall Fields, but we have to get there before they close.' This was September and they closed at three o'clock in the afternoon. We got enough money at Marshall Fields so that I could get on the train for New York. I telegraphed Thurman, just as I was about to step on the train. I ran into this lady across the Pullman aisle. She recognized me and said she was Mrs. Henry Fare from Houston, Texas, a great friend of my mother's. I said I was glad to see her, and I told her that I was running away to get married, and she said, 'Oh, thank God I'm here, it would mean so much to your mother to know that I'm here and to see that you are properly chaperoned.' I thought that was very funny! . . .' "

As part of the further adventures of Frances Arnold and Mrs. Fare they encountered a fine Southern gentleman, Captain James by name, who took the two ladies under his protective wing for the rest of the trip to New York. "Well, we got to New York," Frances continued, "and Thurman was staying at the Commodore. . . . Captain James took us there by cab, and he said, 'Now you say he's registered here?' I said, 'yes,' although I was surprised he had not met the train. Captain James went into the lobby and soon returned, 'Well, they say that he was registered here, but he checked out this morning.' I felt like an awful fool, as you can imagine, and Mrs. Fare looked absolutely floored; she didn't know what to do with me, so we went on over to the Gotham, where she had rooms engaged. . . . We had dinner in the Hotel Gotham. I had no way of getting in touch with Thurman. I didn't know where he was, or what had happened. But in the morning the telephone rang, about six o'clock. It was Thurman; he had just got back from a trip to Plattsburg. I had left my name at the Commodore. Thurman said he would be right over for breakfast!" Mrs. Frances Arnold, Interview, July 21, 1971.

31. "Up almost to the time of my graduation from college my inclination was toward law, but shortly after graduation, I determined to study theology and graduated in 1884." So wrote Professor Paul Van Dyke (1859–1933) in the fiftieth year anniversary publication of his Princeton class. He was a dynamic, dogmatic theologian who wrote several major histories and biographies including: *The Age of the Renascence* (1897); *Renascence Portraits* (1905); *Catherine de Medici*; *Ignatius Loyola, The Founder of the Jesuits* (1926); and *George Washington, the Son of His Country* (1931). Van Dyke made an indelible impression on long lines of Princetonians. From July 1917 to July 1919 he served in Paris with the American University Union, assisting university students and graduates. Since Van Dyke regarded the war as a moral crusade, the enthusiasm and dedication that he demonstrated in this task can well be imagined. Princeton Faculty File, Princeton University Archives; New York *Times*, August 31, 1933; *After Fifty Years, the Record of the Class of 1881* (Princeton, N.J., 1931), 309–16.

32. Major General Charles T. Menoher (1862–1930) retired in 1926 after an illustrious career in the United States Army.

33. The dates of Thurman Arnold's World War I service were May 1917 to June 1919.

34. Years later, in comradeship with many doughboys, Arnold's most acute recollection of the first World War focused on the cold, rain, and mud. In his autobiography he would write, "The chief discomforts were cold and wet, which I will never forget." *Fair Fights and Foul* (New York, 1964), 28.

35. Brilliant and eccentric, or so he seemed to many of his contemporaries, John D. Clark (1884–1963) graduated from the University of Nebraska in 1905. Two years later, after receiving his LL.B. from Columbia University, he began to practice law in Cheyenne. In 1918, he joined the legal staff of Midwest Refining Company; a year elapsed before he was made general counsel. Five years later, he was vice-president and assistant to the chairman of the board of Standard of Indiana. In 1928, in an announcement that startled his friends and associates, he forsook his business career to enter graduate study in the Department of Economics at Johns Hopkins University. Receiving his Ph.D. in 1931, Clark became professor of economics at the University of Denver, 1931–34; professor and dean of the College of Business Administration, University of Nebraska, 1934–37; 1941–46. From 1946 to 1952 he was a member of the Council of Economic Advisors. The comments of his friends today are ample illustration that few came close to understanding this brilliant, complex man. *Midwest Review* VIII (December 1928), 23.

36. "A congenial gentleman, hardboiled banker, or a friendly story-telling host as the occasion required" was the way a former friend and business associate once described Henry Blackmer (1870–1962). Blackmer began his career, which led to fame and fortune, in 1892 at Colorado Springs. Within a decade he had accumulated wealth and a reputation as an extremely competent attorney. By 1902 he had transferred the site of his activities to Denver, where he became president of the International Trust Company and, later, of the Midwest Refining Company. In the latter capacity, he demonstrated a genius for organization and accumulation. When the Teapot Dome and Continental Trading scandals broke, rather than testify, Blackmer fled to Europe. Indicted for income tax evasion in 1928, he later made peace with his government by paying some four million in back taxes in 1949. Harold D. Roberts, *Salt Creek* (Denver, 1956); New York *Times*, May 27, 1962.

37. John McFadyen (1871–1943) was one of the great characters of the Rocky Mountain oil industry. As the hard-driving vice-president of the Marathon Oil Company in the Rockies, "Uncle Jack" discovered millions of barrels of oil for his company, along the way creating a folk hero image. One of the favorite stories of McFadyen's executive ability was related by the late Fred Smith, vice-president of Marathon. McFadyen came onto a night crew asleep in one of the oil derricks in the Salt Creek field. McFadyen fired them on the spot. It so happened that these men were employees of the Midwest Refining Company, not Marathon. When they appeared for their severance pay the next morning, one of the Midwest officers wanted to know why they were quitting. They told him that Jack McFadyen had fired them, to which the Midwest executive replied, "Jack McFadyen is not running the Midwest Oil Company, but if he said you should be fired, you should be." Fred Smith, Interview, February 2, 1963; *Beacon* VII (May 1943), 20–21.

38. John Hay (1864–1951), banker, rancher, politician: there were few activities in the state of Wyoming in which John Hay, at one time or another, was not involved.

39. David C. Howard (1890–1934) received his B.S. degree from Carleton College in 1911, his Master of Arts and law degrees from Harvard in 1914. For three years he taught in the law school of the University of West Virginia. Then he left college teaching to join the Charleston, W.Va., firm of Price, Smith and Spilman.

40. John R. Turner (1882–1960) received his B.S. from Ohio Northern University, 1901, his Ph.D. from Princeton in 1913. He was associated with the Department of Economics, Cornell University, 1913–16. Then he moved to New York University, eventually becoming dean of the Washington Square College. His tenure as president of the University of West Virginia lasted from 1928 to 1935; he then returned to New York as dean of City College of New York.

41. A professor of Latin at the University of West Virginia from 1890 until his death, Frank B. Trotter (1863–1940) occupied the presidency of the University of West Virginia, 1914–28.

42. One of the first men on the Yale faculty to become attracted to Arnold, Leon Green (1888–) has had a long and eminent career in legal education. Professor of law at the University of Texas from 1921 to 1926, Green had two one-year stints, first as professor and dean of the Law School of the University of North Carolina, then as visiting professor at Yale in 1927. In 1928, he joined the law faculty of Northwestern University, where he stayed for the next twenty years, serving as dean from 1929 to 1947. He returned to the country of his birth in 1947, when he was appointed Distinguished Professor in the Law School of the University of Texas.

43. Along with Samuel H. Knight and Wilson Clough, Fred Nussbaum (1885–1958) remained an intimate friend of Thurman's his entire life. One of the "lights" on the University of Wyoming faculty, where he taught from 1925 to 1956, Fred Nussbaum achieved an international reputation as an economic historian. His most widely acclaimed book was *The Triumph of Science and Reason, 1660–1685* (New York, 1953).

44. Born at Jackson, Ohio on January 26, 1880, Royal Hunt Balcom was educated at Kenyon College and the General Theological Seminary of the Episcopal Church in New York. After a period of service at the Episcopal parish at Irvington-on-Hudson, New York, Balcom came to Wyoming in 1915 as supervisor of St. Michael's Mission and School on the Wind River Reservation at Ethete, Wyoming. Following his tenure on the Wind River Reservation, Balcom was appointed archdeacon of Wyoming. Soon Balcom's countenance became familiar to parishoners from Sundance to Evanston. During his term as archdeacon he built the beautiful Chapel of Transfiguration at Moose. In 1929, Balcom left Wyoming to assume the headmastership of the Voorhis School at San Dimas, California. Three years later he became the rector of the Trinity Church in Santa Barbara, a charge that he held until his death in July 1943. Cecil Dunn to Gene M. Gressley, June 21, 1973.

45. Distinguished jurist and educator, Charles Clark (1889–1963) brought Arnold and Yale together. Clark spent his entire professional career in two positions, one on the Yale law faculty from 1919 to 1939, the last ten years as dean. In 1939, he received an appointment as associate judge on the U.S. Court of Appeals, 2nd Circuit; in 1954 he became chief judge. For those interested in an incredible account of the inner workings of our judicial system, replete with petty jealousies, gossip, and downright inanities, the editor recommends Marvin Shick, *Learned Hand's Court* (Baltimore, 1970).

46. Harold C. Havinghurst (1897–), graduate of Harvard Law School class of 1922, practiced law in New York City after graduation, then joined the University of West Virginia Law School in 1928. His move to Northwestern in 1930 became, in retrospect, a crucial decision for him, as he spent the rest of his

academic career there, becoming dean of the Law School when Leon Green moved to the University of Texas.

47. Albert Coates (1896–) could not be budged from the University of North Carolina, where he spent his entire career.

48. The administration of the University of West Virginia Law School finally tapped one of its own law faculty members to take over the deanship: Thomas Porter Hardman, who was appointed April 25, 1931. This was obviously a successful appointment as Dean Hardman retired on June 30, 1956. On the length of his residency, the current dean, Paul Selby, Jr., commented, "In modern terms, such a length of tenure is almost unheard of! Most of us last from five to ten years." Paul Selby, Jr., to Gene M. Gressley, May 18, 1972.

49. One of the giants of American jurisprudence, Roscoe Pound (1870–1965) is remembered with ambivalence by many of his former students. Arnold became quite scornful of Pound's "do-nothingness and vacillation." Benjamin V. Cohen, the human, brilliant drafter of so much New Deal legislation, remembered Pound as "a strange character. I always thought I got more from him in one year at Harvard than anyone else there. I really took two-thirds of my work with him. And I feel I owe him a great deal. And I do know he developed techniques which have been helpful to me from the beginning through all my career; on the other hand if you tried to talk to him about how to use these techniques, you could not really get him to concentrate on where you wanted to take some ideas and apply them. . . . He would only repeat what he had worked out for himself in his writings; his lectures, while he wouldn't read them, were almost verbatim from what he had written." Benjamin V. Cohen, Interview, July 13, 1971.

50. Full of swirling myth and allegory, it is easy to define why James Branch Cabell (1879–1958) remained one of Thurman Arnold's favorite authors. The mixture of Hindu mysticism and Russian folktales, with which Cabell endowed his symbolic figure, Manuel, in *Figures of the Earth* (New York, 1921) captivated Arnold.

51. Clough's poem, commemorating the Armistice and entitled "Ten Years After," was first published in the Laramie *Republican-Boomerang*, and then in the *Literary Digest* C (January 5, 1929), 27.

52. His biographer depicts him as colorful, affable, multifaceted, suave, and an articulate promoter. Glenn Frank (1887–1940) was all of that and more. As a publicist, editor and president of the University of Wisconsin, Frank left an indelible impression on all who chanced to meet him. For a pleasant biography of Frank, the reader is referred to Lawrence H. Larsen, *The President Wore Spats* (Madison, 1965).

53. Born in New York City and educated at Yale, Arthur L. Goodhart (1891–) has devoted his entire career to Cambridge and Oxford Universities, with numerous visiting lectureships at universities in Great Britain and in the United States. His research in English common law has won him an international reputation.

54. This sentence explains more than Arnold's letter to Pound why Arnold turned down the Harvard offer. Yale, with Sturges, Douglas and Robinson, was shaking up the legal world. The last place Arnold wanted to retreat to was a stolid university—he had been there.

55. Felix Frankfurter (1882–1966), an intimate advisor to President Roosevelt and member of the Harvard law faculty, 1914–39, was appointed in 1939 to the U.S. Supreme Court. He was a liberal, brilliant legal theoretician, whose middle-aged conservatism disturbed those who had known the young Frankfurter.

56. E.D. Dickinson, *The Equality of States in International Law* (Cambridge, 1920); *A Selection of Cases and Other Readings on the Law of Nations* (New York, 1929).

57. The anonymous commentator turned out to be Paul Freund (1908–). A favorite student of Frankfurter's, Freund has had a brilliant career in government and as a longtime member of the Harvard Law School faculty. Freund currently holds the Carl M. Loeb University Professorship at Harvard.

58. From Portland, Oregon, Frank P. Kenan (1899–1954) received his bachelor's degree from the University of Oregon and held a Sterling fellowship at Yale, where he was awarded J.D. degree in 1932. He practiced law in Portland and occupied the office of special assistant to the United States attorney in Portland from 1941 to 1949. *The Oregonian*, July 24, 1954.

59. Stuart Chase (1888–), as a certified public accountant, investigator for the Federal Trade Commission, consultant and advisor to numerous other government agencies, has consumed a lifetime commenting on America's economic habits and sociology through the publication of a spate of books; among the best known are: *Men and Machines* (1929); *The Economy of Abundance* (1934); *Rich Land, Poor Land* (1939); *The Tyranny of Words* (1938); *The Proper Study of Mankind* (1949).

60. Bruce Bromley (1893–) decided to accept Arnold's proffer. Bromley remained with Yale Law School as a Sterling lecturer from 1933 to 1938. With the exception of 1949, when he sat as judge on the New York State Court of Appeals, Bromley has been an associate and partner with the Wall Street firm of Cravath, Swaine and Moore.

61. Responding to the plea of some friends and relatives in Laramie, Thurman conceived the idea, which he thought great fun, of organizing (among his Ivy League friends) a lobbying "putsch" for higher education in Wyoming. This Thurman proceeded to do with his usual great gusto; soon Governor Leslie Miller of Wyoming was hearing via letter and phone about the great academic glory of the University of Wyoming, from law faculty members at Harvard and Yale plus assorted government officials in Washington. Whether Arnold's campaign for "The Yale of the West" had a negative or positive effect was a common topic for debate among Arnold's imbibing friends, over the years.

62. Historian, economist and political scientist, Harrison Dale's (1885–1955) friendship with the Arnold family dated from the 1915–20 period, when Dale was a member of the Political Science Department of the University of Wyoming. Dale went on to be dean of the School of Business at the University of Idaho, 1925–28. From Moscow he moved to Oxford, Ohio, where he again was dean of the Business School at Miami University, 1928–37. The University of Idaho called him back as president, a post he occupied from 1937 to 1946. Dale concluded his career as comptroller at Reed College, 1946–50.

63. James Harvey Rogers (1886–1939) was involved in international economics and politics as a consultant and member of the staff of the League of Nations. As an analysis of the international gold crisis, *America Weighs Her Gold* received critical plaudits, moving Rexford Tugwell to write, "A book like this, so clear, so timely and so courageous ought to make us thankful for universities." *New Republic* LXIX (November 25, 1931), 51.

64. Sheridan Downey's father, Colonel Stephen Downey, historically has been dubbed the "father" of the University of Wyoming. Undeniably, as a member of the legislature from Laramie, Stephen Downey enthusiastically supported and endorsed the establishment of a university in the "Gem City." The specific legislation enabling the establishment of a university was drafted by Willis Van Devanter, a Cheyenne attorney, who later, through the good graces of Senator Francis E. Warren of Wyoming, became a member of the United States Supreme Court. Sheridan Downey (1884–1956) achieved something of a reputation for himself as a follower of Upton Sinclair, a "booster" of reclamation and as a U.S. senator from California, 1939–51.

65. Journalist, economist, editor for eons of the *New Republic*, academician and author, George Soule (1887–) was among the galaxy of Progressive-intellectuals with whom Arnold associated during the New Deal era.

66. One of the foremost legal minds of the twentieth century, Jerome Frank (1889–1957) had a remarkably illustrious career. From the moment his book *Law and the Modern Mind* (1930) appeared he was recognized as a leader of the legal realist school; Frank alternated between government service, private practice and the groves of the academe for most of his life. After graduating from the University of Chicago Law School in 1917, Frank engaged in private practice in Chicago for thirteen years. He joined a New York law firm in 1930, practicing until he received a "call" to the New Deal in 1933. From May 1933 until January 1935 he was the peppery, forceful general counsel of the Agricultural Adjustment Administration. After a palace revolution in the Department of Agriculture, Frank moved over as special counsel to the Reconstruction Finance Corporation. Then from 1937 to 1941 he became commissioner of the Securities and Exchange Commission; during the last two years of this service he was appointed chairman. Rewarded by Roosevelt in 1941 with an appointment to the famous U.S. 2nd Circuit Court of Appeals, "Learned Hand's Court," Frank remained on the bench until his death.

67. Attorney, publisher and penologist, Sam Bass Warner (1889–) held positions on the law faculties of the University of Oregon, Syracuse University and Harvard from 1932 until 1945. He was register of copyrights from 1945 to 1950, and publisher of two small-town newspapers until his death. Intrigued with law and the criminal, Warner had a profound influence on Arnold's thought on the interaction between legal institutions and criminology.

68. Warner and Arnold were exchanging views on Arnold's article, "Theories about Economic Theory," *Annals* CLXXI (March 1934), 26-36. In this essay Arnold suggested what he was to later develop in his *Symbols of Government* and *Folklore of Capitalism*: specifically, that what mattered was not realities or principles, but what people thought they thought–creeds, "folklore" were the only "reality."

69. In view of this statement, his good friend Senator Joseph O'Mahoney should not have been shocked at Arnold's approval of President Roosevelt's "court-packing" plan of 1937.

70. *op. cit.* "Theories about Economic Theory."

71. A specialist in international law, Edwin Borchard (1884–1951) claimed membership in the conservative side of the Yale Law School faculty. After receiving the LL. B. degree at the age of nineteen from the New York University Law School, he joined the Columbia law faculty in 1905. Following a term as law librarian at the Library of Congress, he moved to Yale in 1917, where he remained until his death.

72. Political scientist and legal theoretician, Harold D. Lasswell (1902–) has spent most of his academic tenure at the New School for Social Research and Yale University. His psychoanalytic approach to social organizations and to law has been, if not totally accepted, widely debated. A stimulating and provocative teacher, Lasswell has had an enormous impact on the graduates of the Yale Law School.

73. Karl Lewellyn, Review of "Precedent in English and Constitutional Law, by A.L. Goodhart," *University of Pennsylvania Law Review* XXCIII (January 1935), 396–98.

74. Thurman Arnold, Review of "Precedent in English and Constitutional Law by A.L. Goodhart," *Columbia Law Review* XXV (February 1935), 311–15.

75. Jerome Hall (1901–), particularly noted for his work on criminal law and criminology, has been on the faculty of Indiana University since 1935.

76. The Arnold family ranch, located west of Laramie, was referred to then and now as the Millbrook Ranch. Before the ranch was acquired by C.P. Arnold, it had been owned by the notorious Colonel E.J. Bell.

77. Mayor of Detroit, governor general of the Philippines, governor of Michigan, attorney general and finally associate justice of the U.S. Supreme Court, Frank Murphy (1890–1949) had a meteoric, if somewhat enigmatic, rise in government.

78. James R. Angell (1869–1949) achieved eminence as one of the most important figures in the field of twentieth-century psychiatry. Inaugurating his illustrious career at the University of Minnesota in 1893, he was elected president of the Yale Corporation in 1921, where he remained until 1937.

79. Arnold refers to one of the numerous bureaucratic upheavals during the New Deal. A basic clash of philosophies existed between AAA administrator Chester C. Davis and Jerome Frank, general counsel. When Davis left Washington on a field trip in 1935, Frank, without consulting Davis or for that matter other high officials in the AAA, issued a directive which revised the tenant contracts of the AAA to include Southern sharecroppers. When Davis returned to Washington, he was infuriated at what he considered usurpation of administrative power, not to mention downright insubordination. Davis regarded the Frank directive as putting the AAA into the reform arena. Secretary Wallace fired Frank and his entire staff. Roosevelt, insisting that he had the highest opinion of all parties, immediately appointed Frank special counsel to the Reconstruction Finance Corporation. A spirited account of this feud can be found in Arthur Schlesinger, Jr.'s *The Coming of the New Deal* (Boston, 1959), 56–82. An analysis of Frank's thought and life is available in J. Mitchell Roseberg, *Jerome Frank: Jurist and Philosopher* (New York, 1970).

80. Frank Wozencraft (1892–1966) graduated from the University of Texas in 1913, where he received his LL. B. degree a year later. He joined his father's

Dallas law firm in 1914, practicing in that city until associating with the Radio Corporation of America in 1931. He rose to vice-president and general counsel of RCA, but left in 1942 to go into private practice in Washington D.C.

81. A member of the Harvard Law School faculty since 1950, Arthur E. Sutherland (1902–), upon graduating from Harvard with his J.D. degree, entered private practice in Rochester, New York, where he stayed until 1941, with one year out, 1927–28, as law clerk to Justice Oliver Wendell Holmes. Before returning to Harvard in 1950, he had been on the Cornell University faculty.

82. The Supreme Court, in 1935, destroyed the NRA by declaring the poultry code unconstitutional in the famous case of the *United States* v. *A.L.A. Schechter Poultry Corporation*. The government had indicted the Schechter brothers for their violation of the poultry code, specifically for false sales and price reports, plus selling diseased poultry. The last accusation brought the now famous bon mot from General Hugh Johnson, who forever after referred to the case as the "sick chicken case." In its decision the Court made two clear arguments: one, the president had usurped the legislative prerogatives in promulgating the codes; two, the Schechter brothers' poultry was sold and consumed primarily within state boundaries; therefore, it was not subject to interstate commerce regulation. Donald Richberg, *My Hero* (New York, 1954), 189–96; Victor Weybright, "Chickens Come Home to Roost," *Survey Graphic* XXIV (July 1935), 328–32, 364; *Newsweek* X (April 13, 1935), 18; Arthur M. Schlesinger, Jr., *Politics of Upheaval* (Boston, 1960), 277–83.

83. Sheridan Downey, *Onward America* (Sacramento, 1933).

84. William G. Gehri (1895–1946) arrived in Morgantown just a year preceding the Arnolds. Gehri left the Trinity Episcopal Church in Morgantown for Memphis, where he held the pastorate of the Grace and later the Grace–St. Luke's Church from 1938 until his death. A remarkably intelligent minister, Rev. Gehri's interest in the interaction of religion and mental health was well known throughout the Episcopal world. Mrs. Yolando M. Gehri to Gene M. Gressley, June 11, August 1 and 28, 1972.

85. Harold J. Laski (1893–1950) was a noted political theorist whose ideas and polemics shook the academic and non-academic communities. Laski's home base for most of his career was the University of London.

86. In "A Word to the Republicans," Laski, taking a cue from the British *Realpolitik*, warned the Republican party to be, in effect, the "royal opposition," and to refrain from criticizing for criticism's sake. In "The Decline of the Professors " Laski argued for the socialization of the medical and legal professions. As long as these professions sought private gain above public good, they would not fulfill their professional obligations. *Harper's* CLXXI (November 1935), 676–85; *Harper's* CLXXI (October 1935), 513–28.

87. Laski had written a warm letter in praise of *Symbols of Government*.

88. In common with Roscoe Pound, Walter Wheeler Cook (1873–1943) started his academic career at the University of Nebraska; from the Great Plains he fled East and grasped the brass ring of the university carousel with successive law professorships at the University of Wisconsin, University of Chicago, Yale, Columbia, Johns Hopkins and Northwestern universities.

89. He was an intensely opinionated, warm, intelligent human being and intellectual gadfly. Few men in their lifetimes ever championed more unpopular causes.

At one time or another Harry Elmer Barnes (1889–1968) waved the banner for historical revisionism, women's rights, liberal theology (to the point of absence of theology), criminal and prison reform, and the reduction of world population. He was author of half a card catalog drawer-full of books and articles; his most famous and controversial were *Genesis of the World War* (1926); *History of Western Civilization* (1935); *Historical Sociology: Its Origins and Developments* (1948) and *Perpetual War for Perpetual Peace* (1953); New York *Times*, August 28, 1968.

90. Volney J. Tidball (1883–1949), an intimate friend of the entire Arnold family, at the time of his death had been judge of Wyoming's second judicial district for thirty-six years. One of the most revered members of the Wyoming bar, Judge Tidball received his Bachelor of Arts degree from the University of Wyoming in 1905, his law degree from the University of Michigan in 1908. Returning to Laramie, he practiced law with Sheridan Downey until elected judge. *Cheyenne Tribune*, October 13, 1949.

91. Judge John E. Lacey (1848–1936), one of the conservative members of the Wyoming Bar, stood as a veritable foundation stone of the nineteenth and twentieth century "establishment" in Wyoming.

92. Arnold had invited Sutherland to be a judge in one of the cases presented in the Yale Law School moot courts. The moot courts represented one of Arnold's most original contributions to the law school curriculum.

93. Arnold correctly judged the TVA decision as a gossamer victory for the New Deal. By a vote of eight to one, the Court, on February 17, 1936, upheld the constitutionality of the Wilson Dam power production. What the newspaper reporters failed to understand was that the conservative coalition on the Court had validated the right of a stock holder in a private corporation to question the validity of a federal statute. This legal contortion was unrecognized and soon forgotten; the New Dealers' optimistic hopes of a Supreme Court "reformation" were dashed when the Court, a little over a month later, denounced the administrative techniques of the Securities and Exchange Commission, although the Court did stop short of challenging the constitutionality of the SEC.

94. Ferdinand F. Stone (1908–) spent the year of 1936–37 at the University of Wyoming, then went south to Tulane, where he has built a reputation for his outstanding work in comparative law. Stone remained a close friend of the Arnold family, and to this day he returns to Laramie in the summers to stay in his cabin in the Snowy Range.

95. Samuel O. Clark, Jr. (1900–), after graduating from Yale Law School, went into private practice in New York City and New Haven. In 1932 he left for Washington, where he received recognition as an able assistant attorney general in charge of the Tax Division of the Department of Justice.

96. An executive of Union Carbide, 1937–66, and advisor on foreign economic policy, Kenneth Rush (1910–) has been a persuasive leader in international economic affairs for over three decades.

97. Sir Willmott Lewis (1877–1950) was regarded as one of the ablest journalists in New Deal Washington by his competitors, friends, and government officials. Having a career that began with covering the Boxer rebellion, Willmott Lewis was Washington correspondent for the London *Times* from 1920 to his death.

98. The Laski review appeared in the *American Political Science Review* XXX (June 1936), 581–83.

99. *Cases on Trial Judgements and Appeals* (St. Paul, 1936).

100. Fleming James (1904–), with the exception of three years, has been on the Yale law faculty since 1929.

101. Stanley Reed (1884–), a Kentuckian by birth and education. After practicing in Maysville, Kentucky from 1909 to 1929, he became general counsel for the Federal Farm Board, the Reconstruction Finance Corporation, special assistant to the attorney general, solicitor general and, finally, in 1938, associate justice of the Supreme Court. He retired from the Court in 1958.

102. Max Radin (1880–1950) was a specialist in Roman and civil law; except for a brief period at the City College of New York, Radin spent his entire life on the faculty of the University of California Law School.

103. *Harvard Law Review* XLIX (June 1936), 1397–1401.

104. Little is known of the life and times of Oliver M. Thomason, associate editor of the *Industrial Democrat*, the house newspaper of the Llano Del Rio Co-operative colony near Leesville, Louisana. Thomason's editorials reflected the aims of this co-operative which flourished from 1917 to 1929. In its economic heyday, the colony owned 20,000 acres, a sawmill, ice plant, printing plant, box factory, bakery, shoe shop and assorted other enterprises. The depression, the policy of welcoming all comers that appeared at its doors, and internal dissension among the leaders resulted in the Newllano colony passing out of existence in 1938. New Orleans *Times Picayune*, April 17, 1938.

105. In one episodic sketch after another, Sherwood Anderson, with a broad brush, described the confusion in the life of the "common" American in the depression; geographically he concentrated on the South and West in *Puzzled America* (New York, 1935).

106. An engineer for the Royal Aircraft Works, Major Clifford Hugh Douglas (1878–1952) thought it incredible that many improvements in society were possible from an engineering point of departure but were inconceivable from an economic point of view. Douglas insisted, in Keynesian fashion, that the lack of purchasing power was inherent in capitalism. To solve the problem one had not only to increase production but also to redistribute the goods produced. Arnold's fascination with Douglas' sentences is easy to comprehend, for Douglas' ideology meshed teeth for teeth with Arnold's antitrust goals. While Douglas' scheme never had any substantial impact in the United States, Canadian political leaders imported Douglas' message wholesale, wrapped his ideas in a cocoon of Christian fundamentalism and rode to victory. Social Credit, as a political philosophy and party, was especially virulent in Alberta and British Columbia. John Irving, *The Social Credit Movement in Alberta* (Toronto, 1959).

107. An authority on the law of domestic relations, Epaphroditus Peck (1860–1938), according the Bristol *Press* upon his death, was so involved in the community that his activities were "well-nigh a calendar of Bristol's welfare organizations." Bristol (Conn.) *Press*, Oct. 29, 1938; George R. Perry to Gene M. Gressley, March 13, 1973.

108. George Parmly Day (1876–1959) founded the Yale University Press in 1908. For the next thirty years he was president and treasurer of the Press, and from 1940 to 1942 he held the position of treasurer of the Yale Corporation.

109. Thurman Arnold and Mrs. Justice Butler have another association, although more remote. Arnold, Fortas and Porter purchased the Pierce Butler home at 1229 Nineteenth St., N.W., for their offices. The firm is still domiciled at that address, although Arnold and Porter have spread over several buildings across the street.

110. H.L. Mencken, *The American Language* (New York, 1919).

111. The two oil entrepreneurs, Michael L. Benedum (1868–1959) and Foster Parriott (1878–1957) were among the more successful "independents" in the history of the American petroleum industry. Arnold lost the Tex-Penn case; on March 29, 1937, the U.S. Supreme Court upheld the decision of the Third Circuit Court of Appeals. For a *simpatico* biography of Benedum, see Sam T. Mallison, *The Great Wildcatter* (Charleston, W. Va., 1953).

112. Another Yale colleague, Richard J. Smith (1903–), was on the Yale law faculty from 1927 to 1933. Since 1934, Smith has been in private practice in New York City; currently he is a partner in Whitman, Ransom and Coulson.

113. Eugene Davidson (1902–), member of the editorial department of Yale University Press from 1931 to 1959, now lives in Chicago. His byline appears with considerable frequency in such periodicals as: *Foreign Affairs, Yale Review* and *Modern Age,* which he served as editor.

114. Edwin M. Borchard and William P. Lage, *Neutrality for the United States* (New Haven, 1937).

115. *Folklore of Capitalism*.

116. Those who remember Barton Leach (1900–1971) always recall his towering height, a small satchel which he carried (containing a thermos of warm milk to sooth his ulcer), his robust sense of humor, his delightful wit. He had two careers, one as an enormously popular teacher at the Harvard Law School, the other with the United States Air Force, which he served from 1942 until his death. Harvard Law School *Bulletin* (April 1972).

117. American Bar Association *Journal* XXIII (May 1937), 364.

118. Born in General Armstrong Custer's hometown of Monroe, Michigan, Fred S. Caldwell (1876–1967) practiced law in Oklahoma Territory and Colorado.

119. The historical literature on Roosevelt's Supreme Court "packing" plan is profuse, some obtuse, but most of it intriguing. For those interested in following the blow-by-blow exchanges of the participants, there are two general accounts: Joseph Alsop and Turner Catledge, *The 168 Days* (New York, 1938), and Leonard Baker, *Back to Back, The Duel Between FDR and the Supreme Court* (New York, 1967).

For an able dissection of various pieces of the anatomy of the Court plan see William E. Leuchtenberg, "The Origins of Franklin D. Roosevelt's Court Packing Plan," in *The Supreme Court Review*, edited by Philip B. Kurland (Chicago, 1966), 347–95; F. Alan Coombs, "Joseph Christopher O'Mahoney and the New Deal Years," (Ph.D. dissertation, University of Illinois, 1968); Richard T. Ruetten, "Burton K. Wheeler of Montana; a Progressive Between

Wars," (Ph.D. Dissertation, University of Oregon, 1961); Barry A. Crouch, "Dennis Chavez and Roosevelt's 'Court Packing' Plan," *New Mexico Historical Review* XLII (October 1967), 261–80; William E. Leuchtenburg, "Franklin D. Roosevelt's Supreme Court 'Packing Plan'" in *Essays on the New Deal*, edited by Harold M. Hollingsworth and William F. Holmes (Austin, 1969); and Gene M. Gressley, "Joseph C. O'Mahoney, FDR and the Supreme Court," *Pacific Historical Review* XL (May 1961), 183–202.

120. Norman V. Donaldson (1891–1964). An editor with the Yale University Press from 1919 to 1959, the last nine years of his tenure he was president, treasurer and director of the Press.

121. An authority on political theory and constitutional law, Francis W. Coker (1878–1963), after a twenty-year stint at Ohio State University, joined the Political Science Department of Yale University in 1929.

122. Trained in theology and sociology, Robert S. Lynd (1892–1970) and his wife Helen M. Lynd created a "stir" in the 1920s and 1930s with the publication of their pioneering sociological analysis of Muncie, Indiana, entitled *Middletown* (New York, 1929) and *Middletown in Transition* (New York, 1937).

123. "The Jurisprudence of Edward S. Robinson," *Yale Law Journal* XLVI (June 1937), 1282–89.

124. Bryon Patton Harrison (1881–1941) was U. S. senator from Mississippi from 1919 to his death.

125. Tax consultant and chief of intelligence for the Department of the Treasury, 1919–42, E. L. Irey (1888–1948) had enormously broad responsibilities ranging from the Secret Service to Customs, and narcotic to alcohol tax enforcement.

126. Justin Du Pratt White (1869–1939), a partner of White and Case from 1892 until his death.

127. He exemplified the second-level echelon government servant who, through his ability and perseverance, had an enormous impact on both the legal profession and government. Coming to Washington in 1933 as general counsel of the Farm Credit Administration, after a long career as professor at the University of Chicago and Columbia University, Herman Oliphant (1884–1939) stayed on as general counsel to the secretary of the Treasury Department until his demise.

128. A brilliant legal mind, James Landis (1899–1964) was one of the most influential men in twentieth-century legal education and government. Receiving his law degree from Harvard in 1924, he served one year as law clerk to Mr. Justice Brandeis, returning to the Harvard law faculty until 1933, when he became a member of the Federal Trade Commission. A year later he joined the Securities and Exchange Commission, being appointed chairman in 1935. Again going back to Harvard in 1937, this time as dean of the Law School, he stayed at his alma mater until 1946, when he entered private practice.

129. A physician, politician and Methodist, Dr. Royal S. Copeland (1868–1938) specialized in opthalmology, taught at the University of Michigan, becoming commissioner of health in New York City, 1918–25. From 1928 to his passing, he occupied a U. S. Senate seat (Michigan). A fanatic on physical fitness and health, Dr. Copeland wrote several popular books on these subjects.

130. Burton K. Wheeler (1882–), senator from Montana and a vigorous opponent of Roosevelt's Supreme Court "packing" scheme.

131. Porter Sargent (1872–1951), educator, publisher and scientist, became a peppery critic of American education, ethics and morality. He was especially noted for his leadership in preparatory education.

132. Mount Desert Island, Maine, the location of Bar Harbor.

133. Charles Street, local Laramie businessman, who is now retired, having sold his printing establishment several years ago.

134. Levy had written an essay on legal philosophy and *The Folklore of Capitalism*.

135. See Introduction for Arnold's nomination, plus "Nomination of Thurman W. Arnold," *Hearings*, Subcommittee of the Committee of the Judiciary, United States Senate, 75th Cong., 3rd Sess. (Washington, 1938).

136. Rolling out his omnipresent weapons of satire and wit, Arnold replied to Henry Hazlitt, who had, in his New York *Times* review of *Folklore of Capitalism*, ridiculed the thesis of *Folklore* in addition to implying that Arnold was an admirer of Fascism and a "smart aleck" to boot! Arnold categorically denied a reverence for Fascism, and suggested that Hazlitt really exemplified the type of mentality he had depicted in *Folklore*: a man seduced by "righteous moralizing." Hazlitt, in turn, replied that he had not accused Arnold of Fascism, but he was bewildered by so many complimentary references to dictators. Further, Arnold, by dismissing "all law and economics as a 'theology'. . . does not trouble to answer any statement on its merits." "Letters to the Editors," New York *Times*, March 6, 1938; February 13, 1938.

137. Eugene Meyer (1875–1959), banker and government official, had the most impact on the Washington scene as publisher of the Washington *Post* from 1933 to his death.

138. Hamilton Owens (1888–1967) became editor of the Baltimore *Evening Sun* in 1922, staying with the *Sun* papers until his retirement in 1956.

139. Morris Fishbein (1889–), physician and publicist, and as the editor and guiding light of the *Journal of the American Medical Association* from 1913 to 1949, became the "mouthpiece" for American doctors. Hugh Cox recalls a marvelous scene between Thurman Arnold and Attorney General Cummings. Cummings commented, "Thurman, this is the Goddamnedest thing I ever heard. You propose to indict a hospital, a local medical association, and all these doctors? Well, these doctors are leading citizens of their communities, and I play golf with some of them; you know if you do this there's going to be a lot of trouble and somebody's going to catch hell. Now who is it?" Thurman replied, "Well, you will!" Cummings just laughed and waved Thurman out, "All right, go ahead." Hugh Cox, Interview, July 15, 1971.

140. The suit against the American Medical Association focused on the issues of cooperative medicine. The test case selected by the Department of Justice concerned the Group Health Association, Inc., of the District of Columbia. The complaint specifically charged the American Medical Association with a) threatening physicians with expulsion from the A.M.A. if they joined the Group Health Association; b) threatening the District of Columbia doctors who so much as consulted with the Group Health physicians; and charged

Washington hospitals with excluding Group Health doctors. Understandably this suit became one of Arnold's most controversial. An indictment against the American Medical Association and twenty-one doctors was filed December 20, 1938. The case dragged out over the next four years, finally ending up in the U.S. Supreme Court. On January 19, 1943, the Supreme Court upheld the government. The American Medical Association was fined a modest $2,500 and the defendants $1,500 each. The decision had an immediate effect on voluntary health organizations; one entrepreneur, Henry J. Kaiser, pushed ahead with his Kaiser plan. District Court of the United States, *United States of America* v. *American Medical Association et al.* Criminal No. 63221. Baltimore *Sun*, August 3, 1938; New York *Herald*, August 1, 1938; New York *Times*, August 2, 1938; Washington *Star*, January 19, 1943; New York *Times*, May 19, 1939; Cincinnati *Enquirer*, December 22, 1938; New York *News*, January 23, 1939.

141. Gordon E. Dean (1905–58) had a distinguished career in the academic world and in government. Dean of the Duke University Law School, from where he came to Washington in 1934, Gordon Dean held several positions in the Department of Justice until 1940, when he entered private practice in Washington, D.C. After one year as Mr. Justice Robert H. Jackson's assistant at the Nuremberg trials, Dean joined the faculty of the University of Southern California. In 1949 he was appointed to the Atomic Energy Commission, a position he retained until going with Lehman Bros. in 1953.

142. Journalist Frederic William Wile in the Washington *Star*, October 14, 1938, spouted, "None but Harvard, Yale, and Columbia men need apply!" Wile quoted an alleged applicant who appeared at Arnold's office seeking a position. "A personable young job-hunting lawyer turned up the other day and modestly identified himself as a graduate of a certain famed midwestern university. Without mincing words, Arnold told him the antitrust division is hiring only Harvard, Yale and Columbia graduates."

143. Although she had a reserved seat via her ascension to the Reid publishing dynasty, Helen Rogers Reid (1882–1970) assumed a very dynamic role in the direction of the New York *Herald-Tribune*; one of her unhappy tasks was to preside over its demise.

144. Ford and Chrysler, via the consent decree, capitulated on November 15, 1938, to the Department of Justice's bill of particulars in the vital area of auto financing. Under the terms of the decree, dealers would no longer be required to negotiate with one "authorized" finance company. All service and special privileges that were heretofore reserved for one finance company must be made available to all finance agencies. Finally, Ford and Chrysler could no longer advertise on behalf of a specific auto financing company. Ellis Hawley, *The New Deal and the Problem of Monopoly* (Princeton, 1966), 433; Publicity Release, Department of Justice, November 15, 1938, Arnold Coll.; and *Time* XXXII (November 21, 1938).

145. Academician and journalist, Raymond Moley (1886–) came to Washington with the cascade of original "brain trusters," where he remained until his well-publicized break with the New Deal. Most of his public life has been spent as a contributing editor to *Newsweek* and professor of public law at Columbia.

146. Jack Graham, writes a longtime Laramie resident and University of Wyoming faculty member, was "a rather unusual fellow." Born in Scotland, an oil pipeline and refinery employee, Graham was self taught, widely read, an avid chess player, holding firm and original views.

147. Arnold's speech, with the unimaginative title of "Government," began as follows, "My subject this afternoon is Government. I have fourteen minutes in which to explain it." The address delivered at the Waldorf-Astoria on October 26, 1938, was broadcast over NBC. Basically the "informal" remarks contained nothing but a rehash of the ideas Arnold had expressed in *Folklore*.

148. What caused the upheaval among the true believers was a couple of sentences in the first paragraph, "Every organized group must have its established church, or as I have expressed it elsewhere, its folklore. That church must embody the fundamental truths and principles, which *gave* the state its greatness. At the same time that church must not impose ridiculous and unnecessary material sacrifices on the great mass of people." "Government," unpublished manuscript. Arnold Coll.

149. Son of a notable historian, grandson of a famous president of the University of Michigan, James A. McLaughlin (1891–) joined the Harvard Law School in 1924, staying there until his retirement in 1960, when he associated with the Hastings Law College in San Francisco.

150. William L. Chenery (1884–) had one of the most active editorial careers in American journalism. His major positions were with *The Survey* and *Colliers Weekly*, where he held the post of publisher until 1950.

151. Kernan Robson (1872–1956), after taking a series of degrees from Ohio Northern University, Ohio Wesleyan, Harvard and Cambridge, ended up in North Dakota as a teacher. Forsaking the rigorous winters, he moved to San Francisco, where he again entered college, this time at Stanford. After a short time at Stanford, he opened a real estate and investment office in San Francisco, where he was extremely successful. For relaxation he read Latin and Greek and corresponded with political figures across the country. Miss Vivian Moors to Gene M. Gressley, July 17, 1972.

152. The Securities and Exchange Commission in November 1938 proposed to issue subpoenas against the Bank of America officials to determine whether there had been correct reports made to the Comptroller of Currency. The attack on the Bank of America by the SEC represented part of a broad investigation of holding companies, specifically the Transamerica Corporation, which owned forty-two percent of the stock of the Bank of America. The counsel for the Bank, William Stanley, vigorously objected to the investigation as it would do "irreparable" harm to the Bank of America's reputation. Arnold's role in the action consisted of assuring Federal Judge D.M. O'Donoghue that the SEC had the full support of the Department of Justice. Washington *News*, January 30, 1939; New York *World-Telegram*, January 30, 1939; Chicago *Tribune*, January 31, 1939; the San Francisco *Chronicle*, January 31, 1939.

153. Secretary of the Navy, newspaper publisher and Mason, William Franklin Knox (1874–1944) had a lengthy career in the newspaper world, finally as publisher of the Chicago *Daily News*. His service in government extended from the Spanish-American War as a member of Troop D of the lst U.S. Cavalry, to Secretary of the Navy 1940 to 1944.

154. Felix Morley (1894–), a career journalist, has held editorial positions on the Baltimore *Sun*, 1922–29; the Washington *Post*, 1933–40; and *Human Events*, 1940–45. From 1945 until 1950 Morley was president of Haverford College; he was Washington correspondent for *Barron's Weekly* from 1950 to 1954.

155. The Morley editorial that annoyed Arnold appeared in the Washington *Post* July 27, 1939. Entitled, "Boomerang Indictment," Morley admitted that members of the American Medical Association "have their shortcomings." "But those mistakes are no excuse for an arbitrary attempt to dragoon organized medicine into lowering its cherished standards." Arnold heatedly replied that the suit in no way involved standards, "but whether a group of physicians can use specific threats and coercions against other physicians connected with Group Health about whose standards there is no question." T.W. Arnold to Felix Morley, July 28, 1939. Arnold Coll.

156. Arthur Hays Sulzberger (1891–1968) was publisher, president and director of the New York *Times* and its subsidiaries, in addition to being a member of innumerable boards of eleemosynary institutions.

157. "Government 'By Definition'" appeared in the New York *Times*, August 24, 1939.

158. Economist, journalist, college president and publishing executive Dexter Keezer (1896–) had been a friend of Thurman Arnold since the early 1930s. In the Second World War, Keezer was deputy administrator of the Office of Price Administration. With McGraw-Hill since 1945, he recently retired as vice-president, director and economic advisor.

159. Influential journalist and foreign correspondent, Dorothy Thompson (1894–1961) was also an avid member of the Patrons of Husbandry. Her marriage to her second husband, Sinclair Lewis, has received minute examination.

160. An acronym for the International Alliance of Theatrical Stage Employees and Moving Picture Machine Operators of the United States and Canada.

161. Author and political scientist Max Lerner (1902–) had exchanged intellectual jousts with Arnold since 1931. Lerner has floated between the publishing and academic worlds. On the faculty of Sarah Lawrence College, 1932–35, he later became editor of the *Nation*. Then he moved back to the campus by becoming professor of political science at Williams College, 1938–43. Lerner returned to newspaper life as editorial director of *PM*, 1943–48. Since 1949, he has been professor of American civilization at Brandeis University.

162. *Ideas Are Weapons* (New York, 1939).

163. Freda Kirchwey (1911–), associated with the *Nation* since 1918, as editor 1932–55. The name of Freda Kirchwey became synonymous with liberal causes and events for decades. Some of her tremendous energy has been expended in the fields of civil rights, women's rights and international peace.

164. Dorothy Thompson's column, a virulent attack on the dictatorial power of James C. Petrillo, came out in the New York *Herald-Tribune* on January 1, 1940. Among the spicy sentences, one that sparked a quick retort was, "The Musicians's Union and the Stage Hands Union have already contributed more than any single factor to ruin American theatre, from an economic standpoint."

165. J. Fred Essary's column had appeared on the first page of the Baltimore *Sun* for Sunday, June 21, 1940. Essary noted that Attorney General Jackson

had announced that he was not "disposed to direct any sweeping 'crusades' against violators as a class."

166. Of course a great Potomac sport, as contagious as Potomac fever, is gossip among and between the newspaper columnists and the Washington bureaucracy. Arnold probably suffered more from rumors than most; as a freewheeling, noisy prosecutor, he attracted attention—in essence, he was always good copy. Drew Pearson and Robert S. Allen announced in their "Washington-Merry-Go-Round" piece on April 28, 1939, that four of Murphy's key aides were ready to resign. The reason? "It is difficult to get decisions out of the chief. Cases pile up on the Attorney General's desk and don't move. He [Murphy] is out horseback riding or investigating judges. It is difficult for his aides to see Murphy." Whether Arnold supplied Pearson and Allen with their story or not, the column substantially reflected Arnold's discontent.

Again in July 1939 rumors of Arnold's impending resignation hit the newspapers. This time the press discerned Thomas Corcoran's fine Italian hand in the proceedings. Why? Because Corcoran, as a loyal Harvard alumnus, disliked Yaleman Arnold and the former Attorney General Homer Cummings, also an Eli! At least it made for uproarious reading! Chicago *Tribune*, July 30, 1939.

167. Judge Joseph A. Padway, counsel for the American Federation of Labor, sounded the alarm against Arnold off and on for the better part of two years. Padway in a speech in the spring of 1940 referred to Arnold as "the greatest enemy of organized labor in America." Pittsburgh *Press*, April 28, 1940.

168. The editorial headed "Restraints by Unions" attacked the corruption in unions and applauded Arnold's suit.

169. One Pegler observer once commented "Poor Peg, he hated too much." James Westbrook Pegler (1894–1969) undoubtedly had one of the stormiest careers in the history of American journalism. In and out of litigation, tossing off firecracking opinions, he was either the most respected or the most despised columnist in America.

170. Richardson K. Wood (1903–1976) spent his early career in publishing and advertising. He joined *Fortune* in 1937 as a writer and editor. While on the *Fortune* staff he established the *Fortune* Survey of Public Opinion. After 1945 he consulted with numerous cities and regions on their economic development. Since 1969 he has been a special assistant to the president of New College, Sarasota, Florida.

171. Corwin D. Edwards (1904–), an Arnold friend and associate, was an economic consultant and chairman of the Economic Policy Board of the Antitrust Division, 1939–44. Since the mid nineteen-forties he has been a faculty member of Northwestern University, the University of Chicago and the University of Oregon.

172. Frederick Roe (1905–65) was co-founder of the investment firm of Stein, Roe and Farnham in Chicago in the optimistic year of 1932. From 1941 to 1944 he labored in the Office of the War Production Board.

173. November 28, 1940.

174. Volatile and iconoclastic, General Hugh Johnson (1882–1942) was neither modest nor quiet. As an intimate of Bernard Baruch, an official of the Moline Plow Company, the controversial head of the NRA and a journalist, Hugh Johnson had a propensity for making headlines.

175. Johnson praised Arnold's investigation of lumber price fixing, but suggested that there be closer cooperation with Leon Henderson (1895–), who was then administrator of the Office of Price Administration and Civilian Supply.

176. *The Bottlenecks of Business* (New York, 1940).

177. Edward A. Evans (1892–1951) was a journalist, editorial writer and member of the Scripps-Howard editorial board.

178. Refer to the Introduction for a discussion of the Hutcheson case; also see: Thurman Arnold, *Fair Fights and Foul* (New York, 1965), 114–16; *United States* v. *Hutcheson*, 312 U.S. 219 (1941).

179. Indictment, *United States* v. *Associated Plumbing and Heating Merchants et al.*, No. 45270 (1940).

180. Temporary National Economic Committee was headed by Senator Joseph C. O'Mahoney. For an analysis of TNEC activities see a brilliant tome by Ellis C. Hawley, *The New Deal and the Problem of Monopoly* (Princeton, 1966).

181. National Labor Relations Board.

182. "Labor's Hidden Hold-Up Men," *Reader's Digest* XXXVIII (June 1941), 136–40.

183. Managing editor of *Reader's Digest*, 1931–39, its executive editor and vice-president until his death, Kenneth Payne (1890–1962) was a major figure in the phenomenal success of America's most "widely read" periodical. Before he arrived at *Reader's Digest*, Payne had been with the Newspaper Enterprise Association, *People's Home Journal, Popular Science* and *McClure's*.

184. Rockwell Kent (1882–) was known for his achievements as an artist and his enthusiasm for Communism.

185. Kent had requested Arnold's assistance in a deportation case.

186. A native of Wichita, Kansas, Earl Browder (1891–) has been recognized chiefly as one of the leading spokesmen of Marxism in America. He was general secretary of the American Communist Party, 1930–44.

187. C. Warriner's article sans byline appeared in *Fortune* XXVI (August 1942), 103–6; 132–41.

188. Republican, Quaker and journalist, George H. Adams (1885–1949) found employment with various newspapers, all in Minneapolis, from 1906 to 1942, when he went with the advertising agency of Batten, Barton, Durstine and Osborn.

189. This was one of Arnold's favorite examples of the horrors of monopoly in the country. On July 7, 1938, he asked a grand jury in Chicago to investigate numerous instances of restraints in trade in the dairy industry. After four months of deliberation and millions of words of testimony the grand jury returned two indictments against about everybody connected with the dairy industry, including milk distributors, unions, cooperatives, urban leaders, and manufacturers of ice cream equipment. *Newsweek* XXXII (November 28, 1938), 44; *Business Week* n.v. (November 19, 1938), 55 and *Time* XXXII (November 21, 1938), 55.

190. Editor, director of the Twentieth Century Fund 1928–53, and member of the editorial board of the New York *Times,* Evans Clark (1888–) has been involved

in numerous philanthropic and educational ventures, including: Film Council of America, Council for Democracy, Advertising Council and New York State's Citizen's Council.

191. Before the Second World War, Donald Marr Nelson (1888–1959) was known chiefly for his highly successful business career in merchandising. In 1942 Nelson left his post as chairman of the executive committee of Sears, Roebuck & Co. to take over the chairmanship of the War Production Board. After the war he became involved with the manufacture of pressure containers and in producing independent movies.

192. War Production Board.

193. John Lord O'Brian (1874–1973) came (until shortly before his death) to his office every day at Covington and Burling in Washington, D.C. His long and remarkable career in law has been distinguished not only by success in private practice but by service to his government in both World War I and World War II.

194. Ambassador to France 1957–61, and executive of the Corning Glass Works, Amory Houghton (1899–) left the War Production Board in 1942 to go with the Mission for Economic Affairs as deputy chief. Since the Second World War Houghton has spent most of his time with philanthropy and the Corning company.

195. At the time Arnold wrote this memorandum, Philip Reed (1899–) occupied the office of chief of the Industries Division, War Production Board. Reed spent most of his business career with General Electric, where he was chairman of the board, 1940–42 and 1945–58.

196. A native of Willow Lake, South Dakota, Zay Jeffries (1888–1965) achieved eminence as one of the great metallurgists of the twentieth century. He spent almost his entire business career with General Electric, 1914–49. In the Second World War he served as technical advisor to a number of boards.

197. Hugh Cox, in 1942, left the Antitrust Division and went to London on an assignment for the Board of Economic Warfare. When Cox left, he and Thurman were reading Ernest Haycox's newest Western, "Action by Night," which ran in *Colliers* for ten successive weeks beginning August 8, 1942. Cox recalled, "I wrote to Thurman from London asking him to tell me how the story ended and Thurman's letter was written in response to my request. It was delayed some time in British censorship; I always assumed that the delay was because the letter was being passed around among the censors for their amusement." The editor is indebted to Mr. Cox for providing a copy of this wonderful example of Arnold's humor. Hugh Cox to Gene M. Gressley, March 14, 1972.

198. President Roosevelt wrote Arnold upon his leaving the Antitrust Division.

THE WHITEHOUSE
WASHINGTON

*January 8, 1943*

*Dear Thurman:*

As you know, I am going to send your nomination to be an Associate Justice of the United States Court of Appeals for the District of Columbia to the Senate. This letter is just a personal note to thank you for all you have done for this Administration. You have been Assistant Attorney

General in charge of the Antitrust Division since 1938. In the intervening years you have brought to the Department of Justice a vigor, an intelligence and an economic understanding which has resulted in a consistent and telling enforcement of the antitrust laws. You have surrounded yourself with unusually able men. I believe that not the least of your achievements has been the educational effect of your enforcement campaign on the public; it has brought to the people a clear understanding of the inherent dangers to democracy of monopoly growth.

I know you leave your post in the Department of Justice with mingled feelings. You, of course, have keen regret at leaving the body of men in the Antitrust Division among whom you have built such an excellent esprit de corps. I know also that you can leave them with the assurance that the same vigorous enforcement of the antitrust laws will continue.

I hate to see you go but I know that you want to and I, therefore, bid you Godspeed and great success in your new career. The same qualities of intellect and of heart which you brought to the Department of Justice will serve you in your new career on the bench.

Of course, I shall want to see you for a few minutes before you wrap that robe around you!

Very sincerely yours,

s/ *Franklin D. Roosevelt*

HONORABLE THURMAN W. ARNOLD
ASSISTANT ATTORNEY GENERAL
DEPARTMENT OF JUSTICE
WASHINGTON, D.C.

199. Erwin D. Canhan's (1904–) total career in journalism, beginning in 1925, has been with the *Christian Science Monitor*. Author of numerous tomes, participant in dozens of civic organizations, Canhan has been especially active in supporting the United Nations.

200. Arnold considered Duncan Lawrence Groner (1873–1957) an able judge, both for his legal ability and his common sense. In private practice in Norfolk, Virginia from 1884 to 1901, Groner had the unique distinction of being elected a delegate from Virginia to the Republican National Convention on five successive occasions; (Arnold always insisted that this was because Groner was the only Republican in Virginia). President Harding appointed Groner judge of the Eastern District of Virginia in 1921; ten years passed and President Hoover appointed Groner to the U.S. Circuit Court of Appeals for the District of Columbia, where he became chief judge in 1938.

201. A testimonial dinner honoring Thurman Arnold upon his departure from the Antitrust Division was held in the Presidential Room of the Statler Hotel in Washington, D.C. on March 9, 1943. An enormous affair, some two hundred fifty guests were seated at sixty-two tables. The guest list read like a "Who's Who" of Washington society; among those present and accounted for were: Senator Robert La Follette; Speaker Sam Rayburn; Senator Alben Barkley; Senator Joseph C. O'Mahoney (Toastmaster for the evening); Attorney General Francis Biddle; Mr. Justice Hugh Black; Henry Kaiser, et al. Thurman wrote his Wyoming friend, Fred Nussbaum, "A nauseous odor permeated

the murky room, and remorse on the part of all who attended will settle on all the heads, along with ice packs on the morning after." Thurman Arnold to Fred Nussbaum, March 14, 1943; "A Tribute From His Friends and Associates of the Antitrust Division."

202. Thurman received the following communication from Homer Cummings,

*March 10, 1943*

*Dear Thurman:*

Well, it was a grand banquet and you have every right to feel proud and happy—proud of your friends who came to honor you and pleased with the richly deserved praises they showered upon you and Frances.

You certainly went out, or shall I say "up", in a blaze of glory—up to the higher realm of judicial "security." It reminded me of the ascension of Elijah: "And it came to pass, *as they still went on and talked*, that, behold there appeared a chariot of fire and parted them asunder and Elijah went up by a whirlwind into heaven."

Look down occasionally, old friend, to comfort us; and also to keep an eye on Elisha to make certain that he is wearing your mantle with proper respect.

Affectionate remembrances to you and Frances, in which Julie joins me.

Faithfully yours,

s/ *Homer Cummings*

HON. THURMAN ARNOLD
DEPARTMENT OF JUSTICE
WASHINGTON, D.C.

203. The flavor of Eleanor Medill "Cissy" Patterson cannot be caught in a few sentences. Iconoclastic, opinionated, spoiled and a semi-tragic figure, "Cissy" Patterson helped to keep the social life on the Potomac in an uproar from the time she arrived as publisher of the Washington *Times-Herald* until her demise. A biography that probably comes as close as any will to photographing "Cissy" is Alice Hoge, *"Cissy" Patterson* (New York, 1966).

204. An incredible character, Cal Carrington managed "Cissy" Patterson's ranch in the Jackson Hole country for over twenty years. Rudely and roughedly independent, with speech as native as the wilds of the Teton wilderness, to meet Cal was to remember him forever. He was an authentic Western "primitive." One of the editor's unforgettable experiences was seeing Cal Carrington down on his hands and knees, crawling around the floor, describing the movement and imitating the sounds of wild life that he had encountered on a Patterson safari in Africa!

205. A devoted fan of Hergsheimer (1880–1954), Thurman particularly liked to read and re-read *Java Head* (1919) and *From an Old House* (1925). Like Mencken, Hergsheimer joined that small coterie of literati which Arnold cultivated and enjoyed; in turn, his friendship was valued and reciprocated.

206. The "Sage of Emporia" (which caught on primarily because it translated as a non sequitor to so many), had an unrivalled impact on the twentieth-century

social and political scene. An extremely prolific writer of ten books and thousands of editorials, White was simply a very shrewd, decent and profound human being. Above pettiness, his crusades and observations continually came across the Delphic overtones.

207. A reference to the recent book by William Allen White's son, William L. White, *Queens Die Proudly* (New York, 1943).

208. "Labor Against Itself," *Cosmopolitan* CXV (November 1943), 28–35.

209. T. R. Powell, "Insurance as Commerce–In Constitution and Statute," *Harvard Law Review* LVII (September 1944), 43–56.

210. Robert W. Woodruff (1889–), long an executive of his family's company, Coca Cola. It was Woodruff's retainer who helped emancipate Arnold from the U.S. Circuit Court of Appeals.

211. A liberal, independent-minded governor of Georgia from 1943 to 1947, Ellis Arnall (1907–) has been an insurance executive, involved with the motion picture industry, and in private practice in Atlanta since 1947. He instituted a freight rate discrimination suit against the Pennsylvania Railroad in which two former colleagues of Arnold's, William McGovern and Hugh Cox, were opposing counsels, Cox for the Pennsylvania Railroad, McGovern for the State of Georgia. Georgia lost the suit.

212. Arnold found Frank's *Fate and Freedom* mechanistic. *Saturday Review of Literature* XXVIII (June 23, 1945), 10.

213. The author was Arne Wiprud, the Introduction by Thurman Arnold.

214. For the next several years political columnists would gossip, from time to time, about Arnold's political ambitions. Drew Pearson, whose daughter, Ellen, had married Arnold's son, George, stated flatly, "The most interesting Senate race of the year is shaping up in Wyoming, where Judge Thurman Arnold, the trust-busting former Assistant Attorney General, plans to challenge one of the businessmen in the state, GOP Senator Edward V. Robertson." Washington *Post*, January 24, 1948. The *Rocky Mountain News* forecast that if Governor Lester Hunt bowed out of the primary for the Senate, Arnold would enter. February 5, 1948. "Washington Party Line" in *Colliers*, April 3, 1948, also repeated the same rumors on Arnold's political aspirations.

215. A maverick in politics, Maury Maverick (1895–1954) was mixed up in Texas and national politics for thirty years. A recent biography is Richard B. Henderson's *Maury Maverick, A Political Biography* (Austin, 1970).

216. See the Introduction for the Pullman Company contest with Robert Young.

217. *From an Old House* (New York, 1926).

218. Humbug! Arnold was enamoured with tradition and the past; his enthusiasm for the Lafayette house, which he purchased in Alexandria, Virginia, is but one example.

219. *Balisand* (New York, 1925).

220. One, in the tide of literary expatriates, who found life, amusement, and excitement on the European continent during the 1920s and 1930s, Matthew Josephson (1899–), has written some fifteen volumes, among the best known of which are: *Zola and His Time* (1928); *The Robber Barons* (1934); *The*

*Politicos* (1938); *Edison* (1959); *Life Among the Surrealists* (1962) and *The Infidel in the Temple* (1967). Today the Josephsons live among the rolling hills of western Connecticut, in the literary colony of Sherman. Up the road a piece are the Alfred Vagts, daughter and son-in-law of the Charles Beards, striking off to the northeast is Mrs. Van Wyck Brooks, and so on.

221. A friend from Arnold's Wyoming days.

222. Edward S. Corwin (1878–1963), noted constitutional scholar, who taught at Princeton from 1906 to 1948.

223. A distant cousin of the Arnolds, living in Germany.

224. An acquaintance of Arnold since the days of the Temporary National Economic Committee, Leon Henderson (1895–) occupied a succession of important posts in the New Deal and the Second World War periods. In recent years he has been an economic consultant operating out of New York City.

225. James F. Byrnes (1879–1973) held a remarkable number of governmental posts in his long lifetime: Member of Congress, associate justice of the U.S. Supreme Court, 1941–42; director of economic stabilization, 1942–43; director of war mobilization, 1943–45; secretary of state, 1945–47 and governor of South Carolina, 1951–55.

226. For background on this letter the reader is cited to the Introduction.

227. Geoffrey Parsons (1908–) was a journalist, war correspondent, editor of the European edition of the New York *Herald Tribune*, 1944–50, and director of public relations for NATO, 1950. Since 1957, Mr. Parsons has been vice-president of Northrup International.

228. Originally conceived as a letter to the editor of the New York *Times*, Arnold eventually sent it to *Harper's*. Quoted and requoted, Arnold's "Ten Commandments" were bantered around Capitol Hill throughout the McCarthy era. "How Not to Get Investigated," *Harper's* CLXVII (November 1948), 61–63.

229. Leon E. Aylesworth (1869–1961) received his B.A. degree from the University of Nebraska in 1900; after receiving an M.A. from the University of Wisconsin, he returned to Nebraska to teach political science from 1906 until his retirement in 1941.

230. Andrew Heiskell (1915–) has been a Time, Inc. man for most of his life. He is now chairman of the board and chief executive officer.

231. The Philadelphia *Bulletin* sponsored a "Forum on World Affairs," March 22–23, 1949. Thurman Arnold was invited to participate on a panel, "Are Congressional Hearings on Communism in the Public Interest?" Senator Karl E. Mundt was the opposing speaker with Owen J. Roberts as moderator. Intriguingly enough in light of later events, Owen Lattimore also appeared on the same program offering his observations on "Asia and the Cold War."

232. Civil libertarian and internationalist, the Rev. John Haynes Holmes (1879–1964) was pastor of the Community Church of New York from 1907 to 1949.

233. A professor emeritus of law at Harvard since 1958, George K. Gardner (1891–) joined the Law School faculty in 1928.

234. On the Dorothy Bailey case, please see the Introduction.

235. E.B. Prettyman (1891–), then associate, now chief judge of the U.S. Circuit Court of Appeals for Washington, D.C.

236. Henry White Edgerton (1888–1968), associate judge of the U.S. Circuit Court of Appeals for Washington, 1938; chief judge, 1955–58. For more on Judge Edgerton in this time, the reader is referred to the Introduction.

237. Orrin Keepnews, then an associate editor of Simon and Schuster.

238. President of the American Potash and Chemical Company, Peter Colefax was incensed over alleged untruths in Arnold's article, "The Crash—and What it Meant," in Isabel Leighton's *The Aspirin Age*, a between-the-wars history of the twenties and thirties. In one lengthy paragraph Arnold traced the corporate history and the inter-connections between potash companies. He then labelled the American Potash and Chemical Company as one price fixing firm, with European financial associations. Colefax wrote to Keepnews stating, "American Potash is not controlled by the Germans; it is not operated by Gold Fields; there is no connection between Borax Consolidated and American Potash to fix prices or otherwise violate the antitrust laws." Arnold's reply is this letter. Isabel Leighton, *The Aspirin Age* (New York, 1949), 214–31; Peter Colefax to Orrin Keepnews, March 17, 1950. Arnold Coll.

239. Hugh Cox responded in kind as follows:

*23 March, 1951*

THURMAN ARNOLD, ESQ.
ARNOLD, FORTAS & PORTER
1200 EIGHTEENTH STREET, N.W.
WASHINGTON 6, D.C.

*Dear Thurman:*

I am grateful to you for your letter dated 24 February 1951. Our friendship is of such long standing, however, that I think I can safely point out to you that to be courteous it is not necessary to indulge in flattery. I know that I am not as good a lawyer as James J. Laughlin. I am not even as good a lawyer as you or Stammler, considered either separately or together, that being after Laughlin, the next rank in what our old friend McDougal would undoubtedly call "the hierarchy of legal excellence."

On the second point you are absolutely right. I have been having dizzy spells, ringing in the ears and a touch of the bends. The horrid thing is that I notice nothing unusual. If it goes on, however, I may have to call upon your day and night service.

Sincerely yours,

s/ *Hugh B. Cox*

240. An excellent example of the philosophical range of Arnold's friends, Joseph N. Pew (1907–), a conservative leader of a conservative family.

241. Thurman Arnold, "Mob Justice and Television," *Atlantic Monthly* CLXXXVII (June 1951), 68–71.

242. A cousin of Thurman Arnold's.

243. In January 1952, Cinema Amusement, Inc., a company operating the Broadway Theatre and three drive-in theatres in Denver, brought an antitrust suit against RKO, Twentieth Century-Fox and Metro-Goldwyn-Mayer, charging them with conspiracy with the intent to drive Cinema Amusement out of business. In his closing argument Arnold noted that ninety-five percent of the motion pictures produced in the United States did not sell or had not attempted to sell their product to the Broadway Theatre. After an exhausting seven weeks trial, the jury awarded damages in favor of the plaintiff. Denver *Post*, Jan. 6, 15; Feb. 20, 27, 1952.

244. Will Shafroth (1894–), member of a prominent Denver family, whose father, John Shafroth, was elected senator from Colorado, received the J.D. degree from the University of California in 1916. After a year in the army and a year practicing law in Denver, Shafroth returned to Europe to work with relief agencies. Since 1940, he has been an administrative official with the U.S. Courts in Washington, D.C.

245. Arthur M. Schlesinger, Jr. (1917–) is an able historian who has involved himself in political affairs as an avid supporter of the Americans For Democratic Action and for a time was a prominent member of the John Kennedy entourage.

246. C.R. Smith (1899–) is one of the most successful entrepreneurs in American aviation. His career began with the origins of American Airlines, where he retired as chairman of the board in 1971.

247. A practicing attorney in Cincinnati since 1903, Murray Seasongood (1878–) has had a long and prominent career in government at the city, county, state and national levels. From being mayor of Cincinnati, 1926–30, he went on to participate as a member and consultant for numerous commissions and advisory boards in Washington, including the U.S. Civil Service Loyalty Review Board, 1947–53, and the advisory committee to the U.S. Supreme Court on criminal procedure.

248. After a career as professor of economics at Swarthmore, Patrick H. Malin (1903–64) became vice-director of the Intergovernmental Commission on Refugees, 1943–47. Three years later he assumed the position of executive director of the American Civil Liberties Association.

249. Charles Fahy (1892–), in law practice in Washington, D.C. and Santa Fe, New Mexico, 1914–33. Fahy then occupied a diversified number of government posts in the Department of Interior, the Petroleum Administration Board, the National Labor Relations Board and as solicitor general. President Truman appointed him to the U.S. Circuit Court of Appeals in 1949.

250. Born in Dallas, Texas, William D. Neary (1931–) has been a member of the law firm, Thompson, Knight, Wright & Simmons in Dallas since 1955, with the exception of a three-year period when he served as associate counsel for the Naval Petroleum and Oil Shale Reserve in Washington, D.C. William D. Neary to Gene M. Gressley, April 17, 1973.

251. William D. Neary, "Constitutional Law–Person, Civil, and Political Rights–Perjury–the effect of the First Amendment on an Indictment for Perjury for Lying about One's Sympathies–*United States* v. *Lattimore*, 112 F. Supp. 507 (D.C., 1953)," *Texas Law Review* XXXII (April 1954), 450.

252. Philip L. Graham (1915–64), after graduation from Harvard Law School, began his career as law secretary to Mr. Justice Reed; he then had the

unusual distinction of serving another year as secretary to Mr. Justice Frankfurter. The year, 1946, dates his association with the Washington *Post*, where he stayed until his demise.

253. Leo Rover (1888–1960) practiced law in Washington, D.C. from 1910 until his death. He was appointed U.S. attorney for two terms and chief judge of the Municipal Court of Appeals for one term.

254. Judge Youngdahl's response is in the Introduction.

255. The background of the Peters' case is provided in the Introduction.

256. William M. Oman (1911–) has been active in the publishing world since 1934, when he joined Oxford University Press. Oman left Oxford in 1957 to go with Dodd, Mead and Company as vice-president and director.

257. Eugene C. Gerhart, *America's Advocate! Robert H. Jackson* (Indianapolis, 1958).

258. Warren P. Hill (1924–) has taught in the law schools of Northwestern University, Ohio State University and the University of Pennsylvania. He returned to private practice in 1959; currently he is a supervising attorney for the Legal Services program of the Office of Economic Opportunity in Chicago.

259. Warren P. Hill, "The Psychological Realism of Thurman Arnold," *University of Chicago Law Review* XXII (Winter 1955), 377–86.

260. Alexander T. Schenck (born 1889 in Princeton, New Jersey), a graduate of Harvard Law School, lived his entire life in Newark, New Jersey, where he practiced as a corporate lawyer, specializing in real estate, bankruptcy, labor relations and administrative law. Schenck was a classmate of Thurman Arnold at the Harvard Law School.

261. Joseph J. Daniels (1890–) has practiced law in Indianapolis since 1914. He currently is a counsel in the firm of Baker and Daniels. His major legal activity has centered on Panhandle Eastern Pipeline Co., where he has been general counsel. Daniel's appeal concerns support for the Harvard Law School.

262. Frank C. Waldrop (1905–) is now a breeder of registered cattle, but from 1928 to 1953 he was one of America's outstanding journalists. Most of his career was with the Washington *Times-Herald* (1933–53), where Waldrop was successively reporter, editorial writer, manager of the editorial page, and managing editor.

263. Arnold's review of Fred Rodell's republished *Woe Unto You Lawyers* (New York, 1957) appeared in *Progressive* XXI (October 1957), 35. Arnold got around his discomfiture by ignoring most of Rodell's book and thesis.

264. This letter became the basis for Arthur Krock's column of March 4, 1958, on the problems of labor and antitrust legislation. The views expressed by Krock are very similar to those outlined by Arnold twenty years previously.

265. "Labor's Hidden Hold-Up Men," *Reader's Digest* XXXVIII (June 1941), 136–40; "Labor Against Itself," *Reader's Digest* XLIV (June 1944), 37–41. The latter article was originally published in *Cosmopolitan* for November 1943.

266. David L. Bazelon (1909–) is currently judge of the U.S. Circuit Court of Appeals for the District of Columbia. Judge Bazelon ascended to the bench in 1949 after fourteen years in private practice and government service. Judge Bazelon has been especially concerned with the legal implication of psychiatry.

267. Charles David Ginsburg (1912–) has been a member of the law firm of Ginsburg and Feldman since 1946. He has also held innumerable government positions including a year as legal secretary to Mr. Justice William O. Douglas in 1939.

268. Author and editor, Oliver Jensen (1914–) was one of the founders of *American Heritage* in 1954; since 1956 he has been managing editor. Previous to his association with *American Heritage* he had been in advertising and a writer and editor for *Life*.

269. Pertaining to the manuscript for Arnold's "The Law to Make Free Enterprise Free," *American Heritage* XI (October 1960), 52–55, 92–94.

270. A member of the Cowles publishing dynasty, John Cowles (1898–) has devoted his entire life to the Associated Press and the family newspapers, particularly the Minneapolis *Star and Tribune* and the Des Moines *Register and Tribune*. John Cowles had written Arnold that because of freight problems, it was becoming increasingly difficult to send turkeys across the country. Therefore, he wanted to express his regrets and forewarn Arnold that no more Thanksgiving turkeys would be coming from his game farm, "Glendalough." John Cowles to Thurman Arnold, October 27, 1959. Arnold Coll.

271. A specialist in property law, A.J. Casner (1907–) has been on the Harvard law faculty since 1938.

272. So there!

273. Jacob Hyman (1909–) had a variety of government positions before joining the University of Buffalo Law School in 1946, where he has been since, serving as dean 1953–64. Richard D. Schwartz to Gene M. Gressley, April 27, 1973.

274. Henry M. Hart, Jr., "Forward: The Time Chart of the Justices; The Supreme Court, 1958 Term," *Harvard Law Review* LXXIII (November 1959), 99–125. For a description of the contretemps between Arnold and Hart, the reader is referred to the Introduction.

275. Mr. Justice Douglas' article, "The Supreme Court and Its Case Load," appeared in the *Bulletin* of the Cornell Law School, April 8, 1960. The work load of the Supreme Court surfaced as an issue again in 1972. Chief Justice Warren E. Burger complained of the rise in the number of appeals to the Court. Mr. Justice William O. Douglas, reiterating his position of thirteen years previous, insisted that "We are, if anything, underworked, not overworked." Douglas admitted that the number of cases filed at the Court had risen from 1,063 in 1939 to 3,643 in 1971. However, Douglas pointed out that the Court agrees to rule on a very small percentage of these cases. As the result the Court in 1971 delivered eight fewer signed opinions than they did in 1939. Denver *Post*, Dec. 7, 1972.

276. Eustace Seligman (1889–) began practice with the New York firm of Sullivan and Cromwell in 1914, and since 1923 has been a partner in the firm.

277. A student in the Harvard Law School.

278. Myres S. McDougal (1906–) is a specialist in international law and a full professor at Yale since 1939, where he received his doctorate in jurisprudence in 1931. Before returning to Yale, he was on the law faculty of the University of Illinois from 1931 to 1934.

279. John Glenn, a student in the Indiana University School of Law.

280. "Historical Concept of Treason: English, American," *Indiana Law Journal* XXV (Fall 1959), 70–80.

281. Arnold had addressed the Wyoming Bar Association in early September.

282. Managing editor of the Washington *Post,* Alfred Friendly (1911–) is currently London correspondent for the *Post.*

283. Paul R. Ignatius (1920–) since 1969 has been president of the Washington *Post.* Previously he had been undersecretary of the army, assistant secretary of defense, and assistant secretary of the army.

284. The finale to that story went that when the Encyclopedia received Arnold's refusal letter to pay their bill, they wrote a threatening letter suggesting that they would do everything in their power to cancel Mrs. Arnold's credit rating. To which letter Arnold retorted, "My wife has charge accounts in Chicago, St. Louis, Denver and Laramie; you do what you can at that end. I will do what I can at this end."

285. In 1971, Charles A. Reich's (1928–) book, *The Greening of America*, became an instant best seller—a controversial book, with a "message" that cannot be distilled in a footnote. But superficially Reich outlined the future of America as being in the hands of the youth, who were both less corrupted and corruptible than their parents—hardly as startling a thesis as many reviewers would lead their readers to believe. Reich had been an associate with Arnold, Fortas and Porter from 1955 to 1960. He is now on the Yale Law School faculty.

286. Charles A. Reich, "Another Such Victory," *New Republic* CXLVI (April 30, 1962), 8–10.

287. David T. Bazelon, *The Paper Economy* (New York, 1963).

288. Roger M. Blough (1904–) was an executive of the United States Steel Corporation, chairman of the board of directors and chief executive officer from 1952 to 1969; he is now associated with the legal firm of White and Case in New York.

289. Arthur B. Homer (1896–1972) was with Bethlehem Steel Corporation from 1940; Homer was president from 1945 to 1960, when he became chairman of the board.

290. John E.F. Wood (1903–) received his LL.B. from the University of West Virginia in 1927, before Thurman Arnold arrived to take on the deanship. He has been with Dewey, Ballantine, Bushby, Palmer and Wood since 1940.

291. Carl Bode (1911–) has been professor of English at the University of Maryland since 1947. Professor Bode has had a migratory academic tenure, having served as visiting professor at California Institute of Technology, Claremont, Northwestern and Stanford, among others. He is the author of numerous volumes in the field of American literature.

292. Stone Harbor, New Jersey, the Hergsheimer home.

293. An article in the Washington *Star* analyzing the impact of Arnold, Fortas and Porter on the training of young attorneys. "Arnold-Fortas Firm Supplying U.S. Lawyers," Washington *Star,* January 5, 1964.

294. An editorial concerning the carousel antics of Robert G. Baker, President Johnson's protege—until he fell from grace. The *Post* was upset over Baker's silence. Washington *Post*, February 26, 1964.

295. On the Harvard law faculty since 1932, Livingston Hall (1903–) has specialized in various facets of criminal law. His most recent book on the subject was entitled *Modern Criminal Procedure*.

296. The wife of Arnold's partner, Paul A. Porter, Kathleen Winsor (1919–) had just finished her 947-page novel, *Wanderers Eastward, Wanderers West*. Miss Winsor shot onto the literary scene in 1944 with the publication of *Forever Amber*, one of the most whispered-about books published in the forties. Today one wonders why, but of course today is not yesterday.

297. What Arnold knew (and which most reviewers did not know but at least should have surmised) was that Kathleen Winsor had indulged in an enormous amount of historical research for her novel, including a summer sojourn in Montana. This knowledge, coupled with his intense loyalty to his friends, the Porters, produced the above letter. In addition, Arnold personally held many book reviewers in disdain for the clear reason that, as he once told the editor, "All too often, they [reviewers] are totally ignorant about the book they are reviewing."

298. When Arnold and Fortas opened their office in 1946, Willard M. Kiplinger was their third client.

299. Kiplinger's sparkling letter went as follows:

*July 19, 1965*

HON. THURMAN ARNOLD
ARNOLD, FORTAS & PORTER
1229 NINETEENTH STREET, N.W.
WASHINGTON, D.C.

*Dear Thurman:*

I liked your book about Thurman Arnold, mostly the stuff about Arnold, and lesserly the stuff about law, for, like lots of people, I am more interested in what a man is than what he thinks. This, I am told, is a sign of mediocre intelligence.

I was well along in life when you were born. I was five months old. Nevertheless we were fellow travellers of the times. Your father was better heeled than mine, and the proof is that he sent you to Princeton, which to me at the time was out of the ordinary world, and the "natural" thing was to go to the State University. You were a Democrat, affiliated with "that Bryan." My family, being respectable, were Republicans, and when years later in the times of Woodrow Wilson my mother heard that I had turned Democrat, she said she didn't believe a word of it, for "Willard had always been a good boy." You were a prohibitionist. I was worse than that, for I was also WCTU, and named for Frances Willard.

You got a wife from the East. I in the East got a wife from Wyoming—Cheyenne. The trusts played a part in this, for the Eastman trust broke my wife's father, who had invented a superior paper, and made him trek to Washington as paymaster of the Senate. Otherwise my wife would have been an heiress and married to someone other than me. This is why, when you attack the trusts, I speak a good word for them.

That Yale Law School and its air of impudence is terribly interesting, for it has a good smell, although I don't understand all the implications. The New Deal days I ate up, for I knew all those people, and I reported on them, and tried hard to explain them to my "business public," and often got into rows with them because they assumed that a reporter to business was necessarily OF business, which I wasn't any such thing.

You barely touched on Corcoran-&-Cohen, who were the spark plugs of the times. I claim to have discovered them, dug them up out of the obscurity of the RFC, and sold them to Moley. Out of them came Jackson, Reed, Frankfurter and a lot of others. Out of them also came the decline of Morgenthau. The legends are different, but I KNOW, for I was there when some of the deals were made. As a reporter I reported what was going to happen, and they did happen, and I was called "uncanny."

You didn't make enough of "The Folklore of Capitalism." It was an event, not just a book. I well remember the horror that arose about it, and the author, some Yale professor, actually participating in the administration. So I read it, didn't see anything so radical about it, didn't see any horns on the author, and wrote it so, and got the reputation of being a bit soft and tainted by the surroundings, the New Deal upsetters. One day I sat down next to the author at a Press Club luncheon, and told him I thought he was a conservative. I meant it as an insult, but he guffawed and was pleased.

Then you served those years on the bench, which made you respectable, despite your quirks. When you quit, my office thought we ought to have a "regular lawyer" on libel and publishing matters. We talked a bit about whether the reputation of Arnold for wildness would tarnish us, and decided NO. That's how come we connected. We never intended to let the law firm make any money out of us, and that's still our intention.

One incident has become a yarn with me. The wife of the chief economic adviser to the White House was involved in charges of being a commie. We wrote a paragraph about her, and called our lawyers to check on libel. The lawyers reported back that it was OK. At the same time they told us they were her lawyers, and would we like the facts? We would. On the basis of the facts, we killed the story. As reporters, not as clients, we killed the story.

I looked for some reference to journalism in your book, but there was none, and this made me say to myself such things as these: Damn the lawyers. They think they are the cream. They make laws, and they make laws that benefit their own profession, and the practice of it, and the fees in it. They aren't interested in people, they are interested only in themselves, and their precious profession. I say these things to myself, not out loud, not to others. I know there's a flaw in them, but I also think there's a lot of truth in them.

Compare with journalism. We all know the deficiencies of journalism. And yet, somehow, I feel that the ethics of journalism are of a higher order than the ethics of the law, which means the lawyers.

Next time you write a book, get a journalist to be the working editor. It would have ten times the hitting power.

Sincerely,

s/ *Kip*

300. Joseph Featherstone (1950–), a journalist, the major part of whose career has been spent with the *New Republic*.

301. *Fair Fights and Foul* (New York, 1965).

302. Washington correspondent, managing editor, editor and assistant to the publisher of the New York *Times*, 1933–47, J. Russell Wiggins (1903–) assumed the managing editor spot at the Washington *Post* in 1947. Appointed editor and executive vice-president of the *Post* in 1960, Wiggins left in 1968 to serve as ambassador to the United Nations. He is now publisher and owner of the Ellsworth (Maine) *American*.

303. A cause celebre arose over Professor Monroe Freedman's (1928–) lecture to some forty-five attorneys at George Washington Law School in January 1966. Freedman posed three hypothetical-ethical questions: "Is it proper to cross-examine for the purpose of discrediting the reliability or the credibility of an adverse witness whom you know to be telling the truth?" Two, "Is it proper to put on the stand a witness who you know will commit perjury?" Three, "Is it proper to give your client legal advice when you have reason to believe that the knowledge will tempt him to commit perjury?" Freedman answered yes to all three questions. However, he so qualified and restricted his assent by specific legal boundaries that only in a very unusual case would Freedman condone such legal conduct. When the message of Freedman's classroom performance leaked out, some judges in the Washington, D.C. area expressed incredulity. Judges Alexander Holtzoff and Warren Burger protested to the dean of the George Washington Law School. Freedman, in response, insisted that he was only pointing out the irrationality inherent in the U.S. legal adversary system, where a defense lawyer is constantly caught between adhering to the legal truth and at the same time fighting as hard as he can for his client. Based on complaints brought to the Committee on Admissions and Grievances at the U.S. District Court, a hearing was held on the Freedman case. Eventually, Freedman was cleared of the charges. *Time* LXXXVII (May 13, 1966), 81; Washington *Post*, April 13, 1966.

304. T.A. Larson (1910–) was long head of the history department at the University of Wyoming and is Wyoming's most distinguished historian.

305. *History of Wyoming* (Lincoln, Neb., 1965).

306. Melvin Wulf (1927–) has served with the American Civil Liberties Union from 1958 to the present, first as assistant legal director, and from 1962 as legal director.

307. This refers to an incident that took place during the hearings of a subcommittee of the House Un-American Activities Committee, chaired by Representative Joe Richard Pool of Texas. The hearings ostensibly were aimed at producing a bill that would make it a crime to aid individuals "engaged in hostilities against the United States." A number of students of the "New Left" appeared to testify, and were represented by William Kunstler, Arthur Kinoy and others. The arguments became so heated and spirited that Mr. Pool had the screaming, kicking, five-foot-four-inch, 135-pound Arthur Kinoy bodily ejected from the hearings by three U.S. marshalls.

A professor of law at Rutgers, and an attorney who had defended the "New Left" before, Mr. Kinoy was booked for disorderly conduct, fined $50 and suspended by Judge Harold Greene. The ACLU and other attorneys around the nation denounced the Greene decision claiming that no one could unearth a legal precedent for the arresting of a lawyer on disorderly conduct charges while representing a client. New York *Times*, August 18, 19, 20, 1966.

308. After engaging in private practice in Minneapolis from 1930 to 1962, John de J. Pemberton, Jr. (1919–) was elected executive director of the ACLU.

309. House Un-American Activities Committee.

310. After one more exchange Arnold finally gave up and wrote Pemberton on September 14, 1966:

*September 14, 1966*

MR. JOHN DE J. PEMBERTON, JR.
EXECUTIVE DIRECTOR
AMERICAN CIVIL LIBERTIES UNION
156 FIFTH AVENUE
NEW YORK, NEW YORK 10010

*Dear Mr. Pemberton:*

I have your letter of September 12. There is no use arguing the point further. My only observation is that you are setting out to sea in a leaky boat which is already in very shallow water and sinking mighty fast.

Sincerely,

s/ *Thurman Arnold*

311. Author of innumerable tomes on American constitutional law and biographies of the molders of American legal history, Alpheus T. Mason (1899–) has been in the political science department of Princeton University since 1925.

312. A fighting attorney from Brooklyn, Frank Serri (1889–1968) allotted a lifetime to the espousal of unpopular causes. Charging out of the normalcy atmosphere of the Harding era, Serri campaigned for state attorney general of New York in 1920. Twenty-eight years passed; he again entered the political arena, this time as the American Labor Party candidate for the House of Representatives. His most prominent notoriety came when he was designated by the court as the attorney for sixteen Communist leaders charged with conspiracy to overthrow the government.

313. The Introduction contains a lengthy discussion of Arnold's controversial speech at Valparaiso University on April 28, 1967.

314. Lewis C. Feuer, "The Elite of the Alienated," New York *Times Magazine* (March 26, 1967), 22–23; 74–77.

315. Ernest Gruening (1887–) is a journalist, political figure, onetime governor of Alaska (1938–53), and senator from Alaska (1956–58, 1958–69). Senator Gruening has written several volumes on Alaskan history and politics.

316. This refers to "The Committee for Peace with Freedom in Vietnam," which Douglas served as organizing chairman. The committee opposed unilateral withdrawal; instead, they advocated mutual de-escalation and sponsored the cause of land reform in Southeast Asia. Paul H. Douglas, *In the Fullness of Time* (New York, 1972).

317. Otis L. Graham (1935–) has been on the faculty of the University of California at Santa Barbara since 1966. In 1967, Oxford University Press published his book, *An Encore For Reform: Old Progressives and the New Deal.*

318. A bright, cantakerous, somewhat humorless and occasionally influential individual was Alexander Holtzoff (1886–1969), who occupied the title of special assistant to the attorney general from 1924 to 1945. Under the New Deal, Holtzoff has been primarily remembered for his spotlight task in drafting Social Security legislation and the Supreme Court "packing" bill of 1937. Among the old New Dealers in Washington today, there are those who insist that Roosevelt never forgave him for bungling the phraseology and the premises of the court bill. Arnold, although an admirer of Holtzoff's legal ability, found his absence of humor too much of a challenge. There are innumerable stories of Arnold-Holtzoff verbal encounters in the Department of Justice dining room. Alexander Holtzoff became Judge Holtzoff in 1945, when he received an appointment to the District Court for the District of Columbia.

319. News Release, American Civil Liberties Union, April 24, 1968. In reading this release, it is difficult to discern the rationale for Arnold's anger.

320. A member of the New York legal firm of Spence, Hotchkiss, Parker & Duryea, 1938–54, Ernest Angell (1889–1973) had a long-standing interest and participation in civil liberties and constitutional questions.

321. The son of Arnold's old friend and sociologist Robert Lynd, Staughton Lynd (1929–) took an active role in the "radical" historians' movement of the late sixties. His battle for tenure at Yale and his extra-curricular activities were well publicized within and without the historical guild.

322. William Sloane Coffin, Jr. (1924–), chaplain at Yale University, and Dr. Benjamin Spock (1903–), pediatrician; both received heavy publicity for their intense opposition to the Vietnam War.

323. A social (?) club formed by Mr. Justice Douglas, Thurman Arnold, and other assorted personages while Douglas and Arnold were at Yale together. The club's activities, membership and purposes are as hidden and mysterious today as they were in 1935.

324. Abraham Ribicoff (1910–), after receiving his law degree in 1933 from the University of Chicago, devoted his entire life to politics: governor of Connecticut from 1955 to 1961; secretary of health, education and welfare, 1961–62; and senator from Connecticut since 1962.

325. Ralph Nader had testified before the Subcommittee on Executive Reorganization, March 26, 1969, on Senate Bill 860, a bill to establish a Department of Consumer Affairs. Mr. Nader lashed out at those lobbyists who are part of the "infra-structure that undermines and continues to undermine any consumer activity for Government." Nader aimed his words at three Washington law firms: Covington and Burling, Hogan and Hartson, and Arnold and Porter— ". . . they are masters of the *ex-parte* contract, the private deals and trade-offs, the greasing of the corporate wheels and the softening of bureaucratic will."

326. Nathan M. Pusey (1907–), president of Lawrence College 1944–53; was elected president of Harvard in 1953, resigning in 1971.

327. Julian M. Sturtevant (1908–) has been a member of the Yale faculty since 1931.

# Index